MW00845474

MY SCIENCE, MY RELIGION

MY SCIENCE, MY RELIGION

Academic Papers
(1994–2009)

MICHAEL A. CREMO

TORCHLIGHT
PUBLISHING

Readers interested in the subject matter of this book are invited to correspond with the author at:

Bhaktivedanta Book Publishing Inc.
9701 Venice Blvd. Apt. 3
Los Angeles, CA 90034, USA
or mail@mcremo.com

Published by Bhaktivedanta Book Publishing, Inc. Science Books Division

Exclusively distributed by Torchlight Publishing, Inc.
P. O. Box 52, Badger, CA 93603, USA
www.torchlight.com

Library of Congress Cataloging-in-Publication Data

Cremo, Michael A., 1948-
  My science, my religion : academic papers (1994-2009) / Michael A. Cremo.
    p. cm.
  ISBN 978-0-89213-395-6
1. Religion and science--Congresses. I. Title.
  BL240.3.C747 2012
  201'.65--dc23
                        2012010498

I dedicate this book to the scientists and scholars
who have accepted my papers for presentation
at major international conferences on archeology,
anthropology, history of science, and religious studies,
who have listened to me at those conferences,
who have reviewed my books in their professional journals,
and who have invited me to speak at their
universities and institutes.

CONTENTS

INTRODUCTION

This book is a collection of papers that I have presented at major international conferences on archeology, anthropology, consciousness studies, history of science, and history of religion. Presenting the papers has been an interesting experience for me, as well as for many of the scientists and scholars who have heard me. It is not every day that one sees someone like me making presentations at science conferences. I don't have a PhD, and I openly position myself as someone who looks at the world of science from a religious perspective.

There are many people who believe that science and religion are two entirely separate domains. This is especially true of those influenced by positivism, which holds that real knowledge can only be obtained through positive verification of ideas by material sense evidence. According to positivists, and similar schools of thought, science and religion should not mix. I disagree with that point of view. Science and religion have often mixed, as many historians of science are now recognizing. In their preface to *Science in Theistic Contexts: Cognitive Dimensions,* historians of science John Hedley Brooke, Margaret J. Osler, and J. M. van der Meer say (2001, p. vii): "As recently as twenty years ago, when scholars were in the thrall of positivism in its various forms, they emphasized the separateness of science and religion. . . . Today the history of science is no longer dominated by positivist assumptions. Social, cultural, economic, political, philosophical, and religious factors have all been shown to be intimately connected with the growth, support, and even conceptual development of science." It is a modern myth that religion and science have nothing to do with each other. Einstein (1954, p. 46) famously said, "Science without religion is lame, religion without science is blind."

To speak generically of "science" and "religion" as things that really exist on their own, and in some general opposing relationship, is not really justified. If we look at the history of science and religion, we see that there have been many scientific views of the world, and similarly we find that there is a great variety of expressions of religion. We also find that many times the two overlap, but not always in the same way. Historians of science John Hedley Brooke and Geoffrey Cantor (1998, p. 45), in their book *Reconstructing Nature: The Engagement of Science and Religion,* propose that "the perceived relation between science and religion depends on how both of these terms are defined, when, and by whom." They remind us that in discussions of science and religion we must always ask "whose science?" and "whose religion?" And that is why I have titled this book *My Science, My Religion.* Scientists and historians of science can take this book as a case study of how a particular individual with a particular religious perspective has integrated that perspective into his presentations to members of scientific disciplines concerned with human origins, history, and culture, at professional gatherings of those disciplines. This collection of papers certainly demonstrates that religious perspectives on scientific questions do have a presence in contemporary scientific discourse.

So what exactly are my science and my religion, and what is their relationship? As a start to providing some necessarily incomplete answers to those questions, let me offer a few brief and selective autobiographical reflections. In terms of religion, I was born in the United States of America, in an Italian-American family, and I was raised as a Roman Catholic. I was baptized and confirmed in the Church. Most of my education, however, was in secular schools. My father was an officer in the United States Air Force, and our family moved from base to base in the continental United States and abroad. In the early 1950s, I lived in Hawaii. In my elementary school classrooms there, I was exposed to children from a wide variety of racial, cultural, and religious backgrounds. I see that as a key formative experience.

From 1962 to 1965, I lived in Wiesbaden, Germany, and attended the American military high school there. I was not much interested in science. Although I took the required science and math courses, I was more interested in foreign languages, literature, and history. My father was at the time an intelligence officer. The parents of some of my friends were also employed in civilian or military intelligence services or in the diplomatic service. When thinking about a future career and the education necessary for it, I naturally thought of the diplomatic service or one of the intelligence services. I also had ambitions to be a writer, a novelist or poet. I did not think deeply about or question the main features of the modern scientific worldview, such as the theory of evolution by natural selection.

In 1966, I entered the George Washington University in Washington, D. C., in the program for international relations. In addition to taking courses in foreign languages and political science, I took courses in philosophy and literature. My faith, career ambitions, and educational plan did not survive my exposure to the growing antiwar and counterculture movements of the time. Although I never renounced my Catholicism, my spiritual interests turned to Eastern religions and the more esoteric manifestations of Western religion. I could no longer imagine myself entering government service. I also became dissatisfied with the knowledge factory aspects of the formal university education system, which I left after a couple of years. I wanted to discover truth within myself by some meditative process, and then find some way to exist in the world, with the help of a personal guide. I was not questioning any particular scientific theories, but I felt a general aversion to an exclusive materialism.

After some time, in 1973, I took up a process of meditation (Hare Krishna mantra meditation) from one of the religious traditions in India. As recommended by this tradition, I also began studying one of the main texts of Indian spirituality, the *Bhagavad-gita,* which propounds a theistic worldview, encompassing not just spiritual realities but also the relationship of such realities to the world of matter. I became a disciple of a guru in this tradition, His Divine Grace A. C. Bhaktivedanta

Swami Prabhupada (1896–1977). Bhaktivedanta Swami had founded a society (the International Society for Krishna Consciousness), which included temple and ashrama communities for students of the tradition. I began living in these communities. Part of life in the Society is devotional service, according to one's talents. Because I had some talent as a writer, I was invited to participate in the publishing activities of the Society. I wrote articles (for *Back to Godhead,* the Society's magazine) and helped write some jointly authored small books on topics such as meditation (*Chant and Be Happy*), spiritual vegetarianism (*The Higher Taste*), reincarnation (*Coming Back*), and spiritual ecology (*Divine Nature*) for the Bhaktivedanta Book Trust (BBT).

In 1984, the BBT managers asked me to assist Richard L. Thompson, another disciple of Bhaktivedanta Swami, in producing publications giving the tradition's spiritual perspective on scientific questions. Thompson had a PhD in mathematics from Cornell University. He was a founding member of the Bhaktivedanta Institute, which Bhaktivedanta Swami had set up in 1974 to examine scientific questions from the perspective of the tradition. This perspective is rooted in India's Vedic literature, which includes not only the original four *Vedas* but also related works such as the *Vedanta Sutra*, the *Upanishads*, the *Puranas,* and epic works such as the *Mahabharata.* I worked with Richard to produce a publication called *Origins: Higher Dimensions in Science.*

Prior to this, I had been aware that Bhaktivedanta Swami opposed many features of the modern scientific worldview, especially the idea that life comes from chemicals, the Darwinian theory of evolution, the Big Bang theory of the origin of the universe, and the idea that consciousness is produced by the brain. But I had not been very interested in these things, preferring to focus on what seemed to me to be the more purely spiritual aspects of the tradition. However, my involvement in this new project caused me to give more attention to the relationship of the tradition to modern science.

Thompson had for years thought deeply about this, and had produced some scientific writings expressing his ideas, such as his book *Mechanistic and Nonmechanistic Science.* The BBT managers wanted me to put these ideas into language more suitable for general readers. My method was to sit with Thompson and question him deeply about his ideas on various science topics. From Thompson I learned—in considerable detail—about the latest scientific ideas on the origin of the universe, life, and consciousness. I also absorbed from him his views of the shortcomings of these ideas. Beyond that he proposed alternative ideas consistent with the teachings of the tradition, as it was represented by Bhaktivedanta Swami. We had lengthy discussions about the importance of these scientific topics within the intellectual framework of our spiritual tradition. And then I wrote articles, which he reviewed, for inclusion in *Origins.* The process of producing *Origins* took about a year from beginning to end. For me, it amounted to an intensive course in science and religion supervised by a scientist who was also a religionist.

Thompson wanted to expand each of the articles I wrote for *Origins* into a book. I was given the topic of the fossil evidence for human origins to work on first. According to modern science, humans like us first came into existence less than 200,000 years ago. However, the *Puranas,* the historical writings of the Vedic tradition, present a picture of extreme human antiquity, with a human presence going back many millions of years to the very beginnings of life on earth. According to traditional sources, as given and represented by Bhaktivedanta Swami, the statements of the Vedic literature, including the *Puranas*, are to be accepted literally, except when the statements are presented in the texts themselves as allegorical. The statements about extreme human antiquity are not presented in the texts as allegorical.

So, accepting that there are statements in the *Puranas* about extreme human antiquity, and accepting that these statements should be taken literally, there arises a question: Is there any physical evidence for such extreme human antiquity? This question arises primarily in the context of the modern scientific account of human origins. If I were discussing human antiquity in a gathering of coreligionists, who accepted the authority of the statements of the *Puranas*, I could, as evidence for extreme human antiquity, simply give statements from the *Puranas*.

According to the Vedic tradition, there are three main kinds of evidence: *pratyaksha* (sense evidence), *anumana* (logical inference), and *shabda* (authoritative testimony, i.e. scriptural statements). *Shabda* literally means "sound." Vedic knowledge, according to the traditional sources that inform my work, originally exists in the form of eternal sound, which enters the material world, where it may be expressed in written form, texts. Some of the Vedic statements are about the spiritual domain of reality, beyond sense evidence and logic. But some of the Vedic statements are about material reality, the domain of sense evidence and inference. Sense evidence is uncertain because of the imperfect nature of the senses. Inference is also uncertain, because of the tendency of the human mind to commit mistakes, become illusioned, and cheat or become the victim of cheating. Because *shabda* emanates, according to the tradition, from an omniscient source, it is considered trustworthy. Therefore the statements in the Vedic texts about material reality are ultimately more reliable than sense evidence and logical inference, according to Bhaktivedanta Swami and teachers in the line of the tradition to which he belonged (Gaudiya Vaishnavism). There are other opinions, within the broader Vedic tradition and within the academic world, about the authority of texts like the *Puranas* with reference to material reality. But here I am representing the voices within the tradition that have informed "my science, my religion."

In the realm of modern science, scriptural statements are not accepted as evidence. Modern science relies primarily on *pratyaksha* and *anumana*, sense evidence and logical inference. A scriptural statement can, however, be presented in scientific circles, not as evidence itself but as an idea that can be tested by sense evidence and logical inference. In science, it should make no difference what the source of the idea is, just as long as it is justified on the basis of sense evidence and appropriate logical inferences from this evidence.

The idea that I was trying to justify in terms of physical evidence and inference was the idea of extreme human antiquity, as found in the *Puranas*. I spent eight years researching the primary scientific literature dealing with human origins. I found in the primary scientific literature, from the time of Darwin up to the present, many credible cases of archeological evidence for extreme human antiquity, which I collected and compiled. The result was the book *Forbidden Archeology*. During those eight years of study, I discussed the results of my research on a regular basis with Thompson. And gradually I produced a manuscript. On completing it, I showed it to Thompson, and he reviewed it, after which I made some modifications. Thompson's contribution was such that I thought he should be coauthor, although he had originally suggested to me that I should be the sole author. Thompson told me that my work in producing the book was in some ways similar to writing a doctoral dissertation, with him as advisor.

The book was intended for a scientific audience. It was reviewed in many of the professional journals of archeology, anthropology, and history of science. Although some reviewers were harshly critical, some were appreciative. The book was intended to open a dialog between modern scientists and representatives of the religious tradition to which I belong. And to some limited extent it succeeded in doing that.

I also decided to personally enter into the scientific arena, to present the ideas in the book. One may wonder why I thought I should enter the world of science at all, attempting to justify scriptural statements in terms of material evidence and inference. The simple answer is that my guru, Bhaktivedanta Swami, said it should be done. I am not a professional scientist or academic, but I seem to know just enough about their discourse to be able to communicate with them, just as one might know a foreign language just well enough to get along. It is a credit to the community of modern scientists that they are open to including nonprofessionals with a religions orientation in their discourse, as long as such persons justify their ideas with sense evidence and logic rather than just scriptural authority.

My first presentation at a scientific conference was my paper "Puranic Time and the Archaeological Record." I read this paper in a section on time and archeology at the World Archaeological Congress 3, held in 1994 in New Delhi, India. The paper was selected for inclusion in a peer-reviewed conference proceedings volume, published by Routledge (Cremo 1999). It was a good beginning for this part of my work. In the following years, I presented many such papers, based on my research into archeological evidence for extreme human antiquity, at conferences on archeology and history of science. Most of the papers in this volume are of this type. There is some repetition of material in them.

Some of the reviewers of *Forbidden Archeology* faulted the book for not offering an alternative to the Darwinian theory of evolution. Therefore I offered a sketch of an alternative in my book *Human Devolution: A Vedic Alternative to Darwin's Theory.* This alternative is based on a worldview different from that of the modern scientific worldview.

A worldview involves four elements: (1) an ontology, an account of what things really exist; (2) a cosmogony, an historical account of how the things that exist have come into being; (3) an epistemology, an account of how things that exist can be known; and (4) an ethic, a way of living that takes into account the other three elements of the worldview.

The ontology of the modern scientific worldview recognizes only the existence of ordinary matter and material forces. This is true either in terms of an absolute ontological naturalism, according to which—some scientists believe—vital forces, the soul, and God do not exist, or in terms of a methodological naturalism, according to which scientists should purposely ignore "supernatural" elements such as a soul or God or vital forces, in order to explain things as far as possible in terms of matter and material forces. However, we see that at various times in the history of Western science, scientists have accepted things such as subtle material elements, a nonmaterial soul, and God as part of their explanations of life and the universe.

Ontology is important. It very much determines the nature of the other three elements of a worldview. For example, if an ontology is materialistic, this leads to cosmogonies that do not allow deliberate creation, intelligent design, or the unfolding of preexisting information. Such an ontology will allow only accounts of how matter combines in natural ways, the study of which reveals certain regularities. Epistemologically, such regularities can only be discovered and known by sense evidence and logical inference. Finally, such an ontology will support an ethic that values material consumption, material production, and material happiness.

In *Human Devolution*, I presented and justified an ontology that includes not only ordinary matter and material energy, but also vital forces, nonmaterial conscious selves (souls), and a superior conscious self (God) capable of guiding and controlling matter and material energy in ways that would not happen without such guidance and control. This ontology supports a cosmogony, an historical account of the origin of the universe and life forms within it, different from that provided by materialistic science or by a theism that simply adds God to the materialistic account, without changing that account in any way. The ontology I presented would also support an epistemology that gives a role to revelation in knowing things of this world, and an ethic that encourages the pursuit of nonmaterial values. Some of the papers in this volume are presentations of various aspects of the worldview that I put forward and justified in *Human Devolution*.

The remaining papers in this volume are concerned with some of my other academic interests, such as the history of archeology in India, the Vedic system of architecture called *vastu*, education policy, and sacred places. I have arranged the papers chronologically. I am presenting this collection of papers as part of my individual, personal project of introducing Vedic concepts into modern scientific discourse. Although I am affiliated with the International Society for Krishna Consciousness, the Bhatkivedanta Book Trust, and the Bhaktivedanta Institute, and other related groups, I do not hold any administrative positions in them and I am not officially representing them in these papers. If one takes the trouble of going through the papers in this book, one will get some idea of what I mean by "my science, my religion."

I am grateful to the Bhaktivedanta Book Trust for its ongoing support of my work. I also acknowledge Alister Taylor, my publisher, and his staff at Torchlight Publishing. My research assistant Lori Erbs has also been helpful in many ways.

Michael A. Cremo
September 26, 2010
Los Angeles

Works cited:

Brooke, John and Cantor, Geoffrey (1998) *Reconstructing Nature: The Engagement of Science and Religion.* Oxford: Oxford University Press.

Brooke, John Hedley, Osler, Margaret J., and Van der Meer, J. M. (2001) Preface to *Science in Theistic Contexts: Cognitive Dimensions. Osiris* Second Series, Volume 16. University of Chicago Press Journals Division, pp. vii–xii.

Cremo, Michael A. (1999) Puranic time and the archaeological record. In Tim Murray, ed. *Time and Archaeology.* London: Routledge, pp. 38–48.

Einstein, Albert (1954) *Idea and Opinions.* New York: Crown.

Note on spelling:: In this book I will spell Sanskrit words phonetically, instead of using the system of diacritics. I use "archeology" in preference to "archaeology," except in the case of names of organizations and quoted passages.

Note on Illustrations: In this book, the illustrations are in plates at the end of the main text of the book. In the text, references to illustrations will be given in bold and in brackets: [**see Plates VIII-XI**], [**see Figure 2, Plate III**], etc.

1

Puranic Time and
the Archeological Record

I presented this paper at the World Archaeological Congress 3, held December 4–11, 1994, in New Delhi India. The World Archaeological Congress is an international organization of archeologists. It holds a congress every four years in a different city in the world. This is the first paper I presented at a scientific conference. I read this same paper, with some minor changes, at the conference Revisiting Indus-Sarasvati Age & Ancient India, sponsored by the Greater Atlanta Vedic Temple Society in cooperation with the Hindu University of America and other organizations. The conference was held in Atlanta, Georgia, USA, October 4–6, 1996. A version of the WAC paper was later included in a peer-reviewed WAC conference proceedings volume for a major scientific publisher: Michael A. Cremo (1999) Puranic time and the archaeological record. In Tim Murray, editor, Time and Archaeology. *Routledge, London, pp. 38–48.*

The practically employed time concept of the modern historical scientist, including the archeologist, strikingly resembles the traditional Judaeo-Christian time concept. And it strikingly differs from that of the ancient Greeks and Indians.

This observation is, of course, an extreme generalization. In any culture, the common people may make use of various time concepts, linear and cyclical. And among the great thinkers of any given period, there may be many competing views of both cyclical and linear time. This was certainly true of the ancient Greeks. It can nevertheless be safely said that the cosmological concepts of several of the most prominent Greek thinkers involved a cyclic or episodic time similar to that found in the Puranic literatures of India. For example, we find in Hesiod's *Works and Days* a series of ages (gold, silver, bronze, heroic, and iron) similar to the Indian *yugas*. In both systems, the quality of human life gets progressively worse with each passing age. In *On Nature* (Fragment 17) Empedocles speaks of cosmic time cycles. In Plato's dialogues there are descriptions of revolving time (*Timaeus* 38 a) and recurring catastrophes that destroy or nearly destroy human civilization (*Politicus* 268 d ff). Aristotle said in many places in his works that the arts and sciences had been discovered many times in the past (*Metaphysics* 1074 b 10, *Politics* 1329 b 25) In the teachings of Pythagoras, Plato, and Empedocles regarding transmigration of souls, this cyclical pattern is extended to individual psychophysical existence.

When Judaeo-Christian civilization arose in Europe, another kind of time became prominent. This time has been characterized as linear and vectorial. Broadly speaking, this time concept involves a unique act of cosmic creation, a unique appearance of the human kind, and a unique history of salvation, culminating in a unique denouement in the form of a last judgement. The drama occurs only once. Individually, human life mirrored this process; with some exceptions, orthodox Christian theologians did not accept transmigration of the soul.

Modern historical sciences share the basic Judaeo-Christian assumptions about time. The universe we inhabit is a unique occurrence. Humans have arisen once on this planet. The history of our ancestors is regarded as a unique though unpredestined evolutionary pathway. The future pathway of our species is also unique. Although this pathway is officially unpredictable, the myths of science project a possible overcoming of death by biomedical science and mastery over the entire universe by evolving, space-traveling humans. One group, the Santa Fe Institute, sponsor of several conferences on "artificial life," predicts the transferal of human intelligence into machines and computers displaying the complex symptoms of living things (Langton 1991, p. xv). "Artificial life" thus becomes the ultimate transfiguring salvation of our species.

One is tempted to propose that the modern human evolutionary account is a Judaeo-Christian heterodoxy, which covertly retains fundamental structures of Judaeo-Christian cosmology, salvation history, and eschatology while overtly dispensing with the scriptural account of divine intervention in the origin of species, including our own. This is similar to the case of Buddhism as Hindu heterodoxy. Dispensing with the Hindu scriptures and God concepts, Buddhism nevertheless retained basic Hindu cosmological assumptions such as cyclical time, transmigration, and karma.

Another thing the modern human evolutionary account has in common with the earlier Christian account is that humans appear after the other life forms. In *Genesis*, God creates the plants, animals, and birds before human beings. For strict literalists, the time interval is short—humans are created on the last of six of our present solar days. Others have taken the *Genesis* days as ages. For example, around the time of Darwin European scientists with strong Christian leanings proposed that God had gradually brought into existence various species throughout the ages of geological time until the perfected earth was ready to receive human beings (Grayson 1983). In modern evolutionary accounts, anatomically modern humans retain their position as the most recent major species to occur on this planet, having evolved from preceding hominids within the past 100,000 or so years. And despite the attempts of prominent evolutionary theorists and spokespersons to counteract the tendency, even among evolution scientists, to express this appearance in teleological fashion (Gould 1977, p. 14), the idea that humans are the crowning glory of the evolutionary process still has a strong hold on the public and scientific minds. Although anatomically modern humans are given an age of about 100,000 years, modern archeologists and anthropologists, in common with Judaeo-Christian accounts, give civilization an age of a few thousand years, and, again in common with Judaeo-Christian accounts, place its earliest occurrence in the Middle East.

I do not here categorically assert a direct causal link between earlier Judeao-Christian ideas and those of the modern historical sciences. Demonstrating that, as Edward B. Davis (1994) points out in his review of recent works on this subject, needs much more careful documentation than has yet been provided. But the many common features of the time concepts of the two knowledge systems suggest these causal links do exist, and that it would be fruitful to trace connections in sufficient detail to satisfactorily demonstrate this.

I do, however, propose that the tacitly accepted and hence critically unexamined time concepts of the modern human sciences, whether or not causally linked with Judaeo-Christian concepts, pose a significant unrecognized influence on interpretation of the archeological and anthropological record. To demonstrate how this might be true, I shall introduce my own experience in evaluating this record from the alien standpoint of the cyclical time concepts and accounts of human origins found in the *Puranas* and *Itihasas* of India.

My subjective path of learning has led me to take the Vaishnava tradition of India as my primary guide to life and the study of the visible universe and what may lie beyond. For the past century or so, it has been considered quite unreasonable to bring concepts from religious texts directly into the realm of the scientific study of nature. Indeed, many introductory anthropology and archeology texts make a clear distinction between "scientific" and "religious" ways of knowing, relegating the latter to the status of unsupported belief, with little or no utility in the objective study of nature (see, for example, Stein and Rowe 1993, chapter 2). Some texts even go so far as to boast that this view has been upheld by the United States Supreme Court (Stein and Rowe 1993, p. 37), as if the state were the best and final arbiter of intellectual controversy. But I propose that total hostility to religious views of nature in science is unreasonable, especially for the modern historical sciences. Despite their pretensions to nonreligious objectivity, practitioners unconsciously retain or incorporate into their workings many Judaeo-Christian cosmological concepts, especially concerning time, and implicitly employ them in their day to day work of observation and theory building. In this sense, modern evolutionists share some intellectual territory with their fundamentalist Christian antagonists.

But there are other ways to comprehend historical processes in nature. How this is so can be graphically sensed if one performs the mental experiment of looking at the world from a radically different time perspective—the Puranic time concept of India. I am not alone in suggesting this. Gene Sager, a professor of philosophy and religious studies at Palomar College in California, wrote in an unpublished review of my book *Forbidden Archeology* (Cremo and Thompson 1993): "As a scholar in the field of comparative religion, I have sometimes challenged scientists by offering a cyclical or spiral model for studying human history, based on the Vedic concept of the *kalpa*. Few Western scientists are open to the possibility of sorting out the data in terms of such a model. I am not proposing that the Vedic model is true….However, the question remains, does the relatively short, linear model prove to be adequate? I believe *Forbidden Archeology* offers a well researched challenge. If we are to meet this challenge, we need to practice open-mindedness and proceed in a cross-cultural, interdisciplinary fashion" (personal communication, 1993). The World Archaeological Congress provides a suitable forum for such cross-cultural, interdisciplinary dialogue.

This cyclical time of the *Puranas* operates only within the material cosmos. Beyond the material cosmos lies the spiritual sky, or *brahmajyoti*. Innumerable spiritual planets float in this spiritual sky, where material time, in the form of *yuga* cycles, does not act.

Each *yuga* cycle is composed of 4 *yugas*. The first, the Satya-yuga, lasts 4800 years of the demigods. The second, the Treta-yuga, lasts 3600 years of the demigods. The third, the Dvapara-yuga, lasts 2400 years of the demigods. And the fourth, Kali-yuga, lasts 1200 years of the demigods (*Bhagavata Purana* 3.11.19). Since the demigod year is equivalent to 360 earth years (Bhaktivedanta Swami 1973, p. 102), the lengths of the *yugas* in earth years are, according to standard Vaishnava commentaries, 432,000 years for the Kali-yuga, 864,000 years for the Dvapara-yuga, 1,296,000 years for the Treta-yuga, and 1,728,000 years for the Satya-yuga. This gives a total of 4,320,000 years for the entire *yuga* cycle. One thousand of such cycles, lasting 4,320,000,000 years, comprises one day of Brahma, the demigod who governs this universe. A day of Brahma is also called a *kalpa*. Each of Brahma's nights lasts a similar period of time. Life is only manifest on earth during the day of Brahma. With the onset of Brahma's night, the entire universe is devastated and plunged into darkness. When another day of Brahma begins, life again becomes manifest.

Each day of Brahma is divided into 14 *manvantara* periods, each one lasting 71 *yuga* cycles. Preceding the first and following each *manvantara* period is a juncture (*sandhya*) the length of a Satya-yuga (1,728,000) years. Typically, each *manvantara* period ends with a partial devastation. According to Puranic accounts, we are now in the twenty-eighth *yuga* cycle of the seventh *manvantara* period of the present day of Brahma. This would give the inhabited earth an age of about two billion years. Interestingly enough, the oldest undisputed organisms recognized by paleontologists—algae fossils like those from the Gunflint formation in Canada—are just about that old (Stewart 1983, p. 30). Altogether, 453 *yuga* cycles have elapsed since this day of Brahma began. Each *yuga* cycle involves a progression from a golden age of peace and spiritual progress to a final age of violence and spiritual degradation. At the end of each Kali-yuga, the earth is practically depopulated.

During the *yuga* cycles, human species coexist with other humanlike species. For example, in the *Bhagavata Purana* (9.10.20) we find the divine *avatara* Ramacandra conquering Ravana's kingdom Lanka with the aid of intelligent forest dwelling monkey men who fought Ravana's well-equipped soldiers with trees and stones. This occurred in the Treta-yuga, about one million years ago.

Given the cycle of *yugas*, the periodic devastations at the end of each *manvantara*, and the coexistence of civilized human beings with creatures in some ways resembling the human ancestors of modern evolutionary accounts, what predictions might the Puranic account give regarding the archeological record? Before answering this question, we must also consider the general imperfection of the fossil record (Raup and Stanley 1971). Hominid fossils in particular are extremely rare. Furthermore, only a small fraction of the sedimentary layers deposited during the course of the earth's history have survived erosion and other destructive geological processes (Van Andel 1981).

Taking the above into account, I propose the Puranic view of time and history predicts a sparse but bewildering mixture of hominid fossils, some anatomically modern and some not, going back tens and even hundreds of millions of years and occurring at locations all over the world. It also predicts a more numerous but similarly bewildering mixture of stone tools and other artifacts, some showing a high level of technical ability and others not. And, given the cognitive biases of the majority of workers in the fields of archeology and anthropology over the past 150 years, we might also predict that this bewildering mixture of fossils and artifacts would be edited to conform with a linear, progressive view of human origins. A careful investigation of published reports by myself and Richard Thompson (1993) offers confirmation of these two predictions. What follows is only a sample of the total body of evidence catalogued in our lengthy book. The citations given are for the single reports that best identify particular finds. Detailed analysis and additional reports cited elsewhere (Cremo and Thompson 1993) offer strong confirmation of the authenticity and antiquity of these discoveries.

Incised and carved mammal bones are reported from the Pliocene (Desnoyers 1863, Laussedat 1868, Capellini 1877) and Miocene (Garrigou and Filhol 1868, von Dücker 1873). Additional reports of incised bones from the Pliocene and Miocene may be found in an extensive review by the overly skeptical de Mortillet (1883). Scientists have also reported pierced shark teeth from the Pliocene (Charlesworth 1873), artistically carved bone from the Miocene (Calvert 1874), and artistically carved shell from the Pliocene (Stopes 1881). Carved mammal bones reported by Moir (1917) could be as old as the Eocene.

Very crude stone tools occur in the Middle Pliocene (Prestwich 1892) and from perhaps as far back as the Eocene (Moir 1927, Breuil 1910, especially p. 402). One will note that most of these discoveries are from the nineteenth century. But such artifacts are still being found. Crude stone tools have been reported from the Pliocene of Pakistan (Bunney 1987), Siberia (Daniloff and Kopf 1986), and India (Sankhyan 1981). Given the current view that toolmaking hominids did not leave their African center of origin until about 1 million years ago, these artifacts are somewhat anomalous, what to speak of a pebble tool from the Miocene of India (Prasad 1982).

More advanced stone tools occur in the Oligocene of Europe (Rutot 1907) [see Plates VIII-XI], the Miocene of Europe (Ribeiro 1873 [see Plates I-VII], Bourgeois 1873, Verworn 1905), the Miocene of Asia (Noetling 1894), and the Pliocene of South America (F. Ameghino 1908, C. Ameghino 1915). In North America, advanced stone tools occur in California deposits ranging from Pliocene to Miocene in age (Whitney 1880) [see Plates XII-XV]. An interesting slingstone, at least Pliocene and perhaps Eocene in age, comes from England (Moir 1929, p. 63).

More advanced artifacts have also been reported in scientific and nonscientific publications. These include an iron nail in Devonian sandstone (Brewster 1844), a gold thread in Carboniferous stone (*Times* of London, June 22, 1844), a metallic vase in Precambrian stone (*Scientific American*, June 5, 1852), a chalk ball from the Eocene (Melleville 1862), a Pliocene clay statue (Wright 1912, pp. 266–69), metallic tubes in Cretaceous chalk (Corliss 1978, pp. 652–53), and a grooved metallic sphere from the Precambrian (Jimison 1982). The following objects have been reported from Carboniferous coal: a gold chain (*The Morrisonville Times*, of Illinois, U.S.A., June 11, 1891), artistically carved stone (*Daily News*, of Omaha, U.S.A., April 2, 1897), an iron cup (Rusch 1971), and stone block walls (Steiger 1979, p. 27).

Human skeletal remains described as anatomically modern occur in the Middle Pleistocene of Europe (Newton 1895, Bertrand 1868, de Mortillet 1883). These cases are favorably reviewed by Keith (1928). Other anatomically modern human skeletal remains occur in the Early and Middle Pleistocene of Africa (Reck 1914, L. Leakey 1960, Zuckerman 1954, p. 310; Patterson and Howells 1967, Senut 1981, R. Leakey 1973), the Early Middle Pleistocene of Java (Day and Molleson 1973), the Early Pleistocene of South America (Hrdlička 1912, pp. 319–44), the Pliocene of South America (Hrdlička 1912, p. 346; Boman 1921, pp. 341–42), the Pliocene of England (Osborn 1921, pp. 567–69), the Pliocene of Italy (Ragazzoni 1880, Issel 1868), the Miocene of France and the Eocene of Switzerland (de Mortillet 1883, p. 72), and even the Carboniferous of North America (*The Geologist* 1862). Several discoveries from California gold mines range from Pliocene to Eocene (Whitney 1880). Some of these bones have been subjected to chemical and radiometric tests that have yielded ages younger than suggested by their stratigraphical position. But when the unreliabilities and weaknesses of the testing procedures are measured against the very compelling stratigraphic observations of the discoverers, it is not at all clear that the original age attributions should be discarded (Cremo and Thompson 1993, 753–794).

Humanlike footprints have been found in the Carboniferous of North America (Burroughs 1938), the Jurassic of Central Asia (*Moscow News* 1983, no. 4, p. 10), and the Pliocene of Africa (M. Leakey 1979). Shoe prints have been reported from the Cambrian (Meister 1968) and the Triassic (Ballou 1922).

In the course of negotiating a fashionable consensus that anatomically modern humans evolved from less advanced hominids in the Late Pleistocene, scientists gradually rendered unfashionable the considerable body of compelling contradictory evidence summarized above. It thus became unworthy of discussion in knowing circles. Richard Thompson and I have concluded (1993) that the muting of this evidence was accomplished by application of a double standard, whereby favored evidence was exempted from the severely skeptical scrutiny to which unfavored evidence was subjected.

One example from the many that could be cited to demonstrate the operation of linear progressive preconceptions in the editing of the archeological record is the case of the auriferous gravel finds in California. During the days of the California Gold Rush, starting in the 1850s, miners discovered many anatomically modern human bones and advanced stone implements in mineshafts sunk deeply into deposits of gold-bearing gravels capped by thick lava flows (Whitney 1880) [**see Plates XII–XV**]. The gravels beneath the lava were from 9 to 55 million years old, according to modern geological reports (Slemmons 1966). These discoveries were reported to the world of science by J. D. Whitney, state geologist of California, in a monograph published by the Peabody Museum of Comparative Zoology at Harvard University. From the evidence he compiled, Whitney came to a nonprogressivist view of human origins—the fossil evidence he reported indicated that the humans of the distant past were like those of the present.

To this W. H. Holmes (1899, p. 424) of the Smithsonian Institution replied: "Perhaps if Professor Whitney had fully appreciated the story of human evolution as it is understood today, he would have hesitated to announce the conclusions formulated, notwithstanding the imposing array of testimony with which he was confronted." This attitude is still prominent today. In their college textbook, Stein and Rowe assert that "scientific statements are never considered absolute" (1993, p. 41). But they also make this very absolute statement: "Some people have assumed that humans have always been the way they are today. Anthropologists are convinced that human beings...have changed over time in response to changing conditions. So one aim of the anthropologist is to find evidence for evolution and to generate theories about it." Apparently, an anthropologist, by definition, can have no other view or purpose. Keep in mind, however, that this absolute commitment to a linear progressive model of human origins, ostensibly nonreligious, may have deep roots in Judaeo-Christian cosmology.

One of the things Holmes found especially hard to accept was the similarity of the purportedly very ancient stone implements to those of the modern Indians. He wondered (1899, pp. 451–52) how anyone could take seriously the idea that "the implements of a Tertiary race should have been left in the bed of a Tertiary torrent to be brought out as good as new, after the lapse of vast periods of time, into the camp of a modern community using identical forms?" The similarity could be explained in several ways, but one possible explanation is the repeated appearance in the same geographical region of humans with particular cultural attributes in the course of cyclical time. The suggestion that such a thing could happen is bound to strike those who see humans as the recent result of a long and unique series of evolutionary changes in the hominid line as absurd—so absurd as to prevent them from considering any evidence as potentially supporting a cyclical interpretation of human history.

It is noteworthy, however, that a fairly openminded modern archeologist, when confronted with the evidence catalogued in my book, himself brought up, in a somewhat doubting manner, the possibility of a cyclical interpretation of human history to explain its occurrence. George F. Carter, noted for his controversial views on early man in North America, wrote to me on January 26, 1994: "If your table on p. 391 were correct, then the minimum age for the artifacts at Table Mountain would be 9 million [years old]. Would you think then of a different creation— [one that] disappeared— and then a new start? Would it simply replicate the archeology of California 9 million years later? Or the inverse. Would the Californians 9 million years later replicate the materials under Table Mountain?"

That is exactly what I would propose—that in the course of cyclic time, humans with a culture resembling that of modern North American Indians did in fact appear in California millions of years ago, perhaps several times. "I find great difficulty with that line of reasoning," confessed Carter. But that difficulty, which encumbers the minds of most archeologists and anthropologists, may be the result of a rarely recognized and even more rarely questioned commitment to a culturally acquired linear progressive time sense.

It would, therefore, be worthwhile to inspect the archeological record through other time lenses, such as the Puranic lens. Many will take my proposal as a perfect example of what can happen when someone brings their subjective religious ideas into the objective study of nature. Jonathan Marks (1994) reacted in typical fashion in his review of *Forbidden Archeology:* "Generally, attempts to reconcile the natural world to religious views end up compromising the natural world."

But until modern anthropology conducts a conscious examination of the effects of its own covert, and arguably religiously derived, assumptions about time and progress, it should put aside its pretensions to universal objectivity and not be so quick to accuse others of bending facts to fit religious dogma.

Om Tat Sat

References

Ameghino, C. (1915) El femur de Miramar. *Anales de Museo nacional de historia natural de Buenos Aires,* 26: 433–450.

Ameghino, F. (1908) Notas preliminares sobre el *Tetraprothhomo argentinus,* un precursor de hombre del Mioceno superior de Monte Hermoso. *Anales de Museo nacional de historia natural de Buenos Aires,* 16: 105–242.

Ballou, W. H. (1922) Mystery of the petrified "shoe-sole" 5,000,000 years old. *American Weekly* section of the *New York Sunday American,* October 8, p. 2.

Bertrand, P. M. E. (1868) Crane et ossements trouves dans un carriere de l'avenue de Clichy. *Bulletin de la Societe d'Anthropologie de Paris (Series 2),* 3: 329–335.

Bhaktivedanta Swami, A. C. (1973) *Shrimad-Bhagavatam (Bhagavata Purana),* Canto Three, Part Two. Los Angeles: Bhaktivedanta Book Trust.

Boman, E. (1921) Los vestigios de industria humana encontrados en Miramar (Republica Argentina) y atribuidos a la época terciaria. *Revista Chilena de Historia y Geografia,* 49(43): 330–352.

Bourgeois, L. (1873) Sur les silex considérés comme portant les margues d'un travail humain et découverts dans le terrain miocène de Thenay. *Congrès International d'Anthropologie et d'Archéologie Préhistoriques, Bruxelles 1872, Compte Rendu,* pp. 81–92.

Breuil, H. (1910) Sur la présence d'éolithes a la base de l'Éocene Parisien. *L'Anthropologie,* 21: 385–408.

Brewster, D. (1844) Queries and statements concerning a nail found imbedded in a block of sandstone obtained from Kingoodie (Mylnfield) Quarry, North Britain. *Report of the British Association for the Advancement of Science, Notices and Abstracts of Communications,* p. 51.

Bunney, S. (1987) First migrants will travel back in time. *New Scientist,* 114(1565): 36.

Burroughs, W. G. (1938) Human-like footprints, 250 million years old. *The Berea Alumnus.* Berea College, Kentucky, November, pp. 46–47.

Calvert, F. (1874) On the probable existence of man during the Miocene period. *Journal of the Royal Anthropological Institute of Great Britain and Ireland,* 3: 127.

Capellini, G. (1877) Les traces de l'homme pliocène en Toscane. *Congrès International d'Anthropologie et d'Archéologie Préhistoriques, Budapest 1876, Compte Rendu.* Vol.

1, pp. 46–62.

Charlesworth, E. (1873) Objects in the Red Crag of Suffolk. *Journal of the Royal Anthropological Institute of Great Britain and Ireland*, 2: 91–94.

Corliss, W. R. (1978) *Ancient Man: A Handbook of Puzzling Artifacts.* Glen Arm: Sourcebook Project.

Cremo, M. A., and Thompson, R. L. (1993) *Forbidden Archeology: The Hidden History of the Human Race.* San Diego: Bhaktivedanta Institute.

Daniloff, R., and Kopf, C. (1986) Digging up new theories of early man. *U. S. News & World Report*, September 1, pp. 62–63.

Davis, Edward B. (1994) Review of Cameron Wybrow (Editor): *Creation, Nature, and Political Order in the Philosophy of Michael Foster (1903–1959); The Classic* Mind *Articles and Others, with Modern Critical Essays,* and Cameron Wybrow: *The Bible, Baconism, and Mastery over Nature: The Old Testament and Its Modern Misreading. Isis* 53(1): 127–129.

Day, M. H. and Molleson, T. I. (1973) The Trinil femora. *Symposia of the Society for the Study of Human Biology*, 2: 127–154.

De Mortillet, G. (1883) *Le Préhistorique.* Paris: C. Reinwald.

Desnoyers, J. (1863) Response à des objections faites au sujet d'incisions constatées sur des ossements de Mammiferes fossiles des environs de Chartres. *Compte Rendus de l'Académie des Sciences*, 56: 1199–1204.

Garrigou, F. and Filhol, H. (1868) M. Garrigou prie l'Académie de vouloir bien ouvrir un pli cacheté, déposé au nom de M. Filhol fils et au sien, le 16 mai 1864. *Compte Rendus de l'Académie des Sciences*, 66: 819–820.

The Geologist, London, 1862 Fossil man, 5: 470.

Gould, S. J. (1977) *Ever Since Darwin.* New York: W. W. Norton.

Grayson, Donald K. (1983) *The Establishment of Human Antiquity.* New York: Academic Press.

Holmes, W. H. (1899) Review of the evidence relating to auriferous gravel man in California. *Smithsonian Institution Annual Report 1898–1899*, pp. 419–472.

Hrdlička, A. (1912) *Early Man in South America.* Washington, D. C.: Smithsonian Institution.

Issel, A. (1868) Résumé des recherches concernant l'ancienneté de l'homme en Ligurie. *Congrès International d'Anthropologie et d'Archéologie Préhistoriques, Paris 1867, Compte Rendu*, pp. 75–89.

Jimison, S. (1982) Scientists baffled by space spheres. *Weekly World News,* July 27.

Keith, A. (1928) *The Antiquity of Man.* Vol. 1. Philadelphia: J. B. Lippincott.

Langton, C. G. (1991) Preface. *In* Langton, C. G., *et al.*, eds. *Artificial Life II: Proceedings of the Workshop on Artificial Life Held February, 1990 in Santa Fe, New Mexico.* Santa Fe Institute Studies in the Sciences of Complexity, Proceedings Volume X. Redwood City: Addison-Wesley, pp. xiii–xv.

Laussedat, A. (1868) Sur une mâchoire de Rhinoceros portant des entailles profondes trouvée à Billy (Allier), dans les formations calcaires d'eau douce de la Limagne. *Compte Rendus de l'Académie des Sciences*, 66: 752–754.

Leakey, L. S. B. (1960) *Adam's Ancestors*, 4th edition. New York: Harper & Row.

Leakey, M. D. (1979) Footprints in the ashes of time. *National Geographic,* 155: 446–457.

Leakey, R. E. (1973) Evidence for an advanced Plio-Pleistocene hominid from East Rudolf, Kenya. *Nature,* 242: 447–450.

Marks, J. (1994) Review of *Forbidden Archeology: The Hidden History of the Human Race,* by Michael A. Cremo and Richard L. Thompson. 1993. San Diego: Bhaktivedanta Institute. *American Journal of Physical Anthropology,* 93: 140–141.

Meister, W. J. (1968) Discovery of trilobite fossils in shod footprint of human in "Trilobite Bed"—a Cambrian formation, Antelope Springs, Utah. *Creation Research Society Quarterly,* 5(3): 97–102.

Melleville, M. (1862) Note sur un objet travaillé de main d'homme trouve dans les lignites du Laonnais. *Revue Archéologique,* 5: 181–186.

Moir, J. R. (1917) A series of mineralised bone implements of a primitive type from below the base of the Red and Coralline Crags of Suffolk. *Proceedings of the Prehistoric Society of East Anglia,* 2: 116–131.

Moir, J. R. (1927) *The Antiquity of Man in East Anglia.* Cambridge: Cambridge University Press.

Moir, J. R. (1929) A remarkable object from beneath the Red Crag. *Man,* 29: 62–65.

Newton, E. T. (1895) On a human skull and limb-bones found in the Paleolithic terrace-gravel at Galley Hill, Kent. *Quarterly Journal of the Geological Society of London,* 51: 505–526.

Noetling, F. (1894) On the occurrence of chipped flints in the Upper Miocene of Burma. *Records of the Geological Survey of India,* 27: 101–103.

Osborn, H. F. (1921) The Pliocene man of Foxhall in East Anglia. *Natural History,* 21: 565–576.

Patterson, B. and Howells, W. W. (1967) Hominid humeral fragment from Early Pleistocene of northwestern Kenya. *Science,* 156: 64–66.

Prasad, K. N. (1982) Was *Ramapithecus* a tool-user. *Journal of Human Evolution,* 11: 101–104.

Prestwich, J. (1892) On the primitive character of the flint implements of the Chalk Plateau of Kent, with reference to the question of their glacial or pre-glacial age. *Journal of the Royal Anthropological Institute of Great Britain and Ireland,* 21(3): 246–262.

Ragazzoni, G. (1880) La collina di Castenedolo, solto il rapporto antropologico, geologico ed agronomico. *Commentari dell' Ateneo di Brescia,* April 4, pp. 120–128.

Raup, D., and Stanley, S. (1971) *Principles of Paleontology.* San Francisco: W. H. Freeman.

Reck, H. (1914) Erste vorläufige Mitteilungen über den Fund eines fossilen Menschenskeletts aus Zentral-afrika. *Sitzungsbericht der Gesellschaft der naturforschender Freunde Berlins,* 3: 81–95.

Ribeiro, C. (1873) Sur des silex taillés, découverts dans les terrains miocène du Portugal. *Congrès International d'Anthropologie et d'Archéologie Préhistoriques, Bruxelles 1872, Compte Rendu,* pp. 95–100.

Rusch, Sr., W. H. (1971) Human footprints in rocks. *Creation Research Society Quarterly,* 7: 201–202.

Rutot, A. (1907) Un grave problem: une industrie humaine datant de l'époque oligocène. Comparison des outils avec ceux des Tasmaniens actuels. *Bulletin de la Société Belge de Géologie de Paléontologie et d'Hydrologie,* 21: 439–482.

Sankhyan, A. R. (1981) First evidence of early man from Haritalyangar area, Himalchal Pradesh. *Science and Culture,* 47: 358–359.

Senut, B. (1981) Humeral outlines in some hominoid primates and in Plio-pleistocene hominids. *American Journal of Physical Anthropology,* 56: 275–283.

Slemmons, D. B. (1966) Cenozoic volcanism of the central Sierra Nevada, California. *Bulletin of the California Division of Mines and Geology,* 190: 199–208.

Steiger, B. (1979) *Worlds Before Our Own.* New York: Berkley.

Stein, Philip L. and Rowe, Bruce M. (1993) *Physical Anthropology.* Fifth Edition. New York: McGraw-Hill.

Stewart, Wilson N. (1983) *Paleobotany and the Evolution of Plants.* Cambridge: Cambridge University Press.

Stopes, H. (1881) Traces of man in the Crag. *British Association for the Advancement of Science, Report of the Fifty-first Meeting,* p. 700.

Van Andel, T. H. (1981) Consider the incompleteness of the geological record. *Nature,* 294: 397–398.

Verworn, M. (1905) Die archaeolithische Cultur in den Hipparionschichten von Aurillac (Cantal). *Abhandlungen der königlichen Gesellschaft der Wissenschaften zu Göttingen, Mathematisch-Physikalische Klasse, Neue Folge,* 4(4): 3–60.

Von Dücker, Baron (1873) Sur la cassure artificelle d'ossements recuellis dans le terrain miocène de Pikermi. *Congrès International d'Anthropologie et d'Archéologie Préhistoriques. Bruxelles 1872, Compte Rendu,* pp. 104–107.

Whitney, J. D. (1880) The auriferous gravels of the Sierra Nevada of California. *Harvard University, Museum of Comparative Zoology Memoir* 6(1).

Wright, G. F. (1912) *Origin and Antiquity of Man.* Oberlin: Bibliotheca Sacra.

Zuckerman, S. (1954) Correlation of change in the evolution of higher primates. *In* Huxley, J., Hardy, A. C., and Ford, E. B., eds. *Evolution as a Process.* London: Allen and Unwin, pp. 300–352.

2

The Reception of *Forbidden Archeology:* An Encounter Between Western Science and a Non-Western Perspective on Human Antiquity

I presented this paper at the Sixth Annual Interdisciplinary Conference on Science and Culture, organized by the Kentucky State University Institute of Liberal Studies. The conference was held in Frankfort, Kentucky, March 30 – April 1, 1995.

In 1993 my book *Forbidden Archeology*, coauthored with Richard L. Thompson (Cremo and Thompson, 1993), was published. In his foreword, ethnomethodological sociologist Pierce J. Flynn, of California State University at San Marcos, noted:

> *Forbidden Archeology* does not conceal its own positioning on a relativist spectrum of knowledge production. The authors admit to their own sense of place in a knowledge universe with contours derived from personal experience with Vedic philosophy, religious perception, and Indian cosmology. Their intriguing discourse on the 'Evidence for Advanced Culture in Distant Ages' is light years from 'normal' Western science, and yet provokes a cohesion of probative thought. In my view, it is just this openness of subjective positioning that makes *Forbidden Archeology* an original and important contribution to postmodern scholarly studies now being done in sociology, anthropology, archeology, and the history of science and ideas. The authors' unique perspective provides postmodern scholars with an invaluable parallax view of historical scientific praxis, debate, and development.

In my own introduction to *Forbidden Archeology*, I noted:

> Richard Thompson and I are members of the Bhaktivedanta Institute, a branch of the International Society for Krishna Consciousness [ISKCON] that studies the relationship between modern science and the world view expressed in the Vedic literature. This institute was founded by our spiritual master, His Divine Grace A. C. Bhaktivedanta Swami Prabhupada, who encouraged us to critically examine the prevailing account of human origins and the methods by which it was established.

> From the Vedic literature, we derive the idea that the human race is of great antiquity. To conduct systematic research into the existing scientific literature on human antiquity, we expressed the Vedic idea in the form of a theory that various humanlike and apelike beings have coexisted for a long time.

To further contextually position myself, I offer that in 1976 I was initiated by Bhaktivedanta Swami Prabhupada (1896–1977) into the Brahma-Madhva-Gaudiya branch of Vaishnavism. The lineage of Gaudiya Vaishnavism, of which ISKCON is a modern institutional expression, extends back thousands of years, but the most recent representatives, of the nineteenth and twentieth centuries, are most important for this paper (see Goswami, S. D., 1980).

In the nineteenth century, India's British rulers offered Western education to Indian intellectuals. Their goal was to create a cadre of English speaking and English thinking Indians to assist them in their program of military, political, economic, religious, and cultural domination. This educational program successfully induced many Indian intellectuals, including Gaudiya Vaishnavas, to abandon their traditional culture and wisdom for Western modes of science and theology.

But in the middle of the nineteenth century, Kedarnatha Dutta (1838–1914), an English-speaking magistrate in the colonial administration, became interested in Gaudiya Vaishnavism. After his initiation by a Gaudiya Vaishnava guru, he inaugurated a revival of Gaudiya Vaishnavism among the intelligent classes, in Bengal and throughout India.

The central goal of Gaudiya Vaishnavism is cultivation of *bhakti*, or devotion to the Supreme Personality of Godhead, known by the name Krishna, "the all-attractive one." The *bhakti* school also incorporates a strong philosophical tradition, grounded in a literal, yet by no means naive, reading of the Vedic and Puranic texts, including their accounts of history and cosmogony.

Kedarnatha Dutta, later known by the title Bhaktivinoda Thakura, communicated Gaudiya Vaishnava teachings not only to his Indian contemporaries but also to the worldwide community of intellectuals. He reached the latter by publishing several works in English, among them *Shri Chaitanya Mahaprabhu: His Life and Precepts*, which appeared in 1896.

In the early twentieth century, Bhaktivinoda Thakura's son Bimala Prasada Dutta, later known as Bhaktisiddhanta Sarasvati Thakura (1874–1936), carried on the work of his father, expanding Gaudiya Vaishnavism in India and sending a few disciples to England and Germany. The European expeditions did not, however, yield any permanent results, and the missionaries returned home.

In 1922, my own spiritual master, then known as Abhay Charan De, met Bhaktisiddhanta Sarasvati Thakura in Calcutta, India. A recent graduate of Scottish Churches College in Calcutta and follower of Gandhi, De was somewhat skeptical of this very traditional guru. But he found himself won over by Bhaktisiddhanta Sarasvati's sharp intelligence and spiritual purity. At this first meeting, Bhaktisiddhanta Sarasvati requested De to spread the Gaudiya Vaishnava teachings throughout the world, especially in English. In 1933 De became the formal disciple of Bhaktisiddhanta Sarasvati, and in 1936, the year of Bhaktisiddhanta's death, he received a letter from him renewing his request that De teach in the West. In 1965, at the age of 69, De, now known as Bhaktivedanta Swami, came to New York City, where a year later he started ISKCON, the institutional vehicle through which the teachings of Gaudiya Vaishnavism were to spread quickly around the world.

Among these teachings were those connected with the origin of life and the universe. To scientifically establish these teachings, Bhaktivedanta Swami in 1975 organized the Bhaktivedanta Institute. Bhaktivedanta Swami envisioned the process of introducing Gaudiya Vaishnava teachings on the origin of life and the universe as one of direct confrontation with prevailing Western scientific ideas, such as Darwinian evolution.

My own involvement in the Bhaktivedanta Institute, as a Western convert to Gaudiya Vaishnavism, can thus be seen in the historical context of the larger cultural interaction between Western science and an Asian Indian knowledge tradition with vastly different views on natural history.

The Vedic and Puranic texts speak of a divine origin and spiritual purpose to life. According to the *Puranas*, humans have existed on this planet for hundreds of millions of years, and did not evolve from more apelike ancestors. The *Puranas* do, however, tell of intelligent races of apelike beings who coexisted with humans over vast periods of time.

In the 900 pages of *Forbidden Archeology*, my coauthor and I documented a great deal of scientifically reported evidence that, consistent with Puranic texts, extends the antiquity of our species millions of years into the past. This evidence was accumulated during eight years of research into the history of archeology and anthropology since the time of Darwin. We also documented how this evidence was systematically suppressed, through a social process of "knowledge filtration," by the adherents of an emerging consensus among Western scientists that humans were a fairly recent production of an evolutionary process.

Using the word archeology in Foucault's sense (Foucault, 1972), *Forbidden Archeology* is an archeology of archeology. It investigates the formation of archeological discourse over time, illuminating the subjects, objects, situations, themes, and practices of this discourse, including its practices of exclusion and suppression.

The primary goal of this paper is not to convince readers of *Forbidden Archeology's* picture of extreme human antiquity but to analyze the reception of *Forbidden Archeology* in various knowledge and discourse communities. Nevertheless, just to give an idea of the kind of evidence advanced in *Forbidden Archeology,* I shall provide two examples (much abbreviated from Cremo and Thompson, 1993).

In 1880, Harvard University's Peabody Museum published a massive work by J. D. Whitney, State Geologist of California, on the geology of the gold mining regions of California (Whitney 1880). In this book, Whitney catalogued hundreds of artifacts [see **Plates XII-XV**] and human skeletal remains found by miners, mining engineers, and mine supervisors deep inside gold mines at dozens of locations. All of the evidence gathered by Whitney indicated that the objects could not have entered from other levels. The gold-bearing gravels from which the objects were taken are, according to modern geological reports, anywhere from 10 to 50 million years old (Slemmons, 1966). Given current doctrine that anatomically modern humans came into existence about 100,000 years ago, the evidence reported by Whitney is quite extraordinary.

Whitney's evidence was dismissed, however, by William H. Holmes of the Smithsonian Institution, who said (Holmes, 1899), "Perhaps if Professor Whitney had fully appreciated the story of human evolution as it is understood today, he would have hesitated to announce the conclusions formulated, notwithstanding the imposing array of testimony with which he was confronted." So here we find a credible report of evidence for extreme human antiquity dismissed principally because it contradicted the emerging scientific consensus that humans evolved fairly recently.

Such "knowledge filtration," with theoretical preconceptions governing the acceptance and rejection of evidence, continued to the twentieth century. In 1979, Mary Leakey discovered at Laetoli, Tanzania, a set of footprints indistinguishable from anatomically modern human footprints (Leakey, 1979). These were found in solidified volcanic ash deposits about 3.6 million years old. Fossils of the foot bones of the early hominids of that time do not fit the Laetoli prints. At present, human beings like ourselves are the only creatures known to science that can make prints like those found at Laetoli. Nevertheless, most scientists, because of their theoretical preconceptions, are not prepared to consider that humans like ourselves may have made the Laetoli prints 3.6 million years ago.

Multiply the above two examples a hundred times, and one will get some idea of the quantity of evidence for extreme human antiquity contained in *Forbidden Archeology*.

Having set the stage for the appearance of *Forbidden Archeology*, let us place ourselves in the position of its principal author and imagine his feelings as the book began to make its way out into the world of reactive language. How would it be received, especially given his "openness of subjective positioning"? I was, of course, hopeful. In particular, I hoped my book would have some impact on the community of scholars practicing the sociology of scientific knowledge (SSK).

With this in mind, I sent a copy of *Forbidden Archeology* to SSK scholar Michael Mulkay, who replied in a handwritten letter dated May 18, 1993:

> I have not yet read your manuscript; nor can I at present see a space in which I would have time to read it. I realise this must be extremely irritating to you, after all your effort and your hope of making an impact. But your potential audience, including me, are all obsessively involved in their own affairs. It takes a long time for academic books to have any effect. Sometimes it takes years for them to be reviewed. What I regard as my two best books met with a profound silence. I hope you do much better than that. But I cannot at this moment comment on your text.

Mainstream Archeology and Anthropology

So were the 900 pages of *Forbidden Archeology* to be met with the profoundest of academic silences? I contemplated the prospect of no comment on my text in dark and dreary interior monologues worthy of a narrator of a tale by Edgar Allen Poe. Fortunately, the silence was soon broken, not by a tapping at my door but by a review (Marks, 1994) appearing in the January 1994 issue of *American Journal for Physical Anthropology (AJPA)*. Apparently, *Forbidden Archeology* posed a challenge that could not be ignored.

In a perceptive essay, A. J. Greimas offered a semiotic exploration of a challenge's narrative dimension (Greimas, 1990). "A challenge," he said, "is a confrontation that is perceived as an affront." *Forbidden Archeology* was certainly perceived as such by Jonathan Marks, book review editor for *AJPA*.

Arrogating to himself the reviewing of *Forbidden Archeology* (instead of assigning it to an outside reviewer), Marks (1994) adopted a combative and derisive stance, characterizing the book as "Hindu-oid creationist drivel" and "a veritable cornucupia of dreck."

Why did Marks respond at all? According to Greimas (1990), a challenge consists of a challenging subject inviting a challenged subject to carry out a particular narrative program while at the same time warning the challenged subject "as to his modal insufficiency (his 'not-being-able-to-do') for the carrying out of that program." The sending of *Forbidden Archeology* to the book review editor of *AJPA* was consciously intended as just such an invitation for physical anthropologists to carry out their narrative program (of establishing their truth of human evolution)—with the implication they would not be able to do so in the face of the evidence documented in *Forbidden Archeology*.

A challenge may further be classed (Greimas, 1990) as a "constraining communication." In other words, "When faced with an affirmation of his incompetence, the challenged subject cannot avoid answering because silence would inevitably be interpreted as an admission of that incompetence" (Greimas, 1990). Marks obviously felt constrained to respond to *Forbidden Archeology*, thus accepting its challenge contract and thereby placing the challenged subject (Marks, *AJPA*, physical anthropology, Western science) and the challenging subject (Cremo, *Forbidden Archeology*, Bhaktivedanta Institute, Gaudiya Vaishnavism) on an equal subjective footing. As Greimas (1990) noted, "If the challenge is to work properly there must be an objective complicity between the manipulator [i.e. the challenging subject] and the manipulated [i.e. the challenged subject] . . . It is unthinkable for a knight to challenge a peasant, and the converse is unthinkable also."

Marks's response to the challenge of *Forbidden Archeology* contained elements of bravado, showing him an able defender of physical anthropology, but also elements of unconscious fear, showing him as a threatened member of an unstable discipline in danger of dismemberment by dark forces within and without.

Regarding the latter, Marks (1994) first alluded to "the Fundamentalist push to get 'creation science' into the classroom." The Christian fundamentalist enemy is apparently alive and kicking, still "pushing" to get into territory physical anthropology regards as its own ("the classroom").

Marks (1994) then admitted that "the rich and varied origins myths of all cultures are alternatives to contemporary evolution." His use of the present tense ("are alternatives") instead of the past tense ("were alternatives") is a reflection that physical anthropology, in the postcolonial era, feels once more threatened by living alternative cosmologies that not long ago were securely categorized as cognitively dead myths. In other words, it is not only the Christian fundamentalists who are enemies, but all alternative cosmologies and (Marks 1994) "all religious-based science, like the present volume" (i. e. *Forbidden Archeology*).

Marks (1994) also alluded to "goofy popular anthropology" and its literature. These pose a secular, populist threat to modern physical anthropology and archeology (as in the case of the ongoing reports of Bigfoot and transoceanic diffusionist contacts between North America and the ancient civilizations of Asia, Africa, and Europe).

Of greatest concern to Marks, however, were traitors in the ranks of the academic community itself. Marks (1994) described sociologist Pierce Flynn, who contributed a foreword to *Forbidden Archeology*, as "a curious personage." He went on to castigate Flynn for "placing this work within postmodern scholarship."

In short, Marks identified *Forbidden Archeology*, quite correctly in my view, with an array of perceived enemies at the boundaries of his discipline, and within the walls of the disciplinary sanctuary itself. These enemies included fundamentalists, creationists, cultural revivalists, religion-based sciences (especially Hindu-based), populist critiques of science, purveyors of anomalies, and finally, the postmodern academic critics of science in the fields of sociology, history, and philosophy, what to speak of in anthropology itself. Later, I shall suggest how we might see archeology and anthropology as disciplinary partners of their perceived enemies, sharing a common discursive domain.

After Marks's review appeared, I exchanged some letters with Matt Cartmill, editor of the *AJPA* regarding a rejoinder (I asserted that Marks had misrepresented the substance of the book). But Cartmill declined to allow a rejoinder, saying finally in a letter dated August 30, 1994, "In short, I still think that Dr. Marks's review, despite its derisive tone (to which you have a right to take exception), was essentially accurate... My decision of May 20 accordingly stands."

All in all, I was pleased with Marks's response to *Forbidden Archeology*. The provocation had been designed to evoke just such a response, which I anticipated would be tactically useful. And it was. First, Marks's refusal to come to grips with the substance of the book, namely the factual evidence, lent support to the book's theme of knowledge suppression. Second, his derisive name-calling helped get media attention for the popular edition of *Forbidden Archeology*, titled *The Hidden History of the Human Race*. Excerpts from Marks's review were prominently featured in the book, and when seen alongside positive reviews, gave the impression of a serious work that was stirring considerable controversy. Third, I envisioned that Marks's remarks would provide material for scholarly papers such as this one. And the main news for this paper is that Marks's review objectifies a cognitive clash between a science informed by Gaudiya Vaishnava teachings and traditional Western science, with the clash manifested in the privileged textual space of Western science itself.

If the pages of a discipline's journals are one locus of privileged discourse, the conferences of a discipline are another. A few months after the *AJPA* review, the publishing branch of the Bhaktivedanta Institute took a book display table at the annual meeting of the American Association of Physical Anthropologists. Eight physical anthropologists purchased copies of *Forbidden Archeology* on the spot, and I assume others ordered later from sales materials they took with them.

Also in 1994, Kenneth L. Feder reviewed *Forbidden Archeology* in *Geoarchaeology: An International Journal* (Feder 1994). Feder's tone was one of amazement rather than derision:

> *Forbidden Archeology: The Hidden History of the Human Race* is not the usual sort of publication reviewed in this or, for that matter, any other archeology or anthropology journal. Neither author is an archeologist or paleoanthropologist; one is a mathematician, the other a writer. So far as I can tell neither has any personal experience with the process of archaeological field work or laboratory analysis.

Nevertheless, *Forbidden Archeology* rated a four-page review in *Geoarcheology*, one of the prominent archeology journals.

What was going on here? I submit that Feder and the editors of *Geoarchaeology* were reacting to *Forbidden Archeology* in much the same way as some art critics of the 1960s reacted to the Brillo box sculptures of Andy Warhol. The Brillo boxes were not art, it appeared to some critics, but these critics could not help commenting upon them as if they were art (Yau, 1993). And thus the boxes were, after all, art, or as good as art. I suppose it is true, in some sense, that *Forbidden Archeology* is not real archeology, and that I am not a real archeologist (or historian of archeology). And, for that matter, neither is this paper a "real" paper, and neither am I a "real" scholar. I am an agent of Gaudiya Vaishnavism, with an assigned project of deconstructing a paradigm, and this paper and *Forbidden Archeology* are part of that project. And yet *Forbidden Archeology* is reviewed in *AJPA* and *Geoarchaeology*, and this paper is read by me at an academic conference on science and culture, just like Warhol's Brillo boxes were displayed in galleries for purchase by collectors rather than stacked in supermarkets for throwing out later.

Perhaps what was so disconcerting about Warhol's Brillo boxes was that their idiosyncratic artificial reality somehow called into question the hitherto naively accepted "natural" supermarket reality of the ubiquitous everyday Brillo boxes, and hence of all everyday public culture "things." The same with *Forbidden Archeology*. Its intended artificialness, its not quite seamless mimicry of a "genuine" text, called fascinated attention to itself as it simultaneously undermined the natural artifactlike impression of the so-called "real" archeology texts. But there is a difference between *Forbidden Archeology* and Warhol's Brillo boxes. If you open up a Warhol Brillo box, you won't find any Brillo pads, but if you open up *Forbidden Archeology* you will find archeology, although of an unusual sort.

After all, I am not simply a literary pop artist who delights in producing artificial archeology text surfaces; there is some substantiality to the project. I am a representative of Gaudiya Vaishnavism, and my purpose is to challenge some fundamental concepts of Western science. This did not escape Feder, who wrote: "The book itself represents something perhaps not seen before; we can fairly call it 'Krishna creationism' with no disrespect intended."

Feder (1994), sustaining his mode of amazement, then wrote about this new invasion, this "something perhaps not seen before":

> The basic premises of the authors are breathtaking and can be summarized rather briefly:
>
> • The prevailing paradigm of human evolution . . . is wholly untenable.
>
> • There is what amounts to a passive conspiracy (the authors call it a "knowledge filter") to suppress a huge body of data that contradicts our prevailing paradigm.
>
> • These suppressed data include archaeological evidence in the form of incised bones, lithics, and anatomically modern human skeletal remains that date to well before the commonly accepted appearance of *Australopithecus*.
>
> • This purported evidence indicates that "beings quite like ourselves have been around as far back as we care to look—in the Pliocene, Miocene, Oligocene, Eocene and beyond (p. 525). The authors cite "humanlike footprints" in Kentucky dating to about 300,000,000 (not a misprint) years ago (p. 456).
>
> • All evidence of human evolution from an apelike ancestor is suspect at best and much of it can be explained as the fossil remains of nonancestral hominids or even extinct apes (some *Homo erectus* specimens, it is proposed, might represent an extinct species of giant gibbon [p. 465]).
>
> • Some of these nonancestral hominids have survived into the present as indicated by reports of Bigfoot, Yeti, and the like.
>
> • There is evidence of anomalously advanced civilizations extending back millions of years into the past.

I very much appreciated this accurate representation of the "breathtaking" substance of *Forbidden Archeology* (as compared with Marks's calculated misrepresentation). Feder (1994) further noted:

> While decidedly antievolutionary in perspective, this work is not the ordinary variety of antievolutionism in form, content, or style. In distinction to the usual brand of such writing, the authors use original sources and the book is well written. Further, the overall tone of the work is far superior to that exhibited in ordinary creationist literature. Nonetheless, I suspect that creationism is at the root of the authors' argument, albeit of a sort not commonly seen before.

In the above passage, the Brillo box phenomenon again displays itself. The technically convincing imitation of a well written archeology text somewhat disarmed Feder. But like the critics of Warhol, he showed he was not to be fooled by surface appearances and could see what the artist/author was really up to. He knew what was meant. However, I propose the "meaning" lies not so much beneath the surface of the *Forbidden Archeology* text as in the temporal and spatial continuities and discontinuities of this textual surface with other textual surfaces, not excluding Feder's review and this paper.

Feder (1994) then addressed the Gaudiya Vaishnava element of the *Forbidden Archeology* text:

> When you attempt to deconstruct a well-accepted paradigm, it is reasonable to expect that a new paradigm be suggested in its place. The authors of *Forbidden Archeology* do not do this, and I would like to suggest a reason for their neglect here. Wishing to appear entirely scientific, the authors hoped to avoid a detailed discussion of their own beliefs (if not through evolution, how? If not within the last four million years, when?) since, I would contend, these are based on a creationist view, but not the kind we are all familiar with.

Here Feder is being somewhat unfair. The authors were not avoiding anything. The book as conceived would have introduced an alternative paradigm based on Gaudiya Vaishnava texts. But as I said in the introduction to *Forbidden Archeology* (Cremo and Thompson, 1993):

> Our research program led to results we did not anticipate, and hence a book much larger than originally envisioned. Because of this, we have not been able to develop in this volume our ideas about an alternative to current theories of human origins. We are therefore planning a second volume relating our extensive research results in this area to our Vedic source material.

This book is still in the research and writing stage. But in a paper presented at the World Archaeological Congress (Cremo, 1994) I have outlined in some detail a summary presentation of the Gaudiya Vaishnava account of human origins and antiquity. Furthermore, the relevant source materials are easily available to most readers, many of whom will already know something of Indian cosmology. Feder continued:

> The authors are open about their membership in the Bhaktivedanta Institute, which is a branch of the International Society for Krishna Consciousness, and the book is dedicated to their "spiritual master," the group's founder. They make a reasonable request regarding their affiliation with this organization: "That our theoretical outlook is derived from the Vedic literature should not disqualify it" (p. xxxvi). Fair enough, but what is their "theoretical outlook?" Like fundamentalist Christians they avoid talking about the religious content of their perspective, so we can

only guess at it.

Again, somewhat unfair. The specific religious content of our perspective was openly acknowledged in the introduction to *Forbidden Archeology* (Cremo and Thompson, 1993). Although the detailed development of this perspective was postponed to a forthcoming volume, the pointers to the perspective were clear enough to remove it from the realm of guesswork. Feder (1994) himself did not have to look very far to find out about it:

> Where does Hindu literature say humanity originated and when? According to Hindu cosmology, the cosmos passes through cycles called *kalpas*, each of which corresponds to 4.32 billion earth years (Basham, 1959). During each *kalpa*, the universe is created and then absorbed. Each *kalpa* is divided into 14 *manvantaras*, each lasting 300,000,000 years (the age of the Kentucky footprints), and separated by lengthy periods. Within each *manvantara* the world is created with human beings more or less fully formed, and then destroyed, only to be created once again in the next *manvantara*.

Yes. And I said essentially the same thing in my above mentioned World Archaeological Congress paper (Cremo 1994). Feder (1994) then began to bring his review to a close: "We all know what happens when we mix a literal interpretation of the Judeo-Christian creation myth with human paleontology: we get scientific creationism." We also get scientific evolutionism.

The two are more closely related than the partisans of either would care to admit. As I noted in my World Archaeological Congress paper (Cremo 1994), Judeo-Christian cosmology, based on linear vectorial time, "involves a unique act of creation, a unique appearance of the human kind, and a unique history of salvation, culminating in a unique denouement in the form of a last judgement. The drama occurs only once." I went on to say (Cremo 1994):

> Modern historical sciences share the basic Judeo-Christian assumptions about time and humanity. The universe we inhabit is a unique occurrence. Humans have arisen once on this planet. The history of our species is regarded as a unique though unpredestined evolutionary pathway. The future pathway of our species is also unique. Although this pathway is officially unpredictable, the myths of science project a possible overcoming of death by evolving, space-traveling humans . . . One is tempted to propose that the modern human evolutionary account is a Judeo-Christian heterodoxy, which covertly retains fundamental structures of Judeo-Christian cosmology, salvation history, and eschatology while overtly dispensing with the Biblical account of divine intervention in the origin of species, including our own.

But let us get back to Feder's final words:

> It seems we now know what happens when we mix a literal inter-
> pretation of the Hindu myth of creation with human paleontology; we
> get the antievolutionary Krishna creationism of *Forbidden Archeology*,
> where human beings do not evolve and where the fossil evidence for
> anatomically modern humans dates as far back as the beginning of the
> current *manvantara* (Feder, 1994).

Of course, I did not invent the fossil evidence showing that anatomically modern
humans existed "as far back as the beginning of the current *manvantara*." Abundant
examples are present in the archeological literature of the past 150 years. *Forbidden
Archeology* merely displayed that evidence and demonstrated how it was unfairly set
aside by misapplication of evidential standards.

If I were a scholar trying to make a career in the modern university system, a review like Feder's would be disheartening. But I am not trying to advance an academic
career for myself. I stand outside that system. Indeed, I am part of another system.
And my goal is to engage the system to which Feder belongs in a textual exchange with
the system to which I belong. And in that sense *Forbidden Archeology* can be called
successful. In the privileged textual space of Western science we see the intrusion of
alien texts, not as passive objects of study but as vital resisting and aggressing entities.
There has been a change in the discursive field. A new vortex has formed. The texts of
Gaudiya Vaishnava cosmology, mediated by an array of convincingly contoured archeological textuality (*Forbidden Archeology*), have become displayed in a new textual
space, a space that must now configure itself differently. *Forbidden Archeology* is not a
random event, a ripple that will soon fade, but the foreshock of a tectonic movement of
cultures. Transnationalism and multiculturalism are not merely concepts entertained
by departmental chairs and university administrators; they are brute objective realities.

These realities are reflected in the responses to *Forbidden Archeology* in *AJPA* and
Geoarchaeology. Reviews and brief notices of *Forbidden Archeology* have also appeared
in *L'Homme* (35, 173–174), *Journal of Field Archeology* (21, 112), *Antiquity* (67, 904),
and *Ethology, Ecology, and Evolution* (6, 461). Another full review is forthcoming in
L'Anthropologie.

Responses from individual scholars are also illuminating. In a letter to me dated
November 26, 1993, K. N. Prasad, former director of the Archaeological Survey of
India, praised *Forbidden Archeology* as "an excellent reference book, which will act as a
catalyst for further research on a subject of immense interest." An important audience
for *Forbidden Archeology*, which is an open defense of the reality of India's Puranic literature, is the English-educated Indian elite represented by Prasad. It may be recalled
that *Forbidden Archeology* traces its own lineage to Bhaktivinoda Thakura, the English-
educated magistrate who in the late nineteenth century initiated an effort to reclaim
the Indian intelligentsia from its immersion in nascent Western modernity.

Bhaktivinoda Thakura, as we have seen, also initiated an approach on behalf of
Gaudiya Vaishnavism to the Western intelligentsia itself. *Forbidden Archeology* is part

of that ongoing approach. William W. Howells, one of the major architects of the current paradigm of human evolution, wrote to me on August 10, 1993: "Thank you for sending me a copy of *Forbidden Archeology*, which represents much careful effort in critically assembling published materials. I have given it a good examination. . . . To have modern human beings . . . appearing . . . at a time when even simple primates did not exist as possible ancestors . . . would be devastating to the whole theory of evolution, which has been pretty robust up to now. . . . The suggested hypothesis would demand a kind of process which could not possibly be accommodated to the evolutionary theory as we know it, and I should think it requires an explanation of that aspect. It also would give the Scientific Creationists some problems as well! Thank you again for letting me see the book. I look forward to viewing its impact." I sent *Forbidden Archeology* to Howells, conscious of its relation to the project begun in the last century by Bhaktivinoda Thakura.

And finally a few words from Richard Leakey's letter to me of November 6, 1993: "Your book is pure humbug and does not deserve to be taken seriously by anyone but a fool. Sadly there are some, but that's part of selection and there is nothing that can be done." These words, like those of Jonathan Marks (1994), were reproduced on the cover and in the front matter of the popular edition of *Forbidden Archeology*, inspiring sales and media coverage.

All in all, *Forbidden Archeology*, inspired by Gaudiya Vaishnava teachings on human origins and antiquity, seems to have created a minor sensation within mainstream archeology and anthropology. But that is only part of the story. Indeed, we have only begun to trace the impact of *Forbidden Archeology*.

History, Sociology, and Philosophy

Let us now turn from mainstream science to mainstream science studies—the history, sociology, and philosophy of science.

On November 12, 1993, David Oldroyd of the School of Science and Technology Studies at the University of New South Wales in Australia wrote to the Bhaktivedanta Institute:

> I have been sent a copy of your publication by M. A. Cremo and R. L. Thompson, *Forbidden Archeology*, and have been asked to write an essay review of the book for the journal *Social Studies of Science*.
>
> I have already read the book and have found it exceedingly interesting. However, in order to write a satisfactory review of the book, I should like to know more of its provenance. Could you, therefore, please send me some information about your Institute. . . .
>
> I am myself a historian of science, and my special interest is in the history of geology. Fairly recently, I have been taking more interest in the history of paleoanthropology. I have two students who are also interested in the book.
>
> While I would not, at this stage, wish you to think that I am propos-

ing to offer a ringing endorsement of *Forbidden Archeology*, I think I can fairly say that I shall be able to give it wide notice through a review in a prestigious journal like *Social Studies of Science*. And I think that it should be possible for me to say quite a lot about the implications of the book for studies in the sociology of science and the sociology of knowledge. I do think the book deserves serious consideration.

The promised review has not yet come out [eventually, it was published: Wodak, J. and Oldroyd, D. (1996) 'Vedic creationism': a further twist to the evolution debate. *Social Studies of Science*, 26: 192–213.]. But I did receive a letter (November 12, 1993) from one of Oldroyd's graduate students, Jo Wodak, who was about to begin her thesis:

> I would like to base this on your book, *Forbidden Archeology*, as a case study of the social processes that determine what is "acceptable" within the current paradigm for the "science" of palaeo-archaeology. . . . I have spent part of the last semester reviewing the debate on the origin of modern humans. . . . So I have some familiarity with the field, but I am amazed that I have not come across even a whisper of the material upon which your argument is based! But I have come across enough examples of the suppression of unorthodox views in other sciences to have no doubt about the veracity of your research.

Wodak's readiness to accept the possibility of substantial suppression of controversial evidence and unorthodox views is welcome. From the standpoint of Gaudiya Vaishnavism, *Forbidden Archeology's* deconstruction of modern science involves two issues. The first is the origin and antiquity of the human species. The second is the process by which knowledge of the first issue may best be obtained. In this regard, *Forbidden Archeology* is essentially an argument for the epistemic superiority of received transcendental knowledge to empirically manufactured knowledge. Exposing the shortcomings of the latter increases the viability of the former (the sacred texts of Gaudiya Vaishnavism).

In December of 1994, I attended the World Archaeological Congress 3 in New Delhi, India, where I presented my paper (Cremo, 1994) titled "Puranic Time and the Archeological Record." Several Indian archeologists and anthropologists congratulated me on the paper and requested copies. They found the image of a Western convert to Gaudiya Vaishnavism presenting such a paper at a major scientific gathering intriguing. While standing in one of the lobbies of the Taj Palace Hotel between sessions, I was approached by Tim Murray, an archeologist from La Trobe University in Australia. "Oh, so you're Cremo," he said. He had recognized my name on my badge, and announced to me that he had recently written a review of Forbidden Archeology for *British Journal for the History of Science (BJHS)*. Murray told me that he teaches history of archeology and that he had recommended *Forbidden Archeology* to his graduate students. He told them that if one was going to make a case for extreme human antiquity, *Forbidden Archeology* was the way to do it. I have not yet seen the *BJHS* review. [Later,

I did see it: Murray, T. (1995) Review of *Forbidden Archeology. British Journal for the History of Science,* 28: 377–379.]

At the 1994 annual meeting of the History of Science Society (HSS), A. Bowdoin Van Riper, an authority on the history of human antiquity investigations, requested from a Bhaktivedanta Institute publishing representative a review copy of *Forbidden Archeology.* Van Riper said he sometimes reviewed books for *Isis,* the journal of the History of Science Society. The representative told Van Riper that he was not authorized to give away a free copy. When informed of this later, I personally sent a copy of *Forbidden Archeology* to Van Riper, who replied on January 5, 1995: "The premise is audacious, to say the least, and intriguing to me if only for that reason." I am hopeful he will review the book for *Isis.* There is also a chance for a review of *Forbidden Archeology* in *Bulletin of the History of Archaeology.*

On September 28, 1994, Henry H. Bauer, book review editor for *Journal of Scientific Exploration,* wrote to our publishing branch requesting a copy of *Forbidden Archeology.* Bauer stated:

> We review books on the nature of science and books that describe current scientific knowledge as well as works on unorthodox scientific claims. With respect to the latter, the *Journal* contains material that seeks to "advance the study . . . of any aspect of anomalous phenomena, including . . . 1) Phenomena outside the current paradigms of one or more of the sciences such as the physical, psychological, biological, or earth sciences. 2) Phenomena within scientific paradigms but at variance with current scientific knowledge. 3) The scientific methods used to study anomalous phenomena. 4) The . . . impact of anomalous phenomena on science and society.

I am eagerly looking forward to the reviews of *Forbidden Archeology* in *Social Studies of Science, British Journal for the History of Science,* and *Journal of Scientific Exploration.* Until they come out, it is difficult to gauge the impact the book is having in the science studies community. It is interesting that *Forbidden Archeology* is being treated as both a science text and a science studies text.

Religion Studies

From the beginning, I thought the acknowledged Gaudiya Vaishnava foundation of *Forbidden Archeology* would draw the attention of religion scholars. A review is forthcoming in *Science & Religion News,* published by the Institute on Religion in an Age of Science.

Early in 1994, Mikael Rothstein, of the Institute for the History of Religion at the University of Copenhagen, wrote a major article about *Forbidden Archeology* for publication in *Politiken,* Denmark's largest and most influential newspaper (Rothstein, 1994). In a letter to me dated February 2, 1994, Rothstein said:

The text refers to your points through examples and compares your message to that of the evolutionists at Darwin's time in order to demonstrate how the positions have changed. Today the creationists deliver the provoking news. Previously this was the function of the evolutionists. The article acknowledges your solid argumentation, which is often more than hard to refute, but I do not present any judgement as to whether you are right in your conclusions. . . . However, I find the book amazing in many ways and hopefully I have made my modest contribution to get it sold. . . . For the record: The article is placed in the specific science-section of the paper, and it is entitled (as you may understand after all) "Forbidden Archeology." The subtitle reads: "Religious scientists provoke the theory of evolution." "Religious" because I mention your affiliation with ISKCON and state that you have a religious interest in your otherwise scholarly enterprise.

The *Politiken* article also mentions my affiliation with the Bhaktivedanta Institute, and identifies my spiritual commitment to Vaishnavism. The article resulted in inquiries from one of Denmark's largest publishers about translation rights for *Forbidden Archeology*.

Out of the Mainstream

Up to now, we have been looking at reactions to *Forbidden Archeology* from mainstream scholars and journals. Now let us move out of the mainstream. As we do, you will notice a change in climate, as we encounter some unqualified endorsements of *Forbidden Archeology*.

In the fall 1994 issue of *Journal of Unconventional History*, *Forbidden Archeology* was one of several books discussed in a review essay by Hillel Schwarz:

> *Forbidden Archeology* takes the current conventions of decoding to their extreme. The authors find modern *homo sapiens* to be continuous contemporaries of the apelike creatures from whom evolutionary biologists usually trace human descent or bifurcation, thus confirming those Vedic sources that presume the nearly illimitable antiquity of the human race—all toward the implicit end of preparing us for that impending transformation of global consciousness at which Bhaktivedanta brochures regularly hint. . . . Despite its unhidden religious partisanship, the book deserves a reckoning in this review for its embrace of a global humanity distinct from other primates. . . . Meditating upon our uniqueness (I am here supplying the missing links of the thesis) we may come to realize that what can change (awaken) humanity is no mere biochemical exfoliation but a work of the spirit, in touch with (and devoted to) the ancient, perfect, perfectly sufficient, unchanging wisdom of the Vedic masters (Schwarz, 1994).

William Corliss is the publisher of several "sourcebooks" of well documeted anomalous evidence in different fields of science. Most university libraries have copies. Corliss also sells books by other authors, which he lists in a supplement to his newsletter. In *Science Frontiers Book Supplement Number 89* (September–October 1993), Corliss prominently featured *Forbidden Archeology*:

> *Forbidden Archeology* has so much to offer anomalists that it is difficult to know where to start. One's first impression is that of a massive volume bearing a high price tag. Believe me, *Forbidden Archeology* is a great bargain, not only on a cents-per-page basis but in its systematic collection of data challenging the currently accepted and passionately defended scenario of human evolution. . . . Here are fat chapters on incised bones, eoliths, crude tools, and skeletal remains—all properly documented and detailed, but directly contradicting the textbooks and museum exhibits. . . .The salient theme of this huge book is that human culture is much older than claimed (Corliss, 1993).

I liked having *Forbidden Archeology* in Corliss's catalog. I knew it might generate some sales to university libraries. But more importantly, Corliss was a pipeline to thousands of readers who were deeply interested in the whole subject of anomalous evidence. This audience (the serious scientific anomaly community) was quite prepared to accept that whole areas of science were completely wrong and that evidence was being unfairly suppressed. But this audience was also interested in good documentation for such claims.

Forbidden Archeology has also been reviewed in *Fortean Times* (Moore, 1993), a journal dedicated to the study of "Fortean phenomena" (extreme scientific anomalies); in *FATE* (Swann, 1994), a popular magazine featuring accounts of the paranormal; and in the journals and newsletters of societies focusing on anomalous archeological discoveries and evidence for pre-Columbian contacts between the Americas and the Old World (e. g. Hunt, 1993). Needless to say, the reviews are positive.

In *Forbidden Archeology,* I documented the work of scientists who held positions in mainstream science institutions but who had reported on anomalous archeological discoveries. Some of these scientists, as expected, were very pleased with *Forbidden Archeology.* Virginia Steen-McIntyre, a geologist, had reported a date of over 250,000 years for the Hueyatlaco site near Puebla, Mexico. Thereafter, her career trajectory took a sharp turn downwards. About *Forbidden Archeology,* she said in a letter dated October 30, 1993:

> What an eye-opener! I didn't realize how many sites and how much data are out there that don't fit modern concepts of human evolution. Somewhere down the line the god of the Vedas and the God of the Bible will clash . . . . But until then the servants of both can agree on one thing—human evolution is for the birds! . . . I'm doing my bit getting the publicity out for your book. Have ordered a copy for the local library.

... I'm also sending the book review that appeared in Sept./Oct. *Science Frontiers Book Supplement* to various friends and colleagues (almost 50 so far). I predict the book will become an underground classic. Whether it will break into the mainstream media is questionable—the Illuminati are tightly in control there.

Forbidden Archeology, like a robot surveyor on Mars, was sending back signals to me as it mapped a complex cognitive domain. I am reporting in this paper primarily the preliminary basic mappings of that terrain, but this snippet from Virginia Steen-McIntyre provides a higher resolution look at the mapping process in a confined space. Observe the connections—the copy to the public library, the link with the Corliss newsletter book supplement, the mailing to friends and colleagues (working in geology, archeology, and anthropology), the pointer to other discourse communities (the conspiracy theorists), and reference to the metarelationships among Vedas, Bible, and Science. I shall return to this theme later—*Forbidden Archeology* as robot mapper of alien discourse terrains, prober of new channels and portals of complex border crossing connectivity. For those concerned about the future of scholarly life on this planet, take note—this is where we are heading.

New Age

In *International Journal of Alternative and Complementary Medicine (IJACM),* John Davidson (1994) reviewed *Forbidden Archeology*, saying:

> Michael Cremo and Richard Thompson are . . . to be congratulated on spending eight years producing the only definitive, precise, exhaustive and complete record of practically all the fossil finds of man, regardless of whether they fit the established scientific theories or not. To say that research is painstaking is a wild understatement. No other book of this magnitude and caliber exists. It should be compulsory reading for every first year biology, archaeology and anthropology student—and many others, too!

IJACM can fairly be placed within or on the borders of the New Age scientific discourse community. The same is true of the *Adventures Unlimited 1994 Catalog*, which featured *Forbidden Archeology* in its new book section, with a blurb describing *Forbidden Archeology* as "a thick (nearly 1000 page) scholarly work that confronts traditional science and archaeology with overwhelming evidence of advanced and ancient civilizations." The catalog cover has these subtitles: "Inside...Ancient Wisdom, Lost Cities, Anti-Gravity, Tesla Technology, Secret Societies, Free Energy Science, Exotic Travel... and more!" and "Frontiers in Travel, Archaeology, Science & History." As an author with pretensions to academic respectability, am I embarrassed to find my book in such company? No. I simply notice that *Forbidden Archeology* has mapped both *American Journal of Physical Anthropology* and *Adventures Unlimited 1994 Catalog* as part of its discursive domain. And in addition to simply noting the mapping, I will offer a suggestion that the easy mobility of the exploratory text called *Forbidden Archeology* through the different regions of its domain points to the disintegration of what one might call the Enlightenment consensus. The Enlightment consensus was marked by orogenic episodes that cut an existing domain of discourse (in which Newton could write both his *Principia* and his *Alchemy*) into noncommunicating domains of science and "pseudoscience." All that is now changing, perhaps faster than we can accurately measure.

Barbara and Dennis Tedlock, editors of *American Anthropologist*, have noted (Tedlock and Tedlock, 1995):

> New Age titles in bookstores outnumber anthropological ones, and the kinds of titles we once disliked seeing in the same section with anthropology or archaeology now occupy whole sections of their own— the shamanism, goddess worship, and New Age sections. These shifts reflect social and cultural developments that are well under way not only in this country but all over the world—north or south, east or west. The urban participants in the New Age and related movements have lines of communication that reach into the remotest deserts, jungles, and mountains of our own traditional field research. In some ways these developments look like a privatization of the educational tasks we once saw as our own.

Nonmainstream Religion

In the realm of nonmainstream religion, *Forbidden Archeology* has found its way into many unusual spaces. In a letter to me dated June 28, 1993, Duane Gish of the Institute for Creation Research (ICR), a Christian fundamentalist organization, wrote that he found *Forbidden Archeology* "quite interesting and perhaps useful to us." In 1994, I visited the ICR in Santee, California, and spoke with Gish, who purchased copies of *Forbidden Archeology* for the ICR library and research staff.

During 1994, I appeared on fundamentalist Christian radio and television programs, which were, of course, favorable to the antievolution message of *Forbidden Archeology*. This was true despite the displays of sectarian feeling Christian fundamentalists sometimes manifest in relation to Asian religions, especially those popularly labeled as "new religions."

Siegried Scherer, a microbiologist at a German university and also a young-earth Christian creationist, contributed a jacket blurb for *Forbidden Archeology* even though aware of the Gaudiya Vaishnava backgrounds of the authors.

The Vishwa Hindu Parishad (VHP) is a worldwide Hindu religious and cultural organization. It is generally seen as conservative, even fundamentalist. On August 2, 1993, Kishor Ruperelia, general secretary of the VHP in the United Kingdom, faxed this message to *Back to Godhead,* the bimonthly magazine of the International Society for Krishna Consciousness (ISKCON):

I have just received the May/June 1993 issue (Vol. 27, No. 3) of the magazine *Back to Godhead*, and I am writing with reference to the condensed form article on the book *Forbidden Archeology*, written by ISKCON researchers Michael Cremo and Richard Thompson. . . . Having read the article, I consider it very important that a meeting be held between the authors of the book and some of the Indian scholars who are in the USA at present to participate in a world conference organized by the VHP of America under style of "Global Vision 2000" to take place in Washington DC on Aug 6ᵗʰ, 7ᵗʰ & 8ᵗʰ. . . . Inspired by the Vedic writings and encouraged by His Divine Grace A. C. Bhaktivedanta Swami Prabhupada, the scholarly authors have made a tremendous and painstaking effort to compile and compare umpteen evidences to make archeological scholars rethink about the predominant paradigm on human origin and antiquity.

Of course, this is just the sort of reaction one might expect from a conservative, traditionalist Hindu cultural and religious organization such as the VHP. Less expected would be the extremely favorable review of *Forbidden Archeology* by Islamic scholar Salim-ur-rahman (1994) that appeared in a Pakistani newspaper. Here is an excerpt:

Forbidden Archeology is a serious and thought-provoking book, reminding us that the history of the human race may be far more older than we are led to imagine. . . . In a way, this all ties up with the remarks attributed to the Holy Prophet (PBUH), Hadhrat Ali and Imam Iafar Sadiq in which they said that the Adam we are descended from was preceded by numerous Adams and their progeny.

Forbidden Archeology possesses a remarkable capacity for border crossing—here we find literalist followers of Christianity, Hinduism, and Islam (not always the best of friends in some situations) according a respectful welcome to a text with Gaudiya Vaishnava foundations. And it does not stop there.

Libraries and Media

By having a librarian do an online computer search, I have learned that dozens of university libraries have acquired *Forbidden Archeology* even though the Bhaktivedanta Institute publishing branch has not yet made a systematic approach to them (we have been waiting for some of the forthcoming reviews in academic journals to actually come forth). There have also been some spontaneous requests for inspection copies by university teaching professors, and a search of sales reports from our book trade distributor shows a good number of orders from university bookstores.

Internationally, several publishers have been expressing interest in *Forbidden Archeology* and its popular version *The Hidden History of the Human Race*. A German edition of *Forbidden Archeology* is already in print and selling well. A Mexican publisher has recently acquired Spanish translations rights to *Hidden History*. Inquiries have also been received from Indian, Russian, Slovenian, Indonesian, Dutch, Japanese, French, Belgian, Danish, and Swedish publishers. For example, Monique Oosterhof of the Dutch firm Arena wrote on June 14, 1994:

> We are very interested in the book *The Hidden History of the Human Race* by Michael A. Cremo and Richard L. Thompson. If the Dutch rights are still free, could you please send us a copy of the book? Thank you in advance. Arena is one of the leading Dutch publishers. We publish international literature of high level: Benoit Groult, Viktor Jerofejev, Charles Johnson, Shere Hite, Eduardo Mendoza, Laura Esquivel, Helen Zahavi, Bernice Rubens, Meir Shalev, Klaus Mann, Carmen Martin Gaite, Harold Brodkey, Joan Didion, Kaye Gibbons etc.

During the fall and winter of 1994, I went on an author's tour to promote *Hidden History* in the United States. I was a guest on over 60 radio and television shows, ranging from the sensationalistic *Sightings* television show produced by Paramount to the high brow *Thinking Allowed*, which airs on 80 PBS television stations nationwide. Surprisingly, I found the hosts receptive to the basic message that Western science was not telling the truth about human origins. This was also true of the people who called in on the talk radio shows. Even more surprisingly, I found a great deal of interest in the Gaudiya Vaishnava alternative to the current theory of human evolution. In terms of domain mapping, I found the nationally syndicated radio talk shows of Laura Lee, Art Bell, and Bob Hieronimus to be quite significant. Each host focuses exclusively on scientific anomalies, ranging from UFOs and crop circles to archeological mysteries of the kind found in *Forbidden Archeology*.

As another illustration of the connectivity manifested by *Forbidden Archeology* in its exploratory domain mapping, I offer the following. *Forbidden Archeology* was very positively reviewed in the *Hazelton Standard-Speaker*, a Pennsylvania newspaper (Conrad, 1993). The title of the article, which featured a large blowup of the cover of Forbidden Archeology, was "New book claims man existed on earth long before the apes." On December 18, 1994, Laura Cortner, executive producer of Hieronimus & Co.: 21st Century Media Source, wrote:

> We are very interested in reviewing a copy of your book *Forbidden Archeology* which we read about in an article by Ed Conrad in the *Hazelton (PA) Standard-Speaker*, 11/17/93. We have long been interested in doing a special program on the subject of archeological finds that challenge the earliest recorded history of humans for quite some time, and we are encouraged to learn of an academic book with authors we could interview on the radio. Our programs are designed to educate our listeners on a wide variety of subjects that are usually not covered in the major media, and we know your book will be of interest to them.

Shortly thereafter, I was guest for two hours on the Bob Hieronimus radio show. I returned to the show for another appearance later in 1994. At the request of the show, copies of the abridged version of *Forbidden Archeology* were provided to the show for distribution to other guests appearing on the show. On February 7, 1995, Laura Cortner wrote to me:

> Enclosed is the latest letter of praise we have received from one of our recent guests on 21st Century Radio to whom we have presented a copy [an English zoologist who specializes in "living fossils"]. Thank you very much for supplying us with extra copies to continue this type of promotion. In the last month we have also sent copies to two of the creators of Howdy Doody, and to Peter Occhiogrosso, author of *The Joy of Sects: A Spiritual Guide to the World's Religions* (Doubleday).

Tracking *Forbidden Archeology* can be quite dizzying, as it moves from the pages of *American Journal of Physical Anthropology* to the *Hazelton Standard-Speaker* to the airwaves of 21st Century Radio and then into the hands of an English zoologist and the creators of Howdy Doody.

Cyberspace

Forbidden Archeology has also invaded cyberspace. Not long ago, a friend told me that the introduction to *Forbidden Archeology*, complete with a color image of the book cover, had appeared on somebody's home page on the World Wide Web (WWW). Net surfers can check it out at: http://zeta.cs.adfa.oz.au/Spirit/Veda/Forbidden-Archeology/forbidden-arch.html.

A search through the WWW detected the presence of *Forbidden Archeology* in several online bookstores. *Forbidden Archeology* has also been responsible for some searing flame wars on discussion groups such as Talk.Origins. Anomalous human skeletal remains found in deposits over two million years old at Castenedolo, Italy, in the late nineteenth century were one of the hotter topics. At one point, my chief opponent posted this text (name deleted):

> Subject: Re: Castenedolo (Help!)
> Organization: HAC — Johns Hopkins University, Baltimore
> I have spent the last two days trying to find out as much as I could about the Castenedolo finds. The result is disappointing. I found only one reference that even mentioned Castenedolo, and that was a reference given by [Cremo] . . . [his] post seems impressive, and I am (I admit) not easy to impress. . . . Basically, I've reached a dead-end. . . . It seems that . . . [he] has effectively dealt with my objections. I currently consider . . . [his] Castenedolo post unchallenged on talk.origins. Anyone else willing to give it a try?

Conclusion

It's time to interrupt the transmissions from *Forbidden Archeology* as it continues to map a new terrain of discourse. The preliminary mapping illuminates an ongoing process of global cultural realignment and transition, wherein Western science finds itself retreating, somewhat unwillingly, from its previous position of self-proclaimed epistemic superiority and coming into an intellectual world-space where it finds itself just one of many knowledge traditions.

The responses to *Forbidden Archeology* from within the network of modern science show a degree of resistance to this developing reality and a hope that the system as it is, perhaps with some adjustments, will survive intact.

But, as one can see, the expanding topology of the terrain mapped by *Forbidden Archeology* reaches far beyond artificial interdisciplinary realignments within the modern university system. The familiar unities are dissolving. As foreseen by Foucault (1972, p. 39): "one is forced to advance beyond familiar territory, far from the certainties to which one is accustomed, towards a yet uncharted land and unforeseeable conclusion."

Specifically, *Forbidden Archeology* charts the domain of the discourse of human origins and antiquity. One can no longer hope that this will remain the inalienable property of a certain discipline, such as archeology or anthropology. Neither can salvation be found in forging new interdisciplinary links with other fragmenting disciplines. One cannot even be certain that disciplines such as anthropology can avoid marginalization, a possibility much discussed among anthropologists themselves.

The map generated by *Forbidden Archeology* points to the emergence of a diverse multipolar global intellectual constellation from which may emerge a new academic consensus on human origins. Those participating most effectively in this process will be those who have mastered the techniques of complex boundary crossings, able to move freely with open minds, through scientific disciplines such as anthropology and archeology; the science studies branches of history, philosophy, and sociology; the academic study of religion; the populist purveyors of scientific anomalies; the range of New Age interests; and the whole world of religion-based sciences and cosmologies of traditional spiritual cultures, such as Gaudiya Vaishnavism.

References

Basham, A. L. (1959). *The Wonder That Was India*. New York: Grove Press.

Conrad, E. (1993). New book claims man existed on earth long before the apes. *Hazelton [PA]Standard-Speaker*, November 17.

Corliss, W. (1993) *Forbidden Archeology. Science Frontiers Book Supplement*, 89: 1.

Cremo, M. A. (1994). Puranic time and the archeological record. *Theme Papers: Concepts of Time. World Archaeological Congress-3, New Delhi, December 4–11, 1994*. Bound volume of precirculated papers, issued on behalf of the Academic Committee of WAC 3.

Cremo, M. A., and Thompson, R. L. (1993). *Forbidden Archeology: The Hidden History of the Human Race*. San Diego: Bhaktivedanta Institute.

Davidson, J. (1994) Fascination over fossil finds. *International Journal of Alternative and Complementary Medicine,* (August) p. 28.

Feder, K. L. (1994). Review of *Forbidden Archeology: The Hidden History of the Human Race.* Michael A. Cremo and Richard L. Thompson, 1993, Govardhan Hill Pub., San Diego. *Geoarchaeology: An International Journal,* 9: 337–340.

Foucault, M. (1972). *The Archaeology of Knowledge.* New York: Pantheon.

Goswami, S. D. (1980) *Srila Prabhupada-lilamrta, A Biography of His Divine Grace A. C. Bhaktivedanta Swami Prabhupada, Founder-Acarya of the International Society for Krishna Consciousness. Volume 1. A Lifetime in Preparation, India 1896–1965.* Los Angeles: Bhaktivedanta Book Trust.

Greimas, A. J. (1990). *Narrative Semiotics and Cognitive Discourses.* London: Pinter.

Holmes, W. H. (1899). Review of the evidence relating to auriferous gravel man in California. *Smithsonian Institution Annual Report 1898–1899,* 419–472.

Hunt, J. (1993). Antiquity of modern humans: re-evaluation. *Louisiana Mounds Society Newsletter,* 64: 2–3.

Leakey, M. (1979) Footprints in the ashes of time. *National Geographic,* 155: 446–457.

Marks, J. (1994). Review of *Forbidden Archeology: The Hidden History of the Human Race,* by Michael A. Cremo and Richard L. Thompson. 1993. San Diego: Bhaktivedanta Institute. *American Journal of Physical Anthropology,* 93: 140–141.

Moore, S. (1993). Review of *Forbidden Archeology: The Hidden History of the Human Race,* by Michael A. Cremo and Richard L. Thompson. *Fortean Times,* 72: 59.

Rothstein, M. (1994). *Forbudt Arkaeologi. Politiken,* January 31, section 3, page 1.

Schwarz, H. (1994). Earth born, sky driven: Book review. *Journal of Unconventional History,* 6: 68–76.

Slemmons, D. B. (1966). Cenozoic volcanism of the central Sierra Nevada, California. *Bulletin of the California Division of Mines and Geology,* 190: 199–208.

Salim-ur-rahman (1994) Spanner in the works. *The Friday Times,* April 21.

Swann, I. (1994). Review of *Forbidden Archeology: The Hidden History of the Human Race.* Michael A. Cremo and Richard L. Thompson. *Fate,* January, 106–107.

Tedlock, B., and Tedlock, D. (1995). From the editors. *American Anthropologist,* 97: 8–9.

Whitney, J. D. (1880). The auriferous gravels of the Sierra Nevada of California. *Harvard University, Museum of Comparative Zoology Memoir* 6(1).

Yau, J. (1993). *In the Realm of Appearances: The Art of Andy Warhol.* Hopewell: Ecco.

3

The City of Nine Gates:
A Complex Model for Mind/Body
Dualism from India's *Bhagavata Purana*

I presented this paper at the conference Toward a Science of Consciousness 1996, which was held April 8–13, 1996, in Tucson, Arizona.

Is there a conscious self that is distinct from the physical mechanism of the body? Is there a mind that is distinct from the brain? Those who give positive answers to such questions are called dualists, but they are not numerous in contemporary science and philosophy. Dualistic solutions to the mind/body problem are perhaps hampered, among other things, by the impoverished analogical and allegorical resources of Western thought. Whether we turn to Plato's cave, to the formulations of Descartes, or to the proverbial little green man in the brain, there is apparently not enough substance to inspire the modern consciousness researcher to seriously consider dualism.

But in chapters 25–29 of Canto Four in the *Bhagavata Purana*, a Sanskrit text from India, one finds the elaborate allegory of the City of Nine Gates. The sophistication of the allegory and the potential explanatory power of its elements challenge modern researchers to take a second look at dualism.

The account of the City of Nine Gates is specifically identified as allegorical in the *Bhagavata Purana* itself. It was spoken by the sage Narada Muni, who was questioned by King Prachinabarhishat about the nature of the self, and Narada Muni himself explains all the elements of the allegory in the original text. In other words, it is not that I myself have identified some passages from the *Bhagavata Purana* as allegorical, and myself interpreted the passage in terms of mind/body dualism. The allegorical nature of the passages and their application to a dualist explanation of consciousness are features of the text itself.

In this paper, I will give a summary of the City of Nine Gates, adapted from the Bhaktivedanta Book Trust edition of the *Bhagavata Purana* (published as *Shrimad-Bhagavatam*) along with some hints as to the utility of the allegory in resolving questions that arise in consciousness studies.

The central character in the allegory of the City of Nine Gates is a King named Puranjana. In Sanskrit, the word *puran-jana* means "one who enjoys in a citylike body." Soul/body dualism is thus hinted at in the King's name. King Puranjana originally existed as a spirit soul in a purely spiritual realm in relationship with a supreme conscious being, God. Materialists may oppose the introduction of this transcendental realm, which exists outside the material universe knowable by science. But even the materialist cosmology of modern science incorporates a "transcendental" realm, that is to say, a realm that exists beyond the universe knowable by science, and from which that universe emerged at the time of the Big Bang. This transcendental reality, existing beyond time, space, and ordinary matter, is called the quantum mechanical vacuum, and is pictured as a pure energy field in which particles appear and instantly disappear. From this sea of virtual particles, some go through a process of expansion that keeps them in existence. According to many cosmologists, our universe is one such expansion.

So both the *Bhagavata Purana* and the Big Bang cosmology of modern science have an eternal transcendental existence from which our universe of matter, with its features of time and space, arises. Once this is admitted, we can then decide which version of ultimate reality has the most explanatory power, when applied to the variegated reality of our experience. Modern cosmologists and other theorists have a great deal of difficulty in coaxing a sufficient amount of variety from the rather smooth and featureless universe that, according to theory, expands from the quantum mechanical vacuum. The origin of consciousness also poses a difficult problem. In light of this, an ultimate reality that is itself variegated and conscious might offer a solution.

Having departed from the spiritual world, by misuse of independence, King Puranjana journeys through the material world, accompanied by Avijnata Sakha ("the unknown friend"). The Unknown Friend corresponds to the Supersoul expansion of God. When Puranjana leaves God and the spiritual world, his memory of them becomes covered. But unknown to Puranjana, God accompanies him on his journey through the material world. According to the *Bhagavata Purana,* God accompanies all spirit souls in the material world as their Unknown Friend, who observes and sanctions their activities.

In the Western world, mind/brain dualism is identified with French philosopher René Descartes, who posited the existence of (1) matter extended in space and (2) mind existing outside space. Cartesian dualism is characterized by an interaction between mind and matter, but explaining how this interaction takes place has proved problematic for advocates of the Cartesian model. How, for example, are impressions transmitted from the realm of matter to the completely different realm of mind? Descartes thought the connection between mind and matter occurred in the pineal gland in the brain, an answer most scientists today do not favor.

According to the *Bhagavata Purana*, both matter and the souls in the material world are energies of God, and as such both have a single spiritual source. The *Bhagavata Purana* philosophy is thus both dualist and monist, simultaneously. The interactions of matter and the soul in the material world are mediated by Supersoul, who exists inside each material atom and also accompanies each spirit soul. By the arrangement of Supersoul, impressions of material experience can be channeled to the soul. How this takes place is the subject of the allegory of Puranjana.

Having left the spiritual world, Puranjana, accompanied by Avijnata Sakha (his Unknown Friend, the Supersoul), wanders through the material world. He desires to find a suitable place to enjoy himself. In other words, he searches for a suitable kind of body to inhabit. He tries many kinds of bodies on many planets. Here we note that each species of life consists of a soul inhabiting a particular kind of body. In this respect, the *Bhagavata Purana* account differs from that of Descartes, who held that only humans have souls. For Descartes, animals were simply automatons. If one concedes that animals, with all their signs of life and consciousness, are simply automatons, then why not human beings as well? The *Bhagavata Purana* model avoids this particular weakness of Descartes's system.

Eventually, Puranjana comes to a place called Nava Dvara Pura, the City of Nine Gates. He finds it quite attractive. The City of Nine Gates represents the human male body, with its nine openings—two eyes, two nostrils, two ears, mouth, anus, and the genital opening. As Puranjana wanders through the gardens of the city, he encounters an extremely beautiful woman. Puranjana is attracted to her, and she is attracted to him. She becomes his Mahishi (Queen).

Puranjana, as we have seen, represents the conscious self. The beautiful woman represents *buddhi,* intelligence. According to the *Bhagavata Purana* philosophy, intelligence is a subtle material energy with discriminatory capabilities like those manifested by artificial intelligence machines. The attraction between King Puranjana and the Queen is the root of embodied consciousness. The King, it should be noted, has distinct conscious selfhood, with nonmaterial sensory capability, but this capability becomes dormant when he begins his relationship with the Queen.

The Queen (the subtle material element called intelligence) allows Puranjana (the conscious self) to enjoy the City of Nine Gates (the gross physical body). Employing a computer analogy, we might say Puranjana represents the user, the City of Nine Gates represents the computer hardware, and the Queen represents the software that allows the user to interface with the hardware and use it for practical purposes.

The Queen is not, however, alone but is accompanied by eleven *mahabhatas* (body guards) and a serpent with five heads. The bodyguards comprise the mind and the ten senses. The ten senses are made up of five *jnana-indriyas* (knowledge acquiring senses) and five *karma-indriyas* (working senses). The five knowledge acquring senses are the senses of sight, smell, taste, hearing, and touch. The five working senses are those of walking, grasping, speaking, reproduction, and evacuation. All ten senses are grouped around the mind. The ten senses are considered servants of the mind. Each of these servants has hundreds of wives. The wives are desires for material experience, and the senses act under their pressure. According to this system, the senses are different from the physical sense organs. The senses are part of the invisible subtle material covering of the soul, along with mind and intelligence. The physical organs of sensation (the eyes, nose, tongue, ears, skin, legs, arms, mouth, genitals, and anus) are part of the gross physical body that is visible to the eyes.

The distinction between subtle senses and physical sense organs is important, and offers consciousness researchers a valuable conceptual tool. Let us consider, for example, the problem of phantom limbs. Persons whose legs or arms have been amputated often report that they are able to distinctly feel the missing limb, and even experience quite distinct sensations, such as twinges of pain or itching. The City of Nine Gates allegory provides an explanation for this mysterious phenomenon. Let's take the case of someone whose arm has been amputated but who still feels the presence of the arm. The arm is one of the working senses. It is composed of two elements, the subtle grasping sense and the physical organ of the arm and hand. The process of amputation removes the physical organ through which the subtle sense operates. But the subtle sense itself remains, and therefore its presence may be mentally perceived.

Since the subtle sense is material, it may be able to act upon gross physical matter, without going through the related physical sense organ. This model may therefore explain some of the phenomena reported in connection with ghosts and apparitions, and in connection with mediums, particularly the mysterious movement of physical objects. For a good scientific introduction to these unusual phenomena, one might consult *Thirty Years of Psychical Research*, by Charles Richet, who in 1913 won the Nobel Prize for medicine and physiology.

This model may also explain how persons are able to experience sense data during near death experiences, during which the physical sense organs are incapacitated because of anaesthesia or shock. For a good clinical study of near death experienices, I recommend *Recollections of Death*, by cardiologist Michael Sabom.

The senses are compared to attendants of the Queen. They serve her by bringing information and conducting activity. Together they comprise the array of material intelligence and sensory capabilities, all formed from subtle but nevertheless material energy. They combinedly manufacture a sense of self, with which the King becomes entranced and with which he falsely identifies. The body itself, the City of Nine Gates, is made of gross material energy, of the kind that can be manipulated by ordinary physics and chemistry. It is powered by five subtle airs, listed in the Ayur Veda, the Vedic medical science, as *prana, apana, vyana, samana,* and *udana*. In the Puranjana allegory the five airs, comprising the vital force, are represented by a five-headed serpent.

In the allegory, Puranjana asks about the identity and origin of the Queen and her attendants. The Queen replies, "O best of human beings, I do not know who has begotten me. I cannot speak to you perfectly about this. Nor do I know the names or the origins of the associates with me. O great hero, we only know that we are existing in this place. We do not know what will come after. Indeed, we are so foolish that we do not care to understand who has created this beautiful place for our residence. My dear gentleman, all these men and women with me are known as my friends, and the snake, who always remains awake, protects this city even during my sleeping hours. So much I know. I do not know anything beyond this. You have somehow or other come here. This is certainly a great fortune for me. I wish all auspicious things for you. You have a great desire to satisfy your senses, and all my friends and I shall try out best in all respects to fulfill your desires. I have just arranged this city of nine gates for you so that you can have all kinds of sense gratification. You may live here for one hundred years, and everything for your sense gratification will be supplied."

The King's questioning the Queen represents the self's interrogation of material intelligence for the answers to ultimate questions. The answers provided by the Queen, as well as her fundamental attitude, reflect those of modern science, which prides itself on avoidance of certain questions and the tentativeness of whatever answers it may provide. "I cannot speak to you perfectly about this. . . . We only know that we are existing in this place." Essentially, the Queen provides a monist, materialist answer to the King's questions about his situation.

The *Bhagavata Purana* then provides a more detailed description of the nine gates of the city inhabited by the King and Queen. Seven of the gates are on the surface (the two eyes, two ears, two nostrils, and mouth), and two of the gates are subterranean (the anus and genitals). Five of the gates face east.

The first two gates on the eastern side are called Khadyota (glowworm) and Avirmukhi (torchlight). In order to see, the King would exit these two gates, and go to the city called Vibhrajita (clear vision). On this journey he would be accompanied by his friend Dyuman (the sun, the ruler of the subtle visual sense).

In other words, the King encounters qualia by sensory contact through the physical gates of the body. Qualia are secondary properties of objects, such as color. In consciousness studies, the question of how we perceive qualia is a much debated topic. Do they exist in their own right, in the objects with which they are identified, or, do they exist only in our own minds? According to the *Bhagavata Purana* system, qualia, such as colors, exist as subtle sense objects. They thus have a reality of their own, and are not simply produced within the mind.

That the King goes out through the gates of the eyes to contact subtle sense objects in a city of visual impressions is interesting. This suggests that the seeing process is not simply one of passive reception, but may involve an active process of image acquisition (as in sonar, or radar). This may explain such phenomena as traveling clairvoyance, whereby a subject can mentally journey to a particular location, beyond the range of the physical sense organs, and then accurately report visual impressions. Visual sensations reported during out of body experiences could also be explained by this model. The exact relationships between the physical sense organs, the subtle senses, and subtle sense objects are not easily understood, but could perhaps be clarified by experimental work based on the overall model of the City of Nine Gates.

In the eastern part of King Puranjana's city there are, in addition to the eyes, two gates called Nalini and Naalini, representing the nostrils. The King would go through these two gates with a friend called Avadhuta (representing breathing airs) to the town of Saurabha (odor). The last gate on the eastern side is Mukhya (the mouth), through which the King would go with two friends to the towns of taste sensation and nourishment.

Through the two gates on the northern and southern sides (the ears), the King would go to places where different kinds of sound were heard. Through the gates on the western side of the city, the King would go to the towns where sensations of sexual pleasure and evacuation are experienced. During his journeys, the King would take help from two blind men, Nirvak and Peshakrit, who represent the arms and legs.

In all his activities, the King would follow the lead of the Queen. In other words, the conscious self in the material world becomes conditioned by material intelligence. The *Bhagavata Purana* says: "When the Queen drank liquor, King Puranjana also engaged in drinking. When the Queen dined, he used to dine with her, and when she chewed, King Puranjana used to chew along with her. When the Queen sang, he also sang, and when the Queen laughed, he also laughed. When the Queen talked loosely, he also talked loosely, and when the Queen walked, the King walked behind her. When the Queen would stand still, the King would also stand still, and when the Queen would lie down in bed, he would also follow and lie down with her. When the Queen sat, he would also sit, and when the Queen heard something, he would follow her to hear the same thing. When the Queen saw something, the King would also look at it, and when the Queen smelled something, the King would follow her to smell the same thing. When the Queen touched something, the King would also touch it, and when the dear Queen was lamenting, the poor King also had to follow her in lamentation. In the same way, when the Queen felt enjoyment, he also enjoyed, and when the Queen was satisfied, the King also felt satisfaction."

As noted above, an important question that arises concerning dualist solutions to the mind/body question is how a nonmaterial conscious mind interacts with material sense objects. In this model, there is an answer to this question. As seen above, the interaction is based on illusory identification.

To understand the nature of this illusory identification, we first need to readjust the familiar mind/body dualism to a triadic conception incorporating (1) a nonmaterial conscious self, (2) a subtle material body formed of subtle senses, mind, and intelligence, and (3) a physical body composed of gross matter.

In this model, the mind is a subtle material substance, associated with material intelligence. Mind is at the center of the subtle senses, which are in turn connected to the physical sense organs, which bring to the mind sense data in the form of subtle sense objects. Here yet another question arises.

In consciousness studies, one is faced with the problem of how the various kinds of sense data are presented in an integrated fashion. Even various elements of the visual sense, such as perception of color and movement and form are located in different parts of the brain. Sounds are processed in other parts of the brain. How are all these elements combined?

In the *Bhagavata Purana* model, the integrating function is performed by the subtle mind element, which receives sensory inputs from the subtle senses grouped around it. The mind is not, however, conscious. The mind, might therefore, be compared to multimedia computer software capable of integrating audio and visual materials into a single, integrated display, making use of a variety of inputs and source materials. The material intelligence, represented by the Queen, directs the consciousness of the actual living entity to the integrated display of sense data. Intelligence, as a subtle material energy, is not itself conscious, but it mimics the behavior of consciousness. It thus attracts the attention of the conscious self, causing the self to identify with it, just as we identify with the image of an actor on a movie screen. By identification with material intelligence, which is in turn connected to the mind's integrated display of sense data, consciousness is connected with the sense data. This connection is not direct. The indirect connection of the conscious self with gross matter arises from the self's false identification with the action of a subtle material energy, intelligence. The extremely subtle material element that connects the conscious self with material intelligence is called *ahankara*, or false ego. The whole system is set up and directed by the Supersoul.

According to the *Bhagavata Purana* picture, the conscious self originally experiences nonmaterial sense objects through nonmaterial senses. This takes place in the spiritual world, with God. But having turned from this original situation, the self is placed in a material body in the material world. Identifying with this artificial situation, the self forgets its own nature and that of God. But God remains with the self as Supersoul, the Unknown Friend. If the self tires of the artificial material reality and desires to return to its original position, the Unknown Friend will reawaken the original spiritual senses of the self and reconnect them with their spiritual sense objects.

The whole system of material reality therefore resembles a computer-generated virtual reality. In virtual reality systems, the user's normal sensory inputs are replaced by computer-generated displays. But just as a person can turn off the virtual reality display and return to normal sensory experience, so the conscious self in the artificial sensory environment of the material world can return to its original spiritual sensory experience. The idea of comparing the position of a soul in the material world to a person experiencing a virtual reality generated by a computer first occurred to me in 1986, when I attended a conference on artificial life organized by the Sante Fe Institute. The idea was further developed in discussions with my Bhaktivedanta Institute colleague Richard Thompson, who also attended the conference, and was subsequently presented by us in a Bhaktivedanta Institute video titled "Simulated Worlds."

In the *Bhagavata Purana* allegory, King Puranjana and his Queen enjoy life for some time in the City of Nine Gates. Eventually, however, the City of Nine Gates comes under attack by a king named Chandavega. Chandavega represents time, and his name literally means "very swiftly passing away." Chandavega commands an army of 360 male Gandharva soldiers and their 360 female companions. Together, these represent the days and nights of the year. When Chandavega's army attacks, the five-headed serpent (the vital force) tries to defend the City of Nine Gates. The serpent fights the attackers for one hundred years but eventually becomes weak, causing anxiety for the King and his associates. Finally, the attacking soldiers overwhelm the defenders and set the City of Nine Gates ablaze. As it becomes obvious that the battle is being lost, King Puranjana is overcome with anxious thoughts of his wife and other relatives and associates. Then the commander of the invading forces arrests the King and takes him away along with his followers, including the five-headed serpent. As soon as they are gone, the attackers destroy the City of Nine Gates, smashing it to dust. Even as he is being led away, the King cannot remember his Unknown Friend, the Supersoul. Instead, he thinks only of his wife, the Queen. He then takes another birth, this time as a woman.

In this part of the allegory, we see how the conscious self leaves the gross physical body, accompanied by the intelligence, mind, and subtle senses. When they leave, the gross physical body distintegrates. The conscious self then receives another gross physical body. The kind of body received depends on the condition of the subtle material body, which is composed of intelligence, mind, and subtle senses. The subtle material body is the template upon which the gross physical body is constructed. This model allows one to account for reports of past life memories, such as those researched and verified by Dr. Ian Stevenson of the University of Virginia in his book *Twenty Cases Suggestive of Reincarnation*. In the *Bhagavata Purana* model, the mind is the storehouse of memory, memory of past lives.

In his next life, King Puranjana becomes Vaidarbhi, the daughter of King Vidarbha. When grown, Vaidarbhi becomes the Queen of King Malayadhvaja. At the end of his life, Malayadhvaja retires to the forest and takes up the process of mystic yoga. The *Bhagavata Purana* (4.28.40) informs us: "King Malayadhvaja attained perfect knowledge by being able to distinguish the Supersoul from the individual soul. The individual soul is localized, whereas the Supersoul is all-pervasive. He became perfect in knowledge that the material body is not the soul but that the soul is the witness of the material body." In this state of higher awareness, Malayadhvaja, following the yoga process, deliberately leaves his material body and achieves liberation from material existence.

Queen Vaidarbhi (formerly King Puranjana) is overwhelmed with grief at her husband's departure. At this point, King Puranjana's Unknown Friend (the Supersoul), appears before Vaidarbhi as a *brahmana* sage. The *brahmana* says to Vaidarbhi: "My dear friend, even though you can not immediately recognize Me, can't you remember that in the past you had a very intimate friend? Unfortunately, you gave up My company and accepted a position as enjoyer of this material world. . . . You were simply captivated in this body of nine gates." The *brahmana* then instructs Vaidarbhi further about her original position as a purely spiritual self in the spiritual world.

In this paper, I have extracted only the principal elements of the City of Nine Gates allegory. The complete account is much more detailed, and allows one to make an even more subtle and refined model of self/mind/body interaction. This model does not fit easily into present categories of the mind/body debate. Although dualist, it partakes also of idealism and monism. It does, however, allow one to integrate many categories of evidence from normal and paranormal science, as well as evidence from humanity's wisdom traditions, into a rich synthesis, providing fruitful lines of research confirming and refining a complex dualist model of mind/body interaction.

4

Alfred Russel Wallace and the Supernatural: A Case Study in Reenchanting Reductionistic Science's Hagiography in Light of an Alternative Cosmology

I presented this paper at the Seventh Annual Interdisciplinary Conference on Science and Culture, organized by the Kentucky State University Institute of Liberal Studies. The conference was held in Frankfort, Kentucky, April 18–20, 1996. In 2006, Dr. Charles H. Smith, a professor at Western Kentucky University asked me to submit a version of this chapter for inclusion in a book of academic papers about Alfred Russel Wallace that he was putting together. I did so, but an editor at the company that was to publish the book objected to having anything by me in the book. I had too much of a reputation as a radical.

Modern biology and anthropology texts often contain biographical sketches of Alfred Russel Wallace, co-founder with Charles Darwin of the theory of evolution by natural selection. These idealized sketches routinely ignore Wallace's extensive research into the paranormal and his related conclusions, portraying him instead as a saint of materialism. This slanted hagiography is arguably related to the authors' cultural commitment to materialist, reductionist cosmologies. Adherents of alternative supernatural cosmologies, may, in the course of producing their own science texts, accordingly transform Wallace's biography. In this paper, I will report on such a work of hagiographic transformation in progress, as an example of an interaction of science and culture.

Traditionally, researchers interested in science and culture have focused on the cultural responses of Third World ethnic communities and Fourth World tribal peoples to encroaching modernity, with its characteristic science and technology. For example, cultural anthropologists have extensively reported on how Pacific peoples responded to incursions of modern technological society by integrating some of its salient features into cargo cults (Worsely 1968). By performing certain rituals, members of cargo cults believed that there would someday arrive a large plane or boat bearing abundant Western goods, in sufficient quantities to restore their lost cultural dominance. Generations of anthropologists and sociologists have studied the cargo cults.

But my own case offers a reversal of the usual pattern. I am typical of numerous members of modern, technologically advanced First World countries who have been strongly affected by incursions of Third World cultural and religious elements, adding a globalizing reflexive element to the interaction of science and culture. This phenomenon is worthy of much more attention than it has received.

In the early 1970s, I became a convert to Gaudiya Vaishnavism, a spiritual revivalist movement that originated in Bengal in the late fifteenth and early sixteenth centuries. Its central feature is worship of Vishnu, or Krishna, by *bhakti*, divine love. Shri Chaitanya Mahaprabhu, the leader of the revival, revered as an incarnation of God (Krishna), predicted the movement would spread to every town and village in the world. That began to happen in 1965, when a Gaudiya Vaishnava guru named Bhaktivedanta Swami Prabhupada came to the United States and founded the International Society for Krishna Consciousness.

The spiritual practices of Gaudiya Vaishnavism are founded upon the traditional cosmology of the ancient Vedic and Puranic texts of India. These texts, especially the *Bhagavata Purana,* depict an enchanted universe that is (1) populated with various grades of conscious beings (many with mystical and "supernatural" powers); (2) structured with various levels of ever more subtle material substance, culminating in a purely spiritual dimension; and (3) predominated by a supreme conscious entity. This enchanted universe is greatly different from the universe of modern reductionist science.

Indeed, the texts of modern science laboriously distinguish science and the scientifically described universe from religion and the religiously described universe (particularly the religion and religiously described universe of a tradition that populates the universe with varieties of spirit beings that can interfere with the ordinary physical processes).

Reductionist science distinguishes between natural and supernatural explanations. Natural explanations are scientific. Supernatural ones are not. For me, however, what reductionist science calls supernatural is simply part of the natural. Or one might say the natural of reductionist science is simply a subset of the total natural, This total natural could be the object of a more comprehensive science.

According to the narrative of modern science, however, the past heroes of science exposed part of this larger natural as falsely natural. By driving the falsely natural out of the bounds of the truly natural, the heroes of science improved the lot of humankind. Humanity could now see truth more clearly and experienced new prosperity and liberty.

But as many postmodern critics have observed, that narrative is no longer as convincing as previously. Contraction of the natural has brought spiritual poverty and material degradation to humankind.

My Gaudiya Vaishnava teachers have also told me this, and as part of my cultural project I have been tasked with exposing the inadequacy of cosmological reductionism to members of the larger culture in which I am immersed.

In my attempt to accomplish a reexpansion of the natural and a reenchantment of the reductionist universe, I have journeyed back through time textually, to study carefully the past heroes of science, to see how I might best contend with them and their modern heirs. What I discovered was interesting. Many of the past heroes of science, my adversaries, I thought, were really allies, or at least not as opposed to me as I expected. Pictured in the hagiography of modern science as saints and heroes of reductionism, they were in many cases bearers of truths close to, or even identical to, those I am representing.

The example of Newton is now familiar to many historians of science. Although much is made in modernist scientific texts of his laws of motion and gravity, little is said of his extensive work in alchemy and spirituality. All of that is deliberately excluded from the historical surveys usually included in the first chapters of college textbooks on physics. When we consider everything that Newton wrote, he becomes a much more complex and problematic figure, and this tends to undermine faith in a simple reductionist ("Newtonian") picture of the universe.

Alfred Russel Wallace

The same is true of Alfred Russel Wallace. In a modern textbook on physical anthropology he is depicted as a hero of modern reductionist science, cofounder with Darwin of the theory of evolution by natural selection (Stein and Rowe 1993). In a history of paleoanthropology (Trinkaus and Shipman 1992) he is similarly depicted. Neither text mentions his extensive involvement in paranormal research and the convictions he developed regarding the larger spiritual context in which physical evolution, as he saw it, takes place. Wallace, on the basis of his paranormal research, concluded that the universe is populated with a hierarchy of intelligent conscious beings, who sometimes manipulate matter in "supernatural" fashion so as to guide the formation of the human body and assist humans in a process of spiritual evolution beyond the death of the body.

In the remainder of this paper, I will survey Wallace's extensive paranormal research and provide selections from his works on the larger implications of his findings. This material is taken from a draft chapter of my forthcoming book *Human Devolution: An Alternative to Darwin's Theory*. In my book *Forbidden Archeology* (Cremo and Thompson 1993), I presented extensive evidence that contradicts current accounts of human evolution. This evidence suggests that humans have been present on this planet for hundreds of millions of years, which is consistent with accounts of human antiquity found in the ancient Sanskrit writings of India. *Forbidden Archeology* establishes the genuine need for an alternative account of human origins, but does not itself provide one. In *Human Devolution,* I will provide an alternative account, drawn from the Vedic and Puranic literature. Put in simplest terms, this account holds that humans on this planet have not evolved from the apes but have devolved from an original spiritual position. Wallace's paranormal research provides some empiric support for this account. And I have therefore devoted a chapter in *Human Devolution* to Wallace and his work. But the picture of Wallace found in my work differs substantially from that found in works by mainstream scientists, such as those above cited.

The central feature of Wallace's paranormal research was his belief in spirits and a spirit world. On the basis of personal experiments and reliable reports from other scientists, Wallace concluded that the universe is populated with a hierarchy of spirit beings, some of whom are in contact with the human population on earth, usually through mediums. According to Wallace, the spirit beings lower in the hierarchy, acting through mediums, were responsible for a variety of paranormal phenomena, including clairvoyance, miraculous healings, communications from the dead, apparitions, materializations of physical objects, levitations, etc. More powerful spirit beings may have played a role in the process of evolution, guiding it in certain directions.

Spirits, the kind that can move matter, are the last thing today's evolutionists want to hear about. Such things threaten current evolutionary theory, which depends on philosophical naturalism—the idea that everything in nature happens according to known physical laws. Introduce nonmaterial entities and effects, and the theory of evolution loses its exclusivity as an explanation for the origin of species. Perhaps spirits were involved in the process. If so, one would have to consider "supernatural selection" in addition to natural selection.

In addition to believing in spirits, Wallace also believed that anatomically modern humans were of considerable antiquity. For example, he provisionally accepted the discoveries of J. D. Whitney, which, by modern geological reckoning, place humans in California up to 50 million years ago (Cremo and Thompson, 1993, pp. 368–394, 439–458). [see Plates XII-XV] Wallace noted that such evidence tended to be "attacked with all the weapons of doubt, accusation, and ridicule" (Wallace, 1887, p. 667). Wallace (p. 667) suggested that "the proper way to treat evidence as to man's antiquity is to place it on record, and admit it provisionally wherever it would be held adequate in the case of other animals; not, as is too often now the case, to ignore it as unworthy of acceptance or subject its discoverers to indiscriminate accusations of being impostors or the victims of impostors." Wallace encountered the same kind of opposition when he communicated to scientists the results of his spiritualistic research.

Early Experiences with the Paranormal

Wallace first became interested in paranormal phenomena in 1843. Some English surgeons, including Dr. Elliotson, were then using mesmerism, an early form of hypnotism, to perform painless operations on patients. The reality of this anaesthesia, although today accepted (but not explained), was then a matter of extreme controversy.

At the time, Wallace was teaching school in one of the Midland counties of England. In 1844, Mr. Spencer Hall, a touring mesmerist, stopped there and gave a public demonstration. Wallace and some of his students, greatly interested, attended. Having heard from Hall that almost anyone could induce the mesmeric trance, Wallace later decided to make his own experiments. Using some of his students as subjects, he soon succeeded in mesmerizing them and produced a variety of phenomena. Some were within the range of modern medical applications of hypnotism, while some extended to the paranormal (1896, p. x, pp. 126–128; 1905, vol. 1, pp. 232–236).

One unusual thing witnessed by Wallace was community of sensation. "The sympathy of sensation between my patient and myself was to me the most mysterious phenomenon I had ever witnessed," he later wrote. "I found that when I laid hold of his hand he felt, tasted, or smelt exactly the same as I did. . . . I formed a chain of several persons, at one end of which was the patient, at the other myself. And when, in perfect silence, I was pinched or pricked, he would immediately put his hand to the corresponding part of his own body, and complain of being pinched or pricked too. If I put a lump of sugar or salt in my mouth, he immediately went through the action of sucking, and soon showed by gestures and words of the most expressive nature what it was I was tasting" (1896, pp. 127–128). During such experiments, Wallace took care to "guard against deception" (p. 126). From reports of the mesmeric experiments of other researchers, Wallace concluded that "the more remarkable phenomena, including clairvoyance both as to facts known and those unknown to the mesmeriser, have been established as absolute realities" (p *xi*).

Despite the well-documented observations of numerous competent researchers, the scientific establishment remained hostile to mesmeric phenomena. Eventually, the production of insensibility, behavior modification, and mild delusions would be accepted under the name of hypnotism. But the more extraordinary mesmeric manifestations—such as clairvoyance and community of sensation—were never accepted. In any case, Wallace (1896, p. *x*) found his own experiments of lasting value: "I thus learned my first great lesson in the inquiry into these obscure fields of knowledge, never to accept the disbelief of great men, or their accusations of imposture or of imbecility, as of any great weight when opposed to the repeated observation of facts by other men admittedly sane and honest."

From 1848 to 1862, Wallace traveled widely in the tropics, collecting wildlife specimens and filling notebooks with biological observations. While on an expedition to the East Indies, Wallace learned of paranormal phenomena that went far beyond anything he had witnessed in his experiments with mesmerism. "During my eight years' travels in the East," he later recalled, "I heard occasionally, through the newspapers, of the strange doings of the spiritualists in America and England, some of which seemed to me too wild and outrageous to be anything but the ravings of madmen. Others, however, appeared to be so well authenticated that I could not at all understand them, but concluded, as most people do at first that such things must be either imposture or delusion" (1905, vol. 2, p. 276).

Despite his feelings of disbelief, Wallace suspended judgement. His experience with mesmerism had taught him that "there were mysteries connected with the human mind which modern science ignored because it could not explain" (1896, p. 131). So when Wallace came back to England in 1862, he determined to look carefully into spiritualism.

Initially, Wallace contented himself with studying reports. But in the summer of 1865, he began to directly witness spiritualistic phenomena. His first experiences took place at the home of a friend, described by Wallace as "a sceptic, a man of science, and a lawyer" (1896, p. 132). Wallace, along with his host and members of his host's family, sat around a large, round table, upon which they placed their hands. Wallace (pp. 132–133) observed inexplicable movements of the table and heard equally inexplicable sounds of rapping.

On a friend's recommendation, Wallace then visited Mrs. Marshall, a medium who gave public demonstrations of phenomena stronger than those Wallace had yet seen. Wallace paid several visits to Mrs. Marshall in London, usually in the company of a skeptical friend with a scientific background. Among the numerous physical phenomena he witnessed were levitation of a small table one foot off the ground for a period of twenty seconds, strange movements of a guitar, inexplicable sliding movements of chairs across the floor, and levitation of a chair with a woman sitting upon it.

Wallace noted: "There was no room for any possible trick or deception. In each case, before we began, we turned up the tables and chairs, and saw that there was no connection between them and the floor, and we placed them where we pleased before we sat down. Several of the phenomena occurred entirely under our own hands, and quite disconnected from the 'medium'" (1896, p. 136).

At Mrs. Marshall's, Wallace also saw writing mysteriously appear on pieces of paper placed under the table and heard the spelling out, by raps, of intelligible messages. These messages contained names and other facts of a personal nature, not likely to have been known by the medium. Wallace himself received a message which contained his dead brother's name, the place where he died in Brazil, and the name of the last person to see him alive (p. 137).

As a result of such experiences, Wallace eventually became a convinced spiritualist. Critics suggested that Wallace was predisposed to spiritualism because of religious leanings (Wallace, 1896, p. *vi*). But Wallace, describing his view of life at the time he encountered spiritualism, wrote: "I ought to state that for twenty-five years I had been an utter skeptic as to the existence of any preter-human or super-human intelligences, and that I never for a moment contemplated the possibility that the marvels related by Spiritualists could be literally true. If I have now changed my opinion, it is simply by the force of evidence. It is from no dread of annihilation that I have gone into this subject; it is from no inordinate longing for eternal existence that I have come to believe in facts which render this highly probable, if they do not actually prove it" (p. 132).

"The Scientific Aspect of the Supernatural"

In 1866, Wallace published in a periodical an extended explanation of spiritualism called "The Scientific Aspect of the Supernatural." The heart of the essay was a summary of scientifically documented evidence for psychical phenomena, such as spirit messages. Wallace later brought out the essay in booklet form, and sent it to many of his scientific friends and acquaintances. Some responded with ridicule. For example, Thomas Henry Huxley, who received a copy, replied: "I am neither shocked nor disposed to issue a Commission of Lunacy against you. It may all be true, for anything I know to the contrary, but really I cannot get up any interest in the subject. . . . As for investigating the matter—I have half a dozen investigations of infinitely greater interest to me—to which any spare time I may have will be devoted. I give it up for the same reason I abstain from chess—it's too amusing to be fair work and too hard work to be amusing" (Wallace, 1905, vol. 2 p. 280).

Wallace nevertheless invited leading scientists and other learned persons to witness spiritualist phenomena, advising them that several sittings would be required. This seems reasonable, because most experimental work in science does require repeated trials. Dr. W. B. Carpenter and Dr. John Tyndall came for one sitting each, during which only very mild, unimpressive phenomena occurred. They refused Wallace's requests to attend more sittings (Wallace, 1905, vol. 2, pp. 278–279). Most scientists refused to come at all. G. H. Lewes, for example was "too much occupied and too incredulous to give any time to the inquiry" (p. 279).

Around this same time, Tyndall had called for a single test demonstration that would prove once and for all the true status of spiritualistic phenomena. Wallace replied in a letter to Tyndall that one test, even if successful, would not suffice to convince opponents. Wallace thought it better to amass reports of the numerous credible cases already on record. And to these he added, in his letter to Tyndall, one of his own experiences:

> The place was the drawing-room of a friend of mine, a brother of one of our best artists. The witnesses were his own and his brother's family, one or two of their friends, myself, and Mr. John Smith, banker, of Malton, Yorkshire, introduced by me. The medium was Miss Nichol. We sat round a pillar-table in the middle of the room, exactly under a glass chandelier. Miss Nichol sat opposite me, and my friend, Mr. Smith, sat next her. We all held our neighbour's hands, and Miss Nichol's hands were both held by Mr. Smith, a stranger to all but myself, and who had never met Miss N. before. When comfortably arranged in this manner the lights were put out, one of the party holding a box of matches ready to strike a light when asked.
>
> After a few minutes' conversation, during a period of silence, I heard the following sounds in rapid succession: a slight rustle, as of a lady's dress; a little tap, such as might be made by setting down a wineglass on the table; and a very slight jingling of the drops of the glass chandelier. An instant after Mr. Smith said, "'Miss Nichol is gone." The match-holder struck a light, and on the table (which had no cloth) was Miss Nichol seated in her chair, her head just touching the chandelier.
>
> . . . Mr. Smith assured me that Miss Nichol simply glided out of his hands. No one else moved or quitted hold of their neighbour's hands. There was not more noise than I described, and no motion or even tremor of the table, although our hands were upon it.
>
> You know Miss N.'s size and probable weight, and can judge of the force and exertion required to lift her and her chair on to the exact centre of a large pillar-table, as well as the great surplus of force required to do it almost instantaneously and noiselessly, in the dark, and without pressure on the side of the table, which would have tilted it up. Will any of the known laws of nature account for this? (Wallace 1905, vol. 2 pp. 291–293)

If the facts are as Wallace reported them, it would seem that Miss Nichol herself could not have managed to place herself on the table. If all present at the table were holding hands and did not let go, it would seem that none of them could have lifted Miss Nichol in her chair. That leaves confederates as a possibility. But they should have been exposed by the struck match. Furthermore, it seems any attempt to lift Miss Nichol in complete darkness, either by persons at the table or confederates from outside the room, would have caused much more noise than reported by Wallace. One can propose that Wallace himself deliberately gave a false report. This, however, seems unlikely.

Séances at Miss Douglas's

In 1869, Robert Chambers, author of *Vestiges of Creation*, introduced Wallace to Miss Douglas, a wealthy Scotch lady with an interest in spiritualism. Wallace attended many séances at Miss Douglas's London residence in South Audley Street. There he met many well connected spiritualists, including Darwin's relative Henslcigh Wedgwood. Among the most interesting séances were those with Mr. Haxby, a young postal employee, described by Wallace as "a remarkable medium for materializations." Haxby would sit in a small room separated by curtains from a dimly lit drawing room on the first floor. Wallace gave this account of a typical séance with Haxby:

> After a few minutes, from between the curtains would appear a tall and stately East Indian figure in white robes, a rich waistband, sandals, and large turban, snowy white and disposed with perfect elegance. Sometimes this figure would walk around the room outside the circle, would lift up a large and very heavy musical box, which he would wind up and then swing round his head with one hand. He would often come to each of us in succession, bow, and allow us to feel his hands and examine his robes. We asked him to stand against the door-post and marked his height, and on one occasion Mr. Hensleigh Wedgwood brought with him a shoe-maker's measuring-rule, and at our request, Abdullah, as he gave his name, took off a sandal, placed his foot on a chair, and allowed it to be accurately measured with the sliding-rule. After the séance Mr. Haxby removed his boot and had his foot measured by the same rule, when that of the figure was found to be full one inch and a quarter the longer, while in height it was about half a foot taller. A minute or two after Abdullah had retired into the small room, Haxby was found in a trance in his chair, while no trace of the white-robed stranger was to be seen. The door and window of the back room were securely fastened, and often secured with gummed paper, which was found intact (1905, vol. 2, pp. 328–329).

The usual skeptical explanation for such manifestations is imposture by the medium or a confederate. In this case, the measurements taken rule out imposture by the medium. And the precautions taken to secure the entrances to the back room make the participation of a confederate somewhat doubtful. On the whole, circumstances point to the genuineness of the materialization.

On one occasion at Miss Douglas's, the famous Daniel Dunglass Home was the medium, and Sir William Crookes, a distinguished physicist, was present. Crookes, later president of the Royal Society, was conducting his own research into spiritualistic phenomena. Wallace noted, however, that "his careful experiments, continued for several years, are to this day ignored or rejected by the bulk of scientific and public opinion as if they had never been made!" (1905, vol. 2, p. 293)

At the séance attended by Wallace and Crookes, Home was given an accordion. He held it with one hand, under the table around which he and the witnesses sat. Home's other hand remained on top of the table. On hearing the accordion play, Wallace went under the table to see what was happening:

> The room was well lighted, and I distinctly saw Home's hand holding the instrument, which moved up and down and played a tune without any visible cause. On stating this, he said, "Now I will take away my hand"—which he did; but the instrument went on playing, and I saw a detached hand holding it while Home's two hands were seen above the table by all present. This was one of the ordinary phenomena, and thousands of persons have witnessed it; and when we consider that Home's *séances* almost always took place in private homes at which he was a guest, and with people absolutely above suspicion of collusion with an impostor, and also either in the daytime or in a fully illuminated room, it will be admitted that no form of legerdemain will explain what occurred (1905, vol. 2, pp. 286–287).

Darwin Agrees to Test a Medium

Another scientist who witnessed Home's mysterious accordion playing was Francis Galton, a cousin of Charles Darwin. At the invitation of Crookes, Galton attended three séances with Home and another medium, Kate Fox. Afterwards, in a letter dated April 19, 1872, Galton wrote enthusiastically to Darwin:

> What surprises me is the perfect openness of Miss F. and Home. They let you do whatever you like within certain limits, their limits not interfering with adequate investigation. I really believe the truth of what they allege, that people who come as men of science are usually so disagreeable, opinionated and obstructive and have so little patience, that the seance rarely succeeds with them. It is curious to observe the entire absence of excitement or tension about people at a seance. Familiarity has bred contempt of the strange things witnessed. . . . Crookes, I am sure, so far as is just for me to give an opinion, is thoroughly scientific in his procedure. I am convinced that the affair is no matter of vulgar legerdemain and believe it is well worth going into, on the understanding that a first rate medium (and I hear there are only three such) puts himself at your disposal (Pearson, 1914).

Darwin agreed to see Home, giving Galton a letter to send to him. But by that time

Home had gone on to Russia and never returned to England (Beloff, 1993, pp. 49–50). Who knows what would have happened if Darwin had actually met Home? Perhaps he would have joined Wallace in his spiritualism.

More Experiences

In 1874, Wallace attended a series of séances with the medium Kate Cook. The sittings took place in the London apartment of Signor Randi, a painter. The medium sat in a chair, behind a curtain hung across a corner of a large reception room. Miss Cook always wore a black dress, earrings, and tightly laced boots. A few minutes after she sat behind the curtain, a female figure, wearing white robes, would sometimes come out and stand near the curtain. Wallace offered this description of what happened:

> One after another she would beckon us to come up. We then talked together, the form in whispers; I could look closely into her face, examine the features and hair, touch her hands, and might even touch and examine her ears closely, which were not bored for earrings. The figure had bare feet, was somewhat taller than Miss Cook, and, though there was a general resemblance, was quite distinct in features, figure, and hair. After half an hour or more this figure would retire, close the curtains, and sometimes within a few seconds would say, "Come and look." We then opened the curtains, turned up the lamp, and Miss Cook was found in a trance, in the chair, her black dress, laced-boots, etc., in the most perfect order as when she arrived, while the full-grown white-robed figure had totally disappeared (1905 vol. 2, pp. 327–328).

Wallace had a similar experience with the medium Eglington. The séance took place at a private house, in the presence of about eighteen spiritualists and people inquisitive about spiritualism. The medium was to sit behind a curtain hung across one corner of a room. The space behind the curtain was small, just large enough for the chair on which the medium was to sit. Wallace noted, "I and others examined this corner and found the walls solid and the carpet nailed down" (1905, vol. 2, p. 329). In other words, there was no concealed opening through which a confederate could enter. After Eglington arrived and sat behind the curtain, a robed male figure appeared and walked around the room, in dim light, allowing all of the witnesses to touch his robes and examine his hands and feet. Could the figure have been Eglington in disguise? Wallace gave this description of what happened immediately after the sitting.

> Several of the medium's friends begged him to allow himself to be searched so that the result might be published. After some difficulty he was persuaded, and four persons were appointed to make the examination. Immediately two of these led him into a bedroom, while I and a friend who had come with me closely examined the chair, floor, and walls, and were able to declare that nothing so large as a glove had been

left. We then joined the other two in the bedroom, and as Eglington took off his clothes each article was passed through our hands, down to underclothing and socks, so that we could positively declare that not a single article besides his own clothes were found upon him. The result was published in the Spiritualist newspaper, certified by the names of all present (1905, vol. 2, p. 329).

It is true that on some occasions mediums were exposed in cheating. This should not be surprising, for even in orthodox science there is no shortage of cheating. One notable hoax was Piltdown man, which fooled the scientific world for forty years. And today the manipulation and manufacture of test results in science laboratories is fairly common. So whether we are talking about paranormal science or normal science, we cannot exclude the possibility of cheating and hoaxing. The only thing we can do is examine particular cases and make reasonable judgements about the likelihood of imposture. In the case of Wallace's experience with Eglington, a great deal of care was taken to insure against trickery. In light of this, the apparent materialization of a humanlike figure by Eglington deserves a certain degree of credibility.

The most extraordinary phenomenon witnessed by Wallace was produced by a truly remarkable medium, Mr. Monk. A nonconformist clergyman, Monk had gained a considerable reputation for his séances. In order to study him more closely and systematically, some well known spiritualists, including Hensleigh Wedgwood and Stainton Moses, rented some rooms for Monk in the Bloomsbury district of London. Wedgwood and Moses invited Wallace to come and see what Monk could do. Wallace later gave this account of what happened:

> It was a bright summer afternoon, and everything happened in the full light of day. After a little conversation, Monk, who was dressed in the usual clerical black, appeared to go into a trance; then stood up a few feet in front of us, and after a little while pointed to his side, saying, "Look." We saw there a faint white patch on his coat on the left side. This grew brighter, then seemed to flicker, and extend both upwards and downwards, till very gradually it formed a cloudy pillar extending from his shoulder to his feet and close to his body. Then he shifted himself a little sideways, the cloudy figure standing still, but appearing joined to him by a cloudy band at the height at which it had first begun to form. Then, after a few minutes more, Monk again said "Look," and passed his hand through the connecting band, severing it. He and the figure then moved away from each other till they were about five or six feet apart. The figure had now assumed the appearance of a thickly draped female form, with arms and hands just visible. Monk looked towards it and again said to us "Look," and then clapped his hands. On which the figure put out her hands, clapped them as he had done, and we all distinctly heard her clap following his, but fainter. The figure then moved slowly back to him, grew fainter and shorter, and was apparently absorbed into

his body as it had grown out of it (1905, vol. 2, p. 330).

Broad daylight rules out clever puppetry. That Monk was standing only a few feet from Wallace, in the middle of an ordinary room, rules out the production of the form by stage apparatus. Wedgwood told Wallace that on other occasions a tall, robed, male figure appeared alongside Monk. This figure would remain for up to half an hour, and allowed himself to be touched by Wedgwood and his colleagues, who carefully examined his body and clothes. Furthermore, the figure could exert force on material objects. Once the figure went so far as to lift a chair upon which one of the investigators was seated (Wallace, 1905, vol. 2, p. 331).

Spiritualistic Encounters in America

During the years 1886 and 1887, Wallace traveled in the United States on a scientific lecture tour. In the course of his visit, he also met many American spiritualists, such as Professor William James of Harvard, and attended several séances.

One series of séances took place at the Boston home of Mrs. Ross, a medium famous for materializations (Wallace, 1905, vol. 2, pp. 338–339). To make a space for the medium, a curtain was placed across the corner of a front downstairs room. The sides of this corner were an outside wall of the house and an inside wall, on the other side of which was a back room. The inside wall was occupied by cupboard filled with china. Wallace carefully inspected the walls and floor, from within the front room, the back room, and the basement. He determined that there were no openings through which anyone could enter, other than a sliding door to the back room. This door was sealed with sticking plaster, and the witnesses secretly marked the plaster with pencil, so that if the plaster were moved they would be able to tell. The ten witnesses, including Wallace, sat in dim light in a circle in front of the curtain. The light was sufficient for Wallace to see the hands of his watch and to see the forms of everyone in the room. Under these circumstances, three figures emerged from behind the curtain—a female figure in White, Mrs. Ross dressed in black, and a male figure. When these retired, three female figures, of different heights and dressed in white, came out. These were followed by a single male figure. One of the gentleman witnesses identified him as his son. Later, a figure dressed as an American Indian came out from behind the curtain. He danced, spoke, and shook hands with some of those present, including Wallace. Finally, a female figure holding a baby appeared in front of the curtain. Wallace, on being invited by her, came up and touched the baby, and found it to be real. "Directly after the *seance* was over," wrote Wallace, "the gas was lighted, and I again examined the bare walls of the cabinet, the curtains, and the door, all being just as before, and affording no room or place for disposing of the baby alone, far less of the other figures" (1905, vol. 2, p. 339).

At another séance with Mrs. Ross, attended by William James, Wallace again saw eight or nine figures come out from behind the curtain. One of these was the departed niece of one of the witnesses, Mr. Brackett. Wallace noted that "Mr. Brackett has often seen her develop gradually from a cloudy mass, and almost instantly vanish away"

(1905, vol. 2, p. 339). Wallace himself saw figures known to him.

> One was a beautifully draped female figure, who took my hand, looked at me smilingly, and on my appearing doubtful, said in a whisper that she had often met me at Miss Kate Cook's *séances* in London. She then let me feel her ears, as I had done before to prove she was not the medium. I then saw that she closely resembled the figure with whom I had often talked and joked at Signor Randi's, a fact known to no one in America.
>
> The other figure was an old gentleman with white hair and beard, and in evening-dress. He took my hand, bowed, and looked pleased, as one meeting an old friend. . . . at length I recognized the likeness to a photograph I had of my cousin Algernon Wilson, whom I had not seen since we were children, but had long corresponded with him, as he was an enthusiastic entomologist, living in Adelaide, where he had died not long before. ...These two recognitions were to me very striking, because they were both so private and personal to myself, and could not possibly have been known to the medium or even to any of my friends present (1905, vol. 2, pp. 339–340).

A few months after these events, a group of twelve men came to one of Mrs. Ross's séances with the intention of exposing the materialized spirit forms as imposters. When they executed their plan, the twelve men found themselves unable to detain a single suspect (two men, one woman, two boys, and a little girl) or take a single piece of their paraphernalia. The men declared to a newspaper that the alleged impostors had entered the space behind the curtain through a sliding portion of the baseboard. Upon learning of this, some friends of Mrs. Ross brought her landlord and a carpenter to the scene, where they conducted a thorough inspection. The carpenter testified that there was no opening in the baseboard, and that none had been made and covered up. Wallace sent to the *Banner of Light* a letter stating these facts. He argued that "the utter failure of twelve men, who went for the express purpose of detecting and identifying confederates, utterly failing to do so or to secure any tangible evidence of their existence, is really a very strong proof that there were no confederates to detect" (1905, vol. 2, pp. 340–341).

In Washington, D. C., Wallace, accompanied by a college professor, an army general, and a government official, all spiritualists, attended séances with the medium P. L. O. A. Keeler. Across one corner of the room a black curtain was stretched on a cord, five feet off the floor. In the space behind the curtain was a table, upon which rested a tambourine and a bell. Before the séance, Wallace carefully checked the walls and floor, satisfying himself that there were no hidden entrances. He also checked the curtain, noticing it was one solid piece of cloth, with no openings. Everyone there had the chance to make similar investigations. Keeler and two guests from the audience sat in three chairs in front of the curtain. A lower curtain was then raised in front of them, up to the level of their chests. Keeler's hands were placed on those of the guest sitting next to him.

Wallace observed: "The tambourine was rattled and played on, then a hand appeared above the curtain, and a stick was given to it which it seized. Then the tambourine was lifted high on this stick and whirled round with great rapidity, the bell being rung at the same time. All the time the medium sat quiet and impassive, and the person next him certified to his two hands being on his or hers" (1905, vol. 2, p. 343).

A pencil and notepad were then passed to the hand above the curtain. Behind the curtain, messages were written and these were thrown over the curtain. The messages were signed with names known to certain witnesses, who found the content of the messages intelligible to them. Wallace himself received a message in an extraordinary way. Instead of passing the notepad over the curtain to the hand, he held it himself near the curtain. Wallace then saw a hand with a pencil come through the solid curtain and write a message to him on the pad. On another occasion, Wallace observed a similar occurrence:

> A stick was pushed out through the curtain. Two watches were handed to me through the curtain, and were claimed by the two persons who sat by the medium. The small tambourine, about ten inches in diameter, was pushed through the curtain and fell on the floor. These objects came through different parts of the curtain, but left no holes as could be seen at the time, and was proved by a close examination afterwards. More marvellous still (if that be possible), a waistcoat was handed to me over the curtain, which proved to be the medium's, though his coat was left on and his hands had been held by his companions all the time; also about a score of people were looking on all the time in a well-lighted room. These things seem impossible, but they are, nevertheless, facts (1905, vol. 2, pp. 344–345).

In San Francisco, Wallace, along with his brother John, who lived in California, and Mr. Owen, editor of the *Golden Gate,* attended some slate writing sessions with the medium Fred Evans (Wallace, 1905, vol. 2, pp. 346–349). A physician, a friend of Mr. Owen, also was present. Four folding slates were cleaned with a damp sponge and then handed to the four guests for inspection. The slates were closed and placed on the table. The guests then placed their hands on the slates. When a signal was given, they opened the slates and found writing on all of them. The messages were from departed relatives of Wallace and departed spiritualists. The usual skeptical explanation is that the slates were somehow switched. But Wallace's description of the procedure appears to rule that out, as the witnesses had their own hands on the slates at critical times.

Another set of slates was set on the table. The medium marked one of these slates with a pencil. When opened, this slate was covered with writing in five colors. Wallace observed that the letters were clearly superimposed over the pencil marks. This appears to rule out any clever chemical means of producing the letters.

Wallace's brother had brought a new folding slate of his own. This was placed nearby on the floor for a few minues. Wallace kept the slate in sight the entire time. When the slate was opened, a message was found written upon both sides of it. That it was a new slate, not belonging to the medium, is significant.

Wallace then asked the medium if the writing could be produced on pieces of paper placed between slates. Evans told Wallace to place six pieces of paper from a notepad and place them between a pair of slates. Wallace did so. After a few minutes, the slates were opened. Wallace found portraits of five departed spiritualists and a long dead sister of his drawn in crayon on the six pieces of paper, which had rested one on top of the other between the slates. They had been placed there by Wallace himself, ruling out substitution by the medium. Given the unexpected request by Wallace, the circumstances under which the pieces of paper were placed between the slates, it is hard to see how the medium could have carried out any deception.

Wallace noted: "The whole of the seven slates and six papers were produced so rapidly that the *séance* occupied less than an hour, and with such simple and complete openness, under the eyes of four observers, as to constitute absolutely test conditions. . . . A statement to this effect was published, with an account of the *séance,* signed by all present" (1905, vol. 2, pp. 348–349).

Wallace's Theory of Spiritualism: Analysis and Critique

Summarizing the conclusions he drew from his spiritual researches, Wallace stated: "The universal teaching of modern spiritualism is that the world and the whole material universe exist for the purpose of developing spiritual beings—that death is simply a transition from material existence to the first grade of spirit-life—and that our happiness and the degree of our progress will be wholly dependent upon the use we have made of our faculties and opportunities here" (1892, p. 648).

Such conclusions were drawn solely from facts that had been carefully and repeatedly observed in nature, and they were thus entirely scientific, said Wallace (1885a, p. 809). The observable facts did not, however, warrant extending spiritualist conclusions beyond certain limits. The verifiable facts of spiritualism were, according to Wallace, related to humans and the spirit beings nearest to earthly human existence. He therefore warned: "Speculations on the nature or origin of mind in general as well as those on the ultimate states to which human minds may attain in the infinite future, I look upon as altogether beyond the range of our faculties, and to be, therefore, utterly untrustworthy and profitless" (1885b). Wallace was generally content with the limited conclusions that could be drawn from the observable middle ground of human experience. He himself did, however, sometimes venture into the realm of "untrustworthy" speculation about origins and ultimate states.

Wallace found spiritualism to be a good scientific hypothesis, for it allowed him to intelligibly organize and explain many categories of evidence. For example, spiritualism allowed him to accomodate in one explanatory system the spiritlike daimon that advised Socrates; the Greek oracles; the miracles of the Old and New Testaments; the miracles of saints such as St. Bernard, St. Francis, and St. Theresa; the phenomena of witchcraft; modern Catholic miracles such as Marian apparitions; psychic powers reported in primitive peoples; the efficacy of prayer; and the phenomena of modern spiritualism (Wallace, 1874; cited in Smith, 1991, pp. 87–89). All of these could be attributed to spirits acting through especially sensitive humans to produce unusual physical and mental effects.

If spirits were nonmaterial or made of "the most diffused and subtle forms of matter" (Wallace, 1896, p. 44), how could they act on, or even produce, substantial material objects? Wallace observed that "all the most powerful and universal forces of nature are now referred to minute vibrations of an almost infinitely attenuated form of matter; and that, by the grandest generalisations of modern science, the most varied natural phenomena have been traced back to these recondite forces" (1896, p. 44). Regarding the "almost infinitely attenuated form of matter," Wallace was referring to a space-filling ether. In his system, the spirit beings would act on the ether, and this subtle action would amplify through the forces of nature into action on the level of observable matter. Wallace further proposed:

> Beings of an ethereal order, if such exist, would probably possess some sense or senses . . . giving them increased insight into the constitution of the universe, and proportionately increased intelligence to guide and direct for special ends those new modes of ethereal motion with which they would in that case be able to deal. Their every faculty might be proportionate to the modes of action of the ether. They might have a power of motion as rapid as that of light or the electric current. They might have a power of vision as acute as that of our most powerful telescopes and microscopes. They might have a sense somewhat analogous to the powers of the last triumph of science, the spectroscope, and by it be enabled to perceive instantaneously, the intimate constitution of matter under every form, whether in organised beings or in stars and nebulae. Such existences, possessed of such, to us, inconceivable powers, would not be supernatural, except in a very lmited and incorrect sense of the term. . . . all would still be natural (1896, pp. 47–48).

The space-filling ether of nineteenth century physics is no longer with us. But there are modern scientific concepts that might allow Wallace's basic system to operate. According to deterministic chaos theorists, immeasurably small random perturbances of matter can rapidly propagate into large-scale effects that are not easily predictable. Scientists sometimes give the example of a Caribbean butterfly that by its wings sets off motions of air molecules. These movements might eventually amplify to steer a hurricane from open sea into the American coast. If the butterfly had flapped its wings slightly differently, the hurricane might not have hit land. According to this idea, Wallace's spirit beings might make infinitesimal adjustments on the subatomic level that would quickly propagate into observable spiritualist effects. One might also propose that they are somehow capable of manipulating the curvature of Einstein's space-time continuum. They could thus produce gravitational effects, for gravity is said to be the result of curvature in the continuum. Or one might propose that the spirit beings induce slight changes in the quantum mechanical vacuum, which in some ways resembles an ether. Of course, this approach is limiting, and rather than straining to find ways to explain spiritualist phenomena in conformity with currently accepted physical laws, it may make more sense to come up with a new theoretical system that more naturally incorporates both the normal and paranormal phenomena. Reintroducing a variety of the ether concept might be one way to do it. One could define the ether as a subtle interface between consciousness and matter.

In terms of modern discussion of the mind/body question, Wallace would be a dualist. He accepted the existence of a conscious self distinct from the physical body. Wallace noted that the bodies of organisms, from primitive to advanced, were built up from molecules, arranged in ever increasing complexity. More, however, was needed to explain consciousness.

> If a material element, or a combination of a thousand material elements in a molecule, are all alike unconscious, it is impossible for us to believe, that the mere addition of one, two, or a thousand other material elements to form a more complex molecule, could in any way produce a self-conscious existence. The things are radically distinct . . . There is no escape from this dilemma, —either all matter is conscious, or consciousness is something distinct from matter, and in the latter case, its presence in material forms is a proof of the existence of conscious beings, outside of, and independent of, what we term matter (Wallace 1870; in Smith, 1991, p. 290).

Wallace favored the latter course, but his system has certain puzzling features. Although a dualist, he does not appear to accept the existence of individual conscious entities before their earthly embodiment. According to Wallace, there is an original spiritual mind from which matter is generated. Individual spiritual minds, associated with spiritual bodies (souls), are only developed from and in material bodies, as they come into existence (Wallace, 1885b; in Smith, 1991, p. 100). After death, the individual minds, as above stated, go to "the first grade of spirit life," where they experience progress or the lack of it based on their earthly habits. But if individual spirit souls can exist after earthly embodiment, why not before? And why is there any need at all for earthly embodiment, which is not an altogether pleasant experience? Why not skip that and go directly to "the first grade of spiritual life"?

A system in which there is preexistence of spirit beings offers a solution. According to Wallace, spirit has free will, and as a result suffers or enjoys the consequences of its actions after death. So if we allow that souls exist before their material embodiment, and also possess free will, we could explain the embodiment of some of these souls by misuse of the same free will. Only those souls who misused their free will would suffer embodiment, which does seem to have some unpleasant features, such as inevitable disease and death.

Here is another problem with Wallace's system. In his works, Wallace details reports of varied spiritualistic phenomena, such as levitation, apparitions, and clairvoyance, from his own time and throughout history. But he ignores reports of transmigration of souls, which occur widely in almost all times and places. The reports of transmigration are just as credible as any other category of evidence he considers. The existence of this phenomenon requires, however, certain modifications in Wallace's system. At death, souls would pass not necessarily into the first phase of spiritual existence but perhaps into new material bodies. According to religious systems that incorporate transmigration, such as the Asian Indian system, some souls, because of their strong attachment to their last embodiment, do not attain new material bodies, but remain for some time as ghosts. This actually fits in quite well with the observations of Wallace and other spiritualists, who found that the spirits they contacted often desired to communicate with living friends and relatives.

Wallace's Spiritualism and Evolution

How did Wallace incorporate his spiritualist ideas into his theory of evolution by natural selection? Specifically, how did his spiritualist ideas relate to his theory of human origins? First of all, Wallace believed that evolution was in some sense directed. Although the origin of species was in general governed by natural selection, natural selection was, in his opinion, not sufficient to account for the exact variety of species we encounter today. Some forces, the nature of which were not clearly understood, and which perhaps never could be understood, shaped the path that evolution by natural selection followed.

Stephen J. Gould, an influential modern evolutionary theorist, has proposed that if we "ran the tape" of evolution again we would not get the same result. For example, we might not get human beings. Indeed, we might "run the tape "a thousand different times and get a thousand different sets of species. In other words, there is a certain contingency rather then inevitability to the evolutionary process. There are so many variables that one cannot predict in advance the path evolution will follow. If there are so many paths, each of which is dependent on millions of accidental occurences, great and small, then this leaves open a possibility Gould is certain to dislike—an original Mind could manipulate the process by undetectable adjustments to get a specific manifest result.

Given a certain initial condition and a desired end result, the Mind-directed pathway, mediated by natural selection, might contain a lot of strange features one would not expect from a traditional Creator, but it would nevertheless be guided and intentional. For example, the panda has a thumblike appendage that it uses to grasp bamboo shoots, its favorite food. Gould points out that the so-called thumb is not a real digit but an outgrowth from the panda's wrist. God would never have created the panda's "thumb," says Gould. Only natural selection could account for such a weird, quirky adaptation. But God and natural selection were, for Wallace, not mutually exclusive. The original Mind could have nudged the path of natural selection in a certain direction to get human beings as an end result. And along the way there could have been many unlikely byproducts such as the panda, with its strange thumb.

Let us consider in more detail the source of guidance in Wallace's system of guided evolution. Anticipating Einstein, Wallace (1870) considered matter a transformation of force, or energy. Force existed in two varieties: "The first consists of the primary forces of nature, such as gravitation, cohesion, repulsion, heat, electricity, etc.; the second is our own will force" (Wallace, 1870, in Smith, 1991, p. 290). The ancient question of free will remains an unresolved problem for most philosophers and scientists right up to the present. Foregoing a review of the entire debate, I shall here simply reproduce the main features of Wallace's argument.

Wallace observed that many persons suggest free will is "but the result of molecular changes in the brain" (1870, in Smith, 1991, p. 291). But he countered that no one has ever proved that all force exhibited in a body can be attributed to known primary forces of nature. Accepting the existence of free will as an observed feature of human consciousness, he proposed that its exercise must involve the exertion of a force capable of setting into motion the other natural forces exhibited in organisms. In this sense, the action of natural forces in an organism could be ultimately traced to the action of will force. This led Wallace to conclude: "If, therefore, we have traced one force, however minute, to an origin in our own WILL, while we have no knowledge of any other primary cause of force, it does not seem an improbable conclusion that all force may be will-force; and thus, that the whole universe, is not merely dependent on, but actually is, the WILL of higher intelligences or of one Supreme Intelligence" (1870; in Smith, 1991, p. 291). In other words, all matter and force in the universe are transformations of the will of a Supreme Intelligence, or intelligences.

The will of higher intelligences, according to Wallace, guided the process of evolution by natural selection. Wallace stated:

> . . . a superior intelligence has guided the development of man in a definite direction, and for a special purpose, just as man guides the development of many animal and vegetable forms. The laws of evolution alone would, perhaps, never have produced a grain so well adapted to man's use as wheat and maize; such traits as the seedless banana and bread-fruit; or such animals as the Guernsey milch cow, or the London dray-horse. Yet these so closely resemble the unaided productions of nature, that we may well imagine a being who had mastered the laws of development of organic forms through past ages, refusing to believe that any new power had been concerned in the production, and scornfully rejecting the theory (as my theory will be rejected by many who agree with me on other points), that in these few cases a controlling intelligence had directed the action of the laws of variation, multiplication, and survival, for his own purposes. We know, however, that this has been done; and we must therefore admit the possibility that, if we are not the highest intelligence in the universe, some higher intelligence may have directed the process by which the human race was developed, by means of more subtle agencies than we are acquainted with (1870, pp. 359–360; in Smith, 1991, p. 289).

Wallace believed that certain physiological features of humans could not be explained by natural selection and survival of the fittest alone. He noted that the brains of primitive peoples were as large and developed as the brains of civilized peoples. It appeared, therefore, that the primitive people had brains with capacities far in excess of those demanded by their daily lives. Wallace said that "natural selection could only have endowed the savage with a brain a little superior to that of an ape" (1869; in Smith, 1991, p. 32). Concerning the human hand, Wallace said the savage "has no need for so fine an instrument, and can no more fully utilise it than he could use without instruction a complete set of joiner's tools" (1869; in Smith, 1991, p. 32). Wallace made similar arguments about the human capacity for speech. He took all of this as evidence that some intelligence had "guided the action" of the laws of evolutionary development "in definite directions and for special ends" (1869; in Smith, 1991, p. 33).

Conclusion

It is not that all contemporary scholars are unaware of Wallace's paranormal researches and his cosmological conclusions (see Smith 1992 for a review). Several studies have been done by historians of science and others, including a few with a motive resembling mine (reenchanting the universe). My revisionist view of Wallace, to be included in a forthcoming book, is, however, more thorough and, uniquely, is motivated by and linked to my explicit commitment to a cosmology transmitted to me through a specific wisdom tradition, that of Gaudiya Vaishnavism. I do not, however, stop with Wallace. In establishing a spiritualist cosmology in my book, I shall expand its hagiographic element to include other saints of modern materialism, such as Nobel laureates Sir William Crookes, a president of the Royal Society, and Nobel laureates Charles Richet, and Marie Curie, who also participated in paranormal research. My work thus adds another colorful thread to the complex tapestry of postmodern interaction of science and culture.

References

Beloff, J. (1993) *Parapsychology: A Concise History.* London: Athlone Press.

Cremo, M. A., and Thompson, R. L. (1993) *Forbidden Archeology.* San Diego: Bhaktivedanta Institute.

Pearson, K. (1914) *Francis Galton: Life and Letters.* Vol. 2. London: n. p.

Smith, C. H., ed. (1991) *Alfred Russel Wallace: An Anthology of His Shorter Writings.* Oxford: Oxford University Press.

Smith, C. H. (1992) *Alfred Russel Wallace on Spiritualism, Man, and Evolution.* Torrington, Connecticut: privately published booklet, 72 pp.

Stein, P. L., and Rowe, B. M. (1993) *Physical Anthropology.* 5th ed. New York: McGraw-Hill.

Trinkaus, E., and Shipman, P. (1992) *The Neandertals.* New York: Vintage.

Wallace, A. R. (1869) Sir Charles Lyell on geological climates and the origin of species. *Quarterly Review,* 126: 359–394. Authorship acknowledged after publication.

Wallace, A. R. (1870) *Contributions to the Theory of Natural Selection. A Series of Essays.* London: Macmillan.

Wallace, A. R. (1874) A defence of modern spiritualism. In two parts. *Fortnightly Review,* 15 (new series), no. 89, pp. 630–657; no. 90, pp. 785–807.

Wallace, A. R. (1885a) Are the phenomena of spiritualism in harmony with science? *The Medium and Daybreak,* 16: 809–810.

Wallace, A. R. (1885b) Harmony of spiritualism and science. *Light,* 5: 352.

Wallace, A. R. (1887) The antiquity of man in North America. *Nineteenth Century,* 22: 667–679.

Wallace, A. R. (1892) Spiritualism. *Chamber's Encyclopaedia.* 10 vols. London: William and Robert Chambers, Ltd. Vol. 9, pp. 645–649.

Wallace, A. R. (1896) *Miracles and Modern Spiritualism.* 3rd ed. London: George Redway.

Wallace, Alfred Russel (1905) *My Life: A Record of Events and Opinions.* 2 volumes. London: Chapman & Hall.

Worsely, P. (1968) *The Trumpet Shall Sound: A Study of Cargo Cults in Melanesia.* 2d ed. New York: Shocken Books.

5

Divine Nature:
Practical Application of Vedic Ethical
Principles in Resolving the Environmental Crisis

This paper was presented at Synthesis of Science and Religion, a conference organized by the Bhaktivedanta Institute, in Calcutta, India, January 9–12, 1997. A version of this paper was also presented at the International Symposium on Energy and Environmental Management and Technology, in Newport Beach, California, January 2–30, 1998. This paper was published as: Cremo, M. A. (2001) Vedic Ethical Principles and the Solution to the Environmental Crisis, in T. D. Singh and Samaresh Bandyopadhyay eds., Thoughts on Synthesis of Science and Religion, *Calcutta, Bhaktivedanta Institute, pp. 209–221.*

If there is to be a synthesis of science and religion, there must be a real desire and need for cooperation. And one area in which the need for cooperation between science and religion is most deeply felt is that of concern for the environment.

In 1995, I attended a conference on population, consumption, and the environment, sponsored by the American Association for the Advancement of Science and the Boston Theological Institute.[1] Coming together at the conference were scientists, politicians, environmental activists, and religionists. I was invited as author of the book *Divine Nature: A Spiritual Perspective on the Environmental Crisis,*[2] which had drawn favorable comment from many, including two former environment ministers for the Indian government.[3] *Divine Nature* looks at the environmental crisis from the standpoint of the Vedic teachings of India.

One of the keynote speakers at the conference on population, consumption, and the environment was Bruce Babbitt, Secretary of the Interior for the United States government.[4] For a politician, Babbitt gave a rather remarkable speech. He told of growing up in the town of Flagstaff, Arizona, from which can be seen a large mountain. The mountain inspired in Babbitt a sense of something wonderful, something godlike, in nature. Raised in the Catholic faith, Babbitt asked a priest about the mountain, hoping to gain some clue as to its spiritual significance. But he received no satisfactory answer, perhaps because his priest was used to thinking of God as remote from nature. Later, Babbitt approached a friend his own age. This friend, who happened to be a native American of the Hopi tribe, took Babbitt up to the mountain and explained to him its sacred nature. And from this Babbitt said he developed a sense of God's presence in nature—to a degree that had not been possible for him previously.

Of course, when I heard this, I was reminded of the *Bhagavad-gita,* wherein Lord Krishna says, "Of immovable things I am the Himalayas,[5] of flowing rivers I am the Ganges,[6] of seasons I am the flower-bearing spring."[7] Such expressions of God's immanence in nature are found throughout the *Gita* and other Indian spiritual texts.

Babbitt went on to say that he understood overconsumption was the underlying cause of most environmental problems. There was a general consensus at the conference that the real issue was not overpopulation in the developing world, but overconsumption, particularly in the developed countries and increasingly in the developing countries. Babbitt said that as a politician he could not present to the people a program that would really solve the environmental problem. It would require too much sacrifice from the voters, so much that they would vote against anyone or any party that told them what would really be necessary.

Secretary Babbitt then turned to the religionists present and said only they could bring about the large-scale changes of values needed to reverse the process of environmental degradation.

Also speaking at the conference was Dr. Henry Kendall, professor of physics at MIT and president of the Union of Concerned Scientists. Dr. Kendall said that science can point out the dimensions of the environmental problem, but it cannot solve the problem. Science, he says, has no silver bullet, no technological fix for the environmental crisis. Like Secretary Babbitt, he recognized overconsumption as the cause of environmental degradation, and like Secretary Babbitt he appealed to religion as the only force in the world capable of generating the changes in values needed to restrain humanity's destructive urge to overproduce and overconsume.

This is not the first time such suggestions have been made. In 1990, at the Global Forum of Spiritual and Parliamentary Leaders, held in Moscow, 32 scientists signed a joint declaration appealing to the world's religions to use their immense influence to preserve the environment.[8] The scientists declared that humanity was committing "crimes against Creation." They also said, "Efforts to safeguard and cherish the environment need to be infused with a vision of the sacred."

These statements are somewhat ironic, for it is science itself, or, should I say, a particular brand of science, that is largely responsible for eliminating the sacred from our vision of the universe. Among the signers of the declaration were Carl Sagan and Stephen J. Gould. And I must say it was intriguing to see them endorsing such language as "crimes against Creation." In their writings, both of them are generally quite hostile to the word "creation," as is most orthodox science. It is interesting, however, how science and religion tend to adopt each other's terminology when it suits them, often redefining the terms in the process. One of the tasks before us is to find a common language for science and religion, and use it with integrity for constructive dialogue.

When I use the word science, I mean science as governed by a certain set of metaphysical assumptions. Today's science is governed by a set of metaphysical assumptions that eliminates the sacred from our vision of the universe, if by sacred we mean things connected with a personal God and distinct individual souls. It is quite possible, however, to have a science governed by a set of metaphysical assumptions that would incorporate a genuine vision of the sacred.

But for today's science, governed by its present materialistic assumptions, nature is an object to be not only understood but dominated, controlled, and exploited. And it is science itself that has provided us with the instruments for such domination, control, and exploitation. Of course, I am speaking of technology. Let's consider the automobile. It is certainly a convenience, but it has its downside. It is one of the main contributors to pollution of the atmosphere, and in the United States alone about 50,000 people a year are killed in automobile accidents. For comparison's sake, we can consider that in the entire eight years of the American military involvement in Vietnam, 50,000 American soldiers were killed. The same number of Americans are killed each year on their own highways.

The connection between a materialistic conception of the universe and a materialistic way of life was noted thousands of years ago in the *Bhagavad-gita*. The *Gita* describes materialist philosophers thus: "They say that this world is unreal, with no foundation, no God in control."[9] And what is the practical outcome for people who live in societies dominated by this worldview, which denies the fundamental reality of God and the soul? The *Gita* says, "They believe that to gratify the senses is the prime necessity of human civilization. Thus until the end of life their anxiety is immeasurable."[10] Such people, says the *Gita*, are "bound by a network of hundreds of thousands of desires."[11] And is this not our situation today? Are we not bombarded daily with messages from radio, television, newspapers, magazines, films, and computers, all attempting to entangle us further in hundreds and thousands of desires that can only be satisfied by consuming various products manufactured by our burgeoning industries? The *Gita* warns us that people like ourselves will "engage in unbeneficial, horrible acts, mean to destroy the world." And are we not gradually destroying our world, polluting its air and water and land, and driving hundreds of species into extinction?

This presents humanity with an ethical dilemma. Put simply, ethics is a process for determining what is good, and how to make choices that will establish and preserve what is good. Given the assumptions of modern materialistic science, it is very difficult to construct an ethic for preserving the environment or saving endangered species. According to currently dominant views, our planet, indeed our very universe, is the result of a cosmic accident, a chance fluctuation of the quantum mechanical vacuum. Given this assumption it is very difficult to say that any particular state of our planet's environment is inherently good. Ultimately, there is no reason to say that our earth, with its teeming life forms, is any better than Jupiter or Uranus, both of which, according to modern astronomy, are frozen lifeless planets, with atmospheres composed of elements we would regard as poisonous. Or looking at the history of our own planet, there is no reason to say that our present state of the environment is any better than that of the early earth, which, according to modern geoscience, was a lifeless rock, with a thin reducing atmosphere hostile to today's life forms.

So if we cannot say, on the basis of modern scientific assumptions, that any particular state of the environment is intrinsically good, and thus worthy of preservation, then perhaps we can approach the matter in another way. We can look at nature, at the environment, as an instrumental good, or source of derivative good. In other words, nature is something that yields things of value to living things. Generally speaking we adopt an anthropocentric view, and consider nature to be instrumental to the happiness of our own human species. But according to the asssumptions of modern evolutionary science, our human species is the accidental product of millions of random genetic mutations. So there is nothing special about the human species and its needs. Of course, we might take a larger view and appeal to nature as an instrumental good for an entire ecosystem, comprised of many species. But again, we have the same problem. Why is today's ecosystem any better than the ecosystem that existed during the Precambrian, when, scientists tell us, there was no life at all on land, and in the oceans only jellyfish and crustaceans?

Another way to proceed is to regard the environment as a constitutive good. An acquaintance of mine, Jack Weir, professor of philosophy at Morehead State University in Kentucky, has presented an argument along these lines.[12] Put briefly, given the evolutionary assumptions of modern science we are what we are largely because of our environment. According to this view, we are in a sense constituted by our environmental surroundings. If our environmental surroundings were different, we would not be able to stay as we are. But here again we run into a problem. Given the evolutionary assumptions of modern science, what is so special about our current status as humans? Why should this status, and the environment that constitutes it, be considered worthy of preservation? Why shouldn't we continue on our present course of overconsumption and environmental destruction? Let natural selection continue to operate, as it supposedly has in the past. Let old species perish and let new ones come into existence. Or let them all perish. Given that life itself is an accident of chemical combination in the earth's early oceans, it is difficult to say why there is any particular preference for a planet with life or without life.

Jack Weir backed up his claim that nature was a constitutive good with appeals to "scientific holism and epistemic coherency." But he admitted that "other appeals could be made, such as to "stories and myths, religious traditions, and metaphysical beliefs." Of course, one could also appeal to a different science, founded upon a different set of metaphysical assumptions and perhaps arriving at different conclusions about the origin of life and the universe.

If we look at this history of science, from the time of Newton until the present, we find that scientists have accumulated quite a large body of evidence suggesting there is a vital force operating in living things, a force operating beyond the laws of physics and chemistry as currently understood. All around the world, we find great interest in alternative systems of medicine, such as the one in the Ayur Veda, which are based on the understanding of this vital force, or forces. At the UCLA medical school there is an institute devoted to integrating the insights of traditional Eastern medical systems with Western medicine.

There is also quite an accumulation of evidence suggesting that there is a conscious self that can exist apart from the physical organism. This evidence comes from studies of phenomena ranging from out of body experiences to past life memories. Much of this evidence does not easily fit into the materialistic assumptions of modern science, and is therefore regarded with considerable suspicion. But this body of evidence is increasing daily, and it could be incorporated into the framework of a new science operating with an expanded set of metaphysical assumptions. Aside from the Bhaktivedanta Institute, there are a number of scientific societies attempting this, among them the Scientific and Medical Network in England, the Institute for Noetic Sciences in the United States, the Society for Scientific Exploration, the International Society for the Study of Subtle Energy and Energy Medicine, and others. Furthermore, as scientists carry their research into the biomolecular machinery within the cell, they encounter structures and systems of irreducible complexity, which leads some of them to once more seriously entertain the idea of intelligent design rather than chance evolution as an explanation. In this regard, I can recommend biochemist Michael Behe's various papers or his recent book *Darwin's Black Box*.

This past November I spoke to a gathering of physicists at the department of nuclear physics at the ELTE science university in Budapest, Hungary. I shared the podium with Maurice Wilkins, a British Nobel Laureate in physics, whose discoveries helped in the construction of the atomic bomb during the Second World War. The topic was, as here, science and religion. I chose as my topic physics and the paranormal. I proposed that if there was to be any synthesis of science and religion it would have to be on the mysterious ground of reality that lies between them, and undoubtedly their understanding of this mysterious ground of reality would have to be renegotiated.

In terms of physics it might involve a return to an understanding of reality that had a nonmaterial, nonmechanistic component. I pointed out that Newton wrote just as much about alchemy and spiritual topics as he did about his mathematics, physics, and optics, and that for Newton, his physics, alchemy, and writings about mystical topics were all part of one system, from which modern science has abstracted only the part that suits it. The idea of serious investigation into nonmaterial or paranormal components of physical reality is today taboo, but it has not always been so. In the last century, we find Sir William Crookes, an inventor of the cathode ray tube and president of the Royal Society, conducting extensive research into the paranormal. Nobel laureate physiologist Charles Richet, of France, who himself conducted extensive research into paranormal phenomena, tells us in his book *Thirty Years of Psychical Research* that he was sometimes assisted by Pierre and Marie Curie, who shared the Nobel prize in physics for their discoveries in the field of radioactive elements. For example, we find Marie Curie controlling a famous medium, while Pierre Curie measured the movements of objects moving under apparent psychokinetic influence. I am not bringing up these incidents to prove the reality of the phenonmena but to illustrate the openmindedness of these famous experimental physicists, their willingness to investigate a difficult and troubling phenomenon. But isn't that what science, at its best, is supposed to be about?

After I finished my talk in Budapest, I wondered, of course, how it had been received. I was surprised when the head of the physcis department of a major European university approached me and revealed that in his home he had been privately conducting some telepathic experiments. To his extreme surprise, he had achieved some interesting results, and he asked me if I could put him in touch with others in America who were conducting similar investigations.

Now what does all this have to do with the environment, with nature? It has everything to do with it, because if we are going to formulate an environmental ethic, we first should understand what our environment really is. And from the Vedic, and in particular Vaishnava, standpoint, we would have to say that it is a divine energy, an energy emanating from a transcendent God who is nevertheless immanent in nature, which is itself populated with conscious entities, and structured in a definite way for a definite purpose, namely providing an opportunity for these conscious entities to return to their original pure state. And there is a body of scientific evidence that is consistent with several elements of this view. In other words, religion may be something more than a socially useful set of beliefs that can be harnessed by science to help solve certain problems, such as the environmental crisis. I regard that as a false synthesis of science and religion. It just may be the case that religion has crucial insights into the nature of reality that can be foundational for a true synthesis of science and religion for the benefit of humankind.

With these foundational assumptions it becomes easier to formulate an environmental ethic. Given that, according to Vaishnava teaching, this world is a reflection of a variegated, and essentially gardenlike, spiritual reality, we could say that there is some intrinsic value in attempting to maintain a state of the environment that most closely matches the original. When children learn to write, they are generally asked to copy letters, and if their attempt resembles the original it is said to be good, if it does not it is said to be bad. In the same way, we can propose that there is some intrinsic goodness to a particular state of environmental affairs.

Furthermore, there are certain Vedic principles that contribute in various ways to a viable environmental ethic. The first of these is *athato brahma jijnasa*. This is the opening mantra of the *Vedanta Sutra*. It means that the purpose of human life is cultivation of consciousness, including cultivation of the loving relationship between the individual consciousnesss and the supreme consciousness.

I want to interject here that it is not every religious teaching that leads to a viable environmental ethic. There are many manifestations of religion which, like modern materialistic science, encourage the destructive processes of domination, exploitation, and unending consumption. But the Vedic system emphasizes the study and development of consciousness over the study and development of matter. Matter is not ignored, but it is seen in its connection with the supreme consciousness. In any case, the principle of *brahma jijnasa* encourages an ethic of moderation, which contributes to reasonable levels of economic development and consumption that would not place such a great burden on the ecosystem.

The *Vedanta Sutra* also says *anandamayo 'bhyasat*. We are meant for happiness, and by cultivating consciousness by proper means we can attain nonmaterial satisfaction. And this also sustains an ethic of moderation. The *Gita* says *param drstva nivartate*.[13] When you get the higher taste of developed spiritual consciousness you automatically refrain from excessive material gratification. A proper balance is achieved.

The Vedic principle of *ahimsa*, or nonviolence, also has its application. Nonviolence can be understood in many ways. For example, to encourage people to devote their lives to unrestrained material production and consumption can be considered a kind of violence against the human spirit, and I think we just have to look around us to see the effects of this violence. If we look at Americans at Christmas time crowding into their shiny malls, and instead of heeding the Vedic teaching *athato brahma jijnasa* devoting themselves to the teaching of shop until you drop, I think we see a kind of violence. When we see the young Chinese workers who are crowded into dormitories around the factories that provide most of the Christmas goods found in the American malls, we might also sense that violence to the human spirit.

The principle of *ahimsa* can also be applied to the earth itself. We have recently heard of the Gaia principle, the idea that the earth is in some sense an organism. This principle has long been recognized in Vedic philosophy, and we should try not to commit violence to our planet, by unncessarily poisoning her air, land, and water.

And nonviolence also applies to other living things. Accepting the Vedic teaching of *ahimsa* we will not hunt species to extinction. I will also point out that the killing of animals for food, especially animals raised in factory farms and killed in huge mechanized slaughterhouses, is one of the most environmentally destructive practices in the world today. It is wasteful of precious natural resources. It poisons the land and water.

It can thus be seen that Vedic philosophy provides numerous supports for an ethic of environmental preservation. Similar support can be derived from the teachings of other great religious traditions of the world. But putting this wisdom into practice is difficult. In many areas of ethical concern, we can adopt an objective stance. If we are talking about child molestation, for example, we can feel secure that not many of us are guilty of such a thing, and we can quite comfortably discuss the ethical implications of such behavior, and what steps might be taken to control it without seeming to be hypocrites. But when we speak of the environmental crisis we find that almost all of us are directly implicated. And it is therefore difficult to speak about environmental ethics without seeming to be hypocritical. Nevertheless we must speak. And this engenders in us a sense of humility, and also a sense that even small steps toward the real solution, which must be a spiritual solution, are to be welcomed and appreciated.

Alan Durning, a senior researcher at the World Watch Institute, wrote, "It would be hopelessy naive to believe that entire populations will suddenly experience a moral awakening, renouncing greed, envy, and avarice. The best that can be hoped for is a gradual widening of the circle of those practicing voluntary simplicity."[14]

In this regard, I want to briefly mention that Bhaktivedanta Swami Prabhupada during his life established several intentional rural communities for the specific purpose of demonstrating a life of such voluntary simplicity. Since his departure from this world in 1977, the number of such communities has increased to 40 on five continents, in locations ranging from the Atlantic rain forest region of Brazil to the steppes of Russia.

After I spoke to the physicists in Budapest, I had a chance to visit one of these communities. I have to confess I was rather astonished to find such a rural community founded on Vedic principles in the plains of southwestern Hungary [see **Plate XXVIII**]. The center of the community was a somewhat modernistic temple, but when I inquired I learned that it had been constructed using rammed earth walls and other traditional techniques. No electricity was used in the temple or anywhere else in the community. Along the temple walls I saw brass lamps, which burned oil pressed from locally grown rape seeds. It was a rather cold day in November, and I saw the building was heated with superefficient woodburning stoves, using wood sustainably harvested from a 50 acre plot of forest owned by the community. I was then offered a vegetarian meal, which featured locally grown vegetables, chapatis made from wheat grown and ground in the community, and cheese from the community's cows. I learned that oxen are being trained to do farm work and transport. The people I met did not seem in any way deprived.

I told some of them, "You're doing the right thing." And isn't that what environmental ethics is all about, not just talking about the right thing, but doing it?

To summarize, from the standpoint of Vedic principles, I would say the following elements are necessary for a complete solution to the environmental crisis. (1) a science that recognizes distinct conscious selves, emanating from an original conscious self, as fundamental entities. (2) a religion that goes beyond dogma and ritual to provide actual sources of nonmaterial satisfaction by practice of meditation, yoga, etc. (3) respect for all living things, seeing them as conscious selves like us. (4) an ecofriendly vegetarian diet (5) an economic system founded on villages and small cities, emphasizing local production and self sufficiency. Anything short of this simply will not give the desired result.

Notes:

1. The conference Consumption, Population, and the Environment was held November 9–11, 1995 at the Campion Retreat Center outside Boston.
2. Michael A. Cremo and Mukunda Goswami (1995) *Divine Nature: A Spiritual Perspective on the Environmental Crisis.* Los Angeles: Bhaktivedanta Book Trust.
3. On May 5, 1995, Kamal Nath, then Minister of Environment and Forests, wrote: "At a time when the world's developing countries are tending to let industrial progress take over their economies, oblivious to environmental destruction, *Divine Nature* comes as a welcome breath of relief. The authors have persuasively argued that a return to the original value of humanity's deep spiritual kinship with all living things is the key to achieving pervasive environmental consciousness." And on June 16, 1995, Maneka Gandhi, a former Minister of Environment and Forests, wrote: "This book should be read as a management plan for the economy, especially by politicians and business managers who, having gotten us into the mess we are in by promoting cultural and eating patterns that are destructive, in the mistaken belief that money can be made through devastation, could now truly understand how to repair the earth in a way that all of us can live, not merely exist."
4. The Interior department is in charge of the national park system, and oversees the environmental resource management of large areas of goverment-owned land. The account of his statements is taken from my notes on his speech.
5. *Bhagavad-gita* 10.25. The translations quoted in this paper are from His Divine Grace A. C. Bhaktivedanta Swami Prabhupada, *Bhagavad-gita As It Is,* complete edition, revised and enlarged, Los Angeles: Bhaktivedanta Book Trust, 1989.

6. *Bhagavad-gita* 10.31

7. *Bhagavad-gita* 10.35. After listing numerous manifestations of His presence in nature, Krishna goes on to say in *Bhagavad-gita* 10.41: "Know that all opulent, beautiful, and glorious creations spring from but a spark of My splendor." This indicates that God, although immanent in nature, also transcends nature.

8. The statement was titled "Preserving and Cherishing the Earth: An Appeal for Joint Commitment in Science and Religion." The quotations in this paper are from a machine copy of the original statement.

9. *Bhagavad-gita* 16.8

10. *Bhagavad-gita* 16.11

11. *Bhagavad-gita* 16.12

12. Jack Weir (1995) Bread, labor: Tolstoy, Gandhi, and deep ecology. Presented at the Kentucky State University Institute for Liberal Studies Sixth Annual Interdisciplinary Conference on Science and Culture, Frankfort, Kentucky. Unpublished.

13. *Bhagavad-gita* 2.59

14. Alan Durning (1990) How much Is 'enough.' *World Watch*, November–December, pp. 12–19.

6

The Later Discoveries of Boucher de Perthes at Moulin Quignon and Their Bearing on the Moulin Quignon Jaw Controversy

I presented this paper at the XXth International Congress of History of Science, held in Liège, Belgium, July 19–26, 1997. This paper was later selected for publication in a peer-reviewed conference proceedings volume: Cremo, M. A. (2002) The Later Discoveries of Boucher de Perthes at Moulin Quignon and Their Impact on the Moulin Quignon Jaw Controversy. In Goulven Laurent ed. Proceedings of the XXth International Congress of History of Science (Liege, 20–26 July 1997), Volume X, Earth Sciences, Geography and Cartography. *Turnhout, Belgium: Brepols, pp. 39–56*

My book *Forbidden Archeology*, coauthored with Richard L. Thompson, examines the history of archeology and documents numerous discoveries suggesting that anatomically modern humans existed in times earlier than now thought likely. According to most current accounts, anatomically modern humans emerged within the past one or two hundred thousand years from more primitive ancestors. Much of the evidence for greater human antiquity, extending far back into the Tertiary, was discovered by scientists in the nineteenth and early twentieth centuries. Current workers are often unaware of this remarkable body of evidence. In their review article about *Forbidden Archeology,* historians of science Wodak and Oldroyd (1996, p. 197) suggest that "perhaps historians bear some responsibility" for this lack of attention:

> Certainly, some pre-*FA* [*Forbidden Archeology*] histories of palaeoanthropology, such as Peter Bowler's, say little about the kind of evidence adduced by C&T [Cremo and Thompson], and the same may be said of some texts published since 1993, such as Ian Tattersall's recent book. So perhaps the rejection of Tertiary [and early Pleistocene] *Homo sapiens,* like other scientific determinations, is a social construction in which historians of science have participated. C&T claim that there has been a 'knowledge filtration operating within the scientific community', in which historians have presumably played their part. [Interpolations in brackets are mine.]

I am also guilty of this knowledge filtering. In this paper, I give an example of my own failure to free myself from unwarranted prejudice.

The collective failure of scientists and historians to properly comprehend and record the history of investigations into human antiquity has substantial consequences on the present development of human antiquity studies. Current workers should have ready access to the complete data set, not just the portion marshaled in support of the current picture of the past and the history of this picture's elaboration. The value of historians' work in maintaining the complete archive of archeological data in accessible form can thus be significant for ongoing human antiquity studies. This approach does not, as some have suggested, entail uncritical acceptance of all past reporting. But it does entail suspension of naive faith in the progressive improvement in scientific reporting.

In February of 1997, I lectured on *Forbidden Archeology* to students and faculty of archeology and earth sciences at the University of Louvain, Belgium. Afterwards, one of the students, commenting on some of the nineteenth century reports I presented, asked how we could accept them, given that these reports had already been rejected long ago and that scientific understanding and methods had greatly improved since the nineteenth century. I answered, "If we suppose that in earlier times scientists accepted bad evidence because of their imperfect understanding and methods then we might also suppose they rejected good evidence because of their imperfect understanding and methods. There is no alternative to actually looking critically at specific cases." This is not necessarily the task of the working archeologist. But the historian of archeology may here play a useful role.

The specific case I wish to consider is that of the discoveries of Jacques Boucher de Perthes at Moulin Quignon. This site is located at Abbeville, in the valley of the Somme in northeastern France. In *Forbidden Archeology*, I confined myself to the aspects of the case that are already well known to historians (Cremo and Thompson 1993, pp. 402–404). To summarize, in the 1840s Boucher de Perthes discovered stone tools in the Middle Pleistocene high level gravels of the Somme, at Moulin Quignon and other sites. At first, the scientific community, particularly in France, was not inclined to accept his discoveries as genuine. Some believed that the tools were manufactured by forgers. Others believed them to be purely natural forms that happened to resemble stone tools. Later, leading British archeologists visited the sites of Boucher de Perthes's discoveries and pronounced them genuine. Boucher de Perthes thus became a hero of science. His discoveries pushed the antiquity of man deep into the Pleistocene, coeval with extinct mammals. But the exact nature of the maker of these tools remained unknown. Then in 1863, Boucher de Perthes discovered at Moulin Quignon additional stone tools and an anatomically modern human jaw. The jaw inspired much controversy, and was the subject of a joint English-French commission. To do justice to the entire proceedings (Falconer *et al.* 1863, Delesse 1863) would take a book, so I shall in this paper touch on only a few points of contention.

The English members of the commission thought the stone tools discovered in 1863 were forgeries that had been artificially introduced into the Moulin Quignon strata. They thought the same of the jaw. To settle the matter, the commission paid a surprise visit to the site. Five flint implements were found in the presence of the scientists. The commission approved by majority vote a resolution in favor of the authenticity of the recently discovered stone tools. Sir John Prestwich remained in the end skeptical but nevertheless noted (1863, p. 505) that "the precautions we took seemed to render imposition on the part of the workmen impossible."

That authentic flint implements should be found at Moulin Quignon is not surprising, because flint implements of unquestioned authenticity had previously been found there and at many other sites in the same region. There was no dispute about this at the time, nor is there any dispute about this among scientists today. The strange insistence on forgery and planting of certain flint implements at Moulin Quignon seems directly tied to the discovery of the Moulin Quignon jaw, which was modern in form. If the jaw had not been found, I doubt there would have been any objections at all to the stone tools that were found in the gravel pit around the same time.

In addition to confirming the authenticity of the stone tools from Moulin Quignon, the commission also concluded that there was no evidence that the jaw had been fraudulently introduced into the Moulin Quignon gravel deposits (Falconer *et al.* 1863, p. 452). The presence of grey sand in the inner cavities of the jaw, which had been found in a blackish clay deposit, had caused the English members of the commission to suspect that the jaw had been taken from somewhere else. But when the commission visited the site, some members noted the presence of a layer of fine grey sand just above the layer of black deposits in which the jaw had been found (Falconer *et al.* 1863, pp. 448–449). This offered an explanation for the presence of the grey sand in the Moulin Quignon jaw and favored its authenticity.

Trinkaus and Shipman (1992, p. 96) insinuate, incorrectly, that the commission's favorable resolution simply absolved Boucher de Perthes of any fraudulent introduction of the jaw (hinting that others may have planted it). But that is clearly not what the commission intended to say, as anyone can see from reading the report in its entirety. Here are the exact words of Trinkaus and Shipman:

> In any case, the commission found itself deadlocked. There was only one point of agreement: "The jaw in question was not fraudulently introduced into the gravel pit of Moulin Quignon [by Boucher de Perthes]; it had existed previously in the spot where M. Boucher de Perthes found it on the 28th March 1863." This lukewarm assertion of his innocence, rather than his correctness, was hardly the type of scientific acclaim and vindication that Boucher de Perthes yearned for. [the interpolation is by Trinkaus and Shipman]

But the commission (Falconer *et al.* 1863, p. 452) also voted in favor of the following resolution: "All leads one to think that the deposition of this jaw was contemporary with that of the pebbles and other materials constituting the mass of clay and gravel designated as the black bed, which rests immediately above the chalk." This was exactly the conclusion desired by Boucher de Perthes. Only two members, Busk and Falconer, abstained. The committee as a whole was far from deadlocked.

Their scientific objections having been effectively countered, the English objectors, including John Evans, who was not able to join the commission in France, were left with finding further proof of fraudulent behavior among the workmen at Moulin Quignon as their best weapon against the jaw. Taking advantage of a suggestion by Boucher de Perthes himself, Evans sent his trusted assistant Henry Keeping, a working man with experience in archeological excavation, to France. There he supposedly obtained definite proof that the French workmen were introducing tools into the deposits at Moulin Quignon.

But careful study of Keeping's reports (Evans 1863) reveals little to support these allegations and suspicions. Seven implements, all supposedly fraudulent, turned up during Keeping's brief stay at Moulin Quignon. Five were found by Keeping himself and two were given to him by the two French workers who were assigned by Boucher de Perthes to assist him. Keeping's main accusation was that the implements appeared to have "fingerprints" on them. The same accusation had been leveled by the English members of the commission against the tools earlier found at Moulin Quignon. In his detailed discussion of Keeping, which is well worth reading, Boucher de Perthes (1864a, pp. 207–208) remarked that he and others had never been able to discern these fingerprints. Boucher de Perthes (1864a, p. 197, 204) also observed that Keeping was daily choosing his own spots to work and that it would have been quite difficult for the workers, if they were indeed planting flint implements, to anticipate where he would dig. I tend to agree with Boucher de Perthes (1864a, pp. 194–195) that Keeping, loyal to his master Evans, was well aware that he had been sent to France to find evidence of fraud and that he dared not return to England without it. Evans's report (1863), based on Keeping's account, was published in an English periodical and swayed many scientists to the opinion that Boucher des Perthes was, despite the favorable conclusions of the scientific commission, the victim of an archeological fraud.

Not everyone was negatively influenced by Keeping's report. In *Forbidden Archeology*, I cited Sir Arthur Keith (1928, p. 271), who stated, "French anthropologists continued to believe in the authenticity of the jaw until between 1880 and 1890, when they ceased to include it in the list of discoveries of ancient man."

I also was inclined to accept the jaw's authenticity, but given the intensity of the attacks by the English, in *Forbidden Archeology* I simply noted, "From the information we now have at our disposal, it is difficult to form a definite opinion about the authenticity of the Moulin Quignon jaw." I stated this as a mild antidote to the nearly universal current opinion that the Moulin Quignon jaw and accompanying tools were definitely fraudulent. But because Evans and his English accomplices had so thoroughly problematized the evidence, I could not bring myself to suggest more directly that the Moulin Quignon jaw was perhaps genuine.

Boucher des Perthes, however, entertained no doubts as to the authenticity of the jaw, which he had seen in place in the black layer toward the bottom of the Moulin Quignon pit. He believed it had been rejected because of political and religious prejudice in England. Stung by accusations of deception, he proceeded to carry out a new set of excavations, which resulted in the recovery of more human skeletal remains. These later discoveries are hardly mentioned in standard histories, which dwell upon the controversy surrounding the famous Moulin Quignon jaw.

For example, the later discoveries of Boucher des Perthes rate only a line or two in Grayson (1983, p. 217):

> Evans's demonstration of fraud and the strongly negative reaction of the British scientists ensured that the Moulin Quignon mandible would never be accepted as an undoubted human fossil. The same applied to additional human bones reported from Moulin Quignon in 1864.

Trinkaus and Shipman (1992, p. 96) are similarly dismissive:

> Desperately, Boucher de Perthes continued to excavate at Moulin Quignon. He took to calling in impromptu commissions (the mayor, stray geology professors, local doctors, lawyers, librarians, priests, and the like) to witness the event when he found something, or thought he was about to find something, significant. . . . Soon, the English and French scientists stopped coming to look at his material or paying any real attention to his claims.

Although aware of these later discoveries, I did not discuss them in *Forbidden Archeology*. I thus implicated myself in the process of inadvertent suppression of anomalous evidence posited in *Forbidden Archeology* (Cremo and Thompson 1993, p. 28):

> This evidence now tends to be extremely obscure, and it also tends to be surrounded by a neutralizing nimbus of negative reports, themselves obscure and dating from the time when the evidence was being actively rejected. Since these reports are generally quite derogatory, they may discourage those who read them from examining the rejected evidence further.

The cloud of negative reporting surrounding the Moulin Quignon jaw influenced not only my judgment of this controversial find but also discouraged me from looking into the later discoveries of Boucher des Perthes. So let us now look into these discoveries and see if they are really deserving of being totally ignored or summarily dismissed.

Boucher de Perthes (1864b), stung by the accusations he had been deceived, carried out his new investigations so as to effectively rule out the possibility of deception by workmen. First of all, they were carried out during a period when the quarry at Moulin Quignon was shut down and the usual workmen were not there (1864b, p. 219). Also, Boucher de Perthes made his investigations unannounced and started digging at random places. He would usually hire one or two workers, whom he closely supervised. Furthermore, he himself would enter into the excavation and break up the larger chunks of sediment with his own hands. In a few cases, he let selected workers, who were paid only for their labor, work under the supervision of a trusted assistant. In almost all cases, witnesses with scientific or medical training were present. In some cases, these witnesses organized their own careful excavations to independently confirm the discoveries of Boucher de Perthes.

Here follow excerpts from accounts by Boucher de Perthes and others of these later discoveries. They are taken from the proceedings of the local Société d'Émulation. Most French towns had such societies, composed of educated gentlemen, government officials, and businessmen.

On April 19, 1864 Boucher de Perthes took a worker to the gravel pit, and on the exposed face of the excavation pointed out some places for a worker to dig. Boucher de Perthes (1864b, p. 219) "designated every spot where he should strike with his pick." In this manner, he discovered a hand axe, two other smaller worked flints, and several flint flakes. Then the worker's pick "struck an agglomeration of sand and gravel, which broke apart, as did the bone it contained." Boucher de Perthes (1864b, p. 219) stated "I took from the bank the part that remained, and recognized the end of a human femur." This find occurred at a depth 2.3 meters, in the hard, compacted bed of yellowish brown sand and gravel lying directly above the chalk. In this, as in all cases, Boucher de Perthes had checked very carefully to see that the deposit was undisturbed and that there were no cracks or fissures through which a bone could have slipped down from higher levels (p. 219). Digging further at the same spot, he encountered small fragments of bone, including an iliac bone, 40 centimeters from the femur and in the same plane (p. 219).

On April 22, Boucher de Perthes found a piece of human skull 4 centimeters long in the yellow brown bed. This yellow-brown bed contains in its lower levels some seams of yellow-grey sand. In one of these seams. Boucher de Perthes found more skull fragments and a human tooth (1864b, p. 220).

On April 24, Boucher de Perthes was joined by Dr. J. Dubois, a physician at the Abbeville municipal hospital and a member of the Anatomical Society of Paris. They directed the digging of a worker in the yellow-brown bed. They uncovered some fragments too small to identify. But according to Dubois they displayed signs of incontestable antiquity. Boucher de Perthes and Dubois continued digging for some time, without finding anything more. "Finally," stated Boucher de Perthes (1864b, p. 221), "we saw in place, and Mr. Dubois detached himself from the bank, a bone that could be identified. It was 8 centimeters long. Having removed a portion of its matrix, Mr. Dubois recognized it as part of a human sacrum. Taking a measurement, we found it was lying 2.6 meters from the surface." About 40 centimeters away, they found more bones, including a phalange. They then moved to a spot close to where the jaw was discovered in 1863. They found parts of a cranium and a human tooth, the latter firmly embedded in a pebbly mass of clayey sand (p. 222). The tooth was found at a depth of 3.15 meters from the surface (p. 223).

On April 28, Boucher de Perthes began a deliberate search for the other half of the sacrum he had found on April 24. He was successful, locating the missing half of the sacrum bone about one meter from where the first half had been found. He also found a human tooth fragment in a seam of grey sand. Studying the edge of the break, Boucher de Perthes noted it was quite worn, indicating a degree of antiquity (1864b, p. 223).

On May 1, accompanied for most of the day by Dr. Dubois, Boucher de Perthes found three fragments of human skulls, a partial human tooth, and a complete human tooth (1864b, p. 223). On May 9, Boucher de Perthes (pp. 223–224) found two human skull fragments, one fairly large (9 centimeters by 8 centimeters).

On May 12, Boucher de Perthes carried out explorations in the company of Mr. Hersent-Duval, the owner of the Moulin Quignon gravel pit. They first recovered from the yellow bed, at a depth of about two meters, a large piece of a human cranium, 8 centimeters long and 7 centimeters wide. "An instant later," stated Boucher de Perthes (1864b, p. 224), "the pick having detached another piece of the bank, Mr. Hersent-Duval opened it and found a second fragment of human cranium, but much smaller. It was stuck so tightly in the mass of clay and stones that it took much trouble to separate it."

On May 15, Boucher de Perthes extracted from one of the seams of grey sand in the yellow-brown bed, at a depth of 3.2 meters, a human tooth firmly embedded in a chunk of sand and flint. The tooth was white. Boucher de Perthes (1864b, p. 225) noted: "It is a very valuable specimen, that replies very well to the . . . objection that the whiteness of a tooth is incompatible with its being a fossil." He then found in the bed of yellow-brown sand "a human metatarsal, still attached in its matrix, with a base of flint" (p. 225). In the same bed he also found many shells, which also retained their white color. Boucher de Perthes (1864b, p. 226) observed: "Here the color of the bank, even the deepest, does not communicate itself to the rolled flints, nor to the shells, nor to the teeth, which all preserve their native whiteness." This answered an earlier objection to the antiquity of the original Moulin Quignon jaw and a detached tooth found along with it.

On June 6, Boucher de Perthes (1864b, p. 230) found in the yellow-brown bed, at a depth of 4 meters, the lower half of a human humerus, along with several less recognizable bone fragments. On June 7, he recovered part of a human iliac bone at the same place (p. 231). On June 8 and 9, he found many bone fragments mixed with flint tools, including many hand axes. Later on June 10, he returned with three workers to conduct bigger excavations. He found two fragments of tibia (one 14 centimeters long) and part of a humerus (p. 231). These bones had signs of wear and rolling. They came from a depth of four meters in the yellow-brown bed. Please note that I am just recording the discoveries of human bones. On many days, Boucher de Perthes also found fragments of bones and horns of large mammals. Boucher de Perthes (1864b, p. 232) noted that the human bones were covered with a matrix of the same substance as the bed in which they were found. When the bones were split, it was found that traces of the matrix were also present in their internal cavities (p. 232). Boucher de Perthes (1864b, p. 232) noted that these are not the kinds of specimens that could be attributed to "cunning workers." On this particular day, Boucher de Perthes left the quarry for some time during the middle of the day, leaving the workers under the supervision of an overseer. Boucher de Perthes (1864b, pp. 233–235) then reported:

> In the afternoon, I returned to the bank. My orders had been punc-
> tually executed. My representative had collected some fragments of
> bone and worked flints. But a much more excellent discovery had been
> made—this was a lower human jaw, complete except for the extremity of

the right branch and the teeth.

My first concern was to verify its depth. I measured it at 4.4 meters, or 30 centimeters deeper than the spot where I had that morning discovered several human remains. The excavation, reaching the chalk at 5.1 meters, faced the road leading to the quarry. It was 20 meters from the point, near the mill, where I found the half-jaw on March 28, 1863.

The jaw's matrix was still moist and did not differ at all from that of all the other bones from that same bed. The matrix was very sticky, mixed with gravel and sometimes with pieces of bone, shells, and even teeth.

The teeth were missing from the jaw. They were worn or broken a little above their sockets, such that the matrix that covered them impaired their recognition. The deterioration was not recent, but dated to the origin of the bank.

Although I did not see that jaw *in situ*, after having minutely verified the circumstances of its discovery, I do not have the least doubt as to its authenticity. Its appearance alone suffices to support that conviction. Its matrix, as I have said, is absolutely identical to that of all the other bones and flints from the same bed. Because of its form and hardness, it would be impossible to imitate.

The worker in the trench, after having detached some of the bank, took it out with his shovel. But he did not see the jaw, nor could he have seen it, enveloped as it was in a mass of sand and flint that was not broken until the moment that the shovel threw it into the screen. It is then . . . that it was seen by the overseer.

He recognized it as a bone, but not seeing the teeth, he did not suspect it was a jaw. Mr. Hersent-Duval, who happened to come by at that moment, was undeceived. He signaled the workers and told them to leave it as it was, in its matrix, until my arrival, which came shortly thereafter.

After a short examination, I confirmed what Mr. Hersent had said. It was not until then that the workers believed. Until that moment, the absence of teeth and the unusual form of the piece, half-covered with clay, had caused even my overseer himself to doubt.

I therefore repeat: here one cannot suspect anyone. Strangers to the quarry and the town, these diggers had no interest in deception. I paid them for their work, and not for what they found. . . . Dr. Dubois, to whom I was eager to show it, found it from the start to have a certain resemblance to the one found on March 28, 1863.

On June 17, Hersent-Duval had some workers dig a trench. They encountered some bones. Hersent-Duval ordered them to stop work, leaving the bones in place. He then sent a message for Boucher de Perthes to come. Boucher de Perthes arrived, accompanied by several learned gentlemen of Abbeville, including Mr. Martin, who was a professor of geology and also a parish priest. Boucher de Perthes (1864b, pp. 235–237) stated:

> Many fragments, covered in their matrix, lay at the bottom of the excavation, at a depth of 4 meters. At 3 meters, one could see two points, resembling two ends of ribs.
>
> Mr. Martin, who had descended with us into the trench, touched these points, and not being able to separate them, thought that they might belong to the same bone. I touched them in turn, as did Abbey Dergny, and we agreed with his opinion.
>
> Before extracting it, these gentlemen wanted to assure themselves about the state of the terrain. It was perfectly intact, without any kind of slippage, fissures, or channels, and it was certainly undisturbed. Having acquired this certainty, the extraction took place by means of our own hands, without the intermediary of a worker.
>
> Mr. Martin, having removed part of the envelope of the extracted bone, recognized it as a human cranium. And the two points at first taken as two ends of ribs, were the extremities of the brow ridges. This cranium, of which the frontal and the two parietals were almost complete, astonished us with a singular depression in its upper part.
>
> This operation accomplished, we occupied ourselves with the bones fallen to the bottom of the quarry. They were three in number, covered by a mass of clay so thick that one could not tell the kind of creature to which they belonged. Much later, they were identified by Dr. Dubois as a human iliac bone, a right rib, and two pieces of an upper jaw, perhaps from the same head as the partial cranium, because they came from the same bed.
>
> Having continued our excavation, we found yet another human bone, and we probably would have encountered others, if we had been able, without the danger of a landslide, to carry out the excavation still further.
>
> All of this was recorded by Abbey Dergny, in a report signed by him and professor Martin . . . one of the most knowledgeable and respected men of our town.

On July 9th, a commission composed of the following individuals made an excavation at Moulin Quignon: Louis Trancart, mayor of Laviers; Pierre Sauvage, assistant to the mayor of Abbeville, and member of the Société d'Émulation of that town; F. Marcotte, conservator of the museum of Abbeville, and member of the Société d'Émulation and the Academy of Amiens; A. de Caïeu, attorney, and member of the Société d'Émulation and the Society of Antiquaries of Picardy; and Jules Dubois, M.D., doctor at the municipal hospital of Abbeville, member of many scientific societies (Dubois 1864a, p. 265).

At the quarry they carried out excavations at two sites. Marcotte, who had proclaimed his skepticism about the discoveries, was chosen to direct the digging of the workers. "He had the base of the excavation cleared away until it was possible to see the chalk, upon which directly rested the bed of yellow-brown sand," said Dubois (1864a, p. 266) in his report on the excavation of the first site in the quarry. "After we assured ourselves that the wall of the cut was clearly visible to us and that it was free of any disturbance, the work commenced under our direct inspection." After 15 minutes of digging, Marcotte recovered a bone that Dubois (1864a, p. 266) characterized as probably a piece of a human radius 8 centimeters long. The bone was worn and covered by a tightly adhering matrix of the same nature as the surrounding terrain. The excavation proceeded for a long time without anything else being found until Mr. Trancart found part of a human femur or humerus (p. 267). Some minutes later Trancart recovered a broken portion of a human tibia.

The commission then moved to the second site, about 11 meters away. It is movements like these that remove suspicions the bones were being planted. Dubois (1864a, p. 267) stated: "Here again we had to clear away the base of the section to reveal the actual wall of the quarry. The same precautions were taken to assure the homogeneity of the bed and the absence of any disturbance." At this site, Marcotte found a piece of a human femur, about 13 centimeters long (p. 268). It came from the bed of yellow brown sand which lies directly on the chalk. Boucher de Perthes (1864b, p. 237) noted that two hand axes were also found on the same day.

On July 16, the members of the commission that carried out the July 9 excavation were joined at Moulin Quignon by Mr. Buteux and Mr. de Mercey, members of the Geological Society of France; Baron de Varicourt, chamberlain of His Majesty the King of Bavaria; Mr. de Villepoix, member of the Société d'Émulation; and Mr. Girot, professor of physics and natural history at the College of Abbeville. In additional to the members of the formal commission a dozen other learned gentlemen, including Boucher de Perthes, were present for the new excavations.

Dubois noted in his report that the quarry wall at the chosen spot was undisturbed and without fissures. About the workers, Dubois (1864b, p. 270) stated, "Needless to say, during the entire duration of the work, they were the object of continuous surveillance by various members of the commission." In examining a large chunk of sediment detached by a pick, the commission members found a piece of a human cranium, comprising a large part of the frontal with a small part of the parietal (p. 270). It was found at a depth of 3.3 meters in the yellow-brown bed that lies just above the chalk (p. 271).

Dubois's report (1864b, p. 271) stated:

> Immediately afterwards, one of the workers was ordered to attack the same bank at the same height, but 3 meters further to the left. The other worker continued to dig at the extreme right. Is it necessary to repeat that all necessary precautions were taken to establish the integrity of the bed there and that the two workers each continued to be the object of scrupulous surveillance?
>
> We went a long time without finding anything resembling a bone. The excavation on the far right side yielded no results whatso-

ever. Finally, after about three and a half hours, there came to light the end of a bone, of medium size, situated horizontally in the bed. After its exact position was confirmed, Mr. Marcotte himself took from the sand a complete bone, about 13 centimeters long. . . . It was the right clavicle of an adult subject of small size. . . . Measurements showed it was lying 3 meters from the surface, and 2.3 meters horizontally from our starting point.

Further excavation caused a landslide. The debris was cleared away, however, and the excavation proceeded, yielding a human metatarsal. Several members of the commission, including the geologist Buteux, saw it in place. It was found at a depth of 3.3 meters just above the chalk in the yellow-brown bed. It was situated about 4 meters horizontally from the line where the excavation started (Dubois 1864b, p. 272). According to Boucher de Perthes (1864b, p. 238) the bones from this excavation, and apparently others, were deposited to the Abbeville museum.

I find the account of this excavation extraordinary for several reasons. First of all, it was conducted by qualified observers, including geologists capable of judging the undisturbed nature of the beds. Second, a skilled anatomist was present to identify the bones as human. Third, it is apparent that the workers were carefully supervised. Fourth, some of the human bone fragments were found at points 3 to 4 meters horizontally from the starting point of the excavation and depths over 3 meters from the surface. This appears to rule out fraudulent introduction. Fifth, the condition of the bones (fragmented, worn, impregnated with the matrix) is consistent with their being genuine fossils. I do not see how such discoveries can be easily dismissed.

Summarizing his discoveries, Boucher de Perthes (1864b) stated:

> The osseous remains collected in the diverse excavations I made in 1863 and 1864 at Moulin Quignon, over an area of about 40 meters of undisturbed terrain without any infiltration, fissure, or [p. 239] channel, have today reached two hundred in number. Among them are some animal bones, which are being examined (pp. 238–239).

> Among the human remains, one most frequently encounters pieces of femur, tibia, humerus, and especially crania, as well as teeth, some whole and some broken. The teeth represent all ages—they are from infants of two or three years, adolescents, adults, and the aged. I have collected, in situ, a dozen, some whole, some broken, and more in passing through a screen the sand and gravel take from the trenches (p. 240).

> Doubtlessly, a lot has been lost. I got some proof of this last month when I opened a mass of sand and gravel taken from a bank long ago and kept in reserve. I found fragments of bone and teeth, which still bear traces of their matrix and are therefore of an origin beyond doubt (p. 241).

Armand de Quatrefages, a prominent French anthropologist, made a report on Boucher de Perthes's later discoveries at Moulin Quignon to the French Academy of Sciences. Here are some extracts from the report (De Quatrefages 1864):

> In these new investigations, Boucher de Perthes has employed only a very few workers. In the majority of cases, he himself has descended into the excavation and with his own hands has broken apart and crumbled the large pieces of gravel or sand detached by the picks of the workers. In this manner, he has procured a great number of specimens, some of them very important. We can understand that this way of doing things guarantees the authenticity of the discoveries.
>
> On hearing the first results of this research, I encouraged Boucher de Perthes to persevere, and to personally take every necessary precaution to prevent any kind of fraud and remove any doubts about the stratigraphic position of the discoveries. . . .
>
> As the discoveries continued, Boucher de Perthes sent to me, on June 8, 1864, a box containing several fragments of bones from human skeletons of different ages. I noted: 16–17 teeth from first and second dentitions; several cranial fragments, including a portion of an adult occipital and the squamous portion of a juvenile temporal; pieces of arm and leg bones, some retaining their articulator ends; pieces of vertebrae and of the sacrum. The specimens were accompanied by a detailed memoir reporting the circumstances of their discovery.
>
> I examined these bones with M. Lartet. We ascertained that most of them presented very nicely the particular characteristics that were so greatly insisted upon in denying the authenticity of the Moulin Quignon jaw. In accord with M. Lartet, I felt it advisable to persuade M. Boucher de Perthes to make further excavations, but this time in the presence of witnesses whose testimony could not in the least be doubted. . . . Among the more important specimens found in these latest excavations are an almost complete lower jaw and a cranium.
>
> All of these finds were made in the course of excavations that were mounted in an on-and-off fashion, without any definite pattern. That is to say, Boucher de Perthes would suddenly proceed to the sites, sometimes alone and sometimes with friends. Doing things like this very clearly renders any kind of fraud quite difficult. During the course of an entire year and more, the perpetrator of the fraud would have had to go and conceal each day the fragments of bone destined to be found by those he was attempting to deceive. It is hardly credible that anyone would adopt such means to attain such an unworthy goal or that his activities would have remained for so long undetected.
>
> Examination of the bones does not allow us to retain the least doubt as to their authenticity. The matrix encrusting the bones is of exactly the same material as the beds in which they were found, a circumstance that

would pose a serious difficulty for the perpetrators of the daily frauds. . . . Because of the precautions taken by Boucher de Perthes and the testimony given by several gentlemen who were long disinclined to admit the reality of these discoveries, I believe it necessary to conclude that the new bones discovered at Moulin Quignon are authentic, as is the original jaw, and that all are contemporary with the beds where Boucher de Perthes and his honorable associates found them.

I am inclined to agree with De Quatrefages that the later discoveries of Boucher de Perthes tend to confirm the authenticity of the original Moulin Quignon jaw.

At this point, I wish to draw attention to a report by Dr. K. P. Oakley on the Moulin Quignon fossils. It is one of the few scientific reports from the twentieth century giving any attention at all to the later discoveries of Boucher de Perthes. Oakley gave the following results from fluorine content testing (Oakley 1980, p. 33). The original Moulin Quignon jaw had 0.12 percent fluorine, a second jaw (the one apparently found on June 10) had a fluorine content of 0.05 percent. By comparison, a tooth of *Paleoloxodon* (an extinct elephantlike mammal) from Moulin Quignon had a fluorine content of 1.7 percent, whereas a human skull from a Neolithic site at Champs-de-Mars had a fluorine content of 0.05 percent. Fluorine, present in ground water, accumulates in fossil bones over time. Superficially, it would thus appear that the Moulin Quignon jaw bones, with less fluorine than the *Paleoloxodon* tooth, are recent.

But such comparisons are problematic. We must take into consideration the possibility that much of a fossil bone's present fluorine content could have accumulated during the creature's lifetime. It is entirely to be expected that the tooth of an animal such as an elephant might acquire a considerable amount of fluorine from drinking water and constantly chewing vegetable matter—much more fluorine than the bone in a human jaw, not directly exposed to water and food. Also, the amount of fluorine in ground water can vary from site to site, and even at the same site bones can absorb varying amounts of fluorine according to the permeability of the surrounding matrix and other factors. Furthermore, fluorine content varies even in a single bone sample. In a typical case (Aitken 1990, p. 219), a measurement taken from the surface of a bone yielded a fluorine content of 0.6 percent whereas a measurement taken at 8 millimeters from the surface of the same bone yielded a fluorine content of just 0.1 percent. As such, Oakley's fluorine content test results cannot be taken as conclusive proof that the Moulin Quignon jaws were "intrusive in the deposits" (Oakley 1980, p. 33).

If the Moulin Quignon human fossils of Abbeville are genuine, how old are they? Abbeville is still considered important for the stone tool industries discovered by Boucher de Perthes. In a recent synoptic table of European Pleistocene sites, Carbonell and Rodriguez (1994, p. 306) put Abbeville at around 430,000 years, and I think we can take that as a current consensus.

Fossil evidence for the presence of anatomically modern humans at Abbeville is relevant to one of the latest archeological finds in Europe. Just this year Thieme (1997, p. 807) reported finding advanced wooden throwing spears in German coal deposits at Schöningen, Germany. Thieme gave these spears an age of 400,000 years. The oldest throwing spear previously discovered was just 125,000 years old (Thieme 1997, p. 810).

The spears discovered by Thieme are therefore quite revolutionary. They are causing archeologists to upgrade the cultural level of the Middle Pleistocene inhabitants of Europe, usually characterized as ancestors of anatomically modern humans, to a level previously associated exclusively with anatomically modern humans. Alternatively, we could upgrade the anatomical level of the Middle Pleistocene inhabitants of northern Europe to the level of modern humans. The skeletal remains from Moulin Quignon, at least some of which appear to be anatomically modern, would allow this. They are roughly contemporary with the Schöningen spears. Unfortunately, not many current workers in archeology are aware of the Moulin Quignon discoveries, and if they are aware of them, they are likely to know of them only from very brief (and misleading) negative evaluations.

Why have historians and scientists alike been so skeptical of the Moulin Quignon finds? I suspect it has a lot do to with preconceptions about the kind of hominid that should be existing in the European Middle Pleistocene. The following passage from Trinkaus and Shipman (1992, p. 97) is revealing:

> That any knowledgeable scientist should take the Moulin Quignon jaw seriously as a human fossil appears difficult to fathom in retrospect. Yet, despite the support for the Neander Tal fossils as an archaic, prehistoric human, few knew what to expect. Clearly, many . . . still expected human fossils to look just like modern humans; it was only a matter of finding the specimen in the appropriately prehistoric context.

It is clear that Trinkaus and Shipman would expect to find only ancestors of the modern human type in the European Middle Pleistocene. And today it would be hard to find a "knowledgeable scientist" who did not share this expectation. It is clear to me, however, that this fixed expectation may have obscured correct apprehension of the human fossil record in Europe and elsewhere. So perhaps it is good for researchers with different expectations to look over, from time to time, the history of archeology.

My own expectations are conditioned by my committed study of the Sanskrit historical writings of Vedic India (the *Puranas*), which contain accounts of extreme human antiquity. In his review of *Forbidden Archeology*, Murray (1995, p. 379) wrote:

> For the practising quaternary archaeologist current accounts of human evolution are, at root, simply that. The "dominant paradigm" has changed and is changing, and practitioners openly debate issues which go right to the conceptual core of the discipline. Whether the Vedas have a role to play in this is up to the individual scientists concerned.

I am hopeful that some individual scientists will in fact decide that the Vedas do have a role to play in changing the conceptual core of studies in human origins and antiquity.

But let us return to the more limited question before us. As far as the finds of human bones at Moulin Quignon are concerned, I would be satisfied if a professor of archeology at a European university, perhaps in France or Belgium, would assign some graduate students to reopen the investigation.

References

Aitken, M. J. (1990) *Science-based Dating in Archaeology.* London: Longman.

Boucher de Perthes, J. (1864a) Fossile de Moulin-Quignon: Vérification Supplémentaire. In Boucher de Perthes, J., *Antiquités Celtiques et Antédiluviennes. Memoire sur l'Industrie Primitive et les Arts à leur Origin (Vol. 3).* Paris: Jung-Treutel, pp. 194–214.

Boucher de Perthes, J. (1864b) Nouvelles Découvertes d'Os Humains dans le Diluvium, en 1863 et 1864, par M. Boucher de Perthes. Rapport a la Société Impériale d'Émulation. In Boucher de Perthes, J., *Antiquités Celtiques et Antédiluviennes. Memoire sur l'Industrie Primitive et les Arts à leur Origin (Vol. 3).* Paris: Jung-Treutel, pp. 215–250.

Carbonell, E. and Rodriguez, X. P. (1994) Early Middle Pleistocene deposits and artefacts in the Gran Dolina site (TD4) of the 'Sierra de Atapuerca' (Burgos, Spain). *Journal of Human Evolution,* 26: 291–311.

Cremo, M. A., and Thompson, R. L. (1993) *Forbidden Archeology: The Hidden History of the Human Race.* San Diego: Bhaktivedanta Institute.

Delesse, A. (1863) La mâchoire humaine de Moulin de Quignon. *Mémoires de la Société d'Anthropologie de Paris,* 2: 37–68.

De Quatrefages, A. (1864) Nouveaux ossements humains découverts par M. Boucher de Perthes à Moulin-Quignon. *Comptes Rendus Hebdomadaires de l'Académie des Sciences,* 59: 107–111.

Dubois, J. (1864a) Untitled report of excavation at Moulin Quignon, on July 9, 1864. Société Impériale d'Émulation. Extrait du registre des procès-verbaux. Séance du 21 Juillet 1864. In Boucher de Perthes, J., *Antiquités Celtiques et Antédiluviennes. Memoire sur l'Industrie Primitive et les Arts à leur Origin (Vol. 3).* Paris: Jung-Treutel, pp. 265–268.

Dubois, J. (1864b) Untitled report of excavation made at Moulin Quignon on July 16, 1864. Société Impériale d'Émulation. Extrait du registre des procès-verbaux. Suit de la séance du 21 Juillet 1864. In Boucher de Perthes, J., *Antiquités Celtiques et Antédiluviennes. Memoire sur l'Industrie Primitive et les Arts à leur Origin (Vol. 3).* Paris: Jung-Treutel, pp. 269–272.

Evans, John (1863) The human remains at Abbeville. *The Athenaeum,* July 4, pp.19–20.

Falconer, H., Busk, George, and Carpenter, W. B. (1863) An account of the proceedings of the late conference held in France to inquire into the circumstances attending the asserted discovery of a human jaw in the gravel at Moulin-Quignon, near Abbeville; including the procès verbaux of the conference, with notes thereon. *The Natural History Review,* 3 (new series): 423–462.

Grayson, D. K. (1983) *The Establishment of Human Antiquity.* New York: Academic Press.

Keith, A. (1928) *The Antiquity of Man.* Philadelphia: J. B. Lippincott.

Murray, T. (1995) Review of *Forbidden Archeology*. *British Journal for the History of Science*, 28: 377–379.

Oakley, K. P. (1980) Relative dating of fossil hominids of Europe. *Bulletin of the British Museum of Natural History (Geology)*, vol. 34.

Prestwich, J. (1863) On the section at Moulin Quignon, Abbeville, and on the peculiar character of some of the flint implements recently discovered there. *Quarterly Journal of the Geological Society of London*, vol. 19, first part, pp. 497–505.

Thieme, H. (1997) Lower Paleolithic hunting spears from Germany. *Nature*, February 27, 385: 807–810.

Trinkaus, E. and Shipman, P. (1992) *The Neandertals*. New York: Vintage.

Wodak, J. and Oldroyd, D. (1996) 'Vedic creationism': a further twist to the evolution debate. *Social Studies of Science*, 26: 192–213.

7

Famous Scientists and the Paranormal: Implications for Consciousness Research

I presented this paper at the conference Toward a Science of Consciousness, held in Tucson, Arizona, April 27–May 2, 1998.

Currently, dualist solutions to the brain/consciousness question are distinctly unpopular in mainstream scientific circles. Most research efforts are dedicated to exploring the "neural correlates of consciousness," the brain circuitry that supposedly produces consciousness. The unremitting reductionism of most consciousness research does not interfere with my personal beliefs in Krishna consciousness, nor with my practice of Hare Krishna mantra meditation, inspired by my years of study of the ancient Sanskrit writings of India, as I have received them from my guru Bhaktivedanta Swami Prabhupada.[1] But I am concerned that this almost unquestioned reductionism prevents many in the world of science from appreciating the true dimensions and characteristics of consciousness, which is something absolute, and not derivable from biochemistry or biophysics. Of course, even today there are researchers who pursue investigations suggesting consciousness is something that cannot be understood by the ordinary laws of physics and chemistry. These investigations come under the general heading of the "paranormal." Most paranormal researchers concern themselves with micro-psycho-kinetic effects (statistically significant intentionally induced variations in the output of random number generators) and mico-ESP events (statistically significant identifications of cards or pictures through remote vision). I find such work of considerable value, but I find even more value in the accounts of famous scientists of the past who recorded instances of macro-psychokinetic and ESP events. These accounts, if true, in my opinion, provide stronger and more direct evidence for the existence of a conscious self, distinct from matter, than statistical summations of micro-effects.

Many modern scientists know that Sir Isaac Newton, the founding father of modern science, wrote extensively on alchemy and esoteric spiritual topics. But the paranormal research of later figures in science are less well known in scientific circles. Indeed, many suppose that research into the paranormal has been the special province of those on the outermost fringes of normal science. This may be true today, but it has not always been so. Some of the greatest minds of modern science have busied themselves with problems that now for many seem taboo. I shall now give a few of the many examples that could be given.

Alfred Russel Wallace was cofounder, with Charles Darwin, of the theory of evolution by natural selection. He conducted decades of research into spiritualistic phenomena, sometimes in the company of Sir William Crookes. Wallace wrote: "I ought to state that for twenty-five years I had been an utter skeptic as to the existence of any preter-human or super-human intelligences, and that I never for a moment contemplated the possibility that the marvels related by Spiritualists could be literally true. If I have now changed my opinion, it is simply by the force of evidence."[2]

Sir William Crookes, a prominent physicist who discovered the element thallium, was elected President of the Royal Society, England's most prestigious scientific body. He gave this account of a séance with D. D. Home (May 22, 1871), attended by himself and Wallace: "The table now rose completely off the ground several times whilst the gentlemen present took a candle, and kneeling down deliberately examined the position of Mr. Home's feet and knees, and saw the three feet of the [3-footed] table quite off the ground. This was repeated, until each observer expressed himself satisfied that the levitation was not produced by mechanical means on the part of the medium or any one else present."[3]

Wallace and Crookes had both seen an accordion play while Home held it with one hand, away from the keyboard. Later, Crookes designed an experiment to further test this phenomenon. To insure that Home was not using sleight of hand, Crookes made a cage, which rested under a table. An accordion was placed in the cage, and Home was allowed to insert one hand into the cage to grasp one end of the instrument. Home was to keep his other hand on the top of the table. This arrangement prevented Home from using his free hand to manipulate the instrument. To guard against a trick accordion, Crookes supplied a brand new one never seen by Home. Crookes reported that even with this arrangement the accordion played as usual. Then Home removed his hand from the cage. Crookes stated: "I and two of the others present saw the accordion distinctly floating about inside the cage with no visible support."[4] Wallace reported a similar experience.[5]

Both Wallace and Crookes reported seeing Home levitate. Crookes reported: "The best cases of Home's levitation I witnessed in my own house. On one occasion, he went to a clear part of the room, and, after standing quietly for a minute, told us he was rising. I saw him slowly rise up with a continuous gliding movement and remain about six inches off the ground for several seconds, when he slowly descended. On this occasion no one moved from their places. On another occasion I was invited to come to him, when he rose 18 inches off the ground, and I passed my hands under his feet, round him, and over his head, when he was in the air."[6] Crookes reported many other instances of Home levitating.

Every student of physics knows the story of the Curies. Their investigations of radioactivity earned them the Nobel Prize in 1903 and helped set physics on its modern course. But hardly anyone knows that they were heavily involved in psychical research. Along with Dr. Charles Richet, and other European scientists of the early twentieth century, they participated in investigations of the Italian medium Eusapia Palladino.

Eusapia was born in Italy in 1854, and her psychic abilities manifested early in life. By the late nineteenth century, she was the object of study for many of Europe's leading scientists. In 1905, she came to Paris, where Pierre and Marie Curie were among those who investigated her.

Pierre Curie, letter to Georges Gouy, July 24, 1905: "We had at the Psychology Society a few séances with the medium Eusapia Palladino. It was very interesting, and truly those phenomena that we have witnessed seemed to us to not be some magical tricks—a table lifted four feet above the floor, movements of objects, feelings of hands that pinched you or carressed you, apparitions of light. All this in a room arranged by us, with a small number of spectators all well known and without the presence of a possible accomplice. The only possible cheating would be an extraordinary ability of the medium as a magician. But how to explain the different phenomena when we are holding her hands and legs, and the lighting of the room is sufficient to see everything going on?"[7]

In another letter to Gouy (April 14, 1906), Curie wrote: "We had a few new séances with Eusapia ... those phenomena exist for real, and I can't doubt it any more. It is unbelievable but it is thus, and it is impossible to negate it after the séances that we had in conditions of perfect monitoring."[8]

Charles Richet, who won the Nobel Prize in physiology in 1913, carried out decades of research into psychical phenomena. He participated with the Curies in the investigations of Eusapia Palladino. Here is one of his accounts of a séance:

"It took place at the Psychological Institute at Paris. There were present only Mme. Curie, Mme. X., a Polish friend of hers, and P. Courtier, the secretary of the Institute. Mme. Curie was on Eusapia's left, myself on her right, Mme. X, a little farther off, taking notes, and M. Courtier still farther, at the end of the table. Courtier had arranged a double curtain behind Eusapia; the light was weak but sufficient. On the table Mme. Curie's hand holding Eusapia's could be distinctly seen, likewise mine also holding the right hand... We saw the curtain swell out as if pushed by some large object ... I asked to touch it . . . I felt the resistance and seized a real hand which I took in mine. Even through the curtain I could feel the fingers ... I held it firmly and counted twenty-nine seconds, during all which time I had leisure to observe both of Eusapia's hands on the table, to ask Mme. Curie if she was sure of her control ... After the twenty-nine seconds I said, 'I want something more, I want *uno anello* (a ring).' At once the hand made me feel a ring ... It seems hard to imagine a more convincing experiment . . . In this case there was not only the materialization of a hand, but also of a ring."[9]

Camille Flammarion (1842–1925), founder of the French Astronomical Society, carried out extensive research into clairvoyance and apparitions. Flammarion concluded: "All these observations prove that a human being does not consist only of a body that is visible, tangible . . . it consists, likewise, of a psychic element that is imponderable, gifted with special, intrinsic faculties, capable of functioning apart from the physical organism and of manifesting itself at a distance with the aid of forces as to the nature of which we are still ignorant."[10]

Lord John William Strutt Rayleigh (1842–1919) received the 1904 Nobel Prize in physics for his discovery of argon. Rayleigh was attracted to psychical research by the writings of Sir William Crookes. He was cautious in drawing conclusions, but he never disavowed any of the positive experiences he recorded. Rayleigh accepted the presidency of the Society for Psychical Research in 1919. In his presidential address he said, "I have never felt any doubt as to the importance of the work carried on by the Society . . . Our goal is the truth, whatever it may turn out to be, and our efforts to attain it should have the sympathy of all, and I would add especially of scientific men."[11]

With Charles Richet, Oliver J. Lodge, a famous English physicist, participated in experiments with Eusapia Palladino and was convinced her phenomena, in this case, were real. During the First World War, his son Raymond was killed on the battlefield. Afterwards, Lodge claimed he was receiving verifiable communications from him through mediums. Lodge wrote: "I have made no secret of my conviction, not merely that personality persists, but that its continued existence is more entwined with the life of every day than has been generally imagined . . . and that methods of intercommunication across what has seemed to be a gulf can be set going in response to the urgent demand of affection."[12]

The testimony of such scientists, noted for their skill in experimental design and observation, when taken in combination with modern parapsychological research, provides good reason to suppose that there is more to the human organism than the physical body visible to our eyes. It would appear that a complete picture of the human being must also take into account subtle mental energies and a conscious self distinct from the body. When embodied the conscious self can make use of subtle mental energies to manipulate matter in ways transcending the normal laws of physics. And when detached from the body, the same self can apparently make use of the same subtle mental energies to communicate with selves still embodied.

Notes:

1. I became the initiated disciple of His Divine Grace A. C. Bhaktivedanta Swami Prabhupada in January, 1976. In 1984, I began work with the Bhaktivedanta Institute, the science studies branch of the International Society for Krishna Consciousness.
2. Wallace, A. R. (1896) *Miracles and Modern Spiritualism.* 3rd ed. London: George Redway, p. 132.
3. William Crookes (1889) Notes of séances with D. D. Home. *Proceedings of the Society for Psychical Research,* vol. VI, pp. 98–127.
4. Sir William Crookes (1874) *Researches in the Phenomena of Spiritualism,* London.
5. Alfred Russel Wallace (1905) *My Life: A Record of Events and Opinions.* 2 volumes. London: Chapman & Hall, vol. 2, pp. 286–287.
6. Sir William Crookes, *Journal of the Society for Psychical Research,* vol. VI, pp. 341–342.
7. Anna Hurwic (1995) *Pierre Curie.* Paris: Flammarion, p. 248.
8. Anna Hurwic (1995) *Pierre Curie.* Paris: Flammarion, pp. 263–264.
9. Charles Richet (1923) *Thirty Years of Psychical Research.* New York: Macmillan, pp. 496–497.

10. Camille Flammarion (1922) *Death and Its Mystery.* Vol. 2. New York: Century, p. 369.

11. Lord Rayleigh (1919) Presidential address. *Proceedings of the Society for Psychical Research,* Vol. XXX, pp. 275–290.

12. Sir Oliver Lodge (1916) *Raymond or Life and Death: With Examples of the Evidence for Survival of Memory and Affection After Death,* New York: George H. Doran, p. 83

8

Forbidden Archeology of the Early and Middle Pleistocene: Evidence for Physiologically and Culturally Advanced Humans

I presented this paper at the World Archaeological Congress 4, which was held in Cape Town, South Africa, January 9–14, 1999.

In our book *Forbidden Archeology*, Richard Thompson and I suggested that commitment to theories of a relatively late origin of anatomically modern humans from *Homo erectus* has prevented archeologists from recognizing possible evidence for an anatomically modern human presence in geological contexts older than the latest Pleistocene. Examples of such treatment of evidence according to disciplinary preconceptions, which constitute a kind of knowledge filtering, can be drawn from the most recent archeological discoveries, as well as discoveries recorded in the archeological literature of the past one hundred and fifty years.

In 1991, 1994, and 1997, expeditions to Flores Island in eastern Indonesia recovered stone tools from the Ola Bula formation at Mata Menge (Morwood *et al.* 1998). Earlier expeditions had also found stone tools on Flores, but the reports have been largely ignored. The stone tools were found *in situ*, along with animal bones (*Stegodon*, crocodile, giant rat), in primary stratified deposits of tuffaceous sandstone, with only slight signs of subsequent reworking. About the tools, Morwood et al. (1998, p. 174) stated:

> The Mata Menge deposits contain pieces of volcanic rock and chert identified as artefacts on the basis of well-defined flake scars, ring cracks, bulbs of percussion and systematic edge damage suggestive of retouch. . . . Of 45 stone pieces recovered in a 1994 excavation, 14 were identified as artefacts according to technological criteria. Of these 14 artefacts, four were subsequently examined under high magnification and found to have edge damage, striations, polishing and residues indicating use in the processing of plant materials.

The deposits containing the tools were dated using the zircon fission track method (Morwood *et al.* 1998). Samples were taken from above and below the tool bearing

99

layers. Sample MM1 from immediately below the tool-bearing layers yielded an age of 880,000 years and sample MM2 from directly above the tool-bearing layers yielded an age of 800,000 years. These ages are consistent with a paleomagnetic date of 780,000 years from a transition layer below the tool-bearing strata and with the Early Pleistocene faunal remains.

Morwood *et al.* (1998, p. 176) concluded, however, "The age of the artefacts also indicates that they were produced by *Homo erectus* rather than *Homo sapiens.*" This is a clear example of the kind of knowledge filtering process posited in *Forbidden Archeology*.

From their conviction that the tools were the work of *Homo erectus*, Morwood *et al.* were compelled to alter their conceptions of that hominin's level of culture.

During the early Pleistocene, the island of Java was sometimes connected with the Southeast Asian mainland (the Sunda paleocontinent), but between Java and Flores there were three deepwater straits. The narrowest of these was at least 19 kilometers wide, even during periods of lowered ocean levels. Morwood *et al.* (1998, p. 176) noted, "The impoverished nature of the fauna on Flores . . . seems to negate a connection with Sunda at any time. The presence of endemic pygmy elephants, giant reptiles and giant rats in the Early Pleistocene also suggests a continued insular context."

The implication of an "insular context" is that *Homo erectus*, or whatever hominin was responsible for the tools, had to have arrived by boat. This would require·a revolutionary upward adjustment of the cultural level of *Homo erectus* to include ocean crossing with vessels. Morwood *et al.* (1998, p. 176) noted:

> Previously ... this capacity was thought to be the prerogative of modern humans and to have only appeared in the Late Pleistocene, with the earliest widely accepted evidence for watercraft being the colonization of Australia by modern humans . . . between 40,000 and 60,000 years ago. Outside this region, the technology to undertake even limited water crossings is not clearly evidenced until much later, at the end of the Pleistocene.

But perhaps instead of elevating *Homo erectus* to a level of culture previously associated exclusively with anatomically modern humans, we should consider the possibility that the Flores hominin may have in fact been fully human. Some reason for this can be found in nearby Java.

In 1891, Eugene Dubois discovered at Trinil a *Homo erectus* skullcap. The following year, he found a femur in the same deposits, at a distance of about 15 meters from the place where the skullcap was found. He nevertheless associated the femur with the skullcap, an association that eventually came to be accepted by most physical anthropologists. During the 1930s, Dubois reported additional hominin femurs in boxes of fossils he had sent from Java.

But subsequently Day and Molleson (1973) concluded that "the gross anatomy, radiological [X-ray] anatomy, and microscopical anatomy of the Trinil femora does not distinguish them significantly from modern human femora." They also said that

Homo erectus femurs from China and Africa are anatomically similar to each other, and distinct from those of Trinil. The layers in which the skullcap and femurs were found have a potassium-argon date of about 800,000 years, roughly contemporary with the Flores finds.

In 1984, Richard Leakey and others described an almost complete skeleton of *Homo erectus* in Kenya. Examining the leg bones, these scientists found that the femurs differed substantially from those of modern human beings. About the Java discoveries, Leakey and his coworkers (Brown *et al.* 1985) stated: "From Trinil, Indonesia, there are several fragmentary and one complete (but pathological) femora. Despite the fact that it was these specimens that led to the species name, there are doubts as to whether they are *H. erectus* with the most recent consensus being that they probably are not." In summary, modern researchers say the Trinil femurs are not like those of *Homo erectus* but are instead like those of modern *Homo sapiens*. What is to be made of these revelations? The Java thighbones have traditionally been taken as evidence of *Homo erectus* existing around 800,000 years ago in the Middle Pleistocene. Accepting their traditional provenance, it now appears we can accept them as evidence for anatomically modern humans existing 800,000 years ago.

Let's now consider a similar case from Europe. Thieme (1997) reported discoveries of artifacts in Middle Pleistocene interglacial deposits uncovered in the course of open-cast coal mining at Schöningen, Germany. The artifact locations are 8-15 meters from the surface.

The oldest level of human occupation (Schöningen I), with stone tools, burnt flint, and animal bones, dates to the earliest Holstein interglacial. Schöningen II, representing the Reinsdorf interglacial, has five cultural levels.

> Level 1 contained numerous flint artefacts and three worked branches of common silver fir, *Abies alba*. The wooden tools . . . have a diagonal groove cut in one end. ... It is postulated that the grooves were for holding flint tools or flakes. If this supposition is correct, these implements represent the oldest composite tools yet discovered (Thieme 1997, p. 808).

In Level 4 of Schöningen II, Thieme found numerous stone tools of advanced type (including points and carefully retouched scrapers) as well as three wooden spears, made from spruce. Thieme (1997, p. 809) noted:

> The spears are made from individual trees, which were felled, and the branches and bark were removed; the tips/distal ends are worked from the base of the three. All three spears, although of different lengths were manufactured to the same pattern, with the maximum thickness and weights at the front; the tails are long, and taper toward the proximal end. In all of these respects, they resemble modern javelins, and were made as projectile weapons rather than thrusting spears or lances.

Thieme gave these spears an age of 400,000 years (during the fourth to the last interglacial, oxygen isotope stage 11). The oldest throwing spear previously discovered, from Lehringen, Germany, was just 125,000 years old (Thieme 1997, p. 810).

The spears discovered by Thieme are therefore quite revolutionary. They are causing archeologists to upgrade the *cultural* level of the Middle Pleistocene inhabitants of Europe, usually characterized as ancestors of anatomically modern humans, to a level previously associated exclusively with anatomically modern humans. Thieme said, "The discovery of spears designed for throwing means that theories of the development of hunting capacities . . . of Middle Pleistocene hominids must be revised."

But just as in the case of the Flores finds, we could upgrade the *anatomical* level of the Middle Pleistocene inhabitants of northern Europe to the level of modern humans. There are skeletal remains from the Moulin Quignon site in Abbeville, France, that would allow this. They are roughly contemporary with the Schöningen spears. Unfortunately, not many current workers in archeology are aware of the Moulin Quignon discoveries, and if they are aware of them, they are likely to know of them only from very brief (and misleading) negative evaluations.

In the 1840s Boucher de Perthes discovered stone tools in the Middle Pleistocene high level gravels of the Somme, at Moulin Quignon and other sites. At first, the scientific community, particularly in France, was not inclined to accept his discoveries as genuine.

Later, leading British archeologists visited the sites of Boucher de Perthes's discoveries and pronounced them genuine. But the exact nature of the maker of these tools remained unknown. Then in 1863, Boucher de Perthes discovered at Moulin Quignon additional stone tools and an anatomically modern human jaw. The jaw inspired much controversy, and was the subject of a joint English-French commission (Falconer *et al.* 1863, Delesse 1863).

The English members of the commission thought the recently discovered stone tools were forgeries that had been artificially introduced into the Moulin Quignon strata. They thought the same of the jaw. To settle the matter, the commission paid a surprise visit to the site. Five flint implements were found in the presence of the scientists. The commission approved by majority vote a resolution in favor of the authenticity of the recently discovered stone tools. Sir John Prestwich remained in the end skeptical but nevertheless noted (1863, p. 505) that "the precautions we took seemed to render imposition on the part of the workmen impossible."

In addition to confirming the authenticity of the stone tools from Moulin Quignon, the commission voted in favor of the following statements:

> The jaw in question was not fraudulently introduced into the gravel pit of Moulin Quignon. . . . All leads one to think that the deposition of this jaw was contemporary with that of the pebbles and other materials constituting the mass of clay and gravel designated as the black bed, which rests immediately above the chalk (Falconer et al. 1863, p. 452).

This was exactly the conclusion desired by Boucher de Perthes. Only two members,

Busk and Falconer, abstained.

Their scientific objections having been effectively countered, the English objectors, including John Evans, who was not able to join the commission in France, were left with finding further proof of fraudulent behavior among the workmen at Moulin Quignon as their best weapon against the jaw. Taking advantage of a suggestion by Boucher de Perthes himself, Evans sent Henry Keeping, a working man with experience in archeological excavation, to France. There he supposedly obtained definite proof that the French workmen were introducing tools into the deposits at Moulin Quignon.

But careful study of Keeping's reports (Evans 1863) reveals little to support these allegations and suspicions. Boucher de Perthes (1864a, pp. 197, 204) observed that Keeping was daily choosing his own spots to work and that it would have been quite difficult for the workers, if they were indeed planting flint implements, to anticipate where he would dig. I tend to agree with Boucher de Perthes (1864a, pp. 194–195) that Keeping, loyal to his patron Evans, was well aware that he had been sent to France to find evidence of fraud and that he dared not return to England without it. Nevertheless, a report by Evans (1863), based on Keeping's account, was published in an English periodical and convinced many scientists that Boucher des Perthes was, despite the favorable conclusions of the scientific commission, the victim of an archeological fraud.

Boucher des Perthes, however, entertained no doubts as to the authenticity of the jaw, which he had seen in place in the black layer toward the bottom of the Moulin Quignon pit. Stung by accusations of deception, he proceeded to carry out a new set of excavations, which resulted in the recovery of more human skeletal remains. These later discoveries are hardly mentioned in standard histories, which dwell upon the controversy surrounding the far more famous Moulin Quignon jaw.

Boucher de Perthes (1864b) carried out his new investigations so as to effectively rule out the possibility of deception by workmen. First of all, they were carried out during a period when the quarry at Moulin Quignon was shut down and the usual workmen were not there (1864b, p. 219). Also, Boucher de Perthes made his investigations unannounced and started digging at random places. He would usually hire just one or two workers, whom he closely supervised. Furthermore, he himself would enter into the excavation and break up the larger chunks of sediment with his own hands. In almost all cases, witnesses with scientific or medical training were present. In some cases, these witnesses organized their own careful excavations to independently confirm the discoveries of Boucher de Perthes. Summarizing his discoveries, Boucher de Perthes stated:

> The osseous remains collected in the diverse excavations I made in 1863 and 1864 at Moulin Quignon, over an area of about 40 meters of undisturbed terrain without any infiltration, fissure, or channel, have today reached two hundred in number (1864b, pp. 238–239).

> Among the human remains, one most frequently encounters pieces of femur, tibia, humerus, and especially crania, as well as teeth, some whole and some broken. The teeth represent all ages—they are from in-

fants of two or three years, adolescents, adults, and the aged. I have collected, *in situ,* a dozen, some whole, some broken, and more in passing
through a screen the sand and gravel take from the trenches (1864b, p.
240).

Doubtlessly, a lot has been lost. I got some proof of this last month
when I opened a mass of sand and gravel taken from a bank long ago
and kept in reserve. I found fragments of bone and teeth, which still
bear traces of their matrix and are therefore of an origin beyond doubt
(1864b, p. 241).

Armand de Quatrefages, a prominent French anthropologist, made a report on
Boucher de Perthes's later discoveries at Moulin Quignon to the French Academy of
Sciences. Here are some extracts from the report (De Quatrefages 1864):

On hearing the first results of this research, I encouraged Boucher de Perthes to persevere, and to personally take every necessary
precaution to prevent any kind of fraud and remove any doubts
about the stratigraphic position of the discoveries. . . .

As the discoveries continued, Boucher de Perthes sent to me, on
June 8, 1864, a box containing several fragments of bones from human
skeletons of different ages. I noted: 16–17 teeth from first and second
dentitions; several cranial fragments, including a portion of an adult oc-
cipital and the squamous portion of a juvenile temporal; pieces of arm
and leg bones, some retaining their articulator ends; pieces of verte-
brae and of the sacrum. The specimens were accompanied by a detailed
memoir reporting the circumstances of their discovery.

I examined these bones with M. Lartet. . . . In accord with M. Lartet,
I felt it advisable to persuade M. Boucher de Perthes to make further
excavations, but this time in the presence of witnesses whose testimony
could not in the least be doubted. . . . Among the more important specimens found in these latest excavations are an almost complete lower jaw
and a cranium.

All of these finds were made in the course of excavations that were
mounted in an on-and-off fashion, without any definite pattern. That is
to say, Boucher de Perthes would suddenly proceed to the sites, sometimes alone and sometimes with friends. Doing things like this very
clearly renders any kind of fraud quite difficult. During the course of
an entire year and more, the perpetrator of the fraud would have had
to go and conceal each day the fragments of bone destined to be found
by those he was attempting to deceive. It is hardly credible that anyone
would adopt such means to attain such an unworthy goal or that his
activities would have remained for so long undetected.

Examination of the bones does not allow us to retain the least doubt as to their authenticity. The matrix encrusting the bones is of exactly the same material as the beds in which they were found, a circumstance that would pose a serious difficulty for the perpetrators of the daily frauds. . . . Because of the precautions taken by Boucher de Perthes and the testimony given by several gentlemen who were long disinclined to admit the reality of these discoveries, I believe it necessary to conclude that the new bones discovered at Moulin Quignon are authentic, as is the original jaw, and that all are contemporary with the beds where Boucher de Perthes and his honorable associates found them.

I am inclined to agree with De Quatrefages that the later discoveries of Boucher de Perthes tend to confirm the authenticity of the original Moulin Quignon jaw.

Oakley (1980, p. 33) gave the following results from fluorine content testing. The original Moulin Quignon jaw had 0.12 percent fluorine, a second jaw had a fluorine content of 0.05 percent. By comparison, a tooth of *Paleoloxodon* from Moulin Quignon had a fluorine content of 1.7 percent, whereas a human skull from a Neolithic site at Champs-de-Mars had a fluorine content of 0.05 percent. Fluorine, present in ground water, accumulates in fossil bones over time. Superficially, it would thus appear that the Moulin Quignon jaw bones, with less fluorine than the *Paleoloxodon* tooth, are recent.

But such comparisons are problematic. We must take into consideration the possibility that much of a fossil bone's present fluorine content could have accumulated during the creature's lifetime. It is entirely to be expected that the tooth of an animal such as an elephant might acquire a considerable amount of fluorine from drinking water and constantly chewing vegetable matter—much more fluorine than the bone in a human jaw, not directly exposed to water and food. Also, the amount of fluorine in ground water can vary from site to site, and even at the same site bones can absorb varying amounts of fluorine according to the permeability of the surrounding matrix and other factors. Furthermore, fluorine content varies even in a single bone sample. In a typical case (Aitken 1990, p. 219), a measurement taken from the surface of a bone yielded a fluorine content of 0.6 percent whereas a measurement taken at 8 millimeters from the surface of the same bone yielded a fluorine content of just 0.1 percent. As such, Oakley's fluorine content test results cannot be taken as conclusive proof that the Moulin Quignon jaws were "intrusive in the deposits" (Oakley 1980, p. 33).

If the Moulin Quignon human fossils of Abbeville are genuine, how old are they? In a recent synoptic table of European Pleistocene sites, Carbonell and Rodriguez (1994, p. 306) put Abbeville at around 430,000 years, and I think we can take that as a current consensus. Thus we have good skeletal evidence for anatomically modern humans at roughly the same time as the throwing spears from Schöningen, Germany. Thieme gave these spears an age of 400,000 years.

The evidence from Schöningen and Moulin Quignon may provide a good reason to revisit several other cases of anatomically modern human skeletal remains (and artifacts generally attributed exclusively to anatomically modern humans) for which anomalously old ages had been claimed by the original discoverers. These Middle and Early Pleistocene ages were later rejected, often on the basis of radiometric and chemical dates that conflicted with stratigraphic evidence. Given the known sources of error in these radiometric and chemical dating methods, it may be wise to carefully review these cases. Here follows a summary list of some notable examples:

(1) Galley Hill, England: In 1888, a relatively complete anatomically modern human skeleton was found at a depth of 8 feet (Keith 1928, pp. 250–66) in Middle Pleistocene deposits roughly contemporary with Swanscombe (Oakley and Montagu 1949, p. 34). Swanscombe is now considered to be about 326,000 years old (Carbonell and Rodriquez 1994, p. 306). Contemporary witnesses saw no signs of intrusive burial and found the overlying strata intact (Keith 1928, p. 255, Newton 1895). Fluorine and nitrogen ages obtained by Oakley and Montagu (1949) and a radiocarbon date obtained by Barker and Mackey (1961) indicated a Late Pleistocene or Holocene age.

(2) Avenue Clichy, Paris, France: Bertrand (1868) reported the discovery of a partial human skeleton at a depth of 5 meters in a quarry, in deposits later researchers believed were broadly contemporary with Galley Hill (Keith 1928). Hamy reported additional human bones from the same site, a depth of 4.2 meters (Bertrand 1868, p. 335).

(3) Ipswich, England: In 1911, a relatively complete anatomically modern human skeleton was found by J. Reid Moir at a depth of 1.38 meters below Middle Pleistocene glacial deposits (Keith 1928, pp. 293–5). These deposits appear to be related to the Gipping Till, which is associated with the Anglian glaciation (Bowen 1980, p. 420). The discoverer verified the undisturbed nature of the strata containing the skeleton, ruling out intrusive burial (Keith 1928, pp. 294–5). This would give the skeleton an age in excess of 400,000 years.

(4) Terra Amata, France. De Lumley (1969) reported post holes, indicating construction of elaborate shelters, circular stone hearths, and an anatomically modern footprint. Also found were a projectile point and bone tools, including one characterized as an awl, used for sewing skins. All of the above are normally associated with *Homo sapiens sapiens*. Terra Amata is considered to be 380,000 years old (Carbonell and Rodriguez 1994, p. 306).

(5) Kanjera, Kenya. In 1932 Louis Leakey (1960) found fragments of five human skulls, characterized as anatomically modern (Groves 1989, p. 291), along with a human femur. The Kanjera fossil beds are equivalent to Olduvai Bed IV (Cooke 1963), giving the Kanjera human bones an age of at least 400,000 years. Oakley (1974, p. 257) reported a fluorine content similar to Kanjeran animal bones, but believed nitrogen and uranium content test results indicated a younger age. But earlier uranium tests by Oakley (1958: 53) indicated no discrepancy in the ages of the animal and human bones.

(6) Hueyatlaco, Mexico. Strata containing numerous stone tools of advanced type, associated exclusively with anatomically modern humans, yielded dates of about 250,000–300,000 years (Steen-McIntyre *et al.* 1981).

(7) Buenos Aires, Argentina. An anatomically modern human skull (Hrdlička 1912, p. 322) was found beneath an unbroken layer of carbonate rock in a drydock excavation, at a depth of 11 meters below the bed of the La Plata river (Hrdlička 1912, p. 318). The layers containing the skull were from the Pre-Ensenadan formation (Hrdlička 1912, p. 321). Modern authorities place the beginning of the Ensenadan at 1.5 million

years (Anderson 1984, p. 41) or 1 million years (Marshall *et al.* 1982, p. 1352). Hrdlička (1912, pp. 2–3) denied any great antiquity to the skull because of its modern form.

(8) Olduvai Gorge, Tanzania. In 1913 Hans Reck (1914a, 1914b) discovered a complete anatomically modern human skeleton in upper Bed II. He looked carefully for signs of intrusive burial and found none. The skeleton had to be removed with chisels from the rock. Uppermost Bed II is given a date of 1.15 million years (Oakley *et al.* 1977, p. 166). The skeleton, except for the skull, was lost from a German museum in World War II. Protsch (1974) obtained a Late Pleistocene radiocarbon date from a bone fragment thought to be from the original skeleton, using a method now considered unreliable.

(9) Gombore, Ethiopia. A humanlike humerus was found at a site described as an encampment with a shelter and stone tools (Chavaillon *et al.* 1977). The humerus was characterized as resembling *Homo sapiens sapiens* (Chavaillon *et al.* 1977, p. 962) in lateral view. Senut (1981b, p. 91) says it "cannot be differentiated from a typical modern human." The site was given a potassium-argon age of 1.5 million years (Senut 1979, pp. 112–13).

(10) Kanam, Kenya. In 1932, Louis Leakey (1960) found a hominin jaw described by some as anatomically modern (Woodward *et al.* 1933, p. 478) in a block of limestone containing Lower Pleistocene faunal remains, equivalent in age to Olduvai Bed I, about 1.7 to 2.0 million years old (Oakley *et al.* 1977, pp. 166, 199). The jaw's fluorine content was the same as that of mammalian bones from the same Early Pleistocene stratum. Uranium content, however, was lower.

(11) Koobi Fora, Kenya. Femurs (ER 1481, 1472) described as anatomically modern (R. Leakey 1973a, p. 450; 1973b, p. 821) were found in a geological context below the KBS Tuff, giving an age of at least 1.9 million years.

(12) Koobi Fora, Kenya. A human talus described as anatomically modern (Wood 1974, p. 135) was found between the KBS Tuff (1.9 million years) and the overlying Koobi Fora Tuff (1.5 million years).

Fuller discussions of the above-mentioned finds, giving arguments in favor of the skeletal remains and artifacts being as old as the Middle and Early Pleistocene strata in which they were found, are given in Cremo and Thompson (1993). These Early and Middle Pleistocene finds are continuous with numerous similar discoveries of anatomically modern human skeletal remains and artifacts extending back through the Pliocene and earlier. Thinking about the nature of Middle and Early Pleistocene hominins should be informed by these discoveries, which may lead to wider acceptance of a considerably greater antiquity for anatomically modern humans as recorded in the ancient Sanskrit writings of India.

References:

Aitken, M. J. (1990) *Science-based Dating in Archaeology.* London: Longman.

Anderson, E. (1984) Who's who in the Pleistocene: a mammalian bestiary. *In* Martin, P. S., and Klein, R. G., eds. *Quaternary Extinctions.* Tucson: University of Arizona Press, pp. 40–90.

Barker, H., Burleigh, R., and Meeks, N. (1971) British Museum natural radiocarbon measurements VII. *Radiocarbon,* 13: 157–88.

Bertrand, E. (1868) Crane et ossements trouves dans une carriere de lavenue de Clichy. *Bulletins de la Societe d Anthropologie de Paris (Series 2),* 3: 329–35.

Boucher de Perthes, J. (1864a) Fossile de Moulin-Quignon: Vérification Supplémentaire. *In* Boucher de Perthes, J., *Antiquités Celtiques et Antédiluviennes. Memoire sur l'Industrie Primitive et les Arts à leur Origin* (Vol. 3). Paris: Jung-Treutel, pp. 194–214.

Boucher de Perthes, J. (1864b) Nouvelles Découvertes d'Os Humains dans le Diluvium, en 1863 et 1864, par M. Boucher de Perthes. Rapport a la Société Impériale d'Émulation. *In* Boucher de Perthes, J., *Antiquités Celtiques et Antédiluviennes. Memoire sur l'Industrie Primitive et les Arts à leur Origin* (Vol. 3). Paris: Jung-Treutel, pp. 215–50.

Bowen, D. Q. (1980) The Quaternary of the United Kingdom. *In* Dercourt, J., ed. *Geology of the European Countries.* Vol. 1. Paris: Bordas, pp. 418–21.

Brown, F., Harris, J., Leakey, R., and Walker, A. (1985) Early *Homo erectus* skeleton from west Lake Turkana, Kenya. *Nature,* 316: 788–93.

Carbonell, E. and Rodriguez, X. P. (1994) Early Middle Pleistocene deposits and artefacts in the Gran Dolina site (TD4) of the 'Sierra de Atapuerca' (Burgos, Spain). *Journal of Human Evolution,* 26: 291–311.

Chavaillon, J., Chavaillon, N., Coppens, Y., and Senut, B. (1977) Présence d'hominidé dans le site oldowayen de Gomboré I à Melka Kunturé, Éthiopie. *Comptes Rendus de l'Académie des Sciences, Series D,* 285: 961–63.

Cooke, H. B. S. (1963) Pleistocene mammal faunas of Africa, with particular reference to Southern Africa. *In* Howell, F. C., and Boulière, F., eds. *African Ecology and Human Evolution.* Chicago: Aldine, pp. 78–84.

Cremo, M. A., and Thompson, R. L. (1993) *Forbidden Archeology: The Hidden History of the Human Race.* San Diego: Bhaktivedanta Institute.

Day, M. H. and Molleson, T. I. (1973) The Trinil femora. *Symposia of the Society for the Study of Human Biology,* 2: 127–54.

De Lumley, H. (1969) A Palaeolithic camp at Nice. *Scientific American,* 220(5): 42–50.

De Quatrefages, A. (1864) Nouveaux ossements humains découverts par M. Boucher de Perthes à Moulin-Quignon. *Comptes Rendus Hebdomadaires de l'Académie des Sciences,* 59: 107–11.

Delesse, A. (1863) La mâchoire humaine de Moulin de Quignon. *Mémoires de la Société d'Anthropologie de Paris,* 2: 37–68.

Evans, John (1863) The human remains at Abbeville. *The Athenaeum,* July 4, pp. 19–20.

Falconer, H., Busk, George, and Carpenter, W. B. (1863) An account of the proceedings of the late conference held in France to inquire into the circumstances attending the asserted discovery of a human jaw in the gravel at Moulin-Quignon, near Abbeville; including the *procès verbaux* of the conference, with notes thereon. *The Natural History Review,* 3 *(new series):* 423–62.

Groves, C. P. (1989) *A Theory of Human and Primate Evolution.* Oxford: Clarendon.

Hrdlička, A. (1912) *Early man in South America.* Washington, D. C.: Smithsonian

Institution.

Keith, A. (1928) *The Antiquity of Man.* Vol. 1. Philadelphia: J. B. Lippincott.

Leakey, L. S. B. (1960) *Adam's Ancestors,* 4th edition. New York: Harper & Row.

Leakey, R. E. (1973a) Evidence for an advanced Plio-Pleistocene hominid from East Rudolf, Kenya. *Nature,* 242: 447–50.

Leakey, R. E. (1973b) Skull 1470. *National Geographic,* 143: 819–29.

Marshall, L. G., Webb, S. D., Sepkoski, Jr., J. J. and Raup, D. M. (1982) Mammalian evolution and the great American interchange. *Science,* 215: 1351–57.

Morwood, M. J., O'Sullivan, P. B., Aziz, F., and Raza, A. (1998) Fission track ages of stone tools and fossils on the east Indonesian island of Flores. *Nature,* 392: 173–76.

Newton, E. T. (1895) On a human skull and limb-bones found in the Paleolithic terrace-gravel at Galley Hill, Kent. *Quarterly Journal of the Geological Society of London,* 51: 505–26.

Oakley, K. P. (1958) Physical Anthropology in the British Museum. *In* Roberts, D. F., ed. *The Scope of Physical Anthropology and Its Place in Academic Studies.* New York: Wenner Gren Foundation for Anthropological Research, pp. 51–54.

Oakley, K. P. (1974) Revised dating of the Kanjera hominids. *Journal of Human Evolution,* 3: 257–58.

Oakley, K. P. (1980) Relative dating of fossil hominids of Europe. *Bulletin of the British Museum of Natural History (Geology),* vol. 34.

Oakley, K. P., Campbell, B. G., and Molleson, T. I. (1977) *Catalogue of Fossil Hominids.* Part I. *Africa,* 2nd edition. London: British Museum.

Oakley, K. P., and Montagu, M. F. A. (1949) A re-consideration of the Galley Hill skeleton. *Bulletin of the British Museum (Natural History), Geology,* 1(2): 25–46.

Prestwich, J. (1863) On the section at Moulin Quignon, Abbeville, and on the peculiar character of some of the flint implements recently discovered there. *Quarterly Journal of the Geological Society of London,* 19 (part one): 497–505.

Protsch, R. (1974) The age and stratigraphic position of Olduvai hominid I. *Journal of Human Evolution,* 3: 379–85.

Reck, H. (1914a) Erste vorläufige Mitteilungen über den Fund eines fossilen Menschenskeletts aus Zentral-afrika. *Sitzungsbericht der Gesellschaft der naturforschender Freunde Berlins,* 3: 81–95.

Reck, H. (1914b) Zweite vorläufige Mitteilung über fossile Tiere- und Menschenfunde aus Oldoway in Zentral-afrika. *Sitzungsbericht der Gesellschaft der naturforschender Freunde Berlins,* 7: 305–18.

Senut, B. (1979) Comparaison des hominidés de Gombore IB et de Kanapoi: deux pièces du genre *Homo? Bulletin et Mémoires de la Société d'Anthropologie de Paris,* 6(13): 111–17.

Senut, B. (1981b) Outlines of the distal humerus in hominoid primates: application to some Plio-Pleistocene hominids. *In* Chiarelli, A. B., and Corrucini, R. S., eds. *Primate Evolutionary Biology.* Berlin: Springer Verlag, pp. 81–92.

Steen-McIntyre, V., Fryxell, R., and Malde, H. E. (1981) Geologic evidence for age of deposits at Hueyatlaco archaeological site, Valsequillo, Mexico. *Quaternary Research* 16: 1–17.

Thieme, H. (1997) Lower Paleolithic hunting spears from Germany. *Nature*, 385: 807–10.

Wood, B. A. (1974) Evidence on the locomotor pattern of *Homo* from early Pleistocene of Kenya. *Nature*, 251: 135–36.

Woodward, A. S., *et al.* (1933) Early man in East Africa. *Nature*, 131: 477–78.

9

Forbidden Archeology of the Paleolithic: How *Pithecanthropus* Influenced the Treatment of Evidence for Extreme Human Antiquity

I presented this paper in a section on history of archeology at the European Association of Archaeologists 1999 annual meeting in Bournemouth, United Kingdom.

Introduction

Archeologists are becoming increasingly introspective, exerting almost as much energy in excavating the epistemological, political, ideological, and social foundations of their discipline as in excavating the physical remains of the past. There is growing recognition that epistemological, political, ideological, and social factors have over time greatly influenced the manner in which the excavated physical remains are archived, displayed, and interpreted. For example, an epistemological commitment to evolutionary biology, solidified at an early point in the history of archeology, has influenced the treatment of evidence for extreme human antiquity by archeologists, past and present.

Over the past two centuries, researchers have found many anatomically modern human skeletal remains and artifacts in geological contexts extending to the Pliocene and earlier (Cremo and Thompson 1993).[1] This evidence is consistent with accounts of extreme human antiquity found in the *Puranas*, the historical texts of ancient India. In the later decades of the nineteenth century, reports of such evidence attained wide circulation among archeologists and researchers in allied fields (geology, paleontology, anthropology), engendering significant, although not universal, acceptance of "Tertiary man." At that early point in the history of archeology, a fixed scheme of human evolution had not yet emerged, and researchers were able to approach evidence for extreme human antiquity with somewhat less theoretical bias than they might today.

Up until the very end of the nineteenth century, the only candidate for an evolutionary ancestor of today's humans was Neandertal man. But the Neandertal bones were considered by most researchers, even evolutionists, to be from primitive or pathologically deformed members of our own human species (Trinkaus and Shipman, 1992). Only with the discovery of *Pithecanthropus erectus,* Java man, in the last years of the nineteenth century, were archeologists and others finally able to construct a credible and widely accepted evolutionary picture of human origins, based on actual fossil finds, with the anatomically modern human type arriving rather late on the scene. Java man was generally placed in the Early Pleistocene. This dating, combined with a gradualistic conception of evolutionary processes, located the origin of our species, *Homo sapiens,* in the latest Pleistocene. Java man was thus influential in causing the accumulated evidence for a human presence in the Early Pleistocene, the Pliocene, and earlier to be gradually dropped from active discourse. The discoveries of Piltdown man, *Sinanthropus,* and *Australopithecus* completed the processes, and the evidence for Tertiary (and Early Pleistocene) man was eventually consigned to an oblivion so complete that many archeologists today are unaware of its existence.

Recognition of this process is not new. About the early Tertiary man discoveries and their suppression subsequent to the Java man discoveries, anthropologist Frank Spencer (1984, pp. 13–14) wrote: "From accumulating evidence, it appeared as if the modern human skeleton extended far back in time, an apparent fact which led many workers to either abandon or modify their views on human evolution. One such apostate was Alfred Russel Wallace (1823–1913). In 1887, Wallace examined the evidence for early man in the New World, and . . . found not only considerable evidence of antiquity for the available specimens, but also a continuity of type through time." Spencer (1984, p.14) noted, however, that the case for extreme human antiquity "lost some of its potency as well as a few of its supporters when news began circulating of the discovery of a remarkable hominid fossil in Java." This was, of course, *Pithecanthropus.* I differ from Spencer in that I desire to resurrect Tertiary man, who was unfairly sacrificed on the altar of evolutionary preconceptions.

Examples from the Nineteenth Century

The California Gold Mine Discoveries

As an example of how the Java man discoveries resulted in the suppression of evidence for extreme human antiquity, we can consider a case mentioned by Wallace in his survey of North American evidence—the California gold mine discoveries [**see Plates XII-XV**]. Hundreds of stone tools and weapons, including obsidian spear points and stone mortars and pestles, and numerous anatomically modern human skeletal remains (quite apart from the notorious Calaveras skull, widely regarded as a hoax), were discovered by miners in the California gold mining region. Many of the finds occurred in deeply buried, basalt-capped Eocene river gravels, ranging from 33 to 55 million years old, according to modern geological studies (Slemmons 1966). These discoveries from the auriferous gravels were reported to the scientific world by J. D. Whitney (1880), state geologist of California. Whitney considered and ruled out the possibility of recent intrusion.

In his discussion of the reports of Whitney and others, Wallace (1887, p. 679) said: "The proper way to treat evidence as to man's antiquity is to place it on record, and admit it provisionally wherever it would be held adequate in the case of other animals; not, as is too often now the case, to ignore it as unworthy of acceptance or subject its discoverers to indiscriminate accusations of being impostors or the victims of impostors."

In Whitney's case, the influential anthropologist William H. Holmes, of the Smithsonian Institution, chose the latter course. Holmes (1899, p. 424) said of Whitney's careful report: "Perhaps if Professor Whitney had fully appreciated the story of human evolution as it is understood today, he would have hesitated to announce the conclusions formulated, notwithstanding the imposing array of testimony with which he was confronted." In other words, if the facts reported by Whitney violated the emerging picture of human evolution, those facts, even an imposing array of them, had to be set aside.

Holmes's opposition to the California gold mine discoveries was to a large degree conditioned by his acceptance of Java man. Holmes (1899, p. 470) suggested that Whitney's evidence should be rejected because "it implies a human race older by at least one half than *Pithecanthropus erectus* of Dubois, which may be regarded as an incipient form of human only."

European scientists followed Holmes in using the Java man discoveries to dismiss the California discoveries. According to archeologist Robert Munro, Fellow of the Royal Society of Antiquaries of Scotland, researchers who accepted evidence that human beings of modern anatomy inhabited California during the Tertiary and manufactured a variety of stone tools and weapons of advanced type were "upholding opinions which, if true, would be absolutely subversive, not only of human evolution, but of the principles upon which modern archaeology has been founded" (Munro 905, p. 106). He cited as evidence the *Pithecanthropus* skull, which he assigned to the Plio-Pleistocene boundary. After introducing Holmes's statement that the California evidence belonged to a period older than that of *Pithecanthropus,* Munro (1905, p. 106) said, "According to these calculations the cranium of a Californian 'auriferous gravel man' would have been of so low a type as to be undistinguishable from that of the Simian progenitor of *Homo sapiens* [i.e., *Pithecanthropus*]. But instead of that we have . . . a skull that could have contained the brains of a philosopher of the present day." Munro was referring to the famous Calaveras skull, surrounded by reports of hoaxing, but Whitney reported several other anatomically modern human skeletons from different locations. In any case, Munro's point was that according to evolutionary expectations an old skull should be anatomically primitive. Therefore, if a skull were anatomically modern, it could not possibly be old. In particular, it could not be older than *Pithecanthropus,* with its prominent brow ridges and shallow cranium. About the artifacts, which included projectile points and mortars and pestles, Munro (1905, p. 108) said that if they were to be accepted "we must, henceforth, delete from archaeological nomenclature such terms as Palaeolithic and Neolithic as having no longer any chronological significance." In other words, neither anatomically modern human bones nor finely worked artifacts could be accepted as genuinely old.

Holmes and Munro of course gave other reasons supporting their dismissals of the California discoveries.[2] But their primary consideration appears to have been their absolute conviction that evidence violating their evolutionary convictions had to be wrong.

The Nampa Image

Holmes also raised the specter of Java man to dismiss the Nampa image. This small human figurine came from just below a layer of clay at the 320-foot level of a well boring at Nampa, Idaho (Wright 1912). According to the United States Geological Survey (private communication, February 25, 1985), the clay layer at that depth is "probably of the Glenns Ferry Formation, upper Idaho Group, which is generally considered to be of Plio-Pleistocene age."[3] Among the layers penetrated by the well boring before reaching the clay was a 15-foot thick layer of basalt lava (Wright 1912). Even critics of the find such as Holmes (1919) did not dispute the human manufacture of the tiny clay statuette, representing a female figure. Instead, Holmes (1919, p. 70) wrote: "The formation in which the pump was operating is of late Tertiary or early Quaternary age; and the apparent improbability of the occurrence of a well-modeled human figure in deposits of such great antiquity has led to grave doubts about its authenticity. It is interesting to note that the age of this object, supposing it to be authentic, corresponds with that of the incipient man whose bones were, in 1892, recovered by Dubois from the late Tertiary or Early Quaternary formations of Java." In other words, Holmes doubted the genuineness of the Nampa image mostly because it was out of synch with the emerging concept of human evolution, founded on acceptance of *Pithecanthropus erectus* as a culturally and physiologically primitive human ancestor incapable of such refined art work.[4]

Examples from the Twentieth Century

The Schöningen Spears and the Later Discoveries of Boucher de Perthes

In the late twentieth century, finds that could be taken as evidence for extreme human antiquity continue to be made. But archeologists often interpret them to fit within the now generally accepted scheme of human evolution. For example, Thieme (1997) recently reported the discovery at Schöningen in northern Germany of wooden hunting spears in soft coal deposits over 400,000 years old. Traditionally, archeologists have identified hunting spears exclusively with humans of our type. But according to the current paradigm, anatomically modern humans were not present in Europe, or anywhere else, 400,000 years ago. Thieme therefore chose to attribute the spears to a culturally upgraded Middle Pleistocene hominid (presumably *Homo erectus* or *Homo heidelbergensis*). But perhaps there is another choice.

As an alternative explanation for the Schöningen spears, we could resurrect the nineteenth century discoveries of anatomically modern human remains by Boucher de Perthes at Abbeville, in deposits also roughly 400,000 years old.[5] These latter discoveries are not well known among working archeologists today.

In the 1840s Boucher de Perthes discovered stone tools in the Middle Pleistocene high level gravels of the Somme, at Moulin Quignon and other sites in and around Abbeville. At first, the scientific community, particularly in France, was not inclined to accept his discoveries as genuine. Some believed that the tools were manufactured by forgers. Others believed them to be purely natural forms that happened to resemble stone tools. Later, leading British archeologists visited the sites of Boucher de Perthes's discoveries and pronounced them genuine. But the exact nature of the maker of these tools remained unknown. Then in 1863, Boucher de Perthes discovered at Moulin Quignon additional stone tools and an anatomically modern human jaw. The jaw inspired much controversy, and was the subject of a joint English-French commission (Falconer et al. 1863, Delesse 1863). The English members of the commission thought the recently discovered stone tools were forgeries that had been artificially introduced into the Moulin Quignon strata. They thought the same of the jaw. To settle the matter, the commission paid a surprise visit to the site. Five flint implements were found in the presence of the scientists. The commission approved by majority vote a resolution in favor of the authenticity of the recently discovered stone tools. In addition to confirming the authenticity of the stone tools from Moulin Quignon, the commission also concluded that there was no evidence that the jaw had been fraudulently introduced into the Moulin Quignon gravel deposits (Falconer et al. 1863, p. 452). The English skeptics, including John Evans, who was not able to join the commission in France, were left with finding further proof of fraudulent behavior among the workmen at Moulin Quignon as their best weapon against the jaw. Evans sent his trusted assistant Henry Keeping to France, where he claimed to have obtained proof that the French workmen were introducing tools into the deposits at Moulin Quignon. But careful study of Keeping's reports reveals little to support these allegations. Nevertheless, a report by Evans (1863), based on Keeping's account, was published in an English periodical and swayed many scientists to the opinion that Boucher des Perthes was, despite the favorable conclusions of the scientific commission, the victim of an archeological fraud in regard to the Moulin Quignon jaw.

Boucher des Perthes (1864), stung by accusations of deception, carried out a new set of excavations, which resulted in the recovery of more anatomically modern human skeletal remains, amounting to over one hundred bones and teeth. These later discoveries are hardly mentioned in standard histories, which dwell upon the controversy surrounding the famous Moulin Quignon jaw. Boucher de Perthes carried out his new investigations so as to effectively rule out the possibility of deception by workmen. First of all, they were carried out during a period when the quarry at Moulin Quignon was shut down and the usual workmen were not there (1864, p. 219). Boucher de Perthes himself supervised the excavations, and in almost all cases witnesses with scientific or medical training were present. In some cases, these witnesses organized their own careful excavations to independently confirm the discoveries of Boucher de Perthes. Armand de Quatrefages (1864), a prominent French anthropologist, reported favorably on Boucher de Perthes's later discoveries at Moulin Quignon to the French Academy of Sciences. These later discoveries tend to validate the original Moulin Quignon jaw and, combined with the recent discoveries of the Schöningen spears, offer good evidence of an anatomically modern human population in northern Europe during the Middle Pleistocene, about 400,000 years ago.

The Laetoli Footprints and the Castenedolo Skeletons

Another case in which rigid commitment to an evolutionary consensus has prevented recognition of possible evidence for extreme human antiquity may be found in the Laetoli footprints, discovered by Mary Leakey in Tanzania in 1979. The prints occurred in layers of solidified volcanic ash 3.7 million years old. Leakey herself (1979, p. 453) said the prints were exactly like anatomically modern human footprints, a judgement shared by other physical anthropologists (Tuttle 1981, p. 91; 1987, p. 517). Tim White said, "Make no mistake about it. They are like modern human footprints" (Johanson and Edey 1981, p. 250).

Attempts to account for the humanlike nature of the prints has varied. Some have suggested that late Pliocene hominids such as *Australopithecus afarensis* could have made the prints. But such proposals are not supported by skeletal evidence in the form of a complete *Australopithecus* foot. White and Suwa (1987) attempted to put together such a foot (using bones from three different hominids of different genera), but such an exercise was, of course, quite speculative.[6]

In 1995, Ron Clarke and Phillip Tobias reported the discovery of a partial *Australopithecus* foot from Sterkfontein (Bower 1995), and in 1998 announced the discovery of a fairly complete australopithecine skeleton, to which the foot bones had originally been attached. The four foot bones reported in 1995 made up a left instep. The big toe was long and divergent, like that of a chimpanzee, with features indicating it was capable of grasping. Like White and Suwa, Tobias and Clarke used bones from East African hominids to reconstruct a complete foot, which Tobias said matched the Laetoli prints (Bower 1995). Physical anthropologist Michael Day at the British Museum asserted that the Sterkfontein foot could not have made the Laetoli footprints and questioned the accuracy of a reconstruction that made use of bones of hominids from different parts of Africa (Bower 1995).

In January 1999, at the World Archeological Congress in Cape Town, South Africa, I saw Clarke attempt to justify how the chimpanzeelike Sterkfontein foot could have made the humanlike Laetoli prints. He explained that chimpanzees sometimes walk with their normally divergent big toes pressed inward so as to align with the other toes. These other toes, although longer than human toes, would have been curled under. But it is highly unlikely that the three individuals who made the trails of prints at Laetoli would have all been walking like that. A similar proposal had earlier been made by Stern and Susman (1983). But others (Tuttle 1985, p. 132, White and Suwa 1987, p. 495) pointed out that the prints showed no knuckle marks, and that surely, in the case of so many prints, representing three individuals, some of the prints would have shown the extended toes. Clarke also appealed to a recent study by Deloison (1997), who claimed, in opposition to almost all previous reporting, that the Laetoli prints displayed distinctly primate (chimpanzoid) features. Others (Tuttle *et al.* 1998) answered, demonstrating that Deloison's observations were "false interpretations based on artifactual taphonomic features, reliance on a partial sample of the . . . first generation casts of the Laetoli prints, and her not accounting for the orientation of the prints on the trackway."

So it would appear reasonable to propose that anatomically modern humans made the Laetoli prints in the late Pliocene. This proposal becomes even more reasonable in the context of other discoveries of evidence for anatomically modern humans in the Pliocene. Fairly complete anatomically modern human skeletons were discovered in Middle Pliocene clays at Castenedolo by the geologist Ragazzoni (1880), who testified that the overlying layers were undisturbed. European archeologists later rejected the discoveries on theoretical grounds. For example, Macalister (1921, p. 183) said, "There must be something wrong somewhere." Considering the anatomically modern character of the skeletons, he proposed (1921, p. 184), "Now, if they really belonged to the stratum in which they were found, this would imply an extraordinarily long standstill for evolution. It is much more likely that there is something amiss with the observations."[7]

Conclusion

So what does this all add up to? It appears that commitment to an evolutionary picture of human origins, put into place with the discovery of *Pithecanthropus,* has resulted in a process of knowledge filtration, whereby a large set of archeological evidence has dropped below the horizon of cognition.[8] This filtering has left current researchers with an incomplete data set for building and rebuilding our ideas about human origins.

Notes

1. Incised and carved mammal bones are reported from the Pliocene (Desnoyers 1863, Laussedat 1868, Capellini 1877) and Miocene (Garrigou and Filhol 1868, von Dücker 1873). Additional reports of incised bones from the Pliocene and Miocene may be found in an extensive review by the overly skeptical de Mortillet (1883). Scientists have also reported pierced shark teeth from the Pliocene (Charlesworth 1873), artistically carved bone from the Miocene (Calvert 1874) and artistically carved shell from the Pliocene (Stopes 1881). Carved mammal bones reported by Moir (1917) could be as old as the Eocene. Very crude stone tools occur in the Middle Pliocene (Prestwich 1892) and from perhaps as far back as the Eocene (Moir 1927, Breuil 1910, p. 402). One will note that most of these discoveries are from the nineteenth century. But such artifacts are still being found. Crude stone tools have recently been reported from the Pliocene of Pakistan (Bunney 1987), Siberia (Daniloff and Kopf 1986), and India (Sankhyan 1981), what to speak of a pebble tool from the Miocene of India (Prasad 1982). More advanced stone tools occur in the Oligocene of Europe (Rutot 1907), the Miocene of Europe (Ribeiro 1873, Bourgeois 1873, Verworn 1905), the Miocene of Asia (Noetling 1894), and the Pliocene of South America (F. Ameghino 1908, C. Ameghino 1915). In North America, advanced stone tools occur in California deposits ranging from Pliocene to Miocene in age (Whitney 1880), and Wright (1912, pp. 262–269) reported a Pliocene clay statuette. An interesting slingstone, at least Pliocene and perhaps Eocene in age, comes from England (Moir 1929, p. 63). Humanlike footprints have been found in the Pliocene of Africa (M. Leakey 1979). Human skeletal remains

described as anatomically modern occur in the Middle Pleistocene of Europe (Newton 1895, Bertrand 1868, de Mortillet 1883). These cases are favorably reviewed by Keith (1928). Other anatomically modern human skeletal remains occur in the Early and Middle Pleistocene of Africa (Reck 1914, L. Leakey 1960, Zuckerman 1954, p. 310; Patterson and Howells 1967, Senut 1981, R. Leakey 1973), the Early Middle Pleistocene of Java (Day and Molleson 1973), the Early Pleistocene of South America (Hrdlička 1912, pp. 319–44), the Pliocene of South America (Hrdlička 1912, p. 346; Boman 1921, pp. 341–42), the Pliocene of England (Osborn 1921, pp. 567–69), the Pliocene of Italy (Ragazzoni 1880, Issel 1868), the Miocene of France and the Eocene of Switzerland (de Mortillet 1883, p. 72), and even the Carboniferous of North America (*The Geologist* 1862). Several discoveries from California gold mines range from Pliocene to Eocene (Whitney 1880). Some of the above mentioned human skeletal remains have been subjected to chemical and radiometric tests that have yielded ages younger than suggested by their stratigraphic position. But when the unreliabilities of the testing procedures are measured against the very compelling stratigraphic observations of the discoverers, it is not at all clear that the original age attributions should be discarded.

2. They pointed out the resemblance of the bones and artifacts to those of recent history and hinted at various ways they could have been introduced into the Tertiary auriferous gravels.

3. My research assistant Stephen Bernath sent to the United States Geological Survey a copy of the drilling record from the well boring, and a geologist replied with the estimated age of the clay layer that yielded the Nampa image.

4. Influenced by this conviction, Holmes (1919, p. 70) was reduced to suggesting that the image "could have descended from the surface through some crevice or water course penetrating the lava beds and have been carried through deposits of creeping quicksand aided by underground waters to the spot tapped by the drill."

5. In a recent synoptic table of European Pleistocene sites, Carbonell and Rodriguez (1994, p. 306) put Abbeville at around 430,000 years, and I think we can take that as a current consensus.

6. White and Suwa used the partial OH 8 foot from Olduvai Gorge, usually attributed to *Homo habilis*, along with *Australopithecus afarensis* toe bones from Lucy and the more robust AL 333-115. The OH 8 and AL 333-115 bones were rescaled to fit those of Lucy.

7. Oakley (1980, p. 40) said the Castenedolo bones had a nitrogen content similar to that of human bones from Late Pleistocene and Holocene Italian sites, and judged them recent. But nitrogen preservation can vary widely from site to site, making such comparisons of little value. Oakley (1980, p. 42) reported a high fluorine content for the bones. Low measures of fluorine in the groundwater indicated a potentially great age for the bones, but Oakley explained this away by positing higher levels of fluorine in the past! The Castenedolo bones also had an unexpectedly high concentration of uranium. A radiocarbon date of less than one thousand years was obtained in 1969 (Barker *et al.* 1971), but the methods employed are now regarded as not adequate to prevent falsely young dates from contamination with recent carbon, a distinct possibility in the case of bones that have lain exposed in a museum for a century. The most

certain age estimate comes from the original stratigraphic observations of Ragazzoni. 8. The original *Pithecanthropus erectus* discovery was based on associating a femur with a skullcap. Considering the historical impact of *Pithecanthropus* on evidence for extreme human antiquity, it is interesting that modern researchers no longer consider the association valid. A reexamination of the femur by Day and Molleson (1973) showed it to be indistinguishable from anatomically modern human femurs and distinct from other *erectus* femurs.

Acknowledgements

I am grateful to the trustees of the Bhaktivedanta Book Trust for their grants in support of my work and to Lori Erbs for her research assistance.

References

Ameghino, C. (1915) El femur de Miramar. *Anales de Museo nacional de historia natural de Buenos Aires,* 26: 433–450.

Ameghino, F. (1908) Notas preliminares sobre el *Tetraprothhomo argentinus,* un precursor de hombre del Mioceno superior de Monte Hermoso. *Anales de Museo nacional de historia natural de Buenos Aires,* 16: 105–242.

Barker, H., Burleigh, R. and Meeks, N. (1971) British Museum natural radiocarbon measurements VII. *Radiocarbon,* 13: 157–188.

Bertrand, E. (1868) Crane et ossements trouves dans un carriere de l'avenue de Clichy. *Bulletin de la Societe d'Anthropologie de Paris (Series 2),* 3: 32–335.

Boman, E. (1921) Los vestigios de industria humana encontrados en Miramar (Republica Argentina) y atribuidos a la época terciaria. *Revista Chilena de Historia y Geografia,* 49(43): 330–352.

Boucher de Perthes, J. (1864) Nouvelles découvertes d'os humains dans le diluvium, en 1863 et 1864, par M. Boucher de Perthes. Rapport a la Société Impériale d'Émulation. In J. Boucher de Perthes (ed), *Antiquités Celtiques et Antédiluviennes. Memoire sur l'Industrie Primitive et les Arts à leur Origin* (Vol. 3). Paris: Jung-Treutel, pp. 215–250.

Bourgeois, L. (1873) Sur les silex considérés comme portant les margues d'un travail humain et découverts dans le terrain miocène de Thenay. *Congrès International d'Anthropologie et d'Archéologie Préhistoriques, Bruxelles 1872, Compte Rendu,* pp. 81–92.

Bower, B. (1995) Hominid bones show strides toward walking. *Science News,* 148: 71.

Breuil, H. (1910) Sur la présence d'éolithes a la base de l'Éocene Parisien. *L'Anthropologie,* 21: 385–408.

Bunney, S. (1987) First migrants will travel back in time. *New Scientist,* 114(1565): 36.

Calvert, F. (1874) On the probable existence of man during the Miocene period. *Journal of the Royal Anthropological Institute of Great Britain and Ireland,* 3: 127.

Capellini, G. (1877) Les traces de l'homme pliocène en Toscane. *Congrès International d'Anthropologie et d'Archéologie Préhistoriques, Budapest 1876, Compte Rendu.* Vol.

1, pp. 46–62.

Carbonell, E. and Rodriguez, X. P. (1994) Early Middle Pleistocene deposits and artefacts in the Gran Dolina site (TD4) of the 'Sierra de Atapuerca' (Burgos, Spain). *Journal of Human Evolution*, 26: 291–311.

Charlesworth, E. (1873) Objects in the Red Crag of Suffolk. *Journal of the Royal Anthropological Institute of Great Britain and Ireland*, 2: 91–94.

Cremo, M. A. and Thompson, R. L. (1993) *Forbidden Archeology: The Hidden History of the Human Race*. San Diego: Bhaktivedanta Institute.

Daniloff, R. and Kopf, C. (1986) Digging up new theories of early man. *U. S. News & World Report*, September, 1: 62–63.

Day, M. H. and Molleson, T. I. (1973) The Trinil femora. *Symposia of the Society for the Study of Human Biology*, 2: 127–154.

Delesse, A. (1863) La mâchoire humaine de Moulin de Quignon. *Mémoires de la Société d'Anthropologie de Paris*, 2: 37–68.

Deloison, Y. M-L. (1997) The foot bones from Hadar, Ethiopia and the Laetoli, Tanzania footprints. Locomotion of *A. afarensis*. *American Journal of Physical Anthropology* supplement no. 24 (AAPA abstracts), p. 101.

De Mortillet, G. (1883) *Le Préhistorique*. Paris: C. Reinwald.

De Quatrefages, A. (1864) Nouveaux ossements humains découverts par M. Boucher de Perthes à Moulin-Quignon. *Comptes Rendus Hebdomadaires de l'Académie des Sciences*, 59: 107–111.

Desnoyers, J. (1863) Response à des objections faites au sujet d'incisions constatées sur des ossements de Mammiferes fossiles des environs de Chartres. *Compte Rendus de l'Académie des Sciences*, 56: 1199–1204.

Evans, J., 1863. The human remains at Abbeville. *The Athenaeum*, July, 4: 19–20.

Falconer, H., Busk, G. and Carpenter, W. B. (1863) An account of the proceedings of the late conference held in France to inquire into the circumstances attending the asserted discovery of a human jaw in the gravel at Moulin-Quignon, near Abbeville; including the *procès verbaux* of the conference, with notes thereon. *The Natural History Review*, 3 *(new series)*: 423–462.

Garrigou, F., and Filhol, H. (1868) M. Garrigou prie l'Académie de vouloir bien ouvrir un pli cacheté, déposé au nom de M. Filhol fils et au sien, le 16 mai 1864. *Compte Rendus de l'Académie des Sciences*, 66: 819–820.

The Geologist (London) (1862) Fossil man, 5: 470.

Holmes, W. H. (1899) Review of the evidence relating to auriferous gravel man in California. In *Smithsonian Institution Annual Report 1898–1899*. Washington, D. C.: Smithsonian Institution, pp. 419–472.

Holmes, W. H. (1919). Handbook of aboriginal American antiquities, Part I. *Smithsonian Institution Bulletin 60*. Washington, D. C.: Smithsonian Institution.

Hrdlička, A. (1912) *Early Man in South America*. Washington, D. C.: Smithsonian Institution.

Issel, A. (1868) Résumé des recherches concernant l'ancienneté de l'homme en Ligurie. *Congrès International d'Anthropologie et d'Archéologie Préhistoriques, Paris 1867, Compte Rendu*, pp. 75–89.

Johanson, D. and Edey, M. A. (1981) *Lucy: The Beginnings of Humankind.* New York: Simon and Schuster.

Keith, A. (1928) *The Antiquity of Man.* Vol. 1. Philadelphia: J. B. Lippincott.

Laussedat, A. (1868) Sur une mâchoire de Rhinoceros portant des entailles profondes trouvée à Billy (Allier), dans les formations calcaires d'eau douce de la Limagne. *Compte Rendus de l'Académie des Sciences,* 66: 752–754.

Leakey, L. S. B. (1960) *Adam's Ancestors,* 4th edition. New York: Harper & Row.

Leakey, M. D. (1979) Footprints in the ashes of time. *National Geographic,* 155: 446–457.

Leakey, R. E., 1973. Evidence for an advanced Plio-Pleistocene hominid from East Rudolf, Kenya. *Nature,* 242: 447–450.

Macalister, R. A. S. (1921) *Textbook of European Archaeology,* Vol. I, *Palaeolithic Period.* Cambridge: Cambridge University Press.

Moir, J. R. (1917) A series of mineralised bone implements of a primitive type from below the base of the Red and Coralline Crags of Suffolk. *Proceedings of the Prehistoric Society of East Anglia,* 2: 116–131.

Moir, J. R. (1927) *The Antiquity of Man in East Anglia.* Cambridge: Cambridge University Press.

Moir, J. R. (1929) A remarkable object from beneath the Red Crag. *Man* 29: 62–65.

Munro, R. (1905) *Archaeology and False Antiquities.* London: Methuen.

Newton, E. T. (1895) On a human skull and limb-bones found in the Paleolithic terrace-gravel at Galley Hill, Kent. *Quarterly Journal of the Geological Society of London* 51: 505–526.

Noetling, F. (1894) On the occurrence of chipped flints in the Upper Miocene of Burma. *Records of the Geological Survey of India,* 27: 101–103.

Oakley, K. P. (1980) Relative dating of fossil hominids of Europe. *Bulletin of the British Museum of Natural History (Geology),* 34.

Osborn, H. F. (1921) The Pliocene man of Foxhall in East Anglia. *Natural History,* 21: 565–576.

Patterson, B. and Howells, W. W. (1967) Hominid humeral fragment from Early Pleistocene of northwestern Kenya. *Science,* 156: 64–66.

Prasad, K. N. (1982) Was *Ramapithecus* a tool-user. *Journal of Human Evolution,* 11: 101–104.

Prestwich, J. (1892) On the primitive character of the flint implements of the Chalk Plateau of Kent, with reference to the question of their glacial or pre-glacial age. *Journal of the Royal Anthropological Insti\tute of Great Britain and Ireland,* 21(3): 246–262.

Ragazzoni, G. (1880) La collina di Castenedolo, solto il rapporto antropologico, geologico ed agronomico. *Commentari dell' Ateneo di Brescia,* April, 4: 120–128.

Reck, H. (1914) Erste vorläufige Mitteilungen über den Fund eines fossilen Menschenskeletts aus Zentral-afrika. *Sitzungsbericht der Gesellschaft der naturforschender Freunde Berlins,* 3: 81–95.

Ribeiro, C. (1873) Sur des silex taillés, découverts dans les terrains miocène du Portugal. *Congrès International d'Anthropologie et d'Archéologie Préhistoriques, Bruxelles 1872, Compte Rendu,* pp. 95–100.

Rutot, A. (1907) Un grave problem: une industrie humaine datant de l'époque oligocène. Comparison des outils avec ceux des Tasmaniens actuels. *Bulletin de la Société Belge de Géologie de Paléontologie et d'Hydrologie*, 21: 439–482.

Sankhyan, A. R. (1981) First evidence of early man from Haritalyangar area, Himalchal Pradesh. *Science and Culture*, 47: 358–359.

Senut, B. (1981) Humeral outlines in some hominoid primates and in Plio-pleistocene hominids. *American Journal of Physical Anthropology*, 56: 275–283.

Slemmons, D. B. (1966) Cenozoic volcanism of the central Sierra Nevada, California. *Bulletin of the California Division of Mines and Geology*, 190: 199–208.

Spencer, F. (1984) The Neandertals and their evolutionary significance: a brief historical survey. In F. H. Smith and F. Spencer (eds), *The Origin of Modern Humans: A World Survey of the Fossil Evidence*. New York: Alan R. Liss, pp. 1–49.

Stern, Jr., J. T. and Susman, R. L. (1983) The locomotor anatomy of *Australopithecus afarensis*. *American Journal of Physical Anthropology*, 60: 279–318.

Stopes, H. (1881) Traces of man in the Crag. *British Association for the Advancement of Science, Report of the Fifty-first Meeting*, p. 700.

Thieme, H. (1997) Lower Paleolithic hunting spears from Germany. *Nature*, 385: 807–810.

Trinkaus, E. and Shipman, P. (1994) *The Neandertals*. New York: Vintage.

Tuttle, R. H. (1981) Evolution of hominid bipedalism and prehensile capabilities. *Philosophical Transactions of the Royal Society of London B*, 292: 89–94.

Tuttle, R. H. (1985) Ape footprints and Laetoli impressions: a response to the SUNY claims. In P. V. Tobias (ed). *Hominid Evolution: Past, Present, and Future*. New York: Alan R. Liss, pp. 129–133.

Tuttle, R. H. (1987) Kinesiological inferences and evolutionary implications from Laetoli biped trails G-1, G-2/3, and A. In M. D. Leakey and J. Harris (eds). *Laetoli: A Pliocene Site in Northern Tanzania*. Oxford: Clarendon Press, pp. 508–517.

Tuttle, R. H., Musiba, C, Webb, D. M., and Hallgrimsson, B. (1998) False impressions from the Laetoli Hominid footprints. *American Journal of Physical Anthropology* supplement 26 (AAPA abstracts), p. 221.

Verworn, M. (1905) Die archaeolithische Cultur in den Hipparionschichten von Aurillac (Cantal). *Abhandlungen der königlichen Gesellschaft der Wissenschaften zu Göttingen, Mathematisch-Physikalische Klasse, Neue Folge*, 4(4): 3–60.

Von Dücker, Baron (1873) Sur la cassure artificelle d'ossements recuellis dans le terrain miocène de Pikermi. *Congrès International d'Anthropologie et d'Archéologie Préhistoriques. Bruxelles 1872, Compte Rendu*, pp. 104–107.

Wallace, A. R. (1887) The antiquity of man in North America. *Nineteenth Century*, 22: 667–679.

White, T. D. and Suwa, G. (1987) Hominid footprints at Laetoli: facts and interpretations. *American Journal of Physical Anthropology*, 72: 485–514.

Whitney, J. D. (1880) The auriferous gravels of the Sierra Nevada of California. *Harvard University, Museum of Comparative Zoology Memoir* 6(1).

Wright, G. F. (1912) *Origin and Antiquity of Man*. Oberlin: Bibliotheca Sacra.

Zuckerman, S. (1954) Correlation of change in the evolution of higher primates. In J.

Huxley, A. C. Hardy, and E. B. Ford (eds), *Evolution as a Process.* London: Allen and Unwin, pp. 300–352.

10
Forbidden Archeology:
The Royal Institution Lecture

What follows is a transcript of a lecture that I gave at the Royal Institution of Great Britain in London, United Kingdom, on May 3, 2000. The Royal Institution, founded in 1799, is one of the most famous scientific institutions in the world. Through the efforts of Ray McLennan, a representative of my publisher in the United Kingdom, I received an invitation to give a lecture on my work there. On May 4, 2000, one of the main English newspapers published an excerpt from my lecture. See http://www.independent.co.uk/ opinion/commentators/the-hidden-history-of-human-evolution-717721.html.

Introduction by Dr. Richard Catlow: Ladies and gentleman, I'd like to welcome you to the Royal Institution to this public lecture. My name is Richard Catlow. I'm the director of the Davy-Faraday Lab here at the Royal Institution. I'm also a visiting professor. The public lectures of course are part of a very rapidly expanding range of events offered by the Royal Institution. These lectures aim to highlight topical areas of science, but particularly those which have a broader impact on society. The topic of this evening's lecture, which concerns human origins, is certainly one of enduring importance and fascination. Exploring this topic, our lecturer, Michael Cremo, will take us on an expedition across five continents to key archeological sites. Michael Cremo is an internationally known expert on the history of archeology and on anomalous archeological evidence for extreme human antiquity. He is a research associate in history of science with the Bhaktivedanta Institute and he is a member of the History of Science Society, the Philosophy of Science Association, and the European Association of Archeologists. He is a very distinguished worker in the field of the topic this evening and we are very fortunate that he's agreed to lecture to us. So it is my great pleasure to invite Michael Cremo to present his lecture on *Forbidden Archeology: The Hidden History of the Human Race.*
[applause]

Michael Cremo: I'd like to thank Professor Catlow for the introduction. I'd also like to thank Professor Susan Greenfield, who's not here tonight. She's the director of the Royal Institution. I'd like to thank her for including me in this season's Wednesday Public Lecture Series. And I thank all of you ladies and gentlemen for coming together this evening in this historic lecture theater to hear something about what I call forbidden archeology.

Lately, archeologists have come to recognize that our interpretations of the past are heavily influenced by our current conceptions, particularly our culturally conditioned concepts of time. Archeologists have therefore come to see some value in inspecting the archeological record through different time lenses. A couple of years ago I presented at the World Archaeological Congress a paper in which I looked at the archeological record through a time lens derived from the Vedic literature of India. That paper has recently come out and appeared in the conference proceedings volume entitled *Time and Archeology*, edited by archeologist Tim Murray, and published by Routledge, here in England. My talk this evening is largely based on that paper.

Now as Professor Catlow mentioned in his introduction, I'm a research associate in the history of science for the Bhaktivedanta Institute, which is the science studies branch of the International Society for Krishna Consciousness. As such, my work is inspired by the ancient Sanskrit writings of India, collectively known as the Vedic literature. The Vedic time concept is somewhat different from the time concept of modern Western science, which is linear and progressive. One could make a case that the time concept of modern science has been more or less unconsciously inherited from the European Judeo-Christian culture, in which modern science has many of its roots. Now, if we look at the Judeo-Christian concept of time, we find there is, first of all, a unique creation event; then there is a unique appearance of the lower species, there is a unique appearance of the human species, there is a unique salvation history, and finally there is a unique denouement in terms of a last judgment. Now, according to the cosmological picture that has been developed by modern western science over the past couple of centuries, we find there are many similarities. We find that there is a unique beginning to the universe in the form of a Big Bang. We find there is a unique origin for the various species of life, a unique origin of human species, which is, according to modern biology, one of the last major species of life to attain a developed state on this planet. You might also say there is a unique salvation history, a promise to deliver human society from ignorance and poverty by science and technology. And to carry the cosmological picture out to its extreme you find some kind of unique end to the whole process. Of course there are many varieties of the Big Bang theory, but most of them involve some kind of end—either a big crunch or heat-dissipation death of the universe.

Now, the Vedic time picture is somewhat different. It is cyclical. There are many creations and destructions. There are some versions of the modern Big Bang theory that also incorporate that. And if we look into the history of Europe, back to the time of the Greeks and Romans, we'll see that many prominent philosophers also had a cyclical concept of time.

The basic unit of cyclical time in the Vedic picture is called the day of Brahma. And it lasts for 4.3 billion years. This is followed by the night of Brahma, which also lasts for 4.3 billion years. The days follow the nights endlessly in succession, and according to these ancient Sanskirt writings, during the days of Brahma life is manifest in the universe, including human life, and in the nights it's not manifest. Now these ancient Sanskrit histories also speak of apemen. The idea of apemen is not something that was invented by European scientists in the nineteenth century. Long ago, the authors of these Sanskrit writings were speaking of apemen, but according to those accounts, alongside these creatures were existing humans like ourselves; in other words, we find a picture of coexistence rather than evolution. And the coexistence, according to these accounts, went on for a considerable period of time. If you look at the ancient Sanskrit calendars you'll find we're now about two billion years into the current day of Brahma. So, if we had a Vedic archeologist, such an archeologist might predict a few things. Such an archeologist might predict that we should find evidence for a human presence on this planet going back almost to the beginning of the current day of Brahma. And there should also be evidence for apemen as well.

Now, the ideas that I've just briefly sketched out for you are, of course, somewhat different than the ideas we've received from Charles Darwin and his modern followers. Recently a friend of mine suggested to me: "Perhaps you're a reincarnation of Charles Darwin and you've come back to correct the little mistake." [laughter] Now, I don't know if I'm going to be able to do that in one lifetime, because he made a very convincing case that still is swaying the minds of many people today, and probably will for quite a long time in the future.

The basic picture that we get of human origins from modern western science goes something like this. Life emerges on this planet somewhere between two and three billion years ago. Two billion years is the age of the oldest undisputed fossil evidence recognized by science (although some paleontologists say there are chemical signs of life earlier than that). It's an interesting coincidence. That would roughly correspond with the beginning of the day of Brahma, according to these ancient Vedic cosmological concepts. In any case, the first primates, the first apes and monkeys, come into existence about forty million years ago; the first hominins, the first apemen, around six million years ago; and finally, humans like ourselves, anatomically modern humans, come into existence between 100,000 and 200,000 years ago. The oldest undisputed skeletal evidence for anatomically modern humans goes back about 100,000 years in South Africa. Generally we're told that all the physical evidence ever discovered by science supports this particular picture or some slight modification of it.

However, when I looked into the entire history of archeology, I found something quite different. I found that over the past 150 years or so, archeologists have uncovered and reported in their scientific literature vast amounts of evidence showing that humans like ourselves have existed for far longer than 100,000 years on this planet. Indeed, the human presence appears to go back to the very beginnings of the history of life on earth.

Now people often ask, "Well, if there is so much evidence that contradicts the current views of human origins then why don't we hear about it so much? That's because of what I call knowledge filtration. The "knowledge filter" represents the current consensus in the scientific community about human origins. Reports of evidence that conform to this consensus will pass through this filter very easily, which means you will read about this evidence in textbooks in universities, you will hear archeologists—and other scientists—talking about this evidence at their conferences, and you will see the objects on display in museums of natural history. But if we have evidence that radically contradicts this current consensus, then that evidence tends to be filtered out—it tends to be set aside, ignored, forgotten, and, in some few cases, actively suppressed.

What I'd like to do this evening is review some representative sample of the types of evidence I'm talking about. And I'm going to start with a few cases that I presented at the World Archaeological Congress in January 1999 in Cape Town, South Africa.

In the 1980s Australian archeologists made some interesting discoveries of stone tools on Flores Island in the Indonesian island chain. Their report was published in *Nature*. The layer in which the artifacts were found was dated using the zircon fission track method, which yielded an age of about 800,000 years. The archeologists had to attribute the stone tools to some hominin. Of course, they decided immediately these creatures couldn't have been human beings like ourselves, because we didn't exist 800,000 years ago. So who existed 800,000 years ago in that part of the world? Well, *Homo erectus*. So they attributed the stone tools on Flores Island to *Homo erectus* living there about 800,000 years ago. But there was a problem with that. They published a map that showed the geography of the area as it was 800,000 years ago. On this map, one can see that the coast of Australia comes much further out than it does today. That land mass is known by paleo-geographers as the Sahul subcontinent. And the coast of Southeast Asia also comes out much further than it does today, during this earlier time of lower sea levels. Paleo-geographers call this land mass the Sunda subcontinent. And we can also see on this map that 800,000 years ago Flores Island was separated from the nearest land by deep sea straits at least 20 kilometers wide. So it became a problem for the archeologists to explain how *Homo erectus* got there.

The archeologists concluded that *Homo erectus* had gotten to Flores Island by some kind of deliberate sea crossing, by either rafting or making some kind of primitive boat. That was quite an extraordinary proposal, because up to that time, deliberate sea crossing was an activity that archeologists had attributed only to human beings like us. And, as a matter of fact, the oldest evidence that they had for any such deliberate sea crossings was the presence of anatomically modern humans in Australia at 50,000 years. So to have that kind of activity going on 800,000 years ago was a bit unusual.

But in Cape Town I proposed that there might be another way to resolve this problem. That takes us to the island of Java. It was in Java in the latter part of the nineteenth century that the very first specimens of *Homo erectus* were discovered by the Dutch physician, Eugene Dubois, at Trinil. He found initially two bones—a very apelike skullcap and a thighbone, or femur, which he regarded as being somewhat primitive. But he put the two together and proclaimed the existence of *Pithecanthropus erectus*, now known as *Homo erectus*. That account you'll find in almost every textbook of archeology or anthropology. What you usually don't see mentioned in these textbooks is that in 1973 two prominent British physical anthopologists, Michael Day and T. I. Molleson, conducted a new study of this femur, and they determined that it was indistinguishable from an anatomically modern human thighbone. They also determined that it was different from any other *Homo erectus* thighbone or femur that had been found subsequently. And they determined that it probably did not belong with the skull at all.

Now, that's interesting, because Dubois said that he found both the skull and the femur in the same stratum, as can be seen in his original drawing of the site's stratigraphy. That stratum was later dated using modern dating methods—the potassium-argon dating method in particular—as being about 800,000 years old. So the evidence suggests that there existed 800,000 years ago in Java two hominins: first, a population of *Homo erectus*, represented by the skull; second, a population resembling anatomically modern humans, represented by the anatomically modern human thighbone found in the same stratum. And I propose it was this population of anatomically modern humans existing on Java 800,000 years ago that was responsible for the sea crossing to Flores Island and for the stone tools that were left there.

Here's a similar case. In the late 1990's, a German archeologist, Thieme, found, at Schöningen in northern Germany, some very nice wooden spears. These spears were shaped exactly like modern javelins—the balance point was one-third of the distance from the tip. They were obviously some type of throwing weapon. And along with the spears were found butchered animal bones, indicating that these spears had been used for hunting. The spears were found in soft coal deposits that were about 430,000 years old. So the European archeologists faced the same dilemma as the Australian archeologists. They had to explain who made and used these weapons. Again, they concluded it couldn't have been humans like us because we didn't exist at that time. So their solution was to upgrade our understanding of the abilities of *Homo erectus*. Up to this point in time, this type of hunting, and the use and manufacture of this type of weapon, was something that archeologists had attributed only to humans of our type. As a matter of fact, the oldest throwing spears they had up to this point in time were somewhat less than 100,000 years old. So again, at the meeting of the World Archaeological Congress in Cape Town, South Africa, I proposed that by looking at the history of archeology we could find another solution to this particular problem.

The solution is connected with some discoveries that were made in the nineteenth century in northeastern France by Jacques Boucher de Perthes, one of the famous figures in the early history of archeology. He was the first to demonstrate a human presence in the glacial epoch—the first to demonstrate a human presence coexistent with ice age mammals. He discovered, at a place called Abbeville, an anatomically modern human jaw. It was a matter of considerable controversy at the time of discovery. He discovered it in a fairly deep layer in his excavations, belonging to the middle Pleistocene. And this layer has been dated using the modern geological methods as being roughly 430,000 years old. Several British scientists of the nineteenth century found it difficult to accept that human beings of our type could have been existing at an early time in the Pleistocene. So a commission of prominent British and French archeologists, geologists, and other scientists met in France. They visited the site, and they concluded that the discovery was genuine.

However, John Evans, one of the British scientists who objected to the discovery, didn't come. He had remained in London, where he began writing articles in the popular press suggesting that Boucher de Perthes was the victim of a hoax. And actually his articles were so convincing that they became the dominant view in archeology. And to this day, if you look at the archeological textbooks, you will find the Abbeville Jaw depicted as a hoax. What we generally don't see mentioned in the textbooks is that, subsequently, Boucher de Perthes, who was somewhat stunned by these accusations, made about a dozen additional excavations at Abbeville. And, in conditions that were without any possibility of hoaxing, he found an additional one hundred anatomically modern human bones and teeth in the same strata. So I proposed at Cape Town that it was this anatomically modern human population, existing in northern Europe at 430,000 years ago, that was responsible for the wooden throwing spears found recently in northern Germany in a stratum that was also roughly 430,000 years old.

Things like this come up repeatedly. Just recently, there have been two cases. In Japan, archeologists have recently uncovered signs of human huts in northern Japan, at a place called Chichibu. The evidence takes the form of post holes that have been drilled into solid rock in a circular pattern. It is obvious that tree trunks were placed in these holes, and that they were covered with something to make a hut. The site has been dated as being about 500,000 years old. And the archeologists are saying now we have to upgrade our understanding of *Homo erectus*—we never thought *Homo erectus* was capable of this. But in northern China, at a place called Liujiang, in the 1960s, anatomically modern human skeletal remains were found in middle Middle Pleistocene cave deposits along with bones of animals that went extinct in the middle Middle Pleistocene. The archeologists who examined the site could not believe that humans of our type were existing at that time, so they concluded that even though the fauna in the cave is middle Middle Pleistocene, the human remains had to have been later. I would just suggest that perhaps those humans that were existing perhaps as much as 500,000 years ago in northern China may have also been responsible for the evidence recently uncovered in Japan.

And just yesterday I heard a BBC report about archeologists—British archeologists in Zambia—uncovering a site where they have evidence of aesthetic paintings going back around 400,000 years. Again, reports say archeologists are puzzling over this, because they had not imagined that hominins of the type *Homo erectus* were capable of such a thing. The oldest evidence for aesthetic paintings that they had previous to this would be from less than 100,000 years ago, and the makers were humans like us. Again, I would propose there might be another solution to this problem. We don't have to try to elevate *Homo erectus* to anatomically modern human cultural status. There may be another solution. There are discoveries showing that anatomically modern humans were present during these times.

In Cape Town, I went through a dozen or more of these cases of evidence for the presence of anatomically modern humans going back roughly about two million years. I'm not going to talk about all of them, but I will go over one or two of them.

Virginia Steen-McIntyre is an American geologist who was involved in some discoveries that took place in Mexico at a place called Hueyatlaco in the middle 1970s. Some American archeologists were working there, and they uncovered many very nice stone artifacts, including projectile points. According to archeologists, these are the types of artifacts that are made and used only by humans like us, anatomically modern humans. This is a picture of the excavations at Hueyatlaco. The artifacts were found in the lower levels of the excavations. Of course, the archeologists were interested in finding out how old they were, so they brought in a team of geologists from the United States Geological Survey, including Virginia Steen-McIntyre. Using four of the latest geological methods—the uranium series method, the zircon fission track method, the tephra hydration method, and one other—they determined that the site was 300,000 years old. When they brought that information to the attention of the archeologists, the archeologists said, well that's impossible, because human beings didn't exist 300,000 years ago—what to speak of in North America, because according to the current thinking, humans like us (well, humans of any type) didn't enter North America any earlier than 30,000 years ago maximum. And most archeologists today are struggling with 12,000 years for a human presence in the Americas, so to have something like this—300,000 years—was not really possible. So what happened? The archeologists refused to publish the dates that the geologists had given them. Instead they published an age of 20,000 years for the site. And where did they get that? They got that from a carbon-14 date on a piece of shell that they found five miles from this particular site.

Now, what happened after that? Virginia Steen-McIntyre in particular was a little upset that the dates that she and her colleagues had obtained were not published, so she endeavored to get them published. In the process, she lost a teaching position that she held at a university in the United States, and she found that a lot of her opportunities for advancement in her chosen field were suddenly blocked off. And, as a matter of fact, she eventually left her profession and went with her husband to live in a little town in the Rocky Mountains of Colorado.

So I found out about her case and wrote about it in *Forbidden Archeology,* and started getting her work some of the attention I think it deserves, and partly as a result of that, in the past year or so, a more open-minded group of archeologists has been revisiting the site, and some of the preliminary reports that I'm getting are suggesting that her original work may be confirmed. So we'll see about that.

An anatomically modern human skullcap was discovered in Buenos Aires early in the twentieth century. It was reported to the scientific world by Florentino Ameghino, who was one of the leading paleontologists of Argentina at the time. The skull was found in an excavation that had proceeded about fifty feet from the surface. At that point the excavators broke through a thick layer of limestone rock, called *tosca* in that region. And the skullcap was found at this level here, which belongs to the Ensenadan formation. According to the modern geological reporting, this formation is roughly one million years old.

An anatomically modern human skull, part of a fairly complete anatomically modern human skeleton, was discovered at Olduvai Gorge by the German paleontologist Hans Reck in 1913. He found it solidly embedded in Upper Bed Two of Olduvai Gorge. He had to take it out with hammers and chisels. According to the modern geological reporting, Upper Bed Two would be 1.15 million years old.

In England, in the early part of the twentieth century, J. Reid Moir—a researcher with the Natural History Society in East Anglia—made some interesting discoveries at Foxhall. He discovered signs of a human presence there, including signs of fire and some fairly advanced stone tools. These artifacts were found in the Red Crag formation, about two million years old. Louis Leakey accepted those discoveries.

Richard Leakey, in the 1970s, made an interesting discovery at Lake Turkana in Kenya. This is a femur, a thighbone, technically called the ER 1481 femur. And he found it in a geological context that he regarded as being roughly 1.9 million years old. He attributed it to *Homo habilis*. And at that time, no one had ever discovered a complete skeleton of *Homo habilis*—paleontologists and archeologists had discovered only isolated bones of this creature. So he had found only the thighbone. Because the thighbone was, according to Richard Leakey, "indistinguishable from that of anatomically modern human being"—those were his exact words—he envisioned *Homo habilis* as looking something like this: fairly human below the neck, over five feet tall, with a somewhat apelike head (based on skull fragments and teeth that had been found elsewhere in Africa). Later on, Johanson, Donald Johanson and some of his coworkers discovered at Olduvai Gorge a creature that they regarded as being a member of the *Homo habilis* species. And it turned out to be something like this: it was very short, very apelike, and the thighbone, the femur, was very much different from that of an anatomically modern human being. So, I think what happened is that Richard Leakey discovered some evidence that anatomically modern humans were present in East Africa up to two million years ago.

That was the paper I presented at Cape Town. What we find is a picture something like this. The normal picture we get of human history, over the past few million years, is that around two to three million years ago, we had *Australopithecus*; around two million years ago, *Homo habilis*; maybe 1.8 million years ago, *Homo erectus*; and then, either the Neandertals, or some primitive form of *Homo sapiens*; and finally, anatomically modern humans like us coming to existence about one or two hundred thousand years ago. But if we actually look at everything that archeologists have uncovered, we find that there is quite a bit of evidence that humans like ourselves were present throughout this entire period of time. So, in Cape Town, I stopped there. I didn't really want to talk about evidence for a human presence going back twenty million years or a hundred million years. I thought that might have been a little extreme.

But we'll go ahead—we'll see how much further we can go with this type of evidence.

Now, this is not a human bone. This is a bone of an extinct South American mammal called the *Toxodon*. It was found at a place called Miramar on the coast of Argentina, in what's called the Chapadmalalan formation. It's a very well known site to paleontologists. There's a very well known Late Pliocene mammalian fauna that comes from there. So this bone would be roughly three million years old. What is interesting about it, is it has solidly embedded in it a flint arrowhead [a murmur ripples through the crowd]. This discovery was reported to the scientific world by Carlos Ameghino, brother of Florentino, in 1915. It was a controversial discovery. There was another South American scientist named Eric Boman, who said: Look, it's perfectly possible that something like this happened. Someone took a fossil *Toxodon* bone from one place, a flint arrowhead from a modern Indian settlement, pounded the flint arrowhead into the bone, and buried it at the site. Around this same time, it was decided that a commission should gather at Miramar to make some excavations to see if there really was evidence for a human presence in the Chapadmalalan formation at Miramar. Eric Boman himself was present, and as a matter of fact, he himself directed some of the excavation work. Carlos Ameghino was also there, and the entire commission consisted of the leading paleontologists, geologists, and archeologists of Argentina at the time. Together they supervised the excavations, which were conducted at Mirarar, at this cliff face here—this is the Chapadmalalan level here. First they found a bola stone solidly embedded in this level. Eric Boman directed the workmen to dig further, and they found additional bola stones here and elsewhere at the site. Now according to archeologists, implements like this were something made and used only by humans of our type, not by any kind of apeman. You know how the bolas work: you put a leather thong around the groove that's carved in the stone, around a few of them, and throw them. They are used to capture small animals or birds. They are still used in some parts of South America even today. So it appears that the skeptic, Eric Boman, was himself responsible for some very interesting discoveries that suggest the presence of humans like us in Argentina millions of years ago. Sometimes a skeptical archeologist demands the presence of trained personnel (geologists, paleontologists, and archeologists), demands that the object be photographed *in situ,* etc. etc. In this case all those conditions were met.

Now, an interesting case from the more recent history of archeology. In 1979, Mary Leakey and her coworkers discovered at a place called Laetoli in the country of Tanzania, East Africa, several dozen footprints. And to quote Mary Leakey, in her original description of them, "They are indistinguishable from anatomically modern human footprints." They are found, however, in layers of solidified volcanic ash that have been dated using the potassium-argon method to 3.7 million years. So, how do orthodox archeologists explain these footprints? Generally, they say there must have existed in East Africa 3.7 million years ago some type of hominid, some variety of *Australopithecus* who had feet exactly like ours, that's how the prints were made. It's an interesting proposal, but at the present moment, there is no physical evidence to support it. Scientists have skeletal remains of *Australopithecus,* including the footbones. And the footbones indicate that the structure of the *Australopithecus* foot was somewhat different from the anatomically modern human foot.

Now this came up for me last January in Cape Town when I was speaking there. Also speaking there was Ron Clarke, who in 1998 announced the discovery of a fairly complete skeleton of *Australopithecus.* It was found in a place called Sterkfontein in South Africa. And this discovery was widely advertised all over the world as being the oldest human ancestor. But I saw a slight problem with that.

And that is the foot structure. Now this is a model of the foot that Ron Clarke produced based on his study of the footbones. It's somewhat apelike, as it should be, because the footbones were somewhat apelike. But one thing you notice is that the first toe (the big toe, as we call it) is rather long, and it moves out to the side, much like a human thumb. Actually, it could be extended further out than you see here in this model. You will notice that the other toes are also quite long—over one and a half times longer than the usual anatomically modern human toes. And the foot has other apelike features as well which we won't go into now.

The deposits in which Clarke found the Sterkfontein *Australopithecus* were roughly the same age as the deposits at Laetoli. The latest age estimate for the Sterkfontein deposits is 3.3 million years. So, after Ron Clarke gave his presentation, I was in the audience, and I posed a question to him. And my question was this: "Why is it that the Sterkfontein foot doesn't appear to match the fully human footprints that were discovered by Mary Leakey, in deposits at Laetoli that were not only the same age, but perhaps even a little bit older than the Sterkfontein deposits?" You see what the problem is. He is claiming to have the oldest human ancestor, but you have evidence from another place in Africa that humans like us were walking around at the same time, or even earlier. So how did he answer my question? Basically, he repeated what he said in his talk, which was this: It was my Sterkfontein *Austrolopithecus* that made those prints at Laetoli, but he was walking with his big toe, which normally extended out to the side, pressed up close to the other ones, and with his other long toes curled under, making them appear shorter, like human toes. And that was his explanation. Now, some of you are smiling a little bit. I was also smiling a little bit, because the one thousand archeologists that were sitting listening to this weren't smiling, they were simply nodding their heads saying: sounds perfectly reasonable to me. [laughter]

Here is a photograph of an anatomically modern human skullcap, part of a whole series of discoveries, comprising skeletal remains of four individuals, found by the Italian geologist Giuseppe Ragazzoni at a place called Castenedolo in northern Italy in the latter part of the nineteenth century. They were found in deposits that are assigned to the Pliocene period, which means they'd be in excess of two million years old. They are generally given an age of three or four million years, belonging to the middle part of the Pliocene period. Skeptical archeologists will say in a case like this: It's perfectly obvious what happened. Only a few thousand years ago, someone died at this level here. His friends dug a grave and placed his skeleton down here. And that's why you think you have found an anatomically modern human skeleton in some very ancient layers of rock. Now that is certainly possible—it does happen. Technically it is called intrusive burial. But in this particular case the discoverer was himself a professional geologist, and he was very much aware of this possibility.

If you study Ragazzoni's reports in the original Italian, you'll see that he said: If it was an intrusive burial, the overlying layers would have been disturbed. He said he looked very carefully, as one of the skeletons was being taken out, and all the overlying layers were undisturbed. They were intact and undisturbed, indicating that the skeletal remains really were as old as the layers in which they were found, in this case, about three or four million years.

One case that's always really fascinated me is the California gold mine discoveries [see **Plates XII-XV**]. During the Gold Rush there in the nineteenth century, miners were digging for the gold at places like Table Mountain [see **Plate XII**] in the Sierra Nevada Mountains, in the gold mining region. And to get the gold they were digging tunnels through solid rock. And sometimes inside these tunnels—up to a thousand or more feet inside them—the miners were encountering human skeletal remains. They were also encountering stone tools and weapons—hundreds of them at many different locations in the gold mining region. This is a photograph of a stone mortar and pestle— one of many dozens of such objects recovered from the Table Mountain gold mines.

What is noteworthy about these discoveries is that the oldest ones occur in layers of rock that date back to the early part of the geological period called the Eocene, which means they would be roughly fifty million years old. Now, going back to something that I was talking about in the beginning, a Vedic archeologist—if we could imagine such a thing—wouldn't be surprised to find evidence for a human presence on this planet going back fifty million years. But according to our current way of looking at things, it's really quite extraordinary, practically impossible to imagine such a thing.

This evidence was reported to the scientific world by Dr. J. D. Whitney, who was the State Geologist of California at the time. His monograph, *The Auriferous Gravels of the Sierra Nevada of California*, was published by Harvard University in 1880. But we don't hear too much about these California gold mine discoveries today. You won't find them mentioned in the current textbooks, at least. And that's because of this process of knowledge filtration that I was mentioning earlier in the talk. And the scientist most reponsible for the filtering in this particular case was Dr. William B. Holmes. He was a physical anthropologist working at the Smithsonian Institution in Washington, D. C. And what he said was this: If Professor Whitney had understood the theory of human evolution as we understand it today, he would have hesitated to announce his discoveries, despite the imposing array of testimony with which he was confronted. Translation: if the facts don't fit the theory, the facts have to be set aside. And that's pretty much what happened in this particular case.

I had my own personal experience of this knowledge filtering process in connection with these California gold mine discoveries a few years ago, when I was a consultant for a television program called the *The Mysterious Origins of Man*, which was hosted by Charlton Heston, and which appeared on NBC, the largest American television network. Of course, the American people, they regard Charlton Heston's word to be as good as the word of God. [laughter] They remember his famous role in the movie *The Ten Commandments*.

But in any case, when this television program was being filmed, I told the producers they should go to the Phoebe Hearst Museum of Anthropology at the University of California in Berkeley because that's where the artifacts from the California gold mines are currently being kept. Of course when they went there, the museum officials denied them permission to film the artifacts. Even though we weren't able to get the new video footage that we desired, we were able to use the photographs that were taken in the nineteenth century and which were included in Professor Whitney's admirable book.

There was really quite a stunning reaction when this program aired on NBC in February of 1996 in the United States. There was quite an outcry from a certain segment within the scientific community there, which I sometimes call the fundamentalist Darwinists. They became even more upset when they learned that NBC was going to broadcast this program a second time, so they began a letter writing campaign to the president of the General Electric Company, which owns the NBC television network, asking the president of General Electric to instruct NBC not to show this program, especially at the time it was being shown, 8:00 pm on Sunday evening, when many innocent children would still be up with their parents watching it. [laughter]

Now I am happy to say NBC didn't bow to that pressure. They did broadcast this program a second time, which inspired another reaction. A group of scientists attempted to get the United States government to punish NBC for having shown the program. This is a letter from Dr. Allison R. Palmer, president of the Institute for Cambrian

Studies, to the Federal Communications Commission, which is the United States government agency that licenses television broadcasting companies in the United States, asking that NBC be censured and punished. He said, "At the very least, NBC should be required to make substantial prime time apologies to their viewing audience. And they should perhaps be fined sufficiently."

So, I think it's interesting that this particular type of reaction—to the public presentation of the kind of evidence I have discussed here tonight—took place. It's not the normal way that I think things should go on, but there it is.

This is the Belgian geologist, Dr. A. Rutot. And in the early part of the twentieth century he made some interesting discoveries in his country. He discovered hundreds of stone tools and weapons in deposits dating back to the geological period called the Oligocene [see Plates VIII-XI]. These would be about thirty million years old. A couple of years ago, I was lecturing at archeology departments at some of the universities in Holland and Belgium. One day I happened to be in Brussels, and I thought I would drop by the Royal Museum of Natural Sciences, where I suspected that Rutot's collection was being kept. The first museum officials that I approached denied any knowledge of the collection. They said they didn't have it. But I finally did find one archeologist who said, well yes, we do have them, and he was kind enough to take me to into the storerooms. These objects, of course, aren't displayed to the public, but they are being kept in the museum there.

Actually, throughout the latter part of the nineteenth century and the early part of the twentieth century, scientists all over Europe were reporting discoveries of roughly the same age. For example, Carlos Ribeiro, head of the Geological Survey of Portugal, reported discovering similar artifacts in Miocene formations near Lisbon—they'd be roughly twenty million years old [see Plates I-VII]. Actually, in July I'm going to Lisbon, and I've been given access to Ribeiro's collections and documents in various geological museums in Lisbon. I intend to look at those and revisit some of the sites where Ribeiro discovered them.

Now, we're getting near the end of our little review here. And up to this point all of the cases that I have brought to your attention were either made by professional scientists or were reported in the professional scientific literature. But I want to suggest something. If this evidence for extreme human antiquity really is there in the layers of the earth, then I think we might expect that people other than professional scientists might be encountering it, and their reports, although they might not be making their way into the pages of the scientific literature, they might be making their way into the pages of other kinds of publications, such as ordinary newspapers. I think that is something we could predict. Obviously, reports like this are of a different category than the reporting that we would find in a scientific publication, but nevertheless, I think we should be aware that such reporting is there. I will just give a couple of examples.

This is a newspaper report from the United States, from the nineteenth century, from Iowa. It tells of some miners who found 130 feet deep in a coal mine in which they were working an unusual slab of stone. According to the report, it was about two feet wide, about one foot high. The surface of it was divided into diamond-like shapes, and inside each diamond-like shape was a carved form of a human head, according to the report. If the object really did belong to the layer in which it was found, it would be roughly three hundred million years old. A Vedic archeologist wouldn't be surprised by that, but I think most everyone else would be quite surprised to find something like that.

Here is another report of that type, from the *Morrisonville Times*, published in 1892 in the town of Morrisonville, Illinois, in the United States. It tells of a woman who was putting a piece of coal into a coal-burning stove. The piece of the coal broke in half, and inside she found a gold chain ten inches long. If this object really belonged to the Carboniferous period, the coal-forming age, it would again be roughly three hundred million years old.

Going back to the scientific literature, in the year 1862, a scientific journal called *The Geologist* published a report of an anatomically modern human skeleton being found ninety feet below the surface of the ground in Macoupin County, Illinois. According to the report, directly above the skeleton was a thick layer of slate rock that extended for dozens of yards in all directions, more or less ruling out the intrusive burial hypothesis. And, according to the modern geological reporting, the layers at this level here, at that particular place, are again about three hundred million years old, the same age as the gold chain found in the same state.

An interesting little report from *Scientific American* (1852) tells of a beautiful metallic vase that came from fifteen feet deep in solid rock, belonging to the Cambrian period, near Boston, Massachusetts. An object belonging in rock of that age would be over five hundred million years old.

And that brings us to the end of our little review. Actually, I could go on for quite a long time. I could keep you here from now until Christmas, going through one case after another from the scientific literature, because there really are hundreds of them, which I have documented in my book, *Forbidden Archeology*. Now, I'd just like to go back to what I said in the beginning, namely, that we're generally told that all the physical evidence ever discovered by science supports the standard evolutionary picture of human origins. I think that's a bit of an overstatement. It's not quite true that all of the physical evidence ever discovered supports this particular view. What I suggested at the World Archaeological Congress is that sometimes it may be valuable to look at the archeological time record through a different lens, because it may give us some different ideas about what's possible in our attempts to explain human origins. So thank you—thank you very much. [applause]

Professor Catlow: Thank you very much for a very stimulating lecture. I'm sure we'll have plenty of questions. Who would like to start?

Question and Answer session

[Question from the audience inaudible]

Michael Cremo: The question was, what was the reaction at the World Archaeological Congress in Cape Town to the presentation I gave there? I gave my presentation in the section on the origin of anatomically modern humans, which was a very well attended section. Now, I hope you'll excuse me for not mentioning names. Before I gave my lecture, a prominent American archeologist working in Africa recognized me and said: "So, you're speaking here?" I said yes I am, and I told him the section and time, and he showed up. But after the lecture, during the question session, he didn't ask any questions. And after that he immediately left. So I emailed him a little later, and I said, "You seem to have been interested in what I was going to say. You came, but you didn't say anything. You left rather quickly afterwards. Therefore, I didn't have a chance to ask you what you thought of the presentation, so I'd like to take the opportunity now to ask you." And he replied by email, "I didn't say anything at the time, because I didn't want to publicly embarrass you. And I'm sure everyone in the room felt exactly the same." So I replied: "I appreciate your chivalrous gesture, but I'm afraid we'll never know who would have been publicly embarrassed." [laughter] And it wasn't true that every person in the room felt exactly as he did, because the day after, I was approached by one of the younger archeologists working at one of the sites in South Africa. And she expressed quite a bit of interest in what I had said, and obtained a copy of my book, *Forbidden Archeology*, and since then we've been corresponding about that.

Now, some time later, I was in Johannesburg, and I was speaking there. And another one of the archeologists who had spoken in the same section with me at Cape Town came to my talk. And he put some questions to me. He said to me: "Why don't you put your money where your mouth is, and come to the University of the Witwatersrand and have a little chat with us there?" And I said, "As soon as I receive a definite invitation I will be happy to do that. I will spend as many days as you wish." He never responded with the invitation that he publicly offered. So there were a variety of responses, as you might well imagine, to the controversial ideas I presented.

Question: No terrific fans?

Michael Cremo: Well, it's interesting. I have received a lot of private correspondence from graduate students of archeology who are often quite amazed that there is such a huge body of evidence that they've never heard about, even to be spoken of negatively. I was in Warsaw last spring. My book has been translated into Polish. I was speaking at a university there. And a Polish archeologist came up to me after the lecture and said: "I don't know a single graduate student of archeology in Warsaw who hasn't read your book, and some say they've been getting into fights with their professors about it." [laughter] So, I don't really know who is my fan or who isn't my fan. I can also recall speaking at the Russian Academy of Sciences in Moscow, at the Institute for the Study of Theoretical Questions. And they were quite interested in what I had to say. What I found really surprising in Russia was that the physicists found out I was there, and they sent a car for me. And they drove me out to Dubno, which was their formerly secret atomic weapons research facility. And about two hundred of the leading physicists attended a two-hour lecture on *Forbidden Archeology* in the lecture hall there and kept me for two hours afterwards for questions. Maybe they absolutely hated everything I had to say. It did not seem so. But I think at this present stage that I'm quite grateful that anyone will even listen, so I thank all of you at least for listening this evening.

Question: If the controversial theory of cataclysmic geology should prove to be correct, what impact would that have on the work that you've detailed in your book? I believe that you are aware of the theory, because it is mentioned in the NBC program, as it was shown in this country.

Michael Cremo: Well, if you're asking me what I believe—do I believe there have been catastrophic episodes in the geological history of this earth?

Question: Which might be called the radical altering of the timeline. It might be that things that are believed to be actually old are in fact half that old or whatever.

Michael Cremo: Well, my working method has been to take the standard geological consensus about the age of various strata. Now those may prove in the future to be wrong, they may be changed. But you have to have some kind of framework for discussion. So my working method is to accept the present general consensus among geologists and earth scientists about the geological history of the earth, the age of the earth's strata, and then simply raise the question, well, how do you explain the presence in these strata of these human skeletal remains or these human artifacts, which are normally attributed to anatomically modern humans? Perhaps in the future all these things may change, but that's been my working method.

Question: In terms of the historical collections of the artifacts, you indicated in Brussels they were stored in some back room. And someone like you got word they were there, and they were found. Are there more instances of that? At the time they were found, were most of these collections of artifacts going into historical museums? And are they just stored there, and people have not reevaluated them because the historiography has gone in some other way? Are they there to be reevaluated physically?

Michael Cremo: So the question is, have collections of artifacts been simply lost, or are they stored away in museums, where they are not now being properly cataloged or reevaluated? The latter appears to be the case. Now there is a movement among the European Association of Archaeologists to go through everything that is now in the collections of the various museums throughout Europe and make comprehensive catalogs, which is an effort I highly applaud. Because otherwise what happens is that if there are categories of evidence that really don't fit at a particular point in time, they tend to be, well, put aside, to such an extent that the next generation of researchers is unaware that this evidence even existed.

Question: You don't have a certain curatorial continuity of people staying there fifty or sixty years—there's so much change.

Michael Cremo: Yes. So, some historians of archeology have congratulated me on what I've done. In other words, what I've done is bring the old archive back into view. And I tell graduate students of archeology: I don't mind what you think of all this, just as long as you're aware of the entire data set that's relevant to your field of study. And you can divide it up however you like—you can say: this is useless, this is useful. But at least be aware of it, and there are some historians of archeology who agree with me on that.

Question: Is it a pretty difficult procedure to date these artifacts directly?

Michael Cremo: Well, there are some methods. Of course, it depends upon what age frame you're talking about. There are thermoluminescence methods that can be used to date physical objects that have been subjected to firing, heat, things like that, going back to the hundreds of thousands of years. There are methods which can be used to date human skeletal remains directly. There are varieties of methods, but the problem is this: If we're going to employ these dating methods, we should know they're all imperfect. If you attend any seminars on dating methods at a conference on archeology, you will find that the scientists (the chemists and the physicists) who explain the dating methods to the archeologists will tell them: These are not perfect methods. You're not going to get perfection out of them. They all have their flaws and shortcomings. And if the evidence is quite anomalous, then the shortcomings of these methods might be ignored. And if the dates are uncritically accepted this may lead in some cases to the attachment of artificially young dates to some of the bones or artifacts.

Professor Catlow: But the geological dating methods—they are potentially reliable methods?

Michael Cremo: Yes, I think so. Now a young earth Christian creationist might have a different opinion.

Question: When you mentioned that humans like ourselves might have existed for two or three or even four million years, surely that's not so difficult to fit into the accepted scheme. When you talk about a hundred million or two or three hundred million, surely that's something quite different.

Michael Cremo: Yes, some of the evidence that I documented in my book, *Forbidden Archeology,* is relatively close to what's now accepted, and then we move on from there. What I find significant is that you've got a fairly continuous chain of discoveries going from a hundred thousand years back to these very, very distant points of time. That's what I find is very interesting. Of course, some of the evidence is going to be closer to what's now acceptable, some more distant. Looking at things from the perspective of this Vedic time lens that I was talking about—the premise is that we have a continuous human presence on this planet going back to these very distant times—then that's what you should expect to see: a range of evidence, some close to what is now expected, some further, some quite distant.

Question: I arrived a little late—I didn't hear you talk about the Vedic time scale, Vedic archeology. I was wondering if you could put that in a nutshell. I also wondered if you think that these discoveries of human existence that we find have been there actually enable us to see how the human species thinks or fails to think. Is it actually shedding light on the process of our understanding of those discoveries and our appreciation of them?

Michael Cremo: Okay, the first question. One would predict from these ancient Sanskrit writings that you should find a human presence going back hundreds of millions of years. So that's the premise that I started out with—just briefly. Now, the second point, which I think is a very important point. Yes, I think the work that I've done, and the reactions to it, do reveal something of how science works. And for that reason, the book *Forbidden Archeology* attracted many reviews in the professional literature of history of science, philosophy of science, and sociology of science. As a matter of fact, there's a twenty-page review article on *Forbidden Archeology* by the noted historian of science David Oldroyd and one of his graduate students in Australia just about that very question. Jo Wodak and David Oldroyd asked: Does this work make any contribution at all to the literature on paleoanthropology? And they said yes, for two reasons. First, no one has really gone into this subject in such depth before. They looked at all the current work in the history of archeology, and they could see that the type of evidence that I'm talking about was completely missing from those discussions. Second, they said the book raises important questions about the nature of scientific truth claims, which is a topic that is of very much interest to the historians, philosophers, and sociologists of scientific knowledge. So they do appreciate the work for the reasons that you were speaking about. This work illuminates how in the scientific community claims like this are accepted or rejected, what influence they have. There are jargon terms like "boundary work in science" that would apply to what you were saying.

Question: At the same time as science meets what appears to be modern-like human man in ancient strata, are there remains of other creatures generally considered to be more recently emerged?

Michael Cremo: My preliminary research says yes, but it took me eight years to go through the entire literature of the past one hundred fifty years on the origin of the human species. And when I began that research I wouldn't have suspected that there was as much evidence as I turned up. I thought I would do eight weeks of research and write a little tract, and that would be it. But the eight weeks turned into eight months, and the eight months turned into eight years, [laughter] because one thing just led into another. So I can't predict in advance what I would find, say, if I looked into—well, the complete literature on elephants, for example. Fossil elephant teeth are found. They fossilize quite easily. They preserve quite well in the geological record. How far does that species really go back in time? I know what the current textbooks say, but I can't predict what would happen if I made a similar effort to the one that I made in *Forbidden Archeology,* looking at the record for a human presence. But I'm only one person, I'm 53 years old, and there are millions of species, so . . . [laughter] . . . maybe that will give me a task for my future lives. [more laughter]

Question: Your theory is that we are not descended from great ape ancestors. If that is the case, then why should our human genome so closely resemble the great ape genomes? It would seem that if we expect humans to go back hundreds of millions of years, then we shouldn't expect any similarity at all.

Michael Cremo: Well, I don't know about that. Most of the human genome is what's called, very affectionately, junk genes. Actually, ninety-seven percent of it. And, even if you consider the supposedly small percentage of difference between the human genome and the chimpanzee genome, for example, it would amount to hundreds of thousands of point mutations, so I don't even know—what's two percent of four billion dollars? [note: I mentioned this because there are 4 billion base pairs in the human genome. Two percent of 4 billion is 80 million base pairs difference] I mean, it's a lot of money. So two percent of such a large number of base pairs resulting in a large number of point mutations is still quite significant. I would also say that the human genome has only just recently been sequenced, and only a tiny percentage of the genes have been read from the sequence. Nor has the chimpanzee genome been completely sequenced, and it is not likely to be sequenced in the near future, because there's not very much to be gained financially from it, it would appear. So these studies that you're referring to—they're the result of some very crude analysis using very crude hybridization techniques. I think we don't know what the exact differences between the human genome and the chimpanzee genome really are at this point of time.

Professor Catlow: Well, I'm sure that there would be many more questions if we had time, but I think we're called to draw things to a conclusion ... [announcements] ... but I'd like to conclude by thanking our lecturer this evening for a very stimulating talk. [applause and standing ovations]

11

Forbidden Archeology:
A Three-Body Interaction Among Science,
Hinduism, and Christianity

I presented this paper at The Sanskrit Tradition in the Modern World conference at the University of Newcastle, England, on May 19, 2000.

The interactions among science, Hinduism, and Christianity are as complex as those in the three-body problem of astrophysics. In practice, astrophysicists select a central body, say the Earth, with a second body, the Moon orbiting it, and then try to determine the perturbations induced in the motion of the Moon by the attraction of the third body, the Sun. There is no general solution for this problem. This means that independent of observations one cannot calculate very far in advance (or very far into the past) the exact position of the Moon relative to the other two bodies. The perturbations of the Moon's orbit, induced by the attractions of the Earth and Sun, are incalculably complex, as are the movements of Hinduism in relation to the twin influences of science and Christianity. The reactions provoked by my book *Forbidden Archeology*,[1] from scientists, scholars, and religionists,[2] provide useful data for examination of a three-body problem in the study of Hinduism, Christianity, and science.

I introduce myself as an American citizen, of Italian Catholic heritage and educated in secular schools, who converted to Gaudiya Vaishnavism in 1973, at age twenty-five. In 1976, His Divine Grace A. C. Bhaktivedanta Swami Prabhupada, founder-*acharya* of the International Society for Krishna Consciousness (ISKCON), accepted me as his disciple. Bhaktivedanta Swami Prabhupada traced his lineage through nine generations of Gaudiya Vaishnava *gurus* to Chaitanya Mahaprabhu, who appeared in the latter part of the fifteenth century. Since 1973, I have strictly followed the ISKCON *bhakti* regimen, including rising before dawn, attending temple worship, hearing readings from *Bhagavata Purana,* practicing *japa* meditation for about two hours a day, and making occasional pilgrimages to sites sacred to Gaudiya Vaishnavas, such as Mayapur, West Bengal—the appearance place of Chaitanya Mahaprabhu—and Vrindavan, Uttar Pradesh—the appearance place of Krishna.

In 1984, I began working with the Bhaktivedanta Institute, the science studies branch of ISKCON. The Institute was founded in 1974 for the purpose of examining (and challenging) materialistic scientific ideas about the origin of life and the universe from the standpoint of Vedic knowledge. I use the term Vedic in its broad Vaishnava sense to include the *Vedas, Puranas,* and *Itihasas.* The Bhaktivedanta Institute, following the teachings of Bhaktivedanta Swami Prabhupada, generally favors a literal reading of the Vedic texts. In the realm of scientific discourse, this means using Vedic texts as sources of hypotheses, which can then be employed to explain evidence. My book *Forbidden Archeology*, which presents abundant scientifically reported evidence consistent with Puranic accounts of extreme human antiquity and documents social factors underlying the exclusion of this evidence from contemporary scientific discourse, was published by the Bhaktivedanta Institute in 1993.

As can be seen from this brief autobiographical sketch, I was pulled from the orbit of modern liberal Christianity and secular science into the orbit of traditional Hinduism. I thus have considerable empathy for the Indian intellectuals of the nineteenth century, the *bhadralok* who were pulled from the orbit of traditional Hinduism into the orbits of modern liberal Christianity and secular science.

As we explore the history of that time, we encounter (along with the Christian missionaries, the British Orientalists, the members of the Brahmo Samaj and the Arya Samaj, and the Theosophists) such personalities as Krishna Mohan Banerjea (1813–1885), the Bengali convert and disciple of Scottish missionary Alexander Duff. Born a *brahmana*, Banerjea became a Christian and underwent a liberal education at Calcutta's Hindu College. Afterwards he flouted the rules of his caste, going so far as to get drunk with some friends and throw pieces of raw beef into the courtyard of a *brahmana's* house, causing considerable uproar in the neighborhood.[3] In writing *Forbidden Archeology* and directing to it the attention of evolutionary scientists, I have performed an act roughly equivalent to throwing beef into a *brahmana's* courtyard. The book, anti-Darwinian as well as religiously inspired, has provoked considerable reaction in orthodox scientific circles.

Among the more emotional respondents to *Forbidden Archeology* was Jonathan Marks, who in his review, published in *American Journal of Physical Anthropology*, called it "Hindu-oid creationist drivel" and "a veritable cornucopia of dreck."[4] Here we find a tonal echo of some of the reactions of early European scholars and missionaries to Hinduism. We may recall, for example, the words of William Hastie, leader of a Scottish missionary organization in Calcutta, who as late as 1882 denigrated India as "the most stupendous fortress and citadel of ancient error and idolatry" and condemned Hinduism as "senseless mummeries, licentiousness, falsehood, injustice, cruelty, robbery, [*and*] murder."[5]

Not all reviewers were so dismissive of *Forbidden Archeology's* scholarly worth. In a lengthy review article in *Social Studies of Science* (provocatively titled "Vedic Creationism: A Further Twist to the Evolution Debate"), Jo Wodak and David Oldroyd asked, "So has *Forbidden Archeology* made any contribution at all to the literature on palaeoanthropology?" They concluded, "Our answer is a guarded 'yes', for two reasons." First, "the historical material . . . has not been scrutinized in such detail before," and, second, the book does "raise a central problematic regarding the lack of certainty in scientific 'truth' claims."[6]

In *L'Anthropologie*, Marylène Pathou-Mathis wrote: "M. Cremo and R. Thompson have willfully written a provocative work that raises the problem of the influence of the dominant ideas of a time period on scientific research. These ideas can compel the researchers to orient their analyses according to the conceptions that are permitted by the scientific community." She concluded, "The documentary richness of this work, more historical and sociological than scientific, is not to be ignored."[7]

And in *British Journal for the History of Science*, Tim Murray noted in his review of *Forbidden Archeology*: "I have no doubt that there will be some who will read this book and profit from it. Certainly it provides the historian of archaeology with a useful compendium of case studies in the history and sociology of scientific knowledge, which can be used to foster debate within archaeology about how to describe the epistemology of one's discipline."[8]

I will not dwell much further upon the academic integrity and utility of the archeological evidence presented in *Forbidden Archeology*. I want to focus instead on how the book fits into the larger history of interactions among science, Hinduism, and Christianity. Although these interactions defy simplistic explanation, it is possible to trace a broad pattern of development.

In the late eighteenth century and early nineteenth century, some European scholars, such as John Playfair, were intrigued by the vast time scales of Vedic histories and attributed considerable antiquity to Hindu astronomical texts. Playfair, for example, put the composition of the *Surya-siddhanta* before the beginning of the *Kali-yuga*, or over 5,000 years ago.[9] And that implied an even longer history of refined astronomical observation. But other European scholars, deeply influenced by Christian chronology, were unhappy with such assertions. John Bentley, for example, put his knowledge of astronomical science to work in discrediting the proposals of Playfair and others.

About one of his opponents, Bentley wrote:

> By his attempt to uphold the antiquity of Hindu books against absolute facts [*Bentley's*], he thereby supports all those horrid abuses and impositions found in them, under the pretended sanction of antiquity, *viz.* the burning of widows, the destroying of infants, and even the immolation of men. Nay, his aim goes still deeper; for by the same means he endeavours to overturn the Mosaic account, and sap the very foundations of our religion: for if we are to believe in the antiquity of Hindu books, as he would wish us, then the Mosaic account is all a fable, or a fiction.[10]

Bentley regarded the vast time periods of Hindu cosmology as a recent imposition by the *brahmanas*, who desired "to arrogate to themselves that they were the most ancient people on the face of the earth."[11] Unable to tolerate a chronology that "threw back the creation [*in the current* kalpa] to the immense distance of 1,972,947,101 years before the Christian era,"[12] Bentley held that the Puranic histories should be compressed to fit within the few thousand years of the Mosaic account.[13] Sir William Jones also brought the expansive Hindu chronology into line with the Biblical time scale.[14]

At the same time Bentley and Jones were using science and textual criticism to dismantle the Hindu chronology, their contemporaries in Europe were using the same methods to dismantle the Biblical chronology. The process accelerated with the advent of Darwinism, leaving only a minority of Christian intellectuals committed to a divine creation of Adam and Eve about six thousand years ago. In India, many Hindu intellectuals, influenced by science and liberal Christianity, similarly gave up the historical accounts of the *Puranas*, which place humans on earth millions of years ago. Today, the Darwinian evolutionary account of human origins remains dominant among intellectuals in India and throughout the world, although the postmodern tendency toward relativism has somewhat weakened its hold.

This is the background against which *Forbidden Archeology* appeared. It has been quite interesting for me to monitor academic reactions to the book, especially the attempts of reviewers to grapple with its Hindu inspiration and relationship with Christian and Darwinian accounts of human origins and antiquity.

In his review of *Forbidden Archeology* for *Geoarchaeology*, Kenneth L. Feder wrote: "The book itself represents something perhaps not seen before; we can fairly call it 'Krishna creationism' with no disrespect intended."[15] After describing the contents of the book, Feder added, "While decidedly antievolutionary in perspective, this work is not the ordinary variety of antievolutionism in form, content, or style. In distinction to the usual brand of such writing, the authors use original sources and the book is well written. Further, the overall tone of the work is superior to that exhibited in ordinary [*i.e., Christian*] creationist literature."[16]

Comparisons between *Forbidden Archeology* and Christian creationist literature are common in the academic reviews of the book. Murray wrote in *British Journal for the History of Science*, "This is a piece of 'Creation Science' which, while not based on the need to promote a Christian alternative, manifests many of the same types of argument."[17] He further characterized *Forbidden Archeology* as a book that "joins others from creation science and New Age philosophy as a body of works which seek to address members of a public alienated from science, either because it has become so arcane or because it has ceased to suit some in search of meaning for their lives."[18]

Some of the comparisons are less polite. Marks acrimoniously wrote in *American Journal of Physical Anthropology*, "The best that can be said is that more reading [*of the scientific literature*] went into this Hindu-oid creationist drivel than seems to go into the Christian-oid creationist drivel."[19] Paleoanthropologist Colin Groves wrote:

> A book like this, simply because it is superficially scholarly and not outright trash like all the Christian creationist works I have read, might indeed make a useful deconstructionist exercise for an archaeology or palaeoanthropology class. So it's not without value. You could do worse, too, than place it in front of a Gishite with the admonition "Look here: these guys show that human physical and cultural evolution doesn't work. Therefore it follows that the Hindu scriptures are true, doesn't it?"[20]

Stripping away the armor of defensive ridicule in such statements, we find a materialistic science not yet totally secure in its ongoing global three-body interaction with unreconstructed Christianity and traditional Hinduism.

Wiktor Stoczkowski, reviewing *Forbidden Archeology* in *L'Homme*, accurately noted, "Historians of science repeat tirelessly that the Biblical version of origins was replaced in the nineteenth century by the evolution theory. In our imaginations, we substitute this simple story for the more complex reality that we are today confronted with a remarkable variety of origins accounts."[21] Among those accounts Stoczkowski included that of the Biblical creationists. "*Forbidden Archeology*," he added, "gives us one more, dedicated to 'His Divine Grace A. C. Bhaktivedanta Swami Prabhupada' and inspired by the Vedic philosophy that disciples study in the United States at the Bhaktivedanta Institute, a branch of the International Society for Krishna Consciousness."[22]

The main text of *Forbidden Archeology* is solely dedicated to documentation and analysis of evidence consistent with Vedic accounts of extreme human antiquity. The religious affiliation of my coauthor and I, and our commitment to Vedic historical accounts, are briefly mentioned in the introduction. Reviewers have therefore taken upon themselves to expand upon these topics for the benefit of their readers. It is somewhat novel to find substantive discourse on *yugas* and *manvantaras*, the Bhaktivedanta Institute and ISKCON, in the pages of mainstream journals of archeology, anthropology, and science studies. Up to this time, such references have largely been confined to the pages of religious studies journals.

In the first few pages of their *Social Studies of Science* review article, Wodak and Oldroyd gave extensive background information on: ISKCON ("a modern variant of the Bhakti sects that have dominated Hindu religious life over the last one and a half millennia"); the teachings of the movement's founder ("for Prabhupada, science gives no adequate account of the origin of the universe or of life"); the Bhaktivedanta Institute (they comment on "the boldness of its intellectual programme"); and Vedic chronology ("partial dissolutions, called *pralaya*, supposedly take place every 4.32 billion years, bringing catastrophes in which whole groups of living forms can disappear"). One also encounters many references to the *Rg Veda*, *Vedanta*, the *Puranas*, the *atma*, *yoga*, and *karma*.[23]

In common with other reviewers, Wodak and Oldroyd draw a connection between *Forbidden Archeology* and the work of Christian creationists. "As is well known," they note, "Creationists try to show that humans are of recent origin, and that empirical investigations accord with human history as recorded in the Old Testament. *Forbidden Archeology* (FA) offers a brand of Creationism based on something quite different, namely ancient Vedic beliefs. From this starting point, instead of claiming a human history of mere millennia, FA argues for the existence of *Homo sapiens* way back into the Tertiary, perhaps even earlier."[24]

Despite the considerable attention Wodak and Oldroyd devoted to *Forbidden Archeology*'s Vedic inspiration, the greater part of their review article focused on the book's substance, about which they commented:

> It must be acknowledged that *Forbidden Archeology* brings to attention many interesting issues that have not received much consider-

ation from historians; and the authors' detailed examination of the early literature is certainly stimulating and raises questions of considerable interest, both historically and from the perspective of practitioners of SSK [sociology of scientific knowledge]. Indeed, they appear to have gone into some historical matters more deeply than any other writers of whom we have knowledge.[25]

Another example of extensive references to ISKCON and Vedic concepts can be found in Feder's *Geoarchaeology* review of *Forbidden Archeology*:

> The authors are open about their membership in the Bhaktivedanta Institute, which is a branch of the International Society for Krishna Consciousness, and the book is dedicated to their "spiritual master," the group's founder. They make a reasonable request regarding their affiliation with this organization: "That our theoretical outlook is derived from the Vedic literature should not disqualify it." (p. xxxvi). Fair enough, but what is their "theoretical outlook?"[26]

Feder, citing Basham's *The Wonder That Was India*, goes on to give a succinct account of Hindu cosmology's *kalpas*, each of which lasts 4.32 billion years and "is divided into 14 *manvantaras*, each lasting 300,000,000 years." Feder then explains how "within each *manvantara* the world is created with human beings more or less fully formed, and then destroyed, only to be created once again in the next *manvantara*."[27]

In the concluding paragraph of his review, Feder gives his own comments on our three-body problem:

> We all know what happens when we mix a literal interpretation of the Judeo-Christian creation myth with human paleontology; we get scientific creationism. It seems we now know what happens when we mix a literal interpretation of the Hindu myth of creation with human paleontology; we get the antievolutionary Krishna creationism of *Forbidden Archeology*, where human beings do not evolve and where the fossil evidence for anatomically modern humans dates as far back as the beginning of the current *manvantara*.[28]

A more favorable estimation of *Forbidden Archeology*'s Vedic roots was offered by Hillel Schwarz in *Journal of Unconventional History*, which, as the title suggests, is situated on the outer edges of respectable scholarship's domain. But it is at such edges that advances in understanding often occur. Schwarz observed: "*Forbidden Archeology* takes the current conventions of decoding to their extreme. The authors find modern *Homo sapiens* to be continuous contemporaries of the apelike creatures from whom evolutionary biologists usually trace human descent or bifurcation, thus confirming those Vedic sources that presume the nearly illimitable antiquity of the human race."[29]

Schwarz was not put off by the authors' underlying motives for writing *Forbid-*

den Archeology. "Despite its unhidden religious partisanship," said Schwarz, "the book deserves a reckoning in this review for its embrace of a global humanity permanently distinct from other primates." He accurately detected the book's implicit thesis, namely, that "humanity is no mere biochemical exfoliation but a work of the spirit, in touch with (and devoted to) the ancient, perfect, perfectly sufficient, unchanging wisdom of the Vedic masters."[30]

One might wonder what the Christian creationists think of Hindu-inspired *Forbidden Archeology.* Perhaps sensing an ally in their battle against Darwinism, they have reacted somewhat favorably. A reviewer of the abridged version of *Forbidden Archeology* stated in *Creation Research Society Quarterly*: "This book is a must reading for anyone interested in human origins." After expressing his surprise over finding the book in a major U. S. chain store, the reviewer noted that its "theoretical outlook is derived from the Vedic literature in India, which supports the idea that the human race is of great antiquity." The reviewer made clear that he did not share this view: "As a recent earth creationist, I would not accept the evolutionary time scale that the authors appear to accept. However," he added, "the authors have shown that even if you accept the evolutionary view of a vast age for the earth, the theory of human evolution is not supported."[31]

Up to this point, mainstream religious studies scholars have not, to my knowledge, published any reviews of *Forbidden Archeology* in their professional journals (although many did receive copies for review). But they have not been totally silent. Historian of religion Mikael Rothstein of the University of Copenhagen wrote in a review article published in the science section of *Politiken,* Denmark's largest newspaper, that in the nineteenth century Darwinism challenged the creationist views of Christian religion. Today, he said, the roles have been reversed. Religion, not science, is the primary source of intellectual provocation. And *Forbidden Archeology* is "in principle just as provoking as *The Origin of Species.*" Rothstein informs his readers that the authors of *Forbidden Archeology* belong to the Bhaktivedanta Institute, the "academic center" for ISKCON, which he correctly characterized as "part of the Vaishnava religion from India." Noting that the authors are Hindu "monks" as well as scholars, he stated, "Their otherwise thorough academic argumentation can thus find support in the Vaishnava mythology, which actually describes the history of man and the geological development of the earth in a way that is compatible with their results." According to Rothstein, people who have grown up with the idea of Darwinian evolution can by reading *Forbidden Archeology* "get a glimpse of the feeling the people of the Church experienced when Darwin's theory was presented."[32]

Gene Sager, a professor of religious studies at Palomar College in California, wrote about *Forbidden Archeology*:

> As a scholar in the field of comparative religion, I have sometimes challenged scientists by offering a cyclical or spiral model for studying human history, based on the Vedic concept of the *kalpa.* Few Western scientists are open to the possibility of sorting out the data in terms of such a model. I am not proposing that the Vedic model is true. . . . However, the question remains, does the relatively short, linear model prove to be adequate? I believe *Forbidden Archeology* offers a well researched

challenge. If we are to meet this challenge, we need to practice open-mindedness and proceed in a cross-cultural, interdisciplinary fashion.[33]

I have not yet seen any reviews of *Forbidden Archeology* in academic journals published in India. But I have gotten responses from Indian scholars in other arenas. When I presented a paper based on *Forbidden Archeology* at the World Archaeological Congress 3, held in New Delhi in 1994,[34] a number of Indian scholars approached me privately and expressed their appreciation of my efforts to uphold the Puranic chronology. My World Archaeological Congress paper also drew me an invitation to speak at a conference on Vedic history in the United States, organized by several Hindu organizations.[35] I earlier received an invitation, which I was not able to accept, from Kishor Ruperalia, general secretary for the Vishwa Hindu Parishad in the United Kingdom, to speak at a conference organized by the VHP. Ruperalia wrote about *Forbidden Archeology*, "Inspired by the Vedic writings and encouraged by His Divine Grace A. C. Bhaktivedanta Swami Prabhupada, the scholarly authors have made a tremendous and painstaking effort . . . to make archeological scholars rethink the predominant paradigm on human origins and antiquity."[36]

Where does all this leave us in terms of our three-body question? In astrophysics, there are some special cases of the three-body problem that do allow for reasonably accurate solutions. If one of the bodies (a manmade earth satellite, for example) can be assigned an infinitely small mass, this simplifies the matter somewhat. In terms of the global interactions among science, Christianity, and Hinduism, as related to any substantive discussion of human origins and antiquity, the three-body problem has been solved, in the minds of many modern intellectuals, by assigning traditional Hindu concepts of human origins and antiquity an infinitely small mass. The problem is then reduced to establishing the relative positions of the accounts of human origins and antiquity offered by modern Darwinian evolutionists and their Christian fundamentalist opponents. And the result is a somewhat stable and predictable system. We find a Christian fundamentalist body revolving in a fixed orbit of perpetual subordination to the central body of a Darwinian consensus negotiated between modern science and liberal Christianity (and liberal Hinduism). But the substantial and widespread reactions to *Forbidden Archeology* suggest that traditional Hindu views of human origins and antiquity have again acquired sufficient mass to cause real perturbations in scientific and religious minds, thus introducing new elements of complexity into the relationships among Hinduism, Christianity, and science.

What predictions might be made about future states of the three-body question I have posed?

We seem to be entering an era when the boundaries between religion and science will, as in times past, no longer be so clear cut. This is especially true in the metaphysical areas of science, i.e., those dealing with phenomena beyond the range of normal experimentation and observation, such as Darwinian evolution. Indeed, Karl Popper, the philosopher of science who established falsifiability as a criterion for the validity of a scientific theory, said: "I have concluded that Darwinism is not a testable scientific theory, but a metaphysical research programme—a possible framework for testable scientific theories."[37] And there may be other such frameworks, perhaps even some derived from the Vedic texts.

In July of 1996, I took part in a roundtable discussion, at the Institute for Oriental Studies of the Russian Academy of Sciences in Moscow. After I made a presentation about *Forbidden Archeology* and another work in progress (establishing the antiquity of the *Rg Veda* at five thousand years), Indologist Evgeniya Y. Vanina made these comments:

> I think that the statement you have made, and your paper, are very important because they touch upon the cooperation of science and religion—not just science and religion but how to look at the texts of the classical tradition as sources of information. There is a tendency among scholars to say whatever the *Vedas*—and the *Puranas,* the *Ramayana,* and the *Mahabharata*—are saying, it is all myth and concoction, and there is no positive information in it . . . . I think that such a negativist attitude toward the ancient and early medieval Indian texts as sources of information should definitely be discarded.[38]

Of course, the most likely persons to search for items of positive information in such texts are those who believe in them. For the past century or so, there has not been much room in the academic enterprise for believers, either in religious studies or the sciences. But this may be changing.

G. William Barnard of the religious studies department at Southern Methodist University suggested that "this all too-frequently found notion, that scholars who have no religious inclinations are somehow more objective and therefore are better scholars of religion than those who are pursuing a spiritual life, is fundamentally flawed."[39] Reflecting on the contribution that could be made by genuine spiritual traditions, Barnard advocated "a scholarship that is willing and able to affirm that the metaphysical models and normative visions of these different spiritual traditions are serious contenders for truth, a scholarship that realizes that these religious worlds are not dead corpses that we can dissect and analyze at a safe distance, but rather are living, vital bodies of knowledge and practice that have the potential to change our taken-for-granted notions."[40]

And in a perceptive article in *American Anthropologist,* Katherine P. Ewing observed: "While espousing cultural relativism, the anthropological community has maintained a firm barrier against belief." But this fear against "going native" has a detrimental effect on the search for truth. "To rule out the possibility of belief in another's reality," said Ewing, "is to encapsulate that reality and, thus, to impose implicitly the hegemony of one's own view of the world."[41] Ewing argued that belief may be a valid stance to take in fieldwork in cultural anthropology.

Even Jonathan Marks, one of *Forbidden Archeology's* most strident critics, admitted that (in theory) "the rich and varied origins myths of all cultures are alternatives to contemporary evolution."[42] And Tim Murray wrote in his review that archeology is now in a state of flux, with practitioners debating "issues which go to the conceptual core of the discipline." Murray then proposed, "Whether the *Vedas* have a role to play in this is up to the individual scientists concerned."[43] This amounts to the smallest and most backhanded of concessions that the Vedas may have some utility in the conceptual reconstruction of modern scientific accounts of human origins and antiquity. But at this point in the three-body interaction among science, Hinduism, and Christianity it must nonetheless be regarded as significant.

Some scholars, particularly those who identify themselves as postmodern, have already recognized the utility of the approach taken in *Forbidden Archeology*. Sociologist Pierce J. Flynn found positive value in the authors' status as believers.

> The authors admit to their own sense of place in a knowledge universe with contours derived from personal experience with Vedic philosophy, religious perception, and Indian cosmology. . . . In my view, it is just this openness of subjective positioning that makes *Forbidden Archeology* an original and important contribution to postmodern scholarly studies now being done in sociology, anthropology, archeology, and the history of science and ideas. The authors' unique perspective provides postmodern scholars with an invaluable parallax view of historical scientific praxis, debate, and development.[44]

I first met Pierce when I was living near the ISKCON temple in the Pacific Beach neighborhood of San Diego, California. He would sometimes bring his classes on field trips to the ISKCON temple, which provided an example of an alternative religious community for his sociology of religion students. I had volunteered to be their guide. During a conversation after one of the field trips, I mentioned to Pierce that I was working on a book that examined the question of human origins and antiquity from the viewpoint of the Vedic histories. He immediately grasped its significance and assured me that the book would be of interest to many scholars. When the book was finished, I therefore asked him to contribute a foreword. Pierce Flynn's remarks, written before the publication of *Forbidden Archeology*, and, before the many reviews in academic and scientific journals corroborated his estimation of the book's potential impact, were quite prescient.

And speaking of prescience, I predict we are moving into a period in which the Vedic texts, and scholars openly professing intellectual commitment to the Vedic texts, are going to be playing a larger role in the three-body interaction among science, Hinduism and Christianity. Although we are not going to immediately see a major realignment of the bodies under consideration, careful observers will note some significant perturbations in their orbits, which may eventually propagate into large scale shifts of the kind that have occurred so often in the history of ideas.

Notes:

1. Michael A. Cremo and Richard L. Thompson, *Forbidden Archeology: The Hidden History of the Human Race,* San Diego: Bhaktivedanta Institute, 1993.

2. Scholarly reviews and notices of *Forbidden Archeology*, in addition to the ones cited in this article, appear in *Journal of Field Archeology* 19: 112; *Antiquity* 67: 904; *Ethology, Ecology, and Evolution* 6: 461; *Creation/Evolution* 14(1): 13–25; and *Journal of Geological Education* 43: 193. *Forbidden Archeology*, and its abridged popular edition *The Hidden History of the Human Race*, have also attracted considerable attention in New Age and alternative science circles. Furthermore, I have appeared on about one hundred radio and television programs, including an NBC television special *The Mysterious Origins of Man* (originally broadcast in February 1996). A collection of academic and popular reviews, along with my academic papers and publications related to *Forbidden Archeology*, selected correspondence, and selected transcripts of radio and television interviews, came out in 1998 under the title *Forbidden Archeology's Impact*.

3. Martin Maw, *Visions of India: Fulfillment Theology, the Aryan Race Theory, and the Work of British Protestant Missionaries in Victorian India*, Frankfurt: Peter Lang, 1990, p. 45.

4. Jonathan Marks, *Forbidden Archeology* (book review), *American Journal of Physical Anthropology*, vol. 93(1), 1994, p. 141. Marks's statements were printed along with other favorable and unfavorable review excerpts just inside the cover of the abridged popular edition of *Forbidden Archeology*, helping to draw media attention to the book.

5. William Hastie, *Hindu Idolatry and English Enlightenment*, 1882. Quoted in Martin Maw, *Visions of India*, p. 8.

6. Jo Wodak and David Oldroyd, Vedic creationism: a further twist to the evolution debate, *Social Studies of Science*, vol. 26, 1996, p. 207. I regard this 22-page review article to be the most significant scholarly response to *Forbidden Archeology*.

7. Marylène Pathou-Mathis, *Forbidden Archeology* (book review), *L'Anthropologie*, vol. 99(1), 1995, p. 159. The cited passage is translated from the French original.

8. Tim Murray, *Forbidden Archeology* (book review), *British Journal for the History of Science*, vol. 28, 1995, p. 379.

9. John Playfair, Remarks on the astronomy of the Brahmins, *Transactions of the Royal Society of Edinburgh*, vol. II, pt. 1, 1790, pp. 135–192.

10. John Bentley, *A Historical View of the Hindu Astronomy*, London: Smith, Elder, and Company, 1825, p. xxvii.

11. John Bentley, *A Historical View of the Hindu Astronomy*, p. 84.

12. John Bentley, *A Historical View of the Hindu Astronomy*, p. 84.

13. John Bentley, *A Historical View of the Hindu Astronomy*, p. 84. Bentley preferred a date of 4225 B.C. for the start of the first *manvantara*.

14. Sir William Jones, *The Works of Sir William Jones*, Vol. I, London: Robinson and Evans, 1799, p. 313. In a table, Jones places the beginning of the first *manvantara* at 4006 B.C. and makes the first Manu a contemporary of Adam.

15. Kenneth L. Feder, *Forbidden Archeology* (book review), *Geoarchaeology*, vol. 9(4), 1994, p. 337. Feder's review contains inaccurate statements about the factual material presented in *Forbidden Archeology*. For example, he says (p. 339) that the authors "do not address the issue of use-wear on any of these unexpectedly an-

cient 'tools.'" But *Forbidden Archeology* cites S. Laing's 1894 report on the Thenay, France, implements: "The inference [that an object is cultural] is strengthened . . . if the microscope discloses parallel striae and other signs of use on the chipped edge, such as would be made by scraping bones or skins, while nothing of the sort is seen on the other natural edges" (*F. A.* p. 235). L. Bourgeois, the discoverer of the Thenay implements, reported such signs of use on them (*F. A.* p. 227). Max Verworn also gives quite detailed attention to wear pattern analysis in connection with the Aurillac implements (*F. A.* p. 252). A detailed response to Feder is included in my book, *Forbidden Archeology's* Impact.

16. Kenneth L. Feder, *Forbidden Archeology*, p. 338.
17. Tim Murray, *Forbidden Archeology*, p. 378.
18. Tim Murray, *Forbidden Archeology*, p. 379.
19. Jonathan Marks, *Forbidden Archeology*, p. 141.
20. Colin Groves, Creationism: the Hindu view. A review of *Forbidden Archeology*, *The Skeptic* (Australia), vol. 14(3), pp. 43–45. This review was forwarded to me electronically by a friend who saw it posted on an Internet discussion group. After *Forbidden Archeology* and its authors were featured on the NBC television special *The Mysterious Origins of Man* in February 1996, hundreds of messages about *Forbidden Archeology*, and its "Krishna creationism," were posted, as part of heated discussions, to Usenet groups such as sci.archeology, sci.anthropology, and alt.origins.
21. Wiktor Stoczkowski, *Forbidden Archeology* (book review), *L'Homme*, vol. 35, 1995, p. 173. Quoted passages are translated from the French original.
22. Wiktor Stoczkowski, *Forbidden Archeology* (book review), p. 173.
23. Jo Wodak and David Oldroyd, Vedic creationism, pp. 192–195.
24. Jo Wodak and David Oldroyd, Vedic creationism, p. 192.
25. Jo Wodak and David Oldroyd, Vedic creationism, p. 198.
26. Kenneth L. Feder, *Forbidden Archeology*, pp. 339–340.
27. Kenneth L. Feder, *Forbidden Archeology*, p. 340.
28. Kenneth L. Feder, *Forbidden Archeology*, p. 340. Of course, one might also propose that we know what happens when we mix the Darwinian myth of transforming species with human paleontology. We get the modern account of human evolution, with ancient apes transforming into anatomically modern *Homo sapiens* in the most recent geological times. The real question, in the game of science played fairly, is which "myth," or theory, best fits all of the relevant evidence.
29. Hillel Schwarz, Earth born, sky driven (collective book review), *Journal of Unconventional History*, vol. 6(1), 1994, p. 75.
30. Hillel Schwarz, Earth born, sky driven, p. 76.
31. Peter Line, *The Hidden History of the Human Race* (book review), *Creation Research Society Quarterly*, vol. 32, 1995, p. 46.
32. Mikael Rothstein, Forbudt arkaeologi, *Politiken*, 31 January, 1994, Section 3, p. 1. Quoted passages are translated from the original Danish.
33. The quoted passage is an excerpt from an unpublished review of *Forbidden Archeology* by Dr. Sager. Another passage from the review is printed with other endorsements in the abridged version of *Forbidden Archeology*.

34. Michael A. Cremo, Puranic time and the archeological record, in: *Theme Papers: Concepts of Time.* D. P. Agarwal, M. P. Leone, and T. Murray, (eds.), New Delhi, Academic Committee of the World Archaeological Congress 3, 1994, pp. 23–35. This is a volume of machine-copied original drafts of papers intended for precirculation to conference participants. It is, however, available in some libraries. The official conference proceedings are to be published by Routledge.

35. International Conference on Revisiting Indus-Sarasvati Age and Ancient India, Atlanta, Georgia, U.S.A., October 4–6, 1996.

36. The quoted passage is from a faxed letter to the editors of *Back to Godhead,* dated August 3, 1993. Ruperalia was writing in response to an article about *Forbidden Archeology* that appeared in the May/June 1993 issue of *Back to Godhead,* the bimonthly magazine of the International Society for Krishna Consciousness.

37. Karl Popper, Darwinism as a metaphysical research programme, *Methodology and Science,* vol. 9, 1976, p. 104. The emphasis is Popper's. The article is taken from Karl Popper's *An Intellectual Biography: Unended Quest.*

38. Dr. Vanina is the Chief of the Department of History and Culture of the Center of Indian Studies of the Institute for Oriental Studies of the Russian Academy of Sciences. Her quoted remarks are transcribed from a tape recording, made with the consent of the participants in the roundtable discussion.

39. G. William Barnard, Transformations and transformers: spirituality and the academic study of mysticism, *Journal of Consciousness Studies,* vol. 1(2), 1994, p. 256.

40. G. William Barnard, Transformations and transformers, pp. 257–258.

41. Katherine P. Ewing, Dreams from a saint: anthropological atheism and the temptation to believe, *American Anthropologist,* vol. 96(3), 1994, p. 572.

42. Jonathan Marks, *Forbidden Archeology,* p. 140.

43. Tim Murray, *Forbidden Archeology,* p. 379.

44. Pierce J. Flynn, Foreword to *Forbidden Archeology,* pp. xix-xx. Jonathan Marks, in his review of *Forbidden Archeology,* labeled Flynn a "curious personage." Concerning Flynn's opinion of *Forbidden Archeology,* Marks stated: "Dr. Pierce J. Flynn . . . places this work within postmodern scholarship. I'd like to think postmodern scholars would distance themselves from it; even in the postmodern era, there has to be a difference between scholarship and non-scholarship."

12

The Discoveries of Carlos Ribeiro: A Controversial Episode in Nineteenth-Century European Archeology

I presented this paper at the European Association of Archaeologists Annual Meeting 2000, in Lisbon, Portugal. The paper was later published in a peer-reviewed archeology journal: Cremo, M. A. (2009) The discoveries of Carlos Ribeiro: a controversial episode in nineteenth-century European archeology. Journal of Iberian Archaeology, vol. 12: 69–89.

Introduction

Because my theoretical approach is informed by the *Puranas,* the historical writings of ancient India, which posit a human presence extending much further back in time than most archeologists today are prepared to accept (Cremo 1999), I was intrigued when I learned of the Miocene stone tools discovered by Carlos Ribeiro, a Portuguese geologist of the nineteenth century [**see Plate I, Figure 1**]. While I was going through the writings of the American geologist J. D. Whitney (1880), who reported evidence for Tertiary human beings in California,[1] I encountered a sentence or two about Ribeiro having found flint implements in Miocene formations near Lisbon.[2] Later, I saw Ribeiro's name again, this time in the 1957 edition of *Fossil Men* by Boule and Vallois, who rather curtly dismissed his work. I was, however, led by Boule and Vallois to the 1883 edition of *Le Préhistorique,* by Gabriel de Mortillet, who gave a favorable report of Ribeiro's discoveries. From de Mortillet's bibliographic references, I went to Ribeiro's original reports. Using all of this material, I wrote about Ribeiro's discoveries and their reception in my book *Forbidden Archeology* (Cremo and Thompson 1993). When I learned last year that the European Association of Archaeologists annual meeting for the year 2000 was going to be held in Lisbon, I proposed this paper on Ribeiro's work for the section on history of archeology. In my research, I visited the Museu Geológico in Lisbon [**see Plate I, Figure 2**], where I studied a collection of Ribeiro's artifacts. The artifacts were stored out of sight, below the display cases featuring more conventionally acceptable artifacts from the Portuguese Stone Ages.[3] After spending a week examining and photographing the artifacts, I went to the library of the Institute of Geology and Mines at Alfragide to study Ribeiro's personal papers,[4] and later I went to visit some of the sites where Ribeiro collected his specimens.[5] These investigations demonstrated how contemporary archeology treats reports of facts that no longer conform to accepted views. Keep in mind that for most current students of archeology, Ribeiro and his discoveries simply do not exist. You have to go back to textbooks printed over forty years ago to find even a mention of him. Did Ribeiro's work really deserve to be so thoroughly forgotten? I think not.

A summary history of Ribeiro's discoveries

In 1857, Ribeiro was named to head the Geological Commission of Portugal, and he would also be elected to the Portuguese Academy of Sciences. During the years 1860–63, he began conducting studies of stone implements found in Portugal. Ribeiro learned that flints bearing signs of human work had been found in Tertiary beds between Carregado and Alemquer, two small towns in the basin of the Tagus River, about 35–40 kilometers north of Lisbon. Ribeiro began his own investigations, and in many localities found "flakes of worked flint and quartzite in the interior of the beds." Ribeiro (1873a, p. 97) said: "I was greatly surprised when I forcefully extracted, with my own hand, worked flints, from deep inside beds of limestone which had been inclined at angles of 30–50 degrees from the horizontal."[6] Ribeiro found himself in a dilemma. The geology of the region indicated the limestone beds were of Tertiary age, but Ribeiro (1873a, p. 97) felt he must submit to the then prevalent idea that humans were not older than the Quaternary.[7]

Ribeiro therefore assigned Quaternary ages to the implement-bearing strata (Ribeiro 1866, Ribeiro and Delgado 1867). Upon seeing the maps and accompanying reports, geologists in other countries were perplexed. The French geologist Edouard de Verneuil wrote to Ribeiro on May 27, 1867, asking him to send an explanatory note, which was read at the June 17 meeting of the Geological Society of France and later published in the bulletin of the Society (Ribeiro 1867). On July 16, de Verneuil wrote once more to Ribeiro, again objecting to his placing the Portuguese formations in the Quaternary:

> I am still a little astonished at the depth of your Quaternary formations and at the following circumstances that you mentioned:
> 1. The Quaternary comprises 400 meters;
> 2. The formations are raised, with the stratification sometimes inclined at angles approaching the vertical;
> 3. They contain masses of hard limestone resembling the limestones of the Secondary;
> 4. Finally, and most curiously, they contain implements made by the hands of humans from flint and quartzite. These implements are found at the base of the formations, which means that after they were made they were covered by a deposit 400 meters deep. (Ribeiro 1871, pp. 53–54, n.1)

Given these facts, de Verneuil thought the formations must be Tertiary. But Ribeiro resisted the suggestion.

During that same year, Ribeiro learned that the Abbé Louis Bourgeois, a reputable investigator, had reported finding stone implements in Tertiary beds in France, and that some authorities supported him (de Mortillet 1883, p. 85). Under the twin influences of de Verneuil's criticism and the discoveries of Bourgeois, Ribeiro overcame his doubts and began reporting that implements of human manufacture had been found in Miocene formations in Portugal (Ribeiro 1871, 1873a, p. 98).

From the standpoint of modern geology, Ribeiro's assessment of the age of the formations in the Tagus River valley near Lisbon is correct. Ivan Chicha (1970, p. 50) said about this region: "The Oligocene beds, prevalently of freshwater continental origin . . . are overlain by beds . . . which are placed in the oldest Miocene—Aquitanian." According to Chicha, these Aquitanian beds are surmounted by limestones and claystones that ascend to the Tortonian stage of the Late Miocene. Another study (Antunes *et al.* 1980, p. 138) showed that Tagus Basin limestones, such as those in which Ribeiro found stone tools, occur in the Middle and Early Miocene. Finally, the current official geological maps of Portugal show the formations at Ribeiro's key sites to be Early to Middle Miocene (Zbyszweski and Ferreira 1966, pp. 9–11). In the area around Lisbon, some of the later Miocene beds are of marine origin. According to Ribeiro, implements of flint and quartzite are absent from these marine beds. They are found only in the lacustrine Miocene formations (Ribeiro 1871, p. 57).

In identifying a stone object as an implement, three questions must be answered: (1) is the specimen really of human manufacture? (2) has the age of the stratum in which it was discovered been properly determined? (3) was the implement incorporated into the stratum at the time the stratum was laid down, or was the implement introduced at a later date? As far as Ribeiro was concerned, he was convinced that he had satisfactorily answered all three questions. The toollike flint objects he studied were of human manufacture, they were found in strata mostly of Miocene age, and many appeared to be in primary position, although some of his specimens were found on the surface.

In 1871, Ribeiro exhibited to the members of the Portuguese Academy of Science at Lisbon a collection of flint and quartzite implements, including those gathered from the Tertiary formations of the Tagus valley, and published a study on them (Ribeiro 1871). During my research in the Museum of Geology in Lisbon, I was able to match artifacts to twenty-one of the 128 drawings of artifacts shown in this study. Artifacts were matched to figures 13, 15, 16, 26, 27, 29, 36, 36b, 43, 45, 46, 55, 62, 63, 64, 73, 74, 77, 80, 82, 94. [**See Plates II-VII.**] The implements described in this study show not only striking platforms, bulbs of percussion, and worked edges, but also signs of use. For example, the implement shown in his figure 7 has edges that show use marks, to the extent that they appear polished (Ribeiro 1871, p. 12).

About the large flint implement shown in his figure 10(a), Ribeiro (1871, p. 13) said, "A great part of the surface appears to have been worn by rubbing. One sees on one side a cavity, about 5 centimeters wide. Its surface, smooth and glossy from wear, appears to indicate that hard substances, such as roots and seeds, were ground upon it." The object came from a sand pit on the Quinta-do-Cesar, a farming estate near Carregado.

Regarding a flint object found in one of the beds comprising the hill at Murganheira, Ribeiro (1871, p. 14) said, "This specimen terminates in a point, and from the wear at this place, it appears to have served as a tool." [see **Plate II, Figure 1.**]

According to Ribeiro (1871, p. 17), "Figure 32 shows a flint flake, six millimeters thick and of greyish color, shading to chestnut brown. It is worked on its two edges, and is notched at the top. It appears to be a tool designed for making grooves with the point, which extends from the top of the notch, and which has been worn with use." The implement came from beds of coarse red Tertiary sandstone between Alemquer and Otta.

Ribeiro (1871, p. 28) said, "Figure 95 is of brownish-yellow quartzite, with a maximum thickness of three centimeters. One side, unworked, shows but a single face. The other side, as shown in the drawing, presents three faces, two of which are naturally fractured and while the third is intentionally worked. The edge *a-b* is sharp and shows marks made by extensive use in cutting." It came from a sandy Pliocene bed near Melides. According to Ribeiro, other implements in the study, including those in figures 37, 39, 54, 80, and 86, also showed signs of use.

In 1872, at the International Congress of Prehistoric Anthropology and Archeology meeting in Brussels, Ribeiro gave another report on his discoveries and displayed more specimens, mostly pointed flakes. Bourgeois found one flint that he thought displayed signs of human work, but unfortunately it had not been found *in situ*. He therefore suspended judgment (de Mortillet 1883, p. 95). A. W. Franks, Conservator of National Antiquities and Ethnography at the British Museum, stated that some of the specimens did appear to be the product of intentional work, but he reserved judgment on the age of the strata in which they had been found (Ribeiro 1873a, p. 99).

To settle this question, Ribeiro himself (1873b, p. 100) addressed the Congress on "the exact geological situation of the beds in which he had found worked flint flakes, the authenticity of which has been recognized by Mr. Franks and other members of the Congress." Ribeiro reported that one of the flints had been found in the reddish-yellow Pliocene sandstone on the left bank of the Tagus, to the south of Lisbon (Ribeiro 1873b, p. 101). "Concerning the other flints which Mr. Franks has declared bear evident traces of human workmanship," said Ribeiro (1873b, p. 102), "they were found in Miocene strata." He explained that on the way north from Lisbon to Caldas da Rainha, between the towns of Otta and Cercal, one comes to the steep hill of Espinhaço de Cão. According to Ribeiro (1873b, p. 102), it was in the lacrustine Miocene sandstone beds of this hill, which lie under marine Miocene strata, that he found "flints worked by the hand of man before they were buried in the deposits." This would indicate the presence of human beings in Portugal at least 10 million years ago and perhaps as much as 25 million years ago.

Ribeiro's Miocene flints made an impressive debut at Brussels, but remained controversial. At the Paris Exposition of 1878, Ribeiro displayed 95 specimens of Tertiary flint tools in the gallery of anthropological science. De Mortillet visited Ribeiro's exhibit and, in the course of examining the specimens carefully, decided that 22 had indubitable signs of human work. De Mortillet, along with his friend and colleague Emile Cartailhac, enthusiastically brought other archeologists to see Ribeiro's specimens, and they were all of the same opinion—a good many of the flints were definitely made by humans. Cartailhac then photographed the specimens, and de Mortillet later presented the pictures in his *Musée Préhistorique* (G. and A. de Mortillet 1881).

De Mortillet (1883, p. 99) wrote: "The intentional work is very well established, not only by the general shape, which can be deceptive, but much more conclusively by the presence of clearly evident striking platforms and strongly developed bulbs of percussion." Leland W. Patterson (1983), an expert in distinguishing artifacts from "naturefacts," believes that the bulb of percussion is the most important sign of intentional work on a flint flake. The bulbs of percussion also sometimes had eraillures, small chips removed by the force of impact. In addition to the striking platform, bulb of percussion, and eraillure, some of Ribeiro's specimens had several long, vertical flakes removed in parallel, something not likely to occur in the course of random battering by the forces of nature.

"There can be no doubt," wrote de Mortillet (1883, p. 99) about Ribeiro's stone implements, adding, "In looking at the collection, one believes oneself to be seeing Mousterian tools, only somewhat coarser than usual." In de Mortillet (1883, pp. 98, 81) one can find an illustration of one of Ribeiro's Miocene tools from Portugal and, for comparision, an illustration of a Mousterian tool of the same general type. They share the typical features of intentional human work on stone: the striking platform, bulb of percussion, eraillure, and parallel removal of flakes. De Mortillet (1883, pp. 99–100) further observed: "Many of the specimens, on the same side as the bulb of percussion, have hollows with traces and fragments of sandstone adhering to them, a fact which establishes their original position in the strata."

Plate 3 in *Musée Préhistorique* (G. and A. de Mortillet 1881) featured illustrations of Ribeiro's Miocene and Pliocene discoveries. One of these depicts both sides of a flint flake recovered from a Tertiary formation at the base of Monte Redondo [**Plate 1, Figure 3**]. This formation is said to belong to the Tortonian stage of the Late Miocene (de Mortillet 1883, p. 102). The Tortonian extends from 11.8 to 15 million years ago (Cicha 1970, p. 97). The ventral surface of the flint flake shows "a large striking platform, bulb of percussion, and eraillure." Sandstone, just like that found at the base of Monte Redondo, adhered to the dorsal surface.

An international committee vindicates Ribeiro

At the 1880 meeting of the International Congress of Prehistoric Anthropology and Archeology, which was held in Lisbon, Portugal, Ribeiro served as general secretary.[8] Although very busy with all of the details of organizing the event, and somewhat ill, he delivered a report on his artifacts and displayed more specimens that were "extracted from Miocene beds" (Ribeiro 1884, p. 86). In his report ("L'homme Tertiaire en Portugal"), Ribeiro (1884, p. 88) stated: "The conditions in which the worked flints were found in the beds are as follows: (1) They were found as integral parts of the beds themselves. (2) They had sharp, well-preserved edges, showing that they had not been subject to transport for any great distance. (3) They had a patina similar in color to the rocks in the strata of which they formed a part."

The second point is especially important. Some geologists claimed that the flint implements had been introduced into Miocene beds by the floods and torrents that

periodically washed over this terrain. According to this view, Quaternary flint implements may have entered into the interior of the Miocene beds through fissures and
been cemented there, acquiring over a long period of time the coloration of the beds
(de Quatrefages 1884, p. 95). But if the flints had been subjected to such transport, then
the sharp edges would most probably have been damaged, and this was not the case.

The Congress assigned a special commission of scientists the task of directly inspecting the implements and the sites from which they had been gathered. In addition
to Ribeiro himself, the commission included G. Bellucci of the Italian Society for Anthropology and Geography; G. Capellini, from the Royal University of Bologna, Italy,
and known for his discoveries of incised Pliocene whale bones; E. Cartailhac, of the
French Ministry of Public Instruction; Sir John Evans, an English geologist; Gabriel de
Mortillet, professor of prehistoric anthropology at the College of Anthropology, Paris;
and Rudolph Virchow, a German anthropologist. The other members were the scientists Choffat, Cotteau, Villanova, and Cazalis de Fondouce.

On September 22, 1880, at six in the morning, the commission members boarded
a special train and proceeded north from Lisbon, getting off at Carregado. By other
means, they proceeded further north to Otta, and two kilometers northeast from Otta
arrived at the southern slopes of the hill called Monte Redondo [see **Plate I, Figure
3**]. At that point, the scientists dispersed into various ravines [see **Plate I, Figure 4**] in
search of flints.[9]

Paul Choffat (1884a, p. 63), secretary of the commission, later reported to the
Congress: "Of the many flint flakes and apparent cores taken from the midst of the
strata under the eyes of the commission members, one was judged as leaving no doubt
about the intentional character of the work." This was the specimen found *in situ* by
Bellucci. Choffat then noted that Bellucci had found on the surface other flints with
incontestable signs of work. Some thought they were Miocene implements that had
been removed from the Miocene conglomerates by atmospheric agencies, while others
thought that the implements were of a much more recent date.

De Mortillet (1883, p. 102) gave an informative account of the excursion to Otta
and Bellucci's remarkable discovery:

> The members of the Congress arrived at Otta, in the middle of a
> great freshwater formation. It was the bottom of an ancient lake, with
> sand and clay in the center, and sand and rocks on the edges. It is on
> the shores that intelligent beings would have left their tools, and it is on
> the shores of the lake that once bathed Monte Redondo that the search
> was made. It was crowned with success. The able investigator of Um-
> bria, Mr. Bellucci, discovered *in situ* a flint bearing incontestable signs
> of intentional work. Before detaching it, he showed it to a number of his
> colleagues. The flint was strongly encased in the rock. He had to use a
> hammer to extract it. It is definitely of the same age as the deposit. In-
> stead of lying flat on a surface onto which it could have been secondarily
> recemented at a much later date, it was found firmly in place on the
> under side of a ledge extending over a region removed by erosion. It is

impossible to desire a more complete demonstration attesting to a flint's position in its strata.[10]

All that was needed was to determine the age of the strata. Study of the fauna and flora in the region around the Monte Redondo site showed that the formations present there can be assigned to the Tortonian stage of the Late Miocene period (de Mortillet 1883, p. 102). "Therefore," concluded de Mortillet "during the Tortonian epoch there existed in Portugal an intelligent being who chipped flint just like Quaternary humans" (1883, p. 102). Some modern authorities consider the Otta conglomerates to be from the Burdigalian stage of the Early Miocene (Antunes *et al.* 1980, p. 139).

Choffat (1884b, pp. 92–93) presented, in the form of answers to four questions, the conclusions of the commission members. The first two questions dealt with the flints themselves:

(1) Are there bulbs of percussion on the flints on exhibition and on those found during the excursion? The commission declares unanimously that there are bulbs of percussion, and some pieces have several.

(2) Are bulbs of percussion proof of intentional work? There are different opinions. They may be summarized as follows: de Mortillet considers that just one bulb of percussion is sufficient proof of intentional work, while Evans believes that even several bulbs on one piece do not give certitude of intentional work but only a great probability of such.

Here it may once more be noted that modern authorities such as Leland W. Patterson (1983) consider one or more bulbs of percussion to be good indicators of intentional work.

The remaining two questions concerned the positions in which the flints were found:

(3) Are the worked flints found at Otta from the interior of the beds or the surface? There are diverse opinions. Mr. Cotteau believes all are from the surface, and that those found embedded within the strata came down through crevasses in the beds. Mr. Capellini, however, believes that pieces found on the surface were eroded from the interior of the beds. De Mortillet, Evans, and Cartailhac believe there are two time periods to which the flints may be referred, the first being the Tertiary, the other being the Old and New Stone Ages of the Quaternary. The flints of the two periods are easy to distinguish by their form and patina.

(4) What is the age of the strata of the worked flints? After only a moments discussion the members declared they were in perfect accord with Ribeiro.

In other words, the strata were Miocene. In the discussion that followed the presentation of Choffat's report, Capellini said: "I believe these flints to be the product of intentional work. If you do not admit that, then you must also doubt the flints of the later Stone Ages" (Choffat 1884b, pp. 97–98). According to Capellini, Ribeiro's Miocene specimens were almost identical to undoubted Quaternary flint implements.

The next speaker, Villanova, was very doubtful, even about the Bellucci find. He said that in order to remove all cause for suspicion one would have to discover an unmistakably genuine implement firmly embedded not in a Miocene conglomerate but in the middle of an undifferentiated Miocene formation and alongside characteristic fossils (Choffat 1884b, p. 99). Of course, it would have been better if the flint had been found in an undifferentiated stratum. But the number of human artifacts found in undifferentiated strata directly alongside characteristic fossils is rather small. Furthermore, sometimes anomalous finds are made in undifferentiated strata alongside characteristic fossils, and then some other means will be found to discredit them. Indeed, as previously mentioned, in his report to the International Congress of Prehistoric Anthropology and Archeology at Brussels in 1872, Ribeiro (1873a, p. 97) did tell of finding flint implements "deep inside" apparently undifferentiated Miocene limestone beds.

Following Villanova, Cartailhac spoke. He said that if the question of the Miocene age of the implements were to be decided on the grounds of actual scientific evidence, the answer would have to be affirmative. Cartailhac believed that the coloration of many of the surface finds indicated they were eroded from Miocene beds, and he pointed out that some specimens had remnants of Miocene sediments adhering to them.

Cartailhac then asked the members to consider a particular specimen from Ribeiro's collection, which he had previously studied at the anthropological exposition in Paris. He stated: "I have seen on it two bulbs of percussion, and possibly a third, and a point that seems to truly be the result of intentional work. It has on its surface not a coloration that could be removed by washing but rather a surface incrustation of Miocene sandstone tightly adhering to it. A chemist would not permit us to say that such a deposit could form and attach itself to a flint lying, for whatever amount of time, on a sandstone surface" (Choffat 1884b, p. 100). In other words, the flint must have been lying within the Miocene bed itself, when it was formed. Cartailhac admitted that natural action might in rare occasions produce a bulb of percussion, but to have two on the same piece would be an absolute miracle. He believed that the many very good specimens discovered on the Miocene surface, where there was absolutely no trace of any other deposit, were really Miocene implements that had weathered out of the rock.

After Cartailhac finished his remarks, Bellucci gave his own account of his discovery of the implement in the Miocene conglomerate at Otta (Choffat 1884b, pp. 101–102). Before extracting it, he had shown it to many members of the commission, who saw that it was firmly integrated into the stratum. It had been so firmly fixed in the Miocene sandstone conglomerate that he needed to use Cartailhac's iron pick to break the sandstone. Bellucci stated that the inner surface of the implement, the one adhering to the conglomerate, had not only the same reddish color as the conglomerate but also incrustations of tiny grains of quartzite that could not be detached even by vigorous washing.

Bellucci further pointed out that the elements composing the intact conglomerate corresponded perfectly with those found loose on the surface. This led Bellucci to conclude that the loose stones found on the surface at Otta were the result of weathering of the conglomerate. This indicated that flint implements found on the surface might also have come recently from the conglomerate, which was of Miocene age (Choffat 1884b, p. 103).

As for the signs of intentional work on the piece found *in situ*, Bellucci noted: "This piece was detached from the surface of a flint core, and it not only has a magnificent bulb of percussion, but also one of its surfaces presents marks showing that another flake had been previously detached, in the same direction, when the implement had been still part of the flint nucleus" (Choffat 1884b, p. 104). Successive parallel flake removal from a core is recognized today by experts in lithic technology as one of the surest signs of intentional work. Patterson stated: "Humans will often strike multiple flakes in series from a single core, usually resulting in the production of some flakes with multiple facets on the dorsal face. In contrast, the removal of a few flakes from cores by random natural forces would not be expected to occur often by serial removals. . . . It is characteristic in human lithic manufacturing processes to use the same striking platform for multiple flake removals" (Patterson *et al.* 1987, p. 98).

Altogether, there seems little reason why Ribeiro's discoveries should not be receiving some serious attention, even today. Here we have a professional geologist, the head of Portugal's Geological Commission, making discoveries of flint implements in Miocene strata. The implements resembled accepted types, and they displayed characteristics that modern experts in lithic technology accept as signs of human manufacture. To resolve controversial questions, a congress of Europe's leading archeologists and anthropologists deputed a committee to conduct a firsthand investigation of one of the sites of Ribeiro's discoveries. There a scientist discovered *in situ* an implement in a Miocene bed, a fact witnessed by several other members of the committee. Of course, objections were raised but upon reviewing them, it does not appear to me that they justify rejection of Bellucci's find in particular or Ribeiro's finds in general.

After Ribeiro

Ribeiro died in 1882. In 1889, his colleague Joaquim Fillipe Nery Delgado conducted some new explorations at Monte Redondo, along with Berkeley Cotter of the Geological Commission of Portugal. Delgado recovered some artifacts, which he displayed at the 10th International Congress of Prehistoric Anthropology and Archeology. The collection was divided into two groups. The specimens in the first group were recovered from four excavations into the Tertiary sandstone and from vertical Tertiary sandstone surfaces exposed in ravines and cliffs cut into the base of Monte Redondo [see Plate I, Figure 4]. The second group included flints that were found loose on the surface of the ground, having weathered out from the Tertiary formations.[11] None of the flints in the first group, from the excavations or the exposures, showed signs of human work.

Delgado (1889, p. 530) therefore declared he had not been able to duplicate Ribeiro's discoveries of worked flints in solid rock. Delgado said, "I have no desire to raise any doubts about the authenticity of his discoveries; nevertheless, the spirit of scientific truthfulness compels me to make my statement" (1889, p. 530).

But Delgado did see signs of human work on the flints found loose on the ground (1889, p. 530). He said that many of these "are incontestably Tertiary and have been naturally separated from the underlying beds solely by the action of atmospheric agencies" (1889, p. 529). He believed that others found lying on the surface were from the Late Pleistocene, perhaps left by the humans responsible for the kitchen midden at Mugem (1889, p. 531).

In the discussion that followed Delgado's talk, de Mortillet said he did not think Delgado's failure to find worked flints in his four excavations was all that significant. He pointed out that even in places very rich in artifacts, such as Chelles and St. Acheul in France, one could go through many cubic meters of sediment without finding any flints showing signs of work (Delgado 1889, p. 532).

In 1905, in a memorial volume dedicated to Ribeiro, Delgado further distanced himself from the conclusions of his departed colleague. He wrote (1905, pp. 33–34): "The question of Tertiary man still remains to be decided. If the discovery made ten years ago by Dubois in the [latest] Pliocene of Trinil, on the island of Java, appears to show the way to a solution for this problem, then it is no less certain that the idea of the existence of a being ancestral to man in the Tertiary has also lost much ground." Delgado appears to be saying that *Pithecanthropus erectus,* a precursor to modern humans, ruled out the existence of humans like us in the Tertiary, anywhere in the world. He also appears to be saying that *Pithecanthropus* made it unlikely that similar precursors to modern humans would be found in the European Tertiary. Southeast Asia, apparently, would be the place to look.

This interpretation of his statement is supported by what he said next. Delgado (1905, p. 34) mentioned his 1889 excavations at Monte Redondo, stating that they failed to yield specimens like those that Ribeiro claimed to have found in the Teritiary rock. He did not, however, mention that he had found weathered out from the Miocene formations many worked flints, which, previously, he himself had claimed to be of Tertiary age (Delgado 1889, p. 529). He then quoted Gaudry as saying, in a 1903 publication, that he despaired of finding any remains of predecessors to Chellean man in the Pliocene of France, because all reports announcing evidence for Tertiary man in Europe had proved incorrect (Delgado 1905).

Delgado concluded (1905, p. 34): "Even though the discovery of Tertiary man, or rather an intelligent precursor to man in the Tertiary epoch, has not been confirmed, the name of our compatriot will not fail to be mentioned in textbooks of prehistory, because the discovery of the flints of Otta, to which his name is inextricably connected, will always remain among the most valuable arguments in favor of this hypothesis." But Ribeiro's name did not remain in the textbooks. And the flints of Otta also disappeared from them, or were given far more recent ages.

In 1942, Henri Breuil and G. Zbyszewski of the Geological Service of Portugal restudied the artifacts collected by Ribeiro. They determined that some of them did not actually display any signs of intentional human work. And, not accepting the Tertiary age of the rest, they reclassified them as corresponding to accepted Pleistocene and

Holocene industries, such as the Clactonian, Tayencian, Levalloisian, Mousterian, Upper Palaeolithic, Mesolithic, and Neo-Eneolithic (Zbyszewski and Ferreira 1966, pp. 85–86, Breuil and Zbyszewski 1942).

Here is one example of such reclassification. Ribeiro (1871, p. 14) described an implement of light brown flint. He said it was one of several extracted (*retirès*) from the series of beds forming the hill called Murganheira. Ribeiro (1866, p. 34) said these beds belonged to group one (*groupe inférieur*) of his classification (1866, p. 2). He originally considered the beds of the *groupe inférieur* as earliest Quaternary, but later classified them as belonging to the Lower Miocene (Ribeiro 1871, pp. 47–48), in line with the modern attribution. The implement from the Miocene beds at Murganheira has worked edges, two of them joining to form a point [see Plate II, Figure 1]. The point shows signs of use. On the tool itself is written "*15.IV.1869 1.5 km N da Bemposta*," indicating the artifact was found on April 15, 1869, 1.5 kilometers north of Bemposta, a locality just south of the Murganheira hill. On the new label prepared by the Geological Service of Portugal during the period of reclassification, the artifact is identified as an Upper Paleolithic flint implement found by Ribeiro at Murganheira, near Alemquer [see Plate II, Figure 1]. Apparently, there was no disputing the artifactual nature of the object, but its age was apparently assigned on the basis of its form rather than its provenance.

Some time after this reclassification of Ribeiro's collection, the artifacts were removed from display at the Museo Geológico in Lisbon. Ribeiro and his artifacts entered into an oblivion from which they have yet to emerge.

Discussion

The history of Carlos Ribeiro's discoveries demonstrates the complex interpretative interplay between geology and archeology and evolutionary theories. During the early 1860s, the prevailing archeological view that human artifacts were confined to the Quaternary caused Ribeiro to classify Tertiary formations containing them as Quaternary. When opposition to this geological classification arose from geologists, Ribeiro at first resisted their suggestions that the terrains were certainly Tertiary. When a short time later archeologists began to seriously consider evidence for human artifacts in the Tertiary, Ribeiro changed his mind. He agreed that the Portuguese formations were Tertiary, and now took the archeological remains found in them as evidence for Tertiary humans. Prominent archeologists and geologists agreed with him, and his work remained a topic of active discussion.

There were two possibilities as to the archeological significance of Ribeiro's work: it provided either evidence for humans like us in the Tertiary, or evidence for a human precursor. De Mortillet, for example, favored the latter interpretation, whereas de Quatrefages and others favored the former.[12]

In any case, at this time, even though most European archeologists were working within an evolutionary framework, the time dimension of the evolutionary process had not been settled, mainly because of the lack of skeletal evidence in appropriate geological contexts. The looseness of the evolutionary framework therefore allowed archeologists to contemplate the existence of Tertiary humans.

That changed in the very last decade of the nineteenth century. With the discovery of *Pithecanthropus erectus,* Darwinists began to solidify an evolutionary progression that led from *Pithecanthropus,* at the Plio-Pleistocene boundary, to anatomically modern humans in the Late Pleistocene. This left no room for Tertiary humans anywhere in the world, and put the spotlight on Southeast Asia as the place to look for Tertiary precursors to *Pithecanthropus.* Ribeiro's discoveries lost their relevance and gradually disappeared from the discourse of human origins.[13]

A century later, things have changed somewhat. Africa is now generally recognized as the place where hominids first arose. For some time, the earliest tools were thought to date back only to the Early Pleistocene. But in recent years archeologists are once more pushing the onset of stone toolmaking well into the Tertiary. Oldowan tools have been found in the Pliocene at Gona, Ethiopia (Semaw *et al.* 1997). The large number of tools, described as surprisingly sophisticated, are about 2.5–2.6 million years old. Therefore, we should expect to find stone tools going back even further into the Tertiary.

Conventional candidates for the Tertiary toolmakers include earliest *Homo* or one of the australopithecines (Steele 1999, p. 25). But there are other possibilities. Footprints described as anatomically modern occur in Pliocene volcanic ash 3.7 million years old at Laetoli, Tanzania (M. Leakey 1979).[14] There is even evidence putting toolmakers close to the Iberian peninsula, in Morocco, in the late Tertiary (Onoratini *et al.* 1990). At the Ben Souda quarry near Fez, stone tools were found in place in the Saissian formation, which had for long been considered Pliocene. Onoratini *et al.* said: "The typological characters are clear enough so as to allow one to propose that this industry should be attributed culturally to the middle Acheulean. This constitutes sufficient reason to anthropically date a formation that could not be dated by any other method." Noting the similarity of the Ben Souda tools to the Acheulean tools from a Middle Pleistocene formation at Cuvette de Sidi Abderrahman in the area of Casablanca, Onoratini *et al.* (1990, p. 330) decided to characterize the part of the Saissian formation containing the tools at Ben Souda as also being Middle Pleistocene. Another possibility that deserves to be considered is that there are tools of Acheulean type in the Tertiary of Morocco.

It may be noted that anatomically modern human skeletal remains have been found in the Tertiary (Pliocene) of Italy at Castenedolo[15] (Ragazzoni 1880, Sergi 1884, Cremo and Thompson 1993, pp. 422–432) and Savona (de Mortillet 1883, p. 70, Issel 1868, Cremo and Thompson 1993. pp. 433–435). There may therefore be some reason, once more, to consider the possibility of Tertiary industries in Portugal.

Such a possibility is not much in favor today, as can be seen in a recent critical survey for evidence for the earliest human occupation of Europe (Roebroeks and Van Kolfschoten 1995).[16] The basic thrust of the book, which is a collection of papers presented at a conference on the earliest occupation of Europe held at Tautavel, France, in 1993, is to endorse a short chronology, with solid evidence for first occupation occurring in the Middle Pleistocene at around 500,000 years. Other discoveries favoring a long chronology, perhaps extending into the earliest Pleistocene (1.8 to 2 million years) are, however, mentioned, although the consensus among the authors of the Tautavel papers is that such evidence is highly questionable. Two kinds of doubts are raised against the evidence for the long chronology: doubts about the age of the sites and doubts about the intentional manufacture of the artifacts found there. The sites and the artifacts are nevertheless mentioned, and are not entirely dismissed. The editors, and authors of individual chapters, simply say, in many cases, that better confirmation of the age of the site and the intentional manufacture of the artifacts are required.

Given this liberal approach, Ribeiro's artifacts should have been mentioned in the chapter on the Iberian peninsula (Raposo and Santonja 1995). In that chapter, the authors give the impression that the oldest reported stone tool industries in Portugal are Early Pleistocene pebble industries documented by Breuil and Zbyszewski (1942–1945). Raposo and Santonja (1995, p. 13) called into question the dating of the pebble tool sites, concluding that they "do not document beyond doubt any Early Pleistocene human occupation." But the main point is this: although the industries reported by Breuil and Zbyszewski were not accepted, they were at least acknowledged. The same is true of other controversial sites indicating a possible Early Pleistocene occupation elsewhere in the Iberian peninsula. Raposo and Santonja did not accept them, but they acknowledged their existence, thus offering current archeologists the option of conducting further research to more firmly establish either the dates of the sites or the artifactual nature of the stone objects found there. Ribeiro's discoveries deserve similar treatment.

One possible objection is that although there is some reason to believe in a possible early Pleistocene occupation of Europe, or even a very late Pliocene occupation, there is none to support a Miocene habitation. But there is a body of evidence that can provide a context in which the Miocene discoveries of Ribeiro might make some sense. Miocene flint tools are reported from Puy de Boudieu, near Aurillac in the department of Cantal in the Massif Central region of France (Verworn 1905). Today, many archeologists will assume that the discoverer, Max Verworn of the University of Göttingen, was deceived as to either the geological context or the artifactual nature of the implements. But Verworn's reports show that he gave extensive attention to both problems. He was not an eolithphile, but a skeptical investigator who employed a rigorous method of analysis.

Concerning the provenance, Verworn (1905, p. 16) noted that the worked flints were found in isolated small groups in layers of sediment, apart from unworked flints. This suggests that the worked flints were not picked out of large masses of broken flint. The worked flints showed little or no signs of transport, indicating they had not moved much since they were deposited, whereas unworked stones from the surrounding areas showed signs of transport and rolling (Verworn 1905, p. 16). The flint implements were found in layers of fluviatile sands, stones, and eroded chalk, along with fossils of a typical Miocene fauna, including *Dinotherium giganteum, Mastodon longirostris, Rhinocerus schleiermacheri,* and *Hipparion gracile.* The implement-bearing layers were covered with basalt flows (Verworn 1905, p. 17). Considering the objection that Miocene fossils from lower layers had been mixed into upper layers with Pleistocene implements, Verworn pointed out that no Pleistocene animal fossils were to be found in the same layers as the Miocene fossils and the flint implements. He also observed that the layers bearing the flint implements of the type he collected were always found in the lowest part of the sequence overlying the Oligocene basement formation (Verworn 1905, pp. 19–20). Paleolithic and Neolithic implements of the standard type are found only in the upper terraces, above the sequence of Tertiary sedimentary and volcanic layers (Verworn 1905, p. 17).

Concerning the artifactual nature of the implements, Verworn (1905, pp. 24–25) considered the various causes of natural flaking, including frost, heat, movement by water, rock falls, glaciers, and so forth, and found they could not account for the objects he found at Aurillac. He believed that even the presence of bulbs of percussion, striking platforms, and apparently intentional flaking were not enough to establish the artifactual nature of a flint object. Retouching of a working edge was a good sign of intentional work, but he recommended very careful study of the individual flake removals on the edge, including their depth, size, similarity of planes of impact, and arrangement in regular rows. But even this was not enough, for him. He especially recommended looking for use marks. Verworn expected that implements used for scraping wood, bones, or skin would display characteristic use marks. He conducted experimental research to help in identifying such marks on working edges of flint implements. (Verworn 1905, pp. 25–26).

Summarizing his methodology, Verworn (1905, p. 29) said:

> Suppose I find in an interglacial stone bed a flint that bears a clear bulb of percussion, but no other symptoms of intentional work. In that case, I would be doubtful as to whether or not I had before me an object of human manufacture. But suppose I find there a flint which on one side shows all the typical signs of percussion, and which on the other side shows the negative impressions of two, three, four or more flakes removed by blows in the same direction. Furthermore, let us suppose one edge of the piece shows numerous successive small parallel flakes removed, all running in the same direction, and all, without exception, are located on the same side of the edge. Let us suppose that all the other edges are sharp, without a trace of impact or rolling. Then I can say with complete certainty—it is an implement of human manufacture" (Verworn 1905, p. 29).

Verworn found about 200 specimens satisfying these criteria, and some of these also showed use marks on the working edges.

Similar discoveries come from various places around the world. They include stone tools from the Miocene of Burma (Noetling 1894), stone tools and artistically carved animal bone from the Miocene of Turkey (Calvert 1874), incised and carved animal bones from the Miocene of Europe (Garrigou and Filhol 1868, von Dücker 1873), stone tools from the Miocene of Europe (Bourgeois 1873), stone tools and human skeletal remains from the Miocene of California (Whitney 1880), and a human skeleton from the Miocene of France (de Mortillet 1883, p. 72). For an extensive review of such evidence from all periods of the Tertiary, from all parts of the world, see Cremo and Thompson (1993).

Much of this evidence, like Ribeiro's evidence, disappeared from active consideration by archeologists because of their commitment to a human evolutionary progression anchored on *Pithecanthropus erectus* (Cremo, forthcoming). For example, the influential anthropologist William H. Holmes (1899, p. 424), of the Smithsonian Institution, rejected the California gold mine discoveries reported by J. D. Whitney by saying: "Perhaps if Professor Whitney had fully appreciated the story of human evolution as it is understood today, he would have hesitated to announce the conclusions formulated, notwithstanding the imposing array of testimony with which he was confronted." Holmes (1899, p. 470) specifically appealed the Java man discovery, suggesting that Whitney's evidence should be rejected because "it implies a human race older by at least one half than *Pithecanthropus erectus* of Dubois, which may be regarded as an incipient form of human only."

Not all of the evidence for toolmakers deep in the Tertiary comes from the nineteenth century. K. N. Prasad (1982, p. 101) of the Geological Survey of India described "a crude unifacial handaxe pebble tool recovered from the late Miocene–Pliocene (9–10 m.y. BP) at Haritalyangar, Himachal Pradesh, India." He added (1982, p. 102), "The implement was recovered *in situ*, during remeasuring of the geological succession to assess the thickness of the beds. Care was taken to confirm the exact provenance of the material, in order to rule out the possibility of its derivation from younger horizons." Describing the tool itself, he said (1982, p. 102): "The quartz artefact, heart-shaped (90mm x 70mm) was obviously fabricated from a rolled pebble, the dorsal side of which shows rough flaking. . . . On the ventral side much of the marginal cortex is present at the distal end. Crude flaking has been attempted for fashioning a cutting edge. Marginal flaking at the lateral edge on the ventral side is visible." Prasad concluded (1982, p. 103): "It is not impossible that fashioning tools commenced even as early as the later Miocene and evolved in a time-stratigraphic period embracing the Astian–Villafranchian."

Conclusion

The discoveries of Ribeiro, and other evidences for Tertiary man uncovered by European archeologists and geologists, are today attributed (if they are discussed at all) to the inevitable mistakes of untutored members of a young discipline. Another possible explanation is that some of the discoveries were genuine, and were filtered out of the normal discourse of a community of archeologists that had adopted, perhaps prematurely, an evolutionary paradigm that placed the origins of stone toolmaking in the Pleistocene. But as the time line of human toolmaking begins to once more reach back into the Tertiary, perhaps we should withhold final judgement on Ribeiro's discoveries. A piece of the archeological puzzle that does not fit the consensus picture at a particular moment may find a place as the nature of the whole picture changes.

As an historian of archeology, I believe that the discoveries of Ribeiro remain worthy of being considered in discussions of the earliest human occupation of Europe. I am pleased that the Museo Geológico in Lisbon is once more considering exhibiting the artifacts.[19] I also encourage new investigations at Monte Redondo and other sites identified by Ribeiro. Ribeiro himself made an appeal, which remains relevant today (1871, p. 57):

> If in spite of all the considerations we have put forward, one still hesitates to accept the Miocene man in Portugal, we invite geologists to explore the escarpments formed by the beds of group (a) [Upper Miocene] in the region of Lisbon, and the beds of group (b) [Lower Miocene] along the routes from Carregado to Caldas and from Villa-Nova-da-Rainha to Rio Maior. It is there they will find the authentic facts and conclusive proofs, which serve to demonstrate the contemporaneity of our species and the Tertiary formations of our land.

Acknowledgements

I thank João Zilhão, director of the Portuguese Institute of Archeology (Instituto Português de Arquelogia) for his helpful introductions; Jose Manuel Brandão of the Geological Museum (Museu Geológico) for permission to study and photograph Ribeiro's artifacts; and M. Magalhães Ramalho, Vice President of the Institute of Geology and Mining (Instituto Geológico e Mineiro) for permission to study Ribeiro's correspondence, maps, and field notes in the historical archives of the Institute's library. Conceição Moura of the Institute library provided much helpful assistance. Lori Erbs was helpful in obtaining research materials for me before and after my research trip to Lisbon. I am grateful to Dhira Krishna Dasa, president of the Lisbon center of the International Society for Krishna Consciousness, for providing me with accommodations and transport during my stay. Paula Maior helped me find several of Ribeiro's sites, some in remote regions that demanded her excellent offroad driving skills. Finally, I am grateful to the trustees of the Bhaktivedanta Book Trust for their grants in support of my work.

Notes:

1. Whitney was a prominent geologist, and his reports on the discoveries were published by the Harvard University Museum of Comparative Zoology. The discoveries included anatomically modern human skeletal remains and stone artifacts, such as mortars, pestles, and projectile points [see Plates XII-XV]. They were found in gold mining tunnels that reached Eocene river channels, sealed under hundreds of feet of Miocene and Pliocene basalt flows in the Sierra Nevada Mountains, at places such as Table Mountain in Tuolumne County, California. See Cremo and Thompson (1993, pp. 370–393, 439–452) for a review and discussion.

2. Whitney (1880, p. 282) mentioned that in 1871 Carlos Ribeiro had published a

report that "cut flints, evidently the work of human hands, have been found in abundance in the Pliocene and Miocene even, of Portugal." Whitney criticized Charles Lyell for omitting this report in *The Antiquity of Man,* his comprehensive survey of evidence for human antiquity.

3. The Museu Geológico is located on the second floor of the 17th-century building in the historic center of Lisbon that also houses the Academia das Ciências de Lisboa (19 Rua da Academia das Ciências, Lisbon 1200 003). The director of the museum, Dr. Jose Manuel Brandão, showed me the collection of Ribeiro's artifacts. They are stored according to the sites (the principal ones being Abrigada, Alemquer, Bemposta, Carregado, Encosta da Gorda, Espinhaço de Cão, Murganheira, and Otta) but are mixed with objects collected by others. Most of Ribeiro's artifacts are, however, recognizable by his handwritten labels affixed to the artifacts, or notes written directly upon the artifacts. Others are attributed to him by old museum labels. I matched twenty-one of these artifacts to the figures in Ribeiro 1871 [see Plates II-VII].

These twenty-one artifacts, along with some others, were photographed for me by an assistant. With the permission of Dr. Brandão, I separated these artifacts in the collection drawers, putting them in individual small boxes along with my own handwritten labels associating each with the corresponding figure and plate numbers in Ribeiro's 1871. Assuming that all of the artifacts figured in Ribeiro's 1871 were originally in the collection, it appears that most are now misplaced or otherwise missing.

4. The Instituto Geológico e Mineiro is located at Estrada de Portela, Apartado 7586, Zambujal, Alfragide, in the newer western suburbs of Lisbon. The library of the Museu Geológico was transferred there from central Lisbon a few years ago. The library contains collections of Ribeiro's field notes. The notes are in small notebooks, written mostly in light pencil and sometimes in more legible ink. In my quick scanning of all the pages of the notebooks, I was disappointed not to find much in the way of exact descriptions of the circumstances of discovery of the stone artifacts collected by Ribeiro. The library has a collection of Ribeiro's correspondence (Arquivo Historico, Armario 1, Prataleira 2, Maço 9, Correpondência de Carlos Ribeiro). The collection includes mostly copies of letters to Ribeiro, with only a few of his replies, most of which appear to be first drafts. The letters did not contain information that revealed anything more about Ribeiro's discoveries than can be found in his publications.

5. The main guide to the localities I visited was Ribeiro's 1866. The localities that I found, with considerable help from Portuguese friends who served as drivers and translators, were: (1) A site at the base of an escarpment that runs along the north side of the road that goes from Carregado to Cadafaes (Ribeiro 1866, p. 28). The site is about half the distance between Carregado and Cadafaes (now spelled Cadafais), and can be reached by a small dirt road going through some vineyards. (2) Quinta de Cesar (Ribeiro 1866, p. 32) in Carregado. (3) The hill called Murganheira, east of Alemquer (Ribeiro 1866, p. 34). (4) Encosta da Gorda (Ribeiro 1866, p. 34), near the eastern side of the Murganheira hill. (5) The site on the right bank of the River Otta, where it passes the village of Otta (Ribeiro 1866, p. 42). (6) Monte Redondo, about 2 kilometers northeast of Otta (Ribeiro 1866, p. 45) [see Plate I, Figures 2 and 3].

6. It appears that the implements were sometimes found in layers of sediment ly-

ing between the layers of limestone. For example, de Mortillet (1883, p. 100) says that implements were found in layers of sandstone running between layers of limestone and clay.

7. Ribeiro's dilemma is also reflected in other writings. In his annual report for the Geological Commission of Portugal (Ribeiro 1865, p. 97), Ribeiro, as director, wrote about his investigations from the Serra de Monte Junto to the left bank of the Tagus River, northeast of Lisbon. He said that the work had resulted in important corrections for the official geological map of Portugal, soon to be engraved and printed. Formations that just three months earlier had been classified as Tertiary were now to be recognized as Quaternary.

In his main report justifying his attribution of these formations to the Quaternary, Ribeiro (1866, pp. 59–62) acknowledged his doubts and reservations. He gave several geological reasons that indicated a Tertiary age for the region in question (Ribeiro 1866, p. 60). The lacrustine deposits were concordant with marine Tertiary formations. The deposits were of great thickness, and in some places were greatly deformed. Furthermore, the normal kinds of Quaternary shells were absent from them. He then said, "It is therefore not very surprising that when we encountered worked flints in these formations, subjacent to the conglomerates of Carregado, we were greatly astonished. But because the authenticity of the discovery was incontestable, and because of the incontestablity of the human remains later encountered at other localities, where the sandy part of the deposit had been greatly eroded, we were forced to refer to the Quaternary all of the sandstone rock that constitutes the surface of the Otta depression, and along with that a great portion of the sandstone rock of the same kind that covers the left side of the Tagus valley" (Ribeiro 1866, p. 60).

In this monograph on the implements he discovered, Ribeiro (1871, p. 52) gave a similar account of his early astonishment: "At first we believed we had become subjected to an illusion. We tried to persuade ourselves that the chipped flints and quartzites presented no signs of human work. But that effort was contradicted by the clear evidence of such signs. As the number of specimens increased, and the conditions of their provenance became better understood, our conviction became stronger and stronger as to the true origin of the objects. Finally, it became necessary to announce the proofs, the inconstestable indications shown by the stone objects, which had been held by human hands before they were covered by the beds from which we extracted them."

8. A most interesting collection of documents related to the Congrès International d'Anthropologie et d'Archéologie Préhistoriques of 1880 can be found in the historical archives of the library of the Institute of Geology and Mining in Alfragide, Lisbon (Armario 6, Prataleira 3, Maço 69, IXe Congresso de Antropologia e Arqueuologia, Lisboa 1880). The documents include numerous drafts of the conference schedules, lists of participants, lists of hotels and restaurants, etc., many apparently in Ribeiro's handwriting. Also to be found are the stenographic copies of papers delivered at the Congress, letters of invitation, and other correspondence. In total, they provide an excellent picture of the whole process of organizing an international scientific conference in nineteenth-century Europe, from the first letters of invitation to the final details of publishing the proceedings. The Congress was held in the ornate main hall of the

library in the building housing the Academia das Ciências, located on the floor below the Museu Geológico. The hall, still there today, is worth a visit.

9. In July, 2000, I retraced the commission's route. There is a road leading east from Otta to Aveiras de Cima. Just as this road leaves Otta, one turns onto a small dirt road leading north, and following it, one eventually comes to Monte Redondo [see Plate I, Figure 3]. Monte Redondo and the surrounding area remain in a natural condition, undisturbed by any construction. The area has, however, been reforested with trees not native to Portugal. Although I suspect the landscape has changed somewhat, ravines on the southern slopes of Monte Redondo, like those described in the report of the conference expedition, are still visible [see Plate I, Figure 4]. Their profiles resemble the one figured by de Mortillet (1883, p. 101).

10. At the Tenth Congress in 1889, Villanova claimed that de Mortillet's figure (1883, p. 101) showing the position of Belluci's discovery at Otta was inaccurate. Villanova maintained that the artifact was not found in the interior of the bed, but on the surface (Delgado 1889, p. 531). But the figure does not show the implement was found inside the bed. It is in fact shown on a surface, the under surface of a ledge, and thus appears to me accurate. De Mortillet was present at Otta when the discovery was made, and his account seems reliable.

11. In the various collections of artifacts from Otta in the Museu Geológico, one can see some bearing numbers with red or blue underlining.

12. De Mortillet stated: "If we see in the flint objects found at Thenay signs of intentional work, we can only conclude it was not the work of anatomically modern human beings but of another human species, probably representative of a genus of human precursors that fills the gap between humans and animals" (de Quatrefages 1884, pp. 81–82). De Mortillet called this precursor genus *Anthropopitheque*, existing in three species, the oldest, that of Thenay, being the link with the apes. Thenay is the site of the early Miocene discoveries reported by Bourgeois (1873). The other two species were the makers of the flint tools found by Ribeiro in Portugal and by Rames at Aurillac, in France (de Mortillet 1883, p. 97). "For de Mortillet," stated de Quatrefages (1884, pp. 82–83), "the existence of *anthropopitheques* in Tertiary times is a necessary consequence of Darwinist doctrines."

13. In the *Pithecanthropus erectus* discovery, Dubois associated a femur with a skullcap. Considering the historical impact of *Pithecanthropus* on consideration of evidence for Tertiary humans, it is noteworthy that modern researchers no longer consider the association genuine. When Day and Molleson (1973) carefully reexamined the femur, they found it not different from anatomically modern human femurs and distinct from all other *erectus* femurs.

14. Leakey herself (1979, p. 453) said the prints were exactly like anatomically modern human footprints, a judgement shared by some physical anthropologists (Tuttle 1981, p. 91; 1987, p. 517). Tim White said, "Make no mistake about it. They are like modern human footprints" (Johanson and Edey 1981, p. 250). Some have suggested that an australopithecine could have made the prints. But such proposals were not supported by a complete *Australopithecus* foot. White and Suwa (1987) attempted to put together such a foot (using bones from three different hominids of different genera),

but the exercise was quite speculative. In 1995, Clarke and Tobias reported the discovery of a partial *Australopithecus* foot from Sterkfontein (Bower 1995), and in 1998 announced the discovery of a fairly complete australopithecine skeleton, to which the foot bones had originally been attached. The partial foot reported in 1995 featured a big toe that was long and divergent, like that of a chimpanzee. Like White and Suwa, Tobias and Clarke used bones from East African hominids to reconstruct a complete foot, which Tobias said matched the Laetoli prints (Bower 1995). However, physical anthropologist Michael Day asserted that the Sterkfontein foot could not have made the Laetoli footprints and questioned the accuracy of a reconstruction that made use of bones from different parts of Africa (Bower 1995). Stern and Susman (1983) proposed that an australopithecine foot with long toes curled under made the prints. But others (Tuttle 1985, p. 132; White and Suwa 1987, p. 495) pointed out that the prints showed no knuckle marks, and that surely, in the case of so many prints some would have shown the extended toes. Deloison (1997) claimed, in opposition to almost all previous reporting, that the Laetoli prints displayed distinctly primate (chimpanzoid) features. Others (Tuttle *et al.* 1998) replied that Deloison's observations were "false interpretations based on artifactual taphonomic features, reliance on a partial sample of the . . . first generation casts of the Laetoli prints, and her not accounting for the orientation of the prints on the trackway."

15. According to Oakley (1980, p. 40), the nitrogen content of the Castenedolo bones was similar to that of human bones from the Italian Late Pleistocene and Holocene. But nitrogen preservation varies from site to site, problematizing such comparisons. Oakley (1980, p. 42) reported a high fluorine content for the bones. Low fluorine levels in local groundwater indicated a potentially great age for the bones, but Oakley explained this away by positing higher levels of groundwater fluorine in the recent past. The Castenedolo bones also had an unexpectedly high concentration of uranium, another indicator of great age. A radiocarbon date of less than one thousand years was obtained in 1969 (Barker *et al.* 1971), using a method not adequate to prevent falsely young dates caused by contamination with recent carbon. Ragazzoni's original stratigraphic observations provide the most reliable age estimate.

16. I received my copy of *The Earliest Occupation of Europe* from Wil Roebroeks in Amsterdam, where he visited me for a conversation about *Forbidden Archeology* in October of 1997. I later gave a lecture to some of his students at the University of Leiden.

17. It is encouraging that Roebroeks and van Kolfschoten (1995, p. 297) at least acknowledge in a very general way evidence of the kind reported by Ribeiro, although they do not mention him directly: "One century ago, Palaeolithic archeologists were involved in a fierce debate over the alleged existence of Tertiary humans in Europe. Eolithphiles, both on the continent and Europe, presented thousands of flints from Tertiary deposits, that in their opinion were human worked implements." Regarding the material from the Iberian peninsula, they say (1995, p. 305): "Iberian river terraces have yielded isolated pieces, whose human manufacture or precise age have been doubted by various researchers. . . . Claims for the existence of Early Pleistocene artefacts and human fossils come from localities in the Gaudix-Baza basin near Orca-Vente Micena, but further fieldwork is necessary to turn these claims into compelling

evidence." Again, the point is that these sites, although controversial and not accepted by the authors, are at least acknowledged.

18. Prasad attributed the tool to *Ramapithecus,* then accepted by some researchers as being the first hominid. Since then, *Ramapithecus* has been dropped from the hominid line.

19. A proposal by me for an exhibit of Ribeiro's artifacts was approved by the organizers of the European Association of Archaeologists 2000 annual meeting in Lisbon, but after an initial expression of interest by the director of the Museu Geológico, the plan was dropped by him for unspecified reasons.

References

Antunes, M. T., M. P. Ferreira, R. B. Rocha, A. F. Soares, and G. Zbyszewski (1980) Portugal: cycle alpin. In J. Delecourt (ed), *Géologie des Pays Européens, Vol. 3.* Paris: Bordas, pp. 103–149.

Barker, H., R. Burleigh, and N. Meeks (1971) British Museum natural radiocarbon measurements VII. *Radiocarbon,* 13: 157–188.

Boule, M. and H. V. Vallois (1957) *Fossil Men.* London: Thames and Hudson.

Bourgeois, L. (1873) Sur les silex considérés comme portant les margues d'un travail humain et découverts dans le terrain miocène de Thenay. *Congrès International d'Anthropologie et d'Archéologie Préhistoriques, Bruxelles 1872, Compte Rendu,* pp. 81–92.

Bower, B. (1995) Hominid bones show strides toward walking. *Science News,* 148: 71.

Breuil, H. and G. Zbyszewski (1942–1945) Contribution á l'étude des industries paléolithiques du Portugal et de leurs rapports avec la géologie du Quaternarie. Vol. I., Les principaux gisements des deux rives de l'ancien estuaire du Tage. *Communicaçöes dos Serviços Geológicos de Portugal,* pp. 23, 26.

Calvert, F. (1874) On the probable existence of man during the Miocene period. *Journal of the Royal Anthropological Institute of Great Britain and Ireland,* 3: 127.

Choffat, P. (1884a) Excursion à Otta. *Congrès International d'Anthropologie et d'Archéologie Préhistoriques, Lisbon, 1880, Compte Rendu,* pp. 61–67.

Choffat, P. (1884b) Conclusions de la commission chargée de l'examen des silex trouvés à Otta. Followed by discussion. *Congrès International d'Anthropologie et d'Archéologie Préhistoriques, Lisbon, 1880, Compte Rendu,* pp. 92–118.

Cicha, I. (1970) *Stratigraphical Problems of the Miocene in Europe.* Prague: Czechslovak Academy of Sciences.

Cremo, M. A. (1999) Puranic time and the archaeological record. In T. Murray (ed). *Time and Archaeology.* London: Routledge, pp. 38–48.

Cremo, M. A., forthcoming. Forbidden archeology of the Paleolithic: how *Pithecanthropus* influenced the treatment of evidence for extreme human antiquity. In A. Martins (ed). *Proceedings of the history of archeology section. European Association of Archaeologists 1999 Annual Meeting, Bournemouth, England.* Oxford: British Archaeological Reports. [Note: the volume was never published.]

Cremo, M. A. and R. L. Thompson (1993) *Forbidden Archeology: The Hidden History of the Human Race*. San Diego: Bhaktivedanta Institute.

Day, M. H. and T. I. Molleson (1973) The Trinil femora. *Symposia of the Society for the Study of Human Biology*, 2: 127–154.

Delgado, J. .F. Nery (1889) Les silex tertiaires d'Otta. *Congrès International d'Anthropologie et d'Archéologie Préhistoriques, Dixième Session, 1889, Paris, Compte Rendu*, pp. 529–533.

Delgado, J. F. Nery (1905) *Elogio Historico do General Carlos Ribeiro*. Associação dos Engenheiros Civis Portuguezes. Lisbon: Imprensa Nacional.

Deloison, Y. M-L. (1997) The foot bones from Hadar, Ethiopia and the Laetoli, Tanzania footprints. Locomotion of *A. afarensis*. *American Journal of Physical Anthropology* supplement no. 24 (AAPA abstracts), p. 101.

De Mortillet, G. (1883) *Le Préhistorique*. Paris: C. Reinwald.

De Mortillet, G. and A. Demortillet (1881) *Musée Préhistorique*. Paris: C. Reinwald.

De Quatrefages, A. (1884) *Hommes Fossiles et Hommes Sauvages*. Paris: B. Baillière.

Garrigou, F. and H. Filhol (1868) M. Garrigou prie l'Académie de vouloir bien ouvrir un pli cacheté, déposé au nom de M. Filhol fils et au sien, le 16 mai 1864. *Compte Rendus de l'Académie des Sciences*, 66: 819–820.

Holmes, W. H. (1899) Review of the evidence relating to auriferous gravel man in California. In *Smithsonian Institution Annual Report 1898–1899*. Washington, D. C.: Smithsonian Institution, pp. 419–472.

Issel, A. (1868) Résumé des recherches concernant l'ancienneté de l'homme en Ligurie. *Congrès International d'Anthropologie et d'Archéologie Préhistoriques, Paris 1867, Compte Rendu*, pp. 75–89.

Johanson, D. and M. A. Edey (1981) *Lucy: The Beginnings of Humankind*. New York: Simon and Schuster.

Leakey, M. D. (1979) Footprints in the ashes of time. *National Geographic*, 155: 446–457.

Noetling, F. (1894) On the occurrence of chipped flints in the Upper Miocene of Burma. *Records of the Geological Survey of India*, 27: 101–103.

Oakley, K. P. (1980) Relative dating of fossil hominids of Europe. *Bulletin of the British Museum of Natural History (Geology)*, p. 34.

Onoratini, G., M. Ahmanou, A. Defleur, and J. C. Plaziat (1990) Découverte, prés de Fès (Maroc), d'une industrie Acheuléense au sommet des calcaires (Saïssiens) réputés Pliocènes. *L'Anthropologie*, 94(2): 321–334.

Patterson, L.W. (1983) Criteria for determining the attributes of man-made lithics. *Journal of Field Archaeology*, 10: 297–307.

Patterson, L. W., L. V. Hoffman, R. M. Higginbotham, and R. D. Simpson (1987) Analysis of lithic flakes at the Calico site, California. *Journal of Field Archaeology*, 14: 91–106.

Prasad, K. N. (1982) Was *Ramapithecus* a tool-user. *Journal of Human Evolution*, 11: 101–104.

Ragazzoni, G. (1880) La collina di Castenedolo, solto il rapporto antropologico, geologico ed agronomico. *Commentari dell' Ateneo di Brescia* April 4, pp. 120–128.

Raposo, L. and M. Santonja (1995) The earliest occupation of Europe: the Iberian peninsula. In W. Roebroeks and T. Van Kolfschoten (eds) *The Earliest Occupation of Europe. Proceedings of the European Science Foundation Workshop At Tautavel (France), 1993. Analecta Praehistorica Leidensia, Vol. 27*. Leiden: University of Leiden, pp. 7–25.

Ribeiro, C. (1865) *Relatorio da Commissão Geologica de Portugal, Correspondente ao Anno Economico de 1864–65. Serviço Geologico Relatorios Annos Desde 1857-ate ao Fin do Anno Economico de 1864–1865.* Instituto Geológico e Mineiro. Núcleo de Biblioteca e Publicaçoes, Lisbon. Arquivo Historico. Armario 1, Prataleira 2, Maço 9, Correspendência de Carlos Ribeiro, Pasta 6.

Ribeiro, C. (1866) *Descripção do Terreno Quaternario das Bacias dos Rios Tejos e Sado. Com a Versão Franceza por M. Dalhunty.* Lisbon: Typographia da Academia Real das Sciencias.

Ribeiro, C. (1867) Note sur le terrain quaternaire du Portugal. *Bulletin de la Socièté Géologique de France,* 2nd series, 24: 692.

Ribeiro, C. (1871) *Description de quelques Silex et Quartzites Taillés Provenant des Couches du Terrain Tertiaire et du Quaternaire des Bassins du Tage et du Sado.* Lisbon: Academia Real das Sciencias de Lisboa.

Ribeiro, C., (1873a) Sur des silex taillés, découverts dans les terrains miocène du Portugal. *Congrès International d'Anthropologie et d'Archéologie Préhistoriques, Bruxelles 1872, Compte Rendu,* pp. 95–100.

Ribeiro, C. (1873b) Sur la position géologique des couches miocènes et pliocènes du Portugal qui contiennent des silex taillés. *Congrès International d'Anthropologie et d'Archéologie Préhistoriques, Bruxelles 1872, Compte Rendu,* pp. 100–104.

Ribeiro, C. (1884) L'homme tertiaire en Portugal. *Congrès International d'Anthropologie et d'Archéologie Préhistoriques, Lisbon, 1880, Compte Rendu,* pp. 81–91.

Ribeiro, C. and J. F. Nery Delgado (1867) *Carta Geologica de Portugal na Escala 1:500000.*

Ribeiro, C. and J. F. Nery Delgado (1876) *Carta Geologica de Portugal na Escala 1:500000.*

Roebroeks, W. and T. Van Kolfschoten, eds, (1995) *The Earliest Occupation of Europe. Proceedings of the European Science Foundation Workshop At Tautavel (France), 1993. Analecta Praehistorica Leidensia, Vol. 27.* Leiden: University of Leiden.

Sankhyan, A. R. (1981) First evidence of early man from Haritalyangar area, Himalchal Pradesh. *Science and Culture,* 47: 358–359.

S. Semaw, P. Renne, J. W. K. Harris, C. S. Feibel, R. L. Bernor, N. Fesseha and K. Mowbray (1997) 2.5-million-year-old stone tools from Gona, Ethiopia. *Nature,* 385: 333–336.

Steele, J. (1999) Stone legacy of skilled hands. *Nature,* 399: 24–25.

Stern, Jr., J. T. and R. L. Susman (1983) The locomotor anatomy of *Australopithecus afarensis. American Journal of Physical Anthropology,* 60: 279–318.

Tuttle, R. H. (1981) Evolution of hominid bipedalism and prehensile capabilities. *Philosophical Transactions of the Royal Society of London B,* 292: 89–94.

Tuttle, R. H. (1985) Ape footprints and Laetoli impressions: a response to the SUNY claims. In P. V. Tobias (ed). *Hominid Evolution: Past, Present, and Future.* New

York: Alan R. Liss, pp. 129–133.

Tuttle, R. H. (1987) Kinesiological inferences and evolutionary implications from La-etoli biped trails G-1, G-2/3, and A. In M. D. Leakey and J. Harris (eds). *Laetoli: A Pliocene Site in Northern Tanzania*. Oxford: Clarendon Press, pp. 508–517.

Tuttle, R. H., C. Musiba, D. M. Webb, and B. Hallgrimsson (1998) False impressions from the Laetoli Hominid footprints. *American Journal of Physical Anthropology* supplement 26 (AAPA abstracts), p. 221.

Verworn, M. (1905) Die archaeolithische Cultur in den Hipparionschichten von Auril-lac (Cantal). *Abhandlungen der königlichen Gesellschaft der Wissenschaften zu Göt-tingen, Mathematisch-Physikalische Klasse, Neue Folge*, 4(4): 3–60.

Von Dücker, Baron (1873) Sur la cassure artificelle d'ossements recuellis dans le terrain miocène de Pikermi. *Congrès International d'Anthropologie et d'Archéologie Préhis-toriques. Bruxelles 1872, Compte Rendu*, pp. 104–107.

White, T. D. and G. Suwa (1987) Hominid footprints at Laetoli: facts and interpreta-tions. *American Journal of Physical Anthropology*, 72: 485–514.

Whitney, J. D. (1880) The auriferous gravels of the Sierra Nevada of California. *Har-vard University, Museum of Comparative Zoology Memoir* 6(1).

Zbyszewski, G. and O. da Veiga Ferreira (1966) *Carta Geológica de Portugal Na Escala 1/50,000. Notícia Explicativa da Folha 30-B Bombarral*. Lisbon: Serviço Geológicos de Portugal. See also the actual map, published separately.

13

Paleobotanical Anomalies Bearing on the Age of the Salt Range Formation of Pakistan: A Historical Survey of an Unresolved Scientific Controversy

I presented this paper at the XXIst International Congress of History of Science, which was held in Mexico City, July 8–14, 2001. As a member of the History of Science Society, I applied for and received a travel grant from the National Science Foundation of the United States of America, administered through the History of Science Society, to attend the conference and give this paper. It is probably one of the few times in its history that the NSF gave a grant to an antievolutionist to present an antievolutionary paper at an academic conference.

Introduction

For well over a century the Salt Range Mountains of Pakistan have attracted the special attention of geologists. Starting in the foothills of the Himalayas in northeastern Pakistan, the Salt Range Mountains run about 150 miles in a westerly direction, roughly parallel to the Jhelum River until it joins the Indus. The Salt Range Mountains then extend some distance beyond the Indus. The southern edge of the eastern Salt Range Mountains drops steeply two or three thousand feet to the Jhelum River plain. In this escarpment and other locations, the Salt Range Mountains expose a series of formations ranging from the earliest Cambrian to the most recent geological periods. Such exposures are rarely encountered and are thus of great interest to geologists and other earth scientists. At the bottom of the series, beneath the Cambrian Purple Sandstone, lies the Salt Range Formation, composed of thick layers of reddish, clayey material (the Salt Marl) in which are found layers of rock salt, gypsum, shale, and dolomite. For centuries, the salt has been mined and traded widely in the northern part of the Indian subcontinent. Ever since professional geologists began studying the Salt Range Mountains in the middle part of the nineteenth century, the age of the Salt Range Formation has been a topic of extreme controversy. Some held that it was of early Cambrian antiquity, while others were certain the Salt Range Formation was far more recent. The controversy intensified in the twentieth century when scientists discovered remains of advanced plants in the Salt Range Formation. In this paper, I shall review the history of the controversy, focusing on its paleobotanical aspect, and then

181

comment on the controversy's importance to historical studies of science and to the study of science and religion.

The History of the Controversy

Scientific investigation of the Salt Range Formation began in the nineteenth century, when Pakistan was part of British India. The Cambrian age of the overlying Purple Sandstone, which contains trilobites, was generally undisputed. But there were various opinions about the age and origin of the Salt Range Formation, usually found beneath the Purple Sandstone. Questions also arose about the relative ages of the Salt Range Formation and the Kohat salt deposits, located to the north of the Salt Range Mountains.

A. B. Wynne (1878, p. 83) surveyed the Salt Range Mountains in 1869–71 and concluded that the Salt Range Formation was a normal sedimentary deposit of Paleozoic age. This view was shared by H. Warth, who had extensive knowledge of the region gathered over twenty years (Wynne 1878, p. 73). Wynne and Warth thought the Kohat salt formations were younger, perhaps Tertiary (Wynne 1875, pp.32–37). These views were shared by W. T. Blanford (Medlicott and Blanford 1879 v. 2, p. 488).

Later, C. S. Middlemiss of the Geological Survey of India (1891, p. 42) proposed that the Salt Marl was not a sedimentary formation. It was instead a secretion from an underlying layer of magma that had intruded beneath the Cambrian Purple Sandstone. R. D. Oldham (1893, p. 112), superintendent of the Geological Survey of India, came to a similar conclusion. This opened up the possiblity that the Salt Range Formation was younger than the overlying Cambrian Purple Sandstone.

The German geologist F. Noetling originally thought the Salt Range Formation was Precambrian (Zuber 1914, p. 334). But in a paper published in 1903 (Koken and Noetling, p. 35), Noetling said the Cambrian Purple Sandstone was the oldest formation in the Salt Range Mountains and assigned the underlying Salt Range Formation a much more recent age, without explicit explanation. Holland (1903, p. 26) reported that Noetling believed that the Cambrian Purple Sandstone and other overlying formations had been pushed over the Salt Range Formation by a massive overthrust. According to this idea, the Salt Range Formation was a normal deposit, the same age as the Eocene salt deposits of the Kohat region, just north of the Salt Range Mountains. This overthrust version was accepted by Zuber (1914).

W. Christie (1914), chemist for the Geological Survey of India, held that the Salt Range Formation was not of igneous origin, as proposed by Middlemiss. He found it to be a normal sedimentary deposit, produced by evaporation of seawater, but he did not say when this occurred.

Murray Stuart (1919) agreed with Christie that the Salt Range Formation was a normal sedimentary deposit. According to Stuart, both the salt deposits in the Salt Range and Kohat regions were both of early Cambrian or Precambrian age. In the Kohat region, the salt lies directly below the "nummulitic" limestones, from the Eocene. Stuart explained this by proposing that an overthrust had removed the Paleozoic and Mesozoic layers, which are found overlying the Salt Range Formation 20 miles away.

In 1920, E. H. Pascoe, in considering all the previous reports, came up with his own conclusion. The Salt Range Formation was a normal sedimentary deposit, of Tertiary (Eocene) age, as was the Kohat salt deposit. Pascoe also believed the Purple Sandstone overlying the Salt Range Formation to be Eocene. The position of the Salt Range Formation and the Purple Sandstone below other formations of Cambrian antiquity was attributed to a massive overthrust.

Robert Van Vleck Anderson (1927) gave the first report of botanical fossil remains from the Salt Range Formation. He noted the presence of "poorly preserved impressions of leaves of a Tertiary or, at earliest, Mesozoic type." The impressions came from shale deposits at Khewra Gorge in the Salt Range. He gave samples to Dr. Ralph W. Chaney of the Carnegie Institution, who said:

"This specimen clearly contains fragments of several specimens of dicotyledonous leaves. This places their age as not older than the Lower Cretaceous when the first dicots appeared. One of the leaves is very probably oak (*Quercus*) and its size and margin strongly suggest the Oligocene species *Quercus clarnensis* from western America. It is of interest to note that I found a closely related species in the Oligocene deposits of Manchuria. Your specimen is almost certainly of Tertiary age" (Anderson 1927, p. 672). From this evidence, Anderson argued for a Tertiary age for the Salt Range Formation as well as the Kohat Salt. The presence of Cambrian layers above the Salt Range Formation was attributed by him to an overthrust.

In 1928, Cyril S. Fox published a study concluding that both the Salt Range and Kohat salt deposits were early Cambrian or Precambrian. He saw no signs of an overthrust. He did not mention Anderson's discoveries.

In his presidential address to the geology section of the Eighteenth Indian Science Congress, G. Cotter (1931, p. 296) disputed Anderson's report of leaf impressions found in the Salt Range Formation. He noted that E. R. Gee had searched the same locality in January 1929 and found no new specimens. Cotter joined Gee for another search in March 1929 and also found no new specimens. Cotter noted that they found "carbonaceous markings, some of which simulated broad leaf impressions." But they were in his opinion "not plant fossils."

Anderson then sent to the Geological Survey of India office his best *Quercus* specimen. Cotter considered it "doubtful." But Pascoe (1930, p. 25) said that the specimen had perhaps been damaged by friction during transit, making it "undeterminable." Pascoe expressed a hope that the specimen had been photographed before it was shipped, but there is no record of such a photograph in Anderson's reports. Some of Anderson's specimens were sent to Professor B. Sahni at Oxford, who, according to Cotter, thought that "the specimens, if they were plants at all, were quite indeterminate."

Cotter (1931, p. 299) also made this interesting observation: "About the year 1924 a large trunk of wood of a modern type and scarcely at all decomposed was found in the salt in the upper tunnel of the Khewra mine. Dr. Dunn, who examined this wood states that the trunk was about 2 ft. in diameter, and that there were several branches associated with it of about 3 to 4 inches in diameter. Prof. Sahni regarded this wood as modern and resembling an *Acacia* now found growing in the Salt Range."

Cotter, after considering all arguments pro and con, said he favored a pre-Cambrian age for the Salt Range Formation (1931, p. 300). But before his paper expressing this view went to press, Cotter examined occurences of nummulites, fossil formanifera typical of the Tertiary, discovered by E. R. Gee in the salt marl at Khewra. Cotter, who had originally thought they had been washed into the Salt Range Formation from younger deposits, decided they were native to the Salt Range Formation. In a footnote added to his paper before publication, Cotter (1931, p. 300) reversed the position stated in the paper and declared the Salt Range Formation to be Tertiary. But he regarded it as intrusive, which would explain its position beneath the Cambrian Purple Sandstone. According to Cotter (1933, p. 151), the plastic salt, of Eocene age, was somehow squeezed by geological pressure and other forces into an abnormal positon.

Cotter (1933, p. 150) said that the Khewra nummulites discovered by Gee "occurred in association with plant fragments." He further noted (Cotter 1933, pp. 150–151) that "plant fragments were also found by Mr. Gee in the Salt Marl at the Nila Wahan." Pascoe (1959, p. 569) cites a 1933 report that at Kalra Wahan, a sample of salt marl "yielded not only carbonised stem fragments but also several small leaves of apparently dicotyledenous type." Pascoe (1930, p. 132) also noted that Gee found a small piece of fossil wood in the reddish marls of the Salt Range Formation.

Gee (1934) gave his own opinion about the age of the Salt Range Formation, which he called "the Saline series." He concluded that both it and the Kohat salt deposits were of the same Eocene age. The Kohat salt was in its normal position, but Gee (1934, p. 461) noted that "a very regular thrust of immense dimensions must be postulated in order to explain the present position of the Saline series beneath the early Paleozoics (or pre-Cambrian)." Concerning foraminifera found by him in Salt Range Formation deposits, he admitted that they might be derived from more recent formations (Gee 1934, p. 463; Fermor 1935, p. 64). But Gee (1934, p. 463) noted, "Plant fragments, however, have been found not only in beds of doubtful age but also in beds which are regarded as being definitely *in situ* in the Saline series." He regarded this as evidence the Salt Range Formation was not Cambrian.

Some years later, B. Sahni, then a paleobotanist at the University of Lucknow, reported the existence of numerous plant microfossils in samples taken from the Salt Range Formation at the Khewra and Warcha salt mines. Previously, doubt had been cast on plant fossils from the Salt Range Formation. Critics, said Sahni (1944, p. 462), had pointed out that "in such a highly soluble and plastic substance as the Salt Marl, extraneous material might have penetrated through solution holes or have been enveloped during relatively modern earth movements."

But deep within the mines, Sahni found deposits where such objections could not apply. The salt in these places ran in layers separated by thin layers of saline earth, locally called "kallar." Sahni (1944, p. 462) noted that "the kallar lies closely interlaminated with the salt, in beds which run continuously for long distances and which, although visibly tilted, show no other visible signs of disturbance."

According to Sahni, the salt layers accumulated from evaporation of sea water in coastal lagoons, whereas the kallar represented dust and dirt blown on to the drying salt by the wind. Sahni guessed that the kallar might contain pollen and other plant microfossils. When he examined specimens, he found this to be so (Sahni 1944, p. 462):

". . . every single piece has yielded microfossils. . . . The great majority are undeterminable as to genus and species, being mainly shreds of angiosperm wood, but there are also gymnosperm tracheids with large round bordered pits, and at least one good, winged, six-legged insect with compound eyes." To Sahni, this meant that the Salt Range Formation must be Eocene rather than Cambrian. Sahni later found plant fragments not only in the kallar, but in associated solid rock layers composed of dolomite and shale.

Around this same time, the Geological Survey of India and an oil company sent a team of geologists to carefully study the Salt Range Formation, and on the basis of their field observations they concluded that it was in normal position below the Cambrian Purple Sandstone and was thus Cambrian in age. This conclusion was announced in a letter to *Nature* (Coates *et al.* 1945). Among the geologists signing the letter was Gee, until recently an advocate of an Eocene age for the Salt Range Formation. The geologists admitted, however, that "our conclusions were arrived at despite certain difficulties, such as the occurrence of minute plant fragments of post-Cambrian age in the dolomites and oil shales, for which we have at present no clear explanation to offer." In other words, it might be possible to explain the presence of plant fragments in the soluble salt layers, but how did they get into solid rock such as dolomite and shale? This line of reasoning is based on the assumption that land plants did not come into being until the Silurian, with advanced plants such as angiosperms not arising until the Cretaceous.

In his presidential address to India's National Academy of Sciences in 1944, Sahni (1945) introduced numerous examples of pollen, wood fragments, and insect parts found in samples of kallar, dolomite, and shale from the Salt Range Formation. In his report, Sahni (1945, p. x) said that "stringent precautions" were taken to prevent contamination of the samples with modern organic remains. He also emphasized that samples were taken from locations where the geological evidence ruled out intrusion from younger strata.

The laboratory techniques employed by Sahni and his assistant, B. S. Trivedi, were rigorous. In a demonstration at a symposium, said Sahni (1945, p. xiv) "a piece of carbonised wood was revealed in a tiny block of dolomite . . . which had been cut and polished on all sides to show it had no pits or cracks visible even with a strong pocket lens. The block was, as usual, passed through a flame and then plunged into a jar of filtered dilute HCl."

In his own address to the National Academy of Sciences, Gee (1945, p. 293) concluded that the Salt Range Formation was a normal sedimentary deposit and in its original position below the Purple Sandstone. This meant it was Cambrian or Precambrian (Gee 1945, p. 305), while Kohat salt was Eocene. This was a change from his earlier opinion that the Salt Range Formation was Eocene (Gee 1934). He saw no compelling evidence for a massive overthrust in the region (Gee 1945, p. 305). Pascoe, formerly a supporter of the idea that the Salt Range Formation was an Eocene deposit covered by an overthrust, placed the Salt Range Formation in the Cambrian section of a new edition of his *Manual of the Geology of India* (Sahni 1947b, p. xxxi).

Gee said that foraminifera of Eocene type found by him in the Salt Range Formation were not *in situ,* as he earlier believed, but were derived from younger formations. Concerning plant fragments, Gee (1945, p. 296) noted: "Further work on the clay containing plant fragments at Katha led to the discovery of one or two small leaf impressions which were identified by Prof. B. Sahni as belonging to *Acacia*, a genus still existing in the Salt Range area, whilst in the case of the Khewra mine occurrences, the existence of an important thrust-fault nearby, running roughly parallel to the seams of rocksalt, indicated an alternative explanation for the occurrence of these plant fragments." Gee thought they might have been introduced into the salt in relatively recent times.

Concerning the Katha finds, Gee relied on the assumption that *Acacia* is quite recent, and could not possibly have existed in the Cambrian. Concerning the Khewra finds, Gee used the existence of a fault to explain the presence of advanced plants in a formation he regarded as Cambrian. But he did not explain how close the thrust fault was to the exact places where he recovered plant fragments nor whether the stratification showed any obvious signs of local disturbance. The fact that the salt was still arranged in seams, apparently unbroken, leaves open the possibility that the plant fragments were found *in situ*.

Gee (1945, p. 297) found Anderson's leaf impressions unconvincing, calling them "unidentifiable brownish markings, possibly organic." Gee (1945, p. 299) saw signs of organic deposits in the shales and dolomites of the Salt Range Formation, but characterized them as "too primitive to include resistant skeletons or woody tissues such as might be preserved."

Gee was, however, seriously troubled by the discoveries of Sahni, which were based on careful observation and laboratory work. Apparently, Sahni had demonstrated the existence of advanced plant remains, including woody tissues, not only in the salt and dolomites of the Salt Range Formation but in other kinds of rock as well, such as shale. About the salt and dolomites, Gee proposed that plant fragments could have been introduced into them by "percolating water." But this explanation would not, said Gee (1945, p. 307) apply to the extremely resistant oil shales, in which Sahni had also found microfossils. Gee (1945, p. 306) noted that if Sahni, on the basis of his plant fossils, was correct in assigning an Eocene age to the Salt Range Formation, "then it will be necessary to modify our views regarding the essential characteristics of normal sedimentary and tectonic contacts." According to standard geological reasoning these indicated a Cambian age.

At the Indian National Academy of Sciences annual meeting for 1945, the Salt Range Formation was once more a topic of extended debate. Sahni (1947a, 1947b) gave reports of additional discoveries of angiosperm and gymnosperm microfossils from the salt marl, the oil shales, and dolomites at all levels of the Salt Range Formation. Microfossils of advanced plants were also recovered from core samples from deep borings in the Khewra salt mine. Sahni (1947b, pp. xxxi–xxxvi) gave convincing evidence that the microfossils were not intrusive contaminations. Furthermore, at scientific gatherings in Great Britain, Sahni (1947b, p. xxxix) demonstrated to geologists his laboratory techniques and obtained "fragments of woody tissue" from samples of the Salt Range Formation's dolomites and oil shales.

Sahni (1947a, p. 243) added that "in a fragment of Mr. Anderson's original material several microfragments of wood have been found." This would tend to support Anderson's identification of leaf imprints in his material from Khewra Gorge. Sahni had accompanied Gee and others to Anderson's site, and had found no similar specimens. Sahni (1947b, p. xx) noted that these circumstances "do not by any means cast a doubt upon the identification of Mr. Anderson's specimen as an oak leaf." Sahni (1947b, p. xx) also noted: "As it turned out, we had been searching at the wrong place." Anderson's oak leaf imprint had come from a spot lower than that searched, and some distance away.

Concerning the advanced nature of the plant and insect microfossils found in the Salt Range Formation, Sahni (1947b, pp. xlv–xlvi) noted: "Quite recently, an alternative explanation has been offered by Mr. Gee. *The suggestion is that the angiosperms, gymnosperms and insects of the Saline Series may represent a highly evolved Cambrian or Precambrian flora and fauna!* In other words, it is suggested that these plants and animals made their appearance in the Salt Range area several hundred million years earlier than they did anywhere else in the world. One would scarcely have believed that such an idea would be seriously put forward by any geologist today."

Gee, by questioning basic evolutionary assumptions about the progression of life forms on earth, introduces another possible solution to the Salt Range Formation controversy. Up to this point, the relatively late appearance of the angiosperms, gymnosperms, and certain insects had been taken for granted. Evidence of their presence in the Salt Range Formation had to be resolved by (1) suggesting they were intrusive into the formation, which was of Cambrian age or (2) suggesting that they were native to the formation proving it was Eocene and invoking a massive overthrust to account for the formation's presence below formations generally accepted as Cambrian. Supporters of the former proposal, including Gee, were troubled, however, by the strength of Sahni's evidence for the *in situ* status of his microfossils. So Gee suggested that perhaps the Salt Range Formation is, after all, Cambrian, as the geological evidence strongly suggested, and the microfossils of angiosperms, gymnosperms, and insects were *in situ*. This could only mean that the angiosperms, gymnosperms, and insects evolved far earlier than allowed by any current evolutionary account. It was a bold proposal, but fell on deaf ears at the time.

Subsequently, evidence for angiosperms and gymnosperms was also found in other beds of Cambrian age overlying the Salt Range Formation. These included microfossils of angiosperms and gymnosperms from the Salt Pseudomorph Beds (Ghosh and Bose, 1947), gymnosperms from the Purple Sandstone (Ghosh, *et al.*, 1948), wood fragments from the Neobolus Shales (Ghosh, *et al.*, 1948), and wood fragments from the Magnesian Sandstone (Ghosh, *et al.*, 1948).

Ghosh and Bose (1950, p. 76) proposed two possible explanations for this evidence of advanced vascular plants in the above-mentioned formations: "1. The geologically known Cambrian beds are of post-Cambrian age. 2. The vascular plants existed in Cambrian or pre-Cambrian times." Ghosh and Bose rejected the first proposal because geologists unanimously agreed that the beds in question were in fact Cambrian. Ghosh and Bose found the second proposal more likely, even though it was "inconsistent with the prevailing concepts of plant phylogeny." They pointed out that there had been discoveries of advanced plant remains in beds of similar age in Sweden (Darrah 1937) and in the USSR (Sahni 1947b, in note following plates).

Ghosh and Bose (1947) reconfirmed the original discoveries by Sahni and his co-workers of advanced plant remains in the Salt Range Formation itself. They also found fragments of advanced plants in a sample of shale from the Cambrian or pre-Cambrian beds of the Vindhyans of northern India (Ghosh and Bose 1950b) and in a sample of Cambrian rock from Kashmir (Ghosh and Bose 1951). In some cases, Ghosh and Bose (1951b, pp. 130–131; 1952) found fragments of advanced plants (coniferous) in Cambrian rock samples that also contained trilobites. The samples were from the Salt Pseudomorph beds of the Salt Range and the shales of the Rainwar locality in Kashmir.

Other researchers confirmed the work of Ghosh and his associates (Jacob *et al.* 1953), finding evidence for advanced vascular plants, including gymnosperms, in Cambrian rock samples from the Salt Range and other sites in India. Jacob and his coworkers also called attention to similar Cambrian paleobotanical discoveries in Sweden, Estonia, and Russia, as reported by S. N. Naumova, A. V. Kopeliovitch, A. Reissinger, and W. C. Darrah (Jacob *et al.* 1953, p. 35).

German researchers (Schindewolf and Seilacher, 1955) took samples of rock from the Salt Range to Germany, where specialists found no evidence of plant remains. But in his discussion, Schindewolf mentioned that he personally witnessed an Indian scientist obtain plant microfossils from a Cambrian Salt Range rock sample in India. After this, active discussion of the controversy diminished. It is quite possible that this was the result of the partition of India and Pakistan. After partition, members of the Geological Survey of India may not have had such easy access to the Salt Range in the newly independent Islamic state of Pakistan.

In recent years, petroleum geologists have conducted extensive studies of the Salt Range region, with no reference or only slight reference to the debates that took place earlier in the century. Although modern geological reports acknowledge overthrusts in the Salt Range, they unanimously declare the Salt Range Formation to be Eocambrian (Yeats *et al.* 1984, Butler *et al.* 1987, Jauné and Lillie 1988, Baker *et al.* 1988, Pennock *et al.* 1989, McDougall and Khan 1990). One paper (Butler *et al.* 1987, p. 410) mentions discoveries of wood fragments in the salt deep in the mines at Khewra. The authors propose these are intrusive, but neglect to discuss the extensive reporting by Sahni and others ruling out such an explanation for the microfossils discovered in various kinds of rock from the Salt Range Formation.

Discussion

In the early stages of the debates about the nature and age of the Salt Range Formation, fossil evidence did not play a major role. Geological considerations dominated the discussion. With the introduction of paleobotanical evidence by Sahni and others in the 1930s and 1940s, the Salt Range controversy became interesting from a paleontological perspective. Sahni, along with his coworkers and supporters, believed that microfossils of advanced plants and insects, along with a few plant macrofossils (pieces of wood and leaf imprints), indicated an Eocene age for the Salt Range Formation. They explained the presence of the Salt Range Formation below undisputed Cambrian beds (the Purple Sandstone, the Neobolus beds, the Magnesian Sandstone, and the Salt Pseudomorph Beds) as the result of a massive overthrust.

Advocates of a Cambrian age for the Salt Range Formation challenged Sahni's conclusions on two fronts.

First, they argued that the plant and insect fossils must have been intrusive. But even these opponents acknowledged it would be difficult to explain how such fossils could have intruded into resistant rock such as the oil shales found in the Salt Range Formation. Overall, it seems there is fairly good evidence for the presence of plant and insect microfossils and even some macrofossils in the Salt Range Formation. Sahni and his coworkers presented good arguments against possible contamination of their rock samples, either *in situ* or in the laboratory.

Second, the advocates of a Cambrian age for the Salt Range Formation argued against Sahni's hypothesis of a massive overthrust that covered the Eocene Salt Range Formation with Cambrian formations. Opponents disputed the overthrust hypothesis, citing signs of normal contact between the Salt Range Formation and the overlying beds. Modern geological opinion partly favors Sahni. There is evidence of thrust faulting in the Salt Range. But modern geological opinion is also unanimous in assigning the Salt Range Formation to the Eocambrian.

If we stop at this point, the controversy remains unresolved. There still appears to be a conflict between the geological evidence and the paleobotanical evidence. The conflict may, however, be resolved if we adopt the approach taken by Gee, who proposed that an advanced land flora and insect fauna may have existed in the Cambrian or Precambrian. This, of course, challenges accepted views on the evolution of life on earth. But it seems to be the most reasonable way to bring all categories of evidence into harmony.

Support for the existence of advanced vascular plants (including gymnosperms and and angiosperms) in the earliest Paleozoic is supported by (1) reports by Ghosh and his coworkers of microfossils of gymnosperms and angiosperms in the Cambrian beds overlying the Salt Range Formation and in Cambrian beds elsewhere in the Indian subcontinent; (2) contemporary reports from researchers in other parts of the world giving evidence for advanced vascular plants in the Cambrian (see Leclerq 1956 for a review); (3) modern reports placing the existence of the angiosperms as far back as the Triassic (Cornet 1989, 1993). According to standard views, angiosperms originated in the Cretaceous. Cornet's work places them in the Triassic, providing a step between the standard view of a Cretaceous origin for the angiosperms and Sahni's evidence showing an angiosperm presence in the Cambrian. According to standard views, the gymnosperms originated in the Devonian, and the first land plants appeared in the mid-Silurian.

Furthermore, a review of scientifically reported evidence related to human origins and antiquity has revealed signs of a human presence on this planet extending back hundreds of millions of years, at least as far back as the Cambrian (Cremo and Thompson, 1993). Appreciation of the existence, extent, and significance of this body of evidence is hampered by uncritical acceptance of current evolutionary conceptions about the origin and development of life. In their review of Cremo and Thompson's work, in *Social Studies of Science*, J. Wodak and D. Oldroyd (1995, p. 207) said it is important for two reasons. First, it treats many incidents in the history of archeology in much greater depth than previously. And, second, it raises important issues regarding scientific truth claims. Wodak and Oldroyd advised evolutionists to be more cautious in their claims that evolution is an absolute fact. In any case, the book by Cremo and Thompson (*Forbidden Archeology)* did succeed in bringing about serious discussion of the evidential foundations and certainty of truth claims for human evolution. This present paper is an attempt to initiate similar discussion in plant evolution. It would thus appear that historical studies of science may have a role to play in the active work of a scientific discipline.

In my introduction to *Forbidden Archeology,* I acknowledged that the authors were inspired and motivated by their commitment to Vedic and Puranic accounts of the origin and development of life. This attracted the attention of several reviewers (for example, Wodak and Oldroyd 1995, Murray 1995, and Feder 1994). This paper is similarly inspired and motivated. According to Vedic and Puranic accounts, the earth passes through phases of manifestation and devastation known as *kalpas,* or days of Brahma. Each day of Brahma is 4.32 billion years long. During the day, life is manifest on earth. At the end of each day of Brahma, there is a devastation, during which the earth is submerged in cosmic waters. The period of devastation is called a night of Brahma, and is of the same length as a day of Brahma. At the end of the night of Brahma, the earth emerges from the waters of devastation, and life again becomes manifest. Each day of Brahma consists of 14 *manvantara* periods, each composed of 71 *yuga* cycles, each *yuga* cycle lasting 4.32 million years. According to Puranic accounts, we are now in the 28th *yuga* cycle of the 7th *manvantara* period of the current day of Brahma. In other words, we are roughly 2 billion years into the current day of Brahma. Before that, there would be 4.32 billion years of devastation, with the earth submerged in cosmic waters. According to current accounts, the earth formed about 4 billion years ago (within the latter part of the last night of Brahma), and life first appeared about 2 billion years ago (during the first part of the current day of Brahma). This is an interesting temporal parallel between the modern scientific and ancient Puranic cosmologies. But in Puranic accounts, we also find evidence of humans, plants, and animals existing in the first *manvantara* period of the current day of Brahma. The evidence reported in this paper, in my book *Forbidden Archeology* (Cremo and Thompson, 1993), and in a paper presented at the World Archeological Congress (Cremo 1995) are consistent with the Puranic view.

Conclusion

Paleobotanical and geological evidence from the Salt Range in Pakistan suggests that advanced plants, including gymnosperms and angiosperms, as well as insects, existed in the early Cambrian, consistent with historical accounts in the *Puranas*. When considered in relation to extensive evidence for an anatomically modern human presence extending back to the same period, the evidence from the Salt Range suggests the need for a complete reevaluation of current ideas about the evolution of life on this planet. One possible outcome of this reevaluation could be the abandonment of the Darwinian evolutionary hypothesis in favor of a model for life's origin and development drawn from the Vedic and Puranic texts.

References

Anderson, R. V. V. (1927) Tertiary stratigraphy and orogeny of the northern Punjab. *Bulletin of the Geological Society of America*, 38: 665–720.

Baker, D. M., Lillie, R. J., Yeats, R. S., Johnson, G. D., Yousuf, M., Zamin, A. S. H. (1988) Development of the Himalayan frontal thrust zone: Salt Range, Pakistan. *Geology*, 16: 3–7.

Butler, R. W. H., Coward, M. P., Harwood, G. M., and Knipe, R. J. (1987) Salt control on thrust geometry, structural style and gravitational collapse along the Himalayan Mountain Front in the Salt Range of Northern Pakistan. In Lerche, I., and O'Brian, J. J., eds. *Dynamical Geology of Salt and Related Structures*. Orlando: Academic Press, pp. 339–418.

Christie, W. A. K. (1914) Notes on the salt deposits of the Cis-Indus Salt Range. *Records of the Geological Survey of India*, 44: 241–264.

Coates, J., Crookshank, H., Gee, E. R., Ghost, P. K., Lehner, E., and Pinfold, E. S. (1945) Age of the Saline Series in the Punjab Salt Range. *Nature*, 155: 266–277.

Cornet, B. (1989) The reproductive morphology and biology of *Sanmiguela lewisii*, and its bearing on angiosperm evolution in the Late Triassic. *Evolutionary Trends in Plants*, 3(1): 25–51.

Cornet, B. (1993) Dicot-like leaf and flowers from the Late Triassic Tropical Newark Supergroup Rift Zone, U.S.A. *Modern Geology*, 19: 81–99.

Cotter, G. de P. (1931) Some recent advances in the geology of North-West India. Presidential address, section of geology. *Proceedings of the Eighteenth Indian Science Congress, Nagpur, 1931 (Third Circuit)*. Calcutta: Asiatic Society of Bengal, pp. 293–306.

Cotter, G. de P. (1933) The geology of the part of the Attock District west of longitude 72° 45' east. *Memoirs of the Geological Survey of India, Volume 55, Part 2*. Calcutta: Geological Survey of India.

Cremo, M. A. (in press) Puranic Time and the Archeological Record. Paper delivered at the World Archaeological Congress, December 1994, New Delhi. To be included in conference proceedings, published by Routledge. [Later published.]

Cremo, M. A. and Thompson, R. L. (1993) *Forbidden Archeology*. San Diego: Bhaktive-danta Institute.

Darrah, W. C. (1937) Spores of Cambrian plants. *Science*, 86: 154–155.

Feder, K. (1994) *Forbidden Archeology*. Book review. *Geoarchaeology*, 9(4): 337–340.

Fermor, L. L. (1935) General report of the Geological Survey of India for the year 1934. *Records of the Geological Survey of India, Volume 69, Part 1*, pp. 1–108.

Fox, Cyril S. (1928) A contribution to the geology of the Punjab Salt Range. *Records of the Geological Survey of India, Part 2*, pp. 147–179.

Gee, E. R. (1934) The Saline Series of north-western India. *Current Science*, 2: 460–463.

Gee, E. R. (1945) The age of the Saline Series of the Punjab and of Kohat. *Proceedings of the National Academy of Sciences, India. Section B. Volume 14*, pp. 269–310.

Ghosh, A. K, and Bose, A. (1947) Occurrence of microflora in the Salt Pseudomorph Beds, Salt Range, Punjab. *Nature*, 160: 796–797.

Ghosh, A. K., and Bose, A. (1950) Microfossils from the Cambrian strata of the Salt Range, Punjab. *Transactions of the Bose Research Institute Calcutta*, 18: 71–78.

Ghosh, A. K., and Bose, A. (1950b) Microfossils from the Vindhyans. *Science and Culture*, 15: 330–331.

Ghosh, A. K., and Bose, A. (1951) Recovery of vascular flora from the Cambrian of Kashmir. *Proceedings of the Indian Science Congress, Part III*, pp. 127–128.

Ghosh, A. K., and Bose, A. (1951b) Evidence bearing on the age of the Saline Series in the Salt Range of the Punjab. *Geological Magazine*, 88: 129–132.

Ghosh, A. K., and Bose, A. (1952) Spores and tracheids from the Cambrian of Kashmir. *Nature*, 169: 1056–1057.

Ghosh, A. K., Sen, J., and Bose, A. (1948) Age of the Saline Series in the Salt Range of the Punjab. *Proceedings of the Indian Science Congress, Part III*, p. 145.

Holland, T. H. (1903) *General Report on the Work Carried Out by the Geological Survey of India for the Year 1902/03*. Calcutta: Geological Survey of India.

Jacob, K, Jacob, C., and Shrivastava, R. N. (1953) Evidence for the existence of vascular land plants in the Cambrian. *Current Science*, 22: 34–36.

Jaumé, S. C. and Lillie, R. J. (1988) Mechanics of the Salt Range-Potwar Plateau, Pakistan: a fold-and-thrust belt underlain by evaporites. *Tectonics*, 7: 57–71.

Koken, E., and Noetling, F. (1903) Geologische Mittheilungen aus der Salt Range. No. 1. Das permische Glacial. *Centralblatt für Mineralogie, Geologie, und Päleontologie*, (?): 45–49

Leclerq, S. (1956) Evidence for vascular plants in the Cambrian. *Evolution*, 10: 109–114.

McDougall, J. W. and Khan, S. H. (1990) Strike-slip faulting in a foreland fold-thrust belt: the Kalabagh Fault and Western Salt Range, Pakistan. *Tectonics*, 9: 1061–1075.

Medlicott, H. B. and Blandford, W. T. (1879) *Manual of the Geology of India, Part 2*. Calcutta: Geological Survey of India. Cited in Fox, 1928, p. 149.

Middlemiss, C. S. (1891) Notes on the geology of the Salt Range, with a reconsidered theory of the origin and age of the Salt Marl. *Records of the Geological Survey of India*, 24: 19–42.

Murray, T. (1995) *Forbidden Archeology*. Book review. *British Journal for the History of Science*, 28: 377–379.

Oldham, R. D. (1893) *A Manual of the Geology of India*. Second edition. Calcutta: Geological Survey of India.

Pascoe, E. H. (1920) *Petroleum in the Punjab and North West Frontier Province. Memoirs of the Geological Survey of India*, 40(3). Calcutta: Geological Survey of India.

Pascoe, E. H. (1930) General report for 1929. *Records of the Geological Survey of India, Volume 63*. Calcutta: Government of India Central Publications Branch, pp. 1–154.

Pascoe, E. H. (1959) *A Manual of the Geology of India and Burma, Volume II*. Calcutta: Geological Survey of India.

Pennock, E. S., Lillie, R. J., Zaman, A. S. H., and Yousaf, M. (1989) Structural interpretation of seismic reflection data from Eastern Salt Range and Potwar Plateau, Pakistan. *The American Association of Petroleum Geologists Bulletin*, 73: 841–857.

Sahni, B. (1944) Age of the Saline Series in the Salt Range of the Punjab. *Nature*, 153: 462–463.

Sahni, B. (1945) Microfossils and problems of Salt Range Geology. *Proceedings of the National Academy of Sciences, India, Section B, 1944, Volume 14*, pp. i–xxxii.

Sahni, B. (1947a) The age of the Saline Series in the Salt Range (Second Symposium). Concluding remarks. *Proceedings of the National Academy of Sciences, India, 1945, Section B, Volume 16*, pp. 243–247.

Sahni, B (1947b) Microfossils and the Salt Range Thrust. *Proceedings of the National Academy of Sciences, India, 1945, Section B, Volume 16*, pp. i–xlx.

Schindewolf, O. H. and Seilacher, A. (1955) Beiträge zur Kenntnis des Kambriums in der Salt Range (Pakistan). *Akademie der Wissenschaften und der Literatur. Abhandlungen der Mathematisch-Naturwissenschaftlichen Klasse, Nr. 10*. Wiesbaden: Verlag der Akademie der Wissenschaften und der Literatur in Mainz, in Kommision bei Franz Steiner Verlag.

Stuart, M. (1919) Suggestions regarding the origin and history of the rock-salt deposits of the Punjab and Kohat. *Records of the Geological Survey of India*, 50: 57–97.

Wodak, J. and Oldroyd, D. (1995) 'Vedic creationism': a new twist to the evolution debate. *Social Studies of Science*, 28: 192–213.

Wynne, A. B. (1875) The Trans-Indus Salt Range in the Kohat District, with an appendix on the Kohat Mines or Quarries, by H. Warth. *Memoirs of the Geological Society of India, Volume 11, Part 2*. Calcutta: Geological Survey of India.

Wynne, A. B. (1878) On the Geology of the Salt Range in the Punjab. *Memoirs of the Geological Survey of India. Volume 14*. Calcutta: Geological Survey of India. Cited in Christie (1914, p. 253) and Fox (1928, pp. 147–148).

Yeats, R. S., Khan, S. H., and Akhtar, M. (1984) Late Quaternary deformation of the Salt Range of Pakistan. *Geological Society of America Bulletin*, 95: 958–966.

Zuber, Rudolf (1914) Beiträge zur Geologie des Punjab (Ostindien). *Jahrbuch der Geologischen Reichsanstalt*, 64: 32–356.

14

The Discoveries of Aimé Louis Rutot at Boncelles, Belgium: An Archeological Controversy from the Early Twentieth Century

This paper was accepted for presentation at the XXIVth Congress of the International Union for Prehistoric and Protohistoric Sciences, which was held at Liège, Belgium, September 2–8, 2001.

Why Do I Choose Boncelles?

From July 31 to August 5, 1909, the Archeological and Historical Federation of Belgium held its 21st Congress in Liége. The Congress met in the Museum of the Archeological Institute at the Maison Curtius, on the Quai de Maestricht, not too far from where we sit today. One of the principal attractions of the Congress was to be a lecture on archeological discoveries at Boncelles, presented by Aimé Louis Rutot (1847–1933) **[see Plate VIII, Figure 3]**, conservator of the Royal Museum of Natural Sciences in Brussels, who would also guide an excursion to the site.[1]

Boncelles is a small town about 10 kilometers south of Liège. In 1906, Émile de Munck, a collector of archeological materials, explored a sandpit near here **[see Plate VIII, Figure 1]**, and found some crude flint implements in an Oligocene stratum. In those days, the idea of Tertiary man was still current among many European archeologists, so Oligocene implements were not outside the realm of possibility. The Boncelles artifacts therefore could have been yet another eolithic industry, the earliest of a series that had already been found in the Pliocene and Miocene. ("Ah, yes, the eoliths," archeologists today will sigh, remembering with an air of sad superiority the strange delusion that had infected the minds of some of their illustrious predecessors, in the pre-scientific era of their discipline.) De Munck reported his initial discoveries to Rutot.[2] Among the first specimens gathered by de Munck, there were many flint flakes showing signs of fine retouching and utilization.[3] "It was these implements, including a scraper with a clear bulb of percussion and nicely retouched sharp edge, which convinced me that at the place pointed out by de Munck there existed a deposit of Tertiary eoliths that deserved to be explored and studied," said Rutot.[4] Rutot and de Munck collected additional artifacts from Boncelles, and in 1907 Rutot wrote up the discoveries in a report titled "A Grave Problem."[5] Rutot called the Boncelles industry the Fagnian, after the name of the region, Hautes-Fagnes. The extreme antiquity of the

Fagnian artifacts from Boncelles did pose a grave problem to archeologists of the early twentieth century, and the gravity of the problem has influenced me, as an historian of archeology in the early twenty-first century, to select this particular case for the topic of this paper. Why? Because in my heart, I would like it to be true that hominids (perhaps even humans of our type) used stone tools at Boncelles in the early Tertiary.

Method and Outlook

As I have mentioned in several of my works, I am a kind of creationist, a kind of anti-evolutionist, but a rare one—some have called me a Hindu creationist, others a Vedic creationist, still others a Krishna creationist.[6] I accept all of these designations. My work as an historian is indeed influenced by the historical texts of ancient India, the *Puranas*, which tell of a human presence on this planet going back hundreds of millions of years, to the very beginning of life's history.[7] It is this Vedic perspective that has caused me to select Rutot's report on Boncelles as a topic of inquiry and governs my interpretation of it. The Oligocene age attributed to the artifacts by Rutot is a clear sign to most historians of archeology and archeologists that Boncelles is not of interest, and that something is definitely wrong (the oldest hominids could be no more ancient that the early Pliocene, according to currently dominant ideas). For me, the Oligocene age attributed to the artifacts is a signpost that attracts my interest, and I think, "Maybe there's something to it." Furthermore, Boncelles is not an isolated case. There are hundreds of cases of archeological evidence for extreme human antiquity, consistent with Vedic historical accounts, in the scientific literature of the past 150 years, as documented in my book *Forbidden Archeology*.[8]

Although I am guided in my historical research by my Vedic theoretical perspective, it is not that I uncritically accept every archeological discovery that happens to be consistent with Puranic accounts of extreme human antiquity. My procedure, as an historian of archeology, is to consult primary published works, and to also, whenever possible, visit the sites, examine the collections of artifacts, and research the archives, for correspondence, field notes, and maps. Then I make my judgment, which may be yes, no, or undecided.

This method naturally brings me in contact with working archeologists, and in my interactions with them, I obtain, directly and indirectly, their perspectives on the objects of my historical investigations. These current workers are as much the objects of my study as the persons who studied prehistory and protohistory in the past, such as Rutot. Therefore, I will not avoid speaking about my contacts with them. In this sense, this paper is an ethnographic study of contemporary archeologists in their museum habitat as well as an exercise in history of archeology.[9] Regarding my sociological outlook, I am influenced by the ethnomethodology of Harold Garfinkel.[10]

I was introduced to ethnomethodology by sociologist Pierce J. Flynn, author of *The Ethnomethodological Movement: Sociosemiotic Interpretations*.[11] Pierce visited me several times in the early 1990s, when I was writing and researching *Forbidden Archeology* in Pacific Beach, California. We had a number very productive discussions, and he agreed to write a foreword to the book. Flynn lists eight distinctive concerns of the ethnomethodological research program: 1. indexical expressions, 2. reflexivity, 3. membership, 4. accountability, 5. local practices and social order, 6. situatedness, 7. unique adequacy of methods and becoming the phenomenon, 8. scenic display.[12] My style of work therefore requires that I become familiar with and be able to reproduce, to a sufficient extent, the indexical expressions, local practices, and scenic displays of archeologists (and historians of archeology). I must to some extent also engage in their practices of membership and accountability in the situatedness of their disciplines. But, at the same time, I remain an outsider, although I do manage through some unique ethnomethodological methods to effectively succeed in "becoming the phenomenon" under study.

The ethnomethodologists are linked to an earlier group of radical scholars, the ethnographic surrealists, with whom I also identify. Flynn states: "Ethnographic surrealism refers to a historical disposition toward the empirical world that was founded originally in Paris by members of André Breton's surrealist movement in 1925. Ethnography was wedded to surrealism when in 1929 members of the surrealist movement, including Georges Bataille, Robert Desnos, Michael Leiris, Antonin Artaud, Raymond Queneau and others began a journal *Documents*, that was expressly dedicated to questioning prevailing social categories through the use of 'ethnographic evidence' taken from both anthropological and amateur researchers. . . . The enthnographic surrealists' aesthetic position was to begin with reality deep in question and to attempt to juxtapose exotic and strange cultural practices and objects in order to find new human alternatives that could be assembled into new cultural forms."[13] My own work, which involves injecting strange Vedic historical concepts and extreme archeological anomalies into the current discourse of the discipline, is similarly motivated.

Inevitably, history of science intersects with philosophy of science. Philosophically, I confess to being a constructivist, although ultimately I shy away from total relativism. We can agree to know at least something. Furthermore, I go along with those who prefer a naturalized philosophy of science, one grounded in, but not artificially limited by, the current and past practices and theories of the discipline in question. I also am influenced by the reflexive approach to science studies, as should be clear from the style of this paper. Other labels that might be applied to me are antimaterialist, antireductionist, and, to some extent, antirealist.

I oppose a rigid professionalization of scientific and scholarly inquiry, and value a multicultural approach. As Ian Hodder of Cambridge University says (1997, pp. 699–700): "Day by day it becomes more difficult for a past controlled by the academy. The proliferation of special interests on the 'fringe' increasingly challenges or spreads to the dominant discourse itself . . . . Within this unstable kaleidoscope, it is no longer so easy to see who is 'in' the academy and who is 'outside.'"[14] Finally, I believe that historians of science should not always avoid a normative stance. After saying all this, how, therefore, would I identify myself? I would call myself a Krishna creationist masquerading as an historian of archeology (and sometimes as an archeologist).[15]

What am I doing? What I am getting at in this paper is the indexical nature of archeological artifacts as signs, which are perceived quite differently by different research groups over time, in the context of different theoretical conceptions current in the membership of a discipline. I am also getting at the procedures whereby such perceptions are continually maintained within a certain knowledge community, and how the knowledge community itself is maintained by such processes.

A History of My Boncelles Studies

I first became interested in Rutot's report on Boncelles when I was researching my book *Forbidden Archeology*. At that time, I read Rutot's 1907 report and found it quite convincing. In October 1997, I was on a lecture tour of universities in the Netherlands and Belgium. One of my stops was the Catholic University of Louvain. My audience there was composed of archeologists Pierre Vermeersch and Philip Van Peer and their students. I mentioned the Boncelles artifacts, and was later assured by Van Peer and Vermeersch that they were false. In fact, they said they sometimes used artifacts collected by Rutot from Boncelles in classroom exercises, during which archeology students had to visually separate real from false stone tools. So the Boncelles objects were false. How could it be otherwise?

Still, I thought it would be good to have a look myself. I made some inquiries at the Royal Belgian Institute of Natural Sciences and was put in touch with archeologist Ivan Jadin. I made an appointment, and met him in the Institute's reception area. The scientific research sections of the Institute are housed in a twenty story glass, brick, and steel tower that was erected in front of the old museum buildings where Rutot had worked in the early twentieth century. The archeology section is at the top of the building. On the elevator ride up, Jadin told me that this arrangement—the molluscs on the bottom floors, humans on the top—was deliberate on the part of a former director of the Institute, reflecting the evolutionary progression of the development of life. After we arrived on the nineteenth floor, Jadin took me into the storage rooms of the archeology department. We pulled out a few large wooden trays of Rutot's artifacts, and loaded them into a trolley designed for transporting these trays. We wheeled the trolley into the archeology lab. There I set the heavy trays on tables, and went through them for about three hours, in a preliminary way, taking a few pictures with my digital camera. Jadin also showed me in the storage rooms a large drawer containing a collection of Rutot's correspondence. That stuck in my mind, because I wanted someday to go through that collection. I mentioned to Ivan that I had heard Rutot was involved in psychical research. It was true, he said. He showed me an essay Rutot had written on the topic.[16] He promised to copy it for me and mail it to me. Toward the end of my visit, we exchanged cards. I said I would like to come again to do further research. He said I would be quite welcome, and that I could stay in the Institute guest house nearby. Then it was time to go.

Three years later, in November 2000, Ana C. N. Martins, archeologist and vice president of the Portuguese Association of Archaeologists, invited me to give a paper at the symposium on the history of archeology that she was organizing for this Congress.[17] I immediately decided to do it on Rutot.

After the proposed paper was accepted by her and the Congress program committee, I tried to get in touch with Ivan Jadin at the Royal Belgian Institute of Natural

Sciences, to arrange for a second research visit. But I received no reply. I later learned from Anne Hauzeur, of the archeology section, that Ivan was not then at the Institute because of illness, but she said I was welcome to come and study the artifacts and papers of Rutot if I would first get formal permission from the director, Daniel Cahen.

Of course, I was wondering how that would go, because I do have a little bit of a reputation in history of science and archeology circles for my Vedic creationist views.[18] My formal request included acknowledgment of my affiliation with the Bhaktivedanta Institute, and I directly said that I intended to look at Rutot's work at Boncelles in light of the Vedic historical writings. Cahen replied that he had no objection.

I reported that to Anne, who then informed me that Vanessa Amormino, a graduate student from the prehistory department at the University of Liège, working under Marcel Otte, had been cataloguing Rutot's papers. Anne wanted me to get her permission to look at Rutot's papers. So I wrote to Vanessa, mentioning that I was planning on looking into Rutot's documents, including his correspondence. She had no objection and sent me a copy of her database, which included entries for maps, illustrations, and manuscripts, but no correspondence. She said she wasn't aware of the box of correspondence that Jadin had shown me. I wondered if I could have been mistaken.

On July 19, 2001, I showed up once more in the archeology section of the Royal Belgian Institute of Natural Sciences, accompanied by a photographer assistant. Anne Hauzeur received me, and I began my work by looking through a box of Rutot's miscellaneous papers. Among them I found his collection of calling cards, several hundred of them, including those of most of the leading European and American archeologists of the day. And I was happy to see the box of correspondence was also waiting for me on a trolley in the lab. At this time, Anne was busy preparing a paper on a neolithic site in Luxemburg, which she was presenting over the weekend at a conference in France. She said that Dominic Bosquet, another staff archeologist could help me in her absence.

Finding the Sandpit at Boncelles

I had my own plans for the weekend. I mentioned to Anne and Dominic that I intended to search for the site at Boncelles. Both Anne and Dominic were discouraging, telling me that the area had been extensively developed with factories and shopping centers, and that the site would most probably have been eradicated. Nevertheless, I was determined to give it a try.

In his report, Rutot provided the following information about the location of the main site: "The discovery of the eoliths in question here were made by de Munck in a sandpit situated alongside the main road from Tilft to Boncelles, about 500 meters before arriving at the crossroads, at the place called Les Gonhir."[19] Through friends in Antwerp, I found a young man who was willing to spend a day driving my assistant and me to Boncelles to search for the sandpit. We arrived in Boncelles in the late morning, and located the Tilft road. We did find a crossroads (a small traffic circle), and stopped nearby. From previous experience locating the sites of Ribeiro in Portugal, I had learned that a good way to proceed is to find an elderly inhabitant to ask for directions. Fortunately, we immediately spotted an elderly gentleman walking up the road. My

Belgian friend inquired from him, and we learned that the very place we were standing was still called Les Gonhir. In fact, the surrounding land was owned by the gentleman. We asked about the sandpit. He indicated that there was indeed a sandpit up the road a few hundred meters. We asked him to draw a map, and he did so, showing on it the entrance road, which he said was blocked with a gate. We drove back up the Tilft road and found the small unpaved road. Parking the car on the Tilft road, we walked some distance down the little road and found the sandpit. A nearly vertical exposure about 15-20 meters high extended for about two hundred meters [see Plate VIII, Figure 1]. In one place, it was apparently still being worked a little. I compared the layers visible in the exposure at this place to the drawing of the strata in Rutot's report, and it was clear to me that we were seeing the exact same layers.[20] Unfortunately, minor slumping had covered the implement-bearing layer of flint at the base of the series.

Studying the Boncelles Collection

On returning to the Institute the next week, I once again met Anne Hauzeur, who had returned from her conference. Together we went into the storage rooms and pulled out several trays of Rutot's artifacts from Boncelles, loaded them into a trolley, and wheeled the trolley back into the archeology lab, where Anne gave me and my photographer assistant some space to work. I began going through the trays of artifacts, thousands altogether. One of my goals was to match some of them to the illustrations in Rutot's report. Somehow or other, I was able to match about a dozen of them.

Dominic happened to have come out from his office to the lab, so I showed him how I had matched some of the artifacts to the illustrations. I then mentioned that I had found the sandpit at Boncelles. He asked, "Did you find any artifacts?" This is an indexical expression, one that acquires meaning according to the context. Taking the expression semantically at face value, it is a simple question that requires an answer, yes or no. But in the context of Belgian archeologists working in the archeology laboratory of the Royal Belgian Institute of Natural Sciences, the expression takes on another value. It is not a question to be answered, but an ironic comment on the falsity of the whole phenomenon of Rutot. The ironic comment is not intended to draw a yes or no answer, but a knowing smile or laugh, or a further contribution to the joke. However, I chose to respond in a different way. I explained, in all seriousness, that Rutot's artifact-bearing flint bed at the base of the section was covered. "I was just joking," said Bosquet. "Oh, yes, of course," I replied. I might also have replied that "I also was just joking, or playing along."

This "joking" is an example of disciplinary shop talk. The attitude that underlies such joking is part of the phenomenon under study, the phenomenon of the disciplinary suppression of uncomfortable evidence. The discomfort is removed by the attitude of not taking the evidence seriously. This "not taking seriously" is accomplished by various means, including the jokes and ironic comments exchanged from time to time within the membership of the community that finds the evidence uncomfortable or embarrassing.

Belgian Archeologists Embarrassed by Rutot

Belgian archeologists, particularly those connected with the museum housing Rutot's collection, do have some interest in characterizing the Boncelles artifacts as false. Once, Anne Hauzeur, came up to me as I was working. I suggested that it might be good to do something special with the specimens I had matched to the illustrations in Rutot's report on Boncelles. She provided me with some plastic bags and some cards for labeling. After bagging and labeling the specimens with the figure numbers in Rutot's 1907 report, I replaced them in their original trays. At this time, she remarked casually to me, "You know, it is a false collection." I infer that she somehow did not quite understand why I was spending so much time with the collection, even though I had indicated that my interest was merely historical. Although I assume she assumed that I did in fact know the collection was false, or had the reputation of being false, there was perhaps some nagging doubt. So she delivered her remark to me in an offhand way. She casually referred me to a report by Marguerite Ulrix-Closset, comparing the Rutot collection, unfavorably, of course, to accepted middle paleolithic specimens.[21]

There is a tradition of Belgian archeologists putting Rutot in his place, sometimes with good reason.[22] Rutot in the course of his career as a naturalist was quite a collector himself, and during his tenure as conservator at the Royal Museum, was equally energetic in acquiring the collections of others. It is undoubtedly true that some of his acquired collections, such as the Dethise collections, were false, in the sense that they included forgeries or frauds.[23] But we should not be too quick to adopt a condescending attitude toward Rutot. In a recent editorial in *Antiquity,* we learn of the possibility that "more than 1200 fake antiquities are displayed in some of the world's leading museums."[24] Nevertheless, the forgeries identified in collections acquired by Rutot, perhaps combined with negative attitudes towards Rutot's involvement in psychical research, resulted in an almost total rejection of Rutot's entire body of archeological work.[25] But it seems to me that the dismissals may have been too extreme, with some good being thrown out with the bad. No one has claimed that the Boncelles artifacts are forgeries, or that any fraud was involved in their discovery or acquisition.

Admittedly, the eoliths of Boncelles are, if genuine, quite crude, but industries of similar crudeness have won provisional acceptance among archeologists, even though there may be remaining questions about the artifactual nature of some of the specimens, or even the entire collection. For example, in a recent volume of papers on the earliest occupation of Europe, Raposo and Santonja, in connection with lithics found in the Gaudix-Baza depression in the Iberian peninsula, comment on "doubts relating to the artifactual character of the finds" reported by Carbonell *et al.*[26] References to crude lithics accepted by some researchers and rejected by others can be found throughout the same volume. I believe the reason that they are mentioned in that book, and given some serious consideration, is because they date back only as far as the Early Pleistocene. If the Boncelles implements had been found in an Early Pleistocene context instead of an Oligocene context, it is likely that they would also have been mentioned in a contemporary discussion about the earliest occupation of Europe.

A key issue in philosophy of science is the theory-laden nature of observation.

Given that most contemporary archeologists accept practically without question that the very first hominins came into existence only about 5–6 million years ago, it is no wonder that some such archeologists will find it necessary to debunk, in some fashion, to the satisfaction of their peers, a collection from perhaps 30 million years ago in the Oligocene. And it is natural that the pressure to debunk would be most strongly felt by Belgian archeologists who have to deal with the fact that Rutot was a prominent figure in the history of Belgian archeology, and that his collections are still taking up space in the storage rooms of their main museum of natural history, where he was once conservator.

The Belgian archeologists are not alone in having to deal with such things. In the case of Carlos Ribeiro, head of the geological Survey of Portugal in the nineteenth century, I found that he originally displayed artifacts from Portuguese sites with Miocene age attributions in the Museum of Geology in Lisbon [see Plates I-VII]. Early in the twentieth century, museum officials, without disputing the human manufacture of the artifacts, changed the age attributed to them (from Miocene to well within the Pleistocene), apparently to fit them within the developing paradigm of human evolution. Later the objects were removed from display.[27] In a paper I presented at the European Association of Archaeologists meeting in 1999, I documented several other cases in which scientists had dismissed evidence for Tertiary humans simply because it contradicted the developing concepts of human evolution.[28] For example, in the nineteenth century, J. D. Whitney, the state geologist of California, reported anatomically modern human skeletal remains and stone implements of advanced type (mortars and pestles) [see Plates XII-XV] from geological contexts now recognized as early Eocene.[29] William B. Holmes of the Smithsonian Institution dismissed the finds primarily on theoretical grounds: "Perhaps if Professor Whitney had fully appreciated the story of human evolution as it is understood today, he would have hesitated to announce the conclusions formulated, notwithstanding the imposing array of testimony with which he was confronted."[30] He therefore tried to cast doubt on the provenance of the artifacts. In my 1999 paper, I proposed that the acceptance of *Pithecanthropus erectus* of Dubois as a genuine human ancestor in the early Pleistocene placed a limit on the age of any evidence for anatomically modern humans. Holmes suggested that Whitney's Tertiary evidence from California should be rejected because "it implies a human race older by at least one half than *Pithecanthropus erectus* of Dubois, which may be regarded as an incipient form of human only."[31]

Boncelles: The Provenance Seems Good

In the case of Rutot's finds at Boncelles, the provenance of the artifacts seems solid. We are not talking about surface finds, but about artifacts recovered from a deposit of flint resting on Devonian sandstone beneath 15–20 meters of Oligocene sand deposits. The sand at the pit from which artifacts were first recovered did not contain any fossils, but at another pit 500 meters to the northwest, the sand above the artifact-bearing flint bed yielded fossils of an assemblage of shells generally accepted as Late Oligocene. The most common species was *Cytherea beyrichi*. Rutot stated: "This shell is characteristic of the Late Oligocene of Germany, notably the beds at Sternberg, Bünde, and Kassel. . . . The other recognizable species (*Cytherea incrassata, Petunculus obovatus, P. philippi, Cardium cingulatum, Isocardia subtransversa, Glycimeris augusta,* etc.) are all found in the Late Oligocene."[32] Rutot's interpretation of the stratigraphy at Boncelles is upheld by other authorities. Maurice Leriche in 1922 and Charles Pomerol in 1982 both characterize the sands of Boncelles as Chattian, or Late Oligocene.[33]

Schweinfurth quotes Rutot on the geological history of the Boncelles region: "On the plateau (between the Maas and Ourtherivers), the primary stone was covered with flint-bearing chalk, and during the Eocene period the chalk was eroded away, leaving behind heaps of flint that later formed the flint beds. At the beginning of the Late Oligocene a marine intrusion covered the flint beds, depositing 15 meters of fossil-bearing sands over them."[34]

Are the Boncelles Objects Really Artifacts?

Given the noncontroversial provenance of the Boncelles industry, Belgian archeologists have rejected it by challenging its artifactual nature. My sense is that the attempts to do this have not been met with any very critical evaluation. The debunkings of Rutot have been seen as necessary, and have been all too readily accepted by those who have a strong interest in doing so. After all, he was talking about tool using hominids in the Oligocene. That is quite impossible, is it not? Something therefore has to be wrong, and if someone takes on the duty of pointing out something wrong, who is going to offer any objection, or subject the debunking to any heavy scrutiny?

Rutot, a veteran of the eolith wars, was himself prepared for challenges to the artifactual nature of the Boncelles collection. According to Rutot, the Boncelles tools were very simple ones. The Oligocene inhabitants just picked up pieces of flint that appeared suitable for various tasks, modified them slightly (to improve the working edge or make them easier to hold in the hand), and then used them for various purposes. For Rutot, therefore, the principal signs that the objects were artifacts rather than "naturefacts" were chipping to improve gripping with the hand, chipping to make the working edges more suitable for their task, and use marks on the working edges.

Among the Boncelles artifacts, Rutot found "numerous examples of all the various Eolithic types, that is to say *percuteurs* (choppers), *enclumes* (anvils), *couteaux* (cutters), *racloirs* (side scrapers), *grattoirs* (end scrapers), and *perçoirs* (awls)."[35]

Among the *percuteurs,* Rutot identified several subtypes: the *percuteur simple, percuteur tranchant,* the *percuteur pointu,* the *tranchet,* and the *retouchoir.* The most common type was the *percuteur tranchant,* the sharpened chopper. "The sharpened choppers collected at Boncelles," wrote Rutot, "are as fine and characteristic as possible. Clearly evident is the fact that most of the flaking from usage is angled to the left, as always happens when an implement is gripped in the right hand. The opposite occurs when it is employed with the left hand."[36]

I found among the Boncelles *percuteurs* a particularly convincing example of a *tranchet,* with obvious removal of cortex and unifacial flaking to form the working edge.[37] [**See Plate VIII, Figure 4.**] Searching through thousands of Boncelles artifacts,

I also found among the *percuteurs* the *retouchoir* shown by Rutot in figure 7 of his report.[38] **[See Plate IX, Figure 1.]** The *retouchoir*, as its name implies, is a small percussion implement used in retouching the edges of other stone tools. In his caption, Rutot says that the edges clearly show use marks, and these can indeed be seen on the artifact.

In his report on Boncelles, Rutot gave this description of *couteaux*: "One can see that *couteaux* are made from relatively long flakes of flint, blunt on one side and sharp on the other. The blunt side generally retains the flint's cortex. Prolonged usage of the blade turns the rectilinear edge into a sawlike edge, with small irregular teeth. This is caused by chipping of the edge when the blade is pressed against the irregularities of the surface of the object being cut. The *couteaux* were not retouched. They were used for a long time, until blunted by usage and polishing. It was rare that they were employed until completely unusable. At Boncelles one finds *couteaux* of a very characteristic type."[39] I happened to find in my research the *couteau* shown in Rutot's figure 9.[40] **[See Plate IX, Figure 3.]**

In his report, Rutot described the *racloir*, or side scraper. The *racloir* was ordinarily made from an oval flake, produced either naturally or by deliberate flaking, with one of the longitudinal edges blunt and the opposite edge sharp. After retouching for a suitable grip, the blunt edge was held in the palm of the hand, and the sharp edge of the implement was moved along the length of the object to be scraped. During this operation, series of small splinters were detached from the cutting edge of the implement, thus dulling it. Rutot stated: "The characteristic feature of the *racloir*, used as such, is the presence along the working edge of a series of small chip marks, all arranged in the same direction and located on the same side. When the implement became unusable, it was possible to restore its edge with the retoucher stone, allowing it to be further used."[41] In the Boncelles collection, I found the *racloir* pictured in Rutot's figure 10.[42] **[See Plate IX Figure 4.]** Rutot's caption said it had a bulb of percussion and obvious use marks on the working edge. The bulb of percussion indicates that this particular flake may have been deliberately struck from a core.

Rutot described another type of *racloir* discovered at the Boncelles sites: "Frequently the working edge is not straight; it is finished by means of retouching into one or more concave notches, probably for the purpose of scraping long round objects. This is the notched *racloir* (*racloir à encoche*). Some are made from natural flakes, others from flakes derived from deliberate percussion."[43] I found in the Boncelles collection at the Royal Institute of Natural Sciences the *racloir à encoche* shown in figure 13 of Rutot's report.[44] **[See Plate IX, Figure 2.]** I also found other implements of this type that look quite convincing.

The next type of implement discussed by Rutot was the *grattoir*, another broad category of scraper. According to Rutot, the *grattoir* differed from the *racloir* "in that its working edge is employed longitudinally in relation to the direction of the force of application, whereas the *racloir* is held between the thumb and forefinger in such a manner to set the working edge transverse to the direction of the force. When being used, the working edges of the *racloir* and the *grattoir* are thus situated perpendicular to each other."[45] Rutot observed that in order to help the user direct and push the cutting edge of the *grattoir*, these implements in many cases had special notches to accommodate the thumb and forefinger. One such *grattoir* is shown in his figure 26. I managed to find this *grattoir* in the Boncelles collection[46] [**see Plate X, Figure 1**]. I also located the large *grattoir* shown in Rutot's figure 27[47] [**see Plate X, Figure 2**] and the notched *grattoir* (*grattoir à encoche*) shown in Rutot's figure 29[48] [**see Plate X, Figure 3**].

Rutot then described *perçoirs* (awls or borers). "These instruments, also called *poinçons,*" he stated, "are characterized by the presence of a sharp point, obtained by intentional modification of a natural flake that already has a somewhat pointed shape."[49] I located in the Boncelles collection two *perçoirs* shown in Rutot's figures 32 [**see Plate X, Figure 4**] and 33[50] [**see Plate XI, Figure 1**].

According to Rutot, the Boncelles toolmakers had two ways of modifying a naturally pointed flake to make an awl: "Sometimes the chipping on the two edges making the point was done on just one side of the flake. But sometimes one edge was chipped on the flake's front side, and the other edge was chipped on the flake's back side. This procedure is convenient because it allows all the blows to be struck in the same position and the same direction. In effect, when the first edge is chipped, one flips the implement and chips in the same place on the other edge to make a point."[51] Rutot showed a find with this kind of chipping, unlikely to have occurred naturally, in his figure 34. I was able to locate this artifact in the collection[52] [**see Plate VIII, Figure 5**]. Rutot found other objects that he characterized as throwing stones (*pierres de jet*) and flints for lighting fires (*briquets*).

Comparison With Tasmanian Artifacts of Undisputed Human Manufacture

Rutot's principal reponse to anticipated objections about the artifactual nature of the Boncelles discoveries was to compare the Boncelles collection to a collection of implements from Tasmania. Rutot said: "Hesitation is no longer possible after the discovery of an industry fashioned by recently living Tasmanians, which has been brought to our attention through the research conducted by Dr. F. Noetling. The bringing to light of this industry is, as it were, providential, because it demonstrates quite positively that eoliths are a reality. The discovery shows that scarcely sixty years ago human beings were making and using implements that are, according to competent and impartial observers, absolutely of Eolithic type."[53] Rutot then said about the Tasmanian industry: "We are . . . astonished to see its extraordinarily primitive and rudimentary character. So the truth, after direct comparison, is that the two industries [Boncelles and Tasmanian] are exactly the same and that the Tasmanians, now annihilated, but still in existence just sixty years ago, were at the same level of culture as the very primitive inhabitants of Boncelles and the Hautes Fagnes. Only the materials from which the Tasmanian tools were made were different—quartzite, diabase, granite, and similar types of rock rather than flint."[54]

In his report, Rutot compared illustrations of specific Tasmanian tools to illustrations of specific Boncelles pieces. It can be seen that the Boncelles pieces are in fact quite similar to the Tasmanian tools. I believe that Rutot used this comparative method quite effectively to establish the artifactual nature of his Boncelles collection. Of course, looking at drawings is one thing, and looking at the actual implements is another. As always, the best thing is to hold the implements in your own hands and look at them with you own eyes.

Fortunately, the Tasmanian collection is in the anthropology section of the Royal Institute in Brussels. Anne Hauzeur had part of the collection brought to the archeology lab for me to inspect and photograph. Lying on one of the trays were some of the original museum exhibition panels, letters brown with age. Hauzeur told me that it was good that these were there, because in many cases, they provide the only available information about some of the old collections in the museum. She told me that previous directors had thrown out much of the documentation connected with these collections.

In this Tasmanian collection I found some of the artifacts illustrated by Rutot in his report. For example, I found the Tasmanian *grattoir* in Rutot's figure 51[55] [**see Plate XI, Figure 2**]. In his caption, Rutot describes it as a natural flake used as a *grattoir*. It is therefore analogous to most of the Boncelles implements, which are also natural flakes, slightly modified for use as *grattoirs, racloirs,* etc. The Tasmanian *grattoir*, although smaller, is a good match for the Boncelles *grattoir* shown by Rutot in his figure 27.[56] I also found the Tasmanian notched *grattoir* (*grattoir à encoche*) in Rutot's figure 57[57] [**see Plate XI, Figure 3**], which Rutot compared to the Boncelles notched *grattoir* in his figure 29.[58] A Tasmanian *perçoir*, illustrated by Rutot in his figure 60[59] [**see Plate XI, Figure 4**] is, according to him, comparable to the Boncelles *perçoirs* in his figure 32.[60]

Rutot's comparison method was very effective. In other writings, he replied to the standard objections to eoliths, namely that they could be produced by the random action of natural forces, such as the contact of rocks in fast moving streams, the action of waves, glaciers, pressure of overlying strata, etc. He found ways to distinguish between intentional and accidental chipping of stone.[61]

Support for Rutot from his Correspondents

Rutot's report on Boncelles, although controversial, received support from several authorities, as can be seen from his correspondence with other researchers, whose letters to Rutot contained: (1) favorable responses to his report on Boncelles, (2) requests for specimens to display in museums, (3) discussions related to Rutot's upcoming presentations at scientific conferences, and (4) promises to assist in raising money for future excavations at Boncelles.

William J. Sollas, professor of geology at Oxford University, wrote to Rutot on July 22, 1907, after a visit to Belgium: "I am now again settled in my customary work, but with my mind filled with pleasant images of the many things I have seen and studied in Belgium, not the least delightful among them being the wonderful series you so kindly and generously showed me of your ancient implements. These have made a deep impression on me and I now understand the full strength of your arguments in favor of eoliths. But I have learned much besides this and can only very inefficiently express my thanks for the many lessons you have taught me."[62]

It seems that Sollas may have visited Boncelles with Rutot. In a letter to Rutot, in connection with the upcoming Congress of the Archeological and Historical Federation of Belgium in Liège, Marcel de Puydt, referred to a passage from a letter by Rutot to him: "Your letter of 30 August touched on other points of interest to our Congress. '25 very nice pieces,' you wrote, were found at Boncelles during your visit with an Englishman from the University of Oxford, etc."[63]

On January 20, 1910, Sollas wrote to Rutot, who had sent him a collection of specimens from Boncelles: "Thank you for your kind letter informing me of the dispatch of your generous present. The box reached me yesterday and I have greatly admired its contents. I am arranging an exhibition for all specimens relating to the appearance of man in the stratified rocks and shall give a prominent place to the eoliths of Boncelles. I am very much impressed with some of the characters these specimens display and await with great interest the further developments of your discovery."[64]

American anthropologist Frederick Starr of the University of Chicago wrote to Rutot on December 29, 1908: "I have received the copy of 'Un grave problème' and have read it with care and interest. I am now making an effort to raise the money that you suggest. I cannot of course know what success I shall meet. I feel sure I shall accomplish something. . . . Thank you for the collection sent me. I shall be glad indeed to have it. I will acknowledge its receipt when it comes."[65]

Florentino Ameghino, a geologist and archeologist from the National Museum of Buenos Aires, Argentina, received from Rutot a copy of his report on Boncelles and wrote a letter back to Rutot on August 16, 1910. After carefully studying the drawings and descriptions of the implements, Ameghino concluded: "It remains for me absolutely certain that during the Middle or Upper Oligocene there was in Europe an intelligent being who intentionally broke stones."[66] Ameghino had himself published reports of stone tools, hearths, and cut bones from Miocene sites in Argentina.[67]

My Disagreements with Rutot

I disagree with Rutot on two central points—the level of workmanship displayed in the Boncelles implements and the identity of their users.

Rutot believed that all of the Boncelles implements were simply natural pieces or flakes of flint that were picked up and used as tools, with only minor modification to improve the gripping surface or the working edge or edges. It appears to me, however, that Rutot's own observations demonstrate that some of the flakes or pieces of flint may have been deliberately struck from cores for further modification into tools.

Rutot noted: "In the case of *grattoirs* as well as *racloirs,* there are some that bear very well marked bulbs of percussion."[68] For example, Rutot says the *grattoir* in his figure 24, which displays nice use marks, is made on a flake with a bulb of percussion.[69] "I do not, however," said Rutot, "consider these flakes to have been intentionally made for use as implements. I believe that the flakes with the bulb of percussion were detached involuntarily from the edges of stone anvils while they were being struck by hammer stones. These detached flakes were usable as tools just as were the sharp natural flakes found nearby. And they were in fact used like them, but they were not deliberately struck for this purpose."[70]

I wonder how Rutot could say with such certainty that the flakes made into implements were not deliberately struck for that purpose, especially the ones with bulbs of percussion. Many authorities on lithic technology, such as Leland W. Patterson, take bulbs of percussion to be a clear sign of intentional controlled flaking.[71]

I submit that Rutot was fitting the physical evidence to his own framework of evolutionary ideas. He apparently wanted to characterize the makers of the Oligocene industry of Boncelles as more primitive than the makers of later industries in the Tertiary and Quaternary. But leaving aside Rutot's evolutionary expectations, there is good reason to conclude that some of the Boncelles tools were made from flakes intentionally struck for this purpose. Florentino Ameghino, who had done a lot of experimental work in making stone tools himself, was also of this opinion. In his letter to Rutot on the Boncelles discoveries, he described several features of the artifacts, including bulbs of percussion, that led him to conclude: "Natural causes are absolutely incapable of producing similar pieces. The objects present the characteristics of intentional debitage in a manner even more evident than in my quartzite pieces from the broken stone industry of Monte Hermoso."[72]

Let's now consider the identity of the Boncelles toolmaker. In his initial report, Rutot was somewhat ambiguous, stating: "Who was the intelligent being? Was it merely a precursor of the human kind, or was it already human?"[73] But he soon began to favor the idea of a precursor. Dr. Ewald Wüst wrote to Rutot on January 24, 1908, congratulating him on his work at Boncelles. But then he asked: "So who was the user of these Oligocene eoliths? I personally don't have any doubts that it was some kind of intelligent being. . . . But as for a human being in the Middle Oligocene, I cannot think it possible. I think it is about time that it be seriously and rationally investigated, as to whether or not living apes use eoliths."[74] In other words, he was suggesting that perhaps it was some kind of apeman who made and used the Boncelles implements.

I found a reply written by Rutot to Wüst on 5 January 1908 on stationary of the Musée Royal d'Histoire Naturelle de Belgique.[75] On the question of the intelligent being that used the eoliths at Boncelles, Rutot referred Wüst to the recent work of Florentino Ameghino, who believed that the first appearance of intelligent beings capable of using instruments was relatively ancient (at least Eocene).[76] Rutot summarized Ameghino's views thus: "All the apes, including the anthropoid apes, came into existence during the Miocene and their brutish descendants come from a stock with only the most primitive intelligence. Therefore, it is not among the apes that one should search for the precursor of humans, because the precursor is more ancient than the apes."

In his later works, Rutot very definitely identified the human precursor who used the Boncelles implements with a creature related to the *Pithecanthropus erectus* of Dubois. For example in *La Prehistoire*, Rutot says: "Are we able to conceive the external form of the precursors of humans in the Tertiary epoch? It would be proper to answer this question negatively, because no skeletal remains from the primitive beings of that age are yet known to us. Nevertheless, we do have a partial cranium and another bone from *Pithecanthropus* of Java, who is without a doubt very closely related to the race of precursors."[77] Rutot also commissioned the sculptor L. Mascré to make a life-sized bust of the Tertiary human precursor of Boncelles [see Plate VIII, Figure 2] as part of an entire series of busts showing the various stage of human evolution.[78] The busts are still in the storage rooms of the Laboratory for Anthropology and Prehistory at the Royal Belgian Institute of Natural Sciences in Brussels.

In his identification of the makers of the Boncelles tools, Rutot was influenced by his evolutionary ideas. But if he could call the Oligocene tools identical to those made by anatomically modern humans in Tasmania during the Holocene, it is not apparent to me why the makers of the Boncelles tools could not have been physiologically identical to the modern Tasmanians. Therefore, it would be best to return to Rutot's original conclusion, which leaves open the possibility that the toolmakers of Boncelles could have been human: "When we take into consideration the analogies, or rather the identities, between the Oligocene eoliths of Boncelles and the modern eoliths of the Tasmanians, we find ourselves confronted with a grave problem—the existence in the Oligocene of beings intelligent enough to manufacture and use definite and variegated types of implements. Who was the intelligent being? Was it merely a precursor of the human kind, or was it already human? This is a grave problem—an idea that cannot but astonish us and attract the attention and the interest of all those who make the science of humanity the object of their study and meditation."[79]

Conclusion

A couple of years ago in Los Angeles, I attended an advance screening of a remake of the film *Godzilla*. During the screening it appeared at one point late in the film that the monster Godzilla was dead. Everyone breathed a sigh of relief. But suddenly Godzilla jumped to life again, and the thrills continued. The false ending is a common Hollywood scriptwriter's technique. And it would seem that Belgian archeologists have perhaps written a false ending to the Boncelles script. I do not think that the story of the Oligocene artifacts from Boncelles is finished.[80]

Future researchers may note: (1) The principal Boncelles sandpit site still exists, and can be further explored. (2) The Rutot collection is still being carefully kept in the archeology department of the Royal Belgian Institute of Natural Sciences, and can be further studied. In that collection one can now easily find the specific implements illustrated by Rutot in his 1907 report on Boncelles. (3) There are letters in Rutot's correspondence drawer at the Royal Belgian Institute of Natural Sciences that relate to the Boncelles discoveries. (4) The Boncelles implements do in themselves display good signs of intentional work. (5) The Boncelles implements do convincingly resemble crude stone tools admitted to be of human manufacture, i.e. the tools in the Tasmanian collection in the anthropology department. (6) Rutot did give convincing replies to those who thought eoliths were in all cases the product of natural forces only. (7) Belgian archeologists and other archeologists are perhaps too heavily committed to orthodox views on hominin evolution to fairly consider the possibility of Oligocene stone tools. (8) Rutot's own evolutionary conceptions prevented him from seriously considering the possibility that the makers of his Boncelles tools were fully human. The Oligocene implements of Boncelles therefore remain "*un grave problème.*"

Acknowledgments

I thank Daniel Cahen, director of the Royal Belgian Institute of Natural Sciences, for his permission to study the Rutot artifacts and documents in the Institute's collections. I thank Anne Hauzeur and the staff of the archeology department for giving me and my photographer assistant space to work in the archeology laboratory, and for making all the practical arrangements for me to study the artifacts and documents of interest to me. I thank my photographer, who wishes to remain anonymous. I am grateful to Lori Erbs, my research assistant, for obtaining documents from various libraries around the world. For financial assistance I am grateful to the Trustees of the Bhakivedanta Book Trust. I also thank Ana C. N. Martins for inviting me to give this paper.

References and Notes

1. See the letters to Rutot from Marcel de Puydt, president of the Congress section for prehistory and protohistory. The letters can be found in the Rutot correspondence drawer, in a folder labeled "De Puydt," in the storage room of the archeology department (in the Laboratory of Anthropology and Prehistory) on the nineteenth floor of the Royal Belgian Institute of Natural Sciences at Rue Vautier 29, Brussels, B-1000 Belgium. The letters of special interest are dated August 18, September 16, and December 18, 1908.

2. Rutot had long been a supporter of the eolithic industries from the Miocene of Cantal, in France; from the Pliocene of the Kent Plateau in England, and from the Pliocene of St. Prest in France. He also identified a series of eolithic industries in the Early Pleistocene of Belgium—the Reutelian, Mafflian, and Mesvinien. For a review see Rutot, A. (1918) *La Préhistoire. Prèmiere Partie*. Brussels: Les Naturalistes Belges.

3. Rutot, A. (1907) Un grave problème. Une industrie humaine datant de l'époque oligocène. *Bulletin de la Socièté Belge de Géologie de Paleontologie et d'Hydrologie. Tome XXI*: 439–482, this note p. 442.

4. Rutot, A. (1907) Un Grave Problème, pp. 442–443.

5. For another early report on Boncelles, see Rutot, A. (1909) Une industrie éolithique antérieure à l'Oligocene supérieur ou Aquitanien. *Congrès préhistorique de France. Compte-rendu. IVe Session Chambery, France, 1908*. Le Mans, pp. 90–104.

6. Feder, Kenneth L. (1994) *Forbidden Archeology* (book review). *Geoarchaeology*, 9(4): 37–340. Feder (p. 337) wrote, "The book itself represents something perhaps not seen before; we can fairly call it 'Krishna creationism' with no disrespect intended." Feder added, "While decidedly antievolutionary in perspective, this work is not the ordinary variety of antievolutionism in form, content, or style. In distinction to the usual brand of such writing, the authors use original sources and the book is well written. Further, the overall tone of the work is superior to that exhibited in ordinary creationist literature." Marks, Jonathan (1994) *Forbidden Archeology* (book review). *American Journal of Physical Anthropology*, 93(1): 140–141. Marks (p. 141)

described my work as "Hindu-oid creationist drivel." Wodak, Jo, and Oldroyd, David (1996) Vedic creationism: a further twist to the evolution debate. *Social Studies of Science*, 26: 192–213. Wodak and Oldroyd (p. 207) said: "*Forbidden Archeology* (*FA*) offers a brand of Creationism based on something quite different, namely ancient Vedic beliefs. From this starting point, instead of claiming a human history of mere millennia, *FA* argues for the existence of *Homo sapiens* way back into the Tertiary, perhaps even earlier." The full texts of these reviews and many other responses to *FA* can be found in Cremo, M. A. (1998) *Forbidden Archeology's Impact*. Los Angeles: Bhaktivedanta Book Publishing, along with papers by me outlining in greater detail my Vedic creationist background.

7. Cremo, M. A. (1999) Puranic Time and the Archeological Record. *In* Murray, Tim, ed. *Time and Archaeology*. London: Routledge, pp. 38–48.

8. Cremo, M. A., and Thompson, R. L. (1993) *Forbidden Archeology*. San Diego: Bhakivedanta Institute.

9. As a Vedic creationist, I have arrived on the shores of archeology, much as Malinowski arrived on the shores of the Trobriand Islands. I have learned enough of the language and customs to establish contact and gain some slight entry to the life of the natives. Nevertheless, as a visiting Vedic creationist, I have my own intellectual "tent" in which I live, a recondite inner shelter of traditions and cultural ways alien to those of the archeologists in whose midst I sometimes find myself. For me, "going native" would be to become an assistant professor of archeology. But that is not my purpose. What is my purpose? That may be as difficult for a professional archeologist to ascertain as for a Trobriand Islander to have ascertained the true purpose of a Malinowski. Of course, I am not just arriving physically on the island of archeology, by becoming personally present at archeological sites, archeological laboratories, archeological museums, and archeological conferences, such as this one. Beyond that, my texts, including this paper, are arriving into the community of archeological texts. And how will this text be received by the native texts? Will my text be ignored, or attacked? Will it win some little grudging external toleration, or will there perhaps be some rare instances in which my text is allowed entrance into the hidden cultural textways of the archeologists? In other words, will this text become enmeshed in archeological intertextuality, perhaps by appearing in a conference proceedings volume along with native archeological texts and being drawn into the even deeper realm of citation?

10. Garfinkel, Harold (1967) *Studies in Ethnomethodology*. Englewood Cliffs, N.J.: Prenctice Hall.

11. Flynn, Pierce J. (1991) *The Ethnomethodological Movement: Sociosemiotic Interpretations*. Berlin: Mouton de Gruyter.

12. Flynn, Pierce J. (1991) *The Ethnomethodological Movement*, p. 27.

13. Flynn, Pierce J. (1991) *The Ethnomethodological Movement*, p. 250.

14. Hodder, Ian (1997) 'Always momentary, fluid, and flexible': toward a reflexive excavation methodology. *Antiquity* 71: 691–700.

15. I wrote in a paper presented at a conference on science and culture: "[Archeologists and others] were reacting to *Forbidden Archeology* in much the same way as some

art critics of the 1960s reacted to the Brillo box sculptures of Andy Warhol. The Brillo boxes were not art, it appeared to some critics, but these critics could not help commenting upon them as if they were art. And thus the boxes were, after all, art, or as good as art. I suppose it is true, in some sense, that *Forbidden Archeology* is not real archeology, and that I am not a real archeologist (or historian of archeology). And, for that matter, neither is this paper a 'real' paper, and neither am I a 'real' scholar. I am an agent of Gaudiya Vaishnavism [one of the branches of Hindu religion], with an assigned project of deconstructing a paradigm [modern scientific concepts of human evolution], and this paper and *Forbidden Archeology* are part of that project. And yet *Forbidden Archeology* is reviewed in *AJPA* [*American Journal of Physical Anthropology*] and *Geoarchaeology*, and this paper is read by me at an academic conference on science and culture, just like Warhol's Brillo boxes were displayed in galleries for purchase by collectors rather than stacked in supermarkets." Page 22 in Cremo, M. A. (1998) The Reception of Forbidden Archeology: An Encounter Between Western Science and a Non-Western Perspective on Human Antiquity. Presented at Kentucky State University Institute of Liberal Studies, Sixth Annual Interdisciplinary Conference: Science and Culture, Frankfort, Kentucky, March 30–April 1, 1995. *In* Cremo, M. A., ed. *Forbidden Archeology's Impact.* Los Angeles: Bhaktivedanta Book Publishing, pp. 14–40.

16. Rutot, A. (1928) *Spiritisme, Métapsychisme, Energétisme, Néovitalisme.* Brussels. H. Wellens, W. Godenne, and Co. Rutot also published other writings on this topic, and had an extensive correspondence on parapsychology. For a time, Rutot served as president of the Belgian Council for Metapsychical Research. His combination of research into archeological anomalies and the paranormal is highly interesting to me.

17. I presented a paper in Ana's section at the 1999 European Association of Archeologists Annual meeting in Bournemouth, England. The paper ("Forbidden archeology of the Paleolithic: how *Pithecanthropus* influenced the treatment of evidence for extreme human antiquity") is to be included in a forthcoming conference proceedings volume edited by Ana for British Archaeological Reports. I presented another paper in Ana's section at the European Association of Archeologists 2000 meeting, which was held in Lisbon. The Lisbon paper was on the Miocene archeological discoveries of the nineteenth-century Portuguese geologist Carlo Ribeiro ("The discoveries of Carlos Ribeiro: a controversial episode in nineteenth-century European archeology").

18. In terms of my ethnomethodological research orientation, I regard my request to study the Rutot collection at the Royal Belgian Institute of Natural Sciences (and my presence at this Congress) as a "breaching" technique. Flynn (1991, *The Ethnomethodological Movement*, pp. 253–254) says, "Both the surrealists and ethnomethodological movement utilized idiosyncratic devices and means to 'breach' the normal routines of social reality in order to render them strange. . . . For the ethnographic surrealists, concrete cultural objects, whether foreign or local, were used to play a disruptive, illuminatory role . . . objects sauvages were a source of the surrealist's disposition toward forcing a breach of perception and encouraging

'making the familiar strange.' Garfinkel has utilized similar 'breaching' procedures for rendering the commonplace society 'anthropologically strange.' . . . He led students in 'incongruity experiments' such as inventing new rules during a TickTack-Toe game; engaging friends in conversation and insisting that the person clarify the meaning of common place remarks; entering stores and treating customers as if they were clerks or a maitre d." I detected that my two weeks of research in the archeology laboratory of the Royal Belgian Institute of Natural Science, during which an assistant and I were continually preoccupied in the tasks of examining and photographing the Boncelles artifacts, regarded as false by the staff, did breach the normal routines and appearance of the lab, inducing a degree of strangeness for the staff. Still, my presence was tolerated, for I have, however imperfectly, mastered the techniques of "becoming the phenomena." Mehan and Wood (Mehan, Hugh and Wood, Houston [1975] *The Reality of Ethnomethodology.* New York: John Wiley and Sons. 1975, p. 227) say, "If the purpose of the research is to know the reality of the phenomenon, then the researcher must begin by *first becoming the phenomenon.*" The purpose of my research in this case was, and is, to know the phenomenon of disciplinary suppression of anomalous evidence in archeology. The only way to do this was, and is, to establish myself as part of the phenomenon.

19. Rutot (1907) Un grave problème, p. 442.
20. Rutot (1907) Un grave problème, fig. 1, p. 443.
21. In my *Forbidden Archeology,* I examined the phenomenon of the definitive debunking report: "In paleoanthropology, we sometimes encounter the definitive debunking report—a report that is repeatedly cited as having decisively invalidated a particular discovery or general category of evidence" (p. 151). ". . . researchers who share a certain bias (in this case a prejudice against evidence for Tertiary humans) cooperate by citing a poorly constructed 'definitive debunking report' (in this case by Breuil) as absolute truth in the pages of authoritative books and articles in scientific journals. It is a very effective propaganda technique. After all, how many people will bother to dig up Breuil's original article . . . and, applying critical intelligence, see for themselves if what he had to say really made sense" (p. 164). "Barnes's 1939 paper is typical of the definitive debunking report, which can be conveniently cited again and again to completely resolve a controversial question, making any further consideration of the matter superfluous. But on close examination, it appears that Barnes's definitive debunking report may be in need of some debunking itself" (p. 168).
22. For a review of the orthodox opinion of Rutot held by the generations of archeologists that immediately followed him, see Stockmans, F., (1966) Notice sur Aimé Louis Rutot. *Annales de l'Académie royale de Belgique,* 132e année. Stockmans said, "For those of my generation, who came to know of him toward the end of his life, his name invariably evoked the image of a credulous but honest man fooled by forgers and who talked with the dead" (p. 24). Rutot's interest in psychical research damaged his overall scientific credibility.
23. De Heinzelin, Jean (1959) Déclassement de la collection Dethise. *Bulletin de l'Institut Royal des Sciences naturelles de Belgique* 35(11). See also De Heinzelin, J.,

Orban, R., Roels, D., and Hurt, V. (1993) Ossements humains dits néolithiques de la région de Mons (Belgique), une évaluation. *Bulletin de l'Institut Royal des Sciences naturelles de Belgique* 63: 311–336.

24. Stoddart, Simon, and Malone, Caroline (2001) Editorial. *Antiquity* 75(288): 233–245, p. 238, citing Muscarella, O. W. (2000) *The lie became great: the forgery of Ancient Near Eastern cultures.* Groningen: Unesco/Styx Publications.

25. De Heinzelin, Jean (1957) Fagnien, Reutelien, Strépyien, Mesvinien, Flénusien, Spiennien, Omalien. *Lexique stratigraphique international.* Vol. 1, fasc. 4b, Paris.

26. Raposo, L, and Santonja, M. 1995. The earliest occupation of Europe: the Iberian peninsula. *In* W. Roebroeks and T. Van Kolfschoten (eds) *The Earliest Occupation of Europe. Proceedings of the European Science Foundation Workshop At Tautavel (France), 1993.* Analecta Praehistorica Leidensia, Vol. 27. Leiden: University of Leiden, pp. 7–25. Carbonell, E., Canal, J., and Sabchiz, N. (1982) Cueva Victoria (Murcia, España): lugar de ocupación más antiguo de la Peninsula ibérica. *Endins* 8: 47–57. Palma de Mallorca.

27. Cremo, M. A. (2000) The Discoveries of Carlos Ribeiro: A Controversial Episode in Nineteenth-Century European Archeology. European Association of Archaeologists Sixth Annual Meeting, Lisbon, Portugal. September 10–16. Unpublished, but available on request.

28. Cremo, M. A. (forthcoming) Forbidden Archeology of the Paleolithic. European Association of Archaeologists Fifth Annual Meeting. Bournemouth, England, Sept. 15–18, 1999. Selected for publication in a conference proceedings volume edited by Ana C. N. Martins for British Archaeological Reports.

29. Whitney, J. D. (1880) The auriferous gravels of the Sierra Nevada of California. *Harvard University, Museum of Comparative Zoology Memoir* 6(1). See Cremo and Thompson (1993) *Forbidden Archeology* pp. 368–394 and pp. 439–451 for a review and discussion.

30. Holmes, W. H. (1899) Review of the evidence relating to auriferous gravel man in California. In *Smithsonian Institution Annual Report 1898–1899*: 419–472. Washington, D. C.: Smithsonian Institution, p. 470.

31. Holmes, W. H. (1899. Review of the evidence relating to auriferous gravel man in California, p. 470.

32. Rutot (1907) Un grave problème, p. 447.

33. Leriche, M. (1922) Les terrains tertiaires de la Belgique. *Congrès Géologique International (13e, Bruxelles), Livret-Guide des Excursions en Belgique,* A4:1–46. p. 10. Pomerol, C. (1982) *The Cenozoic Era.* Chichester: Ellis Horwood.

34. Schweinfurth, G. (1907) Über Rutot's Entdeckung von Eolithen in beligischen Oligocän. *Zeitschrift für Ethnologie,* 39: 958–959, p. 959.

35. Rutot (1907) Un grave problème, p. 444.

36. Rutot (1907) Un grave problème, pp. 452–453.

37. Tray 2768 Box 4 (my numbers 25A, 25B). The trays are shelved in the archeology storage rooms of the Laboratory for Anthropology and Prehistory on the 19th floor of the Royal Belgian Institute of Natural Sciences building at Rue Vautier 29, B-1000 Brussels, Belgium. The rows of boxes within each tray do not have num-

bers on them. I took the box at the top left of the tray to be the first, and mentally numbered the boxes from left to right in the top row. I then went down to the next row, and again mentally numbered the boxes from left to right. Lying among the artifacts in the boxes are labels indicating the tool type (*grattoir, racloir, percuteur,* etc.). Some of the labels are quite old, apparently from the original exhibitions of the artifacts in the Royal Belgian Museum of Natural Sciences organized by Rutot himself. Other labels appear to be more recent. "My numbers" refers to the artifact identification numbers shown in my 35mm slides.

38. Tray 2678, Box 5 (my number 26A), matches Rutot (1907) Un grave problème, fig. 7, p. 454. I placed all artifacts matching Rutot's figures in plastic bags, along with identifying labels, before returning them to their boxes in the trays, making it easier to find them.

39. Rutot (1907) Un grave problème, p. 456.

40. Tray 2766, Box 5 (my numbers 5A, 5B, 5C), matches Rutot (1907) Un grave problème, fig. 9, p. 456.

41. Rutot (1907) Un grave problème, p. 458.

42. Tray 2766, Box 5 (my numbers 7A, 7B, 7C), matches Rutot (1907) Un grave problème, fig. 10, p. 458.

43. Rutot (1907) Un grave problème, p. 459.

44. Tray 2769, Box 6 (my number 30), matches Rutot (1907) Un grave problème, fig. 13, p. 458.

45. Rutot (1907) Un grave problème, p. 462.

46. Tray 2770, Box 11 (my number 31), matches Rutot (1907) Un grave problème, fig. 26, p. 463.

47. Tray 2767, Box 2 (my number 19), matches Rutot (1907) Un grave problème, fig. 27, p. 463.

48. Tray 2767, Box 2 (my numbers 16A, 16B), matches Rutot (1907) Un grave problème, fig. 29, p. 463.

49. Rutot (1907) Un grave problème, p. 464.

50. Tray 2767, Box 8 (my numbers 23A, 23B), matches Rutot (1907) Un grave problème, fig. 32, p. 465; Tray 2767, Box 8 (my numbers 22A, 22B), matches Rutot (1907) Un grave problème, fig. 33, p. 465.

51. Rutot (1907) Un grave problème, pp. 464–465.

52. Tray 2767, Box 8 (my numbers 21A, 21B), matches Rutot (1907) Un grave problème, fig. 34, p. 465.

53. Rutot (1907) Un grave problème, pp.448–449.

54. Rutot (1907) Un grave problème, p. 468. Rutot may have exaggerated the similarities. It is likely that the Tasmanian industry as a whole included some pieces more advanced than the typical specimens of Boncelles. Nevertheless, the Tasmanian industry does contain a good many implements that are quite similar to those of Boncelles, as I have seen in my firsthand study of the collections of the two industries at the Royal Belgian Institute of Natural Sciences.

55. Tasmanian collection, unmarked tray, Box 1 (my number 41A), matches Rutot (1907) Un grave problème, fig. 51, p. 475. Resembles my number 19. Trays of Tas-

manian implements are from the anthropology section of the Laboratory of Anthropology and Prehistory at the Institute.

56. Boncelles collection, Tray 2767, Box 2 (my number 19), matches Rutot (1907) Un grave problème, fig. 27, p. 463.
57. Tasmanian collection, Tray 3246, Box 4, (my numbers 34A, 34B), matches Rutot (1907) Un grave problème, fig. 57, p. 476.
58. Boncelles collection, Tray 2767, Box 2 (my numbers 16A, 16B), matches Rutot (1907) Un grave problème, fig. 29, p. 463.
59. Tasmanian collection, Tray 3246, Box 7 (my numbers 36A, 36B), matches Rutot (1907) Un grave problème, fig. 60, p. 476.
60. Boncelles collection, Tray 2767, Box 8 (my numbers 23A, 23B), matches Rutot (1907) Un grave problème, fig. 32, p. 465.
61. See for example: Rutot, A. (1902) Les industries primitives. Défense des éolithes. Les actions naturelles possibles sont inaptes a produire des effets semblables à la retouche Intentionelle. *Bulletin de la Société d'Anthropologie de Bruxelles.* Tome XX, Memoire n. III, pp. 1–68; Rutot, A. (1906) Éolithes et pseudo-éolithes. *Bulletin de la Société d'Anthropologie de Bruxelles.* Tome XXV, Memoire n. I, pp. 1–29; Rutot, A. (1909), Un homme de science peut-il, raisonnablement, admettre l'existence des industries primitives, dites éolithiques? *Bulletins et Mémoires de la Sociéte d'Anthropologie de Paris.* Ve Series, Tome X, pp. 447–473. In *Forbidden Archeology,* I also reviewed and critiqued attempts to debunk eoliths and other crude stone tool industries by appealing to natural forces (see pp. 151–177, for example).
62. Rutot Correspondence Drawer, Folder "Correspondents S."
63. Rutot Correspondence Drawer, Folder "De Puydt."
64. Rutot Correspondence Drawer, Folder "Correspondents S."
65. Rutot Correspondence Drawer, Folder "Correspondents S."
66. Rutot Correspondence Drawer, Folder "Ameghino."
67. See for example Ameghino, F. (1908) Notas preliminaires sobre el *Tetraprothomo argentinus,* un precursor del hombre del Mioceno superior de Monte Hermoso. *Anales del Museo nacional de historia natural de Buenos Aires,* 16: 105–242.
68. Rutot (1907) Un grave problème, p. 462.
69. Boncelles collection, Tray 2767, Box 2 (my numbers 15A, 15B), matches Rutot (1907) Un grave problème, fig. 24, p. 462.
70. Rutot (1907) Un grave problème, pp. 462, 464.
71. Patterson, L. W. (1983) Criteria for determining the attributes of man-made lithics. *Journal of Field Archaeology,* 10: 297–307.
72. F. Ameghino to A. Rutot, August 16, 1910. Rutot Correspondence Drawer, Folder "Ameghino."
73. Rutot (1907) Un grave problème, p. 480.
74. Rutot Correspondence Drawer, Folder "Correspondents W."
75. Rutot Correspondence Drawer, Folder "Correspondents W." This is the only copy of a letter by Rutot that I found in the collection. It could be a letter that for some reason was not sent by Rutot, or it could be a copy or first draft of a letter that was sent.
76. Boule, M., and Vallois, H. V. (1957) *Fossil Men,* London: Thames and Hudson, p.

491: "Ameghino also recorded facts of the same kind from more ancient deposits dating, according to him, from the Oligocene and even from the Eocene." Ameghino, F. (1912) L'age des formations sedimentaires tertiaires de l'Argentine en relation avec l'antiquité de l'homme. *Anales de Museo nacional de historia natural de Buenos Aires*, 22: 45–75. In this work (p. 72) Ameghino referred to "eoliths, which we find in our formations at the close of the Eocene and which differ from those of Boncelles in Belgium in that they are of much smaller size."

77. Rutot, A. (1918) *La Préhistoire. Première Partie.* Brussels. Les Naturalistes Belge, p. 24, see also figures 19 and 20, p. 23. Rutot's statement that there were no discoveries of human bones from the early Tertiary is not entirely true. J. D. Whitney reported anatomically modern human skeletal remains from formations in Calfornia that are now given an Eocene age. Whitney, J. D. 1880. The Auriferous Gravels of the Sierra Nevada of California. *Harvard University, Museum of Comparative Zoology Memoir* 6(1). My *Forbidden Archeology* documents additional reports of discoveries of anatomically modern human skeletal remains from the Tertiary and even earlier.

78. For photographs of the entire series see Rutot, A. (1919) *Un Essai de Reconstitution plastique de quelques Races humaines primitives.* Brussels. Hayez, Imprimeur de l'Académie Royale de Belgique. For photographs and description of the Tertiary human precursor, identified with the Boncelles industry, see pp. 11–14, fig. 1, and plate 1.

79. Rutot (1907) Un grave problème, pp. 480–481.

80. And they are not alone. Rutot concluded that eoliths from other Belgian sites were also of Oligocene age, such as eoliths found at Baraque Michel and in a cave at Fonds de Forêt, north of the cavern at Bay Bonnet. Rutot (1907) Un grave problème, p. 479.

15

The Nineteenth Century California Gold Mine Discoveries: Archeology, Darwinism, and Evidence for Extreme Human Antiquity

I presented this paper in a session on history of archeology, of which I was co-chairperson, at the World Archaeological Congress 5, which was held June 21–26, 2003 at Washington, D.C. Reporter Alexandra Alter wrote an article about my presentation, which was distributed by Religious News Service (What's a creationist doing bashing Darwin at the World Archaeological Congress? July 3, 2003), and published under different headlines in several newspapers. Here is a brief excerpt: "Michael Cremo, a research associate at the Bhaktivedanta Institute . . . in California, is not picketing outside. He's arguing that human civilization may have existed millions of years before the accepted dates, making the self-described Hindu creationist something of a unique voice in the ongoing debate between Darwinists and creationists. Cremo, who has spent more than 20 years looking for evidence of ancient human civilizations, is now pressing the scientific community to be more tolerant of different metaphysical views. In a radical departure from both Darwin's theory and Christian creationism, Cremo comes at the question of evolution from the Hindu understanding of time as cyclical. It was his study of the Puranas–sacred Sanskrit texts that speak of ancient civilizations–that led him to search for evidence of extreme human antiquity. While presenting his paper . . . to a group of seasoned archaeologists last week (June 26), Cremo told his rapt audience that archaeologists have overlooked a large body of evidence that contradicts Darwinian evolution."

Introduction

Philosopher of science Karl Popper (1976, p. 168) was partially right when he wrote in his autobiography "Darwinism is not a testable scientific theory, but a metaphysical research programme." While I agree that Darwinism is a metaphysical research program, I believe that particular Darwinist theories (of human origins, for example) are empirically testable. There is therefore nothing wrong in principle with anthropologists and archeologists serving Darwinism's metaphysical research program in the name of empirical science, so long as they admit that this is what they are actually doing and also admit that other anthropologists and archeologists might choose to serve other metaphysical research programs in the name of science.

The engagement of anthropology and archeology in the service of Darwinism, and its metaphysical assumptions, goes back to the nineteenth century and continues to the present day. Darwinism's background assumption of unguided materialism, combined with the assumption that species developed over time from a simple initial life form, are now expressed in Darwinist anthropological beliefs that humans evolved fairly recently, in a line emerging from African Miocene primates and continuing through a variety of Pliocene and Early Pleistocene hominids. Darwinists often assert that all of the physical evidence known to science supports this basic picture. The identification of Darwinism with anthropology and archeology is now so complete that it is difficult to get many modern practitioners, especially in America, to admit that there could possibly be a difference between the two. In their university level textbook on anthropology, Stein and Rowe (1993, p. 41) make this unqualified profession of faith: "Anthropologists are convinced that human beings . . . have changed over time in response to changing conditions. So one aim of the anthropologist is to find evidence for evolution and to generate theories about it." To be an anthropologist is to be convinced of evolution. The purpose of an anthropologist is therefore to find evidence (skeletal, cultural, genetic, etc.) for evolution, and not evidence against evolution, and to generate theories about evolution, and not theories that contradict evolution. Anthropologists (including archeologists) must therefore, by definition, serve Darwinism.

If the aim of a researcher in human origins is "to find evidence for evolution," then how will such a researcher react to evidence that radically contradicts evolutionary expectations? In this paper, I give a case study showing how commitment to Darwinism operated in the treatment of archeological discoveries from the gold mining region of California in the nineteenth century [see Plates XII-XV]. The discoveries indicated the existence of anatomically modern humans in the Tertiary. I propose to show that this evidence was eliminated from archeological discourse primarily because it contradicted an emerging Darwinist consensus on human origins, with humans evolving from more apelike hominids in the late Pleistocene. I also wish to show how Darwinists today continue to try to keep this evidence out of active scientific discussion and out of presentations to the general public (as shown by their reactions to inclusion of such evidence in the NBC television special *The Mysterious Origins of Man*). Finally, I will discuss the results of my own continuing research into the California gold mine discoveries.

Before entering into my discussion, I think it fair that I give some clues about my own metaphysical commitments so that these can be taken into account. My work in the history of archeology is guided by my studies in the Vaishnava cosmology of India, which posits a supreme being who manifests life forms, including human forms, in universes which undergo repeated events of creation and destruction over vast periods of cyclical time (Cremo 1999). The basic unit of cyclical time in the Vaishnava cosmology is the day of Brahma, which lasts for 4.32 billion years. The current day of Brahma began about 2 billion years ago. The day of Brahma is composed of 14 subcycles called *manvantara* periods, each lasting about 300 million years. Humans are manifested in each *manvantara* period. Although the Vaishnava cosmology recognizes the existence of beings with apelike bodies and humanlike intelligence, humans of our type existed alongside them. I would therefore expect that human artifacts and skeletal remains could be found in Tertiary deposits.

The California Gold Mine Discoveries from Table Mountain

In 1849, gold was discovered in the gravels of ancient riverbeds on the slopes of the Sierra Nevada Mountains in central California. At first, solitary miners panned for flakes and nuggets in the auriferous gravels that had found their way into the present stream beds. But soon gold-mining companies brought more extensive resources into play, sinking shafts into mountainsides, following the gravel deposits wherever they led. The miners found hundreds of stone artifacts, and, more rarely, human fossils.

The artifacts from these deep mine shafts and tunnels were apparently of great antiquity. Some of the more significant discoveries were made at Table Mountain in Tuolumne County [see Plate XII]. There miners dug vertical tunnels that penetrated through layers of volcanic deposits to reach the auriferous gravels. Or they dug horizontal tunnels that ran below the volcanic deposits. The auriferous gravels lay in old river channels. Norris and Webb (1990, pp. 90–93) give the geological history of the region. During the Eocene, rivers cut channels into the bedrock of the Sierra Nevada. These channels became filled with gravels containing gold. In the late Oligocene, the Eocene river channels were covered with thick deposits of rhyolitic volcanic ash, which now forms a pinkish rock. New rivers cut channels into these deposits. At Table Mountain in Tuolumne County, the new river channel was filled by a flow of latite (some earlier geologists called it basalt). This flow occurred in the Miocene. Geologists obtained potassium argon dates of about 9 million years for the Table Mountain latite. Later, the softer material on the sides of the latite flow was worn away by erosion, leaving the harder volcanic deposits. So at Table Mountain we have three hundred feet of Miocene latite covering Oligocene rhyolitic tuffs, which in turn cover the old Eocene river channels containing the auriferous gravels. According to Slemmons (1966, p. 200), the auriferous gravels are at least 30 million years old. If the gravels belong to the early Eocene, they could be as much as 50–55 million years old. The principal discoveries of human bones and artifacts came from the very lowest levels of the auriferous gravels near the bedrock.

Darwinists routinely assert that humans like ourselves appeared fairly recently on this planet, between 150,000 and 100,000 years ago. The California gold mine discoveries provide a counterexample, but they are not an isolated anomaly. In my book *Forbidden Archeology*, coauthored with Richard Thompson, I document numerous other cases showing that human beings like ourselves have existed on this planet for tens of millions, even hundreds of millions of years. This is consistent with the historical accounts found in the ancient Sanskrit writings of India. But among all the discoveries of evidence for extreme human antiquity, I find the ones from the California gold mines to be exceptionally fascinating.

The most significant artifacts and human bones were reported to the scientific community by J. D. Whitney, then the state geologist of California. His detailed reports can be found in his book *The Auriferous Gravels of the Sierra Nevada of California,* published by Harvard University's Peabody Museum of Comparative Zoology in its series of monographs in 1880. Artifacts were discovered at many locations in the gold mining region [see Plates XIII–XV], but I will concentrate on those found at Table Mountain in Tuolumne County. Whitney personally examined a collection of Table Mountain artifacts belonging to Dr. Perez Snell, of Sonora, California. Snell's collection included spearheads and other implements. One of these was, wrote Whitney (1880, p. 264), "a stone muller, or some kind of utensil which had apparently been used for grinding." Dr. Snell informed Whitney "that he took it with his own hands from a car-load of 'dirt' coming out from under Table Mountain." In another case, Mr. Albert G. Walton, one of the owners of the Valentine claim, found a stone mortar, 15 inches in diameter, in gold-bearing gravels 180 feet from the surface and also beneath the latite cap (Whitney 1880, p. 265).

In 1870, Oliver W. Stevens submitted the following notarized affidavit: "I, the undersigned, did about the year 1853, visit the Sonora Tunnel, situated at and in Table Mountain, about one half a mile north and west of Shaw's Flat, and at that time there was a car-load of auriferous gravel coming out of said Sonora Tunnel. And I, the undersigned, did pick out of said gravel (which came from under the basalt and out of the tunnel about two hundred feet in, at the depth of about one hundred and twenty-five feet) a mastodon tooth. . . . And at the same time I found with it some relic that resembled a large stone bead, made perhaps of alabaster." The bead, if from the gravel beneath the latite cap, is at least 9 million years old and could perhaps be far older, from the Eocene. The bead came into the collection of C. D. Voy (1874, p. 50), who described it as "about two inches long and two inches in circumference."

In his book, Whitney (1880, p. 373) included the following statement by James Carvin: "This it to certify that I, the undersigned, did about the year 1858, dig out of some mining claims known as the Stanislaus Company, situated in Table Mountain, Tuolumne County, opposite O'Byrn's Ferry, on the Stanislaus River, a stone hatchet . . . with a hole through it for a handle. Its size was four inches across the edge, and length about six inches. It had evidently been made by human hands. The above relic was found about sixty to seventy-five feet from the surface in gravel, under the basalt, and about 300 feet from the mouth of the tunnel. There were also some mortars found, at about the same time and place."

Llewellyn Pierce found a mortar at Table Mountain, and gave this notarized statement: "This is to certify that I, the undersigned, have this day given to Mr. C. D. Voy, to be preserved in his collection of ancient stone relics, a certain stone mortar, which has evidently been made by human hands, which was dug up by me, about the year 1862, under Table Mountain, in gravel, at a depth of about 200 feet from the surface, under the basalt, which was over sixty feet deep, and about 1,800 feet in from the mouth of the tunnel. Found in the claim known as the Boston Tunnel Company" (Whitney 1880, p. 267).

The following is not one of the cases reported by Whitney in his book, but it is quite similar to them. On August 2, 1890, J. H. Neale signed the following statement about discoveries made by him: "In 1877 Mr. J. H. Neale was superintendent of the

Montezuma Tunnel Company, and ran the Montezuma tunnel into the gravel underlying the lava of Table Mountain, Tuolumne County. The mouth of the tunnel is near the road which leads in a southerly direction from Rawhide camp, and about three miles from that place. The mouth is approximately 1,200 feet from the present edge of the solid lava cap of the mountain. At a distance of between 1,400 and 1,500 feet from the mouth of the tunnel, or of between 200 and 300 feet beyond the edge of the solid lava, Mr. Neale saw several spear-heads, of some dark rock and nearly one foot in length. On exploring further, he himself found a small mortar three or four inches in diameter and of irregular shape. This was discovered within a foot or two of the spear-heads. He then found a large well-formed pestle" (Becker 1891, pp. 191–192).

Neale's affidavit continued: "All of these relics were found . . . close to the bed-rock, perhaps within a foot of it. Mr. Neale declares that it is utterly impossible that these relics can have reached the position in which they were found excepting at the time the gravel was deposited, and before the lava cap formed. There was not the slightest trace of any disturbance of the mass or of any natural fissure into it by which access could have been obtained either there or in the neighborhood" (Becker 1891, p. 192). The position of the artifacts in gravel close to the bedrock at Tuolumne Table Mountain indicates they were of Eocene age, at least 33 million years old.

William H. Holmes, a prominent anthropologist at the Smithsonian Institution, dismissed Neale's finds (and the other finds reported by Whitney) as either intrusions or hoaxes. But in a paper read before the American Geological Society, geologist George F. Becker said (1891, pp. 192–193): "It would have been more satisfactory to me individually if I had myself dug out these implements, but I am unable to discover any reason why Mr. Neale's statement is not exactly as good evidence to the rest of the world as my own would be. He was as competent as I to detect any fissure from the surface or any ancient workings, which the miner recognizes instantly and dreads profoundly. Some one may possibly suggest that Mr. Neale's workmen 'planted' the implements, but no one familiar with mining will entertain such a suggestion for a moment. . . . The auriferous gravel is hard picking, in large part it requires blasting, and even a very incompetent supervisor could not possibly be deceived in this way. . . . In short, there is, in my opinion, no escape from the conclusion that the implements mentioned in Mr. Neale's statement actually occurred near the bottom of the gravels, and that they were deposited where they were found at the same time with the adjoining pebbles and matrix."

Becker (1891, p. 193) also noted that in the spring of 1869, geologist Clarence King, of the United States Geological Survey, was conducting research at Table Mountain. At that time, he found a stone pestle firmly embedded in a deposit of gold-bearing gravel lying beneath the cap of basalt, or latite. The gravel deposit had only recently been exposed by erosion. King did not report the discovery at the time he made it, but did provide details to Becker, who stated (1891, p. 194): "Mr. King is perfectly sure this implement was in place and that it formed an original part of the gravels in which he found it. It is difficult to imagine a more satisfactory evidence than this of the occurrence of implements in the auriferous, pre-glacial, sub-basaltic gravels." From this description and the modern geological dating of the Table Mountain strata, it is apparent that the object, if found in situ, was over 9 million years old.

Even Holmes (1899, p. 453) admitted that the King pestle, which was placed in the Smithsonian Institution, "may not be challenged with impunity." Holmes searched the site very carefully and noted the presence of some modern Indian mealing stones lying loose on the surface. He stated (1899, p. 454): "I tried to learn whether it was possible that one of these objects could have become embedded in the exposed tufa deposits in recent or comparatively recent times . . . but no definite result was reached." If Holmes had found any definite evidence of recent embedding, he would certainly have used it to discredit King's discovery. Instead he could only express wonder "that Mr. King failed to publish it—that he failed to give to the world what could well claim to be the most important observation ever made by a geologist bearing upon the history of the human race, leaving it to come out through the agency of Dr. Becker, twenty-five years later" (Holmes 1899, p. 454). But Becker noted in his report (1891, p. 194): "I have submitted this statement of his discovery to Mr. King, who pronounces it correct."

In addition to human artifacts, human bones were also found in the California gold mining region. On January 1, 1873, the president of the Boston Society of Natural History read extracts from a letter by Dr. C. F. Winslow about a discovery of human bones at Table Mountain in Tuolumne County. Winslow stated: "During my visit to this mining camp I have become acquainted with Capt. David B. Akey, formerly commanding officer of a California volunteer company, and well known to many persons of note in that State, and in the course of my conversation with him I learned that in 1855 and 1856 he was engaged with other miners in running drifts into Table Mountain in Tuolumne County at the depth of about two hundred feet from its brow, in search of placer gold. He states that in a tunnel run into the mountain at the distance of about fifty feet from that upon which he was employed, and at the same level, a complete human skeleton was found and taken out by miners personally known to him . . . He thinks that the depth from the surface at which this skeleton was found was two hundred feet, and from one hundred and eighty to two hundred feet from the opening cut or face of the tunnel. The bones were in a moist condition, found among the gravel and very near the bed rock, and water was running out of the tunnel. There was a petrified pine tree, from sixty to eighty feet in length and between two and three feet in diameter at the butt, lying near this skeleton. Mr. Akey went into the tunnel with the miners, and they pointed out to him the place where the skeleton was found. He saw the tree in place and broke specimens from it" (Winslow 1873, pp. 257–258).

The gravel just above the bedrock at Table Mountain, where the skeleton was found, is of Eocene age. This should be the age of the skeleton unless it was introduced into the gravels at a later time, and I am not aware of any evidence indicating such an intrusion. In another case, Winslow himself collected some human fossils, which he sent to museums in the eastern United States. A human skull fragment was dispatched by Winslow to the Museum of the Natural History Society of Boston. The fossil was labeled as follows: "From a shaft in Table Mountain, 180 feet below the surface, in gold drift, among rolled stones and near mastodon debris. Overlying strata of basaltic compactness and hardness. Found July, 1857. Given to Rev. C. F. Winslow by Hon. Paul K. Hubbs, August, 1857." Another fragment, from the same skull, and similarly labeled, was sent to the Museum of the Philadelphia Academy of Natural Sciences.

Upon learning of this discovery, J. D. Whitney began his own investigation. He learned that Hubbs was a well-known citizen of Vallejo, California, and a former State Superintendent of Education. Whitney got from Hubbs a detailed written account of the discovery, which occurred in the Valentine Shaft, south of Shaw's Flat. Whitney (1880, p. 265) stated: "The essential facts are, that the Valentine Shaft was vertical, that it was boarded up to the top, so that nothing could have fallen in from the surface during the working under ground, which was carried on in the gravel channel exclusively, after the shaft had been sunk. There can be no doubt that the specimen came from the drift in the channel under Table Mountain, as affirmed by Mr. Hubbs." The skull fragment was found in a horizontal mine shaft (or drift) leading from the main vertical shaft, at a depth of 180 feet from the surface. Hubbs stated that he "saw the portion of skull immediately after its being taken out of the sluice into which it had been shoveled" (Whitney 1880, p. 265). Adhering to the bone was the characteristic gold-bearing gravel. As mentioned above, a stone mortar was found in the same mine.

When examining a collection of stone artifacts belonging to Dr. Perez Snell, J. D. Whitney (1880, p. 264) noted the presence of a human jaw. The jaw and artifacts all came from gold-bearing gravels beneath the lava cap of Tuolumne Table Mountain. The gravels from which the jaw came are at least of Miocene antiquity, and could be from the Eocene.

C. D. Voy (1874, pp. 52–53) gives this description of the jaw and accompanying artifacts: "About the year 1862 or 1863, while at Sonora, Dr. P. Snell, an old and well known resident there and whose life, or a greater part of it, has been spent in the development of American antiquities, showed me some relics which he said were found near Table Mountain. The relics consist of an immense jaw bone entire, including many of the teeth, and the thigh bones. These had the appearance of great age. They were found 340 feet below the surface under Table Mountain. This jaw is 5-1/2 (five and a half inches) at the widest place, and is immensely strong . . . . Near these human remains were found some curious stone implements, one probably designed as a pendant. It was hollow on one side and covered on the other. Or as there were little notches on the end, for tying fast, it is possible it may have been used as a shuttle. This implement was of siliceous slate. There were also one or two spearheads about 6 or 8 inches long, and somewhat round, and broken off where the holes were made to fasten to the wood. These were also made of a siliceous slate, also one or two scopes [scoops], or ladles made of steatite, and with well formed handles, somewhat resembling the little horn scopes made by druggists. . . . Some of the above stone relics are now or were recently in the Smithsonian Institute, and came at Yale College Museum. All these implements differ entirely from anything found now in the possession of the present Indians of the Pacific Slope, as far as can be ascertained. I have heard of other relics, being found at different times, under this mountain, some distance from where these were found, but it is so long ago I cannot get any trace of them. They are probably lost or destroyed."

It is not easy to justify the sustained opposition to the California finds by Holmes (1899), Sinclair (1908), and other scientists of their time. Although they often spoke of fraud, they uncovered no actual evidence of it in these cases. And their suggestions that Indians might have carried portable mortars and spearheads into the mines are not credible. A modern historian, W. Turrentine Jackson of the University of California at Davis, points out (personal communication to my research assistant Steve Bernath, March 19, 1985): "During the gold rush era the Indians were driven from the mining region, and they seldom came into contact with the forty-niners from the mining region."

One might therefore ask why Holmes was so determined to discredit Whitney's evidence for the existence of Tertiary humans. The following statement by Holmes (1899, p. 424) provides an essential clue: "Perhaps if Professor Whitney had fully appreciated the story of human evolution as it is understood today, he would have hesitated to announce the conclusions formulated, notwithstanding the imposing array of testimony with which he was confronted." In other words, if the facts do not fit the favored theory, the facts, even an imposing array of them, must go. A more reasonable approach was taken by Alfred Russel Wallace, cofounder of the theory of evolution by natural selection. Wallace (1887, p. 679) said about the reports of Whitney: "The proper way to treat evidence as to man's antiquity is to place it on record, and admit it provisionally wherever it would be held adequate in the case of other animals; not, as is too often now the case, to ignore it as unworthy of acceptance or subject its discoverers to indiscriminate accusations of being impostors or the victims of impostors."

Holmes's opposition to the California gold mine discoveries was to a large degree conditioned by his acceptance of Java man and its key position in Darwinist accounts of human evolution. Holmes (1899, p. 470) suggested that Whitney's evidence should be rejected because "it implies a human race older by at least one half than *Pithecanthropus erectus* of Dubois, which may be regarded as an incipient form of human only." European scientists followed Holmes in using the Java man discoveries to dismiss the California discoveries. According to archeologist Robert Munro, Fellow of the Royal Society of Antiquaries of Scotland, researchers who accepted Whitney's conclusions that anatomically modern humans existed in the Tertiary were "upholding opinions which, if true, would be absolutely subversive . . . of human evolution" (Munro 1905, p. 106). He cited as evidence the somewhat apelike *Pithecanthropus* skull, which he assigned to the Plio-Pleistocene boundary. After introducing Holmes's statement that the California evidence (which included anatomically modern human skeletal remains) belonged to a period older than that of *Pithecanthropus,* Munro (1905, p. 106) said, "According to these calculations the cranium of a Californian 'auriferous gravel man' would have been of so low a type as to be undistinguishable from that of the Simian progenitor of *Homo sapiens.*" About the artifacts, which included projectile points and mortars and pestles, Munro (1905, p. 108) said that if they were to be accepted "we must, henceforth, delete from archaeological nomenclature such terms as Palaeolithic and Neolithic as having no longer any chronological significance." In other words, according to Darwinist evolutionary expectations, neither anatomically modern human bones nor finely worked artifacts could be accepted as genuinely Tertiary.

In America, Sinclair (1908) offered similar theoretical objections to Whitney's reports. For example, he wrote (1908, pp. 129–130): "The occurrence in the older auriferous gravels of human remains . . . would necessitate placing the origin of the human race in an exceedingly remote geological period. This is contrary to all precedent in the history of organisms." Sinclair (1908, p. 130) also argued that Whitney's discoveries "would mean that man of a type as high as the existing race was a contemporary of the three-toed horse and other primitive forms of the late Miocene and early Pliocene, a thesis to which all geological and biological evidence is opposed."

So in connection with the California gold mine discoveries we find not only evidence for extreme human antiquity but also evidence illuminating the processes by which dominant groups in science exclude controversial facts from scientific discussion and public attention. These processes, which I collectively refer to as the "knowledge filter," are a powerful factor in removing certain kinds of evidence from scientific discourse and research. Because of the very effective knowledge filtering efforts of Holmes, Sinclair, and other scientists in the late nineteenth century and the early twentieth century, the California gold mine discoveries from Table Mountain are hardly known today.

Darwinists React to the NBC Television Special *The Mysterious Origins of Man*

In February 1996 the California gold mine discoveries from Table Moutain and other cases from my book *Forbidden Archeology* were featured in an NBC television special called *The Mysterious Origins of Man*. It was produced and directed by Bill Cote and his associates at BC Video. During the filming of *The Mysterious Origins of Man* [*MOM*], I suggested to the producer that he film stone artifacts discovered in California gold mines during the nineteenth century. Geological evidence indicates that these objects are of Eocene age. The artifacts are stored at the Phoebe Hearst Museum of Anthropology at the University of California in Berkeley. The responses from the museum officials were interesting.

"At first we were told they could not make the time," wrote producer Bill Cote in a letter to me (August 26, 1996). "We countered saying we had plenty of time and could wait three or four months." Museum officials responded with a letter claiming they had a shortage of staff and funds. The producers said they would pay all the costs involved in bringing the artifacts out of storage for filming, including overtime pay for the workers. The museum refused this offer. The producers continued to seek permission through various channels. "We patiently went all the way to the head of publicity for the University," explained Bill Cote in his letter, "but it seems the museum director has final say and she said no." Instead of new film of the California gold mine objects, the producers used the original nineteenth century photographs included by Whitney in his book.

The final program contained, in addition to segments based on *Forbidden Archeology*, segments based on the works of others dealing with such topics as Atlantis, the age of architectural monuments in Egypt and South America, and other material not related to the human evolution question. But it was principally the human evolution material, including the California gold mine discoveries, that provoked a storm of protest from Darwinist scientists.

An advance internet press release by NBC (February 21, 1996) drew the attention of Darwinists even before the program aired. The press release said, "Could it be that man has made the climb from the Stone Age to civilization more than once, and that present-day man is just the latest in this cycle? That's just one of the many compelling theories to be addressed by *The Mysterious Origins of Man,* a one-hour special from the Emmy-winning producers of NBC's *Mystery of the Sphinx.* Airing Sunday, February 25, 7/6 p.m., the special challenges accepted beliefs about prehistoric man. . . . Is Darwin's theory of evolution correct? . . . Narrated by Charlton Heston, this is one mind-expanding special you won't want to miss."

On the same day as the NBC internet news release, archeologist John R. Cole sent an alert to proevolution internet discussion groups: "(Sun) NBC TV will broadcast a special on the 'Mystery' of human origins, apparently with a lot of antievolutionist overtones. Narr[ated] by C Heston! . . . NBC PR sounds a lot like Krishna Kreationism as opposed to ICR." The ICR (Institute for Creation Research) promotes a Christian young-earth geology, limited to ten thousand years. The term "Krishna Kreationism," used here in a derogatory fashion, comes originally from a review of *Forbidden Archeology* by Ken Feder in *Geoarchaeology.* Feder (1994, p. 337) had said about *Forbidden Archeology,* "The book itself represents something perhaps not seen before; we can fairly call it 'Krishna creationism' with no disrespect intended." The prebroadcast publicity for *The Mysterious Origins of Man* mentioned time periods of millions of years for human existence. Cole was familiar with *Forbidden Archeology.* I had once debated him on a radio show. Cole is associated with the National Center for Science Education, a small but vociferous proDarwinism organization. The name of the Center misleadingly implies governmental affiliation. Cole had this to say in a letter to internet discussion groups on February 26, 1996, just after *Mysterious Origins of Man* was broadcast on NBC: "From preview info, I suspected and predicted that this show was going to hew to the line of the Hare Krishna book, *Forbidden Archaeology* more than the ICR line. Boy, was I right!" These and other communications related to Darwinist reactions to *The Mysterious Origins of Man* are collected in my book *Forbidden Archeology's Impact* (Cremo 1998).

The broadcast of *The Mysterious Origins of Man* marks one of the few times a major American television network has aired a program challenging Darwinian explanations of human origins. An article in *Science,* the journal of the American Association for the Advancement of Science (March 8, 1996, p. 1357), said, "The claims of creationists . . . routinely send biologists into fits. But those fits pale before the indignation spilling out, mostly over the Internet, since Sunday evening, 25 February, when a major U.S. television network ran a 'special' suggesting that humans coexisted with the dinosaurs, and that the scientific establishment was suppressing the evidence." A report released by B.C. Video on March 4, 1996 reproduced messages from scientists calling the producers "morons or liars" and demands that "you should be banned from the airwaves."

On February 26, archeologist William Doleman of the University of New Mexico at Albuquerque, wrote to *Mysterious Origins of Man's* producer Bill Cote: "The portrayal of legitimate scientists such as myself as constituting a cabal of evil, evidence-suppressing conspirators is unforgivable. But the worst of your crimes lies in the failure to offer the public a balanced view that compares the overwhelming evidence in favor of evolution theory and conventionally-derived dates for man . . . with the dubious and poorly documented 'evidence' the whackos [sic] cite. The average citizen knows the difference between fantasy entertainment such as *The X Files* and documentary presentations. To present fantasy and unsubstantiated pseudo-science to the public in documentary format is a pernicious form of anti-science propaganda." In other words, he wanted to suppress the evidence. Here I want to say a few words about how the knowledge filtering process operates. It is not that "legitimate" (i.e. Darwinist) scientists believe that they are hiding "true" evidence from the public and other scientists. Rather, when Darwinists encounter evidence that radically contradicts their expectations about human origins, they simply assume that such evidence must be "unsubstantiated . . . dubious and poorly documented" and that the purveyors of such evidence must be "whackos." So even though there is no satanic conspiracy to suppress evidence, the result is that archeological evidence for extreme human antiquity is in fact dropped from active scientific discourse.

In a message to archeology discussion groups on the internet (Sci.Archeology, Alt. Archeology) dated February 28, 1996, Darwinist geologist Paul Heinrich responded directly to the Table Mountain evidence presented in *Mysterious Origins of Man*: "While listening to the NBC documentary *The Mysterious Origins of Man (MOM)*, I came across some really mind-boggling distortions of the facts concerning an archaeological controversy. Early in the show, they talked about the Calaveras skull controversy. In this case, a geologist, Dr. J. D. Whitney, was given artifacts and a skull that the miners said were found several hundred feet below beneath Table Mountain in Tertiary, gold-bearing gravels that they were mining. Because the age of these gravels were about Pliocene age, these finds . . . caused a very public controversy. . . . The miners had played a very elaborate prank on him." However, the Calaveras skull was discovered not at Table Mountain in Tuolumne County, California, but at Bald Hill, in Calaveras County. If the skull was a prank, the joke was not on Whitney, but on the mine owner who found the skull in his mine at Bald Hill.

"Anyway," Heinrich continued, "after a very brief and selective summary of the controversy, which strangely omits mention of the skull, the name *Calaveras*, and its resolution, Charlton Heston said: 'This bizarre evidence seems to have been well documented. Yet, the general public and many within the scientific community are unaware of these controversial finds.' The last statement is completely incorrect. When I took my beginning, undergraduate course in North American, this case was mentioned and discussed. The archaeologists specializing in Paleo-Indians who I have as colleagues, know about this case."

Mysterious Origins of Man "omits mention of the skull" and "the name Calaveras" because the case discussed in the program was not that of the well known Calaveras skull, but that of the Table Mountain discoveries reported by Whitney, which are far less well known, as indicated by Heinrich's own ignorance of them. Obviously, he did not learn about them in his undergraduate courses or from specialist archeologists. Therefore Heston's statement is in fact true. The discoveries are not well known either among the general public or scientists.

Heinrich went on to say: "Charlton Heston's next statement is: 'The question is why haven't we heard of these discoveries before?' My answer to this question is: 'You have not heard of these discoveries because the writers for *The Mysterious Origins of Man* (*MOM*) failed to do their homework.' Had they taken the time and trouble to do any sort of research concerning the archaeology of California, anybody would have heard about this controversy." The person who failed to do his homework was Heinrich, who relying on standard Darwinist versions of the archeology of California, was unaware of the Table Mountain discoveries reported by Whitney in his Harvard University monograph.

Finally, Heinrich said, "After that statement [by Heston, above], *MOM* had the authors of *Forbidden Archeology,* which is archaeology as seen through a Hindu creationist knowledge filter, complain about how this controversy was a perfect example of the censorship practiced by archaeologists who they claim have buried more sites than they have excavated. The problem is that no censorship occurred in this controversy, which in my opinion exposes the falsehood of their censorship claims." Apparently, some censorship did occur, and some sites were "buried," because Heinrich did not learn about the Table Mountain finds either through his university courses or from his specialist colleagues. They were eliminated from active discourse in archeology over a century ago, principally because they contradicted Darwinist expectations about human origins. However, the Calaveras skull has remained a part of current discourse, because a hoax (if that is in fact what it is) involving evidence for extreme human antiquity serves some useful purpose, in furthering the belief that all evidence contradicting Darwinist expectations must be of the same type.

"The real problem," said Heinrich, "is that modern archaeology fails to conform to certain Hindu creation myths and *Forbidden Archeology* is an explanation through the authors' knowledge filters of why modern archaeology fails to support these beliefs. . . . Note: *Forbidden Archeology* was published by the Bhaktivedanta Institute of the International Society for Krishna Consciousness." It is true that my *Forbidden Archeology* coauthor and I were looking at modern archeology through a Vaishnava (Hindu) knowledge filter. But it is also true that Heinrich was looking at modern archeology through the filter of Darwinism. It is clear that Heinrich's filter resulted in considerable distortion of the evidence reported in *Mysterious Origins of Man.* He mistakenly identified a case of which he was completely ignorant with a case that he did know about. This misidentification is obvious in his final question, "If there has been the 'massive coverup' as *MOM* claims, how come I was taught about the Calaveras controversy and instantly recognized what they w[ere] talking about although they had mangled the details of the controversy?" The reason for Heinrich's instant misidentification is that knowledge filtering by previous generations of Darwinists had eliminated the Table Mountain discoveries from the knowledge base of modern archeology, leaving only the residue of a possible hoax.

On March 22, 1996, in a letter to several internet discussion groups (Talk.Origins, Sci.Archaeology, Alt.Archaeology, Sci.Anthropology, and Sci.Anthropology.Paleo), I responded to some of the misrepresentations of the *Forbidden Archeology* material included in *Mysterious Origins of Man:* "First, I do not agree with everything that was presented on that show. For example, I have studied the case of the Paluxy man tracks and decided it is not possible to conclude whether or not they are genuine human tracks. . . . Neither do I subscribe to the views that the show presented on Atlantis, massive rapid displacements of the entire crust of the earth, etc. But I will stand behind the material that came from *Forbidden Archeology* and the conclusions that can be drawn from it. In brief, there is a lot of scientifically reported archeological evidence that puts the existence of anatomically modern humans back tens of millions of years. . . . In examining the treatment of the reports of this anomalous evidence, there appears to be a pattern of unwarranted dismissal, based not so much on the quality of the evidence itself but on its out-of-bounds position relative to orthodox paradigms of human origins. I have presented academic papers on this topic at the World Archeological Congress 3 in New Delhi, in December 1994, and at the Kentucky State University Institute for Liberal Studies Sixth Annual Interdisciplinary Conference on Science and Culture, April 1995. I am quite pleased that not everyone in the scientific world is reacting to the book with the kind of conditioned negative response that seems so prevalent in the messages posted recently to this group. For example, Tim Murray, archeologist and historian of archeology at La Trobe University, said in a recent review of *Forbidden Archeology* in *British Journal for the History of Science* (1995, vol. 28, pp. 377–379): 'I have no doubt that there will be some who will read this book and profit from it. Certainly it provides historians of archaeology with a useful compendium of case studies in the history and sociology of scientific knowledge, which can be used to foster debate within archaeology about how to describe the epistemology of one's discipline.' Tim also guardedly admitted that the religious perspective of *Forbidden Archeology* might have some utility: 'The dominant paradigm has changed and is changing, and practitioners openly debate issues which go right to the conceptual core of the discipline. Whether the Vedas have a role to play in this is up to the individual scientists concerned.'"

The reactions to *The Mysterious Origins of Man* extended beyond individual expressions of negative opinions to the producers. Dr. Jim Foley organized a letter campaign directed at the executives of NBC and the sponsors of the program, which included: Coca-Cola, McDonalds, Olive Garden, Toyota, Chevron, Kelloggs, J. C. Penney, Honda, Wendy's, General Motors, LensCrafters, Folger's Coffee, and M&M Candy.

The outrage among Darwinist scientists increased when they saw the following headlines from an internet press release from NBC, dated May 29, 1996: "Controversy Surrounds *The Mysterious Origins of Man* . . . University Profs Want Special Banned from the Airwaves. . . . Program That Dares To Challenge Accepted Beliefs About Pre-Historic Man Will Be Rebroadcast June 8 on NBC." Amazingly, NBC was using their objections to promote another broadcast of the show.

The text of the press release stated: "NBC's *The Mysterious Origins of Man* sparked heated controversy within the academic community when originally broadcast February 25, 1996, and will be rebroadcast on Saturday, June 8 (8–9 p.m. ET). Professors of science and anthropology from some of the nation's most prestigious colleges and universities voiced strong opinions about some of the theories in the special, which challenged long-accepted beliefs about man's beginnings. The program presented startling evidence suggesting man may have made the climb from Stone Age to civilization more than once; that present-day man is just the latest in this cycle, and that Darwin's

Theory of Evolution has serious flaws."

Producer Bill Cote was quoted in the NBC press release as follows: "Our goal was simply to present the public with evidence which suggests an alternative view to some of our most accepted theories. We questioned fundamental issues that they (some scientists) felt should not be questioned. The bottom line is, the world is bigger than scientists can explain, and some of them want us to believe they can explain everything.

"We expected some controversy when we produced this show," Cote continued, "but no one was prepared for the enormous cry of outrage from members of the scientific community. While many viewers, including some scientists, praised the production as 'a great accomplishment and contributing to public education,' many scientists expressed outrage and criticism."

Dr. Jere H. Lipps, a Darwinist paleontologist at the University of California at Berkeley, wrote by email to producer Bill Cote on May 30, 1996 (sending copies to various scientific discussion groups on the internet): "I appreciate the advance notice of your press release about the reshowing of *The Mysterious Origins of Man*. Can you please provide me a list of the news organizations you sent your release to? As you expected I am appalled that you and NBC would once again represent that program as the way science in America is done. It does not do you, NBC, or the sponsors any honor whatsoever. It indicates to scientists a large degree of ignorance about how science works. You seem to think that scientists object to the theories presented. Not in most cases, because everything in the program has been dealt with by legitimate science already. . . . As its writer and director, I can appreciate your desire to use our objections to promote it once again. It is, however, a pathetic way to make a buck, when honesty is so much better and profitable."

As far is honesty is concerned, I hope no one will be deceived into thinking that Lipps and other scientists of his type did not object to the antiDarwinist theories presented in *The Mysterious Origins of Man*. They did object. As for the claim by Lipps that the show mispresented how science works, I believe the show and the reactions to it provided a very good representation of how the Darwinist element in science really does work in practice. Some Darwinists do try to block discussion of controversial evidence, both in the world of science itself and among the public in general.

On the same day he sent his letter to Bill Cote, Lipps made this general appeal to scientists: "NBC is now proposing to reshow their scientific travesty *The Mysterious Origins of Man*, using the objections of the scientific community as a selling point. This is a major disservice to the general public and misrepresentation of the majority of the scientists' objections. . . . If you are worried about science in America, tell your local NBC station, NBC, and its various sponsors that you object to the portrayal of this program as science. America must get smart and we can make a difference!" Lipps demanded: "I challenge to NBC and its program producers to have an introduction to the reshowing of this program by a real scientist." This "real" (i.e. Darwinist) scientist would, said Lipps, "tell the viewers that the program may be entertainment, but it is not science." Others proposed boycotts, as shown in this internet message posted to internet discussion groups for archeologists and anthropologists by C. Wood on May 31, 1996: "Anybody know who the sponsors are? I would like to get an early start boycotting them. There's always the off chance that some of them will pull their sponsorship." Still others proposed pressuring the executives of General Electric, the company that owns NBC, to stop the reshowing of the program.

In the 1950s, the McCarthylike campaign of intimidation waged by Lipps and other Darwinists might have been sufficient to keep NBC from airing the program again. At least, NBC may have been forced to accept Darwinist demands that the rebroadcast of *Mysterious Origins of Man* begin with a segment in which a Darwinist dictated to the public how they should see the show. That NBC had the courage to stand up to the intimidation and the audacity to use the protests from Darwinists to promote the rebroadcast of the unchanged original show to the public was a refreshing sign that intellectual freedom was alive and well in America.

But representatives of Darwinist science did not see things that way. They thought NBC should be severely punished for daring to air the show a second time. On June 17, 1996, Dr. Allison R. Palmer, president of the Institute for Cambrian Studies, wrote to the Federal Communications Commission, the government agency that grants licenses to television broadcasting companies: "This e-mail is a request for the FCC to investigate and, I hope, seriously censure the National Broadcasting Company for crassly commercial irresponsible journalism that seriously violates the trust the public should have in materials that are touted as credible by a major network. . . . Last February they produced a program *Mysterious Origins of Man* that purported to be scientifically based, and received massive negative reactions from responsible scientists representing numerous areas of science. Following this response . . . they chose to use the reactions of the reputable and responsible science community to generate viewer interest by distributing PR announcements implying that the content of their show was science that the 'establishment' did not want brought before the public." It is, however, patently clear that the "establishment" did indeed not want the antiDarwinist scientific content of the NBC show brought before the public, and Palmer's letter to the FCC is excellent proof of this. Palmer's protest was based on the identification of science with Darwinism, and the parallel identification of scientist with Darwinist.

Palmer continued: "At the very least NBC should be required to make substantial prime-time apologies to their viewing audience for a sufficient period of time so that the audience clearly gets the message that they were duped. In addition, NBC should perhaps be fined sufficiently so that a major fund for public science education can be established." Copies of Palmer's letter were sent to the executives of NBC and were widely distributed on the internet to Darwinist scientists, who were invited to send their own letters of support to the FCC. Palmer's attempt to get the FCC to punish NBC failed, but the very fact that such an attempt was made should tell us something

New Research on the Table Mountain Discoveries

As an historian of archeology concentrating on evidence for extreme human antiquity, my practice is to not only study reports in the primary published scientific literature, but to also (1) study original field notes, maps, and other archival documents; (2) to locate and study artifacts in museum collections; and (3) to relocate and revisit the sites of the discoveries. I have done this type of work on the Miocene human artifacts discovered by Carlos Ribeiro, the chief government geologist of Portugal in the late nineteenth century. In addition to studying his published reports, I visited the Museum of Geology in Lisbon to study and photograph his artifacts [see Plates I-VII], and I also visited the museum library's archives to study his original correspondence, field notes, and maps. Using this information, I was able to locate and revisit several of the sites of his discoveries [see Plate I, Figures 3 and 4]. The results of this research were presented in a paper read at the annual meeting of the European Association of Archeologists held in Lisbon in the year 2000. I did similar work regarding the Oligocene artifacts discovered by the Belgian geologist Aime Louis Rutot early in the twentieth century. I studied and photographed the artifacts in the archeology collection of the Royal Museum of Natural Sciences in Brussels [see Plates VIII-XI], and also studied his correspondence and other documents. I used this information to relocate the Boncelles site, where Rutot discovered the Oligocene artifacts [see Plate VIII, Figure 1]. I presented the results of this research in a paper accepted for presentation at the XX-IVth Congress of the International Union for Prehistoric and Protohistoric Sciences in Liege, Belgium, in 2001. This comprehensive kind of study contributes not only to the history of archeology, but also provides current workers with information that could lead to further practical research.

In the spring of 2002, I decided I would like to present a paper on the California gold mine discoveries at the WAC5. My first step was to schedule an appointment to study the catalog of the Phoebe Hearst Museum of Anthropology at the University of California at Berkeley. I flew to Berkeley, and on the day of the appointment, I went to the museum, and was shown to the catalog room, where I did my work. Artifacts were catalogued on cards filed according to county, and sites within counties. I compiled a list of artifacts I wished to study. Mostly they were from a collection of artifacts made by C. D. Voy. The collection was given to the museum in the nineteenth century.

While going through the card catalog, I came upon an interesting artifact, a granite pestle (museum number 1-67275, accession number 854) collected by Thomas N. Hosmer in the year 1885 at Volcano Canyon, the middle fork of the American River, in Placer County, California. On the back of the card there was a handwritten copy of a letter from Thomas N. Hosmer, dated May 9, 1892: "Volcano Canon is a tributary of the Middle Fork of the American River. It was gold bearing, but it is now worked out. The Basin or Gouge Hole where the pestle was found was filled with large boulders, gravel & sand, and so firmly cemented together that it was difficult to loosen it with pick. . . . That this cemented gravel should have remained so long without being worked was on account of this hardness and small pay. In 1885 myself and company determined to work this basin and out from top to bottom. It was somewhat about 30 feet long, about 20 feet wide, and 10 to 15 feet deep. The pestle was found at or near the bottom, where no modern man or pick had ever penetrated before. It was covered with a coating of sand [and cement, in former letter] and so firmly did it adhere that I used a steel scraper to remove and cleanse it. It seems that the pick struck it, as the indentation shows. In this section there is no granite formation, but the pestle is granite."

While working in the catalog section, I also spoke to Leslie Freund, the collections director, who informed me about the details of submitting a request to study artifacts in the museum collection. Freund told me that requests are not granted automatically, but go through a review by the museum's academic staff, who take into account the qualifications of the researcher and the nature of the proposed research project.

Having completed my work in the catalog room, I visited anthropology department library and the Bancroft Library to do some further research. For example, I found in the Bancroft Library a handwritten book manuscript by C. D. Voy, which summarized his research into the artifacts in his collection. The book contained descriptions of discoveries from Tuolumne Table Mountain that I have not found in other sources.

For example, Voy wrote (1874, p. 48): "In 1858, James Riley and H. B. Hurlbut dug out a stone mortar, holding about two quarts, from under Table Mountain under the lava, at a depth of over 300 feet, below the surface in auriferous gravels. Found in what is known as the Excelsior Tunnel Co. next above what is known as the Boston Tunnel Co."

On June 19, 2002, I sent to Leslie Freund a formal request to study the California gold mine artifacts. I asked for permission to see and photograph objects from the C. D. Voy collection (accession number 91, museum catalog numbers 1-4197 through 1-4215). I found in the museum card catalog during my June visit cards for objects with catalog numbers 4197, 4198, 4199, 4202, 4203 a-b, 4204 a-b, 4205, 4206, 4208 a-b, 4209, 4211, 4212, 4214, 4215. I asked to see those objects, plus any other objects in the series that might be available even though not found by me in the card catalog. The objects were stone mortars and pestles, stone dishes, and stone beads, mostly from Table Mountain, Tuolumne County. The collection apparently included some original labels for the artifacts. I also asked to see those. I also asked to see a few additional artifacts not part of the original C. D. Voy collection: (1) Museum no. 1-4558, Acc. no. 166, small round perforated stone, from near Crimea House, Tuolumne Co., collector C. D. Voy, donor D. O. Mills. (2) Museum no. 1-67275, Acc. no. 854, granite pestle, collector Thomas N. Hosmer, 1885, donor Estate of Ellinor C. Davidson. (3) Museum no. 1-11594, stone, possibly a muller or acorn cracker, location Montezuma tunnel, collector possibly Mrs. P. A. Hearst. (4) Museum no. 1-4556, acc. no. 166, very small paint mortar, location near Georgetown, El Dorado Co., collector C. D. Voy, donor D. O. Mills.

After listing the artifacts I wanted to examine, I explained the purposes of my research: "I wish to examine and photograph the above objects for a paper I am presenting at the World Archaeological Congress in Washington, D. C. in June 2003. . . . The paper will examine the history of the California gold mine discoveries reported by J. D. Whitney, state geologist of California, in his book *The Auriferous Gravels of the Sierra Nevada,* published by Harvard University in 1880. Today, many archeologists have become interested in looking at archeological evidence through different cultural lenses. I will be looking at Whitney's discovery through a Vedic cultural lens. The Tertiary antiquity attributed by Whitney to the artifacts makes little sense when looked at through a Western cultural lens, but might make sense when looked at through a Vedic cultural lens, which can accommodate Tertiary humans. Although I am an independent scholar and my approach is somewhat unconventional, it has gotten a hearing in professional forums and publications." I listed some of my papers presented at academic conferences of archeology and history of science, some of which were published in peer reviewed conference proceedings volumes (Cremo 1999, Cremo 2002).

On September 2, 2002, I received an email letter from Leslie Freund informing me that I would be welcome to come to the museum on October 8 and 9 to study and photograph the artifacts I had listed in my research proposal. I arrived in Berkeley with a photographer assistant and my research assistant Lori Erbs. On the morning of October 8, my photographer and I met Leslie Freund at the offices of the Phoebe Hearst Museum of Anthropology. After we filled out the requisite forms, Leslie Freund took us to an off-campus warehouse where the California gold mine artifacts are stored. Over the course of two days, we had a chance to study and photograph most of the artifacts I had asked to see [see Plates XIII-XV]. Throughout, Leslie Freund was courteous, friendly, and helpful. While my photographer and I were doing our work, my research assistant Lori Erbs was looking for old maps of the California gold mining region in the Bancroft Library map collection. She did manage to locate and copy some. She also obtained a copy of the current United States Geological Survey topographical map of the Tuolumne Country region. With the maps in hand, we then drove to the town of Sonora in Tuolumne County, with the goal of locating some of the old mines where artifacts had been discovered. Our first stop was the Tuolumne County Museum and History Center, where we consulted records and maps related to the nineteenth century gold mines in the region. That afternoon, we did some initial explorations along the western side of Table Mountain, a long ridge, with a flat top, oriented in a generally north south direction. The western side of the mountain appeared to be generally free of development, being occupied by a few isolated ranch houses. A dirt track led along the base of the western side of Table Mountain. We did not drive too far on the track, not wishing to risk damage to our rental car. So we left the car and began to walk. The lower slopes of Table Mountain were forested, but the upper third of the elevation was vertical, being composed of sheer walls of latite [see Plate XII, Figure 1]. We found that the general region of some of the old mines was on U.S. government land rather than private property. We walked several miles, but did not locate any of the mines, and turned back as night was falling. The next day, we visited the county tax assessor's office, and searched there for further information about the exact locations of the old mining claims. The office staff were quite helpful. One of the staff (Richard Lundin) turned out to be a consulting archeologist, with experience in mining. As I explained to him the nature of my research, he became increasingly interested, and in the end volunteered to help us locate some of the old tunnels. He met us later in the day with his four wheel drive vehicle, and we drove up to the point we had left off our search the day before. We located an old trail leading up the slope from the dirt track, and we followed it up to a terrace below the latite escarpment. There we found first one [see Plate XII, Figure 2] and then a second tunnel carved into the solid rock. According to our old maps, tunnels of the old Montezuma mining claim should have existed in this area. In the time that we had, it was not possible to conduct any further research. But I was satisfied that we had located tunnels that appeared to be from the nineteenth century, although they could also have been worked after that. Lundin, although quite helpful in the search, got a good laugh when I told him that human bones and artifacts had been discovered in such mines.

My work involves what might be called an archeology of archeology, and this part of this paper might be compared to a report on a season's work at an archeological site. In this case, the "site" is the California gold mine discoveries. My first season's work, some years ago, involved research into the original reports of the discoveries by Dr. Josiah Dwight Whitney, a respected professional geologist. The reports were reliable and answered the usual skeptical objections, such as hoaxing, intrusion, etc. My second season's work involved research into the reactions of Darwinist scientists to attempts to bring this evidence to the attention of the public through a documentary broadcast on a major television network. My third season's work involved getting access to some of the artifacts and relocating some of the places where they were discovered. But work on this "site" is ongoing. My future research goals are: (1) To locate the human skull fragments found in the auriferous gravels below the latite at Table Mountain and later sent to the Boston Museum of Natural History and the Philadelphia Museum of Natural History. (2) To locate the King pestle, found by geologist Clarence King in auriferous gravels below the latite at Table Mountain. This object should be in the collections of the Smithsonian Institution. (3) To search archives of these institutions for further documents related to these discoveries. (4) To organize archeological research to relocate more of the old mining tunnels at Table Mountain, and to conduct excavations in the tunnels and outside the tunnels to establish the times at which the tunnels were worked and to search for additional human artifacts and skeletal remains in the tunnels. (5) To conduct similar archival, museum, and field research in relationship with other archeological sites (other than Table Mountain) documented by Whitney in the California gold mining region.

Discussion

Darwinism has dominated archeology for over a century, and this commitment to a Darwinist perspective has influenced how evidence is treated by archeologists. The process is not simplistic, and depending on the historical moment and the particular Darwinist commitments of researchers, there are several ways that Darwinism may influence the treatment of evidence for extreme human antiquity:

(1) In the early history of archeology, scientifically trained observers whose theoretical preconceptions did not prevent them from seriously considering evidence for extreme human antiquity might find such evidence and report it in some detail. In the late nineteenth and early twentieth centuries, many scientists did in fact publish such detailed reports documenting evidence of a human presence extending as far back as the Miocene and Eocene (Cremo and Thompson 1993). Most of these scientists were Darwinists, but until the discovery of the Java ape-man in the 1890s (in an early Pleistocene geological context), there was not a very firm time line for the human evolutionary process. So before the 1890s, these scientists, Darwinists and nonDarwinists alike, were prepared to encounter evidence for anatomically modern humans or other tool-using hominids in the Pliocene and earlier.

(2) In both the early and more recent history of archeology, scientists with Darwinist preconceptions have opposed, on primarily theoretical grounds, evidence for extreme antiquity that radically contradicts their expectations, given their commitment to particular time lines for human evolution.

(3) Scientists today, with Darwinist theoretical preconceptions that prevent them from seriously considering evidence for extreme human antiquity, might nevertheless find it and perhaps report it without considering its radical implications for the current paradigm. The Laetoli footprints provide an example of this. Scientists discovered footprints consistent with the presence of anatomically modern humans 3.6 million years ago, but because of theoretical preconceptions, could not entertain this possibility (Leakey 1979, discussion in Cremo and Thompson 1993).

(4) In rare instances, "maverick" scientists today might find anomalous evidence and report it in detail, giving attention to how it contradicts the dominant Darwinist consensus. This reporting, one might predict, would not attain wide circulation and the reporting scientists might be subjected to inhibiting social pressures. The case of Virginia Steen-McIntyre, who reported anomalously old dates for the Hueyatlaco site in Mexico and suffered professionally because of it, provides an example (Steen-McIntyre *et al.* 1981, discussion in Cremo and Thompson 1993, pp. 354–366).

(5) Nonprofessionals might also encounter such evidence, and give reports, published in nonscientific literature, that are somewhat incomplete.

Concerning the California gold mine discoveries, we find several of the above patterns. Most of the cases were first reported by mine owners, mining supervisors, and miners. These cases were brought to the attention of professional scientists, including J. D. Whitney, who, after carefully investigating and documenting the discoveries, reported them in a monograph published by Harvard University's Peabody Museum of Comparative Zoology. Whitney, as far as I can tell, was not opposed in principle to the concept of evolution. However, at the time that he originally reported the California gold mining discoveries, the time line for human evolution was not very well fixed, and therefore Whitney had no reason to oppose on theoretical grounds the evidence for extreme human antiquity that he encountered. Whitney published his report in 1880, and his authority carried some weight. But by the end of the nineteenth century, William Holmes, influenced by the discovery of *Pithecanthropus* in the early Pleistocene formations of Java, suggested that if Whitney had been aware of this discovery, then he would not have pronounced in favor a fully human presence in the Tertiary. That may be true. But at the historical moment in which Whitney found himself, he did pronounce in favor of the existence of Tertiary humans on the basis of a considerable amount of well documented evidence. For a modern researcher like myself, with a nonDarwinist perspective that allows for extreme human antiquity, the evidence reported by Whitney is interesting. Whitney's qualifications and reputation as a scientist were quite high. His reporting was thorough, and his conclusions reasonable based on the evidence. He considered and gave good reasons for rejecting the usual skeptical counterexplanations such as hoaxes, intrusion, and so on. And his reports were published by a major American scientific institution. Although no archeological evidence is perfect, the evidence reported by Whitney seems to me credible. And I have therefore cited it in favor of the Vedic picture of extreme human antiquity, both in scientific circles and in presentations to the general public. Some Darwinists have reacted strongly to this, in a way that reveals that their main objection to the evidence is that it violates their theoretical expectations and radically contradicts their current consensus on human origins. I call Darwinists of this type fundamentalist Darwinists, indicating that their commitment to Darwinism has a strong ideological and political flavor to it. Such Darwinists tend to be associated with organizations dedicated to identifying science with materialism and to keeping any other metaphysical perspectives out of science. Such organizations include the National Center for Science Education in the United States and various skeptics societies. Fundamentalist Darwinists wish to eliminate epistemological pluralism in science, education, and in public discussion of science, by enforcing a rigid commitment to Darwinist metaphysics, methodology and conclusions. But not all Darwinists are of the fundamentalist variety. In archeology and among historians of science, I have encountered many Darwinists who are willing to allow researchers with nonDarwinist metaphysical commitments to participate in the discourse of archeology, and history of archeology, and facilitate their research activities. Their commitment to Darwinist metaphysics is flexible and tolerant. I have found that the World Archaeological Congress is a model of such flexibility and tolerance. Also, in the year 2002, I received through the History of Science Society a National Science Foundation grant for travel to the XXIst International Congress for History of Science to present a paper against Darwinism. This is another small sign that Darwinist hegemony in science and science studies is beginning to weaken. Also, during a recent visit to Russia, I lectured against Darwinism at the Darwin Museum in Moscow. After my talk, a couple of the museum staff who had invited me told me that the official policy of the Darwin Museum is that it represents only one of several possible scientific perspectives on the origin of species, including a creationist perspective. I also gave several radio and television interviews in Moscow. During one television interview, I asked that alternatives to Darwinism be presented in the education system. Afterward, the interviewer told me that he had recently had on his show one of Russia's education officials (Larissa Yevgyenyevna Rodionova, of the government education department of the southeast region of Moscow), who said that this was now the policy of the government. As an American, I found it interesting that in Russia there is some degree of official tolerance of a variety of metaphysical perspectives in science education, whereas in America Darwinists enjoy a government enforced monopoly that rigidly excludes such alternative perspectives.

Conclusion

As demonstrated by the California gold mine discoveries, the engagement of archeology in the service of Darwinism and its metaphysical assumptions has influenced the treatment of archeological evidence, causing evidence that radically contradicts Darwinist theoretical assumptions to be eliminated from archeological discourse primarily for that reason. The remedy is not the elimination of Darwinism, but encouragement of tolerance for a variety of metaphysical perspectives in all areas of archeology, including education, field research, museum collections, museum displays, and outreach to the public through the media. Archeologists working in institutions that rely on public funds have a greater responsibility to insure diversity of perspectives than those working in private institutions. For example, archeologists working in museums supported by public funds have a much greater responsibility to reflect a variety of perspectives on human origins in their displays than archeologists working in private museums. The same is true of archeologists working in educational institutions supported by public funds. They have an obligation to reflect a variety of perspectives in the textbooks they author and the lectures they present. This tolerance of a variety of metaphysical perspectives does not rule out the chance of resolving disputes among researchers operating within these perspectives by appeal to evidence, objectively evaluated according to some commonly accepted set of principles for judging evidence. But it does mean that we do have to be careful to see whether the resolutions that have been historically reached in disputes about the reality of evidence for extreme human antiquity actually meet this standard.

References

Becker, G. F. (1891) Antiquities from under Tuolumne Table Mountain in California. *Bulletin of the Geological Society of America,* 2: 189–200.

Cremo, M. A. (1998) *Forbidden Archeology's Impact.* Los Angeles: Bhaktivedanta Book Publishing.

Cremo, M. A. (1999) Puranic time and the archeological record. In Tim Murray, ed. *Time and Archaeology.* London: Routledge, pp. 38–48.

Cremo, M. A. (2000) The discoveries of Carlos Ribeiro: a controversial episode in nineteenth century European archeology. Presented at the history of archeology session of the European Association of Archeologists Annual Meeting, September 11–15, 2000, Lisbon, Portugal. Unpublished. [Later published]

Cremo, M. A. (2001) The discoveries of Belgian geologist Aimé Louis Rutot at Boncelles, Belgium: an archeological controversy from the early twentieth century. XXIVth Congress of the International Union for Prehistoric and Protohistoric Sciences, Liège, Belgium, September 2–8, 2001. Unpublished.

Cremo, M. A. (2002) The later discoveries of Boucher de Perthes at Moulin Quignon and their impact on the Moulin Quignon jaw controversy. In Goulven Laurent, ed. *Proceedings of the XXth International Congress of History of Science (Liege, 20–26 July 1997), Volume X, Earth Sciences, Geography and Cartography.* Turnhout, Belgium: Brepols Publishers, pp. 39–56.

Cremo, M. A., and Thompson, R. L. (1993) *Forbidden Archeology: The Hidden History of the Human Race.* San Diego: Bhaktivedanta Institute.

Feder, K. L. (1994) Review of *Forbidden Archeology. Geoarchaeology,* 9: 337–340.

Holmes, W. H. (1899) Review of the evidence relating to auriferous gravel man in California. *Smithsonian Institution Annual Report 1898–1899,* pp. 419–472.

Leakey, M. D. (1979) Footprints in the ashes of time. *National Geographic,* 155: 446–457.

Munro, R. (1905) *Archaeology and False Antiquities.* London: Methuen.

Murray, T. (1995) Review of *Forbidden Archeology. British Journal for the History of Science,* 28: 377–379.

Norris, Robert M. and Webb, Robert W. (1990) *Geology of California.* Second edition. New York: John Wiley & Sons.

Popper, K. (1976) *Unended Quest.* London: Fontana Books, Wm. Collins & Co.

Ribeiro, C. (1873) Sur des silex taillés, découverts dans les terrains miocène du Portugal. *Congrès International d'Anthropologie et d'Archéologie Préhistoriques, Bruxelles 1872, Compte Rendu,* pp. 95–100.

Rutot, A. (1907) Un grave problem: une industrie humaine datant de l'époque oligocène. Comparison des outils avec ceux des Tasmaniens actuels. *Bulletin de la Société Belge de Géologie de Paléontologie et d'Hydrologie,* 21: 439–482.

Sinclair, W. J. (1908) Recent investigations bearing on the question of the occurrence of Neocene man in the auriferous gravels of the Sierra Nevada. *University of California Publications in American Archaeology and Ethnology,* 7(2): 107–131.

Slemmons, D. B. (1966) Cenozoic volcanism of the central Sierra Nevada, California. *Bulletin of the California Division of Mines and Geology,* 190: 199–208.

Steen-McIntyre, V., Fryxell, R., and Malde, H. E. (1981) Geologic evidence for age of deposits at Hueyatlaco archaeological site, Valsequillo, Mexico. *Quaternary Research,* 16: 1–17.

Stein, Philip L. and Rowe, Bruce M. (1993) *Physical Anthropology.* Fifth edition. New York: McGraw-Hill.

Voy, C. D. (1874) *Relics of the Stone Age Found in California Comprising the Results of Extensive Travels and Explorations of Different Parts of the State by C. D. Voy.* Handwritten manuscript, 185 pp. Manuscript and Map Collections. Bancroft Library. University of California at Berkeley.

Wallace, A. R. (1887) The antiquity of man in North America. *Nineteenth Century,* 22: 667–679.

Whitney, J. D. (1880) The auriferous gravels of the Sierra Nevada of California. *Harvard University, Museum of Comparative Zoology Memoir* 6(1).

Winslow, C. F. (1873) The President reads extracts from a letter from Dr. C. F. Winslow relating the discovery of human remains in Table Mountain, Cal. (Jan 1). *Proceedings of the Boston Society of Natural History,* 15: 257–259.

16

The Mayapur Pilgrimage Place, West Bengal, India: A Mandala of Peace and Ecological Harmony

I presented this paper at the 19th World Congress of the International Association of History of Religions, held in Tokyo, Japan, March 24–30, 2005. The session in which I presented the paper was called Pilgrimage and Sacred Places: Canon of Peace and Ecological Harmony.

Introduction

The Mayapur pilgrimage place is sacred to the Gaudiya Vaishnava sect of India, centered in West Bengal. This paper will examine the history of the pilgrimage place and its present importance to Gaudiya Vaishnavas. With the spread of Gaudiya Vaishnava teachings throughout the world in the latter part of the twentieth century, the site has become internationally known, and each year Gaudiya Vaishnava converts from many countries make the pilgrimage to Mayapur, joining the Bengali and other Indian Gaudiya Vaishnavas in the beautiful rural surroundings [**see Plate XVII**]. I myself am an American convert to Gaudiya Vaishnavism. I was initiated into the Gaudiya Vaishnava *sampradaya*, or disciplic succession, in 1976 by His Divine Grace A. C. Bhaktivedanta Swami Prabhupada (1896–1977), a Gaudiya Vaishnava *guru* and founder-*acharya* of the International Society for Krishna Consciousness.[1] My approach in this paper is thus that of a practitioner as well as a scholar.

Location

The Mayapur pilgrimage place is located in West Bengal near the town of Navadvipa, which lies on the west bank of the Bhagirathi River (a major channel of the Ganges) about 90 miles north of Kolkatta. The pilgrimage zone contains sites on both banks of the river. The most important central site is the appearance place of Chaitanya Mahaprabhu. Called the Yoga Pitha, it lies within the rural settlement of Mayapur, comprising scattered villages and small townships on the east bank of the Bhagirathi, north of the confluence with the Jalangi. The Mayapur area is a flat tropical flood plain, rich with rice fields, coconut trees, mango trees, papaya trees, and vegetable gardens. Domesticated animals are mostly water buffalo, cows, and goats. Seasonal flooding is some-times aggravated by releases of water from dams upstream during the rainy season. In the midst of this predominantly rural landscape one finds the temples and *ashramas* of several Gaudiya Vaishnava organizations.

Chaitanya Mahaprabhu

Chaitanya Mahaprabhu appeared in Mayapur in the year 1486 AD.[2] Gaudiya Vaish-navas recognize Chaitanya Mahaprabhu [see Plate XVI, Figure 1] as an *avatara* of Krishna, the supreme deity and source of all *avataras*. A more esoteric understanding characterizes him as the combined form of Krishna and Krishna's consort Radha, the personification of divine love of God. Specifically, Chaitanya Mahaprabhu is Krishna adopting the complexion and mood (although not the outer female form) of Radha in order to experience for himself what she experiences as the topmost example of lov-ing devotion to Krishna.[3] His advent was for two purposes, one external and the other internal. The first (external) purpose was to spread the *yuga-dharma*, or prescribed method of God realization and self realization for the present Kali-yuga. This method is called *sankirtana*, the congregational chanting of the holy names of the Lord, par-ticularly the Hare Krishna mantra. The second (internal) purpose was to personally taste and demonstrate divine love of Krishna, in the mood of Radha. At times, Chai-tanya Mahaprabhu displayed to his more confidential followers, such as Ramananda Raya, his dual form as Radha and Krishna. The color of Krishna's form is usually bluish, whereas that of Radha is golden. When Krishna appeared as Chaitanya Mahaprabhu, adopting the mood of Radha, he appeared with her golden complexion. Therefore Cai-tanya Mahaprabhu is sometimes called the Golden Avatara.

Gaudiya Vaishnava scholars have found in various texts a number of references predicting the appearance of Chaitanya Mahaprabhu. For example, the *Bhagavata Purana* (11.5.32), in a description of the *avatara* for the Kali-yuga, says:

> *krishna-varnam tvishakrishnam*
> *sangopangastra-parshadam*
> *yajnaih sankirtana-prayair*
> *yajanti hi su-medhasah*

The *avatara* for this age will be a form of Krishna, who will chant the name of Krishna. Although Krishna usually comes in a form that is blackish in complexion, this *avatara* will be another color (golden). He will come along with his associates. Those who are intelligent will worship this *avatara* by *sankirtana,* the congregational chanting of the holy names of the Lord.

Caitanya Mahaprabhu stayed for the first twenty-four years of his manifest pres-ence in Mayapur. At an early age, he married Lakshmipriya, and after she succumbed to a snake bite, he took another wife, Vishnupriya. Both are considered incarnations of his internal potencies (*shaktis*).[4] At age twenty-four, Chaitanya Mahaprabhu entered the renounced order of life, *sannyasa,* and moved to the temple center of Jagannatha

Puri in Orissa. From there he journeyed all over South India, spreading his *sankirtana* movement among the general public and communicating his esoteric teachings to his more confidential associates. After returning to Jagannatha Puri, he journeyed to Vrindavan, located on the banks of the Yamuna River between today's cities of New Delhi and Agra. Vrindavan is the place where Krishna appeared. Lord Chaitanya and his principal followers, the Six Goswamis, rediscovered many of the places of Krishna's pastimes, increasing the importance of Vrindavan as a place of pilgrimage. Returning to Jagannatha Puri, he remained there until his disappearance in 1534. However, Mayapur, because it is the place of Chaitanya Mahaprabhu's appearance is more important to the Gaudiya Vaishnavas.

The Place of Gaudiya Vaishnavism in Indian Religion

The number of Gaudiya Vaishnavas is not easy to calculate. According to the 2001 government census, out of 1.028 billion people in India, 828 million, or 80.5 percent are Hindu. The official census does not break this down any further, but scholars estimate that seventy percent of Hindus consider themselves Vaishnava. That would be roughly 580 million. The Gaudiya Vaisnavas are concentrated in West Bengal. I estimate there are about 12 million Gaudiya Vaishnavas in West Bengal.[5] Taking into account Gaudiya Vaishnava elements in the populations of the nation of Bangladesh, the Indian states of Orissa, Manipur, and other neighboring areas might increase the regional total to 22 million.[6] When we add Gaudiya Vaishnavas living in other parts of India (I noticed a Gaudiya Vaishnava community in Varanasi, for example), then the number might increase even further, perhaps up to 24 million. We also have to take into account the recent expansion of Gaudiya Vaishnavism throughout the world, including émigré communities and such missionary manifestations as the International Society for Krishna Consciousness. Furthermore, many Hindus are not exclusively identified with particular sects, and along with other commitments might simultaneously have a strong affinity for Gaudiya Vaishnavism. When all is taken in account, it would seem that a conservative estimate for Gaudiya Vaishnavas worldwide would be about 25 million, and perhaps, with more generous assumptions in India, up to 30 or 40 million. This lack of certainty does point to the need for better surveys.

Also, although Gaudiya Vaishnavas are a small group within Vaishnavas in India as a whole, perhaps 5 percent, they do share with other Vaishnavas a basic cosmological outlook, a common scriptural canon, and a common core set of rituals. A major difference is the emphasis that the Gaudiya Vaishnavas place on the personality and teachings of Chaitanya Mahaprabhu, and the emphasis on *bhakti*, or devotion, as the principal means of approaching God. Still we must take into account that many secular scholars and Vaishnava religionists recognize Chaitanya Mahaprabhu as an apostle of *bhakti* and also that many Vaishnavas, just like the Gaudiya Vaishnavas, follow the path of *bhakti* and perform *kirtana*, including Hare Krishna mantra *kirtana*. Even more generally, Gaudiya Vaishnavism shares the element of devotional love of God with other monotheistic religions worldwide.

The Rediscovery of the Birthplace of Chaitanya Mahaprabhu

Each year, on the anniversary of the appearance day of Chaitanya Mahaprabhu, pilgrims from around the world come to visit the place of his appearance in Mayapur. There is a temple at the spot, called the Yoga Pitha. But this temple was constructed only in the early part of the twentieth century, at a place identified by the Gaudiya Vaishnava *guru* Bhaktivinoda Thakura (1838–1915) late in the nineteenth century. In the years following the time of Chaitanya Mahaprabhu, the actual places of his appearance and pastimes had been lost because of the shifting course of the Ganges and movement of settlements.

Bhaktivinoda Thakura, born Kedarnatha Dutta, was a convert to Gaudiya Vaishnavism.[7] Educated in English, he also served as a magistrate in the British administration of India. Eager to find the exact place of Chaitanya Mahaprabhu's appearance, he sought and finally received a transfer to Krishnanagara, a town near Mayapur. He then began his historical and geographical research.

In 1888, Bhaktivinoda Thakura was staying at the Rani Dharmasala in Navadvipa. In his autobiography, he reported:

> One night . . . I went up on the roof in order to look around. It was 10 o'clock, and was very dark and cloudy. Across the Ganga, in a northerly direction, I saw a large building flooded with light. . . . In the morning I looked carefully at the place from the roof . . . and I observed that there was one Tal [palm] tree in that location. When I asked others about this place they said that this distant place was known as Ballal-dighi. . . . I returned to Krishnanagar and the following Saturday I went back to Ballal-dighi. I saw that wonderful phenomenon in that place again at night, and the next day I went to see the area on foot. Upon inquiring with the elderly people of that place (Muslims), I was informed that this was the birthplace of Shriman Mahaprabhu.[8]

The name Mayapur does not occur in the earliest biographies of Chaitanya Mahaprabhu. These biographies say that Chaitanya Mahaprabhu appeared in the town of Navadvipa. At the time of Bhaktivinoda Thakura, the town of Navadvipa was (and still is) on the west bank of the Ganges (on the other side of the river from Ballal-dighi). In earlier times, the town of Navadvipa was called Nadia (spelled variously, Nuddea, Nudia, etc.). Bhaktivinoda Thakura found that maps from the seventeenth century show Nuddea (Nadia) on the east bank of the Ganges, north of the confluence with the Jalangi.[9] This corresponds to the present day location of Mayapur. Subsequently, maps showed that Nadia had moved to the west side of the Ganges.[10] In his identification of Lord Chaitanya's birthplace with Mayapur, Bhaktivinoda Thakura also relied on geographical descriptions given in the *Chaitanya-bhagavata*, *Bhakti-ratnakara*, and other Gaudiya Vaishnava scriptures. He also invited the great Gaudiya Vaishnava saint Jagannatha Dasa Babaji to come to the site. At this time, Jagannatha Dasa Babaji was over 120 years old. Unable to walk, he had to be carried. But when he arrived at the site, he became overwhelmed with ecstasy, and jumped up, proclaiming loudly that it was the place of Chaitanya Mahaprabhu's birth.[11] Bhaktivinoda Thakura discovered many other places of Chaitanya Mahaprabhu's pastimes in Navadvipa.

In 1892, Bhaktivinoda Thakura set up a society dedicated to the rehabilitation of the pastime places of Chaitanya Mahaprabhu in Navadvipa.[12] The society took up the construction of a small temple at the Yoga Pitha, and Bhaktivinoda Thakura personally went door to door in Calcutta to collect funds for this project. The temple was officially opened on March 21, 1895, on the anniversary of Caitanya Mahaprabhu's appearance.[13] Later, a larger temple was constructed, under the guidance of Bhaktisiddhanta Sarasvati Thakura, the son of Bhaktivinoda Thakura. In 1934, during the construction of this temple, a small deity of Adhoksaja Vishnu was found in an excavation.[14] This was identified as the household deity of Jagannatha Mishra, Chaitanya Mahaprabhu's father, and was taken as further confirmation that the site was indeed the birthplace of Chaitanya Mahaprabhu. The Yoga Pitha temple was inaugurated by Bhaktisiddhanta Sarasvati Thakura in 1935, on the appearance day of Chaitanya Mahaprabhu. The Yoga Pitha temple houses deities of Chaitanya Mahaprabhu along with his consorts Lakshmipriya and Vishnupriya. There is also a replica of the house of Jagannathta Mishra near a *nim* tree. Chaitanya Mahaprabhu's biographers say that because he was born beneath a *nim* tree he was sometimes called Nimai. Throughout the Navadvipa area, Bhaktisiddhanta Sarasvati Thakura and his disciples constructed many temples at places connected with Chaitanya Mahaprabhu.

Bhaktisiddhanta Sarasvati Thakura ordered one of his disciples, Abhay Charanaravinda De, to spread the teachings of Chaitanya Mahaprabhu to the world outside India. De accomplished this after he took *sannyasa,* the renounced spiritual order of life, adopting the name Bhaktivedanta Swami. Known to his reverent disciples as Shrila A. C. Bhaktivedanta Swami Prabhupada, he began the construction of a world headquarters for his International Society for Krishna Consciousness (ISKCON) near the Yoga Pitha. With the ISKCON center's yearly influx of pilgrims from all over the world, it has radically transformed the character of Mayapur, putting it on the map as an international pilgrimage destination. The popularity of ISKCON in India itself has also drawn increasing numbers of Indians from all parts of the country to Mayapur.

Gaura-Mandala: The Sacred Geography of Mayapur/Navadvipa.

According to Vaishnava cosmology, the highest spiritual planet, the dwelling place of Krishna, is called Goloka. The earthly Vrindavan is a replica manifestation of this topmost spiritual abode or *dhama*. It is therefore called Vrindavan-dhama. According to Gaudiya Vaishnava *acharyas*, Navadvipa is part of Goloka. Bhaktivinoda Thakura says:

> Just how glorious is Shrimati Radharani as the personification of Shri Krishna's internal spiritual potency, and how glorious is Her magnificent love? Krishna also desires to know how She alone fully relishes the wonderful qualities in Him, and the happiness She feels when She

realizes the sweetness of His love. Longing to fulfill these desires, the Supreme Lord Shri Krishna, in His eternal form of Shri Chaitanya Mahaprabhu, the Absolute Divinity of *audarya*, or magnanimity, performs manifold pastimes and savors the loving moods in an exclusive section of Goloka known as Shri Navadvipa-dhama, the highest realm of the Vaikuntha planets and the playground of the Supreme Lord.[15]

Radharani herself manifested Navadvipa-dhama in this exclusive section of Goloka.[16]

This Navadvipa-dhama is also manifest on earth, and Mayapur is the center of it.[17] Navadvipa literally means "nine islands," and the earthly Navadvipa comprises nine islands, originally bounded by channels of the local rivers. The central island is called Antardvipa, and Mayapur, the appearance place of Chaitanya Mahaprabhu is located there. The other eight *dvipas* are arranged around Antardvipa, like the petals of a lotus. Additional sacred places form an outer ring of one hundred petals. This ring, centered on the Yoga Pitha, has a diameter of 58 miles and a circumference of 168 miles.[18] Because of its connection with Chaitanya Mahaprabhu, one of whose names is Gaura, Navadvipa-dhama is sometimes called Gaura-mandala. A *mandala* is a sacred circle of cosmographical significance.

According to Gaudiya Vaishnava *acharyas,* the nine islands represent the nine processes of devotional service to Krishna.[19] These nine processes are enumerated in the *Bhagavata Purana* (7.5.23). Here are the nine processes along with the islands associated with each process: (1) *shravanam* (hearing about the Lord), Simantadvipa; (2) *kirtanam* (chanting about the Lord), Godrumadvipa; (3) *smaranam* (remembering the Lord), Madhyadvipa; (4) *pada-sevanam* (serving the lotus feet of the Lord), Koladvipa; (5) *archanam* (worshiping the form of the Lord in the temple), Ritudvipa; (6) *vandanam* (offering prayers to the Lord), Jambudvipa; (7) *dasyam* (adopting the mood of a loving servant of the Lord), Modadrumadvipa; (8) *sakhyam* (adopting the mood of loving friendship toward the Lord), Rudradvipa; and (9) *atma-nivedanam* (surrendering everything to the Lord, Antardvipa.[20]

There is an intimate connection between Mayapur and Vrindavan. They are considered to be nondifferent from each other, just as Krishna and Chaitanya Mahaprabhu are considered nondifferent.[21] But Caitanya Mahaprabhu is considered to be more merciful than Krishna, and Gaudiya Vaishnavas believe that one approaches Krishna through Chaitanya Mahaprabhu. In the same way, visiting Mayapur (or Navadvipa) prepares one to enter Vrindavan.[22]

The sacred rivers and sacred cities of India can all be found in Navadvipa-dhama.[23] The *dhama* reveals its spiritual identity to those with perfected spiritual vision. The rivers, the trees, and land are all composed of *chintamani*, spiritual touchstone. To those with proper vision, all the inhabitants of the *dhama* reveal their spiritual forms. But all this remains hidden to those with material vision.[24]

The spiritual geography is unchanging, but it is reflected through its temporal material covering in various ways. Bhaktivinoda Thakura wrote: "Following the desires of the Lord, sometimes the streams dry up, and then again by His wish they flow with water; by the Lord's wish sometimes places become covered with water, and by His wish they again become visible. In this way the *dhama* endlessly enacts its *lila*, but the same *dhama* remains always manifest to the fortunate living entity. If a devotee has an acute desire in his heart, all the islands and rivers will be visible. By devotion, the *dhama* is sometimes visible in dreams, meditation, or to the naked eye."[25]

Predictions

Caitanya Mahaprabhu said that his teachings would be spread to every town and village in the world.[26] And Bhaktivinoda Thakura later envisioned how this would happen. In 1885, in an article in his journal *Sajjana Tosani,* he wrote:

> Oh, for that day when the fortunate English, French, Russian, German and American people will take up banners, *mridangas* [drums] and *karatalas* [hand cymbals] and raise *kirtana* [chanting of God's name] through their streets and towns. When will that day come? Oh, for the day when the fair-skinned men from their side will raise up the chanting of *jaya sachinandana, jaya sachinandana ki jaya* [All Glories to Lord Chaitanya! All Glories to Lord Chaitanya!] and join with the Bengali devotees. When will that day be? On such a day they will say, "Our dear Brothers, we have taken shelter of the ocean of Lord Chaitanya's Love; kindly embrace us."[27]

Two predictions are evident in Bhaktivinoda Thakura's words: (1) that people in nations outside India would take up Chaitanya Mahaprabhu's movement of congregational chanting of the holy names of God (especially in the form of the Hare Krishna mantra), and (2) that such people would join in such chanting with the Bengali Gaudiya Vaishnavas, evidently in Bengal. Both predictions have come true. This is connected with another prediction made by Bhaktivinoda Thakura, who wrote in 1896: "A personality will soon appear to preach the teachings of Lord Chaitanya and move unrestrictedly over the whole world with His message."[28] 1896 was the year of the birth of Srila A. C. Bhaktivedanta Swami Prabhupada, by whose efforts the chanting of the Sanskrit holy names of God was spread around the world, in the form of the International Society for Krishna Consciousness.[29]

Another interesting prediction about Mayapur can be found in Bhaktivinoda Thakura's *Navadvipa-dhama-mahatmya.* Therein Nityananda Prabhu, one of Chaitanya Mahaprabhu's principal associates, said in the sixteenth century:

> The Ganges water will almost cover Mayapur for a hundred years, and then the water will again recede. For some time only the place will remain, devoid of houses. Then again, by the Lord's desire, this place will become prominent, and people will live in Mayapur as before. All these *ghatas* on the bank of the Ganges will again be manifest, and the devotees will build temples of the Lord. One exceedingly wonderful temple

will appear from which Gauranga's [Chaitanya Mahaprabhu's] eternal service will be preached everywhere.[30]

Some take this wonderful temple (*adbhuta mandir*) to be the Yoga Pitha temple erected by Bhaktisiddhanta Sarasvati, and others take it to be the massive temple envisioned by Shrila A. C. Bhaktivedanta Swami Prabhupada, yet to be constructed as part of the Mayapur world headquarters of his International Society for Krishna Consciousness.

In the nineteenth century, after his retirement from active government service, Bhaktivinoda Thakura built a house on Godrumadvipa in the Navadvipa area. Nitai Dasa, a disciplie of A. C. Bhaktivedanta Swami Prabhupada, wrote:

> It is said that Shrila Thakura Bhaktivinoda, standing on the balcony of his house in Godruma years ago, looked across the River Jalangi toward the birthsite of Shri Caitanya Mahaprabhu and predicted that one day there would be a shining city filled with devotees of Lord Chaitanya from all over the world. If today one visits the house of Thakura Bhaktivinoda and goes to that balcony, he will see directly before him, fulfilling the prediction of Shrila Thakura Bhaktivinoda, the ISKCON Mayapura-Chandrodaya Mandira, ISKCON's world center at the birthplace of Shri Chaitanya Mahaprabhu.[31] [**See Plate XVI, Figure 2.**]

The Pilgrimage Process

Each year, around the time of Chaitanya Mahaprabhu's appearance, Gaudiya Vaishnava pilgrims come to Mayapur, for organized pilgrimage processions (*parikramas*). For the purpose of this paper, I will focus on the ISKCON pilgrimage, joined by Indian and international participants from North America, South America, Europe, Africa, and Asia, numbering two or three thousand [**see Plate XVII**].

Chaitanya Mahaprabhu was an opponent of caste discrimination. He welcomed into his movement all kinds of people, including those of lower caste and non-Hindus, such as Buddhists and Islamics. The International Society for Krishna Consciousness, a modern manifestation of Chaitanya Mahaprabhu's movement, follows this example by accepting people of all racial, national, class, and religious backgrounds into its membership.

Although it emphasizes *bhakti* (love of God) as the goal of life and *sankirtan* (chanting of the holy names of God) as the principal means to achieve this goal, modern Gaudiya Vaishnavism does not claim exclusivity and recognizes the validity of other genuine spiritual paths. For example, Shrila A. C. Bhaktivedanta Swami Prabhupada said:

> We don't say that you chant Krishna. You chant the holy name of God. If Allah is approved name of God, you chant it. That is our request. We don't force you that you chant the name of Krishna. No, we don't say

that. If somebody says Jehovah is the name of God, that's all right, you chant Jehovah. . . . We simply request that you chant the holy name of God. That's all.[32]

This program of chanting the holy names of God, in all languages, is a platform for peace and cooperation among all genuine spiritual communities. In practice, Gaudiya Vaishnavas welcome all people to join them in the chanting of the names of Krishna, but if people are not attracted to do this, Gaudiya Vaishnavas encourage them to chant the name of God as it is known to them from their own tradition. As they go from place to place in Navadvipa-*dhama,* the ISKCON pilgrims from around the world chant the names of God while playing drums and cymbals.

The pilgrimage takes place the week before the appearance day of Chaitanya Mahaprabhu, which occurs on the full moon in the month of Phalguna.[33] This full moon usually occurs in March. During this time of the year, the weather is usually very pleasant in Mayapur, with cool nights and warm days.

The pilgrimage route follows the outline of the pilgrimage described in the *Navadvipa-dhama-mahatmya* of Bhaktivinoda Thakura, which tells the story of a pilgrimage taken in the sixteenth century.[34] Walking is usually done barefoot, as this increases contact with the *dhama.* Before the pilgrimage, the pilgrims purchase needed supplies at the shops in the ISKCON world headquarters. They also receive instruction about the spiritual purpose of the pilgrimage, including instructions on avoiding offenses to the *dhama* and its residents. On the first day of the pilgrimage, the pilgrims leave the ISKCON property and go in procession to the Yoga Pitha. Over the next seven days they proceed through the four dvipas on the east bank of the Ganges and then through the five dvipas on the west bank of the Ganges, in the order prescribed in the *Navadvipa-dhama-mahatmya.* Finally, they return to the Yoga Pitha at Mayapur in Antardvipa. After the pilgrimage they celebrate the appearance day of Chaitanya Mahaprabhu at the ISKCON center near the Yoga Pitha.

The pilgrims camp in tent villages, or sleep in schools or *ashramas.* They rise early each morning for a program of worship, meditation, and hearing scriptural lectures. After this they take breakfast, and then proceed on procession, chanting the Hare Krishna mantra and other mantras and songs to musical accompaniment. At temples and other sacred sites, they stop and hear discourses about their history and meaning. In the early afternoon they stop at their next camp. They take lunch, and afterwards do their washing and other tasks. In the evening there is a program of dramas or music, attended by pilgrims as well as local people. The purpose of all of this is to allow the pilgrim to enter more deeply into spiritual perception of the *dhama.* For the Gaudiya Vaishnavas, this means entering more deeply into the pastimes of Lord Chaitanya and understanding how they are nondifferent from the pastimes of Radha and Krishna in Vrindavan.

Ecological Considerations

The *dhama*—including the land, the rivers, the plants, the animals, and the people— is considered sacred. The *dhama* is not to be polluted, either spiritually or materially.

The Gaudiya Vaishnava cosmology, with roots in Vedic cosmology generally, is favorable to ecological values.[35] The modern scientific cosmology, however, does not provide a very firm foundation for maintaining any particular ecological state. Its stark materialism and denial of intelligent design and control leave little room for saying that any particular state of the environment is to be preferred over another. For example, there is little reason to say that the earth's current environmental conditions are preferable to the lifeless conditions that, according to today's scientists, are found on the moon or Saturn or Jupiter, or on the earth early in its history. Life itself is considered to be an accident, and there is little within the worldview of modern science that would allow us to say life's disappearance would be a matter of much concern.

However, according to the Gaudiya Vaishnava cosmology, this earth, with its rivers and forests, its plants and animals, is a reflection of an eternal spiritual reality, which also has its rivers and forests, and plants and animals. Therefore it can be said that there is a preferred state of environmental affairs. It is worthwhile trying to make this world as much like the spiritual world as possible. According to the Gaudiya Vaishnava cosmology, life is not an accident. The bodies of plants, animals, and humans are vehicles for eternal souls, which are meant to return to their original spiritual home. Therefore a Gaudiya Vaishnava sees all living things with equal vision. The earth itself is considered the body of an earth goddess, and the river Ganges is the embodiment of the river goddess Ganga Devi. The Gaudiya Vaishnava therefore perceives everything in relation to spiritual personalities, who all have as their source a supreme spiritual personality.

For the Gaudiya Vaishnava, life's ultimate purpose is to return to the spiritual world. While in this world, we should therefore live as simply and as naturally as possible, so as to give priority to life's spiritual goal. The overwhelming materialism of modern secular, industrial society, with its emphasis on material production and consumption, is destroying the environment in addition to distracting humanity from the real spiritual purpose of life. Gaudiya Vaishnavas in the International Society for Krishna Consciousness have therefore started agrarian communities in various parts of the world, based on voluntary simplicity and commitment to Vedic spiritual principles.

ISKCON's Mayapur project is also meant to demonstrate simple living and high thinking, in combination with developing Mayapur as a worldwide place of pilgrimage.

Conclusion

The Mayapur pilgrimage site is a place where people from all parts of the world gather, appreciating their equality on the spiritual platform. The sense of appreciation extends not just to other humans, but to all the living things in the *dhama* and to the *dhama* itself, its lands and waters. As this sense of appreciation expands from the circle of individual human awareness, to awareness of kinship with all other humans and all living things, and ultimately with God, Mayapur-*dhama* manifests as a *mandala* of peace and ecological harmony on multiple levels.

Acknowledgements:

I thank Dr. Rana B. Singh of Benares Hindu University for inviting me to present this paper. Ferdinando Sardella of Gőteborg University provided useful information about Gaudiya Vaishnava populations in Orissa, Manipur, and Bangladesh. I am grateful to the trustees of the Bhaktivedanta Book Trust for their ongoing support of my research.

Notes and References:

1. See Satsvarupa dasa Goswami's biography *Shrila Prabhupada Lilamrta,* published by the Bhaktivedanta Book Trust, Los Angeles, several editions.
2. The details of his life and teachings may be found in the sixteenth century biographies *Chaitanya-bhagavata* by Vrindavan dasa Thakura (English translation by Bhumipati Dasa, Vrajraj Press, with commentary by Bhaktisiddhanta Sarasvati Thakura) and *Chaitanya-charitamrita* by Krishnadasa Kaviraja Goswami (English translation and commentary by Shrila A. C. Bhaktivedanta Swami Prabhupada, Bhaktivedanta Book Trust, several editions).
3. Krishnadasa Kaviraja Goswami includes in his *Chaitanya-caritamrta (Adi-lila 1.5)* this verse from Svarupa Damodara Goswami:

> *radha krishna-pranaya-vikritir hladini shaktir asmad*
> *ekatmanav api bhuvi pura deha-bhedam gatau tau*
> *chaitanyakhyam prakatam adhuna tad-dvayam chaikyam aptam*
> *radha-bhava-dyuti-suvalitam naumi krishna-svarupam*

Shrila A. C. Bhaktivedanta Swami Prabhupada gives this translation in his edition of the *Chaitanya-caritamrta:* "The loving affairs of Shri Radha and Krishna are transcendental manifestations of the Lord's internal pleasure-giving potency. Although Radha and Krishna are one in Their identity, They separated Themselves eternally. Now these two transcendental identities have again united, in the form of Shri Krishna Chaitanya. I bow down to Him, who has manifested Himself with the sentiment and complexion of Shrimati Radharani although He is Krishna Himself."

4. Lakshmipriya is the *bhu-shakti* and Vishnupriya is the *shri-shakti.* See Bhaktisiddhanta Sarasvati Thakura's commentary on the *Chaitanya-bhagavata* of Vrindavan Dasa Thakura (*Adi-khanda* 1.2).
5. According to the 2001 government of India census, there are 58 million Hindus in West Bengal (out of a total population of about 80 million). Assuming that 70 percent of Bengali Hindus are Vaishnavas, that would be about 40 million. How many of them are Gaudiya Vaishnavas? I would estimate about 15 million. From my personal experience in Bengal, it would seem that Gaudiya Vaishnavas in certain districts would be in the majority. For example, District Nadia, the prime center of Gaudiya Vaishnavism, including Mayapur, its most sacred place of pilgrimage, had according to the 1991 survey 2.8 million Hindus. Assuming 70 percent are

Vaishnava, that would be about 2 million Vaishnavas. I would venture to say that in Nadia at least 1.5 million people would be Gaudiya Vaishnavas. I would also expect to find a lesser but still significant percentage of Gaudiya Vaishnavas in the neighboring Barddaman (Burdwan), Murshidabad, and Birbhum districts. I have not yet seen the 2001 census breakdown for the Bengali districts. But according to 1991 census figures, these three districts had a population of 13.2 million, of which 8.3 million (63 percent) were Hindu. According to the 2001 census, these districts have a population of 15.8 million. Assuming 63 percent are Hindu, that would mean about 10 million Hindus, of which about 7 million should be Vaishnavas. If half are Gaudiya Vaisnavas, that would be 3.5 million. And from that I would estimate a heartland core of 5 million Gaudiya Vaishnavas today. Then among the remaining 35 million Vaishnavas in Bengal, I would guess that 20 percent might be Gaudiya Vaishnavas, about 7 million, for a total of 12 million Gaudiya Vaishnavas in West Bengal.

6. The population of Orissa according to the 2001 government of India census is roughly 37 million, including 35 million Hindus. Assuming 70 percent are Vaishnava, that gives about 25 million Vaishnavas. Recent travelers to Orissa report that many villages are Gaudiya Vaishnava (personal communication Pranava Dasa), and historically Gaudiya Vaishnavism has had a significant presence in Orissa. Conservatively, I would estimate about 20 percent of the Vaishnavas are Gaudiya Vaishnavas, about 5 million. The population of Manipur is about 2 million, of which 1 million are Hindu. Because Manipur has been a stronghold of Gaudiya Vaishnavism, I would estimate that .5 million Gaudiya Vaishnavas reside there. As for the nation of Bangladesh, the population according to the 2001 government census was about 130 million (http://www.banbeis.org/bd_pro.htm). Of these, about 10 percent, or 13 million are Hindu. If 70 percent are Vaishnava, that would be 9 million Hindus. I would estimate that 4 million of these are Gaudiya Vaishnavas.

7. For his biography, see Rupa Vilasa Dasa (1989) *The Seventh Goswami*. Manning: New Jaipur Press.

8. *Svalikhita Jivani* (1916) by Shrila Bhaktivinoda Thakura. Edited by Lalita Prasad Datta. Calcutta: Lalita Prasad Datta. English translation: http://www.bhaktivinoda. co.uk/Svalikhitajivani/.

9. See the sketch map of Van Den Brouck (1660), a tracing of which can be found as figure 2 in K. N. Mukherjee (1984), A historico-geographical study for Shri Chaitanya's birthsite. *The Indian Journal of Landscape Systems and Ecological Studies*, 7(2): 33–56. See 1990 revision at http://bvml.org/contemporary/Yogapitha/PKNM_asfscb.html.

10. Mukherjee (1984) figure 3 is a tracing of the map of J. Rennell (1780), which shows Nuddeah now on the west bank of the Ganges.

11. *The Seventh Goswami*, chapter 18.

12. It was called the Shri Navadvipa-Dhama-Pracharini-Sabha.

13. *The Seventh Goswami*, chapter 21.

14. From an article on the Yoga Pitha temple opening ceremony in the newspaper *Gaudiya*, March 16, 1935.

15. Bhaktivinoda Thakura (1886), *Shri Shikshashtaka, Shri Sanmoda Bhashya* commentary on text 8. Translated by Sarvabhavana Dasa 2003, included in Bhaktivedanta Vedabase.

16. How and when Radharani manifested Navadvipa is told by Shiva to Parvati, in chapter 4 of the second part of the *Shri-Chaitanya-janma-khanda* of the *Ananta-samhita*, cited by Bhaktivinoda Thakura in *Navadvipa-dhama-mahatmya, Pramana-khanda*, chapter 2. Radharani once heard that Krishna was enjoying pastimes with some other girl, and to lure Krishna away from her, Radharani, in the company of Her confidential girlfriends (*sakhis*) such as Lalita and Vishakha, manifested a beautiful garden on an island protected by the waters of the Ganges and Yamuna. When Krishna came there, He was enchanted, and said, "As this place is like an island, or *dvipa*, the wise will call it Navadvipa. By My order, all the holy places will reside here. Because You have created this place for My pleasure, I will live here eternally." Shiva then told Parvati, "Krishna . . . merged with Radha's body and began to reside there eternally. Seeing that . . . form— outwardly of a fair complexion but inwardly Krishna Himself—Lalita gave up her beautiful form for the service of Gauranga [Chaitanya Mahaprabhu]. She took on a male form to suitably receive the affection of Gauranga. Seeing that Lalita had taken such a form, Vishakha and all the other *sakhis* also suddenly took on male forms. At that time the tumultuous vibration of 'Jaya Gaurahari!' filled the four directions. From that time the devotees call this form of Krishna Gaurahari. As Radha is Gauri (fair) and Krishna is Hari, when They combine in one form, They are called Gaurahari. . . . and Vrindavana is Navadvipa."

17. The *Bhakti-ratnakara* contains this verse:

> *navadvipa madhye mayapura name sthan*
> *yathaya janmilen gaurachandra bhagavan*

"In the center of Navadvipa there is a place called Mayapura. At this place the Supreme Lord, Gaurachandra, took His birth." Translation from *The Seventh Goswami*, chapter 18.

18. Bhaktivinoda Thakura, *Navadvipa Dhama Mahatmya, Parikrama Khanda*, chapter 2, Measurement and Form of the Dhama, English translation at http://www.salagram.net/BVT-NDM.html.

19. Shrila A. C. Bhaktivedanta Swami Prabhupada, *Chaitanya-charitamrta, Adi Lila* 13.30, purport: "There are different islands in the Navadvipa area for cultivation of these nine varieties of devotional service." Narahari Dasa, *Bhakti-ratnakara, Twelfth Wave*, cited by Bhaktisiddhanta Sarasvati Thakura in his commentary on *Chaitanya-bhagavata, Adi Khanda* 1.7., English translation by Pundarika Vidyanidhi (2003), in Bhaktivedanta Vedabase: "Navadvipa is famous throughout the universe as the place where the nine types of devotional service, beginning with hearing, shine brilliantly."

20. Shrila A. C. Bhaktivedanta Swami Prabhupada, *Chaitanya-charitamrita, Adi-lila*, 13.30, purport.

21. "The materialist, who is blind to spiritual life, cannot see the deep relationship between Navadvipa and Vraja [Vrindavan], which are simultaneously one and different. Know for certain that this same relationship exists between Gaura ["one with golden complexion," i.e. Chaitanya Mahaprabhu] and Krishna, who are also simultaneously one and different." Nityananda Prabhu to Jiva Goswami, *Navadvipa-dhama-mahatmya, Parikrama-khanda,* chapter 18.

22. "If one lives in Navadvipa and takes shelter of the holy name, his offenses will be destroyed and the qualification for the *rasa* will appear. Love of Krishna will soon shine within his heart and topics of Radha and Krishna will prevail. In this way, by achieving Gauranga's mercy, the living entity attains Vrindavana, the holy abode of Radha and Krishna's nectarean pastimes." *Navadvipa-dhama-mahatmya, Parikrama Khanda,* chapter 17. Gauranga ("golden body") is another name for Chaitanya Mahaprabhu.

23. "Near the Ganges flows the beautiful Yamuna, and the Sarasvati flows within another river. East of the Yamuna are the long streams of the Tamraparni, the Kritamala, and the Brahmaputra. The Sarayu, Narmada, Sindhu, Kaveri, Gomati, and Godavari flow swiftly throughout the breadth of Navadvipa. All these rivers intersect to form the nine different islands of Navadvipa. . . . By the order of Gaurachandra [Chaitanya], the seven holy cities: Ayodhya, Mathura, Maya (Haridvara), Kashi, Kanchi, Avanti (Ujjain), and Dvaraka, are always present in their own places within Navadvipa." Bhaktivinoda Thakura, *Navadvipa-dhama-mahatmya, Parikrama-khanda,* chapter 3, "The Procedure for Parikrama of the Dhama."

24. Nityananda Prabhu, one of the principal associates of Chaitanya Mahaprabhu, tells Jiva Goswami: "You should know that the houses, doors, rivers, streams, forests, and court-yards are all completely spiritual and intensely attractive. . . . Materialistic persons cannot enter the *dhama*, nor is there any material influence here. Maya [the deluding energy of Krishna] has eternally covered the *dhama* with a film of dull matter. People who have no relationship with Krishna Chaitanya simply live on top of that covering, blind to the real truth. Though one is thinking, 'I am in Navadvipa,' . . . Maya happily keeps that person far away from the *dhama*." Bhaktivinoda Thakura, *Navadvipa-dhama-mahatmya, Parikrama-khanda,* chapter 18.

25. Bhaktivinoda Thakura, *Navadvipa-dhama-mahatmya, Parikrama-khanda,* chapter 3, "Procedure for Parikrama of the Dhama."

26.

prithivite ache yata nagaradi grama
sarvatra prachara haibe mora nama

"In every town and village on this earth, the chanting of My name will be heard." (*Chaitanya-bhagavata, Antya-khanda* 4.126).

27. This English translation is given in Brahmananda Swami (1974) How the teachings of Lord Caitanya came to the western world, part 2. *Back to Godhead,* issue number 68.

28. Cited in *The Seventh Goswami,* chapter 22.

29. A few Gaudiya Vaishnava preachers came to the West in the early twentieth cen-

tury but did not attract many followers. See for example Baba Premanand Bharati (1904) *Sree Krishna: The Lord of Love.* New York: The Krishna Samaj. After Srila A. C. Bhaktivedanta Swami Prabhupada attracted large numbers of followers internationally in the years 1965 to 1977, other Gaudiya Vaishnava *gurus* came to the West and also began to attract followers, although in smaller numbers.

30. *Navadvipa-dhama-mahatmya, Parikrama-khanda,* chapter 5.

31. Nitai Dasa (1975) The glories of Shridhama Mayapur. *Back to Godhead,* vol. 10, no. 3.

32. Bhaktivedanta Vedabase, Room conversation with yoga student, March 14, 1975, Tehran, Iran. In making this statement, Shrila A. C. Bhaktivedanta Swami Prabhupada was expressing the content of a verse cited by Chaitanya Mahaprabhu from the *Brihan-naradiya-purana,* as recorded by Krishnadasa Kaviraja in *Chaitanya-charitamrita, Adi-lila* 17.21:

> *harer nama harer nama harer nama eva kevalam*
> *kalau nasty eva, nasty eva, nasty eva gathir anyatha*

"In this Age of Kali there is no other means, no other means, no other means for self-realization than chanting the holy name, chanting the holy name, chanting the holy name of Lord Hari."

33. *Navadvipa-dhama-mahatmya, Parikrama-khanda,* chapter 3.

34. "North of Mayapur lies Simantadvipa. *Sadhu* and *shastra* have explained the rules of *parikrama.* After having *darshana* of Mayapur in Antardvipa, learned devotees go to Simantadvipa. Next one should go south of Mayapur to Godrumadvipa, then one should joyfully go to Madhyadvipa. After seeing these four islands on the east bank, one should reverently cross the Ganges. Having walked around Koladvipa at leisure, then take *darshana* of Ritudvipa. After you have seen the most beautiful Jahnudvipa, go and see Modadrumadvipa and then Rudradvipa. Then again cross the Ganges, and walk back to Mayapur. There, respectfully enter the temple of Jagannatha Mishra and Sachi and take *darshana* of the Lord. This is the procedure of *parikrama* for all times. One who follows this practice will obtain unlimited happiness." *Navadvipa-dhama-mahatmya, Parikrama-khanda,* chapter 3.

35. See Michael A. Cremo and Mukunda Goswami (1995) *Divine Nature: A Spiritual Perspective on the Environmental Crisis.* Los Angeles: Bhaktivedanta Book Trust (released on Earth Day, April 22); and Michael A. Cremo (2001) Divine nature: practical application of Vedic principles for solving the environmental crisis. In T. D. Singh and Samaresh Bandyopadhyay eds. *Thoughts on Synthesis of Science and Religion,* Proceedings of Second World Congress for Synthesis of Science and Religion. Calcutta, India, January 4–6, 1997. Calcutta: Bhaktivedanta Institute, pp. 209–221.

17

Human Devolution: A Consciousness-Based Vedic Alternative to Materialistic Evolution

Enoch Page, an anthropologist at the University of Massachusetts at Amherst, read my book Human Devolution: A Vedic Alternative to Darwin's Theory, *and arranged for me to give a talk about it at the annual meeting of the Society for the Anthropology of Consciousness, which was held at the University of Massachusetts at Amherst, April 13–17, 2005. The Society for the Anthropology of Consciousness is a division of the American Anthropological Association. I later presented a similar paper at a conference in India. That paper was published: Cremo, M. A. (2008) Human Devolution: A Vedic Alternative to Darwin's Theory. In Subhash C. Mishra, M. Chidambaram, and Sudipto Ghosh, eds.* Science and Spiritual Quest. Proceedings of the 4th All India Students Conference, 27–29 December 2008, NIT Tiruchirapalli, TN India. *Kolkata, Bhaktivedanta Institute and Tiruchirapalli, National Institute of Technology, pp. 183–200.*

I am grateful for this opportunity to address the Society for the Anthropology of Consciousness, a division of the American Anthropological Association. First let me put this talk into context. I am not an anthropologist. But for those of you who are anthropologists, let me characterize this talk as a kind of "room service" ethnography. Generally, as anthropologists, you go out into the world to do your ethnographic studies, but in this case, I am saving you the trouble by coming, at your invitation, into your domain with my own contribution to your ethnographic work. You can thus study me without going out into the field.

I myself am doing a kind of ethnographic research. It would be a mistake to think that you, as anthropologists, are not also an object of research. My people, the members of the International Society for Krishna Consciousness, with roots in the Gaudiya Vaishnava culture of Bengal, have often been the object of study for cultural anthropologists and sociologists of religion and psychologists. But we are not passive objects of study. I find you interesting, so I would also like to study and understand you. So I have come into your circle this evening, just as you might come into the circle of some indigenous people, or other social group, somewhere in the world. Typically, as anthropologists, you insert yourselves into the lives of others. This means learning something of the languages and customs of other people. As I understand it, you do not become the other, but you become enough like the other to do your anthropological work. So although I am not an anthropologist, perhaps because I have become enough like one I have gained some limited entry into your midst.

In terms of social science theory, you could say that this talk tonight is an exercise in cultural translation, an attempt to translate some key aspects of Vedic cosmology into a form at least minimally comprehensible to an audience absorbed in the modern scientific cosmology. In pragmatic terms, this talk might also be seen as an exercise in "articulation", which taken in the sense of the social sciences implies the contingent linking of interest groups that at first glance might not seem deeply related (Choy 2005). In other words, if I am able to successfully translate some key aspects of Vedic cosmology, as related to human origins, into terms comprehensible to anthropologists then this might result in some of us seeing some common cause.

If a translation is successful, this might also influence some of you to look into the original Vedic texts, and the culture that produced them, as sources helpful for discerning what might be true about reality. Anthropologist Katherine P. Ewing said (1994, p. 572), "To rule out the possibility of belief in another's reality is to encapsulate that reality and, thus, to impose implicitly the hegemony of one's own view of the world." In *Journal of Consciousness Studies* (1994 v. 1, no. 2), William Barnard, speaking about the world's wisdom traditions, advocated (pp. 257–258) "a scholarship that is willing and able to affirm that the metaphysical models . . . of these different spiritual traditions are serious contenders for truth, a scholarship that realizes that these religious worlds are not dead corpses that we can dissect and analyze at a safe distance, but rather are living, vital bodies of knowledge and practice that have the potential to change our taken-for-granted notions."

Of course, I do not wish to overreach. One thing I am going to be talking about tonight is parapsychological phenomena, or psi phenomena, as they are sometimes called. In this regard, I have learned a little about the history of the Society for the Anthropology of Consciousness [SAC], in relation to transpersonal psychology. Mark Schroll (2005, p. 48) explains it like this: "Transpersonal psychology emphasized the ontological importance of the psi phenomena as real, and had their 1986 application for divisional status in the American Psychological Association rejected. . . . whereas a shift in SAC's ontological position on psi led to their acceptance in 1990 as a[n] AAA division." Apparently, the Society for the Anthropology of Consciousness has chosen not to argue for the reality of psi phenomena but simply to focus on describing "the behavior of persons claiming to experience psi-related phenomena" (Schroll 2005, p. 48). However, Schroll (2005, p. 49) goes on to say that "this perspective fails and even prohibits us from investigating the 'source of religion': experiential encounters with ecstatic mystical experiences, shamanic journeys to other worlds, or states of consciousness and seeing and feeling associated with psychic healing." So for those of you who favor the more conservative approach, you can take this talk as ethnographic data, enabling you to record the behavior of a person attempting to persuade others of the reality of a consciousness-based explanation of human origins with roots in the Vedic cosmology of India, and as for the rest of you, perhaps you will allow yourself to be persuaded that what I am saying is true.

Where do we come from? Today the most common answer is that we are combinations of material elements, and that our human form has come about through a process of evolution by natural selection. However, the Vedic literature (*Brhad-aranyaka Upanishad* 1.4.10) says *aham brahmasmi*, which means "I am spirit." But now, even though we are spirit, we find ourselves entangled in the world of matter. Lord Krishna says in *Bhagavad-gita* (15.7),

> *mamaivamsho jiva-loke*
> *jiva-bhutah sanatanah*
> *manah-shashtanindriyani*
> *prakriti-sthani karshati*

"The living entities in this conditioned world are My eternal fragmental parts. Due to conditioned life, they are struggling very hard with the six senses, which include the mind." In other words, each living entity is originally a conscious spiritual part of the supreme conscious spiritual being, but by misuse of free will some of those conscious spiritual beings now find themselves covered by mind and a body made of material senses, a body designed as a vehicle for the conscious self. This conception involves a tripartite division of matter, mind, and consciousness. Our gross material bodies might be compared to computer hardware. Our minds might be compared to computer software, which provides an interface that allows a user to interact with the computer hardware. Mind under this conception is not conscious, although it does have abilities to structure sense data and logical patterns. Finally, the conscious self might be compared to the user of the computer hardware and software.

So we do not evolve up from matter; rather, in a sense, we devolve, or come down, from a level of pure consciousness, or spirit. This traditional Vedic view can be made intelligible in terms of the scientific evidence available to us, as I show in my book *Human Devolution: A Vedic Alternative to Darwin's Theory* (Cremo 2003). I use the term Vedic in its broadest sense, to include not just the four Vedas but also the derivative literatures such as the *Puranas*, or histories.

Although I offer a Vedic alternative to Darwinism, I acknowledge that it is part of a larger family of spiritual alternatives to Darwinism rooted in various world religions, which I also honor and respect.

Before presenting an alternative to the Darwinian concept of human origins, it is reasonable to show that an alternative is really necessary. One thing that clearly demonstrates the need for an alternative is the archeological evidence for extreme human antiquity. Such evidence actually exists, but, as documented in my book *Forbidden Archeology* (Cremo and Thompson 1993), it has been systematically eliminated from scientific discussion by a process of knowledge filtration. Archeological evidence that contradicts the Darwinian theory of human evolution is often rejected just for that reason.

For example, in the nineteenth century, gold was discovered in California. To get it, miners dug tunnels into the sides of mountains, such as Table Mountain in Tuolumne County. Deep inside the tunnels, in deposits of early Eocene age (about 50 million years old), miners found human bones and artifacts [see Plates XXII-XV]. The discoveries were carefully documented by the chief government geologist of California, Dr. J. D. Whitney (1880), but we do not hear very much about these discoveries today. Anthropologist William Holmes (1899, p. 424) said, "Perhaps if Professor Whitney had fully appreciated the story of human evolution as it is understood today, he would have hesitated to announce the conclusions formulated, notwithstanding the imposing array of testimony with which he was confronted." In other words, if the facts did not fit the theory of human evolution, the facts had to be set aside, and that is exactly what happened.

Such bias continued into the twentieth century. In the 1970s, American archeologists led by Cynthia Irwin Williams discovered stone tools at Hueyatlaco, near Puebla, Mexico. The stone tools were of advanced type, made only by humans like us. A team of geologists, from the United States Geological Survey and universities in the United States, came to Hueyatlaco to date the site. Among the geologists was Virginia Steen-McIntyre. To date the site, the team used four methods—uranium series dating on butchered animal bones found along with the tools, zircon fission track dating on volcanic layers above the tools, tephra hydration dating of volcanic crystals, and standard stratigraphy. The four methods converged on an age of about 250,000 years for the site (Steen-McIntyre *et al.* 1981). The archeologists refused to consider this date. They could not believe that humans capable of making the Hueyatlaco artifacts existed 250,000 years ago. In defense of the dates obtained by the geologists, Virginia Steen-McIntyre wrote in a letter (March 30, 1981) to Estella Leopold, associate editor of *Quaternary Research:* "The problem as I see it is much bigger than Hueyatlaco. It concerns the manipulation of scientific thought through the suppression of 'Enigmatic Data,' data that challenges the prevailing mode of thinking. Hueyatlaco certainly does that! Not being an anthropologist, I didn't realize the full significance of our dates back in 1973, nor how deeply woven into our thought the current theory of human evolution has become. Our work at Hueyatlaco has been rejected by most archaeologists because it contradicts that theory, period." This remains true today, not only for the California gold mine discoveries and the Hueyatlaco human artifacts, but for hundreds of other discoveries documented in the scientific literature of the past 150 years.

There is also fossil evidence showing that the current Darwinian picture of the evolution of nonhuman species is also in need of revision. Beginning in the 1940s, geologists and paleobotanists working with the Geological Survey of India explored formations called the Saline Series in the Salt Range Mountains, now part of Pakistan. They found deep in salt mines evidence for the existence of advanced flowering plants and insects in the early Cambrian period, about 600 million years ago. According to standard evolutionary ideas, no land plants or animals existed at that time. Flowering plants and insects are thought to have come into existence hundreds of millions of years later.

To explain the evidence some geologists proposed that there must have been a massive overthrust, by which Cambrian layers, over 550 million years old, were thrust over much younger Eocene layers (containing the remains of flowering plants and insects), about 50 million years old. Others pointed out that there were no geological signs of such an overthrust. According to these scientists, the layers bearing the fossils of the advanced plants and insects were found in normal position, beneath strata containing trilobites, the characteristic fossil of the Cambrian. One of these scientists, E. R. Gee, a geologist working with the Geological Survey of India, proposed a novel solution to the problem.

Paleobotanist Birbal Sahni (1947, pp. *xlv–xlvi*) noted: "Quite recently, an alternative explanation has been offered by Mr. Gee. The suggestion is that the angiosperms, gymnosperms and insects of the Saline Series may represent a highly evolved Cambrian or Precambrian flora and fauna! In other words, it is suggested that these plants and animals made their appearance in the Salt Range area several hundred million years earlier than they did anywhere else in the world. One would scarcely have believed that such an idea would be seriously put forward by any geologist today." The controversy was left unresolved.

In the 1990s, petroleum geologists, unaware of the earlier controversy, restudied the area. They determined that the salt deposits below the Cambrian deposits containing trilobites were early Cambrian or Precambrian (Yeats *et al.* 1984, Butler *et al.* 1987, Jaumé and Lillie 1988, Baker *et al.* 1988, Pennock *et al.* 1989, McDougall and Khan 1990). In other words, they found no evidence of an overthrust. The salt deposits were in a natural position below the Cambrian deposits. This supports Gee's suggestion that the plant and insect remains in the salt deposits were evidence of an advanced fauna and flora existing in the early Cambrian. This evidence contradicts not only the Darwinian concept of the evolution of humans but of other species as well.

Evidence from biochemistry, genetics, and developmental biology also contradicts the Darwinian theory of human evolution.

Although the origin of life from chemicals is technically not part of the evolution theory, it has in practice become inseparably connected with it. Darwinists routinely assert that life arose from chemicals. But after decades of theorizing and experimenting, they are unable to say exactly which chemicals combined in exactly which way to form exactly which first living thing.

As far as evolution itself is concerned, it has not been demonstrated in any truly scientific way. It remains an article of faith. The modern evolutionary synthesis is based on genetics. Evolutionists posit a relationship between the genotype (genetic structure) of an organism and its phenotype (physiological structure). They say that changes in the genotype result in changes in the phenotype, and by natural selection the changes in phenotype conferring better fitness in a particular environment accumulate in organisms. Evolutionists claim that this process can account for the appearance of new structural features in organisms. But on the level of microbiology, these structures appear to be irreducibly complex. Scientists have not been able to specify exactly how they have come about in step by step fashion. They have not been able to tell us exactly what genetic changes resulted in what phenotypic changes to produce particular complex features of organisms. This would require the specification of intermediate stages leading up to the complex structures we observe today. Biochemist Michael Behe (1996, p. 183) says, "In the past ten years, *Journal of Molecular Evolution* has published more than a thousand papers. . . . There were zero papers discussing detailed models for intermediates in the development of complex biomolecular structures. This is not a peculiarity of *JME*. No papers are to be found that discuss detailed models for intermediates in the development of complex biomolecular structures, whether in the *Proceedings of the National Academy of Science, Nature, Science,* the *Journal of Molecular Biology* or, to my knowledge, any science journal."

So archeology, paleontology, biochemistry, genetics, and developmental biology demonstrate a real need for an alternative to the current Darwinian account of human origins. However, before we even ask the question, "Where did human beings come from?" we should first of all ask the question, "What is a human being?" Today most scientists believe that a human being is simply a combination of the ordinary chemical elements. This assumption limits the kinds of explanations that can be offered for human origins. I propose that it is more reasonable, based on available scientific evidence, to start with the assumption that a human being is composed of three separately existing substances: matter, mind, and consciousness (or spirit). This assumption widens the circle of possible explanations.

Any scientific chain of reasoning begins with some initial assumptions that are not rigorously proved. Otherwise, one would get caught in an endless regression of proofs of assumptions, and proofs of proofs of assumptions. Initial assumptions must simply be reasonable on the basis of available evidence. And it can be shown that it is reasonable, on the basis of available evidence, to posit the existence of mind and consciousness, in addition to ordinary matter, as separate elements composing the human being.

At this point, some may object that it is not standard scientific practice to introduce new substances to explain observations. Modern cosmology offers a counterexample. Through the 1960s, astronomers and astrophysicists attempted to explain their observations of the universe in terms of ordinary matter alone. They found they were not able to do this. For example, they were unable to explain the spiral structure of galaxies. In order to explain what they observe, space scientists introduced a strange new substance, dark matter. More recently, in order to account for their observations of an accelerating rate of expansion of the universe, cosmologists have had to introduce an even stranger new substance called dark energy. Today cosmologists say the universe is composed of 5 percent ordinary matter, 30 percent dark matter, and 65 percent dark energy. I am proposing that we also need to introduce new substances to explain what we observe in biology.

Researchers in both artificial intelligence (AI) and artificial life (Alife) have failed to provide convincing models or replications of living things. Rodney Brooks, of the Artificial Intelligence Laboratory at MIT, wrote in a perceptive article in *Nature:* "Neither AI or Alife has produced artefacts that could be confused with a living organism for more than an instant. AI just does not seem as present or aware as even a simple animal and Alife cannot match the complexities of the simplest forms of life" (Brooks 2001, p. 409). Brooks attributes the failure to something other than lack of computer power, incorrect parameters, or insufficiently complex models. He raises the possibility that "we are missing something fundamental and currently unimagined in our models." But what is that missing something? "One possibility," says Brooks (2001, p. 410), "is that some aspect of living systems is invisible to us right now. The current scientific view of things is that they are machines whose components are biomolecules. It is not completely impossible that we might discover new properties of biomolecules, or some new ingredient. . . . Let us call this the 'new stuff' hypothesis—the hypothesis that there might be some extra sort of 'stuff' in living systems outside our current scientific understanding." And what might this new stuff be? Among the possibilities suggested by Brooks (2001, p. 411) are "some more ineffable entity such as a soul or *elan vital*—the 'vital force.'"

Along these lines, I propose that the "new stuff" should be mind and consciousness. I define mind as a subtle, but nevertheless material, energy, associated with the human organism and capable of acting on ordinary matter in ways we cannot explain by our current laws of physics. Evidence for this mind element comes from scientific research into the phenomena called by some "paranormal" or "psychical." Here we are led into the hidden history of physics. Just as in archeology, there has been in physics a tremendous amount of knowledge filtration. For example, every physics student learns about the work of Pierre and Marie Curie, the husband and wife team who both received Nobel Prizes for their work in discovering radium. The account is found in practically every introductory physics textbook. What we do not read in the textbooks is that the Curies were heavily involved in psychical research. They were part of a large group of prominent European scientists, including other Nobel Prize winners, who were jointly conducting research into the paranormal in Paris early in the twentieth century. For two years, the group studied the Italian medium Eusapia Palladino (sometimes spelled Paladino, or Paladina). Historian Anna Hurwic notes in her biography of Pierre Curie (1995, p. 247), "He thought it possible to discover in spiritualism the source of an unknown energy that would reveal the secret of radioactivity. . . . He saw the séances as scientific experiments, tried to monitor the different parameters, took detailed notes of every observation. He was really intrigued by Eusapia Paladino." About some séances with Eusapia, Pierre Curie wrote to physicist Georges Gouy in a letter dated July 24, 1905: "We had at the Psychology Society a few séances with the medium Eusapia Paladina. It was very interesting, and truly those phenomena that we have witnessed seemed to us to not be some magical tricks—a table lifted four feet above the floor, movements of objects, feelings of hands that pinched you or caressed you, apparitions of light. All this in a room arranged by us, with a small number of spectators all well known and without the presence of a possible accomplice. The only possible cheating would be an extraordinary ability of the medium as a magician. But how to explain the different phenomena when we are holding her hands and legs, and the lighting of the room is sufficient to see everything going on?" On April 14, 1906, Pierre wrote to Gouy: "We are working, M. Curie and me, to precisely dose the radium by its own emanations. . . .We had a few new 'séances' with Eusapia Paladina (We already had séances with her last summer). The result is that those phenomena exist for real, and I can't doubt it any more. It is unbelievable, but it is thus, and it is impossible to negate it after the séances that we had in conditions of perfect monitoring." He concluded, "There is, according to me a completely new domain of facts and physical states of space of which we have no idea."

Such research continues today, although most scientists doing it are concentrating on microeffects rather than the macroeffects reported by Pierre Curie. For example, some years ago, Robert Jahn, head of the engineering department at Princeton University, started to research the effects of mental attention on random number generators. A random number generator will normally generate a sequence of ones and zeros, with equal numbers of each. But Jahn, and other researchers, have found that subjects can mentally influence the random number generators to produce a statistically significant greater number of ones than zeros or vice versa (Nelson and Radin 1996). To me, such results, and many more like them from the hidden history of physics, suggest there is associated with the human organism a mind element that can act on ordinary matter in ways we cannot easily explain by our current physical laws. So if we want to speak about human origins, we have to consider not just the ordinary chemical elements but also the subtle mind element.

Now what about the consciousness element? Evidence for a conscious self that can exist apart from mind and matter comes from medical reports of out of body experiences (OBEs). Dr. Michael Sabom, an American cardiologist, conducted extensive research into out of body experiences. He carefully interviewed heart attack patients who reported such experiences. He then compared their reports with their actual medical records. He found that a statistically significant number of the group gave correct accounts, consistent with the reports of their treatment. This is highly unusual, because according to standard medical opinion, the patients should have been completely unconscious. Could the subjects have manufactured their correct reports from their previous knowledge of heart attack treatment procedures (for example, from watching television hospital dramas)? To control for this, Sabom selected a second group of heart attack patients who did not report OBEs. He asked them to imagine the medical treatment they had undergone while unconscious. None of them was able to give a correct report, and almost all of them made major mistakes. For Sabom, the results from the control group confirmed the genuineness of the OBE reports from the first group. In his book *Recollections of Death: A Medical Investigation* (1982, p. 183), Sabom asked, "Could the mind which splits apart from the physical brain be, in essence, the 'soul,' which continues to exist after final bodily death, according to some religious doctrines?"

Sabom's results have been confirmed by further studies. For example, in February 2001, a team from the University of Southampton, in the United Kingdom, published a favorable study on OBEs in cardiac arrest patients in the journal *Resuscitation* (Parnia *et al.* 2001). The team was headed by Dr. Sam Parnia, a senior research fellow at the university. On February 16, 2001, a report published on the university's web site said that the work of Dr. Parnia "suggests consciousness and the mind may continue to exist after the brain has ceased to function and the body is clinically dead."

Past life memories also give evidence for a conscious self that can exist apart from the body. Dr. Ian Stevenson, a psychiatrist at the University of Virginia medical school, has conducted extensive research into past life memories. Stevenson (1974), and his associates, have focused on past life memories spontaneously reported by very young children. Stevenson prefers working with children because older persons might have the motives and means to construct elaborate past life accounts. His technique is to thoroughly interview the child subjects and thus obtain as many details as possible about the reported past life. Using this information, Stevenson and his associates then attempt to identify the person the child claims to have been in the past life. In hundreds of cases, they have been successful in making such identifications.

Having established that the human organism is composed of the elements matter, mind, and consciousness (or spirit), it is natural to suppose that the cosmos is divided into regions, or levels, of matter, mind, and consciousness, each inhabited by beings adapted to life there. First, there is a region of pure consciousness. Consciousness, as we experience it, is individual and personal. This suggests that the original source of conscious selves is also individual and personal. So in addition to the individual units of consciousness existing in the realm of pure consciousness, there is also an original conscious being who is their source. When the fractional conscious selves give up their connection with their source, they are placed in lower regions of the cosmos predominated by either the subtle material energy (mind) or the gross material energy (matter). There is thus a cosmic hierarchy of conscious beings, a fact attested to in the cosmologies of people from all parts of the world. These cosmologies share many features. They generally include an original God inhabiting a realm of pure consciousness, a subordinate creator god inhabiting a subtle material region of the cosmos along with many kinds of demigods and demigoddesses, and an earthly realm inhabited by humans like us.

Harvard University psychiatrist Dr. John Mack (1999, p. 269), in the course of his studies of the modern UFO and alien abduction phenomenon, concluded: "It appears ever more likely that we exist in a multi-dimensional cosmos . . . . The cosmos . . . appears to be filled with beings, creatures, spirits, intelligences, gods."

The human devolution concept posits the action of superior intelligences in the origin of the human form and the forms of other living things. This depends on the ability of consciousness to more or less directly influence the organization of matter in living things. There is evidence that such paranormal modification and production of biological forms actually occurs.

The first category of evidence comes from laboratory experiments in which human subjects are able to mentally influence the growth of microorganisms. For example, Beverly Rubik conducted laboratory research on "volitional effects of healers on a bacterial system" while director of the Institute for Frontier Sciences at Temple University in Philadelphia, Pennsylvania. She reported the results in a paper included in her book *Life at the Edge of Science* (1996, pp. 99–117). The experiments were performed using the bacterium *Salmonella typhimurium*, a very well studied organism. The chief subject in the study was Olga Worrall, who had demonstrated positive abilities in other experiments. In one set of experiments, culture dishes of bacteria were treated with antibiotics that inhibit the growth of the bacteria. Worrall attempted to influence the bacteria in one set of culture dishes to grow. Another set of culture dishes was kept aside as a control. Compared to the control group, the group of culture dishes mentally acted upon by Worrall all showed an increase in growth. In another set of experiments, bacteria were placed on slides in a solution of phenol sufficient to immobilize but not kill them. The slides of bacteria were then observed under a microscope. In her book,

Rubik (1996, p. 108) stated, "Application of … phenol completely paralyzes the bacteria within 1 to 2 minutes. Worrall's treatment inhibited this effect … such that on the average up to 7 percent of the bacteria continued to swim after 12 minutes exposure to phenol compared to the control groups which were completely paralyzed in all cases."

Distance healing by prayer and other miraculous cures provide another category of evidence for paranormal modification of biological form. In a study published in the *Annals of Internal Medicine* (Astin *et al.* 2000), researchers found that "a growing body of evidence suggests an association between religious involvement and spirituality and positive health outcomes." In support of their conclusion, the Astin group cited over fifty credible positive reports from a variety of scientific and medical journals. Even more striking examples of paranormal modification of biological form come from the reports of the Medical Bureau at Lourdes. Since the nineteenth century, the physicians of the Medical Bureau have carefully documented a series of miraculous cures, some involving the inexplicable regeneration of damaged tissues and organs.

Psychiatrist Ian Stevenson has conducted extensive investigations into birthmarks that appear to have some relationship with wounds a person experienced in a past life. Persons who died of gunshot wounds in previous lives sometimes display on their present bodies birthmarks of appropriate size at the positions of the entry and exit wounds. This suggests that when such a person's soul and mind enter the present body, they carry with them impressions that appropriately modify the body's biological form. Some medical investigators have documented cases of "maternal impressions." These occur when a pregnant woman is exposed to a striking event that causes a strong emotional impression. Somehow the psychological impression leaves its mark on the embryo within her womb. For example, if a woman sees someone with an injured foot and then constantly remembers this, her child might be born with a malformed foot. In *Cyclopaedia of the Diseases of Children* (1890 v. 1, pp. 191–216), W. C. Dabney reviewed sixty-nine reports published between 1853 and 1886 documenting a close correspondence between the mother's mental impression and the physical deformation in her child.

Yet another category of evidence consists of reports by prominent scientists who have witnessed mediums produce human limbs or complete human bodies. A particularly striking case was reported by Alfred Russel Wallace, who was along with Darwin the cofounder of the theory of evolution by natural selection. Wallace became involved in paranormal research. Once, Wallace, accompanied by others, saw a clergyman medium named Monk produce a complete human form. In his autobiography (1905 v. 2, p. 330), Wallace described the event, which took place in an apartment in the Bloomsbury district of London: "It was a bright summer afternoon, and everything happened in the full light of day. After a little conversation, Monk, who was dressed in the usual clerical black, appeared to go into a trance; then stood up a few feet in front of us, and after a little while pointed to his side, saying, 'Look.' We saw there a faint white patch on his coat on the left side. This grew brighter, then seemed to flicker, and extend both upwards and downwards, till very gradually it formed a cloudy pillar extending from his shoulder to his feet and close to his body. Then he shifted himself a little sideways, the cloudy figure standing still, but appearing joined to him by a cloudy band at the height at which it had first begun to form. Then, after a few minutes more, Monk again said 'Look,' and passed his hand through the connecting band, severing it. He and the figure then moved away from each other till they were about five or six feet apart. The figure had now assumed the appearance of a thickly draped female form, with arms and hands just visible. Monk looked towards it and again said to us 'Look,' and then clapped his hands. On which the figure put out her hands, clapped them as he had done, and we all distinctly heard her clap following his, but fainter. The figure then moved slowly back to him, grew fainter and shorter, and was apparently absorbed into his body as it had grown out of it."

At this point, some may still feel doubtful that all this talk of mind over matter influences on random number generators, extrasensory perception, past life memories, etc., really belongs in the world of science. However, even the highly skeptical Carl Sagan, who in his book *The Demon-Haunted World* attacked many claims for the paranormal, said therein, "At the time of this writing there are three claims in the ESP field which, in my opinion, deserve serious study: (1) that by thought alone humans can (barely) affect random number generators in computers, (2) that people under mild sensory deprivation can receive thoughts or images 'projected' at them; and (3) that young children sometimes report the details of a previous life, which upon checking turn out to be accurate and which they could not have known about in any other way than reincarnation" (Sagan 1995, p. 302). I do not agree with Sagan that these are the only categories of such evidence worthy of study, but it is highly significant that even Sagan admitted they are worthy of study. When this evidence, and other categories of such evidence are considered, the assumption that humans are composed of matter, mind, and consciousness, and that we are part of a cosmic hierarchy of beings in a multilevel universe, becomes reasonable enough to serve as the foundation for an alternative research program for explaining human origins.

If the forms of humans and other living things are the result of intelligent manipulation of matter, this suggests that the universe itself may have been designed for human life and other forms of life. Modern cosmology provides evidence for this. Scientists have discovered that numbers representing fundamental physical constants and ratios of natural forces appear to be finely tuned for life to exist in our universe. Astronomer Sir Martin Rees considers six of these numbers to be especially significant. In his book *Just Six Numbers* (2000, pp. 3–4), he says, "I have highlighted these six because each plays a crucial and distinctive role in our universe, and together they determine how the universe evolves and what its internal potentialities are. . . . These six numbers constitute a 'recipe' for a universe. Moreover, the outcome is sensitive to their values: if any one of them were to be 'untuned', there would be no stars and no life." There are three main explanations for the apparent fine tuning of the physical constants and laws of nature: simple chance, many worlds, and some intelligent providential creator. Many cosmologists admit that the odds against the fine tuning are too extreme for a simple "one shot" chance to be offered as a credible scientific explanation. To avoid the conclusion of a providential designer, they have posited the existence of a practically unlimited number of universes, each with the values of fundamental constants and laws of nature adjusted in a different way. And we just happen to live in the one universe with everything adjusted correctly for the existence of human life. But these other universes have only a theoretical existence, and even if their existence could be physically demonstrated, one would further have to show that in these other universes the values of the fundamental constants and laws of nature are in fact different than those in our universe. The Vedic cosmology also speaks of many universes, but all of them are designed for life.

The human devolution concept, tying together the various lines of evidence mentioned above, suggests that we do not evolve up from matter; rather we devolve, or come down, from the level of pure consciousness. Originally, we are pure units of consciousness existing in harmonious connection with the supreme conscious being. When we give up our willing connection with that supreme conscious being, we descend to regions of the cosmos dominated by the subtle and gross material energies, mind and matter. Forgetful of our original position, we attempt to dominate and enjoy the subtle and gross material energies. For this purpose, we are provided with bodies made of the subtle and gross material energies. These bodies are vehicles for conscious selves. They are designed for existence within the realms of the subtle and gross material energies. Conscious selves who are less forgetful of their original natures receive bodies composed primarily of the subtle material energy. Those who are more forgetful receive bodies composed of both the subtle and gross material energies, with the gross material energies predominating.

The process by which a pure conscious self becomes covered by the energies of mind and matter is what I call devolution. But it is a process that can be reversed. There is a process of spiritual re-evolution, by which consciousness can be freed from its coverings and restored to its original pure state. Every genuine religious tradition in the world has some process of prayer, or meditation, or yoga to help us accomplish this. And that is the primary purpose of human life.

References Cited:

Astin, John A., Harkness, Elaine and Ernst, Edzard (2000) The efficacy of "distant healing": A systematic review of randomized trials. *Annals of Internal Medicine,* 132(11) (June 6): 903–911.

Baker, D. M., Lillie, R. J., Yeats, R. S., Johnson, G. D., Yousuf, M., Zamin, A. S. H. (1988) Development of the Himalayan frontal thrust zone: Salt Range, Pakistan. *Geology,* 16: 3–7.

Barnard, William (1994) Transformations and transformers: spirituality and the academic study of mysticism. *Journal of Consciousness Studies,* 1(2): 256–258.

Behe, Michael (1996) *Darwin's Black Box: The Biochemical Challenge to Evolution.* New York: Free Press.

Bhagavad-gita As It Is (1986) Sanskrit text, Roman transliteration, English equivalents; translated with elaborate purports by Bhaktivedanta Swami Prabhupada. Los Angeles: Bhaktivedanta Book Trust.

Brooks, Rodney (2001) The relationship between matter and life. *Nature,* 409 (January

18): 409–411.

Butler, R. W. H., Coward, M. P., Harwood, G. M., and Knipe, R. J. (1987) Salt control on thrust geometry, structural style and gravitational collapse along the Himalayan Mountain Front in the Salt Range of Northern Pakistan. In Lerche, I., and O'Brian, J. J., eds. *Dynamical Geology of Salt and Related Structures*. Orlando: Academic Press, pp. 339–418.

Choy, Timoth K. (2005) Articulated knowledges: environmental forms after universality's demise. *American Anthropologist* 107(1): 5–18.

Cremo, Michael A. (2003) *Human Devolution: A Vedic Alternative to Darwin's Theory*. Los Angeles: Bhaktivedanta Book Publishing.

Cremo, Michael A. and Thompson, Richard L. (1993) *Forbidden Archeology*. Los Angeles: Bhaktivedanta Book Publishing.

Dabney, W. C. (1890) Maternal impressions. In Keating, J. M., ed. *Cyclopaedia of the Diseases of Children*. Vol. 1. Philadelphia: J. B. Lippincott, pp. 191–216.

Ewing, Katherine P. (1994) Dreams from a saint: anthropological atheism and the temptation to believe. *American Anthropologist*, 94(3): 571–583.

Holmes, William H. (1899) Review of the evidence relating to auriferous gravel man in California. *Smithsonian Institution Annual Report 1898–1899*, pp. 419–472.

Hurwic, Anna (1995) *Pierre Curie*. Paris: Flammarion. Quoted passages translated from French by Joseph Cudnik.

Jaumé, S. C. and Lillie, R. J. (1988) Mechanics of the Salt Range-Potwar Plateau, Pakistan: A fold-and-thrust belt underlain by evaporites. *Tectonics*, 7: 57–71.

Mack, John E. (1999) *Passport to the Cosmos: Human Transformation and Alien Encounters*. New York: Random House.

McDougall, J. W. and Khan, S. H. (1990) Strike-slip faulting in a foreland fold-thrust belt: The Kalabagh Fault and Western Salt Range, Pakistan. *Tectonics*, 9: 1061–1075.

Nelson, R. D., and Radin, Dean L. (1996) Evidence for direct interaction between consciousness and physical systems: Princeton Engineering Anomalies Research Laboratory, Princeton University, Princeton, N.J., USA. In *Consciousness Research Abstracts. Toward A Science of Consciousness 1996 "Tucson II"*. Journal of Consciousness Studies, p. 161.

Parnia, S., Waller D., Yeates R., and Fenwick, P. (2001) A qualitative and quantitative study of the incidence, features and aetiology of near death experiences in cardiac arrest survivors. *Resuscitation*, 48 (Feb): 149–156.

Pennock, E. S., Lillie, R. J., Zaman, A. S. H., and Yousaf, M. (1989) Structural interpretation of seismic reflection data from Eastern Salt Range and Potwar Plateau, Pakistan. *The American Association of Petroleum Geologists Bulletin*, 73: 841–857.

Rees, Martin (2000) *Just Six Numbers: The Deep Forces That Shape the Universe*. New York: Basic Books.

Rubik, Beverly (1996) Volitional effects of healers on a bacterial system. In Rubik, B., ed. *Life at the Edge of Science*. Philadelphia: Institute for Frontier Science, pp. 99–117.

Sabom, Michael B. (1982) *Recollections of Death: A Medical Investigation*. New York: Harper & Row.

Sagan, Carl (1995) *The Demon Haunted World*. New York: Random House.

Sahni, Birbal (1947) Microfossils and the Salt Range Thrust. *Proceedings of the National Academy of Sciences, India, 1945.* Section B, Vol. 16, pp. i–xlx.

Schroll, Mark (2005) SAC and transpersonal psychology. *Anthropology News,* February, pp. 48–49.

Steen-McIntyre, V., Fryxell, R., and Malde, H. E. (1981) Geologic evidence for age of deposits at Hueyatlaco archaeological site, Valsequillo, Mexico. *Quaternary Research* 16: 1–17.

Stevenson, Ian (1974) *Twenty Cases Suggestive of Reincarnation,* 2nd edition. Charlottesville: University Press of Virginia.

Wallace, Alfred Russel (1905) *My Life: A Record of Events and Opinions.* 2 vols. London: Chapman & Hall.

Whitney, Josiah D. (1880) The auriferous gravels of the Sierra Nevada of California. *Harvard University, Museum of Comparative Zoology Memoir,* 6(1).

Yeats, R. S., Khan, S. H., and Akhtar, M. (1984) Late Quaternary deformation of the Salt Range of Pakistan. *Geological Society of America Bulletin,* 95: 958–966.

18

Excavating the Eternal: Folk Archeological Traditions in India

I presented this paper at the European Association of South Asian Archaeologists bian-nual conference, held at the British Museum, in London, July 4–9, 2005.

Histories of Indian archeology typically begin with observations by 16th century European travelers. For example, in the introduction to his *History of Indian Archaeology from the Beginning to 1947,* Chakrabarti (2001, p. 1) says, "Without doubt these records constitute the first group of archaeological writings on India." Paddayya (1995, p. 112) states, "My main point of emphasis is that archaeology in India is a European innovation." He goes on, like Chakrabarti, to attribute the beginnings of archeology in India to "[European] travelers and sailors who visited sites like the Elephant [Elephanta] caves, rock-cut temples at Mahabalipuram and the temples of Orissa." The usual history then moves on to the Asiatic Society, the colonial Archaeological Survey, and finally the professional archeologists of independent India. But Indian historical texts, ranging from the *Mahabharata* to local *sthala-puranas,* reveal a rich parallel folk archeological tradition, involving the excavation of lost artifacts, deities, temples, and sacred sites, beginning in the earliest historical times and continuing on into the present. Although isolated references to the Indian folk archeological tradition are to be found in multidisciplinary studies of individual temples (for example, S. Goswami 1996) or in works by historians of religion about individual sacred sites in India (for example, Haberman 1994), they are absent from the more general archeological literature, especially works on history of archeology or works that include substantial sections on history of archeology. In giving notice of this absence, I am not seeking to devalue the useful histories of conventional Indian archeology. But an awareness of the extensive folk archeological tradition could add to our understanding of the history of Indian archeology, especially our appreciation for the variety of motives underlying the archeological quest, in its sacred and secular aspects.

A Case from the *Mahabharata:* Recovering the Gold of King Marutta

According to the *Ashvamedha Parva* of the *Mahabharata* (Dutta 1905), in ancient times King Marutta desired to perform a sacrifice, which required gold vessels. The king's priest, Samvarta, instructed him to go to the Munjaban mountain in the Himalayas and take gold from the mines there. Marutta obeyed, and his artisans turned the gold into sacrificial vessels. After the sacrifice, Marutta distributed some gold vessels to the *brahmanas* and buried some in the earth.[1] According to the *Valmiki Ramayana* (C. Goswami 1973, *Uttara Khanda* 17: 43–44), Marutta lived in the Krita (or Satya) Yuga. A long time later, after the Mahabharata war at the end of the Dvapara Yuga, the sage Vyasa ordered King Yudhisthira to perform an *ashvamedha-yajna,* or horse sacrifice. Much wealth was required for the sacrifice, so Vyasa told Yudhishthira about the gold vessels left by Marutta in the Himalayas. Yudhishthira journeyed to the Himalayas to recover them. Before excavations began, the *brahmanas* accompanying Yudhishthira determined that the time was astrologically auspicious and performed rituals to pacify Shiva along with other gods and spirits. Then the work started.

> The king, placing Vyasa ahead, proceeded towards the place where
> the treasure was buried. Once more worshipping the Lord of treasures
> [Shiva], and bowing unto him with reverence and saluting him properly
> ... the king ... caused that spot to be excavated. Then numerous vessels
> of diverse and delightful forms . . . were dug out by king Yudhishthira
> (Dutta 1905, p. 77).[2]

Before moving on to other examples of folk archeology in India, I want to introduce some theoretical considerations. First, is there any reason to think that there is some factual basis to this account, or is it simply an invention? We do have evidence of ancient people collecting artifacts. For example, Woolley (1950, pp. 152–154) informs us that in the sixth century BC the daughter of King Nebonidus put together a collection of Babylonian artifacts. So it is within the realm of possibility that the *Mahabharata* account of the recovery of the gold of King Marutta has a foundation in actual discoveries. At first glance, this kind of treasure hunting seems quite different from modern scientific archeology. But, at least in the popular mind, there is still some connection between treasure hunting and archeology. And in actual fact, the archeological community itself has established ongoing relationships with treasure hunters, be they avocational users of metal detectors or private companies searching for gold in shipwrecks. Furthermore, the many archeologists who do happen to find golden treasures certainly recognize that they have discovered something quite attractive to the popular mind, something that will draw thousands of visitors to museums and provide material for exciting television shows and books. Holtorf (forthcoming 2006: preface) reminds us: "In many ways the reality of professional archaeology is not entirely different from the stereotypical clichés of archaeology that are so prominent in popular culture. . . . Archaeologists really do find exciting treasures."

Aside from this, how are we to situate a case like the recovery of Marutta's treasure in terms of modern theorizing about the history of archeology? Trigger (1989, p. 28) notes some examples of tribal people collecting artifacts "from the unknown past." For example, North American Iroquois sites from the 15th and 16th centuries contain artifacts made thousands of years earlier. We infer that the Iroquois found these artifacts and saved them. Is this archeology? Trigger (1989, p. 29) says he would not use the word archeology, even "indigenous archeology," to characterize such activity. But I would use the word archeology, because I take it to encompass all human cognitive engagement with physical objects that the discoverers believed were manufactured by or otherwise associated with intelligent beings (whether perceived as human or supernatural) from the past.

However, the recovery of the treasure of Marutta rises above simply finding, by chance, an artifact from "the unknown past" and keeping it. Trigger (1989, p. 29), in recognition of such cases, offers that in some early civilizations artifacts were "valued … as the relics of specific rulers or periods of national greatness and as sources of information about the past." The story of Marutta's treasure meets these criteria. The treasure was regarded as the relic of a specific ruler, and its inclusion in a written historical account shows that it did count as information about the past.

According to Trigger (1989, p. 30) a case like this still would not be real archeology, because, as with similar cases he records, "There was absolutely no awareness that the material remains of the past could be used to test . . . speculations about human origins and the general outlines of human history." But modern archeology has come to include more than using physical remains to test theories about the past. Today, a professional archeologist is much more likely to be working in heritage or cultural resource management (CRM) than in doing excavations exclusively for testing theories. The recovery of Marutta's treasure does appear to have some similarities with modern archeological work in heritage management. In this case, knowledge of an archeologically situated (buried) heritage resource (the gold of King Marutta) was being maintained by Vyasa, a *brahmana* playing a curatorial role on behalf of the Vedic social order. So the excavation conducted by Yudhisthira was not simple treasure hunting. It was carried out to extract a heritage resource for a legimate social purpose. And it was carried out under strict regulations, which involved placating the local population of gods and ancestral spirits. Although modern scientific archeologists are not directly involved in placating the local gods and ancestral spirits, they often do have to take into account, sometimes under the compulsion of government regulations, the indigenous peoples who are in fact concerned with the placation of such beings.

This is not to say that the recovery of the treasure of Marutta and modern scientific archeology are isomorphic. What I am proposing here is that there is just enough of a resemblance here to warrant including both the recovery of Marutta's treasure and the activities of modern scientific archeologists within the boundaries of the term archeology, despite the vast differences in worldviews associated with the respective practices. And therefore it would be legitimate to mention a case like the recovery of Marutta's treasure in a history of archeology in India.

The Excavation of the Shri Rangam Deity

The history of Ranganatha, the principal deity in the famous Shri Rangam temple of Tamil Nadu, is told in various Tamil literatures, including the *Koil Olugu*, the temple chronicle (Hari Rao 1967). The following account is from Das (2001, pp. 110–112) and Auboyer (2000, pp. 11–12). The deity is a reclining form of Vishnu. Originally it was worshiped by the demigod Brahma in the heavenly planet Satyaloka. Ikshvaku, a king of the solar dynasty on earth, performed penances to get the deity. Ranganatha agreed to go to Ikshvaku, who worshiped him in his capital, Ayodhya. After Ikshvaku, the kings in the solar dynasty, including Rama, an incarnation of Krishna, continued to worship Ranganatha. King Dharma Varma, from the Chola dynasty in the south, saw Ranganatha in Ayodhya and desired to have him to worship. He eventually would get his wish. After Rama killed the demon Ravana in Lanka, Ravana's saintly brother Vibhishana returned to Ayodhya with Rama. There Rama gave Ranganatha to Vibhishana. When Vibhishana was carrying Ranganatha back to Lanka, he stopped at an island in the Kaveri River to perform worship of Ranganatha. Among those observing the worship was Dharma Varma. Vibhishana was unable to continue the journey, because Ranganatha wanted to remain there to accept Dharma Varma's service. Dharma Varma built a big temple for Ranganatha. This occurred in the Treta Yuga. Later, a massive flood covered the whole temple with sand, destroying the surrounding city, the capital of the Cholas. The capital was moved, and the whole region was covered by jungle. Much later, at the end of the Dvapara Yuga, a descendant of Dharma Varma was hunting in the jungle and rested under a tree. A parrot told him that this was the place of the fabled old temple. Unable to see anything to confirm this, the king nevertheless began to construct a new temple. Ranganatha then appeared to the king in a dream, and revealed his exact location. The king excavated the deity and remnants of the old temple. He then continued building a new temple to house Ranganatha. The king became known as Kilikanda Chola (the Chola who saw the parrot).

Perhaps this is all invention? Well, perhaps, but perhaps not. Jeannine Auboyer, former chief curator of the Guimet archaeological museum in Paris, in the official temple guide (Auboyer 2000: 12) concedes that "the disappearance of the temple beneath the flood waters, sand, and forest has possibly some historical truth" and that the constructors of the present temple may have "built over earlier foundations, which could now only be discovered by random excavations." Such excavations or nonintrusive surveys with ground penetrating radar (GPR) would be welcome. I am inclined to believe that there is some historical basis for the folk archeological accounts of the rediscovery of the temple, and that test bores or GPR surveys would reveal old foundations. But even if one wishes to say that the accounts are invention, we still have to ask why an archeological form of invention was chosen. I will return to that question in the conclusion to this paper.

The Excavation of the Jaganmohini Keshava Deity at Ryali in Andhra Pradesh

In the village of Ryali in the East Godavari district of Andhra Pradesh, about 35 kilometers north of Rajamundhry, stands the Jaganmohini Keshava Swami temple. I visited the temple in 2002. The *sthala-purana* (place history) of the temple (anon. 2001)[3] traces its origins back to ancient times, when Vishnu turned into Mohini Murti, a divine female form, to bewilder the demons who were battling the demigods, thus favoring the demigods. Later, Shiva desired to see the Mohini Murti, and Vishnu agreed to display it once more. Attracted by the divine form of Mohini Murti, Shiva pursued her. A flower fell from the hair of Mohini, and Shiva stopped to pick it up. The place where the flower fell is called Ryali, after the Telugu word for "fall." At this place Shiva saw Mohini in the process of turning once more into Vishnu. A five-foot tall black stone deity, with the front side showing Vishnu facing forward and the back side showing Mohini from the rear, self-manifested at that time, along with a *shiva-lingam*. The demigod Brahma began the worship of the deities. With the passage of time, they were lost. During the 11th century AD, the locale was covered by wild forest. A Chola king, Shri Raja Vikrama Deva, was hunting in the forest. He took rest under a large tree, and Vishnu appeared to him in a dream, informing him that his shrine was under the ground nearby. Vishnu told the king to drive his chariot around the area until the iron bolt holding one of the wheels fell off. There he was to dig. The king did as he was told, and at the place where the bolt fell, he conducted an excavation and found the deity. The king then built a small temple for the deity and started its worship, which continues today.

The reliance on dreams and visions in such cases of folk archaeology seems quite distinct from modern scientific archeological practice. But even within the modern scientific archeological enterprise, we do find hints of such things. British archeologist Frederick Blight Bond used psychical techniques in his work at Glastonbury Abbey (Bond and Lea 1918). J. N. Emerson, an anthropologist at the University of Toronto, used a psychic to assist him in archeological field work. Emerson (1974) called his technique "intuitive archaeology." In the 1970s, a whole crew of psychic archeologists emerged, including Stephen Schwartz (1978) and Jeffrey Goodman (1977). In mentioning these techniques, I am not here advocating them, rather just pointing out that when we look at the cross cultural history of archeologies, we see some overlapping in praxis. Even if we put aside the deliberate use of psychic methods, we still see that the accounts many archeologists give of their discoveries include the words "hunch" and "luck."

Excavation of Deities and Pastime Places of Krishna in the Vrindavan Region

The *Bhagavata Purana* identifies Mathura as the place where Krishna, accepted by Vaishnava Hindus as God, appeared at the end of the Dvapara Yuga. Soon after his appearance, he was taken to the nearby village of Vrindavan, where he remained through the years of his childhood and youth [**see map Plate XVIII**]. There he engaged in pastimes of divine friendship and love with his cowherd relatives and associates, male and female, as depicted in countless works of art and literature. After Krishna left this world, one of his descendants, Vajranabha, was appointed king of Vrindavan. According to the *Skanda Purana*,[4] he was not happy because the whole place was overgrown with forest, and the pastime places of Krishna were lost. The sage Shandilya showed him the locations of Krishna's pastimes, and to commemorate them Vajranabha established shrines and temples with deities. The four most important temple deities he established were Govindadeva in Vrindavan, Harideva at Govardhana Hill, Keshavadeva in Mathura, and Baladeva in Dauji (Haberman 1994, p. 53). Govinda, Hari, and Keshava are names of Krishna. Baladeva is Krishna's brother. Vajranabha had eight other deities carved and installed, making a total of twelve (Howley 1999, pp. 341–342). Over the course of time, the temples and deities were lost, first under the influence of Buddhism and later under the influence of Muslim invaders.

Madhavendra Puri Excavates the Gopala Deity

Madhavendra Puri was a Vaishnava saint who in the late 15th century journeyed to Vrindavan (Haberman 1994, p. 118). He excavated the Gopala deity, one of the Krishna deities carved and installed by King Vajranabha. The story is recorded in the fourth chapter of the *Madhya-lila* of the *Chaitanya-charitamrita* (Bhaktivedanta 1996).[5] The *Chaitanya-charitamrita*, a Bengali work completed by Krishnadasa Kaviraja in 1615 AD, gives a detailed account of the life and teachings of Chaitanya Mahaprabhu (1486–1532 AD). Chaitanya, a leader of the *bhakti* movement of love for Krishna, was, according to Gaudiya Vaishnava authorities, an incarnation of Krishna in the guise of a devotee of Krishna [see Plate XVI, Figure 1]. Chaitanya recited the story of Madhavendra Puri to his followers. Once Madhavendra Puri was fasting beneath a tree at Govinda Kunda, a pond near the village of Aniyor, at the foot of Govardhana Hill. A cowherd boy approached Madhavendra Puri and offered him some milk. That night the same cowherd boy appeared to him in a dream. Taking Madhavendra Puri by the hand, he led him into an area thick with trees and bushes. Pointing to one of the bushes in this tangle of vegetation, the boy said he had been lying under the ground there for a long time, enduring the extremes of heat and cold. The boy said, "Please bring the people of the village and get them to take Me out of this bush. Then have them situate Me nicely on top of the hill . . . My name is Gopala. I am the lifter of Govardhana Hill. I was installed by Vajra" (*Cc. Madhya.* 4: 37, 40). Gopala explained that a long time ago, his priest had buried him to protect him from an attack by *mlecchas* (Muslims). The first Muslim invasions of the Vrindavan area took place in the early 11th century, when Mahmud Ghazni destroyed many Hindu and Buddhist temples (Kulke and Rothermund 1998, p. 154). Awakening from the dream, Madhavendra understood that the cowherd boy who had brought him milk was Krishna himself. He went into the nearby village and gathered some people. Together, they entered the dense overgrowth, cutting their way through the bushes with choppers (*kuthari*) and uncovering the deity with spades (*kodali*) [see Plate XX, Figure 1]. Under Madhavendra Puri's direction they took the deity to the top of Govardhana Hill and eventually installed it in a new temple [see Plate XX, Figure 2]. In the 17th century, under new threats of Muslim attack by Aurangzeb's forces, the deity was taken to Nathdwar in Rajasthan, where it remains today (Kulke and Rothermund 1998, p. 140), known as Shri Nathji.[6]

The Discoveries of Chaitanya and His Followers

In the early 16th century, Chaitanya Mahaprabhu himself journeyed to Vrindavan. Chaitanya began to search for the places of Krishna's pastimes.[7] In the village of Aritgrama, he asked the people if they could show him Radha Kund and Shyama Kund, two ponds that were important in Krishna's pastimes. The villagers did not know where they were, and neither did Chaitanya's *brahmana* guide. Chaitanya himself then located Radha Kund and Shyama Kund in some rice fields (*Cc. Madhya.* 18.3–5). From that time on, the Kunds were developed as pilgrimage places. Today they are surrounded by temples and *ashramas*, and are visited by tens of thousands of pilgrims yearly.

Chaitanya ordered his principal followers, including Rupa Goswami and Sanatana Goswami, to carry on the work of rediscovering the lost places of Krishna's pastimes in Vrindavan. This is recorded in the *Chaitanya-charitamrita* (*Adi.* 10.90): *lupta tirtha uddharana vrndavane.*[8] Among the definitions for *uddharana* given in Apte's Sanskrit dictionary are "drawing out," "extraction," and "extrication." Krishnadasa Kaviraja Goswami says in *Chaitanya-charitmarita* (*Antya.* 2.128): "Shrila Rupa Goswami and Sanatana Goswami collected many revealed scriptures, and from the evidence in those scriptures they excavated all the lost sites of pilgrimage. Thus they established temples for the worship of Lord Krishna."[9] They began their work around 1515 (S. Goswami 1996, p. 270).

Among the deities discovered by the Gaudiya Vaishnava Goswamis in Vrindavan was the Govindadeva deity. The account is given in the early 18th century *Bhakti-ratna-kara* of Narahari Chakravarti,[10] but is more accessibly retold by Haberman (1994, pp. 32–33), S. Goswami (1996, p. 270), and others. I have taken my version from an English translation of *Bhakti-ratnakara* by Peter Viggiani (1997, pp. 83–84). After receiving the order from Chaitanya to locate the lost pastime places and deities in Vrindavan, Rupa Goswami found many of them but did not find Govindadeva, one of the deities originally installed by King Vajranabha. Once, he sat down beneath a tree on the banks of the Yamuna River, lamenting his failure. A cowherd boy approached and asked why he was unhappy. Rupa Goswami explained the reason. The cowherd boy said, "Don't be anxious at heart. In Vrindavan is a holy place called Gomatila. Every morning a glorious cow with a joyful heart lets her milk flow to the ground at that place. The Deity Shri Govindadeva is hidden at that place." The boy then disappeared, and Rupa Goswami fainted. When he returned to consciousness, he could understand that the cowherd boy had been Krishna. Rupa Goswami and some villagers gathered at Gomatila. Rupa told the villagers that Govindadeva was buried at this place. They began to dig, and found the deity [see Plate XXIV, Figure 2]. This occurred in about 1534 AD (Natha 1996, p. 161; Bahura 1996, p. 199). At first, Rupa Goswami worshiped Govindadeva in a simple hut. Later, in about 1535, he built a small temple, and still later the local Hindu king Man Singh, who was in the service of the Muslim ruler Akbar, built a large and beautiful stone temple for Govindadeva[11] [see Plate XXIV, Figure 1]. Construction began in 1576 and completed in 1590 (Nath 1996: 163). The Govindadeva temple built by Man Singh in Vrindavan was partially destroyed by Muslims at the time of Aurangzeb, and the Govindadeva deity was moved to Jaipur, where it is still worshiped today.

On the north and south sides of the east end of the Govindadeva temple are two attached shrines, one for the goddess Yogamaya and the other for the goddess Vrindadevi. The Yogamaya deity, one of the original Vrindavan deities installed by Vajranabha, was, like Govindadeva, uncovered on the Gomatila hill (Thakur 1996, p. 16). This small stone deity of eight-armed Yogamaya riding a lion is still being worshiped in her shrine at the Govindadeva temple. In this shrine, one can descend some stairs and see the place where the Govindadeva deity was extracted from the Gomatila hill. According to the *Bhakti-ratnakara* (Viggiani 1997, p. 87),[12] the Vrindadevi deity [see **Plate XXV, Figure 1**], also from the time of Vajranabha, was uncovered by Rupa Goswami on the banks of Brahma Kunda [see **Plate XXV, Figure 2**] after she revealed her location to him in a dream. The Vrindadevi deity is now at Kaman, to the west of Vrindavan, on the route that Govindadeva took to Jaipur (Nath 1996, p. 168). Vrindadevi is the presiding goddess of Vrindavan.

The work of the first Gaudiya Vaishnava Goswamis was carried on by Narayana Bhatta Goswami, born in Madurai in south India in 1531. Haberman (1994, p. 55) gives the sources of Narayana Bhatta's history as his own *Vrajotsava Chandrika* (Baba 1960) and a late 17th century biography by his descendant Janaki Prasad Bhatt titled *Narayana Bhatta Charitamrita* (Baba 1957). What follows is based on Haberman (1994, pp. 56–60). Once Krishna appeared to the young Narayana Bhatta and told him to go to Vrindavan to reveal his pastime places. Krishna gave him a small stone deity of himself as a child and said the deity would assist him in this work. Narayana Bhatta arrived in Vrindavan in 1545. There he met Sanatana Goswami and Krishnadasa Brahmachari, who accepted him as a disciple. Over the coming years, he rediscovered dozens of pastime places, including: (1) four important ponds around Govardhana Hill: Manasi Ganga, Kusuma Sarovara, Govindakunda, and Chandra Sarovara; (2) the birthplace of Krishna in Mathura; (3) the sites of Krishna's early childhood pastimes in Gokula, including the house of his parents Nanda and Yashoda; (4) the sites where Krishna killed the many-headed Kaliya serpent and the horse-demon Keshi; (5) Barshana, the town of Krishna's beloved Radha; (6) the place of Krishna's secret forest meetings with Radha; and (7) the locations of the twelve forests of Vrindavan. He laid out the Vrindavan pilgrimage route that is still followed today.

Narayana Bhatta excavated several deities, including one of Balarama (Haberman 1994, pp. 59–60) and one of Radha (Haberman 1994, p. 60). Once Narayana Bhatta followed a cow into the forest south of the village of Unchagaon. The cow came to a place where a beautiful golden boy was sitting. The boy drank the milk that flowed from the cow's udder. Then the boy disappeared. Narayana Bhatta realized he had seen Balarama, the brother of Krishna. At that moment, he fell asleep and in a dream Balarama told him to dig at the spot where he saw the boy [see **Plate XXVI, Figure 2**]. Narayana Bhatta gathered some villagers, and they excavated a deity of Balarama [see **Plate XXVI**, Figure 1], which was installed in a temple in Unchagaon [see **Plate XXVI, Figure 3**], where it can still be seen today, along with the small stone deity of Krishna that Narayana Bhatta carried with him to guide him in his research. Another time, Narayana Bhatta, absorbed in the mood of being a *gopi*, one of Krishna's cowherd girlfriends, was climbing a hill associated with the demigod Brahma, south of Unchagaon. He saw a beautiful young girl, who turned out to be Radha. She told him that there were deities of herself and Krishna hidden nearby, adding that if he came back that night she would tell him exactly where they were. Then she disappeared. Narayana Bhatta returned that night, and following the instructions given by Radha, found the place where the deities of Radha and Krishna were buried [see **Plate XXVII, Figure 2**]. He excavated them and later installed them in the Shriji temple [see **Plate XXVII**,

Figure 1] on the top of the hill at the place now called Barshana.

The followers of Vallabha made similar discoveries, such as this case described by Haberman (1994, pp. 210–211):

> The image of Balarama in the Dauji temple is believed to have been established by Vajranabh to reign over the southern region of Braj but was later hidden to protect it from Muslim invaders. The local account of its rediscovery is that Gokulnath, one of the seven grandsons of Vallabha, heard from some cowherds that a cow was releasing milk on a stone sticking out of the pond named Kshir Sagar. He went to investigate and discovered the image of Balarama. Gokulnath tried to move the image to Gokul, but it refused to budge, as this was the birthplace of Revati, his consort. Thus, a temple was built for Balaram on the shore of the Kshir Sagar; Revati now stands facing him inside the inner chamber of the temple.

Vaudeville (1976) argued, not very convincingly, that there were no lost shrines or temples in the Vrindavan area for the Chaitanyaite Goswamis and followers of Vallabha to rediscover when they came there in the early 16th century. Speaking against this are some things that Vaudeville herself includes in her study. First, the large Keshava temple, housing a deity of Krishna at Krishna's birthplace, existed in Mathura in ancient times, prior to its destruction by Mahmud of Ghazni early in the 11th century (Vaudeville 1976, p. 200). The legends of how Krishna was taken to Vrindavan right after his birth in Mathura were certainly known at this time. For example, the *Bhagavata Purana,* which contains extensive descriptions and glorifications of Krishna's pastimes in Vrindavan, dates back at least as far as the 10th century, according to many scholars (Rocher 1986, pp. 147–148), and Vaishnava tradition says it goes back much further. So it is hard to imagine that there could be a large and popular temple celebrating Krishna in Mathura, and that there would be no contemporary shrines or deities of Krishna in the nearby rural villages of Vrindavan itself, where he spent his entire childhood and youth. Vaudeville (1976, p. 195) notes that some images of Krishna date to the Gupta period (4–6th centuries AD): "The hero is then represented in the pose known as *govardhana dharana,* 'the holding of the Govardhan hill' or *Kaliya-dhamana,* 'the taming of the Kaliya [Naga]'; also as receiving milk or curd from the Gopis." Once more, it is hard to imagine that artists of the region, most likely under royal patronage, were producing images of Krishna directly connected to Vrindavan themes and locales without there being any shrines in the locales themselves. This is especially true, considering that today one can find an abundance of shrines to gods, goddesses, and saints in even the smallest villages in India. Finally, the accounts of excavations of deities recorded by the followers of Chaitanya and Vallabha themselves attest to the rediscovery of lost shrines.

The scope of sustained archeological activity carried out by the Vrindavan Goswamis and the followers of Vallabha is impressive. It goes far beyond the chance finding of isolated artifacts. It was a massive indigenous archaeological undertaking, carried out deliberately and systematically, like the excavation of a Troy or Chatal Hayuk, or a Mohenjodaro or Harappa. Actually, it goes beyond the scale of single towns, because the work of rediscovery of lost sites and deities was carried out over an entire region, including a major urban center and many towns and villages as well as rural locations. In his *Vraja Bhakti Vilasa,* Narayana Bhatta enumerated dozens of linked sites within the Braja-mandala (the circle of Vrindavan), a symbolic lotus with a circumference of 84 *kroshas* or 168 miles (Haberman 1994, p. 59). Some of the Goswamis employed a methodology much like modern Classical or medieval archeologists in Europe, in that historical texts and archeological exploration were both used in an integrated way to bring the past into the present. The purpose of this extensive folk archeological work was not simply to collect artifacts and expose sites, but rather to bring them back to life, so that people could experience what it was (and is) like to be with Krishna in Vrindavan. The work was one of restoring social memory, a collective remembering. However, the restoration of Vrindavan was not an exact recreation, like an open air museum exhibit; new temples were built, adapted for the living use of living people.

Bhaktivinode Thakura Rediscovers the Appearance and Pastime Places of Chaitanya Mahaprabhu at Mayapur

In the late 19th century, the Gaudiya Vaishnava guru Bhaktivinoda Thakura (1838–1915) relocated the site of Chaitanya Mahaprabhu's birth at Mayapur in the region around the town of Navadvipa, West Bengal, beginning its development into a major pilgrimage place [**see Plates XVI-XVII**]. In the centuries following the time of Chaitanya Mahaprabhu, the actual places of his appearance and pastimes had been lost because of the shifting course of the Ganges and movement of settlements. Bhaktivinoda Thakura, educated in English, served as a magistrate in the British administration of India and had extensive dealings with British literary and intellectual figures in Calcutta. One of his philosophical works was reviewed in the journal of the Royal Asiatic Society of London (Dasa 1989, p. 212). Eager to find the exact place of Chaitanya Mahaprabhu's appearance, he sought and finally received a transfer to Krishnanagara, a town near Navadvipa. On one of his first visits to the Navadvipa region, Bhaktivinoda (1916) wrote "seeing the land in all four directions the hair on my body stood on end." He then began his historical and geographical research (Bhaktivinoda 1916; Dasa 1989, pp. 164–165). Each weekend, he would come to Navadvipa, but did not find very much. He was disappointed that the local people did not know much about the pastime places of Chaitanya. One Saturday night in 1888, he was standing on the roof of a guesthouse in the town of Navadvipa. Looking across the Ganges River he saw "a large building flooded with light." Bhaktivinoda's son also saw it, but a hotel clerk standing with them said he saw nothing. "Because of that, I was utterly amazed," wrote Bhaktivinoda. The next morning, he looked out across the river at the place where he had seen the shining building in the night sky. He saw a tall palm tree. Asking some of the local people, he learned that the place was called Ballaldighi. The next Saturday he returned to Ballaldighi. That night, he again had a vision of a shining building there, and the next morning he went on foot to explore the area where it had appeared. Some of the elderly villagers told him this was the birthplace of Chaitanya Mahaprabhu. Bhaktivinoda Thakura confirmed this by carefully studying the geographical descriptions of Mayapur given in the early biographies of Chaitanya (the *Chaitanya-bhagavata* of Vrindavan Dasa Thakura and the *Chaitanya-charitamrita* of Krishnadasa Kaviraja) and other works such as the *Bhakti-ratnakara* of Narahari Chakravarti. He also studied centuries old records and maps by Dutch and British cartographers (Mukherjee 1984). Among these maps was one made on the order of Ganga-Govinda Singh, an official in the late 18th century administration of the British governor Warren Hastings (Dasa 1989, p. 166; Mukherjee 1984). This map had the name "Shri Mayapura" in the area of Balladighi. After he was confident in his identification of the location of Chaitanya's birthplace, Bhaktivinoda Thakura invited the great Gaudiya Vaishnava saint Jagannatha Dasa Babaji to come to the site. At this time, Jagannatha Dasa Babaji was over 120 years old. Unable to walk, he had to be carried. But when he arrived at the site, he became overwhelmed with ecstasy, and jumped up, proclaiming loudly that it was the place of Chaitanya Mahaprabhu's birth (Dasa 1989, pp. 166–167). Bhaktivinoda Thakura discovered many other places of Chaitanya Mahaprabhu's pastimes in Navadvipa, recording them in his book *Navadvipa-dhama Mahatmya,* published in 1890. As in the case of the Goswamis of Vrindavan, his archeological work extended over a vast region, encompassing dozens of sites arrayed throughout a lotus figure, with its center at Chaitanyas birthplace and a diameter of 58 miles.[13]

In 1892, Bhaktivinoda Thakura set up a society dedicated to the rehabilitation of the pastime places of Chaitanya Mahaprabhu in Navadvipa. The society took up the construction of a small temple at Chaitanya's birthplace, which opened in 1895. Later, a larger temple was constructed, under the guidance of Bhaktisiddhanta Sarasvati Thakura, the son of Bhaktivinoda Thakura. In 1934, during excavation for the foundation of this temple, a small (20 centimeter) black stone deity of Adhoksaja Vishnu was found in an excavation (Mukherjee 1984). This was identified as the household deity of Jagannatha Mishra, Chaitanya Mahaprabhu's father, and was taken as further confirmation that the site was indeed the birthplace of Chaitanya Mahaprabhu. Mukherjee (1984) gives reasons for its authenticity. Chaitanya's early biographers say that after he left Mayapur, his mother and wife left the family house, leaving all their possessions behind. Mukherjee noted:

> According to the archeological experts, who are now excavating at the Ballal Dhipi [Ballaldighi], the idol is not a fraudulent one. It is extremely rare and is more than 500 years old. . . . The slightly Mongolian eyes and square jaw indicate that the idol may have been made in the Sylhet area of old Assam from where the Mishra family came to Navadvipa-dhama. Iconologically, the upward tapering back frame (*chala-chitra*) also indicates the idol to be of 15th Century.

Mukherjee, formerly head of the geography department of City College in Calcutta and a specialist in soil analysis, added that he "found the soil in the Mayapura area to be very compact, deep and humus clay, indicating rather old land formation." Mukherjee

(1984) said that in his work on Chaitanya's birthplace he employed "all writings of contemporary biographers and Vaishnava scholars, all surveyed maps, air photographs, travellers accounts with sketches, land use surveys, statistical accounts and records, archeological and historical relics, iconology and field observations (including drainage conditions, ground slope, soil patterns etc.)." Although Mukherjee says in his 1984 study that he is not a Vaishnava, he does mention in his credits that he was then a director of research for the Shri Chaitanya Research Institute in Calcutta, which does seem to indicate some sympathy for Gaudiya Vaishnavism. The conclusion of his study on the location of Chaitanya Mahaprabhu's birthplace supported the identification made by Bhaktivinoda Thakura a century earlier. This rediscovery of the birthplace of Chaitanya Mahaprabhu is interesting, because it in some way represents a confluence of the two streams of the history of archeology in India—the indigenous, or folk, archeological tradition and the European, or modern scientific, archeological tradition.

Conclusion

The accounts of folk archeological discoveries mentioned in this paper could easily be multiplied hundreds, even thousands of times. One can find such examples in practically every Indian town and village. If taken at face value, the reports tell us that physical remains were uncovered. This is plausible. After all, we do know that people other than modern scientific archeologists find artifacts in the ground. And this is especially true in places that are relatively rich in artifacts, such as Israel, Italy, Greece, and India. It would seem natural that chance discoveries would lead to more deliberate searches, guided by local tradition and texts. Even granting this, there still remains another question: why have these accounts of folk archeological discoveries become so thoroughly woven into the fabric of the spiritual lives of the people of the subcontinent?

One of the primary concerns of Indian spirituality is *moksha*, or liberation from *samsara*, the cycle of birth and death. The liberated person is beyond the destructive force of time, and this can be experienced even in this world. In his introduction to Case's volume of papers on the Govindadeva temple in Vrindavan, Kapila Vatsyayan (1996, p. 3), academic director of the Indira Gandhi National Centre for the Arts, wrote: "For the devotee—the person who participates in rituals, rites, fairs and festivals [at the Govindadeva temple]—the monument is neither archeology nor history, not is it sculptural programming. It is a living presence, and abode of the divine, where physical space and finite time are transmuted into a plane of ceaseless eternal play, here and now as also in the beyond."

I suspect that the desire to transcend time and death is one of the motivations that also drives modern scientific archeological work. Shanks and Tilley (1992, p. 7) tell us, suggestively: "The past . . . recedes in an indefinite, perhaps endless series of galleries. Archaeologists wander the winding and seemingly endless corridors, forever unlocking doors . . . picking over the skeletal remnants of past societies, scrutinizing shelves of death." Why? Something more than curiosity seems to be involved. Unfortunately, there have been practically no systematic studies of the psychological motivations of archeologists. This points to a gap in the edifice of archeological theory. A great deal of archeological theory, such as typology and seriation, deals with the classification of the physical evidence itself. Another body of archeological theory examines how and to what extent the material evidence in our hands can tell us something about the lives of the people associated with this evidence in the past. Another body of archeological theory concerns itself with the uses to which archeology is put in the present, in terms of privileging or legitimizing cosmologies, ideologies, polities, classes, genders, and so on. But there is very little, if any, theoretical attention given to the psychological motivations of archeologists. There is a pervasive silence about it that invites investigation. If it is investigated, I have a hunch the trail will lead to a desire for *moksha*, freedom from time in its destructive aspect.

There are, however, two simultaneous and complementary aspects to *moksha*, to transcendence, in Indian spirituality—the diachronic and synchronic aspects. The synchronic aspect provides liberation into the eternal within the here and now. The diachronic aspect reaches back through time to the eternal. This reaching back through time to the eternal is prominent in Indian spiritual culture. When Hindus go to a temple to have some rituals performed on their behalf, the temple priests ask for the *gotra*, the family lineage. The *gotra* is traced back to one of the progenitor sages who existed at the beginning of creation—Gautama, Maitreya, or Atri, for example. One's biological parents are important, but they are also valued for bringing their children into the *gotra*, a seminal line that ultimately goes back to timeless divine beings. If one takes a guru, one inquires after the guru's *parampara* or *sampradaya* (lineage). The guru normally traces his lineage back through a disciplic succession to a divine being, to Vishnu, or Shiva, or Brahma, or Lakshmi, or Durga. The power of the mantra given by the guru is considered enhanced by its having been received through the line of succession. The mantra is eternal sound, coming down from the eternal through time. If the line is broken, it has to be restored, as Krishna tells Arjuna in *Bhagavad-gita* (4.2–3). The Hindu kings, the rulers of society, trace their lineages to divine beings, through the *Surya-vamsha* to the sun god or through the *Chandra-vamsha* to the moon god. And the lineages go back further, to Manu, and then back to Brahma, and eventually to a timeless supreme being, from whom the ruling power and authority ultimately descend. Through the present guru, the present parents, the present royal priest-kings (*rajarshis*), one gets *moksha*, liberation into the eternal. But the potency of those present personalities depends on their unbroken link with the eternal, back through time. Places and deities also have their histories that reach back to the eternal. So in times when the linkages are weakened or broken, there is a need to restore the diachronic feature of *moksha*, by finding lost deities, lost temples, lost sacred sites, which also have linkages with *gotra, sampradaya*, and *parampara*. A rediscovered deity may be perceived as more potent, therefore, than a newly manufactured one.

In the end, the claim that there was no archeology in India prior to the coming of the Europeans is much like the claim that there was no history, no historical sense, in the writings of ancient India. The latter concept has been deconstructed by scholars like Romila Thapar (1984, p. 269), who defined the historical sense "as a consciousness of past events, which events are relevant to a particular society, seen in a chronological framework, and expressed in a form which meets the needs of the society." With a definition like this, we can see that history will take different forms according to the needs and natures of the societies that record past events. It is not required that the historical sense of one culture conform exactly to that of another culture. Western culture has valued history as something distinct from other forms of knowledge, but ancient Indian culture embedded history within cosmology and theology and ethics, and the Indian historical writings such as the *Puranas* reflect this. Although historical consciousness manifests differently in different cultures, and at different times in cultures, still, there are some commonalities that allow us to recognize a sense of history when we see it. In the same way, we can recognize an archeological tradition in ancient India, an indigenous or folk archeological tradition that continues up to the present. The goal of this folk archeological tradition was not simply to give a vicarious experience of the dead past, but to launch people to the timeless reality of the deity's *nitya-lila*, eternal pastimes.

Notes:

1. *Ratnams cha maruttena nihitam prithivitale. Mahabharata, Ashvamedha Parva, Anugita Parva, lxiii, 2.* English translation Dutta (1905: 75), "the riches which Marutta had buried in the earth."

2. *Mahabharata, Ashwamedha Parva, Anugita Parva* 65: 9–16. The key Sanskrit phrase is *khanayamasa cha nidhim* (*Anugita Parva* 65: 11), literally "caused the excavation of the treasure."

3. This is a small booklet sold in the temple, mostly in Telugu, but with a brief English summary.

4. The account of Vajranabha rediscovering the pastime places of Krishna is from the *Bhagavata Khanda* of the *Vaishnava Khanda* of the *Skanda Purana*.

5. The *Chaitanya-charitamrita* is divided into three parts: *Adi-Lila*, *Madhya-lila*, and *Antya-lila*, with each of these three divided into chapters and verses. My citations, from the Bhaktivedanta (1996) edition, will take this form: (*Cc. Adi*.14.36).

6. The followers of Vallabha Acharya, a contemporary of Chaitanya and leader of the Pushti Marga *bhakti* school, have a different version of the discovery of the Shri Nathji deity, told in *Shri Nathaji Prakatya Varta*, attributed to Hariray, a great-great-grandson of Vallabha Acharya who lived in the 17th century. In this account the deity was discovered by a villager looking for his lost cow. Later it was taken out of the ground, and Madhavendra Puri became its priest (Haberman 1994, p. 119). Perhaps because of my own Gaudiya Vaishnava leanings, I prefer the *Chaitanya-charitamrita* version of the history.

7. The Vaishnava guru Vallabha, the founder of the Pushti Marg *bhakti* school, also journeyed to Vrindavan, and rediscovered lost deities and pastime places of Krishna. See Haberman (1994, pp. 66–68).

8. See also *Cc. Madhya.* 23.103, *tumiha . . . mathuraya lupta-tirthera kariha uddhara*: "you should also . . . excavate the lost places of pilgrimage in the district of Mathura." Vrindavan is in the district of Mathura. Some of Krishna's pastimes, including

his birth, took place in Mathura. Excavation of lost pilgrimage places is also mentioned in *Cc. Antya.* 4.80.

9. Another reference to using history books to guide the search for lost pilgrimage
places is found in *Cc. Madhya.* 25.215: *mathura-mahatmya-shastra sangraha ka-
riya/ lupta-tirtha prakata kaila vanete bhramiya.* "Having collected books about
Mathura's glories, Sanatana Goswami wandered through the forests finding lost
places of pilgrimage."

10. Second Wave, 404–477. As his authority, Narahari Chakravarti cites the *Sadhana-
dipika* of Radha-Krishna Goswami.

11. Elsewhere in India, Man Singh built other temples with deities discovered by folk
archeological methods. At Baikatpur, near Patna in Bihar, Raja Mana Simha built a
temple on the spot where his mother was cremated (Asher 1996, pp. 219–220). The
main deity is a *shiva-lingam*, said to have been in the possession of Jarasandha, a
demon-king who fought Krishna in ancient times. Its location was revealed to Man
Singh in a dream. At Baikatpur, Man Singh also had a dream in which the location
of an image of Durga called Shila Mati was revealed to him. He recovered the deity
from a river, and later installed it in a temple at Amber in Rajasthan (Asher 1996,
p. 220).

12. *Bhakti-ratnakara* Second Wave, texts 449–451.

13. Bhaktivinoda Thakura, *Navadvipa-dhama Mahatmya, Parikrama Khanda,* chapter
2, Measurement and form of the *dhama*, English translation at http://www.sala-
gram.net/BVT-NDM.html.

Works Cited:

Anon. (2001) *Sri Jaganmohini Kesava Swamy and Gopala Swamy Temple: Sthala Pura-
nam,* Ryali: np.

Apte, V. S. (1965) *The Practical Sanskrit-English Dictionary,* fourth revised and enlarged
edition, Delhi: Motilal Banarsidass.

Asher, C. B. (1996) Kacchavaha pride and prestige: the temple patronage of Raja Mana
Simha, in Case, M. H., *Govindadeva: A Dialogue in Stone,* New Delhi: Indira Gandhi National Centre for the Arts, pp. 215–238.

Auboyer, J (2000) *Sri Ranganathaswami: A Temple of Vishnu in Srirangam (Tamilnadu,
India),* Srirangam: Srirangam Temple.

Baba, K, ed. (1957) *Narayana Bhatta Charitamrita* of Janaki Prasad Bhatta, Kusumsarovar: Krishnadas Baba.

Baba, K., ed. (1960) *Vrajotsava Chandrika* of Narayan Bhatta, Kusumsarovar: Krishnadas Baba.

Bahura, G. N. (1996) Sri Govinda gatha: service rendered to Govinda by rulers of
Amera and Jayapura, in Case, M. H. ed., *Govindadeva: A Dialogue in Stone,* New
Delhi: Indira Gandhi National Centre for the Arts, pp. 195–213.

Bhaktivedanta Swami Prabhupada, A. C. (1996) *Shri Chaitanya-charitamrita* of Krishnadasa Kaviraja. English translation and commentary, with original Bengali text,
in nine volumes. Los Angeles: Bhaktivedanta Book Trust International.

Bhaktivinoda Thakura (1916) *Svalikhita Jivani.* Calcutta: Lalita Prasad Datta, English translation: www.bhaktivinoda.co.uk/Svalikhitajivani/.

Bond, F. B. and Lea, T. S. (1918). *The Gate of Remembrance: The Story of the Psychological Experiment Which Resulted in the Discovery of Edgar Chapel at Glastonbury.* Oxford: Basil Blackwell.

Chakrabarti, D. K. (2001) *A History of Indian Archaeology from the Beginning to 1947.* New Delhi: Munshirama Manoharlal Publishers.

Das, R. K. (2001) *Temples of Tamilnad.* Mumbai: Bharatiya Vidya Bhavan.

Dasa, R. V. (1989) *The Seventh Goswami.* Manning: New Jaipur Press.

Datta, P. (1920) *Vrindaban Katha.* Calcutta: Manasi Press.

Dutt, Manmatha Nath, ed. (1905) *Mahabharata. Vol. 14. Ashwamedha Parva.* Calcutta: Manmatha Nath Dutt.

Emerson, J. N. (1974) Intuitive archeology: a psychic approach, *Archaic Notes* 3(5): 1–2.

Goodman, J. (1977) *Psychic Archaeology: Time Machine to the Past.* New York: Berkeley Medallion.

Goswami, C. L. (1974) *Shrimad Valimiki-Ramayana, Part III.* Gorakhpur: Gita Press.

Goswami, S. (1996) Govinda darshana: lotus in stone, in Case, M. H. ed., *Govindadeva: A Dialogue in Stone.* New Delhi: Indira Gandhi National Centre for the Arts, pp. 269–277.

Haberman, D. L. (1994) *Journey Through the Twelve Forests: An Encounter with Krishna.* Oxford: Oxford University Press.

Hari Rao, V. N. (1967) *Koil Olugu. The Chronicle of the Srirangam Temple, with Historical Notes.* Madras: Rochouse.

Holtorf, C. (2006) *Archaeology As a Brand.* Oxford: Archaeopress.

Howley, J. (1999) *Spiritual Guide: India.* Vrindavana: Spiritual Guides.

Kulke, H. and Rothermund, D. (1998) *A History of India.* London: Routledge.

Mitchell, G. (1996) 'The missing sanctuary', in Case, M. H., *Govindadeva: A Dialogue in Stone.* New Delhi: Indira Gandhi National Centre for the Arts, pp. 115–122.

Mukherjee, K. N. (1984), A historico-geographical study for Shri Chaitanya's birthsite. *The Indian Journal of Landscape Systems and Ecological Studies,* 7(2): 33–56. See 1990 revision at http://bvml.org/contemporary/Yogapitha/PKNM_asfscb.html.

Nath, R. (1996) Shri Govindadeva's itinerary from Vrindavana to Jayapura, c. 1534–1727, in Case, M. H., ed., *Govindadeva: A Dialogue in Stone.* New Delhi: Indira Gandhi National Centre for the Arts, pp. 161–183.

Paddayya, K. (1995) Theoretical perspectives in Indian archaeology, in Ucko, P, ed., *Theory in Archaeology: A World Perspective.* London: Routledge, pp. 109–137.

Rocher, L. (1986) *The Puranas.* Wiesbaden: Otto Harrassowitz.

Schwartz, S. A. (1978) *The Secret Vaults of Time.* New York: Grosset & Dunlap.

Shanks, M. and Tilley, C. (1992) *Re-Constructing Archaeology.* second edition, London: Routledge.

Thakur, N. (1996) The building of Govindadeva, in Case, M. H., ed., *Govindadeva: A Dialogue in Stone.* New Delhi: Indira Gandhi National Centre for the Arts, pp. 11–68.

Thapar, R. (1984) *Ancient Indian Social History: Some Interpretations.* Hyderabad:

Longman Orient Limited.

Trigger, B. G. (1989) *A History of Archaeological Thought*. Cambridge: Cambridge University Press.

Vatsyayan, K. (1996) Introduction, in Case, M. H., ed., *Govindadeva: A Dialogue in Stone*. New Delhi: Indira Gandhi National Centre for the Arts, pp. 3–8.

Vaudeville, C. (1976) Braj, lost and found, *Indo-Iranian Journal*, 18: 195–213.

Viggiani, P. (1997) *Shri Bhakti-ratnakara*. English translation. Los Angeles: Peter Viggiani.

Woolley, C. L. (1950) *Ur of the Chaldees*. Harmondsworth: Penguin.

19

Beijing Man and the Rockefeller Foundation:
An Episode in the Globalization of Science
in the Early 20ᵗʰ Century

I presented this paper at the 22ⁿᵈ International Congress of History of Science, held in Beijing, China, July 24–30, 2005.

Introduction

Not far from where we speak today, the Beijing Man (*Sinanthropus*) fossils were discovered at Zhoukoudian. Beijing Man was one of the twentieth century's significant fossil discoveries related to the question of human origins. In this paper, I will examine the role of the Rockefeller Foundation in providing financial and institutional support for the key researchers involved in the Beijing Man discoveries, especially anatomist Davidson Black, of the Peking (hereafter Beijing) Union Medical College. The interrelations of Davidson Black, the Beijing Union Medical College, and the Rockefeller Foundation have been explored in the biography of Black by Dora Hood (1964). Although Hood gives detailed attention to the dealings of Black with officials of the College and Foundation, she does not say much about how Black's work related to the Rockefeller Foundation's larger goals. Much work has been done on the Rockefeller Foundation's establishment of the Beijing Union Medical College, such as the comprehensive study by Mary Brown Bullock (1980), and the larger goals of the Rockefeller Foundation in promoting science on a global basis have been examined by researchers such as Gerald Jonas (1989), but these works say very little about Black. So what I wish to do in this paper is put Black's work into the larger context of the goals of the Rockefeller Foundation.

John D. Rockefeller: Baptist, Industrialist, Philanthropist

John D. Rockefeller was throughout his life a strict Baptist. As a result of his Baptist religious training, he believed "a man should make all he can and give all he can" (Fosdick 1952, p. 6). Even as a young clerk, Rockefeller made regular charitable contributions (Chernow 1999, p. 50). When he earned a huge fortune through the Standard Oil Company and other ventures, he continued his lifelong pattern of charity. Not surprisingly, his charity was initially directed toward Baptist churches and missions.

According to Fosdick (1952, p. 6), Rockefeller was at first "giving to a multiplicity of small causes mostly related to his church interests—schools, hospitals, and missions." As a result, he was continually being approached by Baptist ministers and other Baptist petitioners. To relieve himself from having to attend personally to all of these requests, Rockefeller appointed Frederick T. Gates, a former Baptist minister and officer of the American Baptist Education Society, to oversee his charitable contributions. Gates soon organized a system whereby Rockefeller would give a lump sum to a mission board that would distribute the funds in an appropriate fashion.

Rockefeller and Gates later set up a number of charitable trusts, including the Rockefeller Institute for Medical Research, the General Education Board, the International Education Board, the Rockefeller Foundation, and the Laura Spelman Rockefeller Trust. The Rockefeller charities were generous. For example, Rockefeller gave 35 million dollars for building the University of Chicago, which, according to Fosdick (1952, p. 7), started out as "as an idea for a Baptist institution of higher learning, under Baptist auspices and control." In the end, it turned out to be something different, teaching the scientific account of human evolution rather than the Biblical creation story.

At this point, I should say something about my own perspective on evolution. My work in history of science is inspired by my studies in the ancient Sanskrit writings of India, which offer a picture of human origins and antiquity quite different from that of modern evolutionists. The picture is one of coexistence of humans and apemen, rather than the evolution of humans from apemen (Cremo 1999). My views therefore have something in common with the Biblical creationism advocated by many members of the Baptist Church. I am therefore interested in how the Rockefeller Foundation, with its roots in John D. Rockefeller's gifts to Baptist causes, came to be involved in funding scientific research that favored the theory of evolution and challenged a literal reading of the Bible.

Rockefeller's own views on evolution are not easy to discern. I have not been able to find anything in his own words on the question of biological evolution. Furthermore, he stayed in the background of his charitable foundations, which were created late in his life. He left their direction to others, especially Gates, whose views are more directly evident. Gates started out as a typical Baptist but underwent a conversion to a more liberal Christianity. Under the influence of Biblical scholarship critical of a literal reading of the Bible he gave up his exclusive commitment to the Baptist Church and its teachings. While retaining a nonsectarian belief in God, he said he accepted "the spirit and results of modern scientific research," which he believed were reconstructing theology (Jonas 1989, p. 25).

Gates served as a mentor to John D. Rockefeller Jr., who took over the oversight of the Rockefeller charitable enterprises on behalf of his father. The younger Rockefeller followed the lead of Gates in moving away from sectarian Baptist beliefs and organizations. On July 28, 1921, Rockefeller, Jr. wrote to his father against "fundamentalist" Baptists: "These 'Fundamentalists' as you know, believe in the literal interpretation of the Bible and in other kindred doctrines which men of broader minds and wider vision cannot today accept" (Ernst 1994, p. 123). Rockefeller, Jr. would later end his contributions to the main Baptist organization in the northern United States (Ernst 1994, pp. 210–211). Instead, he supported the establishment of the interdenominational Riverside Church. The church, formally opened in 1931, was decorated with statues of scientists, including Darwin (Chernow 1999, p. 641).

Beijing Union Medical College

In 1921, the China Medical Board, a division of the Rockefeller Foundation, opened the Beijing Union Medical College, at huge expense. John D. Rockefeller, Jr. and his entourage attended the opening. It was the largest project of the Foundation outside the United States. Significantly, China was a major market for Standard Oil, the main source of the Rockefeller fortune. Standard Oil entered China during the 1870s, through agreements with Western trading companies (Cochran 2000). From 1883 to 1903, it marketed kerosense through agreements with local Chinese agents. But in 1903 it began to market kerosene through its own direct employees, both Western and Chinese, and introduced its American style management and distribution systems, under the control of its New York headquarters. It also invested in an extensive infrastructure for bulk shipments of kerosene for the lamps of China. Standard Oil used the Chinese name Meifu (beautiful and trustworthy) for its corporate name and products. By 1921, Standard Oil controlled 77 percent of the kerosene sales in China, and China was its largest Asian market. By 1928, Standard Oil controlled 88 percent of the kerosene market in China. After John D. Rockefeller, Jr. attended the opening of the Beijing Union Medical College he journeyed to Shanghai to tour the Standard Oil headquarters there, with its extensive port, storage, and distribution facilities (Bullock 1980, p. 23). So the Rockefellers had a huge economic as well as charitable presence in China.

For years, the Rockefellers had given support to Baptist missionary activities in China. Gates, in furtherance of his desire to spread the gospel of science, originally wanted to create not a medical college but a university in China. But he noted that the "missionary bodies at home and abroad were distinctly and openly, even threateningly hostile to it as tending to infidelity" (Fosdick 1952, p. 81). Furthermore, the Chinese government wanted control, an idea that the Foundation could not support. Charles Eliot, a Rockefeller Foundation official and president of Harvard University, proposed a solution: a medical college, which would serve as an opening to the rest of Western science. Fosdick (1952, p. 81) wrote: "To President Eliot there was no better subject than medicine to introduce to China the inductive method of reasoning which lies at the basis of all modern science. He thought it would be the most significant contribution that the West could make to the East." Here science shows itself a quiet but militant ideology, skillfully promoted by the combined effort of scientists, educators, and wealthy industrialists, with a view towards establishing worldwide intellectual dominance. The medical hospital strategy outlined by Eliot worked. The Chinese government approved establishment of the Beijing Union Medical College under Foundation auspices.

The Rockefeller Foundation Sends Black to China

The College was staffed by professors from the West as well as China. One of them was Davidson Black. Davidson Black graduated from the University of Toronto medical school in 1906. To satisfy his strong interest in anatomy, he took a post at Western Reserve University in Ohio, where he worked with T. Wingate Todd, a noted English anatomist. A forceful advocate of human evolutionary theory, Todd organized at Western Reserve University an extensive skeletal museum, including casts of bones from all known forms of fossil man. Under Todd, Davidson Black therefore had an opportunity to become acquainted with the latest developments in human origins research. In 1914, Black went to Manchester, England, to work under famed anatomist Grafton Elliot Smith, who was then occupied with Piltdown man. Black also developed a friendly relationship with Sir Arthur Keith, accompanying him to the Piltdown site.

After returning to Western Reserve, Black read *Climate and Evolution* by William Diller Matthew. In 1911, Matthew had said in an address to the National Academy of Sciences of the United States: "All authorities are today agreed in placing the center of dispersal of the human race in Asia. Its more exact location may be differently interpreted, but the consensus of modern opinion would place it probably in or about the great plateau of central Asia" (Osborn 1928, p. 192). From the time he first became acquainted with Matthew's ideas in 1915, Black intended to go to northern China to search for the center of human origins. But the First World War delayed his plans.

In 1917, during the First World War, Black joined the Canadian military medical corps. Meanwhile, a friend of Black, Dr. E. V. Cowdry, was named head of the anatomy department at the Rockefeller Foundation's Beijing Union Medical College. Cowdry asked Dr. Simon Flexner, director of the Rockefeller Foundation, to appoint Black as his assistant. After meeting Flexner in New York, Black was accepted and wrote to a colleague: "In addition to my work at the school I shall have the privilege of accompanying such scientific expeditions as may be organized to explore and collect material in central China, Tibet, etc." (Hood 1964, pp. 41–42).

After Rockefeller Foundation officials petitioned the Surgeon General of Canada, Black won his release from the Canadian military and proceeded to Beijing, arriving in 1919. At the Beijing Union Medical College, Black did everything possible to minimize his medical duties so he could concentrate on his real interest—paleoanthropology. In November 1921, he went on a brief expedition to a site in northern China, and other expeditions followed. Black's superiors were not entirely pleased.

In 1921, Dr. R. M. Pearce, the Rockefeller Foundation's advisor on medical education, visited Beijing on an inspection tour. Afterward, Pearce wrote to Black: "If you think of anatomy for nine months out of the year, it is no one's business what you do with the other three months in the summer in connection with anthropology, but for the next two years at least give your entire attention to anatomy" (Hood 1964, p. 55). But gradually the Rockefeller Foundation would be won over to Black's point of view.

Late in 1922, Black submitted a plan for a Thailand expedition to Dr. Henry S. Houghton, director of the medical school. Black expertly related his passion for paleoanthropology to the mission of the medical school. Houghton wrote to Roger Greene, the resident director of the China Medical Board, the branch of the Rockefeller Foundation that funded the medical school: "While I cannot be certain that the project which Black has in mind is severely practical in its nature, I must confess that I have been deeply impressed by . . . the valuable relationship he has been able to establish between our department of anatomy and the various institutions and expeditions which are doing important work in China in the fields which touch closely upon anthropology research. With these points in mind I recommend the granting of his request" (Hood 1964, p. 56). Here can be seen the importance of intellectual prestige—ordinary medicine seems quite pedestrian in comparison with the quest for the secret of human origins. Houghton was clearly influenced. The expedition took place during Black's summer vacation in 1923, but unfortunately produced no results. In 1924, Black took a year's paid leave to travel around the world, visiting early man sites, museums, and scholars in the field of human evolution. Black returned to Beijing determined to give more time to his pet research projects.

Black and the Birth of *Sinanthropus*

In 1926, Black attended a meeting at which J. Gunnar Andersson presented to the Crown Prince of Sweden a report on two hominin molars found by Austrian paleontologist Otto Zdansky in 1923 at a limestone quarry near Zhoukoudian, a village about 25 miles southwest of Beijing. Excited on learning of the teeth, Black accepted a proposal by Andersson for further excavations at Zhoukoudian, to be carried out jointly by the Geological Survey of China and Black's department at the Beijing Union Medical School. Dr. Amadeus Grabau of the Geological Survey of China called the hominin for which they would search "Beijing man."

On October 27, 1926, Black wrote to Sir Arthur Keith about Zdansky's teeth: "There is great news to tell you—actual fossil remains of a man-like being have at last been found in Eastern Asia, in fact quite close to Beijing. This discovery fits in exactly with the hypothesis as to the Central Asiatic origin of the Hominidae which I reviewed in my paper 'Asia and the Dispersal of Primates'" (Hood 1964, p. 84). Black had found what he was looking for.

Hood (1964, p. 85) stated in her biography: "Black's next task was to approach the Rockefeller Foundation through Roger Greene to ask for funds with which to make a large-scale excavation at the caves of Chou-K'ou-tien. To his delight and relief a generous sum was forthcoming. This response showed a marked change in the attitude of the authorities in New York towards Black's efforts to promote research into China's prehistory from his experience in 1921." Roger Greene was the China representative of the Rockefeller Foundation's China Medical Board, the agency that funded the Beijing Union Medical College.

By spring 1927, work was underway at Zhoukoudian. During several months of painstaking excavation, there were no discoveries of any hominid remains. Finally, with the cold autumn rains beginning to fall, marking the end of the first season's digging, a single hominid tooth was uncovered. On the basis of this tooth, and the two previously reported by Zdansky (now in Black's possession), Black decided to announce the discovery of a new kind of fossil hominid. He wrote in *Nature:* "The newly discovered specimen displays in the details of its morphology a number of interesting and unique characters, sufficient, it is believed, to justify the proposal of a new hominid genus *Sinanthropus,* to be represented by this material" (Black 1927, p. 954).

Black was eager to show the world his discovery. Dr. Heinrich Neckles, a friend of Black, later recalled: "One night he came to my office very excited, to show the precious tooth of *homo pekinensis.* He wanted me to advise him about the safest method to take the invaluable find to England (where he was going shortly) safe against loss or theft. I suggested a brass capsule with a screw closure and a ring at the top, with a strong ribbon through it, so he could wear it around his neck. We had a good Chinese mechanic in the Physiology Department who made a very nice capsule for him and he was as happy as a little boy" (Hood 1964, p. 90).

In the course of his travels with his newly found tooth, Black discovered that not everyone shared his enthusiasm for *Sinanthropus.* At the annual meeting of the American Association of Anatomists in 1928, some of the members heavily criticized Black for proposing a new genus on so little evidence. Regarding such criticism of Black's activities, Grafton Elliot Smith wrote: "It had no other effect upon him, beyond awaking his sympathies for anthropologists who are unfairly criticized and to make him redouble his efforts to establish the proof of his claim" (Hood 1964, p. 93).

Black kept making the rounds, showing the tooth to Aleš Hrdlička in the United States and then journeying to England, where he met Sir Arthur Keith and Sir Arthur Smith Woodward. At the British Museum, Black had casts made of the Beijing Man molars, for distribution to other workers. This is the kind of propaganda work necessary to bring a discovery to the attention of the scientific community. This serves to illustrate that even for a scientist political skills are not unimportant.

On returning to China, Black kept in close touch with the excavations at Zhoukoudian. Dynamite was used to blast out sections of rock. Crews of workers then searched through the debris, sending the larger chunks back to Beijing, where any fossils were carefully extracted. The sole aim of the whole project was, of course, to find more Beijing Man remains. For months nothing turned up, but in the end there was success. Black wrote to Keith on December 5, 1928: "It would seem that there is a certain magic about the last few days of the season's work for again two days before it ended Böhlin found the right half of the lower jaw of *Sinanthropus* with the three permanent molars *in situ*" (Hood 1964, p. 97). Now a financial problem loomed. The Rockefeller Foundation grant that supported the digging would run out in April of 1929. In January 1929, Black wrote the Rockefeller Foundation directors, asking them to support the Zhoukoudian excavations by creating and funding a Cenozoic Research Laboratory.

Restructuring of the Rockefeller Foundations

Around this time, the Rockefeller foundations were in a period of change. At the urging of John D. Rockefeller, Jr., a consolidation plan was put into effect in late 1928. All programs in various Rockefeller charities "relating to the advance of human knowledge" were shifted to the Rockefeller Foundation, which was reorganized into five divisions: international health, medical sciences, natural sciences, social sciences, and the humanities (Fosdick 1952, pp. 137–138). Each division was run by a highly competent academic and technical staff who advised the trustees of the Foundation where to give their money. Raymond D. Fosdick, president of the Foundation at the time, said (1952, p. 140) that the year of 1928 marked "the end of an era in philanthropy," and the beginning of a new one.

Dr. Max Mason, a mathematical physicist and former president of the University of Chicago, took over as president of the reorganized Rockefeller Foundation. According to Fosdick (1952, p. 142), Mason "emphasized the structural unity involved in the new orientation of program. It was not to be five programs, each represented by a division of the Foundation; it was to be essentially one program, directed to the general problem of human behavior, with the aim of control through understanding." One naturally wonders—who would be controlling human behavior, and for what purpose?

Black's Propaganda Campaign

Black's research program, with its emphasis on human evolution, fit in well with the goals of the reorganized Rockerfeller Foundation. In April 1929, Black received the funds he desired. With the financial backing of the Rockefeller Foundation for the Cenozoic Research Laboratory secure, Black resumed his travels for the purpose of promoting Beijing Man. In May of 1929, Black arrived in Java, for the Fourth Pacific Science Congress. There he was able to give a report on *Sinanthropus* before an audience that included Grafton Eliot Smith. Black stated: "Elliot Smith's cordial backing after my presentation of the material at the conference made all the difference in the world to its reception there" (Hood 1964, pp. 100–101). Nevertheless, Beijing Man still had not achieved the worldwide celebrity he would later enjoy. While in Java, Smith and Black visited the Trinil site, where Dubois had originally discovered *Pithecanthropus,* the southern relative of *Sinanthropus.*

Black then returned to China, where work was proceeding slowly at Zhoukoudian, with no new major *Sinanthropus* finds reported. Enthusiasm seemed to be waning among the workers. But then on the first of December, at the very end of the season, W. C. Pei (Pei Wenzhong) made an historic find. Pei later wrote: "At about four o'clock next afternoon I encountered the almost complete skull of *Sinanthropus.* The specimen was imbedded partly in loose sands and partly in a hard matrix so that it was possible to extricate it with relative ease" (Hood 1964, p. 104).

In order to protect the skull, Pei immediately wrapped it in paper and cloth soaked with flour paste. He then rode 25 miles on a bicycle to the Cenozoic Research Laboratory, where he presented the skull to Black, who gave him full credit for the discovery. By early 1930, Black had published two preliminary papers on the skull and set about publicizing the find around the world. His secretary, Miss Hempel, recalled: "For weeks and months we did nothing but write letters" (Hood 1964, p. 109).

Black wrote to Dr. Pearce at the Rockefeller Foundation: "Yes, *Sinanthropus* is growing like a bally weed. I never realized how great an advertising medium primitive man (or woman) was till this skull turned up. Now everybody is crowding around to gaze that can get the least excuse to do so and it gets embarrassing at times. Being front page stuff is a new sensation and encourages a guarded manner of speech" (Hood 1964, pp. 110–111). Black worked busily, carefully freeing the skull from its stone matrix and later making a cast of it. Copies of the cast were sent to museums all over the world. The site itself was purchased by the Geological Survey of China.

In September of 1930, Sir Grafton Elliot Smith arrived in Beijing to inspect the site of the discovery and examine the fossils. Smith himself had been a recipient of Rockefeller Foundation funding for his anthropology institute at University College London (Jonas 1989, p. 104). During Smith's stay, Black primed him for an international propaganda blitz on behalf of Beijing Man. Smith then departed, and apparently did his job well. In December, Black wrote an extremely candid letter to Dr. Henry Houghton, director of the Beijing medical school, who was vacationing in America: "You, too, are dripping with the gore of the same hegoat and I love you, for your soul is white if your hood be scarlet and your aid, comfort and participation in the plot from its inception made success possible and doubly enjoyable. . . . You must admit that we have not been any blushing roses when it came to turning our wolf loose (if you don't mind mixed metaphors) —if I blushed every time I thought of the cold-blooded advertising campaign I thought of and G. E. S. has carried through, I'd be permanently purple" (Hood 1964, p. 115).

Cold-blooded advertising campaign? That is not the way most people think scientific discoveries normally make their way into academic acceptance and public notice. Black is to be commended for his forthright statements. In any case, having turned the wolf of *Sinanthropus* loose on the world, he received many honors, including appointments as honorary fellow of the Royal Anthropological Institute and honorary member of America's National Academy of Sciences (Hood 1964, p. 116). Black was later elected a fellow of the Royal Society, Britain's foremost assembly of scientists. His newly won fame also insured continued access to Rockefeller Foundation funds. Black wrote to Sir Arthur Keith: "We had a cable from Elliot Smith yesterday so he is evidently safe home after his strenuous trip. He characteristically has not spared himself in serving the interests of the Survey and the Cenozoic Laboratory and after his popularizing *Sinanthropus* for us in America I should have a relatively easy task before me a year from now when I will have to ask for more money from the powers that be" (Hood 1964, p. 116).

Beijing Man had come at just the right moment for advocates of human evolution. A few years previously, in one of the most famous trials in the world's history, a Tennessee court had found John T. Scopes guilty of teaching evolution in violation of state law, much to the delight of Biblical creationists. Thus any new evidence bearing on the question of human evolution was highly welcome—perhaps to even John D. Rockefeller, Jr., who had expressed his abhorrence of Biblical fundamentalism.

The Experimental Biology Program of the Rockefeller Foundation

Changes in the Rockefeller Foundation science programs continued in a direction favorable to Black and his work. In 1933, the Rockefeller Foundation board of trustees approved a program of research that focused more than ever before on the biological sciences. Warren Weaver, who headed the Rockefeller Foundation's natural sciences division, which funded the Cenozoic Research Laboratory in Beijing, said in a report to the trustees: "The welfare of mankind depends in a vital way on man's understanding of himself and his physical environment. Science has made magnificent progress in the analysis and control of inanimate forces, but it has not made equal advances in the more delicate, more difficult, and more important problem of the analysis and control of animate forces" (Fosdick 1952, p. 157). The Rockefeller Foundation's annual report for the year 1933 (p. 199) asked: "Can we develop so sound and extensive a genetics that we can hope to breed in the future superior men? . . . In short, can we rationalize human behavior and create a new science of man?"

Mason, Weaver, and other foundation officers outlined a coordinated program, approved by the Foundation trustees, to attain this goal. Fosdick (1952, p. 158) stated: "The trustees, in the spring of 1933, voted to make experimental biology the field of primary interest. . . . It was conceived, moreover, as being closely linked with other aspects of the Foundation's program, notably the program in psychiatry of the Medical Sciences division and the social-science program in human relations. Biology is important because it has the potentiality of contributing to the problem of understanding ourselves, and the three programs—in widely separated fields—could be thought of as a unified endeavor to stimulate research in the sciences underlying the behavior of man."

Weaver said of the Foundation's natural sciences program: "It seemed clear in 1932, when the Rockefeller Foundation launched its quarter-century program in that area, that the biological and medical sciences were ready for a friendly invasion by the physical sciences." Weaver believed that the physical sciences gave scientists the tools "for discovering, on the most disciplined and precise level of molecular actions, how man's central nervous system really operates, how he thinks, learns, remembers, and forgets." And such knowledge would allow us to "gain information about our behavior of the sort that can lead to wise and beneficial control" (W. Weaver 1967, p. 203).

Some popular commentators make light of research into the reproductive habits of earthworms and other apparently obscure research projects. But these have their purpose. According to Weaver, "Before we can be wise about so complex a subject as the behavior of a man, we obviously have to gain a tremendous amount of information and insight about living organisms in general, necessarily starting with the simpler forms of life. Experimental biology is the means for such exploration. It furnishes the basis necessary for progress in solving the sequence of problems which begins with the strictly biological and moves through the mental to the social" (Fosdick 1952, p. 158). Here the intent to use science for perfecting methods of social control is stated explicitly.

And what about something as apparently innocent as stargazing through the 200-inch telescope at Mt. Palomar? Fosdick (1952, p. 179) stated: "Superficially the 200-inch and the lesser projects in astronomy which have received Foundation aid would seem to be far removed from the main interest of the Natural Sciences program. What possible relationship can there be between the stars and experimental biology?" Fosdick (1952, p. 180) answered that astronomy gives the first glimmers of regularity in nature, the understanding of which will lead to control of humanity and the universe.

Conclusion

After Black launched Grafton Eliott Smith on his successful world propaganda tour, he continued his work on *Sinanthropus* at the Cenozoic Research Laboratory, funded by the Rockefeller Foundation as part of its experimental biology program. In 1934, Black died of a heart attack late one night while working on his reconstruction of the *Sinanthropus* skull. After a short time, Franz Weidenreich took over the leadership of the Cenozoic Research Laboratory, and with Rockefeller Foundation support continued Black's work until 1938 when excavations stopped during the Japanese occupation of the region. In 1941, the *Sinanthropus* fossils were packed up for shipment out of China, but were lost during transport to the port city of Chingwantao. They have never been found.

The Rockefeller Foundation support for the work that led to the discovery of Beijing man was part of the globalizing of Western science in the early twentieth century. The Rockefeller Foundation pursued a worldwide program of encouraging scientific research, and its support of the Beijing Union Medical College was part of that program. When the Beijing Man discoveries were made in China, Rockefeller Foundation funding insured that they were widely publicized for global impact. The Beijing Man discoveries were helpful for another goal of Rockefeller Foundation officers and board members, such as John D. Rockefeller, Jr., and Frederick T. Gates, namely, reducing the influence of fundamentalist religion.

The Rockefeller Foundation in the early twentieth century was an evangelical organization. Although its roots were in evangelical Christianity, it turned to evangelizing the modern scientific worldview. If the goal of evangelical Christianity was salvation of humanity from sin, the goal of evangelical science was the salvation of humanity from ignorance and self destructive behavior. If the goal of evangelical Christianity was bringing souls to heaven, the goal of evangelical science was to make a heaven on earth. The Rockefeller Foundation in the early twentieth century was not alone in this evangelizing of science, but it was very prominent. And to a large degree it was successful in its goals.

Over the decades since the early twentieth century, science has developed a comprehensive cosmology that explains the origin of human beings as the culmination of a 4-billion-year process of chemical and biological evolution on this planet, which formed in the aftermath of the Big Bang, the event that marked the beginning of the universe some 16 billion years ago. The Big Bang theory of the origin of the universe, founded upon particle physics and astronomical observations suggesting we live in an expanding cosmos, is thus inextricably connected with the theory of the biochemical evolution of all life forms, including human beings. The major foundations, especially the Rockefeller Foundation, provided key funding for the initial research supporting this materialistic cosmology, which has for all practical purposes pushed God and the soul into the realm of mythology—at least in the intellectual centers of modern civilization.

The extent of the Rockefeller Foundation's support of biological research is remarkable. The Foundation funded the fruit fly genetics work of Thomas Hunt Morgan and Theodosius Dobzhansky. Dr. Max Perutz said the Cambridge Medical Research Council Laboratory of Molecular Biology in England owed its existence to the Rockefeller Foundation. The Foundation furnished funds for the Laboratory's X-ray diffraction equipment, which provided critical research results used by Watson and Crick in their pioneering work on DNA's helical structure (W. Weaver 1967, p. 235).

The Foundation was equally supportive of selected projects in the realm of the physical sciences. The Rockefeller Foundation funded the Mt. Palomar Observatory, where much of the work on the Big Bang theory of the origin of the universe took place. The Foundation also gave funds to Ernest O. Lawrence for building the world's early particle accelerators.

If the Big Bang and biochemical evolution represent the Godless and soulless cosmology of the scientific worldview, psychiatry and psychology represent its secular moral code and guidelines for practical behavior. In the early 1930s, around the time the Zhoukoudian excavations were in full swing, the medical division of the Rockefeller Foundation chose psychiatry as its principal focus, establishing schools of psychiatry at major medical colleges.

The Rockefeller Foundation saw in psychiatry a way to influence human social behavior. Dr. Alan Gregg, head of the Medical Sciences Division of the Foundation, wrote: "I should not be satisfied with the definition of psychiatry as that specialty in medicine which deals with mental disorders." He believed its "province is the conduct of man, his reactions, his behavior as an indivisible sentient being with other such beings" (Fosdick 1952, p. 130). Gregg later wrote of "the possibility that through psychiatric understanding our successors may be able to govern human politics and relationships more sagely" (Fosdick 1952, p. 133). The desire to bring about better human relations is certainly laudable. But the Rockefeller Foundation scientists and officials and trustees of the early twentieth century believed this goal could best be achieved by having science establish beneficial control over human society within the worldview established by science.

The Beijing Man discoveries contributed to the establishment of that worldview, a key part of which is the belief that humans have evolved from more primitive ape-like ancestors. However, as I have shown in my book *Forbidden Archeology* (Cremo and Thompson 1993), there is abundant evidence for extreme human antiquity that suggests this belief is not fully justified. I have therefore offered an alternative explanation for human origins in my book *Human Devolution: A Vedic Alternative to Darwin's Theory* (Cremo 2003). This explanation depends on an alternative cosmology, which includes not only matter, but also mind and consciousness, as well as intelligent design. And it suggests a direction for human civilization, away from its current exclusive focus on material production and consumption and towards a focus on the development of consciousness.

Today the goals of the Rockefeller Foundation, as revealed in its annual reports stored on its website, are somewhat different than they were in the early twentieth century. The Foundation now devotes its resources to relieving the plight of "poor and excluded people," in terms of increasing their access to health care, economic development, and the arts. It is a far cry from the scientific evangelism of the early twentieth century. If Davidson Black were applying today for a grant, he might be asked to look elsewhere.

Works Cited

Black, D. (1927) Further hominid remains of Lower Quaternary age from the Chou Kou Tien deposit. *Nature,* 120: 927–954.

Bullock, M. B. (1980) *An American Transplant: The Rockefeller Foundation & Peking Union Medical College.* Berkeley: University of California Press.

Chernow, R. (1999) *Titan: The Life of John D. Rockefeller, Sr.* New York: Vintage Books.

Cochran, S. (2000) *Encountering Chinese Networks: Western, Japanese, and Chinese Corporations in China, 1880–1937.* Berkeley: University of California Press.

Cremo, Michael A. (1998) *Forbidden Archeology's Impact.* Los Angeles: Bhaktivedanta Book Publishing.

Cremo, M. A. (1999) Puranic Time and the Archeological Record. Tim Murray, ed. *Time and Archaeology.* London: Routledge, pp. 38–48.

Cremo, M. A. (2003) *Human Devolution: A Vedic Alternative to Darwin's Theory.* Los Angeles: Bhaktivedanta Book Publishing.

Cremo, M. A., and Thompson, R. L. (1993) *Forbidden Archeology.* San Diego: Bhaktivedanta Institute.

Ernst, J. W. (1994) *"Dear Father"/ "Dear Son".* New York: Fordham University Press.

Fosdick, R. D. (1952) *The Story of the Rockefeller Foundation.* New York: Harper.

Goodman. J. (1983) *The Genesis Mystery.* New York: Times Books.

Hood, D. (1964) *Davidson Black.* Toronto: University of Toronto.

Jonas, G. (1989) *The Circuit Riders: Rockefeller Money and the Rise of Modern Science.* New York: W. W. Norton.

Osborn, H. F. (1928) *Man Rises to Parnassus.* Second edition. Princeton: Princeton University.

Weaver, W. (1967) *U. S. Philanthropic Foundations.* New York: Harper & Row.

20

Forbidden Archeology: Archeological Evidence for Extreme Human Antiquity and Implications for Education Policy

On May 4, 2006, I presented this paper at a meeting of the Faculty of Education, School of Education Studies, University of Kwazulu-Natal, Edgewood Campus, South Africa, in cooperation with the Provincial History Committee.

Ladies and gentleman, this is not my first visit to South Africa. I came in 1999 to Cape Town to present a paper at the World Archaeological Congress 4, which was held that year at the University of Cape Town. During this year's visit, I have spoken already at the University of the Witwatersrand, the University of Pretoria, and the University of Johannesburg. This week, I am speaking at universities in the Durban area, and next week I will be in Cape Town, speaking at universities there.

Over the years, I have had a chance to present my ideas at some of the world's leading scientific institutions, such as the Royal Institution in London, the Russian Academy of Sciences in Moscow, and many others. I have also presented my ideas at international conferences on archeology, anthropology, and history of science, and at universities throughout the world, and I am honored to be here today at the University of Kwazulu-Natal.

My purpose today is not necessarily to persuade you to change your own ideas about human evolution. Rather my purpose is to persuade you that in the fields of archeology and history of science, there are some, including me, who do not accept the current theory of human evolution, or the theory of evolution generally, and that this fact has some significance for education policy on the topic of human origins.

In recent times, archeologists have become interested to see what the science of human origins and antiquity looks like from different cultural perspectives. For a long time, the discipline was dominated by an Anglo-American perspective. But now many archeologists have become interested to see what archeology looks like from an African perspective, an Australian aboriginal perspective, an Asian perspective, and so on. Today I want to offer you a glimpse of what archeology looks like from an Asian Indian perspective. I know that your country is a multicultural country, and that there is an Asian Indian element to the population here.

Since 1973, I have been a member of the International Society for Krishna Consciousness, which has its roots in the spiritual traditions of India, and this has had some influence on my work. My investigations in the field of human origins and antiquity are inspired to some extent by my studies in the ancient Sanskrit writings of India. Among these writings is a group called the *Puranas,* or histories. These histories inform us that humans have existed since the beginning of life on earth. If you are interested in learning more about the Puranic concept of extreme human antiquity and how it relates to physical evidence, you can have a look at my paper "Puranic Time and the Archeological Record," presented at the World Archaeological Congress 3 in New Delhi, in 1994, and later published in the peer reviewed conference proceedings volume *Time and Archaeology* (Routledge, London, 1999) edited by archeologist Tim Murray.

The same message of extreme human antiquity, that humans have been present since the beginning of life on earth, is found in other spiritual traditions, such as Judaism, Christianity, and Islam. Of course this idea is different from the idea of human origins and antiquity supported by the modern followers of Charles Darwin. They say that life began on earth about 2 billion years ago. The first primates, the first apes and monkeys, came into existence about 40 million years ago. The first hominins, ape men, came into existence about 6 million years ago. And finally, they say, humans like us came into existence only about 150,000 years ago. And they say all of the physical evidence supports this evolutionary picture of human origins. But when I did eight years of research into the entire history of archeology, I found something different. Over the past 150 years, archeologists have found much evidence showing that humans have existed since the beginning of the history of life on earth. This evidence takes the form of human skeletal remains, human footprints, and human artifacts many millions of years old.

I documented this evidence in my book *Forbidden Archeology,* with my coauthor Richard L. Thompson. This was a 900-page book, directed toward a scientific audience. It was reviewed in most of the professional journals that deal with human origins and antiquity, such as *American Journal of Physical Anthropology, Geoarchaeology, Journal of Field Archaeology, Antiquity, L'Homme, L'Anthropologie, British Journal for the History of Science, Social Studies of Science,* and *Ethology, Ecology, and Evolution.* Because the antievolutionary thesis of the book was quite controversial, many of the reviews were, as you might expect, not favorable.

But some of the reviewers thought that the book had some value. For example, a noted historian of science, David Oldroyd, and his graduate student, Jo Wodak, wrote a 20-page review article on *Forbidden Archeology* in *Social Studies of Science* (vol 26, no. 1, 1996). At the end of their review (p. 207), they asked: "So has *Forbidden Archeology* made any contribution at all to the literature on palaeoanthropology?" They replied, "Our answer is a guarded 'yes', for two reasons. First . . . much of the historical material they [Cremo and Thompson] resurrect has not been scrutinized in such detail before. Second, . . . Cremo and Thompson do raise a central problematic regarding the lack of certainty in scientific 'truth' claims." Today many scientists claim that their evolutionary theory of human origins is absolutely certain in terms of its truth. Wodak and Oldroyd thought we did a good job in problematizing that claim to absolute certainty.

Forbidden Archeology has also come out in an abridged popular edition called *The*

Hidden History of the Human Race. That book has now been translated into about 20 languages around the world, including German, French, Spanish, Italian, Portuguese, Polish, Russian, Czech, Bulgarian, and Japanese.

The evidence documented in these books is not very well known, either among scientists or the general public, because of what I call a process of knowledge filtration. Here I am not talking about a satanic conspiracy to suppress truth. Rather I am talking about something very well known to historians of science, philosophers of science, and sociologists of science: theoretical preconceptions often determine how evidence is treated. I have just tried to show how this process operates in studies of human origins and antiquity.

The knowledge filter is a metaphor for the currently dominant consensus among scientists on human origins and antiquity. Reports of evidence that conform to this consensus pass through this social and intellectual filter quite easily. This means that students will read about this evidence in their textbooks. People will hear scientists talking about it on television. And when people go to the local museum, they will see the artifacts on display. But reports of evidence that radically contradict the current consensus do not pass through the knowledge filter. And that means students will not read about this evidence in their textbooks, people will not see scientists talking about it on television, and if people go to the local museum they will not see the artifacts, although they might be there in the museum storerooms. Let me now give a few representative examples of the kind of evidence I am talking about.

In the 1970s, American archeologists were excavating a site called Hueyatlaco, near the town of Puebla in central Mexico. They found many stone tools. Of course, they wanted to know how old they were, so they called a team of geologists to date the site. Geologist Virginia Steen-McIntyre and her colleagues used four methods to date the site. Let me mention two of them. In the same layer with the stone tools the archeologists found animal bones with butchering marks on them. The geologists used the uranium series method to date the bones and got an age of about 245,000 years. Above the layer with the stone tools and animals bones was a layer of volcanic ash. The geologists used the zircon fission track method to date the layer of ash and got an age of about 270,000 years. From the results of all four methods they employed, the geologists concluded the age of the site must be at least 250,000 years. But the archeologists did not believe the site could be that old. According to their understanding, human beings capable of making the artifacts did not exist 250,000 years ago—they had not evolved yet. So the archeologists refused to accept the age for the site given by their own team of geologists, and instead assigned a far younger age to the site.

Later, Virginia Steen-McIntyre and her colleagues independently published the true age for the site in the journal *Quaternary Research* (1981, vol. 16, pp. 1–17). On March 30, 1981, Steen-McIntyre wrote to Estella Leopold, one of the editors: "Not being an anthropologist, I didn't realize . . . how deeply woven into our thought the current theory of human evolution has become. Our work at Hueyatlaco has been rejected by most archaeologists because it contradicts that theory, period." If you wish to learn more about the details of this case, you can write to Dr. Steen-McIntyre at this address: dub.ent@ix.netcom.com.

In 1997, a German archeologist (H. Thieme) announced in *Nature* (1997, vol. 385, pp. 807–810) the discovery of wooden spears at a place called Schöningen in northern Germany. The spears were shaped exactly like modern Olympic javelins. They were obviously weapons made for hunting, and animal bones were found in the same Middle Pleistocene layers, which are about 430,000 years old. Who made the spears? According to the current theories, it could not have been humans like us because humans like us had not evolved yet. So archeologists have attributed the spears to *Homo heidelbergensis*, a variety of *Homo erectus* that inhabited Central Europe during the Middle Pleistocene. This was interesting, because before this discovery archeologists did not believe *Homo erectus* made and used throwing spears. In fact, the oldest throwing spears they had were less than 100,000 years old, within the range of the modern human species.

However, there is another answer to the question "who made the spears?" The answer is connected with some discoveries that were made by Jacques Boucher de Perthes at Abbeville in northeastern France. In the 19th century, Boucher de Perthes, one of the founders of modern archeology, discovered an anatomically modern human jaw in one of his excavations. He found it along with flint tools in a Pleistocene layer that modern geologists give an age of about 430,000 years. At the time, the discovery was quite controversial. Many scientists could not believe that humans existed as far back in the Pleistocene as the position of the jaw suggested. Therefore, some of them proposed that Boucher de Perthes had been the victim of a hoax. According to them, someone had obtained a human jaw from some nearby cemetery and planted it in the excavation for Boucher de Perthes to find. And this is the story that you will see in most textbooks today. What you do not read in most textbooks today is that Boucher de Perthes made many additional excavations in the same location, and in those new excavations, he found over one hundred additional anatomically modern human bones and teeth, in the same formation that yielded the original jaw. These new discoveries were made under carefully controlled conditions that ruled out the hoax explanation. These later discoveries show that the original discovery of the jaw was also genuine.

What we have at Abbeville is evidence for an anatomically modern human population existing in northern Europe over 400,000 years ago. I propose it was members of this population who made the spears found by Thieme in Germany. If you would like to know more about the details of this case you can consult my paper on it, published in the peer-reviewed *Proceedings of the XXth International Congress of History of Science* (2002, vol. 10, pp. 39–56).

In 1913, the German scientist Hans Reck found an anatomically modern human skeleton in Upper Bed II of Olduvai Gorge in Africa. According to modern geologists, Bed II of Olduvai Gorge is 1.15 to 1.7 million years old. Because the skeleton was in Upper Bed II, it should be at least 1.15 million years old. Reck said the skeleton was firmly embedded in the rock. He had to take the skeleton out with hammers and chisels. The details of the discovery with citations from original reports can be found in my book *Forbidden Archeology* (pp. 628–649). In 1974 (*Journal of Human Evolution*, vol. 3, pp. 379–385), Reiner Protsch published a radiocarbon dating of a fragment of bone he alleged was from the original skeleton. The original skeleton, except for the skull, was lost during bombing raids in Germany during World War II. The skull itself was considered too valuable to use for samples. Protsch got an age of about 16,000 years for the bone fragment allegedly from the original skeleton. However, not too long ago, Protsch was forced to resign from his position as professor at Frankfurt University after a committee of scientists revealed that he had falsified dozens of radiocarbon dates over the course of his career. His radiocarbon dating of a bone fragment allegedly from the original Reck skeleton is therefore suspect. The most reliable evidence for the true age of the skeleton remains the report of the discoverer, who said it was firmly embedded in Upper Bed II of Olduvai Gorge, which would give it an age of over one million years.

In 1973, Richard Leakey published a report in *Nature* (vol. 242, pp. 447–450) about a femur, or thighbone, found at East Rudolf, Kenya. He described the femur (designated ER-1481) as indistinguishable from anatomically modern human femurs. It was found in a formation 1.8 million years old. So to what kind of creature did the femur belong? According to current theories, it could not have been humans like us, because humans like us did not exist 1.8 million years ago. Leakey attributed the femur to the apeman *Homo habilis*. On the basis of this discovery scientists came up with a picture of *Homo habilis* that was very humanlike in size and proportions. The reconstruction was based not on a complete skeleton, but on isolated bones. However, in 1987 Don Johanson and his coworkers announced the discovery of a fairly complete skeleton of *Homo habilis* at Olduvai Gorge. This individual (designated OH 62) turned out to have an anatomy that was not very humanlike. In particular, the femur was quite different from the humanlike ER 1481 femur. So what did Richard Leakey actually find? He said the ER 1481 femur was indistinguishable from modern human femurs. I believe he found evidence that humans like us were present in Africa 1.8 million years ago.

In 1979, Mary Leakey announced the discovery of footprints at Laetoli in Tanzania. The footprints were found in layers of solidified volcanic ash 3.7 million years old. In her original report in *National Geographic* (1979, vol. 155, pp. 446–457) she said that the footprints were indistinguishable from anatomically modern human footprints. Other scientists agreed. For example, Tim White said, "Make no mistake about it. They are like modern human footprints." This statement is from the book *Lucy* by D. Johanson and M. Edey (1981, p. 250). Mary Leakey did not believe that humans like us were present almost 4 million years ago. So how did she explain the footprints? She proposed that there must have existed at that time some kind of apeman who had feet exactly like modern human feet. That is possible, of course. But at present there is no physical evidence to back up that idea. We have skeletons of the apemen who existed at that time. They are called *Australopithecus*. And the foot structure of *Australopithecus* is different from that of a modern human foot. Perhaps in the future, someone will discover an apeman from 3.7 million years ago with a foot like a modern human foot. But at the present moment, the only creature known to science that has a foot exactly like a modern human foot is a modern human being. So what did Mary Leakey find? I believe she found evidence that humans like us were present in Africa 3.7 million years ago.

In the mid 19th century, Carlos Ribeiro was the chief government geologist of Portugal. Like many geologists of that time, he was also an archeologist. He found in Portugal hundreds of human artifacts in Lower Miocene formations about 20 million years old [see Plates I-VII]. He determined that they could not have entered these formations from more recent levels. Ribeiro displayed the artifacts in the Museum of Geology in Lisbon. But if you go to the museum today, you will not see them. They are kept out of view in cabinets. A few years ago, I was preparing a paper about Ribeiro's discoveries that I presented at a meeting in 2000 of the European Association of Archaeologists, of which I was a member. During my research I went to Lisbon and received permission from the director of the Museum of Geology to study and photograph Ribeiro's artifacts. From my studies of Ribeiro's maps and field notes in the museum archives, I was able to go out into the countryside of Portugal and relocate some of the sites where Ribeiro made his discoveries. One of the sites I relocated was the quarry at Murganheira, where Ribeiro found flint artifacts, including a pointed flint artifact with use marks on the tip. As I said, Ribeiro displayed this artifact, and others, in the Museum of Geology in Lisbon with labels indicating a Lower Miocene age of about 20 million years. After Ribeiro died, his colleagues did something interesting. They left the artifacts on display, but they wrote new labels for them, giving them far younger ages that fit within the accepted theories of human evolution. Finally, the next generation of officials in the museum removed the whole collection from display. You can find a complete account of Ribeiro's discoveries, including citations from original reports in my book *Forbidden Archeology* (pp. 213–226).

In the mid 19th century, gold was discovered in California. To get the gold, miners dug tunnels into the sides of mountains, such as Table Mountain in Tuolumne County [see Plate XII], California. Deep inside the tunnels, in the solid rock, the miners found human bones and human artifacts [see Plates XIII-XV]. The discoveries were made in gold bearing gravels in ancient river channels along with plant and animal fossils characteristic of the early Eocene, which would give them an age of about 50 million years. These ancient Eocene river channels are capped by hundreds of meters of solid volcanic deposits, dated using the potassium-argon method, which gave an age of 20–33 million years. The discoveries were carefully documented by Dr. J. D. Whitney, the chief government geologist of California, in his book *The Auriferous Gravels of the Sierra Nevada of California,* published by Harvard University in 1880. He said that there was no evidence the artifacts could have come from higher, more recent levels. But we do not hear very much about these discoveries today. In the *Smithsonian Institution Annual Report for 1898–1899* (p. 424), anthropologist William Holmes said, "Perhaps if Professor Whitney had fully appreciated the story of human evolution as it is understood today, he would have hesitated to announce the conclusions formulated, notwithstanding the imposing array of testimony with which he was confronted." In other words, if the facts did not fit the theory of human evolution, the facts had to be set aside, and that is exactly what happened.

However, some of the artifacts from the California gold mines are still in the collection of the Phoebe Hearst Museum of Anthropology at the University of California at Berkeley. A few years ago, I was researching a paper about these discoveries, which I later presented at the meeting of the World Archaeological Congress in 2003. I received permission from the museum officials to study and photograph the artifacts [see Plate XIII-XV]. They are not displayed to the public. They are kept in a storage building several miles from the museum itself. By studying Whitney's old maps and documents, I was able to go out to Table Mountain and relocate some of the old nineteenth century gold mining tunnels where the objects were originally found [**see Plate XII**].

So how far back in time can we go with evidence like this? In December of 1862, the following brief but intriguing report appeared in a journal called *The Geologist:* "In Macoupin county, Illinois, the bones of a man were recently found on a coal-bed capped with two feet of slate rock, ninety feet below the surface of the earth. . . . The bones, when found, were covered with a crust or coating of hard glossy matter, as black as coal itself, but when scraped away left the bones white and natural." The coal in which the Macoupin County skeleton was found is at least 286 million years old and might be as much as 320 million years old.

The following report, titled "A Relic of a Bygone Age," appeared in the magazine *Scientific American* (June 5, 1852): "A few days ago a powerful blast was made in the rock at Meeting House Hill, in Dorchester, a few rods south of Rev. Mr. Hall's meeting house. The blast threw out an immense mass of rock, some of the pieces weighing several tons, and scattered fragments in all directions. Among them was picked up a metallic vessel in two parts, rent asunder by the explosion. On putting the two parts together it formed a bell-shaped vessel. . . . On the side there are six figures or a flower, or bouquet, beautifully inlaid with pure silver, and around the lower part of the vessel a vine, or wreath, also inlaid with silver. . . . This curious and unknown vessel was blown out of the solid pudding stone, fifteen feet below the surface. . . .The matter is worthy of investigation, as there is no deception in the case." According to a recent U.S. Geological Survey map of the Boston-Dorchester area, the pudding stone, now called the Roxbury conglomerate, is of Precambrian age, over 600 million years old.

I could keep you here for many months, going through one case after another, because there are hundreds of them in the scientific literature of the past 150 years. I won't do that. But I will ask you to remember one thing. There are many scientists who will claim that all of the physical evidence supports their evolutionary account of human origins, with humans like us coming into existence between 100,000 and 200,000 years ago. But it is not true that all of the physical evidence supports that idea. When we look carefully at all of the evidence in the primary scientific literature (the reports of original investigators) we find a series of discoveries of human bones, human footprints, and human artifacts going back to the very beginning of the history of life on earth, which is consistent with the accounts of human origins found in the *Puranas*, the Bible, the Koran, and the accounts of other spiritual traditions.

What is the significance of this evidence? In a letter dated August 10, 1993, William W. Howells, one of the principal architects of the modern theory of human evolution, wrote to me, "Thank you for sending me a copy of *Forbidden Archeology*, which represents much careful effort in critically assembling published materials. . . . Most of us, mistakenly or not, see human evolution . . . with man emerging rather late. . . . To have modern human beings . . . appearing a great deal earlier, in fact at a time when even simple primates did not exist as possible ancestors, would be devastating . . . to the whole theory of evolution."

In this presentation, I have focused on physical evidence that contradicts the current theory of human evolution. Some will ask, "What about other species?" Is there any physical evidence that contradicts the evolutionary history of other plant and animal species? There is such evidence. Let me mention just a couple of examples.

Until very recently, scientists believed that the mammals that existed during the Mesozoic, the age of the dinosaurs, were very small creatures, about the size of mice. But just last year, scientists in China announced the discovery of a skeleton of a Mesozoic mammal 20 times larger than any previously known from that time. The animal was the size of a large dog, and scientists found evidence that it had been killing and eating small dinosaurs. The report was published in *Nature* (January 13, 2005). Who knows what will be discovered next? Paleontologist Ming Jen of the American Museum of Natural History said, "This new evidence gives us a drastically new picture." A drastically new picture of the history of animal life on this planet. And if the kind of evidence I have presented in *Forbidden Archeology* is considered, our picture of the history of life on earth will be even more drastically new and different.

What about plant life? There is physical evidence that contradicts the current evolutionary history of plants. A few years ago, when things were a little more peaceful in that part of the world, I went to the Salt Range Mountains of Pakistan to visit a site where some interesting paleobotanical discoveries were made. Beginning in the 1940s, geologists and paleobotanists working with the Geological Survey of India, including Birbal Sahni, explored the Salt Range Mountains. They found deep in salt mines at the Khewra Gorge evidence for the existence of advanced flowering plants (angiosperms), evergreens (gymnosperms), and insects in the early Cambrian period, about 600 million years ago. Accounts of the discoveries are found in the proceedings of the National Academy of Sciences of India (1945, section B, v. 16, pp. xlv–xlvi). According to standard evolutionary ideas, no land plants or animals existed at that time. Flowering plants and insects are thought to have come into existence hundreds of millions of years later.

What about genetics and molecular biology? Hasn't evidence from these fields demonstrated the evolutionary origins of modern life forms, including human beings? This is a belief that is strongly held and widely held among scientists. However, the very first thing the supporters of this belief would have to say is that the very first living thing self-organized from chemicals early in the history of the earth. This is asserted in most textbooks. However, no scientist today can tell us exactly which chemicals combined in exactly which way to become exactly what first living thing. Therefore the idea that life self-organized from chemicals remains a belief, not an established fact.

Let us grant, for the sake of discussion, the existence of some first one-celled creature. Then we have to wonder how this single-celled creature transformed into something like a human being, with trillions of cells organized in very complex organs such as the human eye. We are told it happened by evolution. But we have to keep in mind that evolution is today a genetic science. Evolutionists would say that there were genetic changes that resulted in physical changes that made the organism more fit. So if we want to explain the origin of the eye, evolutionists would propose that long ago there existed some primitive animal that did not have a developed eye. They would then have to specify the genetic structure of that animal, and then specify the first change in the genetic structure that led to a more developed eye for the descendants of that creature. And then they would have to specify the second genetic change, and so on. And not only would they have to explain the physical structure of the eye in that way, but also the optic nerve and the neuronal structures in the brain capable of receiving signals from the eye and converting them into a visual display. Evolutionists claim that is what happened—there was a series of genetic changes that led to a series of physical changes that led to the human eye. But if you ask them to specify what those genetic changes were, and how exactly they led to the required physiological changes in the organism, they cannot do it. You can find no such detailed explanation in any scientific publication or collection of scientific publications. That means it could have happened some other way.

So, in summary, there is a lot of physical evidence that contradicts the current theory of human evolution. There is also physical evidence that contradicts the evolutionary accounts of the origin of mammals, insects, and plants. Furthermore, the current evolutionary theories have not been fully demonstrated by genetics and molecular biology.

As I said in the beginning, I am not necessarily trying to persuade you, as educators and education policy makers, to change your personal views on the human evolution question. Everything I have said is, of course, controversial, and there are going to be different opinions about it all, and you may not be persuaded to accept my antievolutionary opinions. But I am hoping to persuade you that there are alternative views on the origin of species that can be supported by physical evidence, and that there are some of us who are representing, as I am, these alternative views in the world of science—making presentations at leading scientific institutions, at scientific conferences, and in scientific publications. If these alternative views are being represented in the world of science, they should also be represented in the classroom.

Now let's be honest about something. The current alternatives to Darwinism are theistic, in one form or another. Creationists of various kinds are quite open about their theistic perspectives. Supporters of the more recent intelligent design theory are not so open, but almost everyone knows that the designer they talk about is God.

Should theistic alternatives to Darwinism be allowed in science classrooms? One thing that educators and education policy makers should consider before answering a question like this is the beliefs of students and their parents. Education, and here I am talking about state supported education, is a public service, funded by the tax money of all the people. It would seem natural that the opinions of the people should be a factor in making decisions about education policy. Surveys have been done on this topic. Because I am from the United States, I will give the results of study from there. In 2005, *Nature* published the results of a survey by the Gallup organization on belief in evolution in the United States among teenagers 13–17 years old. The survey found only 10 percent believed humans came about by evolution from apelike beings without God. About 43 percent believed God created human beings by guiding their evolution from apelike beings. We must keep in mind that the idea that God guided evolution from the beginning to produce humans contradicts the modern scientific idea that evolution is an unguided, natural process relying on random genetic mutations. Finally, the survey found that 38 percent of the teenagers believed that God created humans in the beginning just as they are today (that is the view that I myself favor). What about adults? According to the same Gallup survey, only 35 percent of Americans believe the theory of evolution is well supported by scientific evidence. Educators and education policy makers should take these beliefs of students and their parents into account.

Some educators and education policy makers will naturally raise this question: Should God have any place in the science classroom? Would that constitute a violation of the separation of church and state, which is one of the foundations of the modern secular state? In order to answer this question, we should have a clear understanding of the different roles that the concept of God plays in religion, philosophy, and science. In religion, God is an object of worship. And the state should not dictate to people how they should worship God. And of course, religion, worship of God, has no place in science classrooms. In philosophy, God is a metaphysical principle that many philosophers have arrived at through the exercise of logic and reason. Government should not dictate to philosophers that they cannot use logic and reason to come to the conclusion that there is God. Neither should government forbid philosophy teachers in schools and universities to teach about philosophers who have come to that conclusion. In science, God is an inference arrived at by study of nature. Historically, many scientists have inferred from their study of nature that there must be a supreme intelligent being responsible for the order and complexity visible to us. And government should not forbid scientists to make that inference. Neither should they forbid teachers from teaching about scientists who have inferred the existence of God, an intelligent designer, from the evidence visible to us.

Some educators and education policy makers are under the impression that there has always been, and always should be, a clear separation between God and science. But the best of modern scholarship in the history and philosophy of science demonstrates that this is not true. I refer you to a recent (2001) volume edited by John Hedley Brooke *et al.*, and published by the University of Chicago Press, titled *Science in Theistic Contexts*. The University of Chicago Press description of this book tells us: "It is a widely shared assumption that science and religion are fundamentally opposed to each other. Yet, recent historiography has shown that religious belief [in God] needs to be added to the social, economic, political, and other cultural factors that went into the making of modern science. This new collection shows religious ideas not only motivated scientific effort but also shaped the actual content of major scientific theories." It is a modern myth that God and science have nothing to do with each other.

So what are the practical implications of all this for education policy? First, education policy makers should recognize that today the vast majority of scientists accept the theory of evolution. This is a fact. But it is also a fact that some in the world of science, a small number, do not accept the theory and are proposing theistic alternatives, and education policy makers should recognize this. The proper solution is that the theory of evolution and its supporters should be given most of the time in the classroom and most of the pages in the textbooks. But a small amount of classroom time and a small number of textbook pages should be devoted to neutrally presenting the theistic alternatives to the current theory of evolution. How small? I would suggest 5 percent of the classroom time and 5 percent of the textbook pages. But I will leave it up to you.

Right now, in many parts of the world, especially the United States, educators and education policy makers are participating in a system of intellectual apartheid that is artificially excluding voices that are opposed to the theory of evolution from the education system. We should end this system of artificial exclusion and give fair, proportionate representation to all the views that are there in the world of science. We cannot pretend that there is no debate about these questions in the world of science. Everyone knows there is a debate. It is going in the media, in the courts, in the school systems themselves. Educators and education policy makers here in South Africa can take a leading role in resolving this debate in the fairest way for all concerned

21
Finding Krishna: 16th Century Archeological Activity by Vaishnava Saints in the Braj Mandal Region of Northern India

I presented this paper at the biannual meeting of the European Association of South Asian Archaeologists, held in Ravenna, Italy, July 2-6, 2007. In it, I focus on one of the topics that I included in the paper I presented at the 2005 meeting of the EASAA in London (included in this volume). I presented similar papers at other conferences: (1) Rewriting the History of Indian Archeology, at the World Archaeological Congress intercongress, held in Osaka, Japan, January 12-15, 2006; (2) Excavating the Eternal: An Indigenous Archeological Tradition in India, at the World Archaeological Congress intercongress held in Kingston, Jamaica, May 20-27, 2007; (3) Archeology and Tourism: An Early Example of the Connection from Medieval India, at the World Archaeological Congress 6, held in Dublin, Ireland, July 1-5, 2008; (4) Rewriting the History of Indian Archeology, at the 23rd International Congress of the History of Science and Technology, held in Budapest, Hungary, July 27–August 2, 2009. A version of this paper was published in one of the main archeology journals: Cremo, M. A. (2008) Excavating the eternal: an indigenous archaeological tradition in India. Antiquity, 82: 178–188.

Histories of archeology by Western scholars routinely say that archeology began in India with the reports of European travelers of the 16th century. Trigger (1989, p. 181) says, "Archaeological research in India began in a colonial setting. . . . European travelers began to note ancient monuments as early as the sixteenth century." Even Indian scholars have accepted this perception of the history of archeology in India. About the writings of the early European travelers, Chakrabarti (2001, p. 1) says, "Without doubt these records constitute the first group of archaeological writings on India." But Indian historical texts and oral traditions reveal a parallel indigenous archeological tradition, involving the excavation of lost sacred images and the relocation of sacred landscape features.

Excavation of Sacred Images and Sites in the Braj Mandal Region

The Braj Mandal region of northern India [**see Plate XVIII**] provides a striking example of indigenous archeological activity. The Braj Mandal is famous for its associations with the Hindu god Krishna, a form of Vishnu. Followers of Vishnu, called Vaishnavas, regard Vishnu or any of his selfsame forms, such as Krishna, as the supreme god. In the term Braj Mandal, *braj* means a pasturing place for cows, animals dear to Krishna, and *mandal* means a circular region. The Braj Mandal is about 50 miles in diameter. Its largest town is Mathura, on the west bank of the Yamuna River between New Delhi and Agra. The *Bhagavata Purana* identifies Mathura as the place where Krishna appeared in ancient times. At various locales in the Braj Mandal, such as Vrindavan (a name often used to refer to the whole of the Braj Mandal), youthful Krishna engaged in pastimes of divine friendship and love with his cowherd relatives and friends, as depicted in countless works of Hindu art and literature. After Krishna left this world, one of his descendants, Vajranabha, was appointed king of the Braj Mandal. According to the *Skanda Purana*, the area was overgrown with forest, and the pastime places of Krishna were lost. The sage Shandilya showed Vajranabha the locations of Krishna's pastimes, and to commemorate them Vajranabha established shrines housing images of Krishna. Over the course of time, many of the locales, shrines, and images were lost again and later rediscovered.

Whether or not one accepts the account of Vajranabha in the *Skanda Purana's Bhagavata-mahatmya* section (according to modern scholarly opinion it is a fairly late interpolation), the identification of the Braj Mandal with Vajranabha and Krishna is recorded in other documents. According to Entwistle (1987, p. 60), the core of the Vajranabha story is found in the *Mahabharata*, a Sanskrit epic that modern scholars say reached its final form between 500 BCE and 200 CE. As for Krishna, Megasthenes, a Greek ambassador to the court of the Indian king Chandragupta Maurya in the late 4th century BCE, wrote in his *Indika*: "Herakles was worshiped by the inhabitants of the plains—especially the Sourasenai, an Indian tribe possessed of two large cities, Methora and Kleisobara and who had a navigable river, the Jobares, flowing through its territories." Bryant (2003, xvii–xviii) notes, "There seems little reasonable doubt (and almost all scholars agree) that the Sourasenoi refers to the Surasenas, a branch of the Yadu dynasty to which Krsna belonged; Herakles refers to Krsna, or Hari-Krsna; Methora to Mathura, Krsna's birthplace; and the Jobares to the Yamuna river, where Krsna sported."

What form the worship of Krishna (Hari-Krishna, or Herakles) took is not specified, but there could have been temples housing images of Krishna. Megasthenes tells us in his descriptions of government officers in India that one of their duties was to maintain temples. And Quintus Curtius (Bryant 2003, xviii) says that the front ranks of the Indian army that confronted Alexander the Great's invading forces carried an image of Herakles (Hari-Krishna).

The Indian emperor Ashoka (304 BCE–232 BCE) converted to Buddhism, and under his patronage Buddhism became dominant in northern India, including Mathura, and remained dominant for hundreds of years. Worship of Hindu gods in Mathura diminished but did not completely disappear. Some scholars interpret a first-century CE stone inscription from Mathura as referring to a temple dedicated to Vasudeva (another name for Krishna), and several stone figures of Krishna found in Mathura date to the time of the Kushan dynasty (first and second centuries CE). Examples increase through the Gupta dynasty (250–560 CE). Sharma (1994) gives an overview of Krishna sculpture from Kushan and Gupta times in the collection of the Mathura Museum. When Mahmud of Ghazni (971–1030 CE) sacked Mathura early in the 11th century, there were many Hindu temples, including one large temple of Krishna. Cycles of Hindu temple construction and Muslim destruction followed over the next few centuries.

Discoveries by Chaitanya

In the early 16th century, the *bhakti* movement of devotion to Krishna rose in north India. A central figure of this movement was Chaitanya Mahaprabhu (1486–1533), who appeared in Bengal (known as Gaudadesha) [**see Plate XVI, Figure 1**]. He is regarded by his followers as an avatar of Krishna, or Vishnu. The followers of Chaitanya Mahaprabhu are known as Gaudiya (Bengali) Vaishnavas. Their intense devotion to Krishna inspired a special interest in the Braj Mandal, the place of Krishna's earthly pastimes. Chaitanya Mahaprabhu and other Gaudiya Vaishnavas (and also Krishna worshipers of other Vaishnava sects) sought to revive the importance of the Braj Mandal as a place of pilgrimage. This revival, especially among the Gaudiya Vaishnavas, had an archeological component, involving the deliberate search for lost images of Krishna and lost landscape features.

In 1514, Chaitanya Mahaprabhu journeyed to Vrindavan to find lost pastime places and images, as recorded in the *Chaitanya Charitamrita* of Krishnadasa Kaviraja Goswami (1615) and the *Bhakti Ratnakara* of Narahari Chakravarti (completed ca. 1710–1730). That Chaitanya Mahaprabhu came to the Braj Mandal to restore its importance as a holy place is also accepted by modern scholars. Haberman (p. 36) says, "The development of Braj was clearly inspired by charismatic Vaishnava leaders such as Chaitanya, Vallabha, and others, and was carried out by their diligent followers." A modern Indian scholar, Shrivatsa Goswami, wrote (Goswami 1996, p. 269) that Chaitanya "entered the northern wilds of Mathura and there he discovered, reidentified, revealed and created the heart of Vraja [Braj]." The accounts of Chaitanya's activities in the *Chaitanya Charitamrita* demonstrate their deliberate and arguably archeological nature.

Relocation of Shyama Kund and Radha Kund

The first case of indigenous archeological work by Chaitanya involves the relocation and excavation of a lost landscape feature of the Braj Mandal. In Arit-gram (*gram* means "village"), Chaitanya asked the people if they could show him Radha Kund and Shyama Kund [**see Plate XIX**], two ancient water storage tanks (*kunds*) that were, according to Gaudiya Vaishnava tradition, important in Krishna's earthly pastimes. Shyama is a name for Krishna, and Radha is the name of his beloved consort. The inhabitants of Arit-gram did not know where the *kunds* were, and neither did Chaitanya's *brahmana* guide. Chaitanya himself then located in nearby agricultural fields two shallow ponds that he identified as Radha Kund and Shyama Kund (*Chaitanya Charitamrita, Madhya-lila.* 18.3–5). It is significant that Chaitanya began his search at Arit-gram (the modern Aring-gram), a village near Govardhan Hill. According to traditional sources, Krishna and Radha had excavated their respective *kunds* just after Krishna had killed the bull-demon Aristha. Growse (1890, p. 83) said Aring is "a contraction for *Arishta-ganw*," which, relying on local etymologies, he characterized as "the scene of the combat with the bull [Arishta]." The combat with Arishta is related in the *Bhagavata Purana*, a work traditionalists assign an age of about five thousand years. Recent scholarship (Bryant 2003, xvi) suggests the extant text can be dated to the Gupta period, over a thousand years before Chaitanya's arrival in the Braj Mandal.

After Chaitanya rediscovered the *kunds*, Raghunatha Dasa Goswami, one of his followers, excavated them and developed them as places of pilgrimage. According to a longstanding local account, Raghunatha found ancient images of Radha and Krishna while excavating Radha Kund (Mahanidhi Swami 1995, p. 73). The images found by Raghunatha were installed in the first temple at Radha Kund, now called the Purana Radha Krishna temple (*purana* means old). The discovery of the images suggests that the recovered landscape features actually were ancient *kunds*, because it is a Hindu practice to dispose of damaged or polluted sacred images, in *kunds* or other bodies of water. It is likely, also, that endangered images might be hidden in *kunds*. Early in the twentieth century, during a civic project for cleaning *kunds*, over 600 sculptures were found and given to the Mathura Museum (Sharma 1994, p. 34).

According to traditional histories, the excavation of Radha Kund and Shyama Kund by Raghunatha was not the first. Much earlier they had been discovered and excavated by King Vajranabha. Brahmacari (1999, p. 31), repeating local accounts, says, "After excavating Shyama-kunda, it is said king Vajranabha constructed an eight foot high and sixty foot square sandstone boundary wall around the original *kunda*, wide enough for people to walk along. When Shyama-kunda is periodically emptied for cleaning, or sometimes during the hot summer months when the water level goes down, this sandstone structure can be clearly seen." Brahmacari (1999, p. 36) gives a photo of this feature. This again suggests that Chaitanya reidentified a real landscape feature, an ancient *kund* that was restored by Raghunatha Goswami.

For the purpose of this paper, which is to demonstrate that some indigenous archeological work was carried out by Chaitanya and his followers, it is not necessary to assume that the *kund,* or the structures and images found in it, actually were connected with Vajranabha. It is sufficient to show it is likely that old landscape features and images were recovered, and that this was recorded in texts (like *Chaitanya Charitamrita*) and/or preserved in local oral tradition. How these particular indigenous archeological discoveries relate to the traditional history of the Braj Mandal is another question. Even in modern scientific archeology initial attributions of objects to certain makers or times may change, yet it remains a fact that genuinely old objects or features were recovered.

Radha Kund [**see Plate XIX, Figure 1**] is mentioned by Lakshmidhara in the *Mathuramatmya* section of his *Krtyakalpataru,* which was composed in the late 12th century CE, according to Entwistle (1987, p. 48), who suggests this kund may be the same as the modern Radha Kund. It is possible that at the time of Lakshmidhara, the Radha Kund he mentions was developed as a pilgrimage site, with a stone wall enclosing the *kund,* which was smaller than the one that exists today. It is possible that this site fell into disuse as Hindu pilgrimage numbers declined after the time of the Muslim invasions. And it was this site that was rediscovered by Chaitanya in the 16th century. According to this view, the walled structures visible now when Radha Kund and Shyama Kund are drained, or the water levels decrease sufficiently, are the remains of the kund walls from the time of Lakshmidhara.

Chaitanya Gives the History of an Excavated Image

From Arit-gram, Chaitanya went to the hill of Govardhan, where he saw the image of Krishna called Gopal (cowherd boy) or Nathji (little master). Before coming to the Braj Mandal, Chaitanya had told his followers the history of this image, which involved an excavation. The excavation was carried out by Madhavendra Puri, a Gaudiya Vaishnava saint who came to the Braj Mandal in the late 15th century, before Chaitanya. According to *Chaitanya Charitamrita*, the image, dating from the time of Vajranabha, had been buried by its priests to protect it from Muslim invaders. The location of the image was revealed to Madhavendra Puri in a dream. He then went to the nearby village of Aniyor and gathered some assistants. Together, they entered a bushy area near Govardhan Hill [**see Plate XX, Figure 1**]. They cleared the bushes with choppers (*kuthari*) and uncovered the image with spades (*kodali*). Under Madhavendra Puri's direction they installed the image in a temple on the top of Govardhana Hill [**see Plate XX, Figure 2**]. In the 18th century, under new threats of Muslim attack by Aurangzeb's forces, the Nathji image was taken to Nathdwar in Rajasthan, where it remains today. The followers of Vallabha (the founder of the Pushti Marg Vaishnava sect) give a slightly different account of the image's history, told in *Shri Nathaji Prakatya Varta*. In this account the arm of the image protruding from the ground was seen by a villager looking for his lost cow. Later the image was taken out of the ground, and Madhavendra Puri became its priest before worship was taken over by the followers of Vallabha (Haberman 1994, p. 119).

There is iconographic evidence that a genuinely old image was recovered. The Nathji or Gopal image is in the form of *govardhan-dhari*, Krishna holding Govardhan Hill aloft on one upraised hand. Several early images of Krishna as *govardhan-dhari* have been found throughout India. One of the oldest is in the collection of the Mathura Museum (catalog number D-47). It was found at a place called Gatashram Tila in Mathura. Vaudeville (1980, p. 6) says these images are from the Gupta era (3rd through 6th century CE). According to Vaudeville (1980, p. 6), these ancient images are different from later images in several ways. First the later images show Krishna standing in the open and holding the hill over his head, whereas in the earlier images Krishna is shown within the hollow of a mountain cave, holding his hand up out of the cave. Second, in the later images, the mountain is resting on the upraised little finger of Krishna's left hand, whereas in the earlier images the palm of the raised left hand is upturned with the extended five fingers pressed together, with the palm just about parallel to the plane of the ground. Third, in the later images, Krishna is sometimes in a dancing pose, with one foot flat on the other ground, and the other touching the ground only with the tip of the large toe, whereas in the Gupta era images Krishna is standing with both feet flat on the ground.

And, finally, the Gupta era images show Krishna with his right hand on his hip, whereas this feature is not always present in the later images. Vaudeville (1980, p. 6) says that in Shri Nathji "these characteristics of ancient Mathura iconography are preserved."

Chaitanya Excavates Images at Nandeshvar Hill

After seeing the image of Gopal (Shri Nathji), which was still present at Govardhan Hill during his time, Chaitanya continued on his pilgrimage to a lake called Pavana Sarovara [see Plate XXI, Figure 2]. Afterwards, he climbed the nearby Nandeshvar Hill. He asked villagers if there were any sacred images nearby. The villagers said they had heard some images were in a cave on the hill. The *Chaitanya-charitamrta* (*Madhya* 18.61) says that Chaitanya excavated the cave and found images of Nanda and Yashoda (Krishna's father and mother) along with an image of child Krishna. Later, Sanatana Goswami, one of Chaitanya's followers, established a temple for the images on the top of the hill [see Plate XXI, Figure 1]. This place is called Nandagram or Nandagaon (the village of Nanda). During my visit in November 2005, a temple priest, Shri Hari Vallabh Goswami, told me that beneath the temple the cave where the images were found is still there, but only the temple priests are allowed to enter.

Discovery of the Dauji Deity

At around the same time Chaitanya was in the Braj Mandal, Vallabha was also there. The followers of Vallabha made discoveries like those made by Chaitanya and his followers. One of these cases is described by Haberman (1994, pp. 210–211). An image of Krishna's brother Balarama, called Dauji (a nickname meaning "big brother"), according to traditional sources, was installed by King Vajranabha in ancient times at Baldeo. The image was later hidden in a *kund* to protect it from Muslim invaders. According to Pushti Marg sources, the image [see Plate XXII, Figure 1] was rediscovered by Gokulnath (1551–1647), one of the seven grandsons of Vallabha. Gokulnath learned that a cow was pouring milk on a stone protruding from the ground [see Plate XXII, Figure 3] on the edge of the Kshir Sagar Kund [see Plate XXII, Figure 4]. Gokulnath excavated the image and constructed a temple [see Plate XXII, Figure 2] to house it.

Entwistle (1987, p. 421) says: "The large image of Balarama in the main temple here is certainly ancient, perhaps dating from the Kushana period. R. C. Sharma, while he was director of the museum at Mathura, had a chance to examine it and noted underneath the black patina it had acquired from repeated burning of incense and application of oil, that it is carved from the spotted red sandstone characteristic of early Mathura sculpture." The Kushan period in Mathura goes back to the first and second centuries CE. The attribution of the Baldeo Balarama image to the Kushan period tends to confirm that Vaishnava saints at the time of Chaitanya and Vallabha were recovering genuinely old images. The image of Balarama at Baldeo features a hood of serpent heads, as does a second century CE sandstone Kushan image of Balarama in the collection of the Mathura Museum (no. 14.406, R. C. Sharma 1994, fig. xvii). It came from the Kachahrighat well in Mathura city.

Lokanatha Discovers a Krishna Image

Even before Chaitanya himself came to the Braj Mandal, he sent there one of his followers, Lokanatha Goswami, from Bengal, with instructions to excavate lost sacred images and sacred places of Krishna's pastimes. According to *Bhakti-ratnakara,* he settled near Kishori Kund [see **Plate XXIII, Figure 3**] and found there an image of Krishna called Vinoda [see **Plate XXIII, Figure 1**]. He worshiped it simply, along with an image of Radha. The Radha Vinoda images were later moved to the Radha Gokulananda temple in the town of Vrindavan. At the time of the Muslim attacks during the reign of the Mogul emperor Aurangzeb, the Radha Vinoda images were relocated to Jaipur, where they can be seen in the Vinodlal temple. Today there is a small temple on the banks of Kishori Kund. The temple houses replica images of Radha Vinoda and a shrine to Lokanatha Goswami [see **Plate XXIII, Figure 2**]. According to a document kept in the temple, Krishna informed Lokanath in a dream that an image of him was to be found in the *kund* and Lokanatha excavated it.

Discoveries by Other Followers of Chaitanya

Chaitanya ordered others of his principal followers, including Rupa Goswami and Sanatana Goswami, to carry on the work of rediscovering the lost places of Krishna's pastimes in Vrindavan. This is recorded in the *Chaitanya-charitamrita* (*Adi.* 10.90): *lupta tirtha uddharana vrindavane:* "you should uncover the lost pilgrimage places in Vrindavan." Among the definitions for *uddharana* given in Apte's Sanskrit dictionary are "drawing out," "extraction," and "extrication." Some translators, such as Bhaktivedanta Swami Prabhupada, have used the word "excavate." Krishnadasa Kaviraja Goswami says in *Chaitanya-charitamrita* (*Antya.* 2.128): "Rupa Goswami and Sanatana Goswami collected many revealed scriptures, and from the evidence in those scriptures they excavated all the lost sites of pilgrimage. Thus they established temples for the worship of Lord Krishna." This shows the deliberate nature of their search and reminds one of techniques employed by modern Classical and historical archeologists.

Among the images discovered by Rupa Goswami was the image of Krishna called Govindadeva. The account is given in the early 18th century *Bhakti Ratnakara* of Narahari Chakravarti, and is accessibly retold by Haberman (1994, pp. 32–33). After much searching, Rupa had been unable to find Govindadeva, one of the images originally installed by Vajranabha. Rupa sat on the bank of the Yamuna River, lamenting his failure. According to *Bhakti Ratnakara,* Krishna revealed to Rupa that the image was to be found on the Gomatila hill. Rupa assembled some villagers and conducted an excavation that led to the discovery of the image [see **Plate XXIV, Figure 2**]. This occurred in 1534. Later, a local Hindu king named Man Singh built a large stone temple for Govindadeva [see **Plate XXIV, Figure 1**]. This temple was partially destroyed by Muslims at the time of Aurangzeb, and the Govindadeva image was moved to Jaipur, where it is still worshiped today. The image is a *muralidhara* form, with Krishna holding a flute. Such *muralidhara* images of Krishna can be found in India going back to the 12th century CE (Bhattacharya 1996, pp. 61–62).

Man Singh, who built the temple for Govindadeva, himself discovered sacred images by folk archeological methods. One of these was Shila Mata, an image of Shiva's consort Durga, in the form of Mahishasuramardini—Durga as the killer (*mardini*) of a demon (*asura*) who had taken the form of a buffalo (*mahisha*). Asher (p. 220) says the location of the image in a river was revealed to Man Singh in a dream. Afterwards, he brought the image to his palace in the Amber Fort, in Rajasthan, and built a small temple for it. Asher says (p. 220) the image "appears to be in the Pala-Sena style, dating to about the twelfth century." Although not from the Braj Mandal, this image provides another example of a recovered object being substantially older than the time of discovery, and adds credibility to the archeological discoveries made by Chaitanya and his followers.

Discoveries by Narayana Bhatta

The work of the first Gaudiya Vaishnava Goswamis was carried on by Narayana Bhatta Goswami (Haberman 1994, pp. 56–60). He was born in south India in 1534. According to his biography, while he was still a boy Krishna appeared to him and told him to go to the Braj Mandal to rediscover his pastime places. Narayana Bhatta arrived in Vrindavan in 1545. There he met Gaudiya Vaishnavas such as Sanatana Goswami and Krishnadasa Brahmachari, who accepted him as a disciple. Narayana Bhatta is credited with rediscovering dozens of Krishna's pastime places, including: (1) four important ponds around Govardhan Hill: Manasi Ganga, Kusum Sarovara, Govinda-kund, and Chandra Sarovara; (2) the birthplace of Krishna in Mathura; (3) the sites of Krishna's early childhood pastimes in Gokul, including the house of his parents Nanda and Yashoda; (4) the sites where Krishna killed the many-headed Kaliya serpent and the horse-demon Keshi; (5) Barshana, the town of Krishna's beloved Radha; (6) the place of Krishna's secret forest meetings with Radha; and (7) the locations of the twelve forests of the Braj Mandal. He laid out the Braj Mandal pilgrimage route that is still followed today.

Narayana Bhatta excavated several images (Haberman 1994, pp. 59–60). The location of the Balarama image at Unchagaon was revealed to him in a vision. Narayana Bhatta gathered some villagers, and with his crew excavated the image of Balarama [see **Plate XXVI, Figure 1**], for which he built a temple [see **Plate XXVI, Figure 3**] in Unchagaon, where the image remains today. The *prakata-sthala*, or place of the image's discovery, is said to be at the base of a tree that grows at the rear of the temple [see **Plate XXVI, Figure 2**]. Once Narayana Bhatta was climbing a hill at Barshana, south of Unchagaon. In a vision, Radha revealed to him that images of her and Krishna were buried on the hill. Narayana Bhatta excavated the images and installed them in a temple on the top of the hill [see **Plate XXVII**].

Were There Really Lost Temples and Deities?

Implicit in the accounts I have given is the assumption that there were in fact lost things to be found. Vaudeville (1976) argued that there were no lost shrines in the

Braj Mandal area for the Gaudiya Vaishnavas and followers of Vallabha to rediscover when they came there in the early 16th century. Speaking against this are some things that Vaudeville herself includes in her study. First, a large temple, housing a deity of Krishna called Keshava, existed in Mathura up to the early 11th century, when it was destroyed by Mahmud of Ghazni (Vaudeville 1976, p. 200). The narratives of Krishna's pastimes at various locations throughout the Braj Mandal were certainly known at this time. For example, the *Bhagavata Purana,* which contains extensive descriptions and glorifications of Krishna's pastimes in many locales in the Braj Mandal, dates back at least as far as the 10th century (Rocher 1986, pp. 147–148), and Vaishnava tradition says it goes back much further. So it is hard to imagine that there could be a large and popular temple celebrating Krishna in Mathura, and that there would be no contemporary shrines or images of Krishna in the nearby places associated with Krishna. Vaudeville (1976, p. 195) notes carved stone images of Krishna dating to the Gupta period (4–6th centuries AD) show him holding up Govardhan Hill and killing the multiheaded serpent Kaliya at a place called Kaliyaghat on the Yamuna River in the Braja Mandal. Once more, it is hard to imagine that artists of the region were producing images of Krishna directly connected to Braj Mandal locales without there being any shrines in the nearby locales themselves. Entwistle (1987) cites evidence for a Gupta-era Vaishnava temple near Satoha on the road from Mathura to Govardhan (p. 129) and 12th century Vaishnava temples at Kaman and Mahaban (p. 123) in the Braj Mandal. Finally, the accounts of excavations of images recorded by the followers of Chaitanya and Vallabha themselves attest to the existence of lost shrines and images. It may, however, be true that the shrines in the Braj Mandal region outside Mathura and other large settlements were not monumental. They could have been quite simple. Even today, the hills, forests, ponds, and rivers of the Braj Mandal are themselves considered sacred, not just the shrines and images.

Should This Be Called Archeology?

According to Trigger (1989, p. 30), activities like those carried out by Chaitanya and his followers should not be called archeology, because, as with similar cases he records, "There was absolutely no awareness that the material remains of the past could be used to test . . . speculations about human origins and the general outlines of human history." But modern archeology has come to include more than using physical remains to test theories about the past. Today, a professional archeologist is much more likely to be working in heritage or cultural resource management (CRM) than in doing excavations exclusively for testing theories. The recovery of images and landscape features in the Braj Mandal is similar to modern archeological work in heritage management. In this case, knowledge of a heritage resource (the lost images and sacred sites of the Braj Mandal) was conserved in documents and memories. Chaitanya and his followers, and other Vaishnavas and their followers, used this knowledge to recover and restore this heritage resource for the benefit of Krishna worshipers. Using the term archeology for their activities is thus appropriate.

In this paper I have mentioned only a few of the many examples of the recovery of sacred images and landscape in the Braj Mandal what to speak of other locales in every part of India (Vaudeville 1980, pp. 29–30, note 30). The scope of sustained archeological activity carried out in the Braj Mandal by the followers of Chaitanya, and Vallabha, and other Vaishnava teachers, is impressive. It was an extensive indigenous archeological undertaking, carried out deliberately and systematically. The work of rediscovery of lost sites and images took place over an entire region, including a major urban center and many towns and villages as well as rural locations. In his *Vraja Bhakti Vilasa,* Narayana Bhatta enumerated hundreds of linked sites within the Braj Mandal, a symbolic lotus with a circumference of 168 miles (Haberman 1994, p. 59). Some of the Braj Mandal Goswamis employed a methodology much like that of modern Classical or medieval archeologists in Europe, in that historical texts were used to guide archeological exploration. The purpose of this extensive indigenous archeological work was not simply to collect artifacts and expose sites, but rather to bring them back to life, so that people could experience what it was (and is) like to be with Krishna in the Braj Mandal. The work was one of restoring social memory of the earthly Braj Mandal of the past, thus facilitating present access to the eternal Braj Mandal, which the earthly Braj Mandal replicates.

Conclusion

The claim that there was no archeology or archeological literature in India prior to the coming of the Europeans relies on definitions of archeology that prevent recognition of cognate activities in other cultures. I propose we should define archeology in such a way as to include all human cognitive engagement with material objects that the discoverers understood as having been made by or otherwise associated with past human or humanlike beings. I am not claiming that the recovery of the lost images and sacred sites of the Braj Mandal and modern archeology are exactly the same. What I am proposing is that there is enough of a resemblance to warrant including both within the boundaries of the term archeology.

Works Cited

Apte, V. S. (1965) *The Practical Sanskrit-English Dictionary,* fourth revised and enlarged edition, Delhi: Motilal Banarsidass.

Asher, C. B. (1996) Kacchavaha pride and prestige: the temple patronage of Raja Mana Simha, in Case, M. H., *Govindadeva: A Dialogue in Stone.* New Delhi: Indira Gandhi National Centre for the Arts, pp. 215–238.

Bhaktivedanta Swami Prabhupada, A. C. (1996) *Shri Chaitanya-charitamrita* of Krishnadasa Kaviraja. English translation and commentary, with original Bengali text, in nine volumes. Los Angeles: Bhaktivedanta Book Trust International.

Bhakti-ratnakara of Narahari Chakravarti, Fifth Wave: *Mathura Mandala Parikrama* translation by Pundarika Vidyanidhi (1992) Vrindavan.

Bhakti-ratnakara of Narahari Chakravarti, anon. English translation from the website http://www.russiantext.com/russian_library/library/asiatica/indica/authors/

narahari_cakravarti/br-total.doc

Bhattacharya, S. K. (1996) *Krishna-Cult in Indian Art.* New Delhi: M. D. Publications.

Brahmacari, Rajasekhara Dasa (1999) *The Colour Guide to Radha-kunda.* Vrindavan: Vedanta Vision Publications

Bryant, Edwin (2003) *Krishna: The Beautiful Legend of God (Srimad Bhagavata Purana).* London: Penguin Books (Penguin Classics).

Chakrabarti, D. K. (2001) *A History of Indian Archaeology from the Beginning to 1947.* New Delhi: Munshirama Manoharlal Publishers.

Entwistle, A. W. (1987) *Braj: Centre of Krishna Pilgrimage.* Groningen: Egbert Forsten.

Goswami, S. (1996) Govinda darsana: lotus in stone, in Case, M. H., *Govindadeva: A Dialogue in Stone.* New Delhi: Indira Gandhi National Centre for the Arts, pp. 269–277.

Growse, F. S. (1890) *Mathura: A District Memoir.* 3rd edition. India: Northwestern Provinces and Oudh Government Press. Reprint 1979. New Delhi: Asian Educational Services.

Haberman, D. L. (1994) *Journey Through the Twelve Forests: An Encounter with Krishna.* Oxford: Oxford University Press.

Mahanidhi Swami (1995) *Radha Kunda Mahima Madhuri.* Vrindavan: Mahanidhi Swami.

Rocher, L. (1986) *The Puranas.* Wiesbaden: Otto Harrassowitz.

Sharma, R. C. (1994) *The Splendour of Mathura Arts & Museum.* New Delhi: DK Printworld.

Trigger, B. G. (1989) *A History of Archaeological Thought.* Cambridge: Cambridge University Press.

Vaudeville, C. (1976) Braja, lost and found, *Indo-Iranian Journal* 18: 195–213.

Vaudeville, C. (1980) The Govardhan myth in northern India, *Indo-Iranian Journal* 22: 1–45.

22

The Forbidden Zone:
Archeology and Archeologists in an Invented
Civilization *(Planet of the Apes)*

I presented this paper at the annual meeting of the European Association of Archaeologists, held in Zadar, Croatia, September 18–23, 2007. I presented the paper in a session called Invented Civilizations, organized by archeologists Michael Jasmin and Cornelius Holtorf. It was quite a popular session at the conference. This paper does not have a formal bibliography. Essential reference information is included in the text.

In 1963, the novel *Planet des Singes* by Pierre Boulle appeared. In 1968, the book was turned into a Hollywood film called *Planet of the Apes*, starring Charlton Heston. The film was popular internationally, and generated four film sequels, as well as television programs, comic books, and merchandise. The film is still referenced in popular culture as well as in scientific publications. For example, in September 2006, *Scientific American* published a special edition titled *Planet of the Apes, Becoming Human: Evolution and the Rise of Intelligence.* And in *Journal of Evolutionary Biology* (1999, vol. 12, no. 1, p. 200), we find Richard J. Smith giving the title "Planet of the Apes" to his review of the book *Function, Phylogeny, and Fossils: Miocene Hominoid Evolution and Adaptations* by David R. Begun *et al.* (1997). In the film *Planet of the Apes,* one of the main characters is an ape archeologist, and archeology plays a key role in ape society. An analysis of the role of archeologists and archeology in the invented civilization of the planet of the apes can shed light on the role and practices of archeologists in our own human civilization.

I did not see *Planet of the Apes* in 1968 when it first came out. At that time, I was a twenty-year old student at the George Washington University in Washington, D.C. I was aware of the film, but I was not attracted to see it. Astronauts among apemen on another planet? It sounded like a typical Hollywood fantasy, a popcorn film suitable for children of twelve years or less. I quite deliberately refused to see it. I fancied I had more adult sensibilities. I was regularly going to an art film theater called the Biograph to see films by Antonioni, Fellini, Bergman, Godard, Renoir and others. I was only inspired to see *Planet of the Apes* when I started to think about which invented civilization to pick for my paper in this session on "Invented Civilizations" at this conference of the European Association of Archaeologists. Having now finally seen *Planet of the Apes*, I confess that my 1968 prejudgment was wrong—I find it to be an exceptionally deep, complex, and intellectually stimulating film, as well as being good popcorn fun.

In this paper, I am not going to attempt to sketch an overall theory of archeology based on a comprehensive, consistent analysis of the film. Rather I am just going to capriciously select some scenes from the film that will let me respond in a limited, and perhaps also capricious, way to the following question posed by the organizers of this session in their session proposal: "What are these fictions telling us about the public's interest in the past or about the archaeological way of documenting and exhibiting archaeological sites and finds?"

My selection and explication of events and persons from the film is, of course, going to be governed by my personal point of view, my prejudices, my ontological commitments, my history, etc. Let me give some brief indication of what they are. First, of all, I am a bit of an outsider at this meeting of the European Association of Archaeologists, being, in the strict sense, neither a European nor an archaeologist, although I can say that my grandparents were Italians and I have been peripherally associated with archaeologists for over twenty years through my work. And what might my "work" be? We could call it inter-traditional (or cross-cultural) communication on human origins and antiquity. Therefore one might further ask what tradition I claim to represent. Since the early 1970s, I have been a practitioner of a kind of Hindu devotional mysticism, which I learned from my guru Bhaktivedanta Swami Prabhupada (1896–1877), who introduced these teachings to the world outside India through the International Society for Krishna Consciousness. So I have deeply entered into a tradition different from that into which I was born. My practice has an internal mystical aspect but also an external scholarly aspect to it, which includes study of the ancient Sanskrit literature. One part of this literature, the *Puranas,* contains accounts of human origins (spiritual) and antiquity (extreme) somewhat different from those now prevalent in the knowledge tradition represented by modern scientific archeology. So I have been in dialogue with archeologists, historians of science, and others about this for twenty years, through books like *Forbidden Archeology* (with R. L. Thompson), *Forbidden Archeology's Impact*, and *Human Devolution: A Vedic Alternative to Darwin's Theory,* as well as through presentations of papers at conferences on archeology, anthropology, and history of science (while simultaneously busying myself with my more mystical pursuits).

I regard the whole of what I am doing as a contribution to the program advocated by Paul Feyerabend in his book *Science in A Free Society* (1978, London, Verso Editions, pp. 9–10): "A free society is a society in which all traditions have equal rights and equal access to the centres of power (this differs from the customary definition where individuals have equal rights of access to positions defined by a special tradition—the tradition of Western Science and Rationalism). . . . How can a society that gives all traditions equal rights be realized? . . . People in many countries now realize that the law gives them more leeway than they had assumed; they gradually conquer the free space that has so far been occupied by specialists and they try to expand it further."

With this introduction, I hope that you now have some basis for judging how and why I select and interpret certain scenes from *Planet of the Apes*. I am, of course, vulnerable to criticism of the kind "you picked this scene, which supports your ideas, but neglected to mention this other scene, which does not support your ideas." Or, "You did not mention that the planet of the apes is (as revealed in the film's final scene) really the earth." I plead guilty to all such charges. But I would hope you will not insist on total consistency with the whole of *Planet of the Apes* as an absolute requirement for this little intellectual exercise of mine. (I note, however, that in the original novel, the planet of the apes is in fact a planet different from our earth planet.)

In the 1968 film version of *Planet of the Apes*, an American astronaut named Taylor, played by Charlton Heston, crash lands with his crew in a lake on an unknown planet. They escape from their sinking spaceship, taking a raft to the shores of a desolate mountainous desert, with no sign of life. After crossing the desert, they come to a green, semi-forested area, where they observe humans foraging for food in lush agricultural fields. The astronauts join the speechless humans, who appear to be on the level of animals, in feeding on fruits and vegetables. Suddenly, the humans begin to flee, pursued by bands of intelligent gorillas, clad in dark military dress, riding on horses and armed with rifles. Some of the humans, including Taylor, are captured and taken to an ape city. Because of a wound suffered during his capture, Taylor temporarily loses the ability to speak. In his captivity, Taylor learns that the ape population has three classes—the gorillas, who serve as soldiers and laborers; the orangutans, who serve as administrators; and the chimpanzees, who serve as research scientists and intellectuals. Speechless humans, of a low level of culture, are treated as animals. Mostly they live in the wild, but some are kept as research animals.

During one of his attempted escapes, Taylor runs through an ape museum of natural history. The museum has displays showing the ape version of humans and their history. According to official ape science, humans are now and always have been speechless animals, with a very low level of intelligence. They live in the forests, and sometimes become a nuisance by raiding the apes' agricultural fields. Humans kill other humans, whereas apes never kill other apes. Taylor, running through the museum, frightens an ape mother and child who had been viewing the exhibits. It is as if an australopithecine in a natural history museum on our planet were to break out of his (or her) display and terrorize the Sunday visitors (maybe not a bad idea!).

The presence of the ape mother and child in the museum reminds us that the ape museum is there to educate the ape public. As in many modern museums, authorship of the exhibits is hidden, giving the appearance of bare objective truth. The hidden authors of the displays are, we can infer, ape scientists, acting in concert, we can also infer, with the political leaders of the ape state that funded the building of the public museum.

In his recent book *Archaeology Is A Brand* (2007, p.107), Cornelius Holtorf outlines three approaches to the relationship between science (including archeology) and society: "*The Education Model*, which involves the gaining of reliable knowledge by an elite of scientists and its subsequent distribution to those with knowledge 'deficits' contributing to their enlightenment and competence as citizens. *The Public Relations Model*, which seeks to improve the public image of science in order to secure its license to practice and increase social and political support for science, science spending and science legislation. . . . *The Democratic Model*, which . . . is based on participatory processes in which non-scientists predominate." There is no doubt about which model the ape museum embodies—it is clearly the education model. Like most state-funded museums of natural history in our world, the ape museum presents one point of view in its exhibits. Humans are lower than apes. Apes are superior to humans.

Michael Shanks says in his book *Experiencing the Past* (1992, p. 29) that "different social groups in the present may well develop different pasts." Taylor, the astronaut, sees the museum exhibits differently than the ape woman and child. He is shocked to see the dead, stuffed body of one of his astronaut comrades on display in the museum. In looking at the stuffed astronaut, the ape woman and child would just see another human animal from the planet of the apes. That's how he was displayed—the ape curators were unaware of his astronaut status, and considered him just another specimen of the humans of their experience. But Taylor knows that his dead comrade, now a museum exhibit, was a different kind of human, a human from another planet, a human who once manifested high intelligence and the power of speech. Like Taylor, the exhibited astronaut was a member of a human civilization that sent a vehicle across interstellar space. In short, Taylor does not accept the message that the hidden authors of the exhibits in the ape museum are trying to communicate to their museum visitors—that humans are, and always have been, inferior to apes.

When I enter any modern museum of natural history, and see the usual displays about human evolution, I feel like Taylor in the museum on the planet of the apes. I do not accept the message that the hidden authors of the human evolution exhibits are trying to communicate to their museum visitors. I have my own sense of my present and past. In 2006, I was on a lecture tour of South Africa. I took the chance to visit the Sterkfontein Caves, now a United Nations World Heritage Site, advertised as the Cradle of Humanity. Before visitors are taken down into the caves, they wait in a museum. The first big panel in the small but very well designed museum welcomes visitors with these words superimposed over an x-ray image of a human skull in profile: Discover Your Self. Okay, that sounds good. I want to discover my self. But what kind of self does the museum lead its visitors to discover? Prominently displayed among the exhibits illustrating the evolution of modern humans from earlier hominins is a large panel with a blow up of this well-known quote from the book *The Selfish Gene* by Richard Dawkins: "We are survival machines—robot vehicles programmed to preserve the selfish molecules known as genes." After discovering my self as a robot vehicle, a survival machine, I went on the guided tour to the caves. Led by our guide, we exited the museum and proceeded outdoors along the "evolution walk", a long path lined on either side with boulders containing display fossils showing the evolution of life from single celled organisms up to humans (sort of like the Stations of the Cross). I felt like I was on a religious pilgrimage. We then arrived at the entrance to the caves, and descended into the earth. Deep in one of the caves, we saw the sacred discovery site of the australopithecine named Little Foot, viewing it with as much reverence as pilgrims view the birthplace of the   Christ Child in a cavern beneath the Church of the Nativity in Bethlehem. Coming out, we were led to a bronze bust of one of the saints of evolution studies, Robert Broom, discoverer of some of the original Sterkfontein hominin fossils, and paid our respects.

In their book *Re-constructing Archaeology* (2ⁿᵈ edition, 1992, p. 98), Michael Shanks and Christopher Tilley characterize the museum as "an ideological institution", an institution that sometimes "distorts the past as a means of legitimatizing present sectional interests." In the museum "the present recognizes itself and is justified" (p. 97). The museum, like archeology generally, is more about the present than the past. The museum is active in shaping present values. So what kinds of values emerge from the idea, presented in the Sterkfontein museum, that we are robot vehicles, survival machines, etc.? It would seem that such a starkly material sense of self leads to values that encourage competition for the control and exploitation of matter, and therein, I believe, we have the root of the environmental crisis and the violent struggles for control of material resources like oil. I myself favor an alternative view of human nature and human origins, one that I propose would lead to a different set of values. I do not share the view of the human past presented in the museum at Sterkfontein.

So what is the solution to the problem of how museums should take into account the different pasts of different knowledge traditions? Shanks and Tilley make some interesting suggestions in *Re-constructing Archaeology*, among them (p. 99): "Allow community use of museum artifacts, people constructing and presenting their own pasts in the museum." In other words, let Taylor make his own exhibit in the public museum of natural history on the planet of the apes. Or, to put it in earth terms, why not let some Christian creationists come into a tax supported public museum of natural history on our planet and make a temporary exhibit (Shanks and Tilley suggest all exhibits *should* be obviously temporary) about their Adam and Eve view of human history? Some will object on grounds of separation of church and state. In that case, perhaps we should remove all paintings with Christian themes from state supported art museums. Perhaps we should also remove from state supported museums all paintings and sculptures from classical Greece. We do not want secular state supported museums promoting the religion of paganism, do we? If there is a place for Christian paintings in public art museums, there is a place for Christian exhibits on human origins in natural history museums.

I suspect I am taking the suggestion of Shanks and Tilley further than they intended. But Feyerabend, I think, would have approved, although in *Science In A Free Society* (p. 83) he is careful to point out that what he favors is a political relativism (the idea that all knowledge traditions have equal rights to exist in the state and its institutions) and not a philosophical relativism (the idea that all knowledge traditions are equally true). He just suggests that in a democratic society, the truth value of traditions should be established in fair interactions among the traditions. Today, the conditions for such fair interaction do not exist, because the tradition of modern materialistic science has attained monopoly status as a kind of state-supported religion and now rather zealously excludes alternative knowledge traditions, especially from the state education system. Feyerabend observes (p. 10) that representatives of modern scientific rationalism now have the competitive advantage of "using tax money to destroy the traditions of the taxpayers." He points out (p. 103) that these "traditions can become powerful rivals and can reveal many shortcomings of science if only they were given a fair chance to compete," adding that "it is the task of the institutions of a free society to give them such a fair chance."

One of these institutions is the public, tax supported museum. Directors of public museums using the tax money of all the people should feel obligated to take into account the diversity of knowledge traditions in the tax paying population. Private museums are another question. They can be allowed to represent a specific tradition, like Darwinism, Christian creationism, Australian aboriginal creation accounts, etc. But public museums should be more open to a variety of knowledge traditions.

In his captivity on the planet of the apes, Taylor is studied by Dr. Zira, a chimpanzee scientist who does research in animal (in this case human) psychology. Taylor is one of her lab animals. During his capture, Taylor's throat was wounded, and he lost his ability to speak. So at first he appeared to Zira like an ordinary speechless human animal. By writing messages on pieces of paper, Taylor convinces Zira that he is able to use language. This contradicts one of the main doctrines of ape science, namely that humans are mentally and physiologically incapable of language, of speech. Zira tells her chimpanzee colleague and fiancé Dr. Cornelius, an archeologist, about Taylor's remarkable abilities. Cornelius himself has made some remarkable discoveries related to the history of humans and apes on the planet of the apes. In a cave in the Forbidden Zone, the desert wasteland where Taylor's spaceship crashed, Cornelius had found archeological evidence for an advanced human culture preceding that of the apes. So Zira and Cornelius have two categories of evidence that challenge the orthodox views of ape science on humans. They have evidence that humans can speak and that humans with a culture superior to that of the apes had once existed on their planet.

These ideas about advanced human intelligence and past cultural superiority of humans to apes are quite dangerous to the established ape civilization. Dr. Zaius, an orangutan, who serves as the ape minister of science, cautions Zira and Cornelius. When they persist in trying to draw his attention to the abilities of Taylor, they are called along with Taylor before a government tribunal, which includes Dr. Zaius. Taylor is dismissed as a freak of nature (Zaius threatens to have him neutered and sent to a brain research lab for a lobotomy), and Zira and Cornelius are accused of scientific heresy.

Here a particular scientific party (represented by Zaius) maintains its views with the aid of the state over other scientific views (represented by Zira and Cornelius), with the aim of upholding an ape society that depends on keeping humans, including Taylor, in the status of subordinate animals. We see things like this happening on earth today. A dominant scientific party committed to a particular theory of ape-human relationships (the Darwinian theory of human evolution), seeks to maintain its authority and power by identifying its interests with those of the state and by using the compliant state to suppress alternative views. In recent years in the United States, Darwinist scientists have used the state's judicial system to suppress even the slightest expression of alternative views, such as creationism and intelligent design, in the state education systems.

This sort of thing is also happening in Europe. On June 8, 2007, the Committee on Culture, Science, and Education of the Council of Europe submitted to the Council a "Report on the Dangers of Creationism in Education" along with a draft legislative proposal (www.assembly.coe.int/Main.asp?link=/Documents/WorkingDocs/Doc07/EDOC11927.htm). The draft resolution states: "The teaching of all phenomena concerning evolution as a fundamental scientific theory is . . . crucial to the future of our societies and our democracies. For that reason it must occupy a central position in the curriculum, and especially in the science syllabus." Evolution science and the state are one. The resolution calls on the 47 member states to vigorously oppose the introduction of any alternatives to evolution from other knowledge traditions, especially anything related to creationism or intelligent design. Here we find an attempt to have the state guarantee the position of the Darwinian theory of evolution, over all other views.

What should be done? On May 4, 2006, in a talk to educators and government education officials at the School of Education Studies, University of Kwazulu-Natal, Edgewood Campus, in South Africa, I made the following proposal, "First, education policy makers should recognize that today the vast majority of scientists accept the theory of evolution. This is a fact. But it is also a fact that some in the world of science, a small number, do not accept the theory and are proposing theistic alternatives, and education policy makers should recognize this. The proper solution is that the theory of evolution and its supporters should be given most of the time in the classroom and most of the pages in the textbooks. But a small amount of classroom time and a small number of textbook pages should be devoted to neutrally presenting the theistic alternatives to the current theory of evolution. How small? I would suggest 5 percent of the classroom time and 5 percent of the textbook pages. But I will leave it up to you."

To escape repression by the combined forces of orthodox ape science and the ape state, Zira, Cornelius, and Taylor (with a human female named Nova) escape to the Forbidden Zone. They go to the cave site that had been discovered by Cornelius.

The existence of archeology and archeologists on the planet of the apes raises an important issue about archeology on earth. Cornelius represents an archeological tradition independent of earth archeology. We could call it an indigenous archeology. On our planet, when archeologists speak of indigenous archeology, they usually mean involving indigenous peoples in the work of modern scientific archeology, as stakeholders, assistants, informants, permission givers, owners in full or in part of the finds and research results. It may also mean giving indigenous people the chance to enter universities for archeological training, enlisting them in the ranks of professional archeologists. It seems to me that very little attention is given to the ways that indigenous people relate to the physical remains of the past, independent of modern scientific archeology and their involvement with it. We need a meta-archeology that can accommodate not just modern scientific archeology but the ways of understanding the physical remains of the past practiced by members of other knowledge traditions, which I propose can also be called archeologies. In several (as yet unpublished) papers presented at meetings of the World Archaeological Congress and the European Association of South Asian Archaeologists, I have explored the existence of such an independent indigenous archeological tradition in India. [Note: One of the papers has since been published: M. A. Cremo (2008) Excavating the eternal: an indigenous archaeological tradition in

India. *Antiquity* 82: 178–188. A version of this paper is included in this volume.]

As soon as Taylor, Nova, Zira, and Cornelius arrive outside the cave, which is situated high above them on a seaside cliff, they are intercepted by a squadron of gorilla soldiers led by Dr. Zaius. But Taylor manages to turn the tables by capturing Zaius. Together, Zaius, Taylor, Nova, Zira, and Cornelius go into the cave. Cornelius, the ape archeologist, shows them the excavations. He points out a location where he found ape bones with primitive stone tools. He explains that below that level he had found human bones with signs of a culture much more advanced than that of the ancient apes. At one point, Taylor starts going through some of the objects, and finds some eye glasses and also some metal rings that he recognizes as part of an artificial heart. But the key artifact is a doll, in the form of a human female infant. Amazingly, it has a voice mechanism and speaks simple human words. The archeological evidence, especially the doll, challenges the whole orthodox ape science view of the relationship between humans and apes. It turns out that humans of the past could not only speak but were once technologically superior to apes, thus shaking the ideological foundations of the ape state and culture.

Emerging from the cave, Taylor ties up Dr. Zaius. Then Taylor and Nova, on horseback, decide to journey further into the Forbidden Zone. Taylor asks Zira and Cornelius to come with them, but they refuse. They are part of the ape civilization and do not want to leave their culture behind. As Taylor and Nova ride away, Zira and Cornelius release Dr. Zaius, who tells them that they might have to stand trial but hints they will get off easily. Dr. Zaius then orders the gorilla soldiers to blow up the cave, destroying the archeological evidence in it.

So what lessons can archeologists learn from this popular invented civilization? The popularity of the film shows that depictions of relatively complex relations between archeology and the state, archeology and the public, and archeology and worldviews can be attractive to a good many people. I would say that the film does a better job of communicating these things to people than anything they might encounter in an archeology museum. In their discussion of museums, Shanks and Tilley (p. 98) make this recommendation: "Introduce political content into conventional displays—show how the past may be manipulated and misrepresented for present purposes." *Planet of the Apes* does this; a good many archeological museum displays do not. From *Planet of the Apes*, archeologists can learn how not to present the past to the public in state supported museums. Do not organize such museums on an oppressive education model, do not present just one worldview. As Shanks and Tilley put it (p. 97), "We must oppose professional preservative History with its archaeologist-curator speaking for a monolithic and murdered past." Do not be willing partners with the state in suppressing or marginalizing alternative worldviews. Archeologists should be aware of their role in forming their audience's concept of self, and how concept of self influences the goals people set for themselves individually and collectively. The existence of ape archeology on the planet of the apes should sensitize archeologists to the existence of other archeologies, independent of modern scientific archeology on this planet. Finally, archeologists should be aware that there might be the equivalent of an archeological forbidden zone on this planet, with evidence contradicting current theories of human origins and antiquity.

Postscript

A few years ago, I was a consultant for a television documentary called *The Mysterious Origins of Man*. Produced by American filmmaker Bill Cote, it aired on the National Broadcasting Company (NBC), a major U.S. television network. The program featured, among other things, material from my book *Forbidden Archeology*, and both my coauthor and I appeared in the show. The show was hosted by, of all people, Charlton Heston, who said in one of the opening scenes: "What happens when we find a modern human skull in rock strata far beneath even the oldest of man's ancestors? In their controversial book, *Forbidden Archeology*, Michael Cremo and Dr. Richard Thompson have documented hundreds of these anomalous artifacts." Here we find echoes of *Planet of the Apes*. Charlton Heston was still speaking like Taylor, and I was put into a role like that of Cornelius, speaking about forbidden archeological evidence that challenges conventional accounts of human origins.

A museum also entered the story. When Bill Cote was filming the documentary, I advised him to go to the Phoebe Hearst Museum of Anthropology at the University of California at Berkeley, because I knew that some anomalously old artifacts from the California gold mines were present in the museum collections [**see Plates XIII-XV**]. In the nineteenth century, gold was discovered in California. To get it, miners dug tunnels into the sides of mountains, such as Table Mountain in Tuolumne County [**see Plate XII**]. Deep inside the tunnels, in deposits of early Eocene age (about 50 million years old), miners found human bones and artifacts. The discoveries were carefully documented by Dr. J. D. Whitney, the chief government geologist of California, in his book *The Auriferous Gravels of the Sierra Nevada of California*, published by Harvard University's Museum of Comparative Zoology in 1880. But we do not hear very much about these discoveries today. In the *Smithsonian Institution Annual Report for 1898–1899* (p. 424), anthropologist William Holmes said, "Perhaps if Professor Whitney had fully appreciated the story of human evolution as it is understood today, he would have hesitated to announce the conclusions formulated, notwithstanding the imposing array of testimony with which he was confronted." In other words, if the facts did not fit the theory of human evolution, the facts had to be set aside, and that is exactly what happened.

What happened when Bill Cote went to the museum to get permission to film the artifacts? "At first we were told they could not make the time," he wrote in a letter to me (August 26, 1996). "We countered saying we had plenty of time and could wait three or four months." Museum officials responded with a letter claiming they had a shortage of staff and funds. Cote said he would pay all the costs involved in bringing the artifacts out of storage for filming, including overtime pay for the workers. The museum refused this offer. The producers continued to seek permission through various channels. "We patiently went all the way to the head of publicity for the University," explained Bill Cote in his letter, "but it seems the Museum Director has final say and she said no." Unable to obtain new images of the artifacts for his documentary, Bill Cote used photographs from Whitney's original report.

Then some characters like Dr. Zaius entered the narrative. As far as I know, the broadcast of *The Mysterious Origins of Man* by NBC in February of 1996 was the first time a major American television network had aired a program challenging Darwinian explanations of human origins. This apparently caught the orthodox scientific community in the United States by surprise. They thought they (intellectually) owned the mainstream media. NBC's showing of the documentary seemed to threaten the dominant position that evolution science had attained in the state and the state-licensed media.

Although evolution scientists in America were outraged when the program was first shown, they became even more upset when they saw the following headlines from an internet press release from NBC, dated May 29, 1996: "Controversy Surrounds *The Mysterious Origins of Man* . . . University Profs Want Special Banned from the Airwaves. . . . Program That Dares To Challenge Accepted Beliefs About Pre-Historic Man Will Be Rebroadcast June 8 on NBC."

Scientists organized attempts to influence NBC not to show the documentary again. When these attempts failed, these scientists, like Dr. Zaius on the planet of the apes, wanted to convene a state tribunal to set things right. On June 17, 1996, Dr. Allison R. Palmer, president of the Institute for Cambrian Studies, wrote to the Federal Communications Commission, the government agency that regulates and grants licenses to television broadcasting companies: "This e-mail is a request for the FCC to investigate and, I hope, seriously censure the National Broadcasting Company." Palmer continued: "At the very least NBC should be required to make substantial prime-time apologies to their viewing audience for a sufficient period of time so that the audience clearly gets the message that they were duped. In addition, NBC should perhaps be fined sufficiently so that a major fund for public science education can be established." Palmer's attempt to get the FCC to punish NBC failed, but the very fact that such an attempt was made should tell us something. Palmer's letter was widely circulated to scientists, who were asked to send letters of support to the FCC. So perhaps as Taylor found in the final scene of the 1968 film, the planet of the apes is really our planet.

23

An Insider's View of a Fringe Archeology

I presented this paper at the annual meeting of the European Association of Archaeologists, held in Zadar, Croatia, September 18–23, 2007. I presented the paper in a session called "'Fringe' Archaeologies: 'The Other' Past," organized by archeologists Eleni Stefanou and Anna Simandiraki.

This paper is in the form of a discursive essay, so if you were expecting a neatly developed argument, intricate footnotes, and a formal bibliography, you are going to be disappointed. I will, however, touch on a number of topics related to the title of this paper. And I will give enough hints for you to track down articles and books mentioned in the essay.

First, let me establish my credentials as a "fringe" archeologist, one whose work is concerned with the development of an "other" past. Andrew O'Hehir, in "Archaeology from the Dark Side" (Salon.com, August 6, 2005), said about me, "Cremo is a singular figure on the scientific fringe. He is friendly with mainstream archaeologists and with Graham Hancock [author of *Fingerprints of the Gods*]." I find myself on many lists of "fringe" and "pseudo" archeologists and archeologies. Why? Since 1984, I have been researching archeology and history of archeology from a perspective derived from my studies in the *Puranas*, the ancient historical writings of India, which contain accounts of extreme human antiquity, inconsistent with modern evolutionary accounts of human origins. And for some reason my work has become known in academic circles as well as among the general public. Some archeologists and other scholars find this kind of thing, which they call "fringe" or "folk" archeology, threatening. Why? In his book *From Stonehenge to Las Vegas* (2005, Walnut Creek: AltaMira, p. 12), Cornelius Holtorf offers a possible explanation: "Michael Michlovic (1990) [*Current Anthropology*, 31: 103–107] pointed out that patronizing reactions toward folk archaeology are merely the result of a perceived challenge to archaeology's monopoly on interpretation of the past and the associated state support."

How did my involvement in "folk" or "fringe" archeology from a Puranic perspective come about? When I went to the George Washington University in Washington, D.

C., in 1966 to study international relations, I was very much a part of American Cold War conservative culture. I was contemplating a career in the diplomatic corps or one of the intelligence services. By 1968, I had moved into the American counterculture. I demonstrated against the war in Vietnam, grew my hair to my shoulders. I identified with and participated in leftist causes, political, intellectual, and cultural. However, by the early 1970s I had become just as disillusioned with American counterculture as with American conventional culture. Searching for something that was more satisfying, I left the United States. I traveled widely and investigated many cultures. I found myself attracted to the yoga and meditation systems of India, and became the student of an Indian guru, A. C. Bhaktivedanta Swami Prabhupada (1896–1977), founder of the International Society for Krishna Consciousness, a modern but conservative manifestation of the traditional Krishna-*bhakti*, devotional mysticism centered on the Hindu god Krishna. I shaved my head and moved into an ashram. Now, thirty five years later, I have some hair (whatever's left) back on my head. I am more multicultural, at home in many places and moving across many boundaries.

In the early 1980s, I became associated with the Bhaktivedanta Institute, which Bhaktivedanta Swami established in 1974 to explore the relationships between the Vedic knowledge of ancient India and the worldview of modern science. I use the term Vedic broadly, to include not just the original Vedas, but also the derived texts such as the *Puranas,* or histories. The original Vedas are called *shruti*, that which is directly heard, and the derived texts like the *Puranas* are called *smriti*, that which is remembered. So it is interesting that the Sanskrit texts dealing with the human past are characterized as memory. In *From Stonehenge to Las Vegas* (p. 3), Holtorf says, ". . . our knowledge of the past can be said to be the result of a process of collective remembering. Through memory we re-present the past, and this applies equally to our respective personal past and to that of our culture, region, or species."

In 1984, I began researching the Puranic accounts of human origins and antiquity. The *Puranas,* like the writings of many traditional cultures (including the Christian Bible), put the origin of humanity at the very beginnings of the history of life on earth. I looked into the history of archeology, to see whether or not there was any archeological evidence for such extreme human antiquity, i.e. evidence that humans have been present for longer periods of time than current theories allow (200,000 years or so). Such evidence is absent from current textbooks, but I was surprised to see that there was evidence for extreme human antiquity in the primary archeological literature, the reports by original investigators of the past two centuries. Let me give two examples. My purpose in giving them is not to convince you of the case I make for extreme human antiquity, but rather just to let you know how I am making use of archeological materiality in establishing an "other past," a different collective memory.

In the 1970s, American archeologist Cynthia Irwin-Williams was excavating a site called Hueyatlaco, near the town of Puebla in central Mexico. She and her coworkers found many stone tools, including advanced bifaces. The archeologists called a team of geologists to date the site. Geologist Virginia Steen-McIntyre and her colleagues used four methods to establish the age of the artifact-bearing layers. I will here mention two of them. In the same layer with the stone tools the archeologists found animal bones with butchering marks on them. The geologists used the uranium series method to date the bones and got an age of about 245,000 years. Above the layer with the stone tools and animals bones was a layer of volcanic ash. The geologists used the zircon fission track method to date the layer of ash and got an age of about 270,000 years. From the results of all four methods they employed, the geologists concluded the age of the site must be at least 250,000 years. But the archeologists did not believe the site could be that old. According to their understanding, human beings capable of making the artifacts did not exist 250,000 years ago—they had not evolved yet. Furthermore, according to current ideas, humans did not enter the New World until about 25,000 years ago. So the archeologists refused to accept the age for the site given by their own team of geologists, and instead assigned a far younger age to the site.

Later, Virginia Steen-McIntyre and her colleagues independently published the age they had obtained for the site in the journal *Quaternary Research* (1981, vol. 16, pp. 1–17). On March 30, 1981, Steen-McIntyre wrote to Estella Leopold, one of the editors: "Not being an anthropologist, I didn't realize . . . how deeply woven into our thought the current theory of human evolution has become. Our work at Hueyatlaco has been rejected by most archaeologists because it contradicts that theory, period." Partly as a result of my publishing the history of the case in my books, new archeological investigations have been carried out at the site, as documented by archeologist Chris Hardaker in his book *The First American* (2007, Franklin Lakes, NJ: Career Press).

In the mid 19th century, gold was discovered in California. To get the gold, miners dug tunnels into the sides of mountains, such as Table Mountain in Tuolumne County, California. Deep inside the tunnels, in the solid rock, the miners found human bones and human artifacts. The discoveries were made in auriferous gravels in ancient river channels along with plant and animal fossils characteristic of the early Eocene, which would give them an age of about 50 million years. These ancient Eocene river channels are capped by hundreds of meters of solid volcanic deposits, dated using the potassium-argon method, which gave an age of 20–33 million years. The discoveries were carefully documented by Dr. J. D. Whitney in his book *The Auriferous Gravels of the Sierra Nevada of California,* published by Harvard University's Museum of Comparative Zoology in 1880. Whitney said that there was no evidence the artifacts could have come from higher, more recent levels. But we do not hear very much about these discoveries today. In the *Smithsonian Institution Annual Report for 1898–1899* (p. 424), anthropologist William Holmes said, "Perhaps if Professor Whitney had fully appreciated the story of human evolution as it is understood today, he would have hesitated to announce the conclusions formulated, notwithstanding the imposing array of testimony with which he was confronted." This authoritative pronouncement caused scientists to ignore Whitney's reports, and the discoveries were forgotten.

However, some of the artifacts from the California gold mines are still in the collection of the Phoebe Hearst Museum of Anthropology at the University of California at Berkeley. A few years ago, I was researching a paper about these discoveries, which I later presented at the 2003 meeting of the World Archaeological Congress. I received permission from the museum directors to study and photograph the artifacts [**see Plates XIII-XV**]. And by consulting Whitney's old maps and documents, I was able to go out to Table Mountain and relocate some of the old nineteenth century gold mining tunnels where the objects were originally found [see Plate XII].

My work in "fringe" archeology often takes me into museum collections and archives. Museums around the world have in their storerooms human artifacts and bones to which their discoverers attributed ages that go far beyond what modern theories of human origins allow (for example, the Miocene artifacts of Carlos Ribeiro in the Museum of Geology in Lisbon [see Plates I-VII]; the Oligocene artifacts of A. Rutot in the Royal Museum of Natural Sciences in Brussels [see Plates VIII-XI]; etc.). I propose that museum policies in (1) curation, (2) access by researchers and media representatives, and (3) display, need to take alternative archeologies into consideration. Museums can do this by: (1) insuring that artifacts perceived as "anomalous" are not lost or removed from collections, and that the accompanying documentation is also preserved (an archeologist on the staff of the Royal Museum of Natural Sciences in Brussels informed me that a previous director had ordered documentation related to the discoveries and exhibitions of Rutot thrown out); (2) insuring that access to collections is open to researchers with alternative archeological perspectives, and that access is granted to media (television producers, filmmakers, etc.) who may be presenting things from points of view different from those of mainstream archeologists, and (3) insuring that display policies allow alternative presentations of "other pasts" in state supported museums. If there is to be a real multivocality (and multivisuality) in archeology this should be reflected in archeology museum policies. I am not saying that absolutely anything goes, but I do sense there is a need for greater openness.

I collected hundreds of cases of evidence for extreme human antiquity, mostly from the scientific literature, in my book *Forbidden Archeology,* coauthored with my coreligionist Richard L. Thompson. The book was intended for a scientific audience. Its stated purpose was first of all to start a dialog with archeologists about anomalous archeological evidence for extreme human antiquity, with the further goal of eventually demonstrating that an intellectually defensible case could be made for the alternative picture of human origins and antiquity that emerges from the *Puranas.* One way that I tried to get the dialog going was by submitting the book for review in professional journals. The effort was successful. *Forbidden Archeology* was reviewed in many of the professional journals of archeology, anthropology, and history of science, including: *American Journal of Physical Anthropology, Geoarchaeology, Journal of Field Archaeology, Antiquity, Journal of Unconventional History, L'Homme, L'Anthropologie, British Journal for the History of Science, Social Studies of Science,* and *Ethology, Ecology, and Evolution.*

Given the controversial antievolutionary nature of the book, it drew a variety of responses. Some of the reviewers were downright hostile, expressing their unremittingly negative opinions in crude derogatory language. For example, Jonathan Marks, writing in *American Journal of Physical Anthropology* (1994 v. 93, no. 1, pp. 140–141), called the book "Hinduoid creationist drivel." But other reviewers, although they disagreed with the book's conclusions, expressed their disagreement more politely, and admitted they found the book of at least some academic interest and value. For example, in *Geoarchaeology* (1994 v. 9, pp. 337–338), Kenneth Feder said, "The book itself represents something perhaps not seen before; we can fairly call it 'Krishna creationism' with no disrespect intended . . . While decidedly antievolutionary in perspective, this work is not the ordinary variety of antievolutionism in form, content, or style. In distinction to the usual brand of such writing, the authors use original sources and the book is well written. Further, the overall tone of the work is superior to that exhibited in ordinary creationist literature."

In *L'Anthropologie* (1995 v. 99, no. 1, p. 159), Marylène Pathou-Mathis wrote: "M. Cremo and R. Thompson have willfully written a provocative work that raises the problem of the influence of the dominant ideas of a time period on scientific research. These ideas can compel the researchers to orient their analyses according to the conceptions that are permitted by the scientific community" (my translation from the original French). She concluded, "The documentary richness of this work, more historical and sociological than scientific, is not to be ignored."

And in *British Journal for the History of Science* (1995 v. 28, pp. 377–379), Tim Murray noted in his review of *Forbidden Archeology* (p. 379): "I have no doubt that there will be some who will read this book and profit from it. Certainly it provides the historian of archaeology with a useful compendium of case studies in the history and sociology of scientific knowledge, which can be used to foster debate within archaeology about how to describe the epistemology of one's discipline." He further characterized *Forbidden Archeology* as a book that "joins others from creation science and New Age philosophy as a body of works which seek to address members of a public alienated from science, either because it has become so arcane or because it has ceased to suit some in search of meaning for their lives." Murray acknowledged that the Vedic perspective of *Forbidden Archeology* might have a role to play in the future development of archeology. He wrote in his review (p. 379) that archeology is now in a state of flux, with practitioners debating "issues which go to the conceptual core of the discipline." Murray then proposed, "Whether the *Vedas* have a role to play in this is up to the individual scientists concerned."

The most significant review was a 20-page review article in *Social Studies of Science* (1996 v. 26, pp. 192–213) by graduate student Jo Wodak and historian of science David Oldroyd. In their article, titled "Vedic Creationism: A Further Twist to the Evolution Debate," they asked (p. 207), "So has *Forbidden Archeology* made any contribution at all to the literature on palaeoanthropology?" They concluded, "Our answer is a guarded 'yes', for two reasons." First, "the historical material . . . has not been scrutinized in such detail before," and, second, the book does "raise a central problematic regarding the lack of certainty in scientific 'truth' claims." They also commented (p. 198), "It must be acknowledged that *Forbidden Archeology* brings to attention many interesting issues that have not received much consideration from historians; and the authors' detailed examination of the early literature is certainly stimulating and raises questions of considerable interest, both historically and from the perspective of practitioners of SSK [sociology of scientific knowledge]. Indeed, they appear to have gone into some historical matters more deeply than any other writers of whom we have knowledge."

In the first few pages of their article (pp. 192–195), Wodak and Oldroyd gave extensive background information on the Vedic inspiration for the work. In common with other reviewers, Wodak and Oldroyd drew a connection between *Forbidden Archeology* and the work of Christian creationists. "As is well known," they noted (p. 192), "Creationists try to show that humans are of recent origin, and that empirical investigations accord with human history as recorded in the Old Testament. *Forbidden Archeology* (FA) offers a brand of Creationism based on something quite different, namely ancient Vedic beliefs. From this starting point, instead of claiming a human history of mere millennia, *FA* argues for the existence of *Homo sapiens* way back into the Tertiary, perhaps even earlier."

I collected all of these reviews and related correspondence (among other things) in my book *Forbidden Archeology's Impact*, which got its own set of academic reviews. For example, Simon Locke wrote in *Public Understanding of Science* (1999 v. 8, no. 1, pp. 68–69), "Social constructivism, reflexivity, and all that is postmodern have inspired a variety of experiments in new literary forms to enliven the staid old world of the standard academic study. . . . As attempts to document the social process of knowledge production and capture some of its reflexivity, they are both consistent and courageous. So, too, Michael Cremo's book. The 'impact' the book documents is that of Cremo's earlier work, *Forbidden Archeology*. In this latest book rather than construct his own historical narrative, Cremo opts for the far more interesting strategy of directly reproducing much of the source material from which any such narrative would be constructed. The result is a multi-faceted textual kaleidoscope, in which a wide range of the many discourses surrounding contemporary science reflect and refract each other in fascinating array. . . . Cremo has provided here a resource of considerable richness and value to analysts of public understanding [of science]. . . . It should also make a useful teaching resource as one of the best-documented case studies of 'science wars,' and raising a wide range of issues covering aspects of 'knowledge transfer' in a manner sure to be provocative in the classroom."

As can be seen above, the reviewers of *Forbidden Archeology* have labeled me a Hindu creationist, a Vedic creationist, a Krishna creationist. I accept all the labels. I am a creationist, but not of the usual sort, and perhaps the novelty is what attracts so much attention. I do not accept a young earth or special creation, the idea that God independently created each species or kind. I agree with Darwin that the evidence suggests that species came from a common ancestor in the distant past by a process of descent with modification. But Darwin and I would disagree about the common ancestor. He would say it was the simplest living thing, and I would say it was the most complex. He would say that the process of descent with modification was unguided, and I would say it was intelligently guided. He would see the bodies of living things as no more than complex biological machines. I see them as vehicles for conscious selves that existed before the bodies (yes, I am a dualist). I make a case for all this in my latest book *Human Devolution: A Vedic Alternative to Darwin's Theory.*

Some have objected to me bringing my religion into my science. They say there must be a strict separation between the two. But the best of modern scholarship in the history and philosophy of science demonstrates that a strict separation has never existed. I refer you to a recent (2001) volume edited by John Hedley Brooke *et al.*, and published by the University of Chicago Press, titled *Science in Theistic Contexts.* The

University of Chicago Press description of this book tells us: "It is a widely shared assumption that science and religion are fundamentally opposed to each other. Yet, recent historiography has shown that religious belief needs to be added to the social, economic, political, and other cultural factors that went into the making of modern science. This new collection shows religious ideas not only motivated scientific effort but also shaped the actual content of major scientific theories." It is a modern myth that God and science have nothing to do with each other.

So what are the practical implications of all this for education policy? First, education policy makers should recognize that today the vast majority of scientists accept the Darwinian theory of human evolution, defined as a purely naturalistic process. This is a fact. But it is also a fact that some in the world of science, a small number, do not accept the naturalistic evolution theory and are proposing theistic alternatives. Education policy makers for the life sciences in general, and archeology in particular, should recognize this. The proper solution is that evolutionary theory of human origins and its supporters should be given most of the time in the biology (and archeology) classrooms and most of the pages in the textbooks, including archeology textbooks. But a small amount of classroom time and a small number of textbook pages should be devoted to neutrally presenting the theistic alternatives to the current theory of human evolution. How small? I would suggest 5 percent of the classroom time and 5 percent of the textbook pages. But I will leave it up to you.

Despite my provocative approach to the question of human origins and antiquity, openly based on an antievolutionary "other past" outlined in the *Puranas,* I have received numerous invitations to speak in mainstream academic circles. I have lectured at hundreds of universities around the world. I have probably spent more time in the classroom than many professors. Much to the dismay of some of my more strident critics, I have been invited to give presentations on my book *Forbidden Archeology* at prominent academic institutions such as the Royal Institution in London, the department of anthropology of the Russian Academy of Sciences in Moscow, the department of experimental anthropology and morphology of the Bulgarian Academy of Sciences in Sofia, and the department of archeology of the Ukrainian Academy of Sciences, among others. For these presentations, I am usually given at least an hour, with thirty or more additional minutes for questions and discussion. I have also had a chance to present (within the standard 20 minute time limit) papers about my work and its Vedic inspiration at several meetings of the World Archaeological Congress, the European Association of Archaeologists, the International Union for Prehistoric and Protohistoric Sciences, and the International Congress for History of Science, with some of the papers published. For example, my paper "Puranic Time and the Archeological Record," delivered at the December 1994 meeting of the World Archaeological Congress, was included in the peer reviewed conference proceedings volume *Time and Archeology,* edited by Tim Murray and published by Routledge in its One World Archaeology series in 1999 (pp. 38–48). And my paper "The Later Discoveries of Boucher de Perthes at Moulin Quignon and Their Impact on the Moulin Quignon Jaw Controversy" appeared in *Proceedings of the XXth International Congress of History of Science, Vol. X., Earth Sciences, Geography, and Cartography,* edited by Goulven Laurent and published by Brepols in 2002 (pp. 39–56). As Ian Hodder said, "Day by day it becomes more difficult to argue for a past controlled by the academy. . . . it is no longer so easy to see who is 'in' the academy and who is 'outside'" (*Antiquity* 1997, 71: 699, 700).

Why does the academy have any interest at all in my brand of "fringe" archeology? Partially, I believe, it's because of the novelty of my position. Also, I am relatively nonthreatening. I am not backed up by some huge religious organization or political party. It is just me and my unusual ideas. So there is little harm in inviting me, just to hear what I have to say. Perhaps it is also because I take my academic audience and its standards of discourse somewhat (but not completely) seriously. Although I am an outsider, I have learned something about the language and customs of archeologists, enough to be allowed some entrance into their circle, much like a cultural anthropologist, who, by learning enough of the language and customs of a tribal group, can gain entrance into the tribal circle, as a participant observer. This particular somewhat surrealist "anthropologist" has not become an initiated member of the archeological tribe but he has, it appears, gained enough acceptance to carry out his purpose, which is different from that of most archeologists. So although you will see me around, you do not have to fear that I will be competing with you for a research grant, a university post, or a contract in contract archeology. What then is my purpose? That might seem obscure to you. But I hope that by the end of this paper, you will have the beginnings of an answer to that question.

However, I am not simply interested in communicating with professional archeologists and other mainstream scientists and scholars. I also desire to communicate my "fringe" archeological ideas beyond the academy to a variety of other audiences, audiences that could be called "popular." Even professional archeologists sense the danger and boredom of becoming what Michael Shanks and Christopher Tilley in their *Re-constructing Archaeology* (2002, 2nd ed., New York: Routledge, p. 265) call "simply archaeologists who write for other archaeologists who write for other archaeologists." (It would not be proper for me to write a paper like this without citing Shanks and Tilley, would it?)

In addition to writing papers for academic presentation and publication, I write a column for *Atlantis Rising* magazine, which, as its name suggests, features "fringe" archeological topics. My column is titled "The Forbidden Archeologist." I have also brought out my 900-page *Forbidden Archeology*, intended for an academic audience, in a more accessible abridged edition, titled *The Hidden History of the Human Race*. This book is now out in about 20 languages worldwide, including, among European languages, English, German, Danish, French, Italian, Spanish, Russian, Polish, Czech, Slovenian, Croatian, Bulgarian, Estonian, and Hungarian. When my books are released in different countries, I go there for publicity tours. I do lectures and book signings at bookshops. I appear on national television and radio, and I do interviews for newspapers and magazines. During these tours, in addition to speaking to academic audiences at universities and scientific institutions, I also give auditorium lectures to the general public. But many of my public lectures and media presentations are for special audiences.

Among my audiences are Christian creationists, Islamic creationists, other kinds of creationists, and intelligent design theorists. Phillip E. Johnson, one of the leaders of the intelligent design movement, wrote in his foreword to the 1994 hardcover edition of my book *The Hidden History of the Human Race:* "The authors frankly acknowledge their motivation to support the idea, rooted in the Vedic literature of India, that the human race is of great antiquity. I do not share their religion or their motivation, but I also do not think that there is anything disreputable about a religious outlook which is candidly disclosed. Scientists, like other human beings all have motives, and biases that may cloud their judgment, and the dogmatic materialism that controls the minds of many mainstream scientists is far more likely to do damage to the truth because it is not acknowledged as a bias."

I have spoken at all kinds of esoteric, alternative science, and New Age gatherings. I have spoken at the College of Psychic Studies in London. I have lectured at various branches of the Theosophical Society. This past winter, I was an invited speaker for the Shivananda Yoga Society at its center on Paradise Island in the Bahamas. I have spoken at many UFO conferences and conferences organized by supporters of the ancient astronaut theory. Once I spoke at a crop circle conference in Glastonbury, England. I have spoken at conferences that feature speakers who might be called conspiracy theorists. Two years ago, I spoke about my work at an eco-camp in the countryside outside Brasilia, in Brazil.

I also reach out to my various popular audiences through the internet. My forbidden archeology website (www.mcremo.com) ranks high among archeology sites. If on Google, you type in the search word "archeology," my site ranks amongst the top ten of millions of websites that feature some aspect of archeology. Last time I looked, I was mentioned on thousands of blogs and websites, many of which sell my books. Bootleg videos of my lectures and tv appearances have also popped up on You Tube and other video websites.

So why am I reaching out to so many audiences in so many different ways? In one sense, it could be just crass self-promotion and a mercenary desire to sell books (it is income from my books that allows me to fly to Zadar, pay the registration fees for this conference, and stay in my hotel here—I do not have access to university funds or grants). But, really, there is more to it. For now, let me touch on just one part of that "more" (more "more" later). Rightly or wrongly, I believe that today we, the people of this planet, are in the midst of a fundamental renegotiation of our whole picture of reality. The foundations of the modernist worldview are continuing to crumble, and many are struggling to come up with a new consensus worldview. I characterize that struggle as a renegotiation, and I see many parties to the renegotiation, including mainstream scientists, religionists, paranormal researchers, UFO theorists, creationists, intelligent design theorists, the general public. So I deliberately try to communicate with all of them.

When I speak of a consensus worldview, I do not mean to say that there are not, or should not be, other worldviews, coexisting with it. But in the world today, although there are many languages, English has become by consensus a kind of inter-language, or superlanguage. There are many currencies, but the US dollar, at the moment, seems by consensus to have the widest range of acceptance, and serves as a standard for measuring relative values of other currencies. Any person may have several currencies, and speak several languages, but may still have to function, in some situations, with the realities of English being the international language and the dollar being the international currency. Similarly, we may have commitments to one or more particular local cultural worldviews, but we also seem also to have to simultaneously recognize and deal with the existence of a super-worldview that has somehow achieved worldwide status as the common "modern" or "scientific" worldview. And it is that super worldview, which includes a particular view of the past, that I think is now under renegotiation.

All the parties to this renegotiation, as listed above, have something to contribute, including the "fringe" archeologists. Michael Shanks says in his book *Experiencing the Past* (1992, London: Routledge, p. 114): "Archaeology excavates a hollow. There is an emptiness. The raw existence of the past is not enough, insufficient in itself. . . . What is needed is our desire to fill the hollow, raise the dead. . . . Fringe archaeologies can be read in this context. Leyliners, dowsers, New Age mystics explicitly or implicitly pose the question of the identity of the past, recognizing some element of transcendence, the unsayable, the spiritual. They assert the necessity of a human involvement in perceiving the past. Scientific rationality is conceived as partial at best, harmful or destructive at worst."

By under-emphasizing the role of the human spirit in all its complexity and mystery in comprehending and representing the past, scientific rationalism is creating a void that must be filled somehow. I agree (of course) with Shanks when he says (pp. 114–115): "I do not think that fringe archaeologists should be dismissed out of hand as cranks, weirdos, and hippies. I have tried to show that the impulse to think and mine the subjective and affective, holistic and meaningful aspects of the past is a reasonable one. What is perhaps more unreasonable is a social science which is not very able to deal with these aspects of the past, creating a gap filled by popular, media and fringe archaeologies."

A few years ago, I was invited to address the staff of the archeology department of a museum of natural history in a European country. In my talk, I mentioned some of my alternative ideas, such as my belief in reincarnation. One of the staff archeologists approached me afterwards, and confided to me how in her burial excavations she had uncovered evidence indicating the people of that culture believed in reincarnation. But she had been discouraged from mentioning anything about this in her publications. She had been advised to just stick to the physical aspects of the finds. To do otherwise would be unprofessional, unscientific.

My approach to alternative archeologies is not uncritical. I agree with Shanks when he says (p.115): ". . . the problem with fringe archaeologies, with their mysterious powers in the past, spacemen and catastrophes, is the overwhelming tendency to mysticism and irrationalism. Intuition, inspiration, extra-sensory perception, initiated wisdoms, mystic energies are fertile ground for nonsense." But so also are blind materialism, presumptuous positivism, and superficial scientism a fertile ground for nonsense of another kind.

Shanks perceptively says (p. 115) science does not "have a monopoly on rationality and reason," adding, "I am trying to show how there are reasonable ways of extending science's partial view to include reflection on the vital human dimensions of the past." My project is similarly motivated. One could say I am advocating a rational mysticism or a mystical rationalism. In other words, there can be an archeology informed by a complementary relationship between "initiated wisdoms" and scientific rationality. As Einstein famously said, "Science without religion is lame, religion without science is blind." My commitment to this project is rooted in the history of the *bhakti* school of devotional mysticism that I follow. In its current form, it arose in India in the 16th century, although there were certainly antecedents. In the 16th century, proponents of the *bhakti* school took two different approaches to the rationalistic Vedanta philosophy of India. One group chose to reject Vedanta rationalism completely whereas the other group (mine) chose to incorporate Vedanta rationalism into the devotional mysticism of *bhakti*. A teacher of this latter school, Jiva Gosvami, wrote major philosophical works to accomplish this integration. Ravi M. Gupta explains how this occurred in his book *The Caitanya Vaisnava Vedanta of Jiva Gosvami: When Knowledge Meets Devotion* (2007), recently published by the Routledge Hindu Studies Series in collaboration with the Oxford Centre for Hindu Studies. Gupta says (p. 3) about Jiva Gosvami's approach to the rationalism of Vedanta and the mysticism of bhakti, "The school is remarkable in its ability to engage in Vedantic discourse and at the same time practice an ecstatic form of devotion." Today I see a need to bring into similar productive relationship the rationalistic insights of modern scientific archeology and the mystical insights of what are called alternative, or "fringe" archeologies. They are both parties to the renegotiation of our worldview.

What would I like to see as the result of this renegotiation? Some further clues may be found in my latest book, *Human Devolution: A Vedic Alternative to Darwin's Theory*. My book *Forbidden Archeology* simply documents archeological evidence that contradicts modern accounts of human origins and that is consistent with Puranic accounts of extreme human antiquity. *Human Devolution* briefly reviews this evidence and then moves on to offer an alternative account of human origins. In the book, I propose that before we even ask the question "Where did human beings come from?", we should first ask the question, "What is a human being?" Today many researchers believe a human being is simply a combination of the ordinary material elements, but when I look at all the evidence, I find it is more reasonable to say that a human being is a combination not just of matter but also of a subtle (but nonetheless material) mind element and an irreducible element of nonmaterial consciousness. To put things very simply, we do not evolve up from matter but down from pure consciousness. Consciousness is primary, not matter. But this process of devolution, whereby pure consciousness becomes covered by mind and matter, can be reversed, through disciplines of contemplative prayer, meditation, and yoga. Consciousness can be restored to its original pure state, and this restoration is, or should be, the main purpose of human existence.

To some, this proposal that there may a nonmaterial component to organisms, especially the human organism, may seem outside the bounds of modern scientific inquiry. But perhaps not. Rodney Brooks, of the Artificial Intelligence Laboratory at MIT, wrote in a perceptive article in *Nature* (2001, no. 409, pp. 409–411): "Neither AI [artificial intelligence] or Alife [artificial life] has produced artefacts that could be confused with a living organism for more than an instant. AI just does not seem as present or aware as even a simple animal and Alife cannot match the complexities of the simplest forms of life" (p. 409). Brooks attributes the failure to something other than lack of computer power, incorrect parameters, or insufficiently complex models. He raises the possibility that "we are missing something fundamental and currently unimagined in our models." But what is that missing something? "One possibility," says Brooks (p. 410), "is that some aspect of living systems is invisible to us right now. The current scientific view of things is that they are machines whose components are biomolecules. It is not completely impossible that we might discover . . . some new ingredient. . . . Let us call this the 'new stuff' hypothesis—the hypothesis that there might be some extra sort of 'stuff' in living systems outside our current scientific understanding." And what might this new stuff be? Among the possibilities suggested by Brooks (p. 411) are "some more ineffable entity such as a soul or *elan vital*—the 'vital force.'" Along these lines, I propose that the "new stuff" should be mind and consciousness, understood not as simple byproducts of brain chemistry but as independently existing entities.

As was the case with my earlier books, this latest book, *Human Devolution,* has found its way to various audiences, including the academic audience. When the book first came out, it came into the hands of an anthropologist at a university in the United States, and by his recommendation I was invited to give a two hour presentation about the book at a conference held by the Society for the Anthropology of Consciousness, a division of the American Anthropological Association. The book has begun to attract reviews in academic journals, and I have been invited to speak about it at universities around the world. Of course, I have also given lectures about the book to the other kinds of audiences I have mentioned above.

In October and November of 2006, I went to India for a nationwide lecture and publicity tour about the book, which was available in English-language bookshops, especially the new large national bookstore chains, like Crossword, Oxford, Odyssey, and Landmark. In each city, there were university lectures, media interviews, and bookstore signings. In Kolkata, the book was officially launched at an evening event at the Palladium Lounge in the Bengal Chamber of Commerce and Industry, attended by 150 of Kolkata's leading citizens. I was introduced by Alfred Ford, a member of the Ford auto dynasty, who, like me, is a student of Bhaktivedanta Swami Prabhupada. I was also invited to speak by the anthropology department of Calcutta University. That talk was attended by professors and graduate students of the department. I granted interviews to reporters of all the large papers in Kolkata including the *Times, Hindustan Times, Telegraph,* and *Statesman.* Here are some excerpts from their articles:

> Michael Cremo's book challenges Charles Darwin's theory of evolution in that Cremo believes "we did not evolve from matter, instead we devolved, or came down, from the realm of pure consciousness, spirit." From "The Vedas Versus Darwin," *The Statesman* (Kolkata), October 24, 2006.

> The Darwinian theory should not be enforced by the government in the schools, the author said. "The vast majority [of scientists] believe it is

true so the syllabus must reflect that, but what's the harm in mentioning that there are alternative theories? Let students decide what they want to believe." From "Origin of Species vs. Vedic 'Devolution.'" *The Times* (Kolkata), October 20, 2006.

In Mumbai, there was a book launch at the Oxford Bookstore. I gave an interview to a reporter for the *Free Press Journal*, one of the large Mumbai papers. In Mumbai, I gave talks on my book *Human Devolution* at the Indian Institute of Technology (IIT), and two other universities. The IIT schools have a high reputation in India. One professor who heard the talk bought four copies of the book. The organizers of the IIT talk got written feedback from the audience, including the following:

> Quite compelling. I have never been comfortable with the idea of evolving from an ape and then not going any further. The fact that we are consciousness that devolves into matter is far more interesting. N.S., Ph.D.

> I strongly believe that theory given by Darwin has great limitations. But in Vedic literature one will get perfect knowledge of mechanism of human devolution and finally one is soul and not the body. This type of lectures should be held in series and in more detail. I like to suggest that every University/Institute should seriously think on such topics and classroom time should be made available. S.D.J., Ph.D.

In Bangalore there was a book launch for *Human Devolution* at the Oxford Bookstore in the spectacularly opulent Leela Palace Galleria. Lots of reporters were present, and several articles in the major Bangalore papers appeared, for example an interview with the science reporter for the *Deccan Herald*. I also did an interview for a *Doordarshan* news program (*Doordarshan* is the national tv network). On the academic side of things, I gave a talk on *Human Devolution* at the Indian Institute of Science, one of India's most prominent science schools.

From Bangalore I went to Coimbatore in the far south of India. After some lectures in Coimbatore, I flew to Trivandrum. There I spoke at the University of Kerala, in a lecture for the combined science departments, and had three television interviews. From Trivandrum, I flew to Chennai (formerly Madras). There I spoke at Anna University and the Indian Institute of Technology (IIT Chennai). I also had two bookstore events, at an Odyssey bookstore and another at an Oxford bookstore. Some favorable newspaper articles came out. From Chennai, I flew to Hyderabad, where I spoke at several universities and had two bookstore events. Then I flew to Delhi, where I spoke at universities and gave an interview for the *Times* of India. And that was it.

During my visit to India, in addition to accepting invitations from academic and scientific organizations, I also accepted invitations to speak for more traditional Hindu cultural and religious organizations. This may lead some to wonder if I might be a religious fundamentalist or a Hindu nationalist. My answer is no. Although my work is inspired by my study of key Hindu texts such as the *Bhagavad-gita,* my reading of these texts leads me away from fundamentalism, racism, and nationalism. Of course, any text is subject to multiple readings and misreadings. But my reading of the *Gita* and other texts takes seriously their direct teaching that the actual conscious self, the *atma,* is different from the temporary material body. Therefore, in terms of how we identify ourselves, the conscious self is primary, and the body, with its external designations of gender, race, nation, religion, etc. is secondary—not unreal, or totally unimportant, but secondary. The *Gita* says *panditah sama-darshinah*: a wise person sees all living things equally. I regard nationality as a very superficial level of self-identification, not as important as the equality of all people on the level of the *atma,* the conscious self within. So, no, I am not a Hindu nationalist, or any other kind of nationalist, in the sense of placing the highest value on nationalism in self-identification.

Ultimately, it is a question of proper balance. In modern cosmology, astrophysicists have noticed that the kind of universe we have, with its ordered complex forms, depends on a particular balance between the force of expansion and the force of gravitational attraction. If the force of expansion were much greater than it is, in relation to the force of gravitational attraction, the universe would have by now expanded into a uniform gas. If the force of expansion were much less than it is, the universe would have by now collapsed on itself. Similarly, for there to be proper relationships among people on earth, there must be a proper balance between the appreciation of equality and the recognition of differences. Go too far in the direction of unity, and you wind up with a totalitarian sameness; go too far in the direction of difference, and you wind up unable to recognize other groups as properly human. I believe my alternative archeology contributes to a proper balance. I do not support alternative archeologies (or mainstream archeologies) that lead to extreme forms of nationalism, senseless violence, unjust oppression of minorities, and other such things.

I should mention here that my concept of God is gendered, but not exclusively male or exclusively female. According to the *bhakti* school, God exists eternally in transcendence as a youthful, attractive couple, female and male, given the name Radha-Krishna. Radha is the female person of the pair, and Krishna the male. In the *bhakti* school, meditation upon and participation in their exchanges of spiritual pleasure energies is considered the highest kind of yoga. (See Graham Schweig's *Bhagavad Gita: The Beloved Lord's Secret Love Song,* 2007, New York: HarperCollins, especially pages 272–278, for a good contemporary introduction to the love mysticism of the *Gita.*) Our less perfect and temporary material pleasure exchanges are a pale reflection of this eternal reality. God is love, the saying goes. I regard my forbidden archeology work as an integral part of my yoga, my meditation, my spiritual discipline. It is the way I find and develop my love for the divine. By this work, which as I see as desired by God (love means to satisfy the desire of the beloved), I am engaged in an archeology of the heart, digging to find the lost love for God that is deeply buried in the layers of my forgetfulness.

Interestingly enough, archeology per se (of the digging in the earth kind) has historically been part of the *bhakti* school. In a paper I recently presented at a meeting of the European Association of South Asian Archeologists in Ravenna, Italy ("Finding

Krishna: 16th Century Archeological Activity by Vaishnava Saints in the Braj Mandal Region of North India"), I pointed out that saints of the *bhakti* school in India deliberately excavated lost sacred images of Krishna and relocated lost sacred sites.

In terms of religion, I do not believe in exclusive claims to truth. My particular approach to religion is one of commitment to techniques of contemplation, meditation, and yoga that yield actual transformations of consciousness, rather than commitment to the more external forms of religion, which can be a cause of sectarian religious conflict. A geologist or metallurgist can tell us how to extract gold from its ore, where it is mixed with other less valuable elements. Once the gold is extracted, it can be formed into coins, and the coins can be stamped with the symbols of different nations. But if it is actually gold, it does not matter what symbol is stamped on it. It will be accepted as something valuable. Similarly, if by the above-mentioned spiritual techniques, one can come to a real awareness of the spiritual nature within all humans and other living things, this can and should be recognized as something valuable, no matter what symbols are attached to the processes. In other words, it does not matter if you label the process Hinduism, or Christianity, or Islam, or anything else. If it yields an awareness of the conscious self in oneself and others as part of the spiritual being of God, and fosters love for all, then that is the essence of religion as far as I am concerned. It is that approach to religious experience that my alternative archeology favors, and not exclusive claims to truth that lead to sectarian conflict. I am even tolerant of atheists, although I prefer the kind that can tolerate theists.

So I am among those who would agree with Shanks and Tilley that archeology is really more concerned with the present than the past. They say in *Reconstructing Archaeology* (2nd ed., p. 264): "It is important that archaeology shifts from instituting a series of judgments on the past . . . to becoming a form of 'counter memory', aiming to challenge current modes of truth, justice, rationality, and social and economic organization. In other words, archaeology should be helping us to understand and change the present by inserting it in a new relationship with the past." Or as Cornelius Holtorf, a former student of Michael Shanks, says in his book *From Stonehenge to Las Vegas* (p. 6), "Archaeology . . . remains significant, not because it manages to import actual past realities into the present but because it allows us to recruit past people and what they left behind for a range of contemporary human interests, needs, and desires."

So for what present purposes am I recruiting the past? I believe that modern scientific archeology, with its emphasis on the materiality of the human past and the materiality of human nature at present, is deeply implicated in driving human "interests, needs, and desires" in an overly materialistic direction, with unfortunate consequences. The goals that we set for ourselves, individually and collectively, are to a large extent determined by the answers we give to the fundamental questions, "Who am I?" and "Where did I come from?" If I think I am an American man, I behave as such. Today, through its monopoly in the education system, Darwinian biology, in which modern scientific archeology plays a leading role, dictates to people the answers to those fundamental questions. And the answers dictated are very materialistic. We are just biological machines, combinations of chemicals. And therefore to me it is no surprise that humanity has in general become quite materialistic in its goals, so much so that most people in the developed world act as if they believe the most important purpose of human life is the production and consumption of more and more material things. I hold this to be one of the main causes of environmental destruction, violent competition among nations for scarce material resources, and class conflict for control of wealth within nations. The ultimate purpose of my alternative archeology/anthropology is to derive from the past (and the present) a different set of answers to the questions "Who am I?" and "Where did I come from?" Recognition that within us all is a spark of divine consciousness, emanating from the same source, coupled with the cultivation and experience of inner happiness, could lessen our tendencies to see others as enemies and also decrease our need to seek happiness through the ever-increasing exploitation of matter. Hopefully, such recognition would lead to a simpler and more natural way of life, with less environmental destruction, as outlined in my book *Divine Nature: A Spiritual Perspective on the Environmental Crisis,* coauthored with Mukunda Goswami. Hopefully, the re-cognition of our common spiritual nature would result in a lessening of conflict based on superficial externalities like nationality and race and sectarian religion. So this is where I hope my forbidden archeology, my "fringe" archeology leads. So that is my agenda.

As for being called a "fringe" archeologist, I can accept that, to some extent. The fringe of a fabric is, after all, still part of the fabric, a decorative border that makes it more interesting. But it would be more accurate to call me a promoter of an alternative archeology. Sometimes one finds one needs not just new borders and fringes but a whole new fabric.

24
Temple as Body, Body as Temple

I presented this paper at the World Archaeological Congress 6, held in Dublin, Ireland, July 1, 2008. I presented the paper in a session called Visual Bodies: Exploring the Representation of Identity. I presented a similar paper (House, Temple and City as Body: Body Substitution in Traditional Hindu Architecture) at the European Association of Archaeologists annual meeting, Riva del Garda, Italy, September 15–20, 2009.

Introduction

The body is a popular topic in archeological theory. As noted by Hamilakis *et al.* (2002, p. 5) interest in visual representations of the body has inspired a growing literature. But in discussing future research agendas, Hamilakis *et al.* (2002, p. 11) point to a related topic, body as symbol or metaphor: "The physiological body provides a rich source of symbolism and metaphor which may be used to provide understandings of other features of the natural and cultural world." In this paper, I explore how the image of the body was consciously built into the architecture of the Hindu temple, so that the temple symbolically or metaphorically represents a divine humanlike body. Hamilakis *et al.* (2002, p. 11) remind us, however, that the relationship of symbol or metaphor is "a recursive relationship," adding, "pots become named and treated as bodies, bodies become vessels." So just as the Hindu temple may be seen as body, the human body in Hinduism may also be seen as temple. Johnson (1988, p. 230) says in a study of Japanese Buddhist temples: "Correspondence of form, with respect to the body:temple image means that forms resembling each other *participate* in each other. The equation, then, is not simply body:temple but body:temple = temple:body." Hamilakis *et al.* (2002, p. 11) go on to caution us that "we have to be careful to consider ontologies in which entities including bodies and persons may be understood as presenced—such as the Christian doctrine of transubstantiation or certain sacred Australian paintings—and not simply referred to." This is certainly the case with the Hindu temple. In terms of the ontology of the Hindu worldview, the body is related to the temple not just symbolically or metaphorically but in terms of real co-presence. Thus in seeing a classic Hindu temple of a certain type, one properly knowledgeable is visually encountering the presence of a real body. Then I extend the image of body beyond the temple to other architectural features, such as houses and towns. I will also suggest how knowledge of the body image in Hindu architecture, a topic that properly belongs in art history or historic archeology, may also have a part to play in research into the prehistoric archeology of the Indian subcontinent. Along the way, I also show how the concepts of self and body in Hinduism transcend a simple dualism to allow archeological interpretation within modern analytical frameworks.

My approach to this topic is first of all influenced by my personal commitment to a form of traditional Hindu spirituality—the devotional mysticism of Krishna *bhakti*. In 1975, I was initiated by Bhaktivedanta Swami Prabhupada (1896–1977), a member of one of the traditional Krishna *bhakti* disciplic lineages in India. An important element of Krishna *bhakti* is meditation upon worshipable images of Krishna and related deities in temples. During my many visits to India, I have visited many Krishna temples, and also temples of other Hindu deities. Gradually, I learned, from study of texts and conversations with fellow religionists, local temple priests, and other informants, that the images of gods and goddesses are not the only visual manifestation of (divine) human form in the temples. The temples themselves are constructed according to principles set down in an ancient Hindu architectural system called *vastu*, a Sanskrit word that means, among other things, extended material form, or residence. One element of *vastu* is the concept of the *vastu purusha*, the personal form of *vastu*. The temple is constructed in awareness of the *vastu purusha*. My approach to this topic is also informed by my studies in the modern academic literature on the Hindu temple and *vastu*, as well as the modern archeological literature on the body and archeology.

Vastu Purusha

The principal Sanskrit texts that deal with *vastu* are listed by S. K. Ramachandra Rao (1998, p. 16) as *Manushyalaya-chandrika, Vishvakarma-vastu-shastra, Maya-vastu, Kashyapa-shilpa, Samarangana-sutradhara, Aparajita-priccha, Manasara, Arthashastra, Vastu-kundali, Yukti-kalpatara, Vastu-tattva, Vastu-yoga-tattva, Manasollasa, Vastu-vidya, Vishvakarma-prakasha,* and *Sanatkumara-vastu-shastra*. Almost all of them explain the origin of the *vastu* system of architecture in terms of the *vastu purusha*. There are various accounts of the origin of the *vastu purusha*. One goes like this: At the beginning of creation, there was an *asura* (demon) who opposed the demigods. The demigods led by Brahma pushed the demon down onto the earth's surface, and the demigods took their places on his form to hold him there. Brahma named the demon *vastu purusha*. Offering the *vastu purusha* a kind of redemption, Brahma ordained that anyone building any kind of residence would have to pacify him with sacrifice and worship (Gray 2007, pp. 67–68; Thirumalachar 1998, p. 45; Kramrisch 1976, p. 73).

Another formulation is that the *vastu purusha* is the material energy (*apara prakriti*) of God, or is the universal form (*vishvarupa*) of God, and the demigods take their places in the universal form to assist God (Krishna) in the manifestation of material reality (Gray 2007, pp. 70–71, pl. 76, Kramrisch 1976, p. 21). The visible material world can be meditated upon as the humanlike form of the *vishvarupa*. The *Bhagavata Purana* (2.1.30–33) says that the mountains are the bones of the *vishvarupa*, the rivers are his veins, the ocean his abdomen, the trees his bodily hair, the clouds the hair on his head, the air his breath, his eye is the sun, and so on.

Any building must rest on the *vastu purusha*, and it is the *vastu purusha* that gives shape to the building. The form of the *vastu purusha* is depicted graphically in the *vastu purusha mandala*. The *mandala*, or diagram, is square. According to Kramrisch (1976, pp. 22–28), the square form represents the divine order whereas the circle represents unordered material reality. The *purusha* is depicted as a male, lying face down. The head occupies the northeast part of the *mandala*, and the feet are in the southwest. The right knee and right elbow meet in the southeast corner. The left knee and left elbow meet in the northwest corner. The form of the *vastu purusha* is thus contorted to fit in the confines of the square. The main square of the *mandala* is divided into 64 (8 x 8) or 81 (9 x 9) squares. Each square is inhabited by a demigod, each one taking its place on the form of the body of the *vastu purusha*.

The person who knows the science of *vastu* is the architect. The original divine architects, among them Vishvakarma, were manifested from the chief demigod, Brahma. All subsequent architects, called *sthapatis*, are descended from Vishvakarma. *Sthapati* means "master of what stands or abides" (Kramrisch 1976, p. 11). The building of a temple is an act of sacrifice that the *sthapati* performs on behalf of the *yajamana,* or sponsor of the sacrifice. After the site is leveled, the *vastu purusha mandala* is drawn upon it, thus converting that plot of land into the extent of the universe (Kramrisch 1976, p. 12). Within the context of the *mandala*, the architect will give stable form to matter as a residence for God and humans, thus repeating original acts of creation.

Temple as Body

The temple in its completed state is considered to be a manifestation of the *vastu purusha*. In the beginning of the building of the temple, the *vastu purusha* is seen as a demon held face down by the demigods, supporting the structure. But as the construction is carried out, the *vastu purusha* is also seen as a personality facing upward, reaching toward God, having controlled and transformed the chaos of matter (Kramrisch 1976, p. 78, citing *Vishnusamhita* 12.51, *Agni Purana* 93.3, *Vastuvidya* 4.48, etc.). This is also the story of each individual soul (*jiva*). The *jiva* turns against its spiritual nature and comes under the influence of matter. But encountering the limitations imposed by the higher powers of the gods, it may turn back to its source, through an elevating practice of spiritual discipline (*sadhana*), to which the construction of the temple corresponds (Kramrisch 1976, pp. 82, 84).

The construction of the temple proceeds both horizontally and vertically. The person of the *vasta purusha* is thus reflected not only horizontally, in the form of the *vastu purusha mandala*, but vertically, with the various elements of the temple elevation representing parts of the *vastu purusha* in erect, standing form, moving up toward the divine. Gray (2007, pp. 67–68, p. 71 pl. 75) says, "The elevation was conceived as elements of the standing human body. The summit of the tower, the decorative *amalaka*, is equated to the head, the tower (*shikara)* to the body's trunk. The sanctum (*garbhagriha* or *vimana*) is the nerve center located at the navel (*nabhi*), and houses the soul (*atman*), represented by the consecrated image. The transept projections from the *maha-mandapa* are defined as the outstretched hands (*hasta*) and pillars, and the lower plinth or platform is represented by the feet (*pada*). . . . The human form thus served as a metaphor for both the body of the deity and the temple itself."

The concept of the temple as body is multifaceted. In one sense, the emerging temple structure is the form of the *vastu purusha*. In another sense it is the body of the patron of the temple, the one who is causing the temple to be built. Kramrisch (1976, p. 52) says, "Builder and building are one; the building is a test of the health and probity of the builder, his 'alter ego,' his second body; if the building be a sacred one, a temple, this second body is his sacrificial body born from a second birth."

The temple can also be seen as the body of the main deity worshiped in the temple, the worshipable image of the main deity being the soul of the temple. The image of the main deity is installed in the *garbha griha*, the "womb house", which is the central part of the temple structure. It is a large, thick-walled cube, the interior of which is dark and isolated. The outer structure of the temple is decorated with images of subordinate gods and goddesses, servants of the supreme god within the *garbha griha*. The worshiper comes from outside, from the outer world, into the dark interior of the temple to see the temple image in an act called *darshan*. And from this vision, the process of realization, of return to the spiritual level of reality, begins. It is something that grows from the heart of the worshiper, like the temple has grown, from a seed. And in this sense, the temple can be seen as the body of the ordinary worshiper who visits the temple, reaching through the temple toward transcendence. Kramrisch (1976, p. 163) says, "The *garbha griha* is not only the house of the Germ or embryo of the Temple as *purusha* [God]; it refers to man who comes to the Centre and attains his new birth in its darkness." The new birth means a new or transformed body, related intimately to the temple structure. Kramrisch (1976, p. 253) says, "The architectural rhythms of the Hindu temple. . . . evoke in the devotee (*bhakta*) an adjustment of his person to its structure; his subtle body (*sukshma sharira*) responds to the proportions of the temple by an inner rhythmical movement. By this 'aesthetic' emotion the devotee is one with the temple; and qualified to realize the presence of God."

The body of the worshiper can be considered to be a temple because, according to the tenets of Krishna *bhakti*, within the body of the worshiper is not only the soul of the worshiper but also the Supersoul, an expansion of the supreme god. The *Skanda Upanishad* (10), cited by Savakar (1998, p. 37), says *deho devalaya proktah*: "the body is a temple." My guru wrote in his commentary on *Bhagavad-gita* 9.11, "A devotee should see that because Krishna is present in everyone's heart as Paramatma, every body is the embodiment or the temple of the Supreme Lord; so as one offers respect to the temple of the Lord, he should similarly properly respect each and every body in which the Paramatma dwells" (Bhaktivedanta Swami 1986, p. 470).

Gendered Architecture

Although the *vastu purusha* is depicted as male, there is a female aspect to the temple as well. Baked bricks are the preferred material for the construction of temple, although stone and wood are also acceptable. The bricks are considered female, because they are made of earth (considered feminine) and are laid down with recitation of mantras, Vedic hymns, which are also considered feminine. Both the bricks and Vedic hymns are considered daughters of the sage Angirasa. They are worshiped as goddesses (Kramrisch 1976, pp. 104–105). If the *yajamana*, or patron of the temple construction, is female, the temple, as the sacrificial body of the *yajamana,* is also considered to have a female aspect. And if the deity worshiped in the temple is female, the temple as body of the deity is also considered female (Kramrisch 1976, p. 107).

Interestingly, although the bricks are generally considered feminine, they can also be seen as masculine, feminine, or neuter, according to variations in their size and shape (Kramrisch 1976, p. 107). The flexibility or changeability of gender in Hindu culture is something I will return to later in this paper.

The feminine is also evident in the ceremonies that precede the actual construction of the temple. First there is a ceremony for the laying of the first bricks in a pit. Then comes another ceremony called *garbhadhana.* Kramrisch explains, "Before the temple in the likeness of the *Purusha* is constructed, the rite of *garbhadhana* is performed and a casket which holds the Seed and Germ of the temple is immured in the wall, to the right of the door, above the level of the First Bricks. As to a woman, the ancient rite of *garbhadhana,* of impregnation and steadying of the womb, is performed to the earth; she received the seed (*bjia*) of the building and gives substance (*prakriti*) to the Germ. *Garbha* means germ as well as womb, and the receptacle (*garbhapatra*) which is deposited holds the Seed—the causal stage whence the unmanifest becomes manifest—and is the womb of the temple which is to arise. The sacrificing priest acts as generator, the *guru* who deposits the *garbha* on behalf of the donor, on a night of flawless stars" (Kramrisch 1976, p. 126). The name *garbhadhana* is also given to the ritual that a pious Hindu married couple undergo before conceiving a child. After the *garbhadhana samskara,* the actual construction of the temple begins. The *garbhapatra,* or receptacle, which represents the earth goddess, contains samples of the earth on which the temple is built, precious stones, metals, herbs, grains, flowers, and, in the center, "the symbols of God in the special manifestation in which his presence is invoked in the main image and in the temple itself" (Kramrisch 1976, p. 128). For a temple dedicated to Krishna, the symbols and images would be those of Krishna. So the temple is a body, not only statically in terms of its mature completion, but dynamically in terms of its development, from conception.

The completed temple can be seen in both male and female aspect. The *Ishanashivagurudevapaddhati* (3.12.16), a Shaivite *vastu* text, says, "The Temple is made of the presence of Shiva and Shakti . . . . The concrete form of Shiva is called House of God. Hence one should contemplate and worship it" (Kramrisch 1976, p. 130). Shakti is the feminine energy of Shiva. Translated into the concepts of Krishna *bhakti,* a temple of Krishna can be seen as made of the presence of Krishna and Radha, the personified pleasure energy of Krishna. The energetic and the energy are simultaneously one and different. The energy exists as originally spiritual but can be transformed into material energy, and back again. The construction of the temple represents the material energy being transformed back into its original spiritual nature.

House as Body

The principles of *vastu* are also used in construction of other buildings besides temples. For example, a residential house can be built according to *vastu* principles. The house is considered like a person, like a body. Savarkar (1998, p. 42) says, "Our health is maintained if we follow the rules of diet consistent with the rules of Nature. In the same manner, the health of a building or *vastu* can be maintained if the construction is made giving due regard to the principles of Nature. The limbs in a body should invariably be in their proper places. So much so, the rooms in a house should be designed in their proper places. That will keep the house healthy and thereby the inmates too happy."

There are many kinds of *vastu* house designs. One kind of house constructed according to *vastu* principles can be seen as a human body lying on the ground with the head to the east and feet to the west (R. G. Rao 1998, Figs. 2–3, pp. 154–155). Windows should be on the eastern side, in the head of the house. Because the head is the place of contemplation, the household temple room should be in the east. One of the rules for a traditional house built according to *vastu* principles is that the central part should be kept free. This corresponds to the lungs in the chest (upper trunk) region of the human figure. Thirumalachar (1998, p. 51) says, "Architectural constructions are . . . living organisms and they behave like human beings. Like the living beings, they vibrate and pulsate; they breathe. For such breathing structures, the center space serves as the lungs. If the lungs are filled with substances other than air, what would happen?" Below the lungs in the trunk of the body is the stomach. In the house, this is the dining room. Then, at the western end of the house, come the toilet and washing areas. On either side of the main central (trunk) area of the house are two arms, containing guest rooms, bedrooms, and other kinds of rooms.

The house therefore is a body that the souls of the inhabitants animate. According to Hindu religious principles, the house is also a temple, and therefore the deity is also present animating the house. Therefore a house is not simply a structure in which the inhabitants live. The home is the body of the inhabitants, and they work together as a system. So when archeologists uncover a house in an excavation, they are discovering a dead house, just as much as when they uncover a skeleton, they are uncovering a dead human. There is tendency to see the house as an inanimate stage for the human, whose living identity can perhaps be brought back to life on the stage. But perhaps we need to see that the house was also alive, in a system that incorporated the house along with the animating presences of the *vastu purusha*, the household deity, and the human resident. About the *vastu* design of a residence, Kramrisch (1976, p. 71) says that what is involved is "an identification by transfer of one's own bodily frame into the special design as well as the introduction of that image into the corresponding disposition of one's own body." Similarly, one can say that the body is like a home for the soul, just as one can say the temple is a home for the temple deity.

Town as Body

The principles of *vastu* are also applied in the design and construction of towns.

In an article by the Press Trust of India, published on September 21, 2005, Y. S. Rawal, director of the Archaeological Survey of India, said, without giving much detail, he could detect signs of *vastu* at the Harappan site of Dholavira in the Indian state of Gujarat. In Feburary of 2008, I visited Lothal, another Harappan site in Gujarat. The Lothal site was first excavated during the years 1955–1962 by S. R. Rao (1985). I wanted to see if *vastu* principles were evident in its design. The identification of *vastu* design elements in Harappan sites, if genuine, contributes to the resolution of questions about cultural continuity and change in northwest India during the second and third millennia BC. *Vastu* is generally considered part of Vedic culture, so the presence of *vastu* in Harappan sites would challenge the conventional view that Vedic culture was a post-Harappan import.

At Lothal, I looked at the site and the site plan for Period A, which goes from 2,400 to 1,900 BC (S. R. Rao 1985, p. 3). The plan shows that Lothal was laid out in square form, with sides oriented to the cardinal directions. This corresponds to one of the standard *vastu* grids. K. V. R. Rao (1998, pp. 89) says, "The most important shape used in the initial concept of towns and cities, as per the *Samarangana-sutradhara,* is towards square shape, as it denotes limits to expanding life and also a perfection sans life and ultimately, sans death." According to *vastu* principles, an ideal site for a town is higher in the west and south than in the north and east (Pulipanni 1998, p. 160). At Lothal, there is a definite elevation in the south, sloping down to the north and east. S. K. Ramachandra Rao (1998, p. 22), citing a *vastu* text called *Yukti-kalapataru,* says that "houses facing the four main directions are beneficient, while those facing the corner points forebode evil." At Lothal, all the buildings face the main directions. Roads are oriented north to south, and east to west (S. R. Rao 1985, p. 8), another feature of *vastu* town design (K. V. R. Rao 1998, p. 87). According to *vastu* texts, waste water should drain to the north or east (Pulippani 1998, p. 159). I found that the main water drainage system at Lothal, in the area of the citadel, did drain to the east, as also noted in the site report (S. R. Rao 1985, p. 9).

According to *vastu* principles, the four social classes (workers, merchants, rulers, and priests) should occupy the western, southern, eastern, and northern sides of a town respectively (Kramrisch 1976, p. 42). Workshops are found primarily on the western side of Lothal. The southeastern corner, Lothal's center of trade, is occupied by a structure identified as a warehouse. The site plan shows the acropolis, identified as the residence of the town's rulers (*kshatriyas*), extending from the central part of the site to the site's eastern boundary. In the middle of the northern boundary of Lothal is a structure identified as a public fire altar, which would likely have been attended by priests (*brahmanas*). The principal deity of the northern side of the *vastu purusha mandala* is Soma, the moon, and the quarter over which the moon rules is known as the "quarter of men" (Kramrisch 1976, p. 93). The Lower Town of Lothal, which includes most of the residences, is in the northern half of the site, whereas the southern half of the town is occupied by the warehouse trade area, acropolis government area, and the workshop areas.

The Lothal site plan shows a cemetery outside the northwestern boundary wall, and Rao comments (1985, p. 45), "Considering the large population of Lothal which is estimated at 15,000 the number of skeletons (17) found is very small. It is likely that cremation was also practiced here." The deity of the northwest corner of the 81-square *vastu purusha mandala* is Roga, disease; just below Roga is Papayakshman, consumption; and just below Papayakshman is Shosha, emaciation (Kramrisch 1976, pp. 32–33, 93). A possibility that deserves consideration is that the northwest cemetery burials could represent cases of special burial for persons who suffered from diseases considered particularly inauspicious. Based on the *vastu purusha mandala*, one might venture an archeological prediction, namely that a cremation ground might be found outside the southwest corner of the Lothal settlement walls, near the bank of the now dry river that once ran there. The southern side of the *vastu purusha mandala* is ruled by Yama, the lord of death. The southwest corner specifically is occupied by Pitarah, the lord of the ancestors, or Nirritih, the lord of dying, exiting from life (Kramrisch 1976, pp. 32, 93). This would make sense because the river flowed from north to south, and typically in Hindu towns, the riverside cremation grounds are usually located so that the river carries water away from the inhabited areas of the town.

Body as Town (City) and Some Thoughts on the Embodied Self

Just as the city or town can be seen as the form of the *vastu purusha,* the biological human form can been seen as a city. The *Bhagavata Purana* (in chapters 25 through 29 of the fourth canto) gives an extensive allegory in which the body is depicted as a city of nine gates (the nine gates being the two eye holes, two nostrils, ear holes, mouth, anus, and genital opening). The city of nine gates is the city of the conscious self, or soul. At first this may seem like the familiar Cartesian dualism of Western philosophy. But the picture that emerges from the allegory is actually more complex and may be useful in current archeological debates about the body and self. Morris and Peatfield (2002, p. 112) say, "In their choice of analytical models archaeologists tend to prefer either living cultures that are traditional (or to use a more loaded term 'primitive') or sophisticated complex cultures that are dead. In terms of understanding the body, this is particularly limiting, because it ignores the considerable, and still evolving, exploration of the body, mind and systemic energetic abilities found in the yoga practices of India . . . . for the western analyst they offer a real alternative to Cartesian hierarchical mind/body divisions."

The allegory of the city of nine gates is historical, and in this sense can be seen as an example of what Robb (2002, p. 155) calls "biographical narratives," by which he means "not the life stories of particular notable or ordinary individuals, but a cultural idea of what a human life should be." In the allegory King Puranjana leaves his original home and searches for a new one. He is accompanied, secretly, by a friend, an old *brahmana.* King Puranjana comes to a city with nine gates and enters it. King Puranjana represents the *atma*, the conscious self, or soul, which originally exists in the spiritual world but comes to live in a material body. The very name Puranjana means a person (*jana*) who lives in a city (*pura*). The original spiritual form of the conscious self is a humanlike form with spiritual senses. On this level of reality there is no dualism between conscious self and body. The body and conscious self are spiritually one. It is just that the self has innate spiritual form and senses.

The same is true of God in the theology of Krishna *bhakti*. God also has human-like form and senses and is nondifferent from them. Additional understandings found in the interpretative texts of the Krishna *bhakti* school reveal that God's original form displays both a male and female aspect. Krishna is the male aspect, or *purusha*, and Radha is the personified pleasure energy (*hladini shakti*) of Krishna. They both exist coeternally. Because Krishna comes under the control of Radha, his pleasure potency, Radha is considered superior. In Hindu temples, the divine pair is addressed as Radha-Krishna, giving priority to Radha, the female energy. Both figures are present in image form on temple altars, standing side by side. In esoteric descriptions of the dealings of Radha and Krishna, we find that sometimes Krishna dresses as Radha, or as some other female person, and sometimes Radha dresses as Krishna.

Adding a further level of spiritual gender complexity, sometimes Krishna desires to experience the mood of Radha. In other words, God desires to experience what it is like to be the lover of God. So Krishna, who is normally bluish takes on the golden complexion of Radha, and appears in a golden male form called Chaitanya. It is said *shri krishna chaitanya radha-krishna nahe anya*: Chaitanya is the combined form of Radha and Krishna. Radha and Krishna eternally exist in the spiritual world, but also appear simultaneously in this world in expansions of their spiritual forms. Similarly, Chaitanya also exists eternally in the spiritual world, but manifests in the material world to teach love for Krishna. Once Chaitanya was being questioned by one of his confidential devotees, and revealed his form as both Radha and Krishna. There is thus a high level of complexity in divinity gender in Krishna *bhakti*.

The relationship of the individual spirit soul to Radha-Krishna is also complex, in terms of sex and gender. Each soul has a particular eternal spiritual form, called the *svarupa* ("self-form"), in which it eternally serves Radha-Krishna in a particular loving emotional mood, called a *rasa*. The five principal *rasas* are passive adoration, servitor-ship, friendship, parental love, and conjugal love (either married or unmarried). The forms that experience *rasa* can be considered in terms of sex and gender. The forms of the individual eternal servants of Radha and Krishna are of male and female sex. But all of them are considered ultimately female in gender, because they are manifestations of Krishna's pleasure energy, which is considered female in relationship to Krishna, who in this respect alone is considered *purusha*, or male. Therefore, a soul who is eternally one of Krishna's servants in male form in terms of spiritual body (*svarupa*) is still considered ultimately female in terms of basic ontological gender. Also consider this: a conditioned soul in the material world resides within a material body, forgetting its *svarupa*, its eternal spiritual form. So it is possible, for example, for a soul with an eternally male spiritual body to be identifying with the material body of a biological female, while a soul with an eternally female spiritual body may be identifying in the material world with a biological body that is male. And in the course of reincarnation, a soul with an eternally female form may take on a succession of material forms, some male, some female. All material forms, male and female, are considered to be of falsely male gender (i.e. falsely taking on the role of being *purusha*, independent enjoyer), when in fact, in terms of ultimate spiritual gender, they are meant to be *shakti*, or female, in terms of serving the *purusha*, Krishna. Liberation means to attain one's actual *svarupa*, in which self and bodily form are the same, nondual.

It seems that modern archeology is having a great deal of trouble with the concept of self/body dualism, a dualism from which it cannot seem to escape, no matter how hard it tries. As Pluciennik (2002, p. 229) puts it, "The much criticized (philosophical) mind-body or (theological) soul-flesh distinction still haunts our frameworks and categories." The depth of this frustration can be seen in Hamilakis, who says (2002, p. 122): "Despite all the recent advances in archaeological thinking and practice, we are still missing maybe the most important aspects of human experience in the past, the corpo-reality, the condition of human embodiment. . . . most of the recent theoretical discussion, even when it talks about the human body, embodiment and corporeality, maintains abstract, mentalist notions and schemes, still works within Cartesian logocentric intellectual discourses." Still, it seems that Hamilakis, in his desire to transcend the Cartesian dualism of self and body, in favor of a postmodern monistic concept of self as body, has gotten caught up in another dualism, i.e. trying to resolve the duality between self in body and self as body in favor of self as body. This in itself is a manifestation of a traditionally logocentric practice of supposing that a dichotomy must be seen in either/or terms and resolved in favor of either one or the other of the alternatives. In the *bhakti* worldview, there is another way of resolving dichotomies, such as the dichotomies involved in self and body. Are self and body the same, or are they different? The solution may be that self and body are simultaneously one and different. This philosophical outlook is technically called *achintya bheda-abheda-tattva*, the truth (*tattva*) of being simultaneously and inconceivably (*achintya*) one (*abheda*) and different (*bheda*). This is a position that it is almost impossible for a mind trained in dualistic logics to comprehend, but there are some traditional analogies that point in this direction—sunshine being simultaneously one with and different from the sun, for example.

In the materially conditioned state the material body is different from the actual self, but is the same as the false self or false ego (*ahankara*), the image of the spiritual self reflected in the alien medium of matter. The reflection presents itself as body, and self identifies nondually with body. This kind of view, although in a strict sense ultimately dualistic, is from the standpoint of the experienced state of the conditioned soul in *ahankara* (false ego) not dualistic, because the self in its conditioned state identifies itself interactively with the changing material body that it helps to continually construct. But even so it is a complex nondualism, which can support many visions of changing bodies. Pluciennik (2002, p. 174) says, "Bodies are in many ways malleable in nature and meaning, whether we like to think of them as performed, constructed within discourses, as nodes in social networks, as projects, as signs of presence of agents or as the instruments of individual actors, as temporary vessels, as founded and self-contained, or as only one aspect of a social person."

Self is involved in the construction of body, and body is involved in the experience of self. The kind of self that is experienced in false ego is constructed by the material body in its sensorimotor engagement with material reality. To see how this is accomplished, we return to the allegory of the city of nine gates.

When Puranjana enters the city of nine gates, he finds a garden, and in the garden he encounters a beautiful young woman, who is accompanied by a strong bodyguard, ten assistant bodyguards, a serpent with five heads, and numberless maidservants. In terms of the allegory, the queen represents the material intelligence. The chief bodyguard represents the mind. The ten assistants represent the ten senses, including five knowledge-acquiring senses and five working senses. The knowledge-acquiring senses are the visual sense, touch sense, taste sense, smell sense, and hearing sense. The working senses are the speaking sense (voice), the ambulatory sense (legs), the grasping sense (arms and hands), the evacuation sense, and the genital sense. The maidservants represent the varieties of material desires that motivate the self. And the five-headed serpent represents the five vital airs that power the subtle and gross machinery of the body.

The King marries the Queen. The marriage represents *ahankara*, false ego, which arises from the attractive attachment of the spiritual self to material intelligence, binding them together. This binding causes forgetfulness of the spiritual self and identification with the material body, beginning with the subtle material element of intelligence. Intelligence draws the attention of the consciousness to the mind, which presents proposals to the self based on sensory inputs. According to the allegory, the knowledge-acquiring and working senses (the assistant bodyguards) are grouped around the mind (the chief bodyguard), which integrates them into an interactive sensory display, involving perception and action. The mind synthesizes the input of the senses and presents to the intelligence proposals for accepting and rejecting different courses of action based on the sensory input. For example, a person may be about to cross a street. The mind presents to the self the sensory input giving the situation on the street, including traffic coming from either direction. The mind expresses itself in terms of "should I cross now, or should I wait, should I cross now or should I wait?" Intelligence makes the decision. And then the working senses carry out the action, or refrain from the action.

So it is not a simple ghost in the machine, driver in the car kind of analogy. There is an interactive engagement of the self with the world through the senses. In this state, the self identifies itself with the collectivity of the senses and their inputs and outputs. As Hamilakis (2002, p. 122, interpolation mine) says, "The notion of the embodiment is based on the idea that our subjectivity [in this case the subjectivity of *ahankara*, or false ego] is defined by our sensory experiences, our bodily encounters with the world." Past actions determine current conditions of opportunity and restriction, and current action determines future conditions.

The material intelligence, mind, and senses form the sensorimotor body of the self in material consciousness. The subtle but material senses operate through the organs of the gross physical body. For example, the subtle visual sense normally operates through the physical organs of the eyes, the fleshy balls in the sockets of the skull. According to the allegory, when the King wishes to see, he exits the gates of the eyes with the two persons representing the subtle visual sense and with them goes to the city of visual impressions. There the King acquires visual impressions. According to allegory, and the *sankhya* philosophy of India, there are subtle sense objects that are acquired by each of the senses. The subtle sense objects (the *tan matras*) are visual sensation, auditory sensation, touch sensation, taste sensation, and smell sensation, which are material. The subtle working senses operate through the limbs and organs of the gross material body. For example, the subtle grasping sense operates through the arms and hands of the material body. This may help explain the phenomenon of phantom limbs. Sometimes people who lose limbs report still feeling the presence of the limb. Elsewhere (Cremo 2005), I have offered an extensive scientific justification for the objective reality of the picture of the self presented in the allegory of the city of nine gates.

Hamilakis (2002, p. 122) complains that even archeologists who have adopted the postmodern theoretical perspective of embodiment privilege the visual sense, but as can be seen in the allegory of the city of nine gates, all the knowledge-acquiring and working senses are given appropriate attention. Of course, there is also a socially interactive element to self. The self, with other selves, is literally part of a social body, but although I want to allude to this, it is beyond the scope of this paper to give a full explanation. I simply note that the intellectuals form the head of this body, the administrators form the arms, the agriculturists and traders form the abdomen, and the artisans form the legs.

So, in cooperation with the material intelligence, the material mind, and material senses, the self enjoys life in the city of nine gates. But the period of enjoyment comes to an end. Another king, Kalayavana (time), attacks the city, aided by his 360 white soldiers and 360 black soldiers, the passing of the days and nights. Kalayavana is joined in the attack by his sister Kalakanya, old age. In the embrace of old age, Puranjana loses strength. In the end Kalayavana breaks the city's defenses, burns the city, and takes Puranjana captive. Puranjana is led out if the city with the queen and bodyguards and the rest of his entourage. The king then takes his next birth as a female, the Queen named Vaidarbhi.

Let us consider how this happens, in terms of the worldview of the allegory. The conscious self and the subtle material body, composed of intelligence, mind, and subtle senses, move out of one gross material body, the city of nine gates, and move into another gross material body, another city of nine gates. The *svarupa*, the eternal form of the self, remains the same (although hidden, unseen), while the false (although consciously experienced) material self takes on a new form. The new material body configures itself according to the condition of the intelligence, mind, and subtle senses. This time the body is female. So the material self is not essential. It is a changeable construction, not only in its own material selfhood, but in its relationships with other material selves.

As an example of the complexities of sex and gender in the Hindu worldview, we can consider the following case, summarized from the first chapter of the ninth canto of the *Bhagavat Purana*. In ancient times, Manu desired a son. He asked the sage Vashishta to organize the performance of a sacrifice that would allow him to have a son. But Manu's wife, who desired a daughter, influenced the priest who actually conducted the sacrifice to do so in such a way that a daughter would be born. The girl was named Ila. To satisfy Manu, who was unhappy with this result, Vashistha transformed Ila into a boy named Sudyumna. Later Sudyumna and his male companions rode into a forest sacred to the demigod Shiva. Any male who entered this forest would be turned into a female. Sudyumna was thus transformed into a woman. Sudyumna then accepted Budha (a son of the moon god, not the Buddha of Buddhism) as her husband. They had a son named Pururava. Vashishta later asked Shiva to change Sudyumna back into a man. Shiva then gave Sudyumna a benediction that he would live one month as a woman and one month as a man. Sudyumna then ruled his kingdom, alternating between male and female, finally retiring to the forest and turning the kingdom over to his son Pururava.

Sudyumna thus occupied many positions, as his result of his interactions with persons of various degrees of power. Thomas (2002, p. 38) says, "People are different by virtue of their different positioning within the networks of power and knowledge. We are not free to be what we will, but we realize our potentials differently because of our different opportunities, experiences, access to knowledge . . . . and because we may have been excluded, dominated, or oppressed by others." In the Hindu understanding, the different positionings as male and female in the networks of power and knowledge, in this life and the next, are determined by the self in its interactions with the networks of power and knowledge, i.e. by its *karma*.

In the allegory, Queen Vaidarbhi lives for some time, until her husband dies, and she becomes frustrated with life. At that point, an elderly *brahmana* (sage) approaches her, saying, "I am your old friend." He says that this world is not her real home, that they both once existed in another place, to which he will guide her. We may recall that when Puranjana left his original home he was secretly accompanied by a confidential friend, who remained hidden. In terms of the allegory, this is the Supersoul, a manifestation of God who accompanies the individual soul in its journey through material bodies in the material world.

At this stage, a conscious self may attain the stage called *jivan mukta*, liberation while still in the body, in the world. In such a state one is aware of one's *svarupa* and somewhat detached from the external material body. The *Bhagavata Purana* (3.27.38) says that the material body just goes on its own, and the self remains somewhat unaware of it, as a drunken person remains somewhat unaware of the actions of his body.

In the eternally liberated state, there is no duality between spiritual self and spiritual body, and the self willingly participates in the eternal *lila*, or pastimes, of Krishna and Radha. This participation is enabled and restricted by the *yogamaya* potency of Krishna. One is moved by and moves in this energy, freely, as in a dance. This is in fact the highest realization of Krishna, participation in the *rasa* dance, the dance of the exchange of spiritual emotions of love. The dance is usually depicted with Radha and Krishna in the center, and around them a circle of dancing girls, each an expansion of Radha, each girl accompanied by an expansion of Krishna.

Conclusion

So if someone enters a Radha-Krishna temple in India, constructed according to *vastu* principles, then what is happening? Let us assume for the sake of the discussion that the eternal form of this person is that of a *gopi*, one of the young female associates of Krishna, but that the outer material body of this person is that of a male. Let us assume that he is married, and that he comes to the temple with his wife, with whom he has had several children. This kind of thing can happen. Bhaktivinoda Thakur (1838–1914), one of the predecessors of my *guru,* indicated in some of his poems that his eternal spiritual form was that of a *manjari,* one of the young female servants of the *gopis.* But at the same time, his material body was that of a male, and he had several children with his wife. But let us suppose that the person entering the temple is not in that position of total realization of his eternal identity. He simply suspects that his eternal form might be that of a *gopi* or *manjari.* Before entering the temple, he circumambulates its exterior and sees the *shikara* rising to the sky. He knows that at the base of the temple is the *vastu pursua mandala,* and that the temple structure is a visible manifestation of the bodily form of the *vastu purusha.* He knows that the temple was erected on behalf of a saintly king by an architect who knew the *vastu* principles. The temple remains a visible expression of the spiritually aspiring body of the temple patron, the king. He sees on the sides of the temple carvings of the deities inside. He sees the temple as a visual manifestation of the form of the deity, in this case Krishna. His gaze takes in the carvings of the different kinds of beings inhabiting the lower and higher regions of the material cosmos, moving up to the spire, which is the point where the material merges into the spiritual. And he himself wants to make that journey. And in that sense he sees in the temple the visible form of his own spiritually aspiring body. After circumambulating the temple, he enters. He approaches the *garbha-griha.* Before the *garbha-griha* is the *mandapa,* the temple hall. He joins a group of devotees, chanting and singing *mantras* before the images of Radha and Krishna. His body moves. He sings. He hears the instruments, the drums and cymbals. He meditates upon how he is one of the eternal servants of Radha and Krishna. If he attains pure devotion, he begins to experience his eternal spiritual body, while engaging his present material body in singing and dancing. He smell the incenses. He sees the votive flames offered by the temple priest in circular motions before the sacred images. One of the temple priests, from a small metal spoon, pours into his palm some drops of *charanamrita,* the sweet liquid (a mixture of water, honey, milk, and yogurt) that has been offered to Radha and Krishna in a bathing ceremony. He tastes the *charanamrita.* Almost all of his sensorimotor capacities are engaged, not just his eyes. But this is a paper about the visual body, so I concentrate on the visual. He sees the image of Krishna. He feels one with and different from Krishna. He sees his own body as a temple, because as Supersoul, Krishna is also within his body. He sees the bodies of the other devotees in the temple as also being temples of Krishna. Having taken *darshan,* he leaves the temple. He sees it as the visual body of the *vastu purusa,* the temple patron, the temple deity. He sees how the temple takes its place in a town, also designed according to *vastu* principles, involving the humanlike form of the *vastu purusha.* The townspeople form a social body. And the town is set in a landscape that is also the visible body of God, the *vishvarupa.*

I hope in this paper I have managed to communicate something about the concept of the visual (or envisioned) body in one of the many manifestations of Hindu religion (Krishna *bhakti*), as manifested in material things that are or may become part of the archeological record, i.e. houses, towns, temples, and landscapes.

Works cited:

Bhagavata Purana [*Shrimad-Bhagavatam*] (1976) trans. Bhaktivedanta Swami, A. C. Los Angeles: Bhaktivedanta Book Trust.

Bhaktivedanta Swami, A. C. (1986) *Bhagavad-gita As It Is.* Los Angeles: Bhaktivedanta Book Trust.

Cremo, Michael A. (2003) *Human Devolution: A Vedic Alternative to Darwin's Theory.* Los Angeles: Bhaktivedanta Book Publishing.

Guy, John (2007) *Indian Temple Sculpture.* Chennai, India: Westland Books.

Hamilakis, Yannis; Pluciennik, Mark; and Tarlow, Sarah (2002) Introduction. In Y. Hamilakis, M. Pluciennik, and S. Tarlow eds. *Thinking Through the Body: Archaeologies of Corporeality.* New York: Kluwer Academic, pp. 1–22.

Johnson, Mary Brock (1988) Temple architecture as construction of consciousness: a Japanese temple and garden. *Arch. & Comport./Arch. Behav.* 4(3): 229–249.

Kramrisch, Stella (1976) *The Hindu Temple.* In 2 volumes. New Delhi. Motilal Banarsidass. Reprint of 1946 edition by University of Calcutta.

Morris, Christine, and Peatfield, Alan (200) Feeling through the body: gesture in Cretan Bronze Age religion. In Y. Hamilakis, M. Pluciennik, and S. Tarlow, eds. *Thinking Through the Body: Archaeologies of Corporeality.* New York: Kluwer Academic, pp. 105–120.

Pluciennik, Mark (2002) Bodies in/as material culture: Introduction. In Y. Hamilakis, M. Pluciennik, and S. Tarlow, eds. *Thinking Through the Body: Archaeologies of Corporeality.* New York: Kluwer Academic, pp. 173–177.

Pluciennik, Mark (2002b) Art, artefact, metaphor. In Y. Hamilakis, M. Pluciennik, and S. Tarlow, eds. *Thinking Through the Body: Archaeologies of Corporeality.* New York: Kluwer Academic, pp. 217–232.

Pulipanni, U. S. (1998) Hindu Geomancy. In Vasudev, Gayatri Devi, ed. *Vastu, Astrology, and Architecture.* New Delhi: Motilal Banarsidass, pp. 157–170.

Rao, K. V. Raja (1998) Relevance of ancient Vastu technology to modern town planning. In Vasudev, Gayatri Devi, ed. *Vastu, Astrology, and Architecture.* New Delhi: Motilal Banarsidass, pp. 82–92

Rao, R. G. (1998) Vastu of the heavenly planets in human houses. In Vasudev, Gayatri Devi, ed. *Vastu, Astrology, and Architecture.* New Delhi: Motilal Banarsidass, pp. 152–157.

Rao, S. K. Ramachandra (1998) Vastu vidya. In Vasudev, Gayatri Devi, ed. *Vastu, Astrology, and Architecture.* New Delhi: Motilal Banarsidass, pp. 13–27.

Rao, S. R. (1985) *Lothal.* New Delhi: Archaeological Survey of India.

Robb, John (2002) Time and biography. In Y. Hamilakis, M. Pluciennik, and S. Tarlow, eds. *Thinking Through the Body: Archaeologies of Corporeality.* New York: Kluwer Academic, pp.153–171.

Savarkar, H. A. (1998) The concept of Vastu Purusa Mandala. In Vasudev, Gayatri Devi, ed. *Vastu, Astrology, and Architecture.* New Delhi: Motilal Banarsidass, pp. 37–44.

Thirumalachar, M. S. (1998) The Vastu Purusa. In Vasudev, Gayatri Devi, ed. *Vastu, Astrology, and Architecture.* New Delhi: Motilal Banarsidass, pp. 45–48.

Thomas, Julian (2002) Archaeology's humanism and the materiality of the body. In Y. Hamilakis, M. Pluciennik, and S. Tarlow, eds. *Thinking Through the Body: Archaeologies of Corporeality.* New York: Kluwer Academic, pp. 29–45.

Vasudev, Gayatri Devi, ed. (1998) *Vastu, Astrology, and Architecture.* New Delhi: Motilal Banarsidass.

Index

A

Abbeville, France, 78, 82, 84, 85, 86, 87, 89, 91, 92, 102, 105, 108, 109, 114, 118, 120, 129, 130, 306
A. C. Bhaktivedanta Swami Prabhupada, xii, 13, 31, 35, 74, 96, 143, 147, 150, 243, 247, 249, 250, 253, 255, 257
ahankara (false ego), 42, 362, 363
ahimsa (nonviolence), 72, 73
alchemy, 47, 71, 93
alien abduction, 267
allegory, 37, 38, 39, 40, 43, 44, 360, 362, 363, 364, 365
Alter, Alexandra, 219
Ameghino, Carlos, 132
Ameghino, Florentino, 131, 207, 208
American Association of Physical Anthropologists, 19
American Baptist Education Society, 292
American Geological Society, 223
American Psychological Association, 260
Amormino, Vanessa, 199
anaesthesia, 40, 48
anatomically modern humans, 2, 6, 16, 23, 48, 77, 89, 90, 99, 100, 101, 102, 105–107, 114, 116, 117, 127–129, 130, 132, 137, 139, 148, 168, 202, 209, 220, 226, 231, 237,

238
angiosperms, 185, 187, 189, 190, 263, 310
anthropocentric, 70
anthropology, v, xi, xv, 3, 5, 8, 13, 15, 17, 18, 19, 24, 29, 30, 34, 45, 47, 111, 128, 147, 151, 152, 154, 162, 206, 209, 216, 220, 231, 235, 294, 295, 298, 303, 328, 340, 343, 348, 352
anumana (inference), xiv
apelike ancestors, 15, 301
apemen, 126, 127, 292, 307, 327
apparitions, 40, 48, 59, 61, 95, 265
Archaeological Survey of India, 23, 359, 367
Archaeology Is A Brand, 329
archeological record, 4, 6, 7, 34, 126, 155, 240, 366
Aristotle, 1
artificial intelligence, 39, 264, 347
artificial life, 2, 43, 264, 347
ashrama, xiii
atom, 38
auriferous gravel, 6, 9, 35, 113, 120, 178, 214, 222, 223, 226, 240, 271
Aurillac, France, 11, 122, 154, 169, 170, 175, 180
Australopithecus, 20, 112, 116, 118, 122, 132, 133, 175, 176, 179, 307
automatons, 39
avatara, 4, 244
Avenue Clichy, Paris, France, 106

369

PLATES

Plate I (Chapter 12)

Fig. 1

Fig. 2

Fig. 3

Fig. 4

Fig. 1: Carlos Ribeiro. Fig. 2: Michael Cremo, Museum of Geology, Lisbon. Fig. 3: The hill at Monte Redondo, Portugal. Fig. 4: Ravines on the side of the hill at Monte Redondo.

Plate II (Chapter 12)

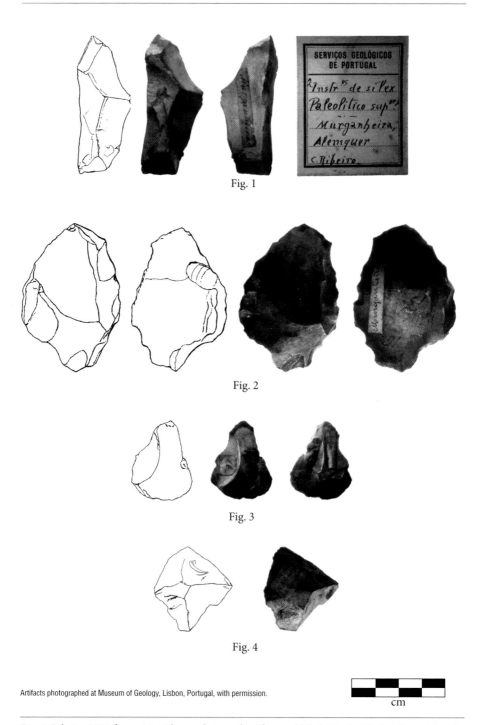

Fig. 1

Fig. 2

Fig. 3

Fig. 4

Artifacts photographed at Museum of Geology, Lisbon, Portugal, with permission.

cm

Fig. 1: Ribeiro 1871 figure 13 with my photos of artifact and label. Fig. 2: Ribeiro figure 15 with my photos. Fig. 3: Ribeiro figure 16 with my photos. Fig. 4: Ribeiro figure 26 with my photo.

Plate III (Chapter 12)

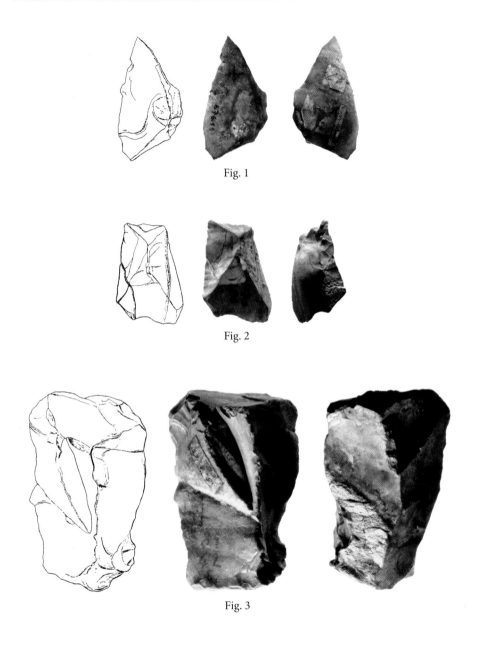

Fig. 1

Fig. 2

Fig. 3

Artifacts photographed at Museum of Geology, Lisbon, Portugal, with permission.

cm

Fig. 1: Ribeiro 1871 figure 27 with my photos of artifact. Fig. 2: Ribeiro figure 29 with my photos. Fig. 3: Ribeiro figure 36 with my photos.

Plate IV (Chapter 12)

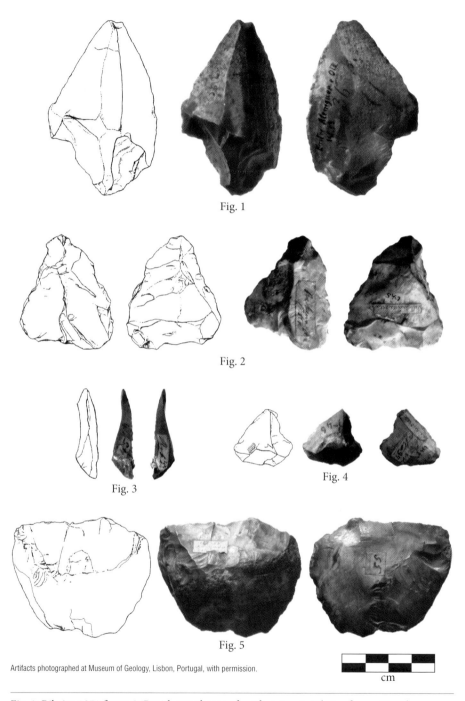

Fig. 1

Fig. 2

Fig. 3

Fig. 4

Fig. 5

Artifacts photographed at Museum of Geology, Lisbon, Portugal, with permission.

cm

Fig. 1: Ribeiro 1871 figure 36B with my photos of artifact. Fig. 2: Ribeiro figure 43 with my photos. Fig. 3: Ribeiro figure 45 with my photos. Fig. 4: Ribeiro figure 46 with my photos. Fig. 5: Ribeiro figure 55 with my photos.

Plate V (Chapter 12)

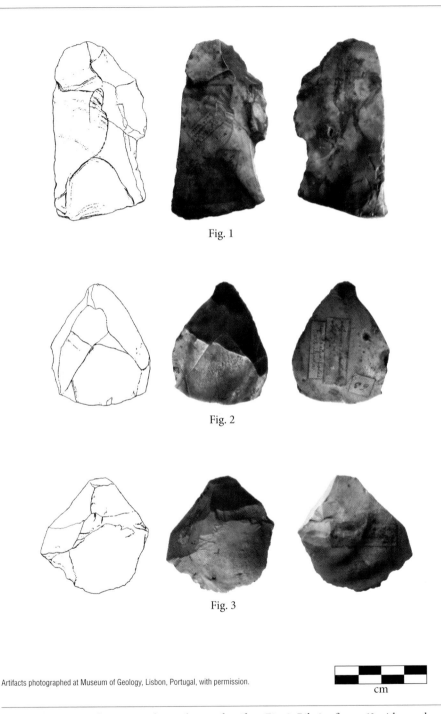

Fig. 1

Fig. 2

Fig. 3

Artifacts photographed at Museum of Geology, Lisbon, Portugal, with permission.

cm

Fig. 1: Ribeiro 1871 figure 62 with my photos of artifact. Fig. 2: Ribeiro figure 63 with my photos. Fig. 3: Ribeiro figure 64 with my photos.

Plate VI (Chapter 12)

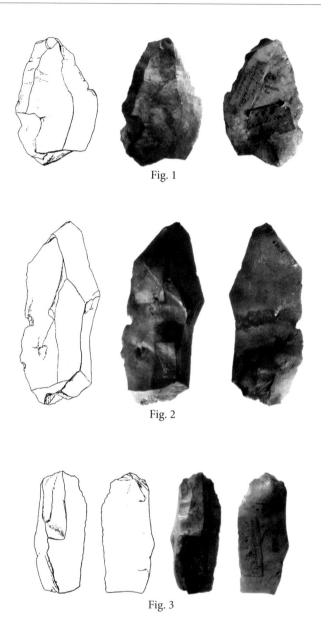

Fig. 1

Fig. 2

Fig. 3

Artifacts photographed at Museum of Geology, Lisbon, Portugal, with permission.

cm

Fig. 1: Ribeiro 1871 figure 73 with my photos of artifact. Fig. 2: Ribeiro figure 74 with my photos. Fig. 3: Ribeiro figure 77 with my photos.

Plate VII (Chapter 12)

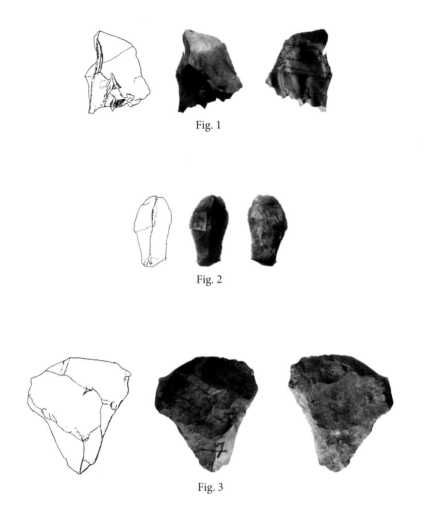

Fig. 1

Fig. 2

Fig. 3

Artifacts photographed at Museum of Geology, Lisbon, Portugal, with permission.

cm

Fig. 1: Ribeiro 1871 figure 80 with my photos of artifact. Fig. 2: Ribeiro figure 82 with my photos. Fig. 3: Ribeiro figure 94 with my photos.

Plate VIII (Chapter 14)

Fig. 1

Fig. 2   Fig. 3

Fig. 4   Fig. 5

cm

Fig. 1: Sandpit at Boncelles, Belgium, where Rutot excavated Oligocene stone tools. Fig. 2: Statue of Boncelles toolmaker commissioned by Rutot. Fig. 3: A. Rutot. Fig. 4: Boncelles artifact with flake removal on working edge. Fig. 5: Rutot 1907 figure 34 with my photos of artifact.

Plate IX (Chapter 14)

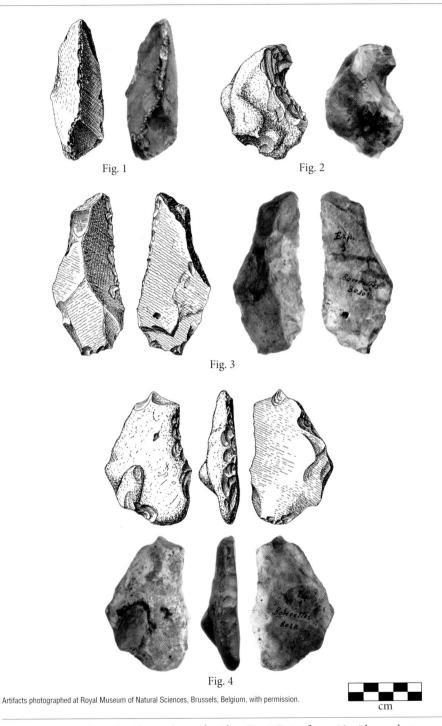

Fig. 1

Fig. 2

Fig. 3

Fig. 4

cm

Artifacts photographed at Royal Museum of Natural Sciences, Brussels, Belgium, with permission.

Fig. 1: Rutot 1907 figure 7 with my photo of artifact. Fig. 2: Rutot figure 13 with my photo.
Fig. 3: Rutot figure 9 with my photos. Fig. 4: Rutot figure 10 with my photos.

Plate X (Chapter 14)

Fig. 1

Fig. 2

Fig. 3

Fig. 4

Artifacts photographed at Royal Museum of Natural Sciences, Brussels, Belgium, with permission.

cm

Fig. 1: Rutot figure 26 with my photo. Fig. 2: Rutot figure 27 with my photo. Fig. 3: Rutot figure 29 with my photo. Fig. 4: Rutot figure 32 with my photos.

Plate XI (Chapter 14)

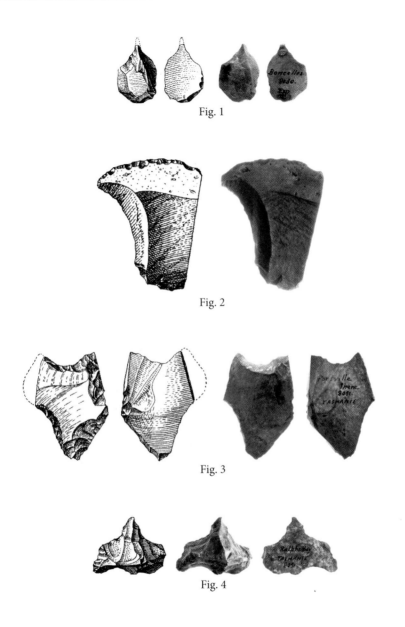

Fig. 1

Fig. 2

Fig. 3

Fig. 4

cm

Fig. 1: Rutot figure 33 with my photos. Fig. 2: Rutot figure 51 of Tasmanian artifact with my photo. Compare Plate III, fig. 2. Fig. 3: Rutot figure 57 of Tasmanian artifact with my photos. Compare Plate III, fig. 3. Fig. 4: Rutot figure 60 of Tasmanian artifact with my photos. Compare Plate III, fig. 4.

Plate XII (Chapter 15)

Fig. 1

Fig. 2

Fig. 1: Table Mountain, Tuolumne County, California. Fig. 2: Gold mining tunnel at Table Mountain.

Plate XIII (Chapter 15)

Fig. 1

Fig. 2

Fig. 3

Fig. 4

Fig. 5

Artifacts photographed at Phoebe Hearst Museum of Anthropology, University of California, Berkeley, with permission. ▰▰▰ cm

Fig. 1: Catalog No. 1-4209, mortar, from auriferous gravel, Table Mountain. Fig. 2: Catalog No. 1-4206, mortar, from auriferous gravel, Gold Springs, Tuolumne County. Fig. 3: Catalog No. 1-4213, mortar, from auriferous gravel, Buckeye Hill, Nevada County. Fig. 4: Catalog No. 1-4215, mortar, from auriferous gravel, American Flat, El Dorado County. Fig. 5: Catalog No. 1-42198, stone dish (broken), from auriferous gravel, El Dorado County.

Plate XIV (Chapter 15)

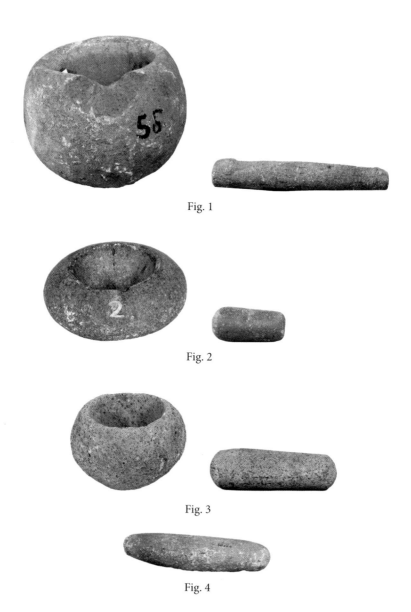

Fig. 1

Fig. 2

Fig. 3

Fig. 4

Artifacts photographed at Phoebe Hearst Museum of Anthropology, University of California, Berkeley, with permission. cm

Fig. 1: Catalog Nos. 1-4208 A & B, mortar and pestle, from auriferous gravel, Kincades Flat, Tuolumne County. Fig. 2: Catalog Nos. 1-4203 A & B, mortar and pestle, from auriferous gravel, Spanish Flat, El Dorado County. Fig. 3: Catalog Nos. 1-4204 A & B, mortar and pestle, from auriferous gravel, El Dorado County. Fig. 4: Catalog No. 1-4210 B, pestle, from auriferous gravel, Forest Home, Amador County.

Plate XV (Chapter 15)

Fig. 1

Fig. 2

Fig. 3

Fig. 4

Fig. 5

Fig. 6

Fig. 1: Catalog No. 1-4207, mortar, from auriferous gravel, Shaw's Flat, Tuolumne County. Fig. 2: Catalog No. 1-4205, mortar, from auriferous gravel, Gold Springs, Tuolumne County. Fig. 3: Catalog No. 1-42556, mortar, from auriferous gravel, near Georgetown, El Dorado County. Fig. 4: Catalog No. 1-4558, perforated stone, from auriferous gravel, near Crimea House, Tuolumne County. Fig. 5: Catalog No. 1-4202, stone ball, from auriferous gravel, Tuolumne County. Fig. 6: Catalog No. 1-4917, stone dish, from auriferous gravel, Tuolumne County.

Plate XVI (Chapter 16)

Fig. 1

Fig. 2

Fig. 1: Chaitanya Mahaprabhu and associates chanting Hare Krishna in Mayapur, West Bengal, India. Fig. 2: View across the Jalangi River to Mayapur, from balcony of the house of Bhakti-vinoda Thakura.

Plate XVII (Chapter 16)

Fig. 1

Fig. 2

Fig. 1: Members of the International Society for Krishna Consciousness (ISKCON) seated beneath a banyan tree while on pilgrimage in Mayapur. Fig. 2: ISKCON members prepare to cross the Ganges River while on pilgrimage in Mayapur.

Plate XVIII (Chapter 21)

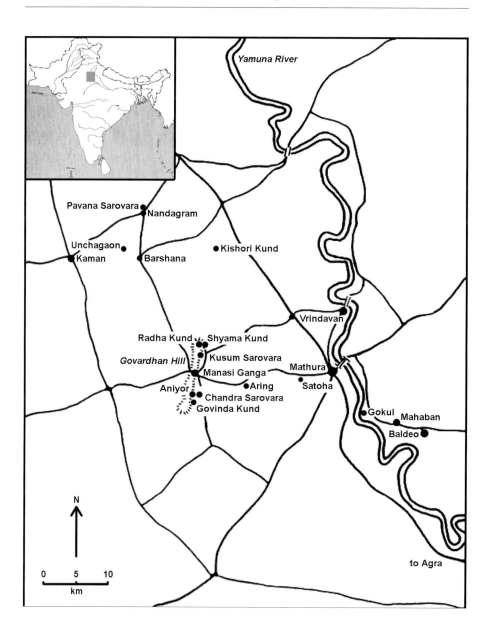

Map of Braj Mandal region, northern India.

Plate XIX (Chapter 21)

Fig. 1

Fig. 2

Fig. 1: Radha Kund, Braj Mandal, India. Fig. 2: Shyama Kund, Braj Mandal, India.

Plate XX (Chapter 21)

Fig. 1

Fig. 2

Fig. 1: Shrine marking the place where Madhavendra Puri excavated the Gopal deity. Fig. 2: Gopal temple (white) on Govardhan Hill, Braj Mandal, India.

Plate XXI (Chapter 21)

Fig. 1

Fig. 2

Fig. 1: Nandagram temple on Nandeshvara Hill, Braj Mandal, India. Fig. 2: Pavana Sarovara, Braj Mandal, India.

Plate XXII (Chapter 21)

Fig. 1

Fig. 2

Fig. 3

Fig. 4

Fig. 1: Deity of Balaram at Baldeo, Braj Mandal, India. Fig. 2: Baldeo temple, Braj Mandal, India. Fig. 3: Painting depicting excavation of Balaram deity on wall at Baldeo temple, Braj Mandal, India. Fig. 4: Kshir Sagar Kund, Braj Mandal, India, where the deity was excavated.

Plate XXIII (Chapter 21)

Fig. 1

Fig. 2

Fig. 3

Fig. 1: Radha Vinoda deities excavated by Lokanath Goswami at Kishori Kund, Braj Mandal, India. They are now located in Jaipur, Rajasthan, India. Fig. 2: Shrine of Lokanath Goswami at Kishori Kund, Braj Mandal, India. Fig. 3: Kishori Kund, Braj Mandal, India.

Plate XXIV (Chapter 21)

Fig. 1

Fig. 2

Fig. 1: Govindaji temple, Vrindavan, India. Fig. 2: In a chamber beneath the altar in the Govindaji temple is the place where the Govindaji deity was excavated by Rupa Goswami.

Plate XXV (Chapter 21)

Fig. 1

Fig. 2

Fig. 1: The Vrindadevi deity excavated by Rupa Goswami at Brahma Kunda, Vrindavan, India. The deity is now in a temple at Kaman, Braj Mandal, India. Fig. 2: Brahma Kund.

Plate XXVI (Chapter 21)

Fig. 1

Fig. 2

Fig. 3

Fig. 1: The Balarama deity (left) excavated by Narayan Bhatt in the 16th century at Unchagaon, Braj Mandal, India. Fig. 2: This tree marks the place where the Balarama deity was excavated. Fig. 3: Temple of Balarama at Unchagaon.

Plate XXVII (Chapter 21)

Fig. 1

Fig. 2

Fig. 1: Temple housing deities of Radha and Krishna excavated by Narayan Bhatt at Barshana, Braj Mandal, India. Fig. 2: This tree marks the place where the deities or Radha and Krishna were excavated.

Plate XXVIII (Chapter 5)

Fig. 1

Fig. 2

Fig. 1: Temple at rural eco community of the International Society for Krishna Consciousness in southwestern Hungary. Fig. 2: Oxen that have been trained to work at the eco community.

Plate XXIX (Chapter 5)

Fig. 1

Fig. 2

Fig. 1: Oil lamps used in temple at rural eco community of the International Society for Krishna Consciousness in southwestern Hungary. Fig. 2: Vegetable garden at the eco community.

Plate XXX (Chapter 5)

Fig. 1

Fig. 1: Wood burning stove in temple at rural eco community of the International Society for Krishna Consciousness in southwestern Hungary.

Forbidden Archeology

By Michael A. Cremo
and Richard L. Thompson

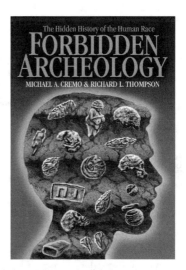

A Remarkable Historical Study of Scientific Controversy About Human Antiquity

After Darwin published his theory of evolution, archeologists and other scientists began searching for fossil evidence of forms linking modern humans with ancient apes. Some of these researchers instead found archeological evidence that anatomically modern humans existed in the very distant past. Cremo and Thompson explore the controversies surrounding these discoveries.

$35

ISBN: 978-0-89213-395-6
6" x 9", hardbound, 408 pages, 32 plates

"Certainly it provides the historian of archeology with a useful compendium of case studies in the history and sociology of scientific knowledge, which can be used to foster debate within archaeology about how to describe the epistemology of one's discipline."
—Archeologist Tim Murray, in
British Journal for the History of Science,
Vol. 28, 1995, p. 379.

"It must be acknowledged that *Forbidden Archeology* brings to attention many interesting issues that have not received much consideration from historians; and the authors' detailed examination of the early literature is certainly stimulating and raises questions of considerable interest, both historically and from the perspective of practitioners of sociology of scientific knowledge."
—Historians of science Jo Wodak and
David Oldroyd, in *Social Studies of
Science*, Vol. 26(1), 1996, p. 196.

Order your copies today!

Available from your local bookseller, or just fill out the order form in back and fax it to **559-337-2354,** or call us toll free at **1-800-443-3361**.

· · · · · · · · · · · · · ·

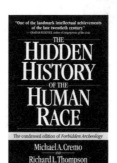

Abridged Version

6" x 9"
Softbound
352 pages

$15.95

ISBN:
978-0-89213-325-3

Forbidden Archeology's
IMPACT

How a controversial new book shocked the scientific community and became an underground classic!

Compiled by Michael A. Cremo

How did the scientific community respond to *Forbidden Archeology*'s challenge to its deeply held beliefs? In this comprehensive compilation of reviews, correspondence, and media interviews, readers get a stunning inside look at the varied reactions the book provoked.

$35.00 ISBN: 978-0-89213-283-6
6" x 9", hardbound, 600 pages

"Cremo has provided here a resource of considerable richness and value . . . . It should also make a useful teaching resource as one of the best-documented case studies of 'science wars,' and raising a wide range of issues covering aspects of 'knowlege transfer' in a manner sure to be provocative in the classroom."

—Sociologist Simon Locke, *Public Understanding of Science*, vol. 8(1), 1999, pp. 68-69

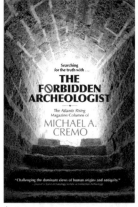

The Forbidden Archeologist

The Atlantis Rising *Magazine Columns of Michael A. Cremo*

"Today, most scientists believe that human beings like us first appeared on earth between 100,000 and 200,000 years ago. But the ancient Sanskrit writings of India, and the writings of other ancient wisdom traditions, tell us that humans like us have existed for many millions of years, going back to the very beginnings of life on earth. Therefore, many of my *Atlantis Rising* columns are about this evidence. They also record my experiences in presenting this evidence at major international scientific conferences, such as the meetings of the World Archeological Congress, the European Association of Archeologists, and the International Congress for History of Science, and my experiences in presenting this evidence to students at university lectures around the world."

—*From the author's introduction.*

$21.95
ISBN: 978-0-89213-337-6
5.5" x 8.5", hardbound
244 pages

Available from your local bookseller, or just fill out the order form in back and fax it to **559-337-2354,** or call us toll free at **1-800-443-3361**.

Human Devolution

A Vedic Alternative to Darwin's Theory

By Michael A. Cremo

In their book *Forbidden Archeology,* Michael A. Cremo and Richard L. Thompson documented evidence showing that humans have existed on earth for tens of millions of years. Such anomalous evidence, contradicting Darwinian evolution, inspired a question: "If we did not evolve from apes then where did we come from?"

Human Devolution is Michael A. Cremo's answer to that question. He says, "We did not evolve up from matter; instead we devolved, or came down, from the realm of pure consciousness, spirit." Basing his response on modern science and the world's great wisdom traditions, including the Vedic tradition of ancient India, Cremo proposes that before we ask the question, "Where did human beings come from?" we should first ask, "What is a human being?"

For a long time, most scientists have assumed that a human being is simply a combination of ordinary physical elements. In *Human Devolution,* Cremo proposes it is more reasonable to assume that a human being is a combination of three distinct substances: matter, mind, and consciousness (or spirit). He shows that scientific evidence for a subtle mind element and a conscious self that can exist apart from the body has been systematically eliminated from mainstream science by a process of "knowledge filtration."

$35.00   ISBN: 978-0-89213-334-5
6" x 9", hardbound, 554 pages

"This controversial book tries to reinterpret the origin of species, and chiefly that of man, in accordance with the truths of the Vedic tradition, by adopting the categories of the paranormal. A 'devolution' of pure spirits to minds and eventually to bodies is assumed. A copious and reliable documentation of paranormal phenomena is presented."

—Giuseppe Sermonti, biologist,
in *Revista Biologia*

Book Order Form

☎ Telephone orders: Call 1-800-HIDDEN-1 (1-800-443-3361).
   Have your credit card ready.

✻ Fax orders: 559-337-2354

✉ Postal orders: Torchlight Publishing, P. O. Box 52,
   Badger, CA 93603, USA

▲ World Wide Web: www.torchlight.com

▲ Email: torchlightpublishing@yahoo.com

Please send the following:

☐ *Forbidden Archeology* — The full, unabridged original edition, 952 pages,
   141 illustrations, 25 tables, hardback, $44.95

☐ *Forbidden Archeology's Impact* — 600 pages, hardback, $35.00

☐ *The Forbidden Archeologist* — 264 pages, hardback, $21.95

☐ *The Hidden History of the Human Race* — The abridged version of
   Forbidden Archeology, 352 pages, 120 illustrations, softback, $15.95

☐ *Human Devolution* — 558 pages, hardback, $35.00

(CA residents add 8.75% sales tax.)

☐ **Please send me your catalog and info on other books by Torchlight Publishing.**

Company_____

Name_____

Address_____

City _____ State_____ Zip_____

(I understand that I may return any books for a full refund—no questions asked.)

Payment: ☐

☐ Check / money order enclosed   ☐ VISA   ☐ MasterCard   AmEx

Card number_____

Name on card_____ Exp. date_____

Signature_____

Shipping and handling:

Forbidden Archeology, Forbidden Archeology's Impact, and Human Devolution — Book rate: USA $6.00 for
first book, $3.00 for each additional book.
The Hidden History of the Human Race and The Forbidden Archeologist — Book rate: USA $4.00 for first book, $3.00
for each additional book. *Surface shipping may take 3–4 weeks. Foreign orders: please phone, e-mail, or fax for details.*